# ENVIRONMENTAL LAW HANDBOOK

## Eleventh Edition

J. Gordon Arbuckle, Mary Elizabeth Bosco,
David R. Case, Elliott P. Laws, John C. Martin,
Marshall Lee Miller, Robert D. Moran,
Russell V. Randle, Daniel M. Steinway,
Richard G. Stoll, Thomas F. P. Sullivan,
Timothy A. Vanderver, Jr., Paul A. J. Wilson

Government Institutes, Inc.
Rockville, MD
1991

## PUBLISHER'S NOTE

This publication is designed to provide accurate and authoritative information with regard to the subject matter covered. It is sold with the understanding that the publisher and authors are not engaged in rendering legal, accounting or other professional service. If legal advice or other expert assistance is required, the services of a competent professional person should be sought.--Adapted from a Declaration of Principles jointly adopted by a Committee of the American Bar Association and a Committee of Publishers.

Publication of this book does not signify that the contents necessarily reflect the views or policies of Government Institutes, Inc.

### ALL RIGHTS RESERVED

Eleventh Edition

March 1991

Published by
Government Institutes, Inc.
Rockville, Maryland 20850
U.S.A.

ii

# SUMMARY OF CONTENTS

ABOUT THE AUTHORS

## Chapter 2  ENFORCEMENT AND LIABILITIES

## Chapter 3  WATER POLLUTION CONTROL

## Chapter 4  SAFE DRINKING WATER ACT

## Chapter 5  EMERGENCY PLANNING AND COMMUNITY RIGHT-TO-KNOW ACT (EPCRA)

## Chapter 6 NATIONAL ENVIRONMENTAL POLICY ACT (NEPA)

## Chapter 7 TOXIC SUBSTANCES CONTROL ACT (TSCA)

## Chapter 8  FEDERAL REGULATION OF PESTICIDES

## Chapter 9 OCCUPATIONAL SAFETY AND HEALTH ACT (OSHA)

## Chapter 10  ASBESTOS

## Chapter 11  RESOURCE CONSERVATION AND RECOVERY ACT (RCRA)

## Chapter 12  UNDERGROUND STORAGE TANKS

## Chapter 13 COMPREHENSIVE ENVIRONMENTAL RESPONSE, COMPENSATION AND LIABILITY ACT (CERCLA OR SUPERFUND)

## Chapter 14 AIR POLLUTION CONTROL

# ABOUT THE AUTHORS

## J. Gordon Arbuckle

J. Gordon Arbuckle is a partner in the Washington, D.C. law firm of Patton, Boggs, & Blow and works in the Denver office. He has practiced environmental and natural resources law for over 20 years and has written and spoken extensively on the Clean Water Act, TSCA, hazardous waste, biotechnology, and other areas of environmental law. In addition, Mr. Arbuckle played a major role in developing and securing enactment of the Deepwater Ports Act and the Deep Seabed Hard Mineral Resources Act, as well as certain provisions of other environmental laws, including RCRA, the Clean Water Act and CERCLA.

In his practice, Mr. Arbuckle has represented clients in petitions filed under RCRA and in hearings on Clean Water Act permits. Among others, he represented the consortium of businesses that formed the Louisiana Offshore Oil Port in the legislative and administrative efforts necessary to obtain governmental approval, complete construction and continue operations. Further, Mr. Arbuckle is an author of the *Environmental Health and Safety Manager's Handbook* and *SARA Title III Law and Regulations,* and has written several articles concerning criminal liability under environmental statutes.

## Mary Elizabeth Bosco

Ms. Bosco is a partner with the law firm of Patton, Boggs & Blow where she specializes in environmental law and litigation. Her experience includes representing clients before EPA in connection with the underground storage tank and used oil regulations, as well as Superfund litigation. She is a contributing author to *Regulation of the Gas Industry,* (Mathew Bender 1989). Ms. Bosco is a 1978 graduate of Yale University and a 1983 graduate of George Washington University Law School with honors.

## David R. Case

Mr. Case is General Counsel for the Hazardous Waste Treatment Council, a trade association of hazardous waste firms in Washington, D.C. He was formerly with the law firm of Crowell & Moring where he specialized in environmental law. He was a chairman of the Environmental Pollution Committee and deputy chairman of the Council of Natural Resources and Lands of the Federal Bar Association. He has authored articles and lectured on environmental regulation under RCRA, Superfund, the Clean Air Act, the Clean Water Act, and other federal and state environmental programs. Mr. Case received his B.A. from Amherst College, his LL.B Cantab. from Cambridge University, and his law degree from the University of Michigan Law School.

### Elliott P. Laws

Mr. Laws is an attorney at Patton, Boggs & Blow in Washington, D.C., specializing in environmental law and litigation. Prior to joining Patton, Boggs & Blow, he was a trial attorney with the Environmental Defense Section in the Justice Department's Land and Natural Resources Division. There he represented EPA in both District Court and appellate cases, and served as trial counsel for other federal agencies involved in environmental litigation. He was formerly an enforcement attorney in the Water Enforcement Division of EPA's Office of Enforcement and Compliance Monitoring, participating in the agency's enforcement and policy development efforts under the Clean Water, Marine Protection Research and Sanctuaries, and Safe Drinking Water Acts. A former prosecutor in New York City, he also has a broad range of criminal experience.

### John C. Martin

Mr. Martin is a partner in the law firm of Patton, Boggs & Blow where he specializes in environmental law and litigation. He was formerly a trial attorney with the Department of Justice's Lands and Natural Resources Division where he litigated a broad spectrum of environmental issues, representing EPA. He was the recipient of a Special Achievement Award for his efforts in Superfund litigation and successfully litigated many penalty cases, including one in which the court rendered the largest judgment ever handed down in an environmental case brought by the federal government. He previously served as an attorney in the Solicitor's Office at the Department of the Interior.

### Marshall Lee Miller

Mr. Miller is an attorney in Washington, D.C., specializing in the areas of environmental law, occupational health and safety, and international transactions. Mr. Miller was previously Special Assistant to the Administrator of the U.S. Environmental Protection Agency, Chief EPA Judicial Officer, Associate Deputy Attorney General in the U.S. Department of Justice, and Deputy Administrator of the Occupational Safety and Health Administration. He was educated at Harvard, Oxford, Heidelberg, and Yale.

## Robert D. Moran

Mr. Moran is a Washington, D.C. lawyer who specializes in occupational safety and health law. For the past fourteen years his practice has included advising and representing business and industry throughout the country in OSHA-related matters. He was a U.S. Wage and Hour Administrator in 1969 and headed the task force that planned the implementation of the Occupational Safety and Health Act and the formation of OSHA. He then served a 6-year term on the U.S. Occupational Safety and Health Review Commission and was its first Chairman. He previously served as Associate Commissioner of Labor and Industries for the Commonwealth of Massachusetts, Chairman of the State Board of Conciliation and Arbitration, and Chairman of the Minimum Wage Commission. He has written and lectured extensively on occupational safety and health law over the past 20 years.

## Russell V. Randle

Mr. Randle is a partner in the Washington, D.C. office of the national law firm of Patton, Boggs & Blow, where his experience includes litigation, counseling, and administrative proceedings under the Clean Water Act, CERCLA, the Clean Air Act, RCRA, the Safe Drinking Water Act, NEPA, and other environmental statutes. He graduated magna cum laude from Princeton University, earned his law degree from Yale Law School, where he was an editor of the Law Journal, and served as law clerk to the Honorable John H. Pratt of the United States District Court for the District of Columbia. Prior to his clerkship, he worked in various capacities for the Environmental Protection Agency, Congressman Gilbert Guale, and the National Commission on Water Quality.

## Daniel M. Steinway

Mr. Steinway is a partner in the Washington, D.C. office of Anderson, Kill, Olick & Oshinsky. He has previously served as minority counsel responsible for environmental matters on the Committee on Science and Technology of the U.S. House of Representatives, and as an attorney-advisor with the Office of Enforcement of the U.S. Environmental Protection Agency. He is also a vice chairman, Subcommittee on Alternate Energy Sources, in the Section of Natural Resources Law of the American Bar Association and is the chairman of the Steering Committee, Environmental Law Committee of the Federal Bar Association. He is a member of the District of Columbia Bar and the State of Michigan Bar. Mr. Steinway received a B.S.E. from the University of Michigan and a J.D. from the George Washington University National Law Center.

## Richard G. Stoll

Mr. Stoll is a partner in the Washington, D.C. law firm of Freedman, Levy, Kroll & Simonds where he specializes in environmental law--primarily in the hazardous waste area. His former positions include Deputy General Counsel of the Chemical Manufacturers Association and Assistant General Counsel of the U.S. Environmental Protection Agency. Previously serving as Vice Chairman, he is currently Chairman of the American Bar Association's Section of Natural Resources, Energy, and Environmental Law. He has served as Chairman of the Section's Solid and Hazardous Waste Committee. Mr. Stoll is a magna cum laude graduate of Westminister College in Missouri and received his law degree from Georgetown University. He has taught a course in environmental law and policy at the University of Virginia for the last eight years.

## Thomas F. P. Sullivan

Mr. Sullivan is an attorney in Washington, D.C. who has been in the forefront of the environmental field since the 1960s. He has a science degree, and he gained experience in industry before practicing law and representing clients in the environmental field. He now has more than 25 years experience, has authored numerous books and is a regular lecturer internationally on environmental topics. He serves as President of Government Institutes, Inc. Mr. Sullivan has undergraduate degrees from Cardinal Glennon College and St. Louis University, and his law degree from Catholic University.

## Timothy A. Vanderver, Jr.

Mr. Vanderver is a partner in the law firm of Patton, Boggs & Blow, located in Washington, D.C. His practice focuses on Superfund, RCRA and other environmental concerns, including the National Environmental Policy Act, water pollution law, air pollution law, solid waste disposal and land development. His previous experience includes government service in senior positions of responsibility where he specialized in environmental law with the Department of the Interior and the Department of Housing and Urban Development. After receiving his undergraduate degree from Washington & Lee University, he was selected as a Rhodes Scholar and received his Masters in law from Oxford University. He obtained his law degree from Harvard.

**Paul A. J. Wilson**

Mr. Wilson is a partner with Patton, Boggs & Blow in Washington, D.C. He holds a B.A. from the University of Massachusetts, an M.A. from Northwestern University, and a J.D. from the University of Virginia, where he was executive editor of the *Virginia Journal of Natural Resources Law*. From 1975 through 1980, Mr. Wilson worked at the U.S. Environmental Protection Agency in the pesticides, mobile source air pollution control and toxic substances programs. While with the EPA, he was twice awarded the agency's Bronze Medal for commendable service. Since entering private practice, Mr. Wilson has practiced in the areas of Superfund, EPCRA, RCRA, TSCA, as well as other major environmental laws.

# Chapter 1


# FUNDAMENTALS OF ENVIRONMENTAL LAW

J. Gordon Arbuckle
Patton, Boggs & Blow
Washington, D.C. and
Denver, Colorado

Thomas F. P. Sullivan, Esq.
Government Institutes, Inc.
Rockville, Maryland

This chapter introduces the Environmental Law field and provides an overall context or roadmap for use in understanding and applying the information provided in the chapters that follow.


## 1.0 ENVIRONMENTAL LAW AS A SYSTEM

Environmental Law is more than simply a collection of laws on environmental subjects. The field is one which cannot be mastered simply by learning the specific requirements of the individual laws and regulations governing conduct impacting the environment. Over the past few decades, "Environmental Law" has evolved into a *system* of statutes, regulations, guidelines, factual conclusions and case specific interpretations which relate one to another in the context of generally accepted principles established during the history (short though it may be) of the field. The system is complex in itself and is made even more challenging by the difficulty of the subject matter to be regulated (man's activities and the environment) and the problems which the law often has in dealing with the scientific issues and uncertainties nearly always faced in environmental cases.

Understanding this Environmental Law System, its unifying principles and the ways in which the individual elements work together to achieve the system's objectives is a challenge for those who either practice or try to comply with environmental laws. This book is intended to provide assistance in meeting that challenge.

## 2.0 DEFINING OUR SUBJECT MATTER--WHAT IS ENVIRONMENTAL LAW?

The key to understanding a system as complex as environmental law is the definition of the subject. The best definition we have found is:

> The Environmental Law System is an organized way of using all of the laws in our legal system to minimize, prevent, punish or remedy the consequences of actions which damage or threaten the environment, public health and safety.

By this definition, the thing that makes a law or regulation a part of the environmental law system is not its label or original function but the purpose for which it is used. It would be a mistake, for example, to assume that a compilation of the federal "environmental statutes" enacted since about 1970 to regulate the various activities which pollute or might pollute the environment would include the entire body of environmental law or even most of it. It would also be a mistake to think that the "Criminal Code" or the "Administrative Procedure Act" does not contain important "Environmental" laws.

When we talk about the Environmental Law System, then, we are referring to all aspects of our Legal System--the Constitution, statutes, regulations, rules of evidence, rules of procedure, judicial interpretations, the common law and, indeed, the criminal law--to the extent that these elements are being applied towards environmental ends. "Environmental Law" is best defined--not as a book or compilation of certain laws, but, instead, as a *system* for using *all* of the laws for environmental, public health and safety purposes. The reader should note that over the years, the term environment has been greatly expanded to also encompass protecting public health and workers' safety.

In summary, environmental law encompasses all the protections for our environment that emanate from the:

(1) United States Constitution and state constitutions,
(2) federal and state statutes and local ordinances,
(3) regulations promulgated by federal, state and local agencies,
(4) court decisions interpreting these laws and regulations and,
(5) the common law.

### 2.1 How a Federal or State Law is Made[1]

Federal and state legislative processes are similar; the federal procedure is used here for illustration. First a bill is introduced in either the House of

---

[1] For a more comprehensive treatment of how laws and regulations are made the reader is referred to Al Coco's, *Finding the Law* (Government Institutes, 1982).

Representatives or the Senate. Each bill is assigned a bill number preceded by S. if in the Senate, H.R. if in the House of Representatives, e.g. S. 100 or H.R. 222. Bills are referred to committee for consideration. The committee(s) in considering a bill, may hold hearings, study, investigate, and issue a report and a recommendation on whether or not the bill should pass. When a bill is reported out of committee, it is placed on a calendar in the respective house, considered, debated, and, if passed, it becomes an act. In the environmental field, the House and Senate generally pass different bills and a conference of House and Senate representatives resolves the differences. After passage in both the House of Representatives and the Senate, the act is sent to the President of the United States. The act will become law if it is signed by the President of the United States or if the act is not vetoed within ten days.

## 2.2 How Regulations Are Made[2]

Environmental statutes generally empower an administrative agency, like the U.S. Environmental Protection Agency (EPA), to develop and promulgate regulations. The President may also empower an executive agency to promulgate regulations through an Executive Order.

The rule-making process is one of publishing proposed regulations in the *Federal Register*; providing opportunity for the public to comment either through submission of written comments or through public hearings that concern the regulations; and publishing final regulations in the *Federal Register* which have the force and effect of law when they become effective. Annually the regulations are combined into the Code of Federal Regulations (C.F.R.).

## 3.0 HOW DOES THE SYSTEM WORK?

Most systems develop characteristic sets of duties and compliance requirements adapted to the subject matter and circumstances being regulated. The Environmental Law System is no exception to this rule. There are about eight generic compliance obligations or regulatory approaches which are utilized, in some combination, by virtually all of the environmental laws discussed in the later chapters of this book. Understanding these duties and obligations, the ways they work together and the ends they are intended to achieve is critical to an understanding of the subject matter of this text.

The eight primary compliance obligations are:

---

[2] *See* Coco, *op. cit.*

## 3.1 Notification Requirements

> -- to advise appropriate authorities, employees and often the public of intended or actual releases of pollutants, violations of discharge limits or other prohibitions and of the commencement of activities, such as resource extraction or construction,which may have significant environmental impacts.

Like our tax laws, the environmental laws place on the regulated community the obligation to provide to the regulators the information required to regulate and to those put at risk the information needed to avoid it. These duties to notify, the cornerstone of virtually all of the environmental statutes, take various forms--requirements to file permit applications before commencing an activity or discharge, periodic monitoring and compliance reports, non-compliance reporting, spill or release reporting, product labeling, exposure notifications, annual inventory reporting and so on.

Since these notification, monitoring and self-reporting requirements are so critical to operation of the environmental law system, they are broadly interpreted and vigorously enforced. The questions of: "Is notice required?" and "How should it be given and kept current?," are central to operation of the system and among the most critical to be faced in environmental law practice and compliance efforts. An understanding of various notification requirements, how they work and what they seek to achieve, is an important part of understanding environmental law.

## 3.2 Point of Discharge or "Waste End" Controls

> -- to prevent or acceptably minimize the release of pollutants into the environment.

These controls, variously referred to as "emission limits", "effluent limitations", "exposure limits", "design, construction and operating standards", "closure requirements" or "discharge prohibitions", are imposed at the point where pollutants are discharged, disposed of or released to the environment. They are probably the oldest and perhaps still the most prevalent type of pollution control requirement. The level of effectiveness or "standard of performance" required to be achieved by these point of discharge controls is generally set by reference to the limits of technological practicability or possibility, health effects levels, environmental effects levels or a combination of all of the above. The process for developing these limits involves the intricacies and uncertainties of risk analysis, difficult scientific issues, an ill-adapted legal system and a lack of public consensus about "how clean is clean?" or "how safe is "safe enough?" The process is and will remain a major challenge to be faced in this field.

## 3.3 Process Oriented Controls and Pollution Prevention

-- to reduce the quantities, prevent the release and minimize the hazardous characteristics of wastes which are generated.

Sometimes it is not practical to directly control the discharge of pollutants and necessary, for that reason, to require protective actions in the plant or process--before the waste is generated. The simplest example of this type of control approach is that used with respect to unanticipated spills. Since these discharges are unanticipated, it is impractical to treat them. We therefore try to prevent them by requiring the adoption of spill prevention and containment programs and by requiring maintenance of tank integrity and leak detection systems. Similarly, if it is impractical to treat plant site run-off, we consider mandating management practices to keep the run-off from becoming contaminated and to minimize its volume. More sophisticated process oriented controls, such as substitution of solvents and other materials used and aggressive reduction in the use of water and other waste generating consumables, are becoming increasingly popular ways of attaining environmental objectives and are sometimes mandated, particularly at the state level.

## 3.4 Product Oriented Controls

-- to assure that products are designed, formulated, packaged or used so that they themselves do not present unreasonable risks to human health or the environment when either used or disposed of.

Environmental effects of use or disposal of a product can be as severe as those of the process by which the products are manufactured. This is clearly true, for example, in the case of the automobile, and it has long been recognized that tailpipe emissions and fuel efficiency are appropriate subjects for environmental regulation. Other products, such as asbestos building materials, have been perceived to be so inherently hazardous as to require a ban on new product sales and regulation of the product in place. Regulation of PCBs under the Toxic Substances Control Act is an example of stringent product control regulation extending to a phasing out and elimination of nearly all existing product uses. Product controls are the primary regulatory mechanism for pesticide products. The states are becoming increasingly active in the development of product and packaging standards focused towards minimization of solid waste generation and disposal problems and we can expect federal law to follow that lead.

## 3.5 Regulation of Activities

-- to protect resources, species or ecological amenities.

In some instances an activity, regardless of the stringency with which its processes, waste streams and products are regulated, cannot take place at a particular location or time, exploit a particular resource or otherwise be conducted without impacts which are arguably unacceptable. The regulatory approaches which seek to protect resources, species or environmental amenities through control or curtailment of activities up to the present have usually focussed on the protection of especially significant areas--like wetlands under the Clean Water Act Section 404 permit program or beaches and coastal margins under the Coastal Zone Management Act--fragile species--like the Northern Spotted Owl and the Arizona Red Squirrel under the Endangered Species Act--or irreplaceable amenities--like "Ancient Forests"--which environmentalists are seeking to preserve through actions under the National Environmental Policy Act, the Endangered Species Act and other laws. These arguments about threatened species, fragile ecosystems and priceless amenities do not find ready compromises, are often not soluble by the expenditure of money or application of technology and almost always involve scientific issues, both real and spurious, on the margins of available knowledge. Procedures to handle these issues are developed in the heat of contention and are often ill adapted to achievement of resolution without frequent resort to courts and the Congress. This kind of focus on direct regulation of activities, rather than merely their consequences, will become more common as the focus of environmental law continues to shift from local issues, like hazardous wastes sites, to problems of the planet, like global warming, species diversity and desertification, which can be dealt with, some argue, only by major and wide scale changes in the way people live and organize their institutions. This form of regulation will likely continue to occupy a place on the cutting edge of the system's development.

## 3.6 Safe Transportation Requirements

-- to acceptably minimize the risks inherent in transportation of hazardous wastes or materials, oil or other potentially harmful substances.

These laws and regulations intended to protect the environment from spills and other incidents occurring during the transportation process are an important part of the environmental law system. These laws include the Hazardous Materials Transportation Act and the formidable regulations thereunder, the Oil Pollution Act of 1990, the Tank Vessel Statutes and implementing Coast Guard regulations, some international agreements and treaties, Sections 311 and 312 of the Clean Water Act, the RCRA manifest requirements and other parts of the system of laws and regulations applicable to transportation. They require, in essence, that covered substances be identified, packed properly in proper containers, labeled, loaded onto a placarded, properly designed, built and maintained truck, tanker, pipeline or other transportation mode and delivered to an appropriate site. Adequate financial responsibility is to be maintained and demonstrated throughout the process and careful records are to be kept of everything picked up and everything delivered to its ultimate destination. In some instances, the ability to respond to a spill must be maintained. In every instance, appropriate notifications, in the event of a spill, must be given.

### 3.7 Response and Remediation Requirements

-- to clean up pollutants which have been released, prevent the threat of release or pay the costs of that clean-up or prevention.

After a release or threatened release is discovered, through notification or otherwise, the response and remediation provisions of laws like section 311 of the Clean Water Act, Sections 106 and 107 of the "Superfund" law governing clean up of abandoned hazardous waste dump sites -- and the closure provisions of the Resource Conservation and Recovery Act' which require "responsible parties" to clean up the problem or authorize the government or private parties to clean up the problem and recover the clean up costs from the responsible parties. These requirements that responsible parties bear the cost of remedying problems alleged to result from their wastes are among the most complicated and controversial in the environmental law system. The critical questions are: "Who is responsible for the release or threatened release?", "What is the technical fix or remedy?" and "How will the costs of the remedy be shared among the responsible parties?"

### 3.8 Compensation Requirements

-- to make responsible parties pay private parties, or groups of them, for damages done to their health or environment or to permit self-appointed representatives of the "public interest" recover for injuries done to public assets.

If all other regulatory approaches are unsuccessful in preventing or remedying damage to health or the environment, we need to examine the possibility of making the responsible party pay for that damage. CERCLA and the Oil Pollution Act of 1990, for example, have provisions creating public rights of action for damage to natural resources. Those laws may also create private rights of action for damages caused by spills. Although these statutory compensation mechanisms are important, an even more pervasive set of mechanisms for enforcing obligations to compensate for damage, including that to the environment, is embodied in the "Common Law" which has been developed by courts and judges through the resolution of cases and controversies that have arisen in the last seven hundred or so years. The compensation cases involve larger dollar amounts, probably more complex scientific issues and perhaps more public attention, than any other category of environmental law cases.

These eight compliance obligations or regulatory approaches: *Notification* requirements, *Discharge* limits, *Process* controls, *Product* controls, *Activity* controls, *Transportation* standards, *Response* requirements and *Compensation* requirements are the vital functional organs of the legal system which is this book's subject. Now we need to look at the laws and governmental institutions that define these organs, make them work and establish the framework within which they operate.

## 4.0 LAWS THAT ESTABLISH COMPLIANCE OBLIGATIONS

The natural resource laws such as the Endangered Species Act and those related to fish, wildlife, oil and gas exploration, forests and more are covered in the *Natural Resources Law Handbook* published by Government Institutes. Although important to protection of our ecology, we have elected to approach these from the natural resource perspective and focus herein on environmental laws.

### 4.1 Major Environmental Laws

Subsequent chapters of this book describe the regulatory programs in place under the major federal environmental statutes of concern to U.S. industry. These environmental laws define most of the substantive compliance obligations of the environmental law system. The major federal environmental statutes do not, however, operate alone. There are other components of "environmental laws" that supplement, complement, or go beyond the programs which the federal environmental statutes establish. These are described in the following sections.

### 4.2 State Statutes and Regulations Implementing the Federal Statutes

Many of the federal statutes, like the Clean Air Act or Clean Water Act, establish federal-state regulatory programs in which the states are given the opportunity to enact and enforce laws, meeting federal minimum criteria, to achieve the regulatory objectives which the Congress has established. In most instances where the states have had the opportunity to take over regulatory programs in their jurisdictions, they have done so. States are generally the primary permitting and enforcement authorities subject to federal intervention only if they do not enforce effectively or rigorously enough.

Generally, the states are not precluded from enforcing criteria more stringent than those required by the federal laws, and are given considerable leeway to follow enforcement interpretations which may not be fully consistent with those applied at the federal level. Thus the laws and interpretations used to apply and enforce the federal laws may vary considerably from state to state and these variations may not be readily apparent. Government Institutes has published a separate state environmental law handbook on each state. Reference should be made to these to fully understand environmental obligations in a specific state.

### 4.3 State Laws Independent of the Federal Requirements

The trend is for states, particularly certain states -- like California and New Jersey -- to take initiatives to provide their citizens and their environments with protections or information beyond that generally available under the federal statutes. Examples of laws generated by this trend include:

-- **Toxic Waste Minimization Laws** - like one in Massachusetts which imposes mandatory waste reduction objectives on companies which use or generate toxic or hazardous wastes.

-- **Environmental Full Disclosure Laws** - like California Proposition 65, which requires extraordinary efforts to make the public aware of health risks associated with products or environments to which they are exposed.

-- **Property Transfer Environmental Laws** - like the New Jersey law, which requires extensive investigation and cleanup of contaminated sites before they are sold or transferred.

-- **State Groundwater Protection Laws** - Although the federal government has not yet adopted comprehensive groundwater protection legislation, many, if not most of the states, have detailed permit programs.

The list could go on, including state citizen's action laws, laws compelling response at hazardous substance sites not on the federal superfund list, facility siting laws, laws governing the operation of publicly owned treatment works and landfills, asbestos abatement and so forth and so on. State laws in many states may be a more important factor in dictating the focus of compliance programs than the laws which exist at the federal level. Commensurate attention is clearly warranted.

### 4.4 Tax Laws

There is a trend at both the state and federal levels towards using the tax laws to create incentives towards environmentally benign products and activities and disincentives against products and activities considered to be environmentally detrimental. Gas guzzler taxes, recycling tax credits, taxes on use of virgin materials, taxes on hazardous waste generation and excise taxes on various products are among the approaches which have been adopted or seriously discussed. These approaches and other economic incentive oriented strategies will clearly be more vigorously promoted over the next few years.

## 4.5 Business Regulatory Laws

The Federal Trade Commission and a number of state attorneys general have initiatives to use their ordinary business regulatory authorities to police environmental claims made for products. The Securities Exchange Commission has for some time required full disclosure of environmental liabilities in statements and reports falling under its jurisdiction.

The innovative abilities of both state and federal officials will continue to be applied towards effective utilization of all the laws in their arsenal in an effort to enforce increasingly stringent standards of protection for health, safety and the environment. The limits on this kind of creativity are yet to be seen and are unlikely to be reached in the immediate future because environmental protection is a political asset.

## 4.6 Local and Municipal Laws

While local governmental entities have not yet been as pervasively involved in environmental regulation as their counterparts at the state and federal levels, the localities do have great powers to control the location and operation of facilities within their jurisdictions and are often able to effectively utilize this authority. Active community involvement and participation in consideration of local ordinances is, for a number of businesses, essential to continued ability to profitably operate. While it is difficult to generalize, issues which warrant particularly careful attention include the operation of the local waterworks and waste treatment plants, local recycling initiatives and associated product initiatives, zoning and noise control ordinances, nuisance laws, air emission requirements, landfill restrictions or closures, local emergency planning and initiatives relating to waste site cleanup. In every instance, the impact of this kind of local action can be as immediate and severe as that of any taken at the state or federal level. From the perspective of an environmental law compliance program, local does not mean trivial. It means immediate, important, largely unreviewable, and deserving of considerable attention. Effective environmental compliance requires acceptance and dealing with these facts of life.

## 4.7 Environmental Law and Judicial Decisions

As the courts interpret the environmental laws and regulations and apply them to specific factual situations, they are continually determining what the law actually means in factual situations. In order to gain the proper understanding of court decisions, a basic knowledge of the United States court system is needed. The courts and their role are described later in this chapter.

## 4.8 Common Law

Underlying the development of legal theory in the United States is a body of rules and principles relating to the government and security of persons and property which had its origin, development and formulation in England.

Brought to the American colonies by peoples of Anglo-Saxon stock, these basic rules were formally adopted in the states in which they were in force after the American Revolution. Known as the "common law," these principles are derived from the application of natural reason, an innate sense of justice and the dictates of conscience. The common law is not the result of legislative enactment. Rather, its authority is derived solely from usages and customs which have been recognized, affirmed and enforced by the courts through judicial decisions.

It is important to realize that "common law" is not a fixed or absolute set of written rules in the same sense as statutory or legislatively enacted law. The unwritten principles of common law are flexible and adaptable to the changes which occur in a growing society. New institutions and public policies; modifications of usage and practice; changes in mores, trade, and commerce; inventions; and increasing knowledge, all generate new factual situations which require application and reinterpretation of the fundamental principles of common law by the courts.

As the courts examine each new set of facts in the light of past precedent, an orderly development of common laws occurs through a slow and natural process. Thus, the basic principles underlying American jurisprudence remain fundamentally constant, evolving slowly and progressively.

The common law, so far as it has not been expressly abrogated, is recognized as an organic part of the jurisprudence of most of the states. The major exception is Louisiana jurisprudence, which is based on Roman law--a relic of French rule prior to the Louisiana Purchase. However, since the state court systems have functioned independently of each other, subject only to federal review in cases of national importance, the common law varies slightly from state to state.

The common law actions that we will discuss in subsequent sections are civil suits in which the plaintiff (the party bringing the lawsuit) seeks to remedy a violation of a right. Civil actions are distinguished from criminal proceedings. Criminal actions are those in which the state seeks to redress a breach of public or collective rights which are established in codified penal law. Subsequent sections of this chapter review the three most frequently used types of common law actions that can be the basis of a lawsuit in the pollution control field: nuisance, trespass, and negligence.

### 4.9 Torts

"Tort" is the word used to denote a common law private wrong or wrongful act for which a civil action can be brought by the injured party.

A tort arises from the existence of a generalized legal duty to avoid causing harm to others, through acts of omission, as well as of commission. Every adult person is obliged to fulfill a duty of care for the personal and property rights of others while engaged in daily life. Carelessness in exercising this responsibility may give rise to a cause of action (a lawsuit) by means of which the injured party may seek restitution. This duty is noncontractual; that is, it does not arise from an explicit promissory agreement between the parties to the action. So a tort is also distinguished from a contract right which is dependent upon the contract itself.

Tens of thousands of tort lawsuits have been filed involving asbestos cases and other toxic chemical litigation. These cases have prompted some writers to allege that the 1990s will be the era of "toxic torts." It is clear that tort law will be of considerable interest to industry in the future as its role expands.

The three types of torts most commonly encountered in the environmental field are: (1) nuisance; (2) trespass, and (3) negligence, which are each described in following sections.

### 4.9.1 Nuisance

Nuisance is defined as "that class of wrongs that arise from the unreasonable, unwarrantable or unlawful use by a person of his own property, either real or personal, or from his own improper, indecent, or unlawful personal conduct, working an obstruction of or injury to the right of another or of the public, and producing material annoyance, inconvenience, discomfort or hurt.[3]

The general rule is that a person may use his land or personal property in any manner he sees fit. However, this rule is subject to limitation: the owner must use his property in a reasonable manner. A nuisance arises whenever a person uses his property to cause material injury or annoyance to his neighbor.

In determining whether a given act constitutes a nuisance, the court considers the nature of the act itself. The discomfort must amount to a material injury or annoyance. It must tangibly affect the physical or mental health of ordinary people under normal circumstances or conditions.

### 4.9.1.1 Noise Nuisance

The most common form of environmental nuisance is noise pollution. Noise produced by human activities is a common environmental problem. In order to constitute a nuisance in the legal sense, generally, noise must be of such magnitude and intensity as to cause actual or psychological discomfort to persons of ordinary sensibilities. Noise from the operation of an industrial plant constitutes an actionable nuisance if it affects injuriously the health or comfort of *ordinary* people in the plant's vicinity to an *unreasonable* extent. The courts and legislatures have had difficulty in setting an absolute standard, so this determination rests on the facts.

*O'Neill v. Carolina Freight Carriers Corp.*[4] is an example of a "noise nuisance" case in which a homeowner was awarded both an injunction and damages against the operators of a nearby business. In this case, the

---

[3] *Black's Law Dictionary* 961 (5th ed. 1979).

[4] 156 Conn. 613, 244 A.2d 372 (1988).

plaintiffs showed that they were ordinary people and that the noise from trucks and loading operations at a terminal located immediately adjacent to their home was unreasonable. It caused them loss of sleep and prevented general enjoyment of their home. The court ruled that the truck terminal noises between 11:00 p.m. and 6:00 a.m. were unreasonable and that every property owner must make reasonable use of his land so as not to cause unnecessary annoyance to his neighbors.

In the *O'Neill* case, the facts lead readily to a conclusion of injury to health because the noise during the night could logically cause loss of sleep and resulting injury to health.

There is no fixed standard as to what degree or kind of noise constitutes a nuisance. The circumstances of each case must be considered independently. Generally, the key determination is whether or not the noise is unreasonable and causes some physical or psychological harm. This determination varies from one community to another and from one period of time to another depending on local attitudes and customs.

### 4.9.1.2 Other Nuisances

Smoke, dust, odors, other airborne pollutants, water pollutants and hazardous substances have also been held to be nuisances.

The *Ozark Poultry Products* case,[5] is an example of an odor being classed as a nuisance. In this Arkansas case, nine homeowners in the vicinity of a rendering plant brought suit to abate the odor nuisance created by operation of the plant. They claimed that odors from the rendering plant caused them to feel nausea and to lose sleep at night. On the witness stand, the plant manager admitted that operation of the plant violated existing law. The court found the plant to be a public nuisance, and the homeowners obtained a court order to close the plant unless conditions causing the nuisance were corrected within a time limit established by the court.

In a New York case, *McCarty v. Natural Carbonic Gas Co.*,[6] the plaintiffs owned a home adjacent to the defendant's manufacturing plant. The plaintiffs claimed that under specific wind conditions, black smoke settled about their home causing them discomfort, annoyance and injury. The court determined that the operation of the manufacturing plant resulted in an unreasonable use of property, because all the damage could be avoided by use of hard coal or by use of some modern emission control systems. Although either would involve an increase in expenses, the court held that the safety of persons, generally, is superior in right to a particular use of a single piece of property by its owner. So the court awarded the decision to the plaintiffs.

---

[5] *Ozark Poultry Products, Inc. v. Garmon*, 251 Ark. 389, 472 S.W. 2d 714 (1971).

[6] 189 N.Y. 40, 81 N.E. 549 (1907).

It should be noted that air pollutants only constitute a nuisance under certain circumstances. Normal air is usually considered as that common to a locality and so varies from one area to another. To be a nuisance, the air pollution must cause harm and discomfort to ordinary people to an unreasonable extent.

In the case of *Chicago v. Commonwealth Edison*[7] the court refused to issue an injunction against alleged air pollution. The court found that although the public had a right to clean air, the notion of pure air has come to mean clean air consistent with the character of the locality and the attending circumstances. The court ruled that "The City has failed to answer the threshold question of whether Commonwealth Edison's Indiana facility causes substantial harm so as to constitute an actionable invasion of a public right. In order to be entitled to injunctive relief a substantial harm or injury must be clearly demonstrated." This case is a strict interpretation of the law of nuisance because it was a request for an injunction to cease operation which would have a broad impact on employment and local economics. If the action had been for damages, the court may have decided it differently by not using a strict interpretation of the law.

In *Harrison v. Indiana Auto Shredders*,[8] the Seventh Circuit Court of Appeals also refused to permanently enjoin operation of an automobile shredding and recycling plant based on a nuisance action. The court held that under the evidence presented and in the absence of an imminent hazard to health or welfare--none of which was established--the defendant could not be prevented from continuing to engage in its operation. In addition, the court believed that the operation should be allowed a reasonable time to correct any defects not posing threats of imminent or substantial harm.

In essence, the courts were not convinced by the evidence presented in these last two cases that harm caused by the alleged nuisance was so great as to justify forcing them to cease operation. If these facilities were shut down, many families would be injured by the forced unemployment. So the weighing of equities by the court resulted in a determination based on all the evidence presented in favor of allowing continued operations. This is generally called "balancing the equities."

An unusual type of nuisance case of considerable notoriety and interest involved the construction of the 110-story Sears building in Chicago.[9] In this case, the plaintiffs requested an injunction to prevent completion of the building which they claimed would constitute a nuisance by distorting television reception in surrounding areas. The court held that Sears had a legal right to

---

[7] 24 Ill. App. 624, 321 N.E. 2d 412, 7 Env't. Rep.Case. (BNA) 1974.

[8] 528 F.2d 1107, 8 Env't Rep. Cas. (BNA) 1569 (7th Cir. 1975).

[9] *People ex rel Hoogasian v. Sears, Roebuck and Co.*, 52 Ill. 2d 301, 287 N.E. 2d 677 (1972), *cert. denied*, 409 U.S. 1001 (1972).

use the airspace above its property, at least as much as it can occupy or use in connection with the land, subject only to legislative limitation.

The Earthline Corporation, a subsidiary of SCA Services, Inc., attempted to operate an industrial waste recovery, treatment, storage and disposal site on a 130-acre site in Illinois. Ninety acres are located within the Village of Wilsonville and the remaining acres adjacent to the village. The operation accepted hazardous wastes and toxic substances. The Village sued Earthline to stop the operation and also to require the removal of those hazardous wastes and toxic substances that had been deposited on the site.[10] The court ruled that the site was a public/private nuisance, issued an injunction against Earthline's further operation of the site and required them to remove all wastes and contaminated soil.

It is most important to note that this case was decided against SCA even though there was no showing that SCA had violated any government regulation. Compliance with government regulations is not a defense against a common law nuisance action. Also, the lower court decision emphasized a nuisance does not require a showing of any negligence on the part of the defendant. Nuisance and negligence are distinct torts and except in the cases of nuisances created by negligence, liability for nuisance does not depend upon the existence of negligence. Negligence is not an essential or material element of a cause of action for nuisance and need not be pleaded or proved especially where the thing complained of is a nuisance per se or a public nuisance or results from ultra-hazardous conduct on the part of the defendant. A nuisance is a condition and not an act or a failure to act on the part of the person responsible for the condition.

### 4.9.1.3    Some Defenses to Nuisance Actions

Nuisance actions have often been decided by balancing the equities (weighing the impact of the injuries to respective parties involved in litigation). In any balancing of the equities, the good faith efforts of the polluter, while not absolving him, would be a factor.[11]

The availability of pollution control devices is, of course, a significant factor that can be considered by the court. For example, in *Renkin v. Harvey Aluminum,*[12] the court noted Harvey Aluminum's failure to keep pace with technological advances in pollution controls. In that case the court ordered adoption of such controls.

In general, courts are moving to strict liability for environmental nuisances so that practically speaking, there are no good defenses. The solution is: do

---

[10] *Village of Wilsonville v. SCA Services, Inc.*, 77 Ill. App. 3d 618, 396 N.E. 2d 522 (1979), aff'd 86 Ill. 2d 1, 426 N.E. 2d 824 (1981).

[11] *McElwain v. Georgia Pacific* , 245 Or. 247, 421 P.2d 957 (1986).

[12] 226 F. Supp. 169 (D. Or. 1963).

not create nuisances. If you have an existing nuisance, you are best advised to abate it.

### 4.9.1.4    Coming to a Nuisance

"Coming to a nuisance" is the phrase used to describe a defense that the complainant or plaintiff affected by the nuisance moved into the area where the "complained about activity" had already been in existence.

An example of "coming to a nuisance" occurs when someone moves onto property near to an airport or industrial complex and then complains of the nuisance that existed prior to his moving there. Generally, the fact that an individual purchases property with the knowledge of the existence of a nuisance or that he came to the nuisance will not defeat his right to the abatement of the nuisance or recovery of damages[13] nor will his right to recovery be affected if the property is sold to another while the lawsuit is pending.[14]

However, some cases have held that if the complainant came to a nuisance, this constitutes a defense to a nuisance lawsuit. This minority view is probably a result of an old axiom of law that one who voluntarily places himself in a situation whereby he suffers an injury will not prevail. The test of liability in these cases is often the knowledge of the plaintiff regarding the consequences of his conduct.

The majority rule, however, is that the fact alone that a person moved into the vicinity of a nuisance by purchasing or leasing property in the area does not bar him from complaining in an action against the continued operation or maintenance of the nuisance.[15] The majority rule is based on the theory that pure air and the comfortable enjoyment of property are as much rights belonging to it as the right of possession and occupancy. If population where there was none before approaches a nuisance, it is the duty of those liable to put an end to it.

### 4.9.2  Trespass

In a general sense, an invasion of another's rights is a "trespass." Usually, trespass is used in a more limited sense. It is to be understood as designating an injury to the person, property, or rights of another which is

---

[13] *Fertilizing Co. v. Hyde Park*, 97 U.S. 659 (1987); *Rentz v. Roach*, 154 Ga. 491, 115 S.E. 94 (1922); *Vann v. Bowie Sewerage Co.*, 127 Tex. 97, 90 S.W. 2d 561 (1936) are a few cases.

[14] *Abbott v. City of Princeton, Texas*, 721 S.W. 2d 872 (Tex.App.-Dallas 1986).

[15] A comprehensive article on this subject is found in 42 A.L.R. 3rd 344 (1972). This article includes a listing of cases by jurisdictions that recognize the majority rule.

the immediate result of some unlawful act.

In order to constitute trespass, unlawful intent is not necessary. Intent or motive with which the act was done is immaterial except as far as it may affect the measure of damages. A person is liable even if they acted in good faith and with reasonable care.

Trespass is commonly divided into three types. These are:

(1) **Trespass to personal property** is an injury to or interference with possession, with or without the exercise of physical force. This includes destruction of personal property as well as taking from the possession of another, or a refusal to surrender possession.

(2) **Trespass to the person** is an unlawful act committed on the person of another such as a vehicle impact or even an unauthorized operation. Mere words are not actionable trespass to the person.

(3) **Trespass to realty** is an unlawful, forcible entry on another's possession. An injury to the realty of another or an interference with possession, above or below ground, is a trespass, regardless of the condition of the land and regardless of negligence.

Trespass to realty is the type of trespass action that is generally used in pollution control cases. In an action for trespass to realty, entry upon another's land need not be in person. It may be made by causing or permitting a thing to cross the boundary of the premises. The trespass may be committed by casting material upon another's land, by discharging water, soot or carbon, by allowing gas or oil to flow underground into someone else's land, but not by mere vibrations or light which are generally classed as nuisances.

In the case of *Martin v. Reynolds Metal Co.*,[16] the deposit on Martin's property of microscopic fluoride compounds, which were emitted in vapor form from the Reynolds' plant, was held to be an invasion of this property -- and so a trespass.

Cases have distinguished between trespass and nuisance and held that encroachment of the space above the land is a nuisance. Generally there must be physical invasion of the property to constitute a trespass.

Some courts have used trespass and private nuisance almost interchangeably. The end result is that the distinction between trespass and nuisance is somewhat clouded.

Negligence and trespass have also been used interchangeably as seen in the case of *Stacy v. VEPCO*.[17] In this case, the court ruled that there was

---

[16] 221 Or. 86, 342 O. 2d 790 (1959), *cert. denied*, 362 U.S. 912 (1960).

[17] 7 Env't. Rep. Cas. (BNA) 1443 (E.d.Va. 1975).

"negligence and/or trespass on the part of VEPCO" because of damage caused to Stacy's trees by emissions from VEPCO's Mount Storm plant. It is interesting to note that the court in this case was convinced by the expert meteorologist's testimony that the emissions could travel the 22-mile distance from the plant to damage the trees. The important point to remember is that courts can and do minimize the concern with the form of the action, namely, whether it is a nuisance, trespass or negligence, but endeavor to do substantive justice based on all the evidence presented.

### 4.9.3 Negligence

"Negligence" is: (a) doing or omitting to do an act, (b) which a person owes to another by virtue of a legal duty imposed upon him by law, (c) thereby causing injury to the plaintiff or to his property. Negligence is that part of the law of torts which deals with acts not intended to inflict injury. If there is intent to inflict injury, then the case becomes one of criminal law.

The standard of care required by law is that degree which would be exercised by a person of ordinary prudence under the same circumstances. This is often defined as the "reasonable man" rule, what a reasonable person would do under all the circumstances.

In order to render the defendant liable, his act must be the proximate cause of injury. Proximate cause is that which in the natural and continuous sequence, if unbroken by an efficient intervening act, produces injury and without which the result would not have happened.

An example of a negligence action in a pollution case is *Burgess v. Tamano*.[18] This case involved the July 1972 spill of over 100,000 gallons of bunker oil from the tank ship *Tamano* into Maine's Casco Bay. Fishermen, boat owners, and property owners allegedly damaged by the spill brought suit against the *Tamano*, while Maine filed suit to recover damages sustained by the state as a result of the spill. Since the federal government has a great deal of money with which to pay damages, plaintiffs contended that the proximate cause of the escape and spread of oil from the *Tamano* was the Coast Guard's negligent conduct of its containment and cleanup operations. The court ruled that the United States, in undertaking any task such as pollution abatement, is liable in tort for the consequences of its negligence to the same extent that a private person would be liable.

The evidence convinced the court that the Coast Guard caused injury, which could be foreseen, by its inadequate containment and cleanup operation. Since this conduct was the proximate cause of injury to the plaintiff, the court held that the Coast Guard was guilty of negligence.

Persons harmed as a result of careless and improper disposal or handling of hazardous waste can recover for their losses under a negligence cause of action. Indeed, state and federal courts have long recognized this common law

---

[18] 5 Env't Rep. Cas. (BNA) 1914 (D.C. Me. 1973) and 6 Env't. Rep. Cas. (BNA) 1380 (D.C. Me. 1974).

theory of recovery against defendants who engage in the negligent disposal of pollutants such as hazardous waste.[19] Where negligence can be established, it is no defense that the negligent action was in full compliance with all government regulations[20] and permit conditions.[21] On the other hand, noncompliance with regulations or a permit in some states may be prima facie evidence (proof without any more evidence) of liability.[22]

### 4.9.3.1 Special Negligence Liability Concepts

Generations of creative lawyers have eased the burden of proving negligence or fault in some circumstances by developing the following negligence doctrines.

### 4.9.3.2 Violation of a Statute or Ordinance Can Be Negligence

Generally, the violation of a statute or ordinance which was passed to promote safety is negligence. But the violation of such law does not of itself give rise to civil liability. The plaintiff must show that the violation of the law was the proximate cause of the injury. The violation of a statute or ordinance, which is not designed to prevent the sort of harm about which the plaintiff is complaining, is not negligence.

An example of the application of this doctrine in an environmental lawsuit is the case of *Springer v. Schlitz Brewing Company*.[23] Mr. and Mrs. Springer owned a large farm downriver from a newly constructed Winston-Salem, N.C., brewery of Schlitz. They sued Schlitz for overloading the city's sewage treatment, causing it to pollute the Yadkin River, resulting in fish kills and so interfering with their riparian rights. In North Carolina, as in many other states, a riparian landowner has a right to the agricultural, recreational and scenic use and enjoyment of the stream bordering his land. A city sewage ordinance prohibited the discharge of pollutants that interfere with the city's waste treatment process.

In this case the plaintiff did not, according to the court's opinion, prove

---

[19] See, e.g., *Knabe v. National Supply Div. of Armco Steel Corp.*, 592 F.2d 841 (5th Cir. 1979).

[20] *Greater Westchester Homeowners Assoc. v. City of Los Angeles*, 26 Cal. 3d 86, 603 P.2d 1329 (1979), 160 Cal. Rptr. 733, *cert. denied*, 499 U.S. 820 (1980).

[21] *Brown v. Petroland, Inc.*, 102 Cal. App. 3d 720, 162 Cal. Rptr. 551 (1980); *Belton v. Wateree Power Co.*, 123 S.C. 291, 115 S.E. 587 (1922).

[22] See *Martin v. Hersog*, 288 N.Y. 164, 126 N.E. 814, 439 N.Y.S. 2d 922 (1920).

[23] 510 F.2d 468, 7 Env't. Rep. Cas. (BNA) 1516 (4th Cir. 1975).

that Schlitz was negligent in the conventional sense. Instead, the Court looked to the theory that violation of a city sewage ordinance is negligence "per se." The appeals court directed that the jury should decide if Schlitz violated the city's ordinance. If the jury decides that the ordinance was violated, then the violation is negligence per se; and if the negligence proximately causes injury, then the industry is liable irrespective of any good faith efforts on the part of the defendant.

So, violations of environmental or pollution control statutes or ordinances which are generally designed to protect the public health or safety could result in a successful negligence lawsuit by the injured party even though there is no factual showing of negligence.

### 4.9.3.3    Dangerous Substances--Strict Liability

Courts have ruled that a landowner keeping a potentially dangerous substance on his land which, if permitted to escape, is certain to injure others, must make good the damage caused by the escape of the substance, regardless of negligence on the defendant's part.

This strict liability theory is very old. It was used in a 1907 case where oil escaped into the Potomac River in Washington, D.C., and resulted in injury to boats in a downstream boathouse.[24] In this case, it was determined that a potentially dangerous substance is anything which, if permitted to escape, is certain to injure others. This description of a potentially dangerous substance is so broad as to include oil in the case under discussion plus thousands of other substances in subsequent litigation.

The reasoning for this strict liability standard is that, when persons suffer loss, no good reason can be found to charge the loss against anyone who did not contribute to it. If the defendant is engaged in an ultra-hazardous or dangerous activity for profit, he should bear the burden of compensating others who are harmed by his activities.

In making the determination of whether an activity is ultra-hazardous, courts have traditionally scrutinized six factors: (1) the existence of a high degree of risk, (2) the likelihood that resultant harm will be great, (3) the ability to eliminate risk by exercising reasonable care, (4) the extent to which activity is not common in the community, (5) the appropriateness of activity to the place where it is carried on, and (6) the activity's value to the community.

Not surprisingly, courts have applied strict liability theories in cases involving the disposal of hazardous waste and hazardous materials management.

The Common Law and the litigation it fosters will continue to be an important factor in determining the rate and direction of the development of the environmental law system.

---

[24] *Brennan Constr. Co. v. Cumberland*, 29 App. D.C. 554 (1907).

## 5.0  LAWS THAT ENFORCE - PERMITS, PROHIBITIONS AND PENALTIES

Although the environmental law's mechanisms for enforcing its mandates are essentially the same as those available in other legal disciplines, there are distinctive aspects to the overall enforcement package -- the ways in which the available mechanisms are used together to effectively compel fulfillment of the environmental compliance obligations.

### 5.1  Permits

Perhaps the most distinctive aspect of environmental enforcement is its extensive and effective use of permitting mechanisms.  Particularly with laws as complex and technical as most of the environmental statutes, it is critical that there be an effective mechanism for bridging from generalities like "Effluents shall be treated in compliance with best available technology" to specifics like:

> Permittee is authorized to discharge from outfall number 001 "x" pounds per day of pollutant "y", subject to the condition that the discharge be monitored in accordance with specified protocols and that periodic reports be provided.

The permit fulfills this need by, in effect, establishing the "law" for a particular discharge or activity.  The requirement to obtain a permit and operate in compliance with it is an individualized and highly effective way of insuring that regulators are notified of releases or activities of which they need to be aware.  It is also an effective way of assuring and demonstrating that the person required to comply is on notice of his obligations.  The role of permits in bridging between the substantive requirements of the environmental laws -- notification, discharge controls and so forth -- and the other enforcement mechanisms discussed below.

Permitting requirements, however, are by no means the only weapon in environmental law's enforcement arsenal.

### 5.2  Enforcement Provisions of the Federal and State Environmental Statutes

Each of the major federal environmental statutes provides an array of enforcement tools to compel compliance with its mandates. Generally, these include:

**Civil Penalties** - ranging from $10,000 to $50,000 per violation or day of violation

**Administrative Orders** - to respond or abate, enforceable by civil and criminal sanctions

**Civil Action for Relief** - including prohibition or mandatory injunction enforced by judicial decree

**Citizens Civil Actions** - to compel compliance with or collect damages for violation of the statute

**Criminal Sanctions** - against organizations and responsible individuals for misrepresentation or knowing or negligent violation of the statutes

There is no doubt that the federal environmental statutes and the regulations under them present a formidable set of reasons for a business or other organization to institute programs for aggressive compliance with the environmental laws. They are supported and complemented by similar enforcement provisions in the state environmental statutes as well as in local laws and ordinances.

## 5.3 General Purpose Heavy Duty Criminal Laws

The last major category of "environmental laws that enforce" are laws from the Criminal Code, originally enacted to punish more traditional crimes, which have been adopted and adapted to the prosecution of crimes which are essentially environmental. The Criminal Code provisions which have proven particularly useful in this connection include:

-- Prohibition Against False Statements to the Federal Government
   -- 18 U.S.C. 1001

-- Mail Fraud Statutes - 18 U.S.C. 1341, 1343

-- Conspiracy Laws--18 U.S.C. 371

Even more traditional criminal laws, such as the murder statutes, have been used, at least at the state level, to successfully prosecute environmental offenses. These non-environmental laws have become almost as important as the environmental statutes in defining the liability of violators.

The environmental law enforcement package, then, is a carefully structured combination of methods--environmental and general purpose, traditional and newly conceived--which work together to bring bad consequences to those who fail to fulfill their environmental compliance obligations. This interaction has been extremely effective and will become even more formidable as the environmental law system matures.

## 6.0 LAWS THAT DEFINE THE ENVIRONMENTAL LAW PROCESS

Having discussed the substantive mandates of the environmental laws and the enforcement methods which make compliance mandatory, we now need to examine the organic and procedural environmental laws --the laws that establish the framework within which the system operates. Although "organic and procedural laws" is not a caption which, at first impression, offers great promise of maintaining the rapt attention of those who would toil in the environmental law vineyard, closer consideration may yield a different conclusion. The fact is that many of the questions which are most critical to successful compliance efforts and most difficult for environmental practitioners to answer fall within this category:

What level of government has authority to regulate?

What institution [branch] of government has authority
to regulate?

What protections are available to the regulated?

Do organizations and individuals have substantive rights?

How do questions of scientific fact get answered?

Who can go to court and who pays for it?

Answers to these and similar questions--critical to the resolution of environmental cases--are found not in the "Environmental" statutes or regulations, but in organic and procedural laws such as Constitutions, federal and state, City Charters, Administrative Procedure Acts, Judicial Codes, Rules of Evidence and Procedure that determine how our overall legal system works in environmental contexts as well as in others. It is, of course, impossible in one chapter of one volume to do much at all in the way of summarizing these important requirements. We may be able, however, to briefly touch a few issues in this context which may be particularly germane to the subject at hand.

### 6.1 The Organic Laws--Constitutions and Charters

In our system, the powers of government and the rights of individuals are defined primarily in the "organic acts" by which governments are created--constitutions, in the case of federal and state governments and, generally, charters in the case of local governmental units like cities and counties. These laws provide the foundation for the environmental law system just as they do for the legal system in general. We look to this foundation to give us answers to the most basic and often most important questions a few of the constitutional or organic issues which have been particularly significant in environmental contexts.

### 6.1.1 Defining Governmental Authority

A set of questions which arises early and often in the development of environmental legal regimes revolves around the decision as to which level of government--state, federal or local--is to play the primary role in regulating particular activities affecting the environment. The federal government is a government of limited authority which may act only through the exercise of the enumerated powers granted to it under the Constitution. In practice, however, the enumerated powers -- particularly the power to regulate interstate and foreign commerce -- have been broadly construed and there are few, if any, recent instances where federal laws enacted to protect the public health and welfare have been held to be in excess of constitutional authority.

Once federal authority has been exercised, and a federal system of regulation has been established, important questions arise about the continuing ability of state and local governments to operate in that same area. While state and local governments have broad "police powers" to do what is necessary to protect the health and safety of their citizens-- that authority may be displaced where a scheme of federal regulation, pursuant to enumerated authority, preempts the field of regulation and precludes the further exercise of state and local authority. The judicial trend in these "preemption cases" is towards upholding continued state authority except where the U.S. Congress has explicitly expressed a clear intention to fully occupy the field and displace state authority to regulate. The trend in the Congress is to explicitly preserve the states' continuing authority to regulate.

A closely related set of constitutional cases dealing with the question of "who can regulate?" involves the issue of whether, even in the absence of preemptive federal action, a state or local law may be unconstitutional because it improperly restrains interstate or foreign commerce.

The Constitution grants to Congress the authority ". . . to regulate Commerce with foreign nations and among the several States and with the Indian Tribes." If state statutes or regulations are found by the courts to be an impermissible burden upon interstate commerce, then they are unconstitutional and unenforceable.

It is well settled that a state regulation validly based on police power does not impermissibly burden interstate commerce where the regulations neither discriminate against interstate commerce nor operate to disrupt its required uniformity. Where there is a reasonable basis to protect the social, as distinguished from the economic, welfare of a community, the courts will not deny this exercise of sovereign power and hold it to violate the Commerce Clause.

For example, one Commerce Clause case involved a challenge against New

Jersey's Waste Control Act[25]. This law barred disposal within the state of solid waste originating or collected outside the state's territorial borders. The U.S. Supreme Court opinion held this statute to violate the Commerce Clause of the Constitution.

The Supreme Court held that all objects of interstate trade merit Commerce Clause protection and none is excluded from the definition of "commerce" including "valueless" out-of-state wastes. The Court ruled that the New Jersey statute was basically an economic protectionist measure, and thus virtually per se invalid, and not a law directed at legitimate local concerns that had only incidental effects on interstate commerce.

Another Commerce Clause case involved the Chicago ordinance banning the sale of detergents containing phosphates.[26] The Seventh Circuit Court of Appeals held that the ordinance did not violate the Commerce Clause because, although it had some minor effect on interstate commerce, the benefits far outweighed these effects and the ordinance was a reasonable method to achieve a legitimate goal of improving Lake Michigan.

A similar result favorable to legislators was reached in Oregon when the constitutionality of the Oregon "bottle-bill" which in essence banned the sale of non-returnable beverage containers was upheld.[27]

The trend is definitely one of the courts tying to uphold environmental legislation with the rationale being based on a balancing of environmental benefits against detrimental effects.

We can expect the debate along these lines to intensify and revitalize as international laws and treaties establishing product standards and regulating activities, like marine transportation, potentially affecting the environment. While questions of "unreasonable burden" may be philosophically the same in the global context as within the national borders, the political dynamics and level of complexity will increase radically and new solutions may indeed be required.

The last category of cases limiting the ability of states and localities to regulate conduct within their boundaries is that dealing with "equal protection".

Section One of the Fourteenth Amendment to the Constitution prohibits the states from denying to any person the equal protection of the laws. This provision has been applied, essentially, to prevent inappropriate discrimination between regulated entities or categories.

Does a state noise law which exempts construction equipment where there

---

[25] *City of Philadelphia v. New Jersey*, 437 U.S. 617 (1978).

[26] *Procter and Gamble Co. v. Chicago*, 509 F.2d 69, 7 Env't. Rep. Cas. (BNA) 1328 (7th Cir 1975), *cert. denied*, 421 U.S. 978 (1975).

[27] *American Can Co. v. Oregon Liquor Control Comm'n*, 15 Or. App. 618, 517 P.2d 691, 4 Env't Rep. Cas. (BNA) 1584 (1973).

is no exemption for mining equipment deny equal protection? The Illinois Supreme Court in a suit, *Illinois Coal Operators Association v. Illinois Pollution Control Board*[28] upheld such a state law.

Courts generally hold that for a classification to violate the constitutional guarantee of equal protection, there must be a showing that there is no reasonable basis for the distinction. A law is presumptively valid. Unless clear and convincing proof demonstrates that a law is arbitrary and unreasonable, the law must be upheld. The result is that few laws are ever held to violate the equal protection clause.

So, effective arguments have been made that there is a need to limit the number of regulators by either giving all power to the states and keeping the federal government out or vice versa. The end result of all these arguments has been continued reaffirmation that, in environmental contexts, federal, state and local governments will continue to exercise concurrent, but not always coordinated, jurisdiction. This fact of life is one of the things that makes this field a challenge.

## 6.2 The Courts' Role

While the organic laws define the authorities of the legislative and executive branches of the government as well as the judiciary, this is an environmental *law* handbook, and to understand the law one must understand at least something about the courts. This may be the appropriate point to begin that discussion.

## 6.2.1 State and United States Court Systems

There are two primary judicial systems in the United States: (1) the state and local courts, established in each state under the authority of the state government, and (2) federal courts, set up under the authority of the Constitution by the Congress of the United States.

The state courts have general, unlimited power to decide almost every type of case, subject only to the limitation of state law. State and local courts are located in every town and county and are the tribunals with which citizens most often have contact. The great bulk of legal business such as divorce, probate of estates, traffic accidents and all other matters except those assigned to the U.S. courts is handled by these state and local courts.

The U.S. courts, on the other hand, have the authority to hear and decide only selected types of cases which are specifically enumerated in the Constitution. The U.S. courts are located principally in the larger cities while state and local courts are found throughout the country.

---

[28] 59 Ill.2d 305, 319 N.E.2d 782, 7 Env't. Rep. Cas. (BNA) 1315 (1974).

### 6.2.2 United States Court System

The structure of the U.S. court system has evolved throughout the historical development of our country. The Constitution merely provides: "The Judicial Power of the United States, shall be vested in one Supreme Court, and in such inferior Courts as the Congress may from time to time ordain and establish." Thus, the only court which is constitutionally indispensable is the Supreme Court. The authority to establish and abolish other U.S. courts is vested in and has been exercised by the Congress.

At the present time, the United States court system is pyramidal in structure with three levels. At the apex of the pyramid stands the Supreme Court of the United States, the highest court in the land. On the second level are the 12 geographically divided United States courts of appeals. On the third level down are the 97 United States district courts.

A person involved in a suit in a U.S. court may proceed through the three levels of decision. Generally, the case will first be heard and decided by one of the courts on the district court level. If either party is dissatisfied with the decision, it will usually have a right of review in one of the courts of appeals. Then, if still dissatisfied, it may petition for review in the Supreme Court of the United States. However, review is granted by the Supreme Court only in cases involving matters of great national importance.

This pyramidal organization of the courts serves two purposes. First, the Supreme Court and the courts of appeals can correct errors which have been made in the decisions of the trial courts. Secondly, the higher courts can assure uniformity of decision by reviewing cases in which two or more lower courts have reached different decisions.

State courts have a similar pyramid structure with a basic court of original jurisdiction, an appellate court and then a supreme court. Often states do not use the same terminology in naming their courts. So, at the state level the nomenclature can be confusing, but the system of a lower court deciding a case in the beginning with opportunity for review of the decision by appellate courts is the same as in the federal system.

### 6.2.3 Courts in Practical Perspective

From a practical viewpoint, when you learn about a judicial decision of interest to you, ask which court decided the case. If the Supreme Court of the U.S. decided the case, it is a very important decision for the entire country. If a local court decided the case, it is generally of little interest nationally but of major interest to that local jurisdiction. However, any decision on a point of law is better than none at all.

Also, be aware that courts do differ in their opinions. There are many examples of two lower courts reaching conflicting opinions on a point of law. This is an extremely difficult concept for many to accept. If you are originally trained in engineering or the sciences, you are probably accustomed to dealing in data and facts. To move into the realm of "ifs" and "yes, but" seems to be like going from the "world of black and white" into a "world of gray." For those who find this troubling, remember that in almost everything, we are talking about degrees of certitude. The field of environmental law may involve a higher degree of uncertitude than most other areas because of its newness and changeability. As a result, you do your best to understand what is the meaning of the laws, regulations and court opinions, and you then take into consideration the degree of certitude involved in a particular legal issue before proceeding to a decision.

Also, keep in mind that your court system, although hailed as one of the fairest systems ever developed by mankind, is subject to human frailties. The judges, lawyers, plaintiffs, defendants and jurors all involve human interactions, another source of uncertainties.

### 6.2.4 Court Jurisdiction and Forum Shopping

The question of which court has jurisdiction can be a complex issue. Also, the question of the specific court in which a case is initiated is generally a key move in the overall strategy for winning a lawsuit. The selection of the specific court as a legal strategy is called "forum shopping." When bringing a case a good lawyer will evaluate which court is more inclined toward his client's position. For example, the judges of the U.S. Courts in the District of Columbia are known for their pro-environmental record. So organizations such as the Environmental Defense Fund (EDF) and Sierra Club are inclined to initiate their lawsuits in the U.S. District Courts for the District of Columbia. Industrial firms are generally more inclined to file a lawsuit in a district court in Louisiana or other such geographic area with a more conservative judicial record.

### 6.2.5 When Can Courts Act and Who May Sue?

While the U.S. Congress has tended towards maximizing the role of the Courts in enforcement and interpretation of the environmental laws through various provisions stating that "any person" may file a petition for review of an agency action or initiate a citizen's suit to enforce a statute or compel performance of mandatory duties, courts are not empowered under the Constitution to act like legislatures and decide all matters which come to their attention. They must act within the context of a justiciable "case or controversy" and, in order for a case or controversy to exist, the party bringing the suit or filing the petition must have "standing" or an appropriate individuated interest in the outcome of the case.

In the context of actions to compel or obtain review of agency actions, the required interest is described in the Administrative Procedure Act.

Under that act, standing exists only when a plaintiff can satisfactorily demonstrate that (a) the agency action complained of will result in an injury in fact and that (b) the injury is to an interest "arguably within the zone of interests to be protected" by the statute in question.

The leading cases addressing the "injury in fact" question are cases involving the National Environmental Policy Act and environmental impact statements. The key case is the Supreme Court decision in *Sierra Club v.*

*Morton.*[29]   This case involved the recreational development of the Mineral King Valley.  The question in *Sierra v. Morton* was, what must be alleged by persons  who claim injury of a non-economic nature to widely shared interests to give them standing.   The court recognized that environmental well-being, like economic well-being, is an important ingredient of our society.   The fact that environmental interests are shared by the many rather than few does not make them less deserving of legal protection.   But the "injury in fact" test, according to the Court, requires that the party seeking review be himself among the injured.   The Sierra Club did not allege and show that it or its members would be affected in any of their activities or pastimes by the development. So, the Court ruled against them.   However, this has since proven to be an easy matter to remedy, by the plaintiffs alleging that an aesthetic or other non-economic interest was injured.   So, the Sierra Club established in this decision that environmental interests could be the basis for standing. This was a major development in the law.

In a subsequent Supreme Court case, *SCRAP v. U.S.*[30] the Supreme Court gave some law students standing to sue the Interstate Commerce Commission (ICC) in a rate increase case involving recyclables.  The Supreme Court ruled that standing to sue was demonstrated by the students, showing that they used forest and streams in the Washington, D.C. area for camping and hiking and that this was disturbed by the adverse environmental impact, caused by the nonuse of recyclable goods, brought on by the ICC rate increase on recyclable commodities.

In its most recent visit to the case or controversy and standing issue the Supreme Court has indicated that environmental organizations do not get a free ride to judgment but must allege and prove individuated injury in fact. In *Lujan v. National Wildlife Federation,*[31] the Supreme Court reversed a decision which held that two affidavits filed on behalf of the National Wildlife Federation had satisfactorily alleged injury in fact, even though they were not specific as to the actual injury.   The affidavits were filed in support of a challenge to a program of the Bureau of Land Management.  The Court stated that "whether one of respondent's members has been, or is threatened to be, 'adversely affected or aggrieved' by Government action--Rule 56(e) is assuredly not satisfied by averments which state only that one of respondent's members uses unspecified portions of an immense tract of territory, on some portions of which mining activity has occurred or probably will occur by virtue of the governmental action."[32]   It is too soon to tell whether this decision portends a

---

[29] 405 U.S. 727 3 Env't. Rep. Cas. (BNA) 2039 (1972).

[30] 412 U.S. 669 (1973).

[31] 110 S.Ct. 3177 (1990).

[32] *Id.* at 3189.

trend towards limiting the role of litigation and judicial activism in environmental cases.[33]

## 6.3 Defining The Rights of the Regulated and Limits of Governmental Authority

While we normally think about "Constitutional Rights" in contexts other than environmental law, there is little doubt that the scope and availability of rights which some regard as "fundamental freedoms" will continue to be matters of vigorous contention in this field. Some of these areas of debate are summarized below.

### 6.3.1 Search Warrants and the Fourth Amendment

The Fourth Amendment of the Constitution provides that:

> The right of the people to be secure in their persons, houses, papers, and effects, against unreasonable searches and seizures shall not be violated, and no Warrants shall issue, but upon probable cause, supported by oath or affirmation and particularly describing the place to be searched and the persons or things to be seized.

The warrant issue arises most frequently in connection with the collection or obtaining of evidence. Evidence is necessary for any civil or criminal enforcement program. However, federal evidence collection is limited by Fourth Amendment prohibitions.

The courts have held that the Fourth Amendment applies to the corporate entity as well as to the private citizen. The Supreme Court has held that the requirement for a search warrant even applies to routine inspections.[34] In the *Camara* case, the Court held that the warrant requirement applied to a municipal health inspector's search of a private residence. A similar conclusion was reached with respect to a fire inspector's attempted search of a commercial warehouse.[35] In these cases, the Court indicated that a lesser degree of "probable cause" would be required for an administrative search warrant than for the typical criminal search warrant. So there can be routine periodic searches of all structures in a given area based on an appraisal of

---

[33] The Court did note that this matter arose in the context of a motion for summary judgment rather than a motion to dismiss on the pleadings as was the case in *Scrap v. U.S.* As such, the evidentiary standards are different. Thus, the Court stated that the *SCRAP* decision and its "expansive expression of what would suffice" to permit review of the government action, "is of no relevance here." *Id.*

[34] *Camara v. Municipal Court of San Francisco*, 387 U.S. 523 (1967).

[35] *See v. City of Seattle*, 387 U.S. 541 (1967).

conditions in the area as a whole rather than on a knowledge of conditions in a particular building. The reasonableness of such inspections is to be weighed against the invasion of rights that the search entails.

Generally warrants are only sought after entry is refused because there is no need for a search warrant when the owner or operator has given his consent.

To avoid this need for search warrants, the Congress has authorized warrantless searches in some statutes. In the famous *Barlow* case[36] the constitutionality of these legislative waivers was reviewed by the Supreme Court. The Court held that Section 8 of the Occupational Safety and Health Act (OSHA) authorizing warrantless inspections violated the Fourth Amendment prohibition against warrantless searches and was unconstitutional. Despite this Constitutional protection, the wisdom of demanding a warrant for a normal inspection is dubious at best. Few businesses challenge inspections without warrants because to do so indicates that a problem probably exists. The warrant requirement does put some minimal restraint on the federal government's ability to conduct repetitive or needless inspections.

The Environmental Protection Agency (EPA) has avoided any test of the constitutionality of the warrantless search authorizations given to them by Congress in the Noise Control Act and the Resource Conservation and Recovery Act by not challenging the issue. If an EPA inspector is refused admission, EPA, as standard procedure, will then obtain a search warrant and not even try to use the statutory authority. This avoids the constitutional confrontation.

It is common, in the field of environmental law, to find exceptions to the general rules. An example of an exception to the search warrant requirement is the so-called "open fields" exception described in the Supreme Court case, *Air Pollution Variance Board v. Western Alfalfa.*[37] In this case, an inspector of a Division of the Colorado Department of Health entered the premises of Western Alfalfa Corporation without its knowledge or consent to make a Ringelmann reading of plumes of smoke being emitted from the company's chimneys. Western Alfalfa Corporation claimed that the inspection violated the Fourth Amendment by entering its property to collect evidence without a search warrant. The U.S. Supreme Court ruled that the inspector was within an exception to the Fourth Amendment and had not violated the rights of Western Alfalfa Corporation. The Court held the general rule to be that the act of conducting tests on a defendant's premises without either a warrant or the consent of defendant constitutes an unreasonable search within the Fourth Amendment. However, in this case the inspector did not enter the plant or offices. Basically he sighted what anyone in the area near the plant could see in the sky. He was on the defendant's property, but there was no

---

[36] *Marshall v. Barlow's Inc.*, 436 U.S. 307 (1978).

[37] 416 U.S. 861, 6 Env't. Rep. Cas. (BNA) 157 1 (1974).

showing that he was on premises from which the public was excluded. The Court held that there is an "open fields" exception to the constitutional requirement for a search warrant which was applicable in this case.

In the vast majority of practical situations, consent is given for collection of evidence. The consent may be oral or written, and is commonly given by employees simply admitting the inspectors to the company premises or giving answers to oral or written questions by government employees.

One method of avoiding the necessity of obtaining a search warrant is to require the owner or operator of the pollution source to get a permit or license to operate. Then, a condition is included in the permit, allowing inspections without warrants. The U.S. Supreme Court has not yet ruled on the constitutionality of this method. Since permit systems are now being used more and more by federal, state and local agencies to control pollution, this method of obtaining desired evidence will be the trend of the future and provides the government with the consent needed.

### 6.3.2  Prohibition Against Self-Incrimination: The Fifth Amendment

The Fifth Amendment to the Constitution prohibits compulsory self-incrimination. The protection applies in criminal cases. If the government agency collecting the evidence will use it only for civil actions, such as fines or injunctions, the Fifth Amendment is not applicable. In addition, the Fifth Amendment applies only to persons and not to corporations or partnerships.

Most environmental statutes provide penalties for both individuals and corporations. Therefore, in a case where the evidence or samples taken might be used in a criminal action, the person in authority at the place where evidence is to be taken should be advised of his rights to remain silent, to an attorney, and that any evidence taken may be used against him in a subsequent criminal action. If these rights are not formally observed, the evidence so collected may not be admissible in a criminal action.

### 6.3.3  Due Process, the Fifth and Fourteenth Amendments

The requirement that government entities provide due process of law is found in the Fifth and Fourteenth Amendments.

The Fifth Amendment to the U.S. Constitution says: "No person shall . . . nor be deprived of life, liberty, or property, without due process of law; nor shall private property be taken for public use, without just compensation."

The Fourteenth Amendment to the U.S. Constitution states: "Section 1 . . . No State shall make or enforce any law which shall abridge the privileges or immunities of citizens of the United States; nor shall any State deprive any person of life, liberty, or property without due process of law; nor deny to any person within its jurisdiction the equal protection of the law."

The Fifth Amendment prohibition applies to federal government and the Fourteenth applies to states.

An example of the application of the legal concept of due process is found in the case, *Construction Industry Ass'n. v. Petaluma.*[38]   In this case the Court held that a city ordinance that limits issuance of new building permits to achieve a goal of preserving "small town" character, open spaces and low density population does not violate the due process clause of the Fourteenth Amendment.

The Court's opinion explained that zoning regulations must find their justification in some aspect of the police power asserted for the public welfare to satisfy the due process mandate.   The Court found that the concept of the public welfare is sufficiently broad to uphold Petaluma's desire to preserve its small town character, open spaces and low density population.The due process argument was used against the beverage container ordinance of the City of Bowie, Maryland.[39]   The Court ruled that there was not a violation of due process since there was not a showing that the police power was exercised arbitrarily, oppressively or unreasonably.   The opinion also reasoned that a law should not be held void, if there are any considerations relating to the public welfare by which it can be supported.

### 6.3.4   Police Power and Due Process

Police power is the inherent right of a government to pass laws for the protection of the health, welfare, morals, and property of the people within its jurisdiction.   Police power may not be bartered away by contract.   It extends to all public needs.   It may be put forth in the aid of what is sanctioned by usage or held by prevailing opinion to be greatly or immediately necessary for public welfare.   By exercise of reasonable police power, government may regulate the conduct of individuals and of the use of their property and, in some instances, take property without compensation.

Although the police power of a state is very broad, it is not without limitation.   It is always within the power of the court to declare a law void which, although enacted as a police regulation, is not justified as such.   In other words, a law enacted as a police regulation must be reasonable.   If the law is unreasonable or exercised in an arbitrary manner, it is taking life, liberty, or property without due process of law.

Two examples of allowable exercise of police powers are given in Section 6.3.3.

---

[38] 522 F.2d 897, 8 Env't. Rep. Cas. (BNA) 1001 (9th cir. 1975), *cert. denied,*  424 U.S. 924 (1976).

[39] *Bowie Inn v. City of Bowie,* 274 Md. 230, 335 A.2d 679, 7 Env't. Rep. Cas. (BNA) 2083 (1975).

Another example of the valid exercise of police power which did not violate the due process principle was in the Supreme Court case, *Village of Belle Terre v. Borass*.[40] In this case a New York village ordinance restricted land use to one-family houses and precluded occupancy by more than two unrelated persons. The Court held this ordinance to be a valid exercise of the city's police power, stating:

> A quiet place where yards are wide, people few, and motor vehicles restricted are legitimate guidelines in a land use project addressed to family needs. The police power is not confined to elimination of filth, stench, and unhealthy places. It is ample to lay out zones where family values, youth values, and the blessings of quiet seclusion and clean air make the area a sanctuary for people.

### 6.3.5 Prohibition Against Taking Property Without Compensation

The Fifth Amendment to the Constitution states that ". . . private property [shall not] be taken for public use, without just compensation."

Despite numerous court opinions on this issue, the line between "takings" which require compensation and valid exercises of "police power" which do not require compensation has never been clearly drawn. It is difficult to predict the outcome when the principles in this area are applied to factual situations.

It may be said that the state takes property by eminent domain because it is useful to the public. This taking requires compensation. When the state takes property because it is harmful, it is done under the police power and does not require compensation. What is useful to one person may be harmful to another. So, the perspective of all the conditions and circumstances is often the determining factor in choosing between useful and harmful.

The problem often comes down to one of degree. In both circumstances damages result. If damage is suffered by many similarly situated and is in the nature of a restriction on use and ought to be borne by the individual as a member of society for the good of the public, it is a reasonable exercise of police power not requiring compensation. However, if the damage is so great to the individual that he ought not to bear it under contemporary standards, then courts are inclined to treat it as a "taking" or unreasonable exercise of police power requiring compensation.

This "taking" issue has been in the forefront of noteworthy litigation. One important case involved the denial of operational drilling permits in the Santa Barbara Channel, *Union Oil v. Morton*.[41] In this case the court reviewed the question of the degree to which government may interfere with enjoyment of private property by exercise of police power without compensation and concluded that there was not a simple answer to this question. The courts

---

[40] 416 U.S. 1 (1974).

[41] 12 F.2d 743, 7 Env't. Rep. Cas. (BNA) 1 587 (9th Cir. 1975).

under a variety of tests have recognized that regulation of private property can become so onerous that it amounts to a taking of that property. The court in this case held that a permanent unconditional suspension of permits to install drilling platforms is a taking that requires compensation or violation of the Fifth Amendment.

Two very recent cases decided by the U.S. Court of Claims confirm that failure to issue permits can constitute a taking. The cases, *Florida Rock Industries, Inc. v. United States*, No. 266-82L (Cl. Ct. July 23, 1990), and *Loveladies Harbor, Inc. v. United States*, No. 243-83L (Cl. Ct. July 23, 1990), both were the result of lengthy administrative proceedings which led to the denial of permits under Section 404 of the Clean Water Act. The major import of the court's decisions is twofold: (1) under certain circumstances, the Government's denial of a permit to fill wetlands under Section 404 of the Clean Water Act is an interference with a property owner's legitimate entitlement to the proposed use of its property, and is thus compensable under the Takings Clause; and (2) in determining the market value of such property following the taking, recreational and/or conservation uses carry minimal value.[42]

A series of cases have held that airport noise can constitute a taking of property rights. In the landmark case of *United States v. Causby*,[43] the Supreme Court held that frequent low flights over the Causby's land by military aircraft landing at a nearby airport operated by the United States constituted a taking of the Causby's property without compensation in violation of the Fifth Amendment of the Constitution. The noise from the aircraft rendered it impossible to continue the property use as a commercial chicken farm. Although the flights did not completely destroy the enjoyment and use of the land, they were held to be so low and frequent as to constitute a direct and immediate interference with the full enjoyment of the land, limiting the utility of the land and causing a diminution in its value, and therefore constituted a taking under the Fifth Amendment.

In another major Supreme Court decision on this issue, *Griggs v. Allegheny County*,[44] the Court held that Allegheny County, which owned and operated the Greater Pittsburgh Airport, was liable for a taking of property under the Fifth Amendment where the noise from taking off and landing at the airport on flight paths over the Griggs' property rendered the property undesirable and unbearable for residential use. The Court saw no difference between the county's responsibility to pay for land on which runways were built and its

---

[42] In *Loveladies*, the court placed such value at $1,000 per acre, while in *Florida Rock* it was set at a "nominal" $500 per acre for "future recreational/water management purposes. . . to a government agency".

[43] 328 U.S. 256 (1946).

[44] 369 U.S. 84 (1962).

responsibility for air easements necessary for airport operation. The glide path for the northwest runway is as necessary for the operation of the airport as is a surface right-of-way, wrote the Court. Several states have interpreted their own constitutions to require compensation under less strict circumstances when noise from aircraft has diminished the market value of the homeowner's property. Interference must be substantial and sufficiently direct in the majority of jurisdictions.

To conclude, while the constitutional rights of individuals and organizations may be more difficult to uphold in contexts where these private rights arguably contend with public rights to a safe and healthy environment, it has often been suggested that constitutional rights are most important in the most unpopular cases and it is here we need to work the hardest to uphold them. The Constitution is, and will continue to be a major aspect of environmental law.

### 6.4 Administrative Law and Procedure

As with most areas of law, the business of environmental law is to find the facts and decide what to do about them. While the substantive and organic laws outlined above will greatly affect the way this business is conducted, the required procedures will be influential in determining the outcomes of cases. In cases where there is significant scientific opinion on both sides of an issue, the critical issue is not what the facts are, but who has the burden of proof and what must be done to carry it. In a case where an administrative agency has made a decision, the issue is not whether the rule or decision is good or bad, but whether it was within the agency's authority, consistent with required procedures and otherwise in accordance with law. The critical questions of environmental practice--the cutting edge issues of science, risk assessment, application of technology and analytical methods--are often resolved, not through the scientific and engineering disciplines, but through argument and procedural determinations. Any detailed discussion of the rules for those determinations is well beyond the scope of this text. However, as we have said before, a few brief comments may be helpful.

Administrative law may not be a favorite course in law school and it is probably not an area in which the average lawyer has much experience. It is probable, however, that administrative law issues are at or close to the heart of somewhere between eighty and ninety-seven percent of all disputes concerning the federal environmental laws and regulations. Following is a thumbnail of the most important things we need to know about administrative law.

-- Administrative Agencies have no inherent or residual authority but can act only pursuant to authority "delegated" to them in the statutes enacted by the Congress. If an agency acts beyond the scope of its delegated authority, its action is illegal and void.

-- Agencies' opinions in interpreting their own regulations and the statutes they administer will, particularly if consistently held over a substantial period of time, be granted deference by the courts.

-- Agencies must act in accordance with the procedures specified in their enabling legislation, or if no other procedures are there specified, in accordance with the Administrative Procedure Act. The required procedures normally entail publication in the *Federal Register*, opportunity for public comment, sometimes a public hearing, response to public comment and final publication.

-- Agencies must act in accordance with their own rules and regulations. Failure to follow those rules results in invalid actions.

-- Agencies must maintain a docket or record in support of their action and there must be evidence in that record to support the agency action. The record must be open for public examination throughout the period when public comments are being received.

-- Agency actions may not be "arbitrary and capricious" ... which means that there must be at least some evidence in the record to support the agency decision. When a statute specifically so requires, agencies must support their decisions with "substantial evidence". Although the difference between "some evidence" and "substantial evidence" is somewhat obscure, agencies hate substantial evidence requirements.

-- Agency decisions may be appealed to the courts either under specific judicial review provisions in the enabling statutes or the general provision in the Administrative Procedure Act. You can't go to court, however, unless you have standing, the issue is "ripe," you have exhausted administrative remedies and a final agency decision has issued.

-- On appeal, administrative agency actions are generally upheld in the absence of some glaring procedural defect or a clearly inadequate record. However, these circumstances occur frequently and successful appeals, while not the rule, are far from a rarity.

There is no doubt that a basic familiarity with the administrative process will substantially improve the effectiveness and understanding of those who deal with environmental law.

### 6.5 Rules of Evidence

Most environmental cases don't get to court, but a few do and of those few probably most involve the issue of causation and most of the rest involve the question of who did it and what does it take to prove it. Some of these questions turn on evidentiary determinations, others on questions of responsibility, liability sharing and contribution. Here is a summary of some of the major concepts.

### 6.5.1   Burden of Proof and Presumptions

Where, as is very often the case, the scientific facts of a controversy are being hotly debated in the scientific community or the facts are otherwise unclear, the outcome of the case may turn on the question of who has the "burden of proof" and the obligation of going forward with the evidence.

Fortunately, in our legal system, plaintiffs in civil cases normally have the burden of proving their cases. They must do so by a "preponderance of the evidence." However, attorneys and courts have developed special liability concepts, like strict liability, to shift the burden to defendants in some circumstances. Since the party with the burden will often lose the case, the question is one of the most contentious issues in civil litigation in the environmental context.

In criminal cases, the prosecutor has the burden of proving guilt "beyond a reasonable doubt" and defendants are presumed innocent until proven guilty, though that presumption is not always reflected in public opinion.

Finally, where the issue involves an effort to set aside an agency regulation or other action, there is a presumption of validity and the contesting party has the obligation of proving conclusively that the action is arbitrary and capricious, unsupported by the evidence or otherwise not in accordance with law.

### 6.5.2  Hearsay

Hearsay is evidence which depends solely for its truth or falsity upon statements of a person other than the witness. Hearsay, in itself, has no evidentiary value. The witness cannot be cross-examined regarding hearsay, because the statements are those of another. Generally, hearsay is inadmissible, but there are numerous exceptions.

Usually in the case of documents, a statute provides for an official custodian or witness who will certify to their authenticity or validity to overcome the hearsay objection.

### 6.5.3  Opinion Evidence

Generally, the testimony of a witness is confined to a statement of concrete facts based upon his own observation or knowledge. However, expert opinion evidence, though often based largely on hearsay, opinions, or conclusions not normally admissible into evidence, is admissible when it concerns scientific or technical matters and is presented by an appropriately qualified expert. Non-expert witnesses may be asked to express an opinion to help understand what was observed, but conjecture is not admissible.

An expert can generally be found for either side of a case. For example, the prosecutor will have his psychiatrist testify that the defendant is sane while the defendant's psychiatrist is testifying he is insane. This type of divergent opinion evidence is common in environmental litigation.

The major issues in these cases are whether scientific evidence is credible, reflective of the weight of scientific opinion and sufficient to support a verdict or submission to a jury. Judicial thinking on these issues varies widely from case to case and is clearly in a transitional, uncertain state.

### 6.5.4 Witnesses

Generally, all persons are competent to testify, but their credibility can be attacked. Leading questions (ones which suggest an answer), may generally only be asked of unwilling witnesses or adverse parties. A witness must answer all questions asked, which will provide information on the issue under investigation--unless this testimony may subject the witness to criminal prosecution. The opposing party has a right to cross-examine the witness. If the witness refuses to answer on cross-examination, his entire testimony may be expunged from the record. Generally, cross-examinations are limited to facts on which a witness testified during direct examination.

### 6.5.5 Privileged Communication and Environmental Audits

Privilege is an exception to the rule that the public has the fight to know every man's evidence. The reason for the exception is public policy.

In environmental lawsuits, the concern is with the attorney-client relationship. It is the duty of a lawyer to preserve his client's confidences. This duty outlasts the lawyer's employment.

The concept of privileged communications can be used not only in lawsuits but also when providing legal advice in connection with environmental audits and assessments.

Thus, though there is no absolute assurance that the privilege can be maintained, it may be useful to have a lawyer supervise the information-gathering process during the audit and establish procedures for controlling access to all documents generated during the audit.

### 6.5.6 Your Own Reports as Evidence Against You

Many of the environmental laws and regulations require reports or data to be filed with the government. The laws governing occupational health, waste and air pollution all require reports. Even the reports to the Securities and Exchange Commission require disclosure of information on pollution. Most of these reports are available to the public and to competitors.

The extent to which the results of an investigation or inspection are available in private liability litigation remains uncertain. A corporation is not protected by the self-incrimination provisions of the Fifth Amendment to the U.S. Constitution. So, it may not object to the production of its books to be used as evidence against it.[45]

---

[45] *Essgee Co. v. U.S.*, 262 U.S. 151 (1923).

### 6.5.7  Samples or Physical Evidence

One of the common evidentiary problems raised in court cases involves physical evidence. In environmental cases, the evidence is often a sample or some data. Some of the key issues normally involved with physical evidence are: (1) has the evidence or data been altered or contaminated, (2) was the equipment used in evidence collection properly calibrated, (3) were scientifically acceptable and standard methods of analysis used in evaluation and (4) who has handled the evidence (chain of custody)?

In order to lay a proper foundation for the admission of evidence, an attorney should be able to present the principals in the "chain of custody" to testify as to their involvement and appropriate expertise in the proper handling of the evidence. The courts will frequently require the parties to stipulate authenticity of evidence to avoid this tedious form of proof. In legal terminology, "to stipulate" is to agree initially on conduct or evidence for the purpose of shortening the legal proceedings.

### 6.5.8  Evidence Collection and Constitutional Rights

A problem that may arise in the collection of evidence concerns the Fourth Amendment or Constitutional rights of corporate entities and private persons.

The Fourth Amendment to the U.S. Constitution prohibits all unreasonable searches and requires a search warrant for most investigations. However, no search warrant is needed in three basic situations: (1) when there is an emergency, (2) when the owner or operator gives his consent, or (3) when the samples could be taken from outside of the property (open fields exception). See the previous section on search warrants.

In most states, search warrants are used for searches for the implements or fruits of a crime and not for mere investigation of conditions which may lead to either civil or criminal penalties. A few states authorize a special kind of search warrant, sometimes called an inspection warrant which may be used to investigate conditions.

The Fifth Amendment prohibition against criminal self-incrimination was described earlier. In evidence collection involving criminal charges against private parties, this Fifth Amendment right must be properly observed or the courts will not allow evidence to be introduced in the case. The Fifth Amendment protections apply only to private persons and not to corporations or partnerships.

## 7.0  JOINT AND SEVERAL LIABILITY AND CONTRIBUTION

The concept of joint and several liability in toxic tort and clean-up cases springs from the extreme difficulty of apportioning liability between, say, numerous contributors to a hazardous landfill. Under this concept one party can be held liable for the entire costs of an action. Then it is the responsibility of the one party to identify others to share the liability. The theory is that the public or the injured party should not bear the risk and cost of sorting out these complex situations but, instead, should rest the burden on those who caused the problems. These issues of contribution and liability sharing were among the most hotly contested issues of the eighties and the dispute will continue into the nineties and perhaps beyond. The "public" may eventually "win" this dispute but then, as usual, will pay for its victory with "transaction costs added" for good measure. There clearly is a need for improved procedures to determine and assess responsibility for environmental harms.

## 8.0 ORGANIZING FOR ENVIRONMENTAL COMPLIANCE

Once a basic understanding of the environmental law system and its requirements is achieved, the next step is to apply that knowledge to attain or maintain an acceptable compliance posture in the organizations you advise or act for. Our approach to the development of appropriate compliance structures rests on the basic premise that:

Aggressive compliance is the most effective protection against aggressive enforcement and other efforts to assess liability.

Books have been written -- notably Government Institutes' *Environmental, Health & Safety Manager's Handbook* and *Environmental Audits* -- discussing and detailing the elements of appropriate compliance organization. The following principles derived from those texts may be instructive:

-- Everyone is responsible for environmental law compliance and, to protect against individual liability, should continually demonstrate due concern and diligent efforts to comply. Providing appropriate education and training plus sufficient informational resources is a good demonstration of concern for compliance.

-- The best answer to the question of what can be done to prevent violations and minimize liability is an appropriate corporate "culture" or management structure formulated with a view to environmental objectives and aggressively implemented.

-- Outside consultants and counsel can help, but can't comply for you any better than they could run your company. The objective of an effective program is to provide the organization's officers and employees with the knowledge, resources and motivation required to meet and exceed requirements.

-- After your compliance system is in place, periodic "audits" to verify compliance and identify areas where compliance can be improved will be helpful. "We had a good program but got sloppy," is not a mitigating factor, but an aggravating admission of failure. Don't start what you don't intend to finish and don't do anything half-way.

## 9.0 ENVIRONMENTAL LAW KNOWLEDGE IS CRUCIAL

The need for a working understanding of the environmental law system is probably more crucial now than it ever has been. Our actions and inactions, what we know, and perhaps most importantly--what we ought to know--can have dramatic effects on the financial well being of organizations as well as the financial and personal futures of the individuals who work for them. Knowledge of and strict adherence to the mandates of the environmental laws is not a luxury for the largest companies and organizations. Financial viability and profitability--the bottom lines for businesses, and personal freedom--the bottom line for individuals, may rest on this knowledge and how we use it. We hope this handbook will be helpful in that connection.

Chapter 2

ENFORCEMENT AND LIABILITIES

Elliott P. Laws and Russell V. Randle
Patton, Boggs & Blow
Washington, D.C.

## 1.0 INTRODUCTION

Enforcement, and to an increasing degree criminal prosecution of responsible corporate officials, is the environmental issue cutting across almost all environmental programs. There are strong institutional and political reasons to believe that enforcement will continue the marked increase shown in the late 1980s well into the 1990s. The basic regulatory programs for air and water pollution control, and for the management of hazardous waste have now been in place for some time. In virtually all instances ample time has passed for good faith compliance efforts to be completed, with industry being well conditioned to the importance of environmental laws and regulations. Those who have failed to comply or to comply adequately will be left with little defense.

Monitoring technology has also dramatically improved since the early 1970s, providing regulatory officials with the ability, should they decide to exercise it, to monitor compliance far more effectively. In particular, improvements in small computers should enable regulatory agencies to focus far more rapidly on compliance problems.

Environmental enforcement is also popular politically. The public perception of companies violating hazardous waste or toxic pollution rules is only slightly more favorable than the public perception of cocaine dealers and child molesters. Additionally, the Bush Administration has apparently come to view stringent enforcement efforts as a more inexpensive way carry out the President's pledge to be the "Environmental President," without supporting expensive new public works programs.[1] The same political calculus applies in

---

[1] While the increase in enforcement actions has been hailed by states and environmentalists, President Bush has also come under fire for preferring

(continued...)

many states.

The prospect of criminal prosecutions and imprisonment for negligent violations of environmental requirements should focus corporate managers minds, attention and corporate resources wonderfully. The enforcement options available to regulatory agencies in the event of a violation are usually these:

(a) do nothing;

(b) widespread publicity;

(c) revocation of existing permits and refusal to renew expiring permits;

(d) administrative penalty proceedings involving smaller penalties and corrective action;

(e) civil actions for monetary penalties and injunctive relief;

(f) criminal prosecution of the violator and sometimes of responsible management personnel.

Even if enforcement officials decide not to act, civil enforcement actions for penalties and injunctive relief may be brought by individuals under most federal environmental statutes. Environmental groups have made effective use of these provisions, especially under the Clean Water Act. These "citizen suits," differ from "toxic tort" actions which are also brought in connection with some environmental violations. In successful citizen suits, penalties are usually to be paid into the federal treasury, and all or some of the group's attorney's fees are paid. In the case of toxic torts, massive damages are sought to be paid to the victims of some environmental problem. A violation of environmental regulations can be a critical issue in toxic tort actions, because in many states such a violation is considered *per se* negligence, conclusively establishing the violator's liability, leaving only the issue of compensatory and punitive damages.

---

[1](..continued)

"cosmetic" rather than "substantive" environmental efforts. For example, for the 20th anniversary of Earth Day in 1990, the Justice Department changed the name of its Land and Natural Resources Division which prosecutes environmental violations, to the Environment and Natural Resources Division. Through this, and other popular actions (such as efforts to elevate EPA to cabinet-level status) President Bush has sought to recoup some of the environmental support he had lost as a result of the Exxon Valdez disaster, disputes about global warming, and inevitable conflicts between the energy and environmental objectives of his administration.

## 2.0 FEDERAL ENFORCEMENT

In most states the greatest environmental enforcement threat today comes from the federal government. Ever since the Superfund scandal of the early 1980s, EPA has been trying to prove to Congress, states, the nation and itself, that the agency can vigorously and fairly enforce the statutes under its jurisdiction. This effort has been marked by a steady increase in the number and diversity of enforcement actions initiated by EPA. The Bush Administration, in order to show quickly that it is serious about environmental protection, has continued that increase.

Both civil and criminal enforcement actions are normally referred by EPA to the Department of Justice. EPA does not have the power to bypass the Justice Department and bring enforcement actions to court.

Civil enforcement, which for years has been the mainstay of this nation's environmental protection effort, has increased markedly since 1982. In FY 1982, EPA referred 112 cases to the Department of Justice for action.[2] Recent FY 1990 statistics indicate a record 375 cases referred to the Justice Department. EPA prefers civil enforcement actions because the burden of proof is easier and other procedural requirements are less demanding.

On the criminal side, with the 1982 [3] establishment of the Environmental Crimes Unit[4] in the Department of Justice's Environment and Natural Resources Division,[5] the federal government made a determined commitment to treat seriously those most serious violations of the environmental statutes

---

[2] All enforcement statistics used in this chapter have been obtained from either the United States Environmental Protection Agency or the United States Department of Justice.

[3] Prior to 1982 there were some criminal prosecutions under the environmental statutes. *See, e.g., United States v. Frezzo Bros.*, 602 F.2d 1123 (3d Cir. 1979) (criminal conviction for discharge of pollutants without a permit under the Federal Water Pollution Control Act); *United States v. Distler*, 671 F.2d 954 (6th Cir. 1981) (criminal conviction for discharge of hazardous substances into a navigable water under the Federal Water Pollution Control Act). In general, prosecutions of this type during the pre-1982 period were in response to distinctively flagrant violations of the law.

[4] In 1987, this unit was upgraded and is now known as the Environmental Crimes Section.

[5] In 1990, the division was redesignated as the Environment and Natural Resources Division. *See* note 1, *supra*.

pursuant to a systematic and coherent federal enforcement policy.[6] FY 1982 saw 20 referrals to the Department of Justice, with an increase to 59 in FY 1988. The results for FY 1990 indicate a record high 65 criminal referrals by the Agency to the Department of Justice. In FY 1983, the Justice Department recorded 40 indictments. FY 1990 showed a record 134 indictments. During its existence, the Environmental Crimes Section has indicted 703 corporations and individuals, while obtaining 517 convictions and guilty pleas.[7] Of most importance, sentences during this nine year period have totalled over $56 million in fines and 316 years of jail time. This portion of the chapter will examine both the criminal and civil authorities available to federal enforcers, along with an analysis of their current and projected use of these powers.

## 2.1 Criminal Enforcement

With the exception of the National Environmental Policy Act (NEPA), virtually every environmental statute now provides some form of criminal liability.[8] Although these provisions have been relatively diverse, however, amendments to RCRA, the Clean Water Act, and most recently to the Clean Air Act, confirm Congress' intention to standardize the penalties that are available to the courts under the criminal provisions of environmental statutes. Broadly, the statutes now provide for three types of criminal liability: that resulting from negligent actions, knowing actions, and from knowing endangerment.

The rationale behind the use of criminal provisions to enforce environmental laws is simple: the threat of jail is more likely to make an individual and thus his organization obey the law. Imprisoning corporate managers for corporate actions that violate environmental statutes can galvanize a company's desire and ability to comply, and strongly deters similar

---

[6] Starr, *Countering Environmental Crimes,* 13 Envt'l Affairs, 379, n.1 at 380 (1986).

[7] Of the 703 indictments, 222 were corporations and 481 were individuals. Of the 517 convictions, 163 were against corporations while 354 were against individuals. Many of these cases are still awaiting trial.

[8] Clean Air Act Section 113(c), 42 U.S.C. § 7413(c); Clean Water Act Section 309(c), 33 U.S.C § 1319(c); Comprehensive Environmental Response, Compensation, and Liability Act Sections 103(b) and (c), 42 U.S.C. §§ 9603(b) and (c); Emergency Planning and Community Right to Know Act Sections 325(b) and (d), 42 U.S.C. § 11045(b) and (d); Federal Insecticide, Fungicide, and Rodenticide Act Section 14(b), 7 U.S.C. § 136l(b); Marine Protection, Research, and Sanctuaries Act Section 105(b), 33 U.S.C. § 1415(b); Resource Conservation and Recovery Act Section 3008(d), 42 U.S.C. § 6928(d); Safe Drinking Water Act Section 1423(b); 42 U.S.C. § 300h-2(b); and Toxic Substances Control Act Section 16(b), 15 U.S.C. § 2615(b).

violations by others. Criminal fines, with the statutory potential to reach many millions of dollars, coupled with the real possibility of the incarceration of responsible corporate managers, provide a potent and effective weapon in the federal government's battle to clean up the environment. In FY 1990, the federal government obtained a record $29 million in criminal fines and penalties under the environmental statutes, including $2.25 million from Ashland Oil for the negligent maintenance of a storage tank which led to the massive oil spill on the Monongahela River in Pennsylvania.

### 2.1.1 Negligent Violations

In some respects, the most onerous potential criminal liability arises from negligent actions or omissions. These acts and omissions, though unintentional, often have grave impacts. Under the Clean Water Act, it is clear from the statutory language that negligent violations can give rise to criminal liability.[9] For example, in *United States v. Pennwalt,*[10] the company was criminally convicted for a negligent discharge of chemicals in violation of the Clean Water Act as a result of the collapse of a 75,000 gallon storage tank. Pennwalt failed to report the spill correctly in violation of CERCLA, and also was guilty of a negligent failure to adequately maintain the storage tank.[11] The company was fined $1.1 million. In a related action, the manager of the Pennwalt plant was fined $5,000 and placed on probation for a period of two years. (Under the new sentencing guidelines, a sentence of imprisonment would now result for such conduct.) This case underlines the importance of both proper and accurate reporting as well as instituting adequate checks to ensure that equipment and plant are maintained in a safe condition. The recently amended Clean Air Act[12] and the 1990 Oil Pollution Act's amendments to section 309 of the Clean Water Act[13] make clear that negligent releases of hazardous air pollutants which endanger others, or oil or hazardous substances discharged to navigable waters, will give rise to criminal liablity.

### 2.1.2 Knowing Violations

Most criminal violations require some element of conscious wrongdoing

---

[9] Clean Water Act, § 309(c)(1).

[10] No. CR88-55T (W.D. Wash. May 2, 1989).

[11] To some extent, Pennwalt was indicted as a result of an investigation of a later incident, where the authorities uncovered evidence which led them to suspect a cover-up.

[12] Clean Air Act Amendments of 1990, § 701, amending § 113(c)(4).

[13] Oil Pollution Act of 1990, § 4301(c), amending § 309(c) of the Clean Water Act, 33 U.S.C. § 1319(c).

or some criminal intent.[14]   *United States v. Park,* a landmark case on the criminal liability of corporate officers, established that a finding of guilt cannot be based solely on an officer's position in the company, but required some measure of "blameworthiness."[15]   The rule that came out of *Park* was that a corporate officer could be held criminally responsible if such officer had, "by reason of his position in the corporation, responsibility and authority either to prevent in the first instance, or promptly to correct, the violation complained of, and that he failed to do so."[16]   This rule should encourage corporate managers to read their job descriptions closely, especially since the Justice Department's policy is to indict not only corporations committing environmental offenses, but also the highest ranking individual in a company against whom a case can be proven.

One criminal prosecution under the Resource Conservation and Recovery Act (RCRA) shows that the appellate courts are interpreting the standards for "knowing" violations in a manner very favorable to the prosecution.   The decision in *United States v. Hayes International Corp.,* followed a decision of acquittal by the trial judge after jury verdicts of guilty.[17]   The appeals court reinstated the jury verdict.   The court rejected several arguments based on the "knowing" element of the statute, arguments which had been raised by the

---

[14] *Mens rea.*

[15] 421 U.S. 658, 673 (1975).   Park, the president of a large food distribution company was convicted of adulteration of food under the Food, Drug, and Cosmetic Act, even though responsibility for compliance with applicable rules had been delegated to others in the company.   Park had received notice that the food being held for sale in the company's warehouse was being adulterated by rat poison.   He had delegated the actual responsibility for remedying the situation to some employees.

[16] *Id.* at 673-74.

[17] 786 F.2d 1499 (11th Cir. 1986), In this case, Hayes International Corp. (Hayes) through its employee Beasley, arranged with Performance Advantage, Inc. to dispose of wastes generated in the operation of Hayes' airplane refurbishing operations.   Under the agreement, Performance Advantage would pay Hayes 20 cents per gallon for jet fuel drained from the airplanes Hayes was refurbishing and, for no charge, would pick up other wastes from Hayes including a mixture of paints and solvents.   Hayes and Beasley contended that they thought these wastes, which were shipped to Performance Advantage eight times between January 1981 and March 1982, would be recycled.   In reality, Performance Advantage illegally disposed of the paint and solvent waste obtained from Hayes in seven illegal disposal sites in Georgia and Alabama. Beasley and Hayes were convicted of eight counts of violations of 42 U.S.C. § 6928(d)(1).

defendants in their successful motion for judgment notwithstanding the verdict. In reinstating the conviction, the appeals court articulated rules under which knowing convictions may be obtained under environmental statutes.

1. Mistake of law, grounded in the argument that defendants had no knowledge that a waste was hazardous within the meaning of the regulations or that a permit was required under the statute, was rejected by the court which stated that "it is completely fair and reasonable to charge those who choose to operate in such [highly regulated] areas with knowledge of the regulatory provisions."[18]

2. The Government need not prove a defendant's actual state of mind in order to establish knowledge that a facility receiving hazardous wastes was unpermitted. This may be proved circumstantially by showing that the defendant "willfully fails to determine the permit status of the facility."[19]

3. Although not supported by the facts here, the court found that a good faith belief in a material fact that proved to be in error would be a defense to a charge that a defendant acted knowingly.[20]

Thus, this case stands for the proposition that public welfare statutes involving toxic chemicals and hazardous waste have significant public health implications, and that the companies subject to these statutes are highly regulated and may be presumed to have knowledge of the applicable regulatory requirements. Second, this presumed knowledge may be used to prove circumstantially that a defendant acted in knowing violation of a statute if he or she fails to act in accordance with the strictures of that statute.

When coupled with the results of an earlier case under RCRA, it is easy to see the far reaching implications of these criminal provisions. In *United*

---

[18] *United States v. Hayes International Corp.,* 786 F.2d 1499, 1503 (11th Cir. 1986). This rule was followed in *United States v. Hoflin,* 880 F.2d 1033, 1038-39 (9th Cir. 1989), *cert. denied,* 110 S.Ct. 1143 (1990).

[19] *Id.* at 1504. "If someone is willing to take away wastes at an unusual price or under unusual circumstances, then a juror can infer that the transporter knows the wastes are not being taken to a permit facility." *Id.*

[20] *See, e.g., United States v. International Minerals and Chemicals,* 402 U.S. 558 (1971).

*States v. Johnson and Towers, Inc.,*[21] the court established some of the expansive limits of individual culpability under RCRA in holding that the provisions of 42 U.S.C. § 6928(d)(2)(A), addressing knowing treatment, storage or disposal of a hazardous waste without a permit, applied to employees as well as owners or operators. The court noted that the definition of "person" in the statute includes individuals as well as other corporate and civil entities.[22] The court concluded that had Congress intended in the criminal sanctions established under the statute to limit the meaning of "person" to owners or operators, it would have done so, thus for purposes of criminal sanctions under 42 U.S.C. § 6928(d)(2)(A), the term "person" would have the meaning applicable to RCRA as a whole.[23] Next, the court reviewed the case law concerning criminal penalties associated with public health and welfare laws, and stated that criminal sanctions in such statutes are generally broadly construed by the courts in order to bring out the regulatory purpose envisioned by Congress.[24] These two factors led the court to rule that "it would undercut the purpose of the legislation to limit the class of potential defendants to owners or operators when others also bear responsibility for handling regulated materials."[25]

The court went on to rule that the government's standard of proof included establishing that the individual defendants knew that the waste was hazardous, knew that a permit was required, and knew that their company had no permit. The court pointed out, however, that since RCRA addresses the public health and welfare a lesser showing is required to demonstrate knowing activity with regard to criminal wrongdoing. "[S]uch knowledge, including that of the permit requirement, may be inferred by the jury as to those individuals who hold the requisite responsible positions with the corporate defendant."[26]

---

[21] *United States v. Johnson and Towers, Inc.,* 741 F.2d 662 (3d Cir. 1984), *cert. denied,* 469 U.S. 1208 (1985), arose when the government appealed the trial court's dismissal of three counts of an indictment addressing individual liability under RCRA. Two employees, Hopkins and Angel, were alleged to have managerial responsibility for various aspects of the corporate operations, and that the two had personally, and others at their direction, improperly discharged hazardous wastes. Hopkins and Angel argued that liaibility under RCRA attached only to owners or operators of a facility.

[22] 42 U.S.C. § 6903(15).

[23] 741 F.2d at 665.

[24] *Id.* at 666-67.

[25] *Id.* at 667.

[26] *Id.* at 670.

Two clear conclusions may be drawn from these cases. One, those corporate employees who participated directly in illegal acts are subject to the criminal provisions of these various statutes. Two, those employees who did not *personally* participate in or have knowledge of illegal activities, but who work in an area that is governed by health and safety related statutes or are in certain managerial positions, can have such knowledge and ultimately liability imputed to them. The message is clear: criminal liability may be passed up to those managers and officials who are ultimately responsible for activities governed by environmental statutes by virtue of their roles in managing, supervising, and/or directing the activities of employees whose duties are regulated by those statutes.[27] Such manager or official will be charged with that knowledge which he or she had or should have had.[28] Further, such managers will face criminal liability even when the government cannot prove direct orders to subordinates to violate the law.[29]

Two recent decisions affirming criminal convictions of federal employees

---

[27] As the Supreme Court, in observing that health and welfare statutes impose certain affirmative duties on corporate officials, noted in the *Park* case: "[t]hus *[United States v.] Dotterweich* [320 U.S. 277 (1943)] and the cases which have followed reveal that in providing sanctions which reach and touch the individuals who execute the corporate mission -- and this is by no means necessarily confined to a single corporate agent or employee -- the Act imposes not only a positive duty to seek out and remedy violations when they occur, but also, and primarily, a duty to implement measures that will ensure that violations will not occur. The requirements of foresight and vigilance imposed on responsible corporate agents are beyond question demanding, and perhaps onerous, but they are no more stringent than the public has a right to expect of those who volutarily assume positions of authority in business enterprises whose services and products affect the health and well being of the public that supports them. 421 U.S. at 672.

[28] *"Ignorantia legis neminem excusat."* Ignorance of the law excuses no one.

[29] The Eleventh Circuit gave a subtle twist to, and in the process a slight expansion of, the holding of the *Hayes* and *Johnson and Towers* cases in *United States v. Greer*, 850 F.2d 1447 (11th Cir. 1988). There the court ruled that the government could establish that a defendant knowingly disposed or caused others to dispose of a hazardous waste even when it could not prove that the defendant actually told another party to dispose of the waste. *Id.* at 1451. "[G]iven Fountain's testimony that Greer had approved of previous dumpings as a way to meet storage squeezes, the jury could infer from the context of the specific discussion . . . that when Greer instructed [Fountain] to 'handle' the truckload of waste . . . he effectively ordered him to dump it." *Id.* at 1451-52.

for environmental violations make clear that neither federal employees nor corporations which engage in federal contracting are immune from such prosecutions. In one highly publicized case the Court of Appeals upheld the convictions of three civilian employees of the Army's Aberdeen Proving Grounds in Maryland.[30] The defendants, who were high-level civil servants, had argued on appeal that they were immune from criminal prosecution under RCRA due to their status as federal employees, in effect attempting to claim the sovereign immunity of the United States for themselves. In rejecting that argument the court first noted that the defendants were "individuals," and that term was included in RCRA's definition of "person." The court then went on to state that "[t]he defendants . . . were . . . convicted as individuals, not as agents of the government. Suffice it to say that sovereign immunity does not attach to individual government employees so as to immunize them from prosecution for their criminal acts."[31] In 1989, the Court of Appeals for the Second Circuit rejected federal employee arguments that they could not be "the person in charge" of military installations, and so upheld a conviction for failure to report a release of hazardous substances from the burial of paint cans.[32] In that case, a two-year prison sentence was imposed.

While the Aberdeen case was decided in the context of federal employees, its reasoning applies with equal if not greater force to government contractors. They will not be protected from criminal prosecution for violation of environmental laws even if the actions are purportedly taken at the direction, behest, or sufferance of the federal government.

### 2.1.3 Knowing Endangerment

There is only one published decision addressing the most serious environmental crime, *i.e.* those involving knowing endangerment.[33] In *United*

---

[30] *United States v. Dee,* 912 F.2d 741 (4th Cir. 1990).

[31] *Id.* at 744. Of course, federal employees and installations are also subject to enforcement by state agencies. Although they are currently immune from civil penalties, there have been serious efforts to expand the range of tools available to enforcers when dealing with the federal government and its employees.

[32] *United States v. Carr,* 880 F.2d 1550 (2d Cir. 1989).

[33] Another decision may be forthcoming based on the first conviction under the Clean Water Act's knowing endangerment provision. In *United States v. Borjohn Optical Technology, Inc.,* Cr. 89-256-WD (D. Mass. Nov. 7, 1990). There the company *and* its president were convicted for illegally discharging nickel plating wastes into the public sewer system of Burlington, MA, and in the process placing their employees in imminent danger of death or

(continued...)

*States v. Protex Industries, Inc.* (Protex), the court upheld defendant's conviction for knowing endangerment under RCRA.[34] Protex, a hazardous waste handling company, was charged with knowingly endangering its workers as a result of its operating procedures: exposing employees to solvents resulting in intoxication and psycho-organic injury.[35] In upholding the conviction, the court stated that "[t]he gist of the 'knowing endangerment' provision of the RCRA is that a party will be criminally liable if, in violating other provisions of the RCRA, it places others in danger of great harm and it has knowledge of that danger."[36]

As the *Protex* decision makes plain, there is only one additional element necessary to distinguish a "knowing violation" from a "knowing endangerment" charge. For example, under the Clean Water Act, the only difference between the two crimes is that knowing endangerment entails knowledge that the knowing violation "places another person in imminent danger of death or serious bodily injury."[37] Taken together with the legal standards necessary to establish other nowing" elements of the crime, as set forth in the *Hayes* and *Towers and Johnson* cases, it may be relatively easy to establish that next element against a corporation. If a manager orders the dumping of a liquid waste containing mercury into a local stream or river, the government may be able to prove, that such act knowing placed another person in imminent danger of death or serious bodily injury by establishing that the water fed directly into a public drinking water system. Thus, with scant more than evidence establishing knowledge of the toxic nature of mercury and the use of the stream as a source of drinking water, a company's liability can be increased dramatically.[38]

In knowing endangerment cases prosecuted against individuals, the government is required by the Clean Water Act, RCRA, and the Clean Air Act

---

[33](..continued)
serious bodily injury. The company's president was recently sentenced to 26 months in prison, and fined $400,000.

[34] 874 F.2d 740 (10th Cir. 1989).

[35] The court sharply rejected the contention that psycho-organic injury did not constitute serious bodily injury: "Appellant's position demonstrates a callousness towards the severe physical effect the prolonged exposure to toxic chemicals may cause or has caused to the three former employees." 874 F.2d 740, 743 (10th Cir. 1989).

[36] *Id.* at 744.

[37] Section 309(c)(3)(A), 33 U.S.C. § 1319(c)(3)(A).

[38] *Compare,* 33 U.S.C. § 1319(c)(2) and 33 U.S.C. § 1319(c)(3)(A).

to demonstrate the accused person's "knowledge." This demonstration may be made with circumstantial evidence that the accused took affirmative steps to shield himself from relevant information:

> In determining whether a defendant who is an individual knew that a violation placed another person in imminent danger of death or serious bodily injury --
>
>> (i) the defendant is responsible only for actual awareness or actual belief possessed; and
>>
>> (ii) knowledge possessed by a person other than the defendant, but not by the defendant, may not be attributed to the defendant;
>
> except that in proving a defendant's possession of actual knowledge, circumstantial evidence may be used, including evidence that the defendant took affirmative steps to be shielded from relevant information.[39]

Thus, while a corporate manager will not be held to possess the actual knowledge of a worker in the plant that illegal activity is ongoing, that manager cannot escape liability by ignoring, refusing to act on, or attempting to avoid information which tends to expose the illegal activity.

### 2.1.4 General Criminal Provisions and Sentencing

In addition to charging violations of a particular environmental statute, federal prosecutors have a broad array of generic criminal statutes that can be used along with the statute specific environmental provisions. Chief among these is a prosecution for making false statements, violation of which may be punished by a substantial fine, five years imprisonment, or both.[40] While often used in prosecutions not involving environmental provisions, courts have held that willful failure to report material facts where there is a legal

---

[39] Clean Water Act, § 309(c)(3)(B); Clean Air Act, § 113(c)(5)(B); RCRA, § 3008(f)(2).

[40] "Whoever, in any matter within the jurisdiction of any department or agency of the United States knowingly and willfully falsifies, conceals or covers up by any trick, silence or device a material fact, or makes or uses any false writing or document knowing the same to contain any false, fictitious or fraudulent statement or entry, shall be fined not more than $10,000 or imprisoned not more than five years, or both." 18 U.S.C. § 1001.

obligation to disclose is violative of this provision.[41]   Other, more general, provisions are also available to federal prosecutors.[42]

Since environmental regulation rests so heavily on self-reporting, there may be reluctance to rely on self-monitoring or self-reporting results as the sole basis for criminal prosecutions.  Indeed, some reporting provisions make it a criminal violation to fail to report and provide that the report is not to be the basis for criminal prosecution except for perjury or false statement.[43]   By the same token, where attempts are made to falsify reports or tamper with monitors, the Justice Department and EPA are much more likely to recommend criminal prosecution, because they view such falsifications as threatening the integrity of the entire reporting system.   In these circumstances, prosecutors may rely primarily on statutes penalizing false statements, perjury, and obstruction of agency proceedings, even though the underlying conduct involved complex environmental regulations.  These general criminal violations may be far easier to prove.

Recent revisions of the federal criminal code -- Title 18 -- increased the monetary penalties available to prosecutors in environmental cases, beyond the severe penalties already provided in the substantive statutes.[44]   Thus, in

---

[41] *United States v. Hernando Ospina,* 798 F.2d 1570 (11th Cir. 1986); *United States v. Puerto,* 730 F.2d 627 (11th Cir. 1984); *United States v. Tobon-Builes,* 706 F.2d 1072 (11th Cir. 1983).   In the environmental arena, *United States v. Gold, reported at,* 8 Env't Rep. (BNA) 1239 (N.D., Ill.1977).

[42] *See,* e.g., 18 U.S.C. § 2 (Aiding or Abetting); 18 U.S.C. § 4 (Misprision of a Felony); 18 U.S.C. § 1341 (Mail Fraud); 18 U.S.C. § 371 (Conspiracy); 18 U.S.C. § 1505 (Obstruction of Agency Proceedings).

[43] *E.g.* Clean Water Act Section 311, 33 U.S.C. § 1311.

[44] 18 U.S.C. § 3571 provides judges with the option of sentencing individuals and corporations to either a fine in the amount as set forth in the specific statute violated or the following alternatives:

Felony: $250,000 / individual and $500,000 / corporation.
Misdemeanor resulting in death: $250,000 / individual and
    $500,000 / corporation.
Misdemeanor: $5,000-$100,000/individual and $10,000-
    $100,000 / corporation.

In addition, if a person derives "pecuniary gain" or the offense results in "pecuniary loss" to another, the defendant can be fined up to the greater of twice the gross gain or loss.  This latter provision can, in effect, serve as an unlimited fine schedule.

*United States v. Orkin Exterminating Company,*[45] the district court fined the company $500,000 under these alternate sentencing provisions because misdemeanor violations of the federal pesticide statute resulted in two deaths.[46] In fact, in the recent amendments to the Clean Air Act, rather than raise criminal penalty amounts from the pre-amendment levels which ranged between $10,000 and $50,000 per conviction, Congress instead chose to subject violators to "a fine pursuant to Title 18 of the United States Code."[47]

For serious environmental violations, corporate exposure for criminal fines can be extremely high. Most environmental statutes make each day of a violation a separate offense. For example, in the case of a Clean Water Act violation, fines of $10,000 per day were provided until February 1987 when they were increased to $25,000 per day. Thus, in the case of a long-standing violation, such as failure to secure a discharge permit until February 1991, a company's maximum exposure would be over $40,000,000, the maximum per day fine under the five year statute of limitations. Moreover, under the proposed corporate sentencing guidelines penalties could range even higher.

Criminal fines double under the Clean Water Act and other environmental statutes for repeat violations. Thus, if a company has multiple plants, a criminal violation at one may increase the compliance stakes substantially at all the others.

Criminal convictions can have severe collateral effects on companies and management in addition to the immediate financial effects. Failures to disclose potential environmental liabilities may give rise to securities law investigations and derivative suits by shareholders. Under the Clean Air and Clean Water Acts, convictions can result in the violator being debarred from government contracts,[48] a death sentence for some companies. Additionally, under the Internal Revenue Code, criminal and civil fines are not a deductible business expense so the financial effect of these fines is increased.

While it is easy to discuss criminal environmental liability in legal terms, the real impact of criminal enforcement can only be measured in personal terms. Those convicted of violating criminal provisions of environmental statutes go to jail. Often they are convicted of felonies, and receive sentences of multiple years incarceration. Following their release from prison,

---

[45] Cr. No. 88-40, (W.D.Va. Nov. 16, 1988).

[46] 3 *Toxics Law Reporter* 818 (Nov. 30, 1988).

[47] *See* Section 701, Clean Air Act Amendments of 1990, *to be codified at* 42 U.S.C. § 7613(c).

[48] Clean Air Act, Section 306, 42 U.S.C. § 7606; Clean Water Act, Section 508, 33 U.S.C. § 1368. The 101st Congress considered legislation to extend such debarment to convictions for RCRA violations. The 102d may do so as well.

these convicted felons are usually placed on probation for a number of years. The impact on a person's mental and physical health; the strain placed on marriages and family life; the loss of income and the drain on financial resources attributable to defense against the charges; the embarrassment and humiliation felt by the convicted person and his or her family all represent real results of enhanced enforcement of criminal environmental statutes.

Corporations and their officers should expect the use of criminal enforcement tools by the federal government to continue. In addition, they should expect more of the individuals convicted to actually go to jail. In part as a result of the federal sentencing guidelines, environmental criminals should expect to be sentenced to a term in excess of one year. As national patience over the length of time necessary to bring pollution under control wears thin, and as 1980s hostility to environmental protection is replaced by the greater receptivity in the 1990s, indictments, trials, and jail sentences will become more commonplace.

## 2.2 Civil and Administrative Enforcement

Even with the increase in activity under criminal statutes, EPA's use of its civil enforcement powers will continue to be the mainstay of the federal enforcement effort. As shown by the 1987 amendments to the Clean Water Act and the 1990 amendments to the Clean Air Act, Congress intends the Agency to continue its aggressive civil enforcement program.[49] As noted above, EPA is meeting the challenge. EPA has consistently been setting new records for civil enforcement. The 375 cases referred to the Department of Justice in FY 1990 represented a new record for the Agency, surpassing the 372 cases referred by the Agency in FY 1988. The cases referred covered a broad range of environmental statutes and indicate either stable or increased civil enforcement in each medium under EPA's jurisdiction.

Perhaps the most noteworthy aspect of recent federal civil enforcement efforts have been the large penalties assessed by the courts in these cases. In FY 1990, the federal government recovered in excess of $1.2 billion in civil penalties, its second straight billion dollar year. Although enforcement is covered in detail in each of the substantive chapters, major civil penalties in the past several years have included:

---

[49] The Water Quality Act of 1987, Pub. L. No. 100-4, 101 Stat. 7 (1987), amended the Clean Water Act by raising the maximum per violation civil penalty to $25,000 per day, from $10,000. Section 313(b) of the Water Quality Act, amending section 309(d) of the Clean Water Act, 33 U.S.C. § 1319(d). The Clean Air Act Amendments of 1990 extensively amended section 113, concerning enforcement, strengthening all of its provisions.

-- a $32,000,000 penalty assessed for Clean Water Act violations committed by a municipal waste treatment authority in Puerto Rico. A number of other penalties in excess of $500,000 have been reported against industrial and municipal dischargers;

-- a $6,000,000 penalty assessed under the Clean Air Act against a refiner in Texas;

-- a $15,000,000 penalty assessed under the Toxic Substances Control Act in settlement of PCB disposal violation by pipeline;

-- a $250,000,000 judgment against Occidental Chemical for the cleanup of the Love Canal Superfund site.

These penalty levels and judgments suggest that the results of civil penalty actions can spell the difference between a profitable and unprofitable year for many companies, and in some cases, the difference between survival and bankruptcy.

Most civil enforcement cases are settled rather than tried. These settlements generally include the payment of significant civil penalties, commitments to correct violations through the installation of additional control equipment, and a schedule of stipulated civil penalties where deadlines in the decree are not met. In one recent steel company case, failure to meet deadlines resulted in a court-ordered shutdown of the plant.

EPA currently has several enforcement initiatives, designed to focus its resources on specific areas of environmental concern, ongoing. Specifically, under the Clean Water Act, the Agency is continuing to focus on pretreatment issues. This is a two-pronged attack whereby EPA concentrates its efforts on bringing Publically Owned Treatment Works (POTWs) into compliance with effluent permits. In turn, the POTWs are required to enforce the pretreatment requirements of their industrial contributors. Additionally, the Agency will begin targetting whole effluent toxicity and chemical-specific effluent limits for direct dischargers. Under RCRA, the Agency has focused on owners of treatment, storage, and disposal facilities who have not met groundwater certification requirements or submitted final permit applications. Under the Safe Drinking Water Act, Class V wells will be targetted. Under the Clean Air Act, EPA is making a major effort to ensure compliance with stationary source requirements associated with asbestos removal and demolition. Multi-media enforcement efforts against single facilities will also be an Agency priority; the first set of these major cases was filed in the fall of 1990. Toxic Release Inventory (TRI) data gathered under EPCRA will give a major boost to enforcement efforts as well.

As civil enforcement cases for monetary penalties and injunctive relief have been before the courts since the early 1970s, the procedural law governing such actions has been relatively stable. In one area, however, the Supreme Court made clear that the right to a jury trial applies in civil penalty cases as it does in criminal cases. In 1987, the Supreme Court decided *Tull v. United States*.[50] Prior to the *Tull* decision, it had been held that Congress could adopt certain statutory remedies that have no analogy to common law, "vesting factfinding in an administrative agency or others without the need for a jury trial."[51] The Supreme Court, however, held that a Seventh Amendment right to a jury trial exists to determine liability when the United States seeks civil penalties and injunctive relief under the Clean Water Act.[52] The rationale probably applies to other statutes which provide for civil penalties for environmental violations, though not necessarily to clean-up costs under the Comprehensive Environmental Response Compensation and Liability Act.[53] Whether alleged violators exercise this right, however, remains to be seen, given the public's strong support for enforcement.

Perhaps the most important development in the civil enforcement arena is the government's increasing reliance on administrative actions and the ability to assess penalties administratively. From FYs 1988 through 1990, EPA issued over 11,000 administrative orders, with over 4,000 in FY 1990 alone. Many of these orders also assessed penalties under authority of RCRA and the Clean Water and Safe Drinking Water Acts.[54] In fact, during that three year period, nearly half of the administrative orders EPA issued, 5,271, were pursuant to the authority of the Clean Water and Safe Drinking Water Acts.

---

[50] 481 U.S. 412 (1987).

[51] *United States v. Tull,* 769 F.2d 182, 186 (4th Cir. 1985), quoting *Republic Industries v. Teamsters Joint Council No.83 of Virginia Pension Fund,* 718 F.2d 628, 642 (4th Cir. 1983), *cert. denied,* 467 U.S. 1259 (1984).

[52] *Tull v. United States,* 481 U.S. at 420. The Supreme Court refused, however, to extend the right to a jury trial to the actual assessment of civil penalties. *Id.* at 422-25.

[53] In *Wehner v. Syntex Corp.,* the court refused to extend the *Tull* rationale to a private CERCLA cost recovery action. The court stated: "CERCLA . . . is intended for the public good; under Section 9607(a)(4)(B) courts act *in the public interest* by restoring the status quo and ordering that which rightfully belongs to plaintiffs. Such action is within the recognized power and within the highest tradition of a court of equity." 682 F.Supp. 39, 40 (N.D. Cal. 1987) (emphasis added).

[54] *See* RCRA Section 3008, 42 U.S.C. § 6928; Clean Water Act Section 309(g) (as amended by section 314 of the Water Quality Act of 1987), 33 U.S.C. § 1319(g); Safe Drinking Water Act Section 1414(g) (as amended by the Safe Drinking Water Act Amendments of 1986), 42 U.S.C. § 300g-3.

When assessing penalties pursuant to these provisions, the Agency has to provide various levels of procedural safeguards, including hearings.[55] However, the processes employed in assessing administrative penalties, which can be as high as $25,000 per day, are much less burdensome on the Agency and provide less protection to recipients than civil actions. Under the Clean Water Act and Safe Drinking Water Act, there are caps on penalties in administrative proceedings at $125,000. New Clean Air Act Section 113(d), added by the 1990 amendments, sets a cap at $200,000, which can be adjusted upward to account for inflation. There is no such cap in RCRA.

## 3.0 STATE AND LOCAL ENFORCEMENT EFFORTS

While the focus of this chapter is enforcement by the federal government, it must be noted that states, cities, and counties often have both the authority and inclination to institute criminal, civil, and administrative enforcement proceedings. Under most federal statutes, states can be delegated, or administer in lieu of, federal environmental programs, including enforcement authorities. Many states enact their laws to become authorized by EPA to enforce the environmental programs within their boundaries. Thus, as a result of enforcement agreements and authorizations worked out between the state and EPA, in many states the only enforcement personnel that a company may encounter will be from state agencies. In some instances state authority is in addition to those requirements of federal law, especially in those instances where federal law allows state environmental laws to be more stringent or broader in scope than the federal provisions.[56]

Historically, states have employed common law nuisance and trespass doctrines to abate environmental problems. But with the expansion of state environmental programs and the delegation of federal programs to state control, states are utilizing more sophisticated and use diverse, media-specific statutes to attack environmental violators. For example, New Jersey's Environmental Cleanup Responsibility Act[57] is widely acknowledged to be one of the most stringent state laws in existence addressing potential hazardous waste sites. The law sets forth stringent cleanup requirements for any "industrial establishment" that is to be closed or undergo a transfer of ownership. Statutes of this type, as well as states' use of federal statutes, has resulted in increased enforcement at this level.

While the threat of state enforcement is real, that does not translate

---

[55] *See, e.g.,* Clean Water Act Sections 309(g)(2)(A) and (B), 33 U.S.C. §§ 1319(g)(2)(A) and (B).

[56] *See, e.g.,* RCRA Section 9008, 42 U.S.C. § 6991(g).

[57] N.J. Stat. Ann., Title 13 , Chapter IK (1988); 1983 N.J. Laws Chapter 330.

into its uniform application. In many states, such as Colorado, Maine, and Ohio, the level of environmental awareness, and hence, environmental enforcement is relatively high. Alaska is, following the Exxon Valdez, another example of a state moved to aggressive enforcement of environmental regulations. Other states, for a myriad of reasons including fiscal constraints, tend to rely on EPA to perform the lion's share of environmental enforcement. What is clear, however, is that state environmental agencies and attorneys general offices can likely play a major role in any company's operations. EPA reported that states issued 12,126 administrative orders in FY 1989, only down slightly from a record high of 12,742 such orders issued in FY 1985.[58] In addition, state environmental agencies referred 714 civil actions to state attorneys general in FY 1989, down from a high of 904 in FY 1988.[59] Thus, gauging the level of concern in state officials and keeping track of local enforcement trends is certainly a worthwhile task for any company.

In addition to states, local and regional entities sometimes institute enforcement actions against violators of environmental standards in connection with hazardous waste sites. While actions from these sources occur with much less frequency than actions by federal or state governments, to discount such entities would be a mistake. For example, New York City has instituted massive civil litigation under CERCLA,[60] and the Kings County (Brooklyn, New York) District Attorney's Office has established an environmental unit to prosecute criminal violations on a local level.

## 4.0  CITIZEN SUITS AND TOXIC TORT ACTIONS

Private individuals, often acting through groups, can initiate litigation seeking redress for alleged violations. These actions can come in two broad forms: citizens suits and private damages actions. Virtually every environmental statute permits some form of citizen suit.[61] Although the scope

---

[58] State administrative order statistics reflect those orders issued pursuant to the Federal Insecticide, Fungicide, and Rodenticide Act (FIFRA), the Clean Water Act, the Clean Air Act, and RCRA, or state counterparts.

[59] Judicial referrals are only under the Clean Water Act, the Clean Air Act, and RCRA, or state counterparts.

[60] *City of New York v. Exxon, et al.,* 85 Civ. 1939 (S.D.N.Y.) (KC) is an action where the City of New York is seeking damages for the clean up of five landfills in the City. Clean up estimates range as high as $700 million.

[61] Clean Air Act Section 304, 42 U.S.C. § 7604; Clean Water Act Section 505, 33 U.S.C. § 1365; CERCLA Section 310, 42 U.S.C. § 9659; Emergency Planning and Community Right to Know Act (EPCRA) Section 326, 42 U.S.C. §

(continued...)

of each of the provisions varies, they generally grant citizens the right to participate in or initiate enforcement of most provisions of the statute and its regulations. Citizens usally cannot begin such litigation without giving notice to the federal government (both EPA and the Department of Justice), the state where the alleged violation occurred, and the alleged violator. This is done mainly to give the primary regulatory authorities the opportunity to initiate an enforcement action of their own, which usually serves to preclude the citizen action, or to allow the alleged violator to correct any infraction.

Citizen suits are a major factor in environmental enforcement litigation. The Supreme Court has addressed the scope of the citizens suit provision of the Clean Water Act in *Gwaltney of Smithfield Ltd. v. Chesapeake Bay Foundation Inc.*[62] and the citizens suit provision in the Resources Conservation and Recovery Act in *Hallstrom v. Tillamook County.*[63] In *Gwaltney* the Court held that citizens may not maintain an action under the Clean Water Act where they allege that violations of the law occurred wholly in the past.[64]

---

[61](..continued)
11046; RCRA Section 7002, 42 U.S.C. § 6972; Safe Drinking Water Act Section 1449, 42 U.S.C. § 300j-8; and Toxic Substances Control Act Section (TSCA) 20, 15 U.S.C. § 2619.

[62] *(Gwaltney)* 484 U.S. 49 (1987). Here, environmental groups brought suit against a meat-packing plant pursuant to an approved NPDES program, authorized by section 402 of the Clean Water Act, 33 U.S.C. § 1342, and adminstered by the Commonwealth of Virginia. Va. Code §§ 62.1 - 44.2 *et seq.* (1950). The environmental groups alleged that Gwaltney "has violated . . . [and] will continue to violate its NPDES permit." *Gwaltney* at 54. Gwaltney moved to dismiss, alleging that section 505 of the Clean Water Act only permitted actions where the complaint "allege[d] a violation occurring at the time [it] is filed." *Id.,* quoting *Hamker v Diamond Shamrock Chemical Co.,* 756 F.2d 392, 395 (5th Cir. 1985). In rejecting that argument, the District Court held that an action could be maintained where the complaint only alleged violations that occurred wholly in the past. *Chesapeake Bay Foundation, Inc. v. Gwaltney of Smithfield, Ltd.,* 611 F. Supp. 1542, 1547 (E.D. Va. 1985). The Fourth Circuit affirmed, rejecting the Fifth Circuit's *Hamker* ruling. Prior to the Supreme Court's consideration of the case, the First Circuit adopted a third position, holding that a section 505 action may be maintained where "the citizen-plaintiff fairly alleges a continuing likelihood that the defendant, if not enjoined, will again proceed to violate the Act." *Gwaltney* at 56, quoting *Pawtuxet Cove Marina, Inc. v. Ciba-Geigy Corp.,* 807 F.2d 1089, 1094 (1st Cir. 1986). The Supreme Court acted to resolve the conflict between the Circuits.

[63] *Hallstrom v. Tillamook County,* 110 S.Ct. 304 (1989).

[64] *Gwaltney* at 56-63.

The Court did, however, rule that citizens could maintain an action where they "make a good-faith allegation of continuous or intermittent violation."[65] This holding was clarified on remand when the Fourth Circuit set forth standards for determining if such a good-faith allegation has been made. If the plaintiffs "prove violations that continue on or after the date the complaint was filed, or . . . adduce evidence from which a reasonable trier of fact could find a continuing likelihood of a recurrence in intermittent or sporadic violations," then an action may be maintained.[66] The penalty was later reduced to $289,822 by the Court of Appeals.[67] Thus, any hope among NPDES permittees that citizen suits would stop or slow down when the Supreme Court ruled, has been greatly tempered by the subsequent lower court opinions on remand.

In the *Hallstrom* case, the Court ruled that failure of a plaintiff bringing an action under the citizen suit provision of RCRA to give the required 60-day notice required the district court to dismiss the action.[68] The Court noted that strict application of this rule furthered the act's purposes by allowing state and federal agencies the opportunity to act first.

The other citizen "enforcement" action is the private damages action, popularly known as a toxic tort suit. These actions, which are becoming increasingly common, seek damages for alleged injuries caused by violations of the environmental statutes. They rely on a variety of theories ranging from negligence to strict liaibilty, trespass, and nuisance, as well as product liability theories.

One of the major issues surrounding this type of litigation is causation. Usually a governmental agency or the company itself (through self-monitoring and reporting) has established liability for the alleged violation. In many states this violation is *per se* negligence, conclusively establishing liability if a causal link between the violation and the damage can be shown. The issue in the toxic tort suit then, is to establish a causal relationship between the violation committed by the company and the injury allegedly suffered by the plaintiff.

Punitive damages will often be sought in toxic tort and other private civil environmental cases. Where a knowing violation of applicable regulations is shown, the possibility of significant punitive damages becomes real. In one recent case involving knowing contamination of an aquifer with salt, the

---

[65] *Id.* at 64.

[66] *Chesapeake Bay Foundation, Inc. v. Gwaltney of Smithfield, Ltd.,* 844 F.2d 170, 171-2 (4th Cir. 1988).

[67] *Chesapeake Bay Foundation, Inc. v. Gwaltney of Smithfield, Ltd.,* 890 F.2d 690, 698 (4th Cir. 1989).

[68] *Hallstrom v. Tillamook County,* 110 S.Ct 304 (1989).

district judge levied punitive damages of $10,000,000, a judgment which was affirmed by the court of appeals.[69] As was explained above in connection with criminal prosecutions, "knowing" violations may be considerably easier to prove than most lay people would assume. In particular, environmental audits may be an important source of such evidence, especially if a company refuses to carry out the recommendations of the audit, and a violation of regulations subsequently injures someone. Similar evidence might be found in corporate budget documents where requests for environmental compliance funding are cut. The obsession with short-term bottom-line performance found in some corporate cultures may infuriate a jury of ordinary citizens where a company has cut corners on compliance and people have been hurt. A jury's response in those circumstances will be a sizable award of punitive damages.

## 5.0 CONCLUSION

A recent survey concluded that the American people viewed environmental offenses as the seventh most serious criminal offense -- ahead of sky-jacking and armed robbery. EPA has publicly stated that it intends to continue to implement its enforcement programs to maximize the deterrent impact of cases brought against serious violators, by recouping economic gain and preventing violators from contracting with the federal government through the agency's contractor-listing program. There is every reason to believe that enforcement will increase.

Corporate managers cannot ignore environmental compliance if they wish to lead their companies well and stay out of jail. No matter how urgent the bottom line may seem, compliance efforts cannot be safely subordinated or postponed any longer if enforcement actions, including criminal prosecutions, are to be avoided. EPA and the Department of Justice, in response to public pressure, are treating certain violations of environmental requirements are *crimes,* punishable by incarceration. Whether it seems fair or not, if presented with the opportunity, the enforcers at EPA and the Department of Justice will dutifully try to send you to jail -- and that prospect is not at all heartening.

> I know not whether laws be right,
> Or whether laws be wrong;
> All that we know who lie in [jail]
> Is that the wall is strong;
> And that each day is like a year,
> A year whose days are long.[70]

---

[69] *Miller v. Cudahy*, 656 F. Supp. 316 (D. Kan. 1987), *affirmed*, 858 F.2d 1449, 1458 (10th Cir. 1988), *cert. denied.*, 109 S.Ct. 3265 (1989).

[70] *The Ballad of Reading Gaol*, 1898, Oscar Wilde.

Chapter 3

# WATER POLLUTION CONTROL[1]

J. Gordon Arbuckle, Timothy A. Vanderver, Jr.,
and Russell V. Randle
Patton, Boggs & Blow
Washington, D.C.

## 1.0   INTRODUCTION--THE HISTORICAL PERSPECTIVE

In 1972, Congress put the basic framework for federal water pollution control regulation in place by enacting the Federal Water Pollution Control Act (FWPCA),[2] as well as the Marine Protection, Research and Sanctuaries Act (MPRSA),[3] to regulate ocean dumping. In 1977, Congress renamed the FWPCA the Clean Water Act (CWA) and changed the regulatory focus to rigorous control of toxic water pollutants.[4]   In 1987, Congress passed extensive amendments to improve water quality in areas where compliance with nationwide minimum discharge standards was insufficient to assure attainment of the CWA's water quality goals.[5]  The MPRSA has also been amended several times, most recently in 1988, so that the offshore dumping of industrial wastes and sewage sludge is effectively prohibited, leaving dredge spoil as the

---

[1] For more information on this subject, readers are referred to the *Clean Water Handbook* by the authors, listed at the back of the book.

[2] 33 U.S.C. §§ 1251-1376, Pub. L. No. 92-500, 86 Stat. 816 (1972).

[3] 33 U.S.C. §§ 1401-1445, Pub. L. No. 92-536, 86 Stat. 1052 (1972).

[4] Pub. L. No. 95-217, 91 Stat. 1567 (1977). The statute was also amended in 1978 to deal more effectively with spills of hazardous substances, Pub. L. No. 95-576, 92 Stat. 2467 (1978), and in 1981 primarily to revise the grant program for publicly-owned treatment works (POTWs). Pub. L. No. 97-117, 95 Stat. 1623 (1981) (Municipal Wastewater Treatment Construction Grant Amendments of 1981).

[5] The Water Quality Act of 1987, Pub. L. No. 100-4, 101 Stat. 76 (1987).

only large volume waste for which ocean dumping is regulated rather than prohibited.[6]

Finally, in August 1990, Congress enacted the Oil Pollution Act.[7] This new statute substantially revised section 311 of the CWA and its proscriptions on oil and hazardous substance discharges, created a one billion dollar clean-up fund, tightened vessel, personnel and equipment standards for oil transport and storage, and dramatically strengthened federal removal authority and the applicable civil and criminal penalties.

The Clean Water Act has five main elements:

(1)  a system of minimum national effluent standards for each industry;

(2)  water quality standards;

(3)  a discharge permit program where these standards are translated into enforceable limitations;

(4)  provisions for special problems such as toxic chemicals and oil spills; and

(5)  a revolving construction loan program (formerly a grant program) for publicly-owned treatment works (POTWs).

Some history makes these program elements more understandable and puts the detailed discussion of them into context. Prior to 1970, the standards, generally set by the states, established allowable concentrations of pollutant parameters for various water bodies. These standards were supposed to be used to formulate individualized permit limitations for each discharger. Although this approach was theoretically attractive, it worked badly in most states. Major problems included:

--  Inability to determine precisely when a discharge violated applicable standards;

--  Inapplicability of federal-state water quality standards to intrastate waters;

--  Lack of state initiative in making load allocations required to set enforceable discharge standards; and

--  Cumbersome enforcement mechanisms and the requirement of state consent for federal enforcement.

---

[6] The 1977 and 1980 amendments prohibited almost all ocean dumping of industrial wastes and sewage sludge after 1981. Pub. L. No. 95-153, 91 Stat. 1255 (1977); Pub. L. No. 96-572, 94 Stat. 3344 (1980).

[7] Pub. L. No. 101-340, 104 Stat. 484 (1990).

Although a few states made the water quality approach work, it was clear by 1970 that an effective nationwide approach required a permit program based on federal minimum "end-of-pipe" effluent criteria enforceable directly against the discharger.

When legislation proposed in 1969 to provide this mechanism failed to pass, and when courts and citizens groups "discovered" that the Refuse Act penalized discharges of pollutants which had not been approved by the Army Corps of Engineers and provided a "bounty" to citizens who provided information for the government to bring actions to enforce those permit requirements, the Nixon administration initiated the Refuse Act permit program in late 1970.[8]

The Refuse Act is an archaic 1899 statute designed to protect navigation. It does, however, prohibit almost all discharges into navigable waters or tributaries thereof, unless a permit is obtained from the Corps of Engineers prior to commencing the discharge.[9] By using this authority to require all industrial dischargers to apply for and obtain permits, the granting or denial of which would be based on environmental factors, the administration was able, for the first time, to pose a credible threat of prosecution. Hundreds of criminal cases were prosecuted under the Refuse Act, as such prosecutions were the only mechanism for enforcement provided by the Refuse Act.

The Refuse Act was not drafted as a comprehensive water pollution control statute. Consequently, the permit program encountered severe problems:

-- The act provided no standards for the grant or denial of permits, nor were any regulations promulgated to provide such standards;

-- As a result of a court decision, *Kalur v. Resor,*[10] environmental impact statements had to be prepared for every permit decision, further taxing the inadequate staff in charge of processing the applications;

-- Penalties under the act were thought by many to be inadequate; and

---

[8] 33 U.S.C. § 407; Ex. Ord. No. 11574, 35 Fed. Reg. 19627 (Dec. 23, 1970).

[9] The only exception recognized by the statute is for "refuse matter . . . flowing from streets and sewers and passing therefrom in a liquid state." Thus, the regulation of stormwater discharges, which has proven controversial under the Clean Water Act, *see* § 6.2 below, is more difficult to address under the Refuse Act, though the stormwater exception is to be narrowly applied, and does not include industrial waste. *Crawford v. National Lead Co.*, 29 ERC 1048, 1054 (S.D. Ohio 1989).

[10] 335 F. Supp. 1 (D.D.C. 1971). The relationship between NEPA and current Clean Water Act permit requirements is explored in the Chapter on NEPA, and in following sections of this Chapter.

-- The relationship of the act to other federal and state water pollution control efforts was unclear, and created considerable confusion.

By late 1971, it was evident that comprehensive legislation was needed for the water pollution control program to work.

In late 1972, over President Nixon's veto, Congress finally passed such legislation, Public Law 92-500.[11] This statute made the Environmental Protection Agency (EPA) responsible for setting nationwide effluent standards on an industry-by-industry basis and required EPA to set such standards on the basis of the capabilities and costs of pollution control technologies to the regulated industry as a whole. EPA had to follow a stringent timetable for setting these standards.

The act continued requirements for water quality standards so that more stringent discharge standards could be imposed where effluent standards were insufficient to assure that the quality of receiving waters did not deteriorate to, or remain at, unacceptable levels. States could take over the administration of the permit program when state control programs met rigorous federal standards.

The basic framework of the 1972 act--national effluent limitations, water quality standards, the permit program, special provisions for oil spills and toxic substances, and a POTW construction grant program--proved reasonably sound and remains so today. Congress significantly amended the act in 1977 in an effort to focus technology-based standards more effectively to control toxic pollutants, and to resolve numerous definitional and policy issues raised by court and EPA decisions. Over President Reagan's veto, Congress passed significant amendments in 1987. These amendments brought the act full circle: discharge standards are now to be tightened beyond technology-based minimums to assure that water quality standards for toxic pollutants are met. The 1990 Oil Pollution Act moved the CWA oil and hazardous substance discharge requirements into the modern era by making prevention, removal, and restoration high priorities of the program, with potent enforcement tools and adequate funds to make these priorities felt by the regulated community.

## 2.0 FEDERAL-STATE WATER POLLUTION CONTROL PROGRAM-- OVERVIEW

The regulatory program established under the Clean Water Act, as amended, has two basic elements--a statement of goals and objectives and a system of regulatory mechanisms calculated to achieve those goals and objectives.

---

[11] 33 U.S.C. § 1251-1376, 86 Stat. 816 (1972).

## 2.1 Goals and Objectives

The act states the objective (Section 101) is to "restore and maintain the chemical, physical and biological integrity of the nation's waters." To achieve that objective, the act establishes as "national goals":

- Achieving a level of water quality which "provides for the protection and propagation of fish, shellfish, and wildlife" and "for recreation in and on the water" by July 1, 1983; and

- Eliminating the discharge of pollutants into United States waters by 1985.

The "no-discharge" goal was written into early drafts of the 1972 act in order to encourage the adoption of sewage treatment systems relying on land application of effluent. The "no-discharge" language remained after the legislative emphasis shifted away from land application, in part to encourage the reuse and recycling of industrial process water and chemicals. Even though they are unattainable in the short run, these national goals significantly affect the stringency of limitations imposed.

## 2.2 Mechanisms for Achieving These Goals and Objectives

The principal means to achieve the act's goals is a system to impose effluent limitations on, or otherwise to prevent, discharges of "pollutants" into any "waters of the United States" from any "point source." This system includes six basic elements:

(1) A two-stage system of technology-based effluent limits establishing base-level or minimum treatment required to be achieved by direct industrial dischargers (existing and new sources) and publicly owned treatment works (POTWs) and a complementary system of pretreatment requirements applicable to dischargers to POTWs. EPA has set these standards and the compliance dates for them have expired. EPA is now in the process of revising standards for a number of industries, or setting standards for industry segments which had no nationally applicable standard.

(2) A program for imposing more stringent limits in permits where such limits are necessary to achieve water quality standards or objectives.

(3) A permit program (the National Pollutant Discharge Elimination System--NPDES) requiring dischargers to disclose the volume and nature of their discharges, authorizing EPA to specify the limitations to be imposed on such discharges, imposing on dischargers an obligation to monitor and report as to their compliance or noncompliance with the limitations so imposed, and authorizing EPA and citizen enforcement in the event of non-compliance.

(4)     A set of specific deadlines for compliance or noncompliance with the limitations so imposed, and authorizing EPA and citizen enforcement in the event of non-compliance.  Citizen enforcement actions have become an important factor in recent years.

(5)     A set of specific provisions applicable to certain toxic and other pollutant discharges of particular concern or special character (e.g., stormwater discharges, spills of oil or hazardous chemicals).  These oil spill provisions were dramatically revised and penalties and cleanup obligations made far more severe by the Oil Pollution Act.

(6)     A loan program to help fund POTW attainment of the applicable requirements.  This loan program replaces the previous grant program as a result of the 1987 amendments, though Congress continues to appropriate more money for the program than the Administration requests.

The act is, of course, far more complex than this six-part framework indicates.  In order to grasp how the act applies in concrete situations, it is essential to understand the definitional and policy decisions which translated these broad legislative directives into reality.

## 3.0     ESTABLISHING TECHNOLOGY-BASED EFFLUENT LIMITATIONS

The CWA mandates a two-part approach to establishing effluent limitations for industrial discharges:  (1) nationwide base-level treatment to be established through an assessment of what is technologically and economically achievable for a particular industry; and (2) more stringent treatment requirements for specific plants where necessary to achieve water quality objectives for the particular body of water into which that plant discharges.  According to some commentators, Congress intended EPA to implement this combination of standards in a way that would force control technology innovation.[12]

### 3.1     Pollutants to be Addressed
Although the CWA broadly defined pollutants subject to regulation and permitting, it furnished little guidance before 1977 with regard to toxic pollutants.  For that reason, and because the 1972 act imposed unrealistic deadlines on EPA's limited staff, EPA focused almost entirely on high-volume "conventional" pollutants such as biochemical oxygen demand (BOD), suspended

---

[12] *See, e.g., Chemical Manufacturers Association v. Natural Resources Defense Council*, 470 U.S. 116, 156 (1985) (Marshall, J. dissenting) (and sources cited therein).

solids (SS) and acidity and alkalinity (pH) when it developed the effluent limitations required by the act. As long as this approach was followed, EPA's basic system of effluent limits and permit requirements failed to address the dangers posed by more toxic pollutants such as chlorinated organic chemicals, heavy metals, pesticides and so forth, and at the same time may have overemphasized removal of solids and oxygen-demanding materials contained in conventional wastes.[13] Regulation of "toxic" pollutants was thought to be the exclusive province of Section 307 (a) of the act, which authorized EPA to identify and regulate, on a chemical-by-chemical rather than industry-to-industry basis, substances which it could prove have toxic effects on identified organisms in affected waters.

Because of the stringent burden of proof and extensive procedures which the pre-1977 Section 307 required, EPA failed to establish a workable program to control the discharge of toxic pollutants. Only a limited number of substances were identified as toxic substances; long delays were encountered before final effluent limits were adopted for any of them.

EPA's failure to develop an effective toxics control strategy under the 1972 act led the Natural Resources Defense Council (NRDC), an environmental organization, to sue the Environmental Protection Agency. That litigation was settled, and in the process of settlement, EPA and NRDC developed a policy which focused all of the regulatory mechanisms provided by the 1972 act upon the effective regulation of toxic or priority pollutant discharges. In developing this policy, the parties identified (1) the pollutants which would be the primary subject of regulation; (2) the industries which would be the primary concern in applying the regulations; and (3) the methods of regulating toxic discharges with the act's existing legal mechanisms. The agreements reached in these negotiations were embodied in a settlement decree,[14] and were adopted by Congress as a blueprint for a toxics control strategy in the 1977 amendments, and to a certain degree in the 1987 amendments.

The decree mandated full use of all the available regulatory tools under the act with a specific focus on the identified "priority pollutants." Pursuant to the decree, EPA was to develop a program to regulate the discharge of 65 categories of "priority pollutants" (now including at least 126 specific chemical substances--see Annex A, at the end of this chapter) by 34 industry categories (see Annex B) which include over 700 subcategories. More than 70 percent of the nation's industries were affected by the decree.

The consent decree required adoption of best available technology effluent limitations for each priority pollutant in each industrial category by 30 June 1983. These limitations had to be applicable to at least 95 percent of the

---

[13] It should be noted, however, that conventional treatment frequently, if unintentionally, removes substantial amounts of the more toxic wastes.

[14] *NRDC v. Train*, 8 E.R.C. 2120 (D.D.C. 1976), *modified*, 12 E.R.C. 1833 (D.D.C. 1979).

point sources in each identified industry category or subcategory. Similar technology-based requirements had to be adopted for new sources and sources discharging into publicly owned treatment works. The basis for excluding a category of point sources from the toxic-focused system of technology-based effluent limitations is quite limited.

In addition to these stringent industry-by-industry toxic effluent limits, the consent decree made specific provision for full implementation of the waterway segment-by-segment approach, discussed below.

The NRDC consent decree provided a judicial mandate for full use of the Clean Water Act's enforcement mechanisms in a carefully tailored effort to reduce discharges of toxic pollutants.

The 1977 amendments largely adopted the technology-based aspects of this mandate and enacted them into federal statutory law. The amendments:

-- Adopted the consent decree list of priority pollutants as the list of toxic substances to be given primary emphasis in the implementation of the Clean Water Act (Annex A);

-- Required adoption of best available technology (BAT) effluent limitations for each listed substance;

-- Permitted EPA to add to or remove from the list of "toxic" substances;

-- Required compliance with BAT effluent limitations for toxic pollutants subsequently added to the list within three years of the establishment of the limitations;

-- Provided a new system for upgrading and enforcing pretreatment regulations based on both the effluent limitations on the discharge from publicly owned treatment works and the intended use of the sludge from the facilities;

-- Authorized EPA to adopt regulations establishing best management practices to control the discharge of toxic pollutants in the form of runoff or other uncontrolled discharges from industrial plant sites, parking lots and so forth.

The 1977 amendments did not, however, fully replace the consent decree. Instead, that decree has been the primary mechanism by which the toxics control program has been modified. The consent decree was amended in 1979 to reflect the changes made by the 1977 amendments and to respond to the operational problems perceived by EPA since the decree was originally issued in 1976.[15] The modification also expanded the permissible bases upon which

---

[15] 12 E.R.C. 1833 (D.D.C. 1979).

EPA may exclude substances from regulation pursuant to the consent decree. Pursuant to the deadlines extended in the decree, EPA has now promulgated effluent limitations for all thirty-four industry categories, or decided for some that insufficient levels of toxic discharge were occurring to warrant such regulation. Challenges to the consent decree have twice been rejected by the courts.[16]

Under the revised consent decree, the Environmental Protection Agency can exclude industry categories from regulation of certain substances where only "trace amounts" of the substance are found. The administrator is also authorized to exclude pollutants from coverage under the direct discharge effluent limitations if the amount and toxicity of such pollutants within a category or subcategory does not, in his judgment, justify the development of regulations having nationwide applicability. Seven industry categories of the thirty-four listed ones have been so excluded.

The basis for excluding pollutants from the applicability of standards was similarly expanded. EPA is authorized to make such exclusions when it finds that the amount and toxicity of all incompatible pollutants discharged by a category or subcategory taken together is so small that regulations of nationwide applicability governing pretreatment of those pollutants is not justified. Three pollutants of the list of 129 have been so excluded.

In the water quality standards area, the modified consent decree has had little effect because of EPA's long delays in identifying the affected wastes and developing a control program. The 1987 amendments put teeth in this portion of the consent decree by imposing a two-year deadline for the states to identify water bodies which fail to meet water quality standards because of toxic discharges by particular point sources, and by requiring the imposition of additional effluent limitations on such responsible point sources, and compliance with them, three years after that.

The consent decree as confirmed by the 1977 and 1987 amendments and modified by the court has transformed the entire Clean Water Act program and focused EPA and industry attention on the most dangerous pollutants. The industry-by-industry technology-based effluent limitations have been transformed from limited requirements focused on three or four conventional pollutants to a very specific system of limitations potentially applicable to 126 or more different pollutants as well as whole effluent toxicity for each industry category. Water quality standards will become far more important to industry, especially now that the technology-based standards have been promulgated, and deadlines set to impose more stringent discharge limitations on the basis of water quality standards.

---

16 *Environmental Defense Fund v. Costle*, 636 F.2d 1229 (D.C. Cir. 1980); *Citizens for a Better Environment v. Gorsuch*, 718 F.2d 1117 (D.C. Cir. 1983), *cert. denied*, 467 U.S. 1219 (1984).

### 3.2 Required Level of Treatment--Technology-Based Limits for "Existing" Direct Discharges

Section 301(b) of the 1972 act provided for the establishment of nationally applicable technology-based effluent limitations on an industry-by-industry basis. These effluent limitations were to establish a nationwide base-level of treatment for *existing* direct discharge sources in every significant industrial category. This level of treatment was to be achieved in two phases. For "existing"[17] industrial discharges, Section 301 directs the achievement:

> by July 1, 1977, of effluent limitations which will require application of the best practicable control technology currently available, and by July 1, 1983, of effluent limitations which will require application of the best available technology economically achievable.

As the time for achievement of best practicable technology (BPT) is long past, its primary relevance now is as a basis for setting subsequent standards or, as discussed below, in regulating discharges of conventional pollutants.[18] EPA defined BPT as the "average of the best existing performance by well-operated plants within each industrial category or subcategory." The word "control" in Section 301 emphasized Congress' expectation that, in establishing the 1977 effluent guidelines, EPA would emphasize end-of-pipe treatment rather than in-plant control measures. EPA did so. However, Section 304(b)(1) of the act makes it clear that the alternative of in-plant process changes may be considered, at least for the purpose of determining whether a proposed effluent limitation is "practicable." Under the statute, the word "practicable," was to be read together with the provisions of Section 304(b)(1)(B), and so required that effluent limitations be justifiable in terms of the "total cost of (industry-wide) application of (the required) technology in relation to the effluent reduction benefits to be achieved." This determination was to take into account a number of specific factors such as the age of the equipment and facilities involved, the process employed, and non-water quality environmental impacts. Thus, in developing the BPT limitations, the Environmental Protection Agency was required to make what amounted to a cost-benefit balancing test that took into account a broad range of specific engineering factors relating to the ability of plants within a category or subcategory to achieve the limits. The BPT definition was essentially unchanged by the 1977 amendments.

---

[17] The act's "existing discharge" provisions will in fact apply to some newly constructed facilities since they cover any source for which a new source performance standard (see Part 3.3) has not been proposed.

[18] EPA recently and successfully invoked the BPT provisions in setting revised standards for the organic chemicals industry. *See Chemical Mfrs. Assn. v. EPA*, 870 F.2d 177 (5th Cir. 1989).

EPA defined best available technology (BAT) as the "very best control and treatment measures that have been or are capable of being achieved." The agency can consider in-plant process changes in addition to end-of-pipe treatment measures in establishing these limitations, which had a 1983 compliance deadline under the 1972 act. Although EPA is required to consider the cost of achieving the required effluent reduction in determining whether a BAT limitation is economically achievable, it is not required to balance cost against effluent reduction benefit as it is in the case of the BPT standards. The engineering factors required to be considered--age of equipment and facility, process employed, process changes, non-water quality environmental impacts and so forth--are the same for BAT as for BPT.

The BAT definition was essentially unchanged by the 1977 and 1987 amendments but its scope of applicability was radically altered and its date for attainment was extended until 1989. The BAT effluent limitations now focus primarily on the priority pollutants listed in the *NRDC* consent decree and on additional toxic pollutants identified pursuant to Section 307(a) of the act. These effluent limitations have now been promulgated--several years late in some cases--for all industry categories listed in the consent decree, or, for some industries, EPA has determined that the industry discharges too few toxic pollutants to warrant regulation under this provision. Compliance is required three years after promulgation or March 31, 1989, whichever is earlier.[19] For pollutants not listed in the consent decree but identified as toxic pollutants under Section 307(a)(1) of the act, compliance with BAT effluent limits is required no later than three years after the date on which the limitations are established.

The "conventional" pollutant measures, which were the primary focus of EPA's pre-1977 BAT effluent limitations, are specifically excluded from the scope of coverage of the BAT limits provided by the 1977 amendments. Those pollutants are subject to an entirely new treatment standard established for the first time in the 1977 amendments--best conventional pollutant control technology.

The best conventional technology (BCT) effluent limitations were, like the BPT and BAT limitations, to be adopted on an industry-by-industry basis but were to apply for each affected industry only to pollutants which were identified as "conventional." The compliance deadline for the BCT limitations was July 1, 1984, now extended by the 1987 amendments to three years after promulgation or March 31, 1989, whichever is sooner. The 1977 amendments specifically included within the definition of "conventional pollutants" biological oxygen demand (BOD), suspended solids (SS), fecal coliform bacteria, and pH.

---

[19] CWA, § 301(b). In the section-by-section analysis of the 1987 Amendments, the bill's managers stated that where EPA delays in promulgation of regulations made the compliance date impossible to meet, EPA should issue the affected source an administrative order requiring compliance as expeditiously as practicable. 1987 *U.S. Code Cong. & Admin News* 19.

EPA is authorized to include additional pollutants within the conventional pollutants definition, but to date has added only oil and grease to the statutory list of conventional pollutants.[20] The act specifically excludes heat from the conventional pollutant definition as there are special statutory provisions for thermal discharges.[21] The BCT limitations were to be adopted by EPA based on a consideration of the reasonableness of the relationship between the cost of attaining a reduction in effluents and the effluent reduction benefits which will result. The cost of providing treatment to comply with these limits was expected by the Congress to be generally comparable to the cost of achieving the secondary treatment limitation for publicly owned treatment works. As with BPT and BAT limits, EPA was required, in adopting best conventional technology effluent limits, to take into consideration factors such as the age of the equipment and facilities involved, the process employed, engineering aspects, process changes and non-water quality environmental impacts (including energy requirements).

The Congress anticipated that EPA, in developing the best conventional technology limits, would review the old BAT limits for conventional pollutants and reduce the stringency of such limits to the extent indicated by the economic justification and cost comparability with secondary treatment requirements.

EPA's first effort at developing BCT regulations was reversed because the agency failed to consider cost-effectiveness adequately in the development of these rules.[22] EPA then promulgated revised regulations and methodology, which are far less costly than the original rules. In most industry categories, EPA's new methodology resulted in BCT limitations no more stringent than those established for BPT.

The last of the three categories of technology-based effluent limits for existing industry direct discharges provided in the 1977 amendments is the system of effluent limitations to be adopted for "nonconventional nontoxic" pollutants. This is essentially an "everything else" category which applies to all pollutants other than those identified as priority pollutants, toxic pollutants or conventional pollutants under the preceding sections of Section 301. To date, only about ten substances have been so regulated; most could probably be regulated just as well as either toxic or conventional pollutants. Compliance is required three years after the date the limitations are established by EPA regulations, or March 31, 1989, whichever is sooner.

---

[20] 40 C.F.R. § 401.16.

[21] CWA, § 316.

[22] *American Paper Institute v. EPA*, 660 F.2d 954 (4th Cir. 1981).

## 3.3 Required Level of Treatment--Technology-Based Limits for "New Source" Direct Discharges

The establishment of effluent limitations for "new sources" (defined as any facility or major modification, the construction of which is commenced "after the publication of proposed regulations" prescribing an applicable standard of performance) is separately dealt with in Section 306 of the act. Although the general approach for establishment of new source performance standards under Section 306 is similar to the approach for the establishment of Section 301 effluent limitations (discussed in the previous section) there are significant differences both as to the level of treatment required and the manner of applying the limitations established. These differences remain important because of EPA's delay in promulgating many BPT and BAT limitations, and because the new source standards will govern the addition or replacement of certain equipment at an existing discharger.[23]

Section 306(a)(1) of the act defines the term "standard of performance" as

"a standard for the control of the discharge of pollutants which reflects the *greatest degree of effluent reduction. . .achievable through application of the best available demonstrated control technology, processes, operating methods, and other alternatives,* including, where practicable, standards permitting no discharge of pollutants" (emphasis added).

The primary difference between this criteria and the Section 301 criteria is the requirement in Section 306 that EPA consider not only pollution control techniques, but also various alternative production processes, operating methods, in-plant control procedures and so forth. Accordingly, in the establishment of Section 306 new source performance standards (NSPS), alternatives or supplements to end-of-pipe treatment will be emphasized. Production process alternatives, which, though less economic, may have a significantly reduced pollution potential may, as a practical matter, be required.

A second major difference regarding criteria for development of new source performance standards is the absence of the kind of requirements for detailed consideration of economic and technological factors which are established by Section 301 for existing source effluent limitations procedures. This absence reflects a presumption that if a source is yet to be constructed, there is greater flexibility to alter total facility design so as to achieve stringent effluent limitations. Thus EPA has greater discretion in the promulgation of new source performance standards than it does with respect to existing sources.

A third, and major, factor to be taken into account when considering the applicability of new source performance standards is that the act provides almost no flexibility for moderating the impact of those standards when applied to specific facilities. The fundamental factors variance and other modification

---

[23] 40 C.F.R. § 122.29(b).

authorities provided by the act are not applicable in the new source situation and, accordingly, strict conformity with the new source performance standards, where applicable, is essential.

Finally, where EPA is the issuing authority, the issuance of a permit for a new source discharge is a federal action subject to the review requirements of the National Environmental Policy Act.[24] Thus, where the issuance of a new source discharge permit is found to be a major action with a significant effect on the environment, an environmental impact statement will be required. The result will be both substantial delay in the issuance of the new source permit and the potential inclusion of stringent requirements in permits which are issued, requirements which may address a host of other environmental issues besides water pollution discharges and the quality of receiving waters.[25]

Because a determination that a facility is a new source significantly affects both the stringency of applicable treatment standards and the length of time required in order to obtain a permit, the question of when a facility "commences construction" for purposes of applying new source performance standards has proven controversial. This issue is addressed in considerable detail by Section 122.29 of EPA's NPDES regulations, court decisions, and opinions of EPA's General Counsel. The question remains difficult because it depends so heavily on the facts of each case. Companies planning new facilities or major modifications of older ones should carefully review these factual and legal issues with counsel early in the planning process.

Section 306 does offer both to new and modified sources one protection which is not available to existing sources under Section 301. Section 306 specifically provides that any new facility constructed to meet all applicable new source standards of performance in effect as of the time it is constructed, may not be subjected to any more stringent standards for ten years from the date construction is completed or for the period of depreciation under the Internal Revenue Code, whichever is shorter. This protection from more stringent standards of performance, as EPA construes the act, is inapplicable to any more stringent permit conditions which are not technology-based, i.e. limitations based on water quality standards, toxic pollutant prohibitions, or to any new permit conditions which govern pollutants not controlled by the applicable new source performance standards with which the facility complied at the time of construction. It should be noted that, on the expiration of the ten-year protection period, immediate compliance with the standards in effect at the time of such expiration will be required. No implementation period for compliance with those standards will be allowed.

---

[24] CWA § 511(c), 40 C.F.R. Part 6.

[25] There are serious questions about the legality of EPA including additional environmental requirements based on NEPA in an NPDES permit. *See Natural Resources Defense Council v. EPA*, 822 F.2d 104 (D.C. Cir. 1987).

### 3.4 Effluent Guidelines for Additional Source Categories

The act requires EPA to make periodic revisions of effluent guidelines for industry categories as technology improves and economics change.[26] The initial set of industry categories was specified in part by section 306(b)(1)(A) and has been expanded with time by EPA.

Section 304(m) was added by the 1987 amendments. This new provision requires EPA to establish and to publish a schedule for the annual review and revisions of existing effluent guidelines.[27] This provision also requires the Agency to identify source categories discharging toxic or nonconventional sources for which effluent guidelines have not been published, and to establish a schedule by which enforceable guidelines for these categories are promulgated. The deadline to promulgate such standards is February 1991.[28]

EPA has published such plans in August 1988 and January 1990. These plans indicate that EPA will issue new or revised guidelines for eight source categories and will study eleven additional source categories for revision of existing standards or promulgation of new standards.[29] The dates for such revisions or additions are as late as 1995 under EPA's published plan. Environmentalists have filed suit challenging the legality of EPA's plan, both because of its extension of the schedule for four or more years beyond the statutory deadline, and because EPA failed to include about 70 source categories for which environmentalists believe effluent guidelines should have been revised. This action, if successful, could result in a substantial speed-up of revisions of effluent guidelines, and the more rapid regulation of a number of additional source categories. As is often the case, EPA is caught here between a rigid statutory mandate and inadequate resources to implement that mandate.

### 3.5 Required Level of Treatment--Technology-Based Limits for Indirect Dischargers (Pre-Treatment)

Industrial facilities that discharge into publicly owned treatment works (POTWs) are regulated not by the requirements governing direct discharges, but rather by comparable treatment requirements--pretreatment standards-- adopted pursuant to Section 307(b) of the act. Pretreatment standards are calculated to achieve two basic objectives: (1) to protect the operation of POTWs; and (2) to prevent the discharge of pollutants which pass through publicly owned treatment works without receiving adequate treatment. The dual objectives of the pretreatment program result in a two-part system of

---

[26] 304(b).

[27] 304(m)(1)(A).

[28] 304(m)(1)(B), (C).

[29] 53 Fed. Reg. 32584 (Aug. 25, 1988); 55 Fed. Reg. 78 (Jan. 2, 1990).

controls under the applicable EPA regulations. General requirements are imposed under 40 C.F.R. Part 403 and requirements specific to particular industries, so-called categorical standards, are developed and imposed together with other effluent limitations governing each such industry.

The first part of the general pretreatment regulation focuses primarily on preventing the discharge into POTWs of pollutants which will interfere with the proper operation of the receiving treatment works. This "protection" standard[30] prohibits the introduction into any publicly owned treatment works of:

(i)     Pollutants which create a fire or explosion hazard in the POTW, including but not limited to, waste streams which meet the RCRA test for characteristic inflammable waste;

(ii)    Discharges with a pH lower than 5.0 unless the works is specifically designed to accommodate such discharges;

(iii)   Solid or viscous pollutants in amounts which obstruct the flow in a sewer system;

(iv)    Discharges, including discharges of conventional pollutants, of such volume and concentration that they upset the treatment process and cause a permit violation (e.g., unusually high concentrations of oxygen demanding pollutants such as BOD); and

(v)     Heat in amounts which will inhibit biological activity in the POTW resulting in interference, but in no case heat in such quantities that the temperature influent at the treatment works exceeds 40° C (104° F) unless the works are designed to accommodate such heat;

(vi)    Petroleum oil, nonbiodegradable cutting oil, or products of mineral oil origin in amounts that will cause interference or pass through;

(vii)   Pollutants which result in the presence of toxic gases, vapors or fumes within the POTW in a quantity that may cause acute worker health and safety problems; and

(viii)  Any trucked or hauled pollutants, except at discharge points designated by the POTW.

These general pretreatment provisions were recently revised and tightened dramatically as a result of the work by Pretreatment Implementation Review

---

[30] 40 C.F.R. § 403.5, as amended, 55 Fed. Reg. 30082 (July 24, 1990).

Task Force.[31]   These changes were intended to assure that the domestic sewage exclusion under section 1004(C) or RCRA did not allow hazardous wastes to escape needed regulation.[32]   Consequently, in addition to the substantive requirements noted above, industrial users of POTWs must now provide written notification to the POTW, the EPA regional Waste Management Division Director, and the state hazardous waste authorities "of any discharge which if otherwise disposed of, would be a hazardous waste under 40 CFR part 261."[33]   Moreover, if the discharge is of more than 100 kilograms a month of such waste -- whether listed or characteristic -- the industrial user is to include information about the hazardous waste constituents, mass, and concentration, and estimate these amounts for the following 12 months.   The industrial user must certify as part of its notification that it has a RCRA waste minimization program in place.  These requirements become effective in February 1991.

As pollutants which are already addressed in existing discharge monitoring reports are exempt from this notification requirement, it is likely that these notifications, when filed, will result in revisions of a number of pretreatment permits and the filing of enforcement actions for discharge of materials not addressed in such permits.   As this new rule has received little attention it seems likely that many industrial users will inadvertently violate it.

The second major objective of the pretreatment regulations--preventing the discharge in the publicly owned treatment works of pollutants which pass through those treatment works without receiving adequate treatment--is to be achieved by "categorical" pretreatment regulations.   These categorical regulations are applicable only to "incompatible" pollutants--e.g., pollutants other than biochemical oxygen demand, suspended solids, pH and fecal coliform bacteria, and which are not adequately treated in the POTW treatment process.[34]   These categorical pretreatment regulations, like the BAT regulations and new source performance standards, focus primarily on the thirty-four industries and sixty-five toxic pollutant categories specified in the *NRDC* consent decree.   For each discharger into a POTW, these categorical standards

---

[31] 55 Fed. Reg. 30082 *promulgating amendments* to 40 C.F.R. Part 403 (July 24, 1990).

[32] *See Comite pro Rescate de la Salud v. Puerto Rico Aqueduct and Sewer Authority*, 30 ERC 1473 (1st Cir. 1989) (restricting scope of domestic sewage exclusion under RCRA).

[33] 55 Fed. Reg. 30131, *promulgating* 40 C.F.R. § 403.12(p)(i) (July 24, 1990).

[34] Additional pollutants may be identified as "compatible" for a particular treatment works if it can be shown that the facility in question adequately treats those pollutants.

are intended to result in the same level of treatment prior to discharge from the POTW as that which would have been required had the industrial facility discharged those pollutants directly to the receiving waters. The stringency of these categorical standards can theoretically be reduced through the mechanism of removal credits, which takes into account the removal of these pollutants consistently achieved by the POTW in question. Removal credits, however, will not be available under the statute until EPA completes promulgation of its sewage sludge regulations under section 405 of the Act.[35]

Accordingly, the industrial facility discharging into a POTW will be required to achieve, in meeting the applicable pretreatment limits, a level of treatment performance equivalent to the applicable BAT effluent limitations or new source performance standards unless the receiving POTW has an approved pretreatment program and requests removal credits against the applicable pretreatment limit. This removal credit is to be based on the POTW's demonstrated capability to consistently remove that pollutant in its treatment process. In order to qualify for a revision, the POTW must provide consistent removal of each pollutant for which a discharge limit revision is sought, and its sludge use or disposal practices must, at the time of the application and thereafter, remain in compliance with all applicable criteria, guidelines and regulations for sludge use and disposal. EPA modified its regulations in an effort to account for process variations by POTWs,[36] but that effort was reversed by the court of appeals.[37]

Pretreatment requirements are directly enforceable by EPA and states with NPDES permit issuance authority, but the EPA regulations contemplate eventual delegation of primary enforcement responsibility to individual POTWs with EPA and the states receding to a backup role.

Under the regulations, any POTW (or combination of POTWs operated by the same authority) having a total design flow greater than five million gallons per day must have developed and implemented a pretreatment program by July 1, 1983, if it receives incompatible industrial waste. A POTW must have an approved pretreatment program in order to grant removal credits although it may grant conditional removal credits while EPA is considering approval of the POTW's pretreatment program. POTW programs must meet funding, personnel, legal, and procedural criteria sufficient to ensure that the POTW's enforcement responsibilities can be carried out. Once the program is developed and approved, the POTW will be responsible for enforcement of the national

---

[35] *Chicago Association of Commerce and Industry v. EPA*, 873 F.2d 1025 (7th Cir. 1989); *Chemical Manufacturers Association v. EPA*, 870 F.2d 177, 257-61 (5th Cir. 1989); *Armco, Inc. v. EPA*, 869 F.2d 975 (6th Cir. 1989).

[36] 40 C.F.R. § 403.7, 49 Fed. Reg. 31221, August 3, 1984.

[37] *Natural Resources Defense Council v. EPA*, 790 F. 2d 289 (3d Cir. 1986), *cert. denied*, 107 S. Ct. 1285 (1987).

pretreatment standards. A POTW may exercise enforcement authority through a number of methods including contracts, joint powers agreements, ordinances, or otherwise.

Finally, pretreatment regulations establish extensive reporting requirements for both industrial users and POTWs in order to monitor and demonstrate compliance with categorical pretreatment standards.

The pretreatment regulations significantly affect industries subject to categorical pretreatment standards, as well as other industrial users of POTWs which will have to comply with general pretreatment requirements.

### 3.6 Variances

The statutory mechanisms to authorize variances from technology-based standards are exceedingly limited. The most broadly applicable of these variances is the fundamentally different factors (FDF) variance. There are also variance mechanisms to recognize use of innovative control technology and in certain limited circumstances from BAT limitations. Other than the FDF variance, there are no variances allowed from toxic pollutant standards and none at all from discharge limitations set to meet water quality standards.

The fundamentally different factors (FDF) variance evolved through EPA and court interpretation, and was codified and tightened by the 1987 amendments.[38] The FDF variance was initially applied to the 1977 BPT effluent limitations through the inclusion in each set of effluent limitations regulations of a variance clause. This clause allowed a discharger to demonstrate that the limitations should not apply to its facility because of the existence of factors which were fundamentally different from those considered by EPA in the process of developing the effluent limitations.

The scope of the required variance clause was expanded in the case of *Appalachian Power Company v. Train*,[39] and EPA's recognition of the necessity of some sort of variance mechanism for "fundamentally different factors" was applauded by the Supreme Court in the *Dupont* case.[40] The need for a fundamental factors variance arises from the process EPA uses to develop industry-wide effluent limitations under the Clean Water Act. It is impossible to consider all of the factors required to be considered by Section 304 in a full and timely fashion for every type of plant in every industrial category. Consequently, there must be some way to weigh factors not fully considered in the regulatory development process when the time comes to apply effluent limitations to a particular facility in the form of an NPDES permit.

Thus, in both the pretreatment regulations and NPDES permit program regulations discussed below, EPA allows dischargers to obtain the fundamental

---

[38] CWA, § 301(n).

[39] 545 F.2d 1351 (4th Cir. 1976).

[40] 430 U.S. 112 (1977).

factors variance. The variance is available with respect to the categorical pretreatment regulations, as well as for all of the technology-based effluent limits for existing sources. It is unavailable for new source performance standards (because a facility yet to be constructed has greater design flexibility) or for water quality-related effluent limitations. The Supreme Court has ruled that the fundamental factors variance is available with respect to toxic pollutants under the Clean Water Act.[41] The 1987 amendments have codified the fundamental factors variance in section 301 (n) and made it more difficult to obtain.[42]

In order to obtain a fundamental factors variance, the discharger must show that factors applicable to this facility are fundamentally different from those considered in the development of the effluent limitations guidelines. Factors which Section 125.31 of the regulations and section 301(n) of the act allow to be considered as fundamentally different are:

(1) The nature or quality of the pollutants contained in the waste load of the applicant's process waste water;

(2) The volume of the discharger's process waste water and effluent discharged;

(3) Non-water quality environmental impacts of control and treatment of the discharger's raw waste load (are these impacts fundamentally more adverse than those considered during the development of national limits?);

(4) Energy requirements of the application of control and treatment technology (are they fundamentally greater than those assessed in developing national limits?); and

(5) Age, size, land availability and configuration as they relate to the discharger's equipment or facilities, processes employed; engineering aspects of the application of control technology.

If it finds that a fundamentally different factor exists, the Environmental Protection Agency may adopt alternative effluent limitations for the facility in question. It should be noted that those limits may be either more or less stringent than the effluent limitations with respect to which the variance is granted.

---

[41] *Chemical Manufacturers Association v. Natural Resources Defense Council*, 470 U.S. 116 (1985).

[42] CWA, § 301(n).

The fundamental factors variance is not available simply because the cost of compliance with BPT limitations would force plant closure.[43] Instead, the costs of BPT compliance are relevant in deciding if fundamentally different factors exist at a plant and, if so, whether the alternate effluent limitations are as cost-effective as those imposed on the industry in general.[44] (The language of the 1987 amendments make it unclear whether cost can be considered at all.)

Under the 1987 amendments, an applicant must show that it raised the fundamentally different factors during the development of the regulation *or* show why it did not have a reasonable opportunity to raise the factors in such process.[45] The only meaningful relief available for improper application of factors actually considered during the development process is an appeal to the courts. Unless this appeal is taken within ninety days after the applicable effluent limits are published in final form, the right to raise these issues may be waived. These procedural rules make it imperative for affected industries to monitor and to participate in the development and revision of effluent standards applicable to the industry lest this variance mechanism become unavailable.

There are two additional variance mechanisms applicable to discharges of non-conventional, non-toxic pollutants. The first is under Section 301(c). Section 301(c) grants the administrator authority to modify the BAT requirements or the related pre-treatment requirements affecting nonconventional, non-toxic pollutants if it can be shown that the economic capability of the discharger necessitates less stringent limitations. A further prerequisite to such a modification is showing that it will result in further progress toward elimination of the discharge of pollutants. Though this basis for granting a variance is reasonably broad, the circumstances in which it can be granted are strictly limited. The Section 301(c) variance does not apply to the "Best Conventional Technology" effluent limitations, and Section 301(l) of the act precludes the modification of any effluent limitation regulating a toxic or priority pollutant.

Section 301(g) is the second variance mechanism applicable to BAT limitations for several nonconventional non-toxic pollutants--ammonia, chlorine,

---

[43] *EPA v. National Crushed Stone Association*, 449 U.S. 64 (1980), CWA § 301(n)(1)(A).

[44] *Weyerhauser Co. v. Costle*, 590 F.2d 1011, 1036 (D.C. Cir. 1978).

[45] CWA, § 301(n). EPA's regulatory guidance suggests that all such variance applications should have been filed by July 3, 1989, unless the request is related to a later revision of effluent standards for a source category, or in the establishment of new effluent standards for a source category which did not previously have industry-specific effluent guidelines. 54 Fed. Reg. 246 (Jan. 2, 1989).

color, iron, and total phenols--but excludes heat. In the case of sections 301(c) and (g), the utility of the variance is limited by its application only to nonconventional, non-toxic pollutants.

The final statutory basis for modification of BAT and BCT effluent limits and pretreatment standards is set forth in Section 301(k). That subsection authorizes the administrator or state issuing authority to issue a permit providing for a compliance date extension of two years if a source seeks to achieve the applicable limits through the use of innovative technology which has the potential for industry-wide application and has a substantial likelihood of achieving greater effluent reduction than the effluent limitations require or will result in significantly lower costs. It is unclear whether this innovative technology variance may be granted for toxic pollutant limits in view of the prohibition against modification of toxic pollutant effluent limitations set forth in Section 301(l).

With respect to the 1977 BPT effluent limits, the act provided only one now-obsolete basis for extending the time for compliance.

### 3.7 Technology-Based Treatment Standards--Publicly Owned Treatment Works

For discharges from publicly owned treatment works (POTWs), Section 301 directed that by 1 July 1977, they achieve effluent limitations based on secondary treatment, as defined by EPA, and any more stringent limitations necessary to comply with water quality standards or treatment standards imposed by state law. The 1977 and 1981 amendments provided for extension of the 1977 secondary treatment and other deadlines where, because of lack of federal funding or otherwise, planned facilities had not been completed. The extension was to the earliest date on which funding can be provided and construction completed, but in no case later than July 1988. Industrial dischargers whose permits require discharge to a treatment works and who had enforceable contracts for such discharge or who were included in a treatment works facility plan filed with a grant application could be granted an extension on much the same basis as the treatment works itself.

EPA defined "secondary treatment" for purposes of Section 301 in 1973 and modified that definition late in 1984.[46] The effluent levels prescribed by these regulations are as follows:

| | % Removal 30 day average | Concentration (mg/1) Monthly Average | Weekly Average |
|---|---|---|---|
| BOD(5 day) | 85 | 30 | 45 |
| Suspended Solids(SS) | 85 | 30 | 45 |
| Coliform | | 200/100 ml. | 400/100 ml. |
| pH | | 6.0 to 9.0 | |

[46] *See* 40 C.F.R. Part 133.

The regulations make special provision for upwards revision of the "secondary treatment" effluent limits (1) where necessary to take into account storm water infiltration into combined sewers during wet weather periods; and (2) where necessary to take into account the fact that the Section 301 and Section 306 effluent limitations applicable to major industrial dischargers into the treatment works (those exceeding 10 percent of the design flow) would permit an industrial user to directly discharge greater concentrations than those set forth in the table. In the latter case, the permitted discharge from the POTW which is attributable to the industrial waste received for treatment may be increased to equal, but not exceed, that which would be permitted, under the applicable effluent limitations, if the industrial facility were discharging directly into a waterway.

In the 1981 amendments, Congress revised the definition of secondary treatment so that such biological treatment facilities as oxidation ponds, lagoons, and ditches and trickling filters are deemed to be the equivalent of secondary treatment.[47] These modes of treatment are considerably cheaper than other treatment modes, especially for small communities. The changes made pursuant to this standard allow trickling filters and stabilization ponds to meet secondary treatment requirements if the discharge meets the following parameters:[48]

|  | % Removal 30 day average | Concentration (mg/1) Monthly Average | Weekly Average |
|---|---|---|---|
| BOD(5 day) | 65 | 45 | 65 |
| Suspended Solids(SS) | 65 | 45 | 65 |
| pH |  | 6.0 to 9.0 |  |

The relative stringency of the POTW effluent limitations and the fact that, under the 1972 act, POTWs were, for the first time, subjected to effective and directly enforceable federal effluent limitations and permit requirements, gave municipal authorities a strong mandate to rigorously enforce flow and concentration limitations on industrial users of their systems. In some cases, the "pretreatment requirements" imposed by municipal authorities pursuant to this mandate have been more stringent than the federal pretreatment standards discussed above. In addition, as noted below, the increasing need for high levels of performance by POTWs result in new or upgraded facilities which can drastically increase the cost to industry of waste treatment services. EPA and the Department of Justice have made compliance with pretreatment program requirements by municipalities an enforcement priority.

---

[47] CWA, § 304(d)(4).

[48] 40 C.F.R. § 133.105.

## 4.0   WATER-QUALITY RELATED EFFLUENT LIMITATIONS

The 1972 act made technology-based effluent limitations the nationwide minimum or base level of treatment. The act provides several mechanisms by which these discharge limitations are to be tightened in order to protect or maintain adequate water quality in specific bodies of water. These more stringent water quality-based limitations are most often an issue along bodies of water where there is a heavy concentration of industrial dischargers (e.g. the Houston Ship Channel), where receiving waters need to be maintained at a very high quality for recreational or other purposes (e.g. a trout stream), or where hydrologic modifications for navigation (e.g. lock and dam systems) have reduced the capacity of receiving waters to assimilate pollutants.

Under the CWA as amended in 1987, the new section 304(l) will be the most important of several statutory mechanisms for tightening discharge standards over the next five years. This new provision requires tightening of priority and toxic pollutant discharge limitations to meet water quality standards. Sections 301(b)(l)(C) and 302 apply to all categories of pollutants and provide the basic mechanisms by which water quality standards are established and modified. Other sections provide for periodic reviews of water quality by the states and reports to EPA, efforts to preserve lakes and estuaries, and efforts to develop controls on nonpoint sources of pollution affecting water quality.

### 4.1   Toxic Water Quality Standards

The *NRDC* consent decree contained several provisions addressing water quality standards as they related to priority pollutants. These provisions required EPA to issue water quality guidance for states to use in setting additional discharge standards for toxic or priority pollutants. In addition, the decree required identification of so-called toxic "hot spots," where the application of technology-based standards would not achieve water quality standards. For a variety of reasons, including EPA's slow pace in issuing the technology-based standards and the inherent scientific complexity of establishing water quality standards, these provisions of the consent decree had little effect at the level of the individual discharger.

The 1987 amendments added Section 304(l) to the CWA, an addition which adopts several concepts from the consent decree and places enforceable deadlines on their implementation at the individual discharger level.

Section 304(l) requires that each state identify waters within the state where the application of technology-based effluent limitations does not result in the achievement of water quality standards for toxic pollutants. Where noncompliance results substantially from point source discharges of toxic pollutants, the state is to determine which point sources are responsible and to develop individual control strategies for each of these point sources to bring the water body into compliance with water quality standards. By February 4, 1989, states had to submit the list of identified water bodies, together with the affected point sources and the individual control strategies. EPA had 120 days--or until June 1989--to approve or disapprove. If EPA approved the strategy, then the affected dischargers had up to three years--or until June 1992--in which to comply. If EPA disapproved the control strategies, or if a state failed to submit them, EPA then had one year in which to promulgate substitute control strategies. Sources then have three years to comply, or June 1993, if EPA acts on schedule.

EPA has issued detailed guidance about implementation of Section 304(l).[49] The assessments of impaired water bodies are to be made primarily on the basis of existing water quality data, as time does not permit substantial additional monitoring to be conducted to identify these water bodies. In addition, EPA's guidance indicates that when individual control strategies are prepared, they should address *all* pollutant parameters creating water quality problems (e.g. ammonia, chlorine and "whole effluent toxicity") not simply the toxic pollutants identified in the NRDC consent decree.

EPA treated implementation of section 304(l) as a high priority, and as a result completed its review of state plans and individual control strategies on time in June 1989. As a result of these reviews, EPA listed 595 water bodies as substantially impaired as a result of toxic discharges from 879 point sources, including 240 POTWs. Individual control strategies--NPDES permit proposals--were established for all these point sources. Many of these plans are now in various administrative appeal stages.

Some environmental groups contend that section 304(l) requires EPA to revise NPDES permits for all discharges of toxic pollutants to impaired waters, an interpretation which would dramatically increase the number of NPDES permits which would have to be revised and tightened for toxic pollutants. The Court of Appeals has agreed with parts of this challenge, holding that section 304(l) requires the listing of many more bodies of water as impaired by toxic pollutants.[50] After the listing of additional impaired water bodies, the Court will allow EPA to reconsider its decision not to impose individual control strategies on many sources. Thus the section 304(l) program may apply to many more sources than those listed in the first round of individual control strategies.

Implementation of Section 304(l) requires that states have water quality standards in place for toxic pollutants. States normally rely on EPA's guidance documents for the pollutant in question, which is offered under Section 304(a). EPA has completed most of the guidance documents for pollutants identified in the *NRDC* consent decree.

The 1987 amendments amended Section 303(c)(3)(B) to require the states to adopt numerical water quality standards for toxic pollutants where possible.

---

[49] 54 Fed. Reg. 1300 (Jan. 12, 1989).

[50] *NRDC v. EPA*, 31 E.R.C. 2089 (9th Cir. 1990).

EPA has now announced that where states fail to adopt either numerical toxic water quality standards or mathematical methods to calculate toxic effluent limitations appropriate for water quality, EPA water quality guidelines will become the new state water quality standard.[51] This policy effectively nationalizes water quality standards unless states act to recognize local variations. Though most states are working to adopt new numerical water quality standards for toxic discharges, most have not completed the task yet.[52]

Where numerical standards are impractical, the amended act now requires EPA to issue guidance on biological monitoring methods and for states to use such methods in setting standards and assessing compliance under the act. EPA issued guidance in December 1989 for biomonitoring using five species, three for fresh water, and two for salt water.[53] EPA is also requiring biomonitoring and whole effluent toxicity testing for POTWs discharging more than one million gallons per day, and smaller, if major industrial discharges are present. Some states (e.g. North Carolina) began implementing such requirements even before EPA's formal guidance was issued. Biological monitoring is a relatively new concept under the CWA, and its implementation is likely to prove highly controversial.

### 4.2 Water Quality Standards Affecting All Pollutants

Section 304(l) is a more tightly focused version of water quality approaches which have been part of the CWA since 1972. The most important of these more general water quality provisions are Sections 301(b)(l)(C) and 302.

Section 301(b)(l)(C) requires industrial dischargers and POTWs to achieve no later than July 1977, any effluent limitations more stringent than the minimum technology-based standards which may be necessary to meet applicable federal-state water quality standards. This requirement is incorporated into permits issued by EPA through the state certification requirement under Section 401 of the act. (See Part 5.2 below.)

Section 302 of the act authorizes EPA directly to establish effluent criteria more stringent than the applicable BAT limits where necessary for the attainment or maintenance in a specific water body of water quality which "shall assure protection of public water supplies, agriculture and industrial uses, and the protection and propagation of a balanced population of shellfish, fish and wildlife, and allow recreational activities in and on the water. . ." EPA has interpreted this Section 302 authority as providing a selective tool for the agency to impose more stringent requirements where necessary to protect important water resources. Although this section has received little use to date, it does have great potential impact in that it authorizes EPA to adopt its

---

[51] 55 Fed. Reg. 14350 (April 17, 1990).

[52] *See id.* for status list of state water quality standards.

[53] 54 Fed. Reg. 50216 (December 4, 1989).

own effluent limitations for any body of water as to which a state fails or refuses to adopt water quality standards sufficient to maintain fishing and swimming uses.

The water quality standards and water quality-related effluent limitations imposed by these two mechanisms can require levels of treatment considerably higher than those required by the technology-related effluent limits, particularly for water bodies with heavy concentrations of dischargers, or exceptionally poor water quality and correspondingly stringent water quality standards, or water bodies with limited assimilative capacity because of hydrologic factors such as dams for navigation and water supply. (These hydrologic modifications are more likely to be a factor with conventional pollutants such as BOD, which break down relatively fast, than for more persistent toxic pollutants.) The potential stringency of these limitations is increased by the absence of any variance provision applicable to Section 301 water quality standards. Section 302 does contain a limited variance mechanism for standards imposed under its mandate, including a potential five-year variance from certain toxic pollutant standards. The requirement for compliance with water quality standards is inflexible and mandatory, thus increasing the importance of carefully following the development of such standards as they apply to particular water bodies and dischargers to them.

The procedures for setting water quality standards are quite complex. States, acting pursuant to the procedures set out in 40 CFR Section 131.20, are to hold public hearings every three years for the purpose of reviewing and revising state water quality standards. Although EPA issues guidance documents about the effects of various pollutants, it does not set specific minimums for state standards; instead the rules require that such standards specify and protect appropriate water uses (e.g., water supply, fish, wildlife),[54] and set specific numerical criteria where possible to attain these ends.[55] The state standards must attain Clean Water Act's goal of fishable, swimmable waters wherever attainable, and, at a minimum must maintain the uses designated in the standards and current uses,[56] unless the state can demonstrate that the designated use is unattainable or infeasible for one of a short list of reasons, primarily concerning other physical or biological aspects of the water body.[57] In addition, no degradation of "outstanding national

---

[54] 40 C.F.R. §§ 131.6, 131.10.

[55] 40 C.F.R. § 131.11.

[56] 40 C.F.R. § 131.10(h).

[57] 40 C.F.R. § 131.10(g).

resource" waters, such as those in national and state parks, is to be permitted.[58]

The pollutants required to be addressed by state water quality standards are primarily the priority pollutants under the NRDC consent decree, conventional pollutants, and listed nonconventional non-toxic pollutants--over 140 substances or parameters in all. Although EPA has now issued guidance for almost all of the pollutants listed in the NRDC consent decree, EPA, Congress, and some states seem to be moving beyond a pollutant-by-pollutant approach to an examination of "whole effluent toxicity" and biomonitoring.

Adoption of water quality criteria and standards for priority pollutants have no effect until these standards are translated into end-of-pipe effluent limitations to be imposed on dischargers. Section 303(e) of the Act requires states to inventory all waters within their jurisdiction, to identify those waters as to which BAT and other technology-based effluent limits are inadequate, to promote and maintain compliance with water quality standards (water quality limited segments), to establish maximum loadings for water quality limited segments, and to provide a system for allocating those maximum loadings among all dischargers to the affected waters. Section 304(l) followed this general pattern and tailored it to toxic pollutant problems with tight enforceable deadlines.

Section 305(b) requires biennial reviews of water quality by the states and reports to EPA. These biennial reviews are intended to be used as part of the periodic update of water quality standards by the states under Section 303, and now 304(l), with resultant tightening of discharge standards where needed. For discharges to water-quality limited segments, the issuing authority cannot issue a permit unless it finds that the facility will not cause or contribute to the violation of water quality standards applicable to the water into which the discharge is made. These requirements result in a system similar to that now applicable to the location of new facilities under the Clean Air Act, where pressure for new industrial growth results in the imposition of increasingly stringent requirements on existing sources in order to permit new facilities to operate without violation of applicable standards.

EPA has borrowed another concept from the Clean Air Act--the "bubble"-- for use in the water pollution context. Under the "bubble" concept, EPA would permit facilities to cumulate the discharges from different outfalls of the plant and meet a single effluent limitation, rather than outfall-by-outfall limitations. So far, the bubble is limited to steel plants.[59] This approach may lead to appreciable cost savings depending on whether it can be used in water-quality limited areas and whether it applies to toxic pollutants. Two

---

[58] § 131.12(a)(3).

[59] 40 C.F.R. § 420.03.

subcategories in the steel industry--cokemaking and cold forming--were not permitted to use the bubble, in part because of toxic pollutant concerns.[60]

In summary, it seems clear that, both as to industrial direct discharge and pretreatment requirements, the 1987 amendments and the revised water quality standards they require can be expected, during the next five to ten years, to increase the stringency of treatment requirements imposed on many industrial and other dischargers. The toxics orientation of the water quality standards, together with the policy changes and enforcement mechanisms discussed above, merit careful consideration by potentially affected companies. Those companies would be well advised to participate actively in state proceedings related to the review and revision of existing water quality standards and the carrying out of the Section 303 and 304(1) planning process.

## 5.0 PERMITTING UNDER THE NATIONAL POLLUTANT DISCHARGE ELIMINATION SYSTEM

The act's primary mechanism for imposing limitations on pollutant discharges is a nationwide permit program established under Section 402 and referred to as the National Pollutant Discharge Elimination System (NPDES). EPA's present regulations are found at 40 C.F.R. Parts 121-125. This section will consider three basic permit program issues--the program's scope and applicability, the procedures followed in permit issuance, and the nature of the conditions normally included in permits.

### 5.1 Program Scope and Applicability

Under the NPDES program, any person responsible for the *discharge of a pollutant or pollutants into any waters of the United States* from any point source must apply for and obtain a permit.

Although the definition of "pollutant" in Section 502(6) of the act includes only the materials specifically listed in that section,[61] the definition is nevertheless quite broad and has been broadly interpreted to include virtually

---

[60] 47 Fed. Reg. 23265-66, 23271-74 (May 21, 1982), 40 C.F.R. 420.03(b)(3).

[61] Dredged spoil, solid waste, incinerator residue, sewage, garbage, sewage sludge, munitions, chemical wastes, biological materials, radioactive materials, heat, wrecked or discarded equipment, rock, sand, cellar dirt and industrial, municipal, and agricultural waste discharged into water.

all waste material, whether or not that material has value at the time it is discharged.[62]

The term "discharge of a pollutant or pollutants" under the act is defined in Section 502(12) to mean the *addition* of any pollutant to waters of the United States from any *point source*. The act's requirement that there must be an *addition* of a pollutant in order for a discharge to be regulated has been successfully used in some situations to preclude the imposition of limitations on the discharge of materials in a waste stream which are present only by reason of presence in intake waters, if the intake water is drawn from the same body of water into which the discharge is made and if the pollutants present in the intake water are not removed by the discharger as part of his usual operations.[63] The term does *not* include discharges of water from dams, even if a dam's operations adversely affect the temperature and dissolved oxygen content of the water.[64]

The *point source* element of the discharge definition has been one of the most difficult aspects of the permit program to implement. Section 502(14) of the act defines the term "point source" to include "any discernible, confined and discrete conveyance, . . . from which pollutants are or *may be* discharged." The "may be" language is important because it means that permits are required for facilities such as surface waste impoundments from which discharges are not normally anticipated, except under unusual but foreseeable conditions such as excessive rainfall. The "discrete conveyance" language of the definition is so comprehensive as to cover a number of types of discharges, such as storm sewers, irrigation flows and the like, which are not efficiently regulated through the issuance of permits. For this reason, a number of statutory and administrative exemptions from the point source definition or the scope of the permit program have been adopted. These include irrigation return flows, the discharge of sewage from vessels regulated under Section 312 of the act, effluent from properly functioning marine engines, certain agricultural and silvicultural discharges, and certain discharges of dredged or fill material regulated under Section 404 of the act. Regulations also exclude from the point source definition stormwater discharges which occur outside urbanized areas, provided that the runoff is not from lands or facilities used for industrial or commercial activities. The 1987 amendments

---

[62] *See Weinberger v. Romero-Barcelo*, 456 U.S. 305 (1982) (bombs dropped on naval target range held to be pollutants); *United States v. Standard Oil Co.*, 384 U.S. 224 (1966) (accidental discharge of gasoline held to be pollutant discharge under the Refuse Act).

[63] 40 C.F.R. § 122.45(h).

[64] *National Wildlife Federation v. Gorsuch*, 693 F.2d 156 (D.C. Cir. 1982).

amend Section 502(14) in order to codify the exclusion of agricultural stormwater discharges from the definition of point source.

The term "waters of the United States" is defined by EPA regulations[65] to include (1) navigable waters; (2) tributaries of navigable waters; (3) interstate waters; and (4) intrastate lakes, rivers and streams (a) used by interstate travelers for recreation and other purposes, or (b) which are a source of fish or shellfish sold in interstate commerce, or (c) which are utilized for industrial purposes by industries engaged in interstate commerce. The intent of this definition is to cover all waters over which the broadest constitutional interpretation would allow the federal government to exercise jurisdiction.[66] The definition clearly covers wetlands, and the Supreme Court has upheld an expansive definition of wetlands under regulations governing dredge-fill activities under section 404 of the act.[67] Few exclusions to the definition have been recognized and those which have been accepted to date seem to be limited to situations where the waterway in question is wholly confined on the property of the discharger, does not result in any flow beyond the property line, and is not available for significant public use.

One remaining major issue is the extent to which discharges to publicly or privately owned sewage systems constitute discharges to waters of the United States so as to be subject to the NPDES permit requirement. A discharge to a sewage system which is not connected to an operable treatment works is a discharge subject to the NPDES program, but a discharge to a publicly owned treatment works which is capable of meeting its effluent limits is excluded from the NPDES permit requirement.[68] All industrial dischargers to POTWs are required to comply with general pretreatment standards[69] and many must also comply with industry-by-industry ("categorical") standards, promulgated together with effluent limitations for each industry. (see Section 3.4 above.) There are flexible permit requirements for discharges to privately owned treatment works which give the Environmental Protection Agency substantial discretion to consolidate or issue separate permits as needed to meet effluent standards. In some cases, EPA seems to contend that regional waste water treatment plants built primarily to treat industrial wastes must nonetheless impose pretreatment requirements, thereby defeating much of the purpose of building such regional plants.

---

[65] 40 C.F.R. § 122.2.

[66] *NRDC v. Callaway*, 392 F. Supp. 685 (D.D.C. 1975).

[67] *United States v. Riverside Bayview Homes, Inc.*, 474 U.S. 121 (1985).

[68] 40 C.F.R. § 122.3(c).

[69] 40 C.F.R. Part 403.

To summarize, though there are important exclusions, the scope of the NPDES permit program is exceedingly broad. The basic intent is to regulate all pollutants discharged from all facilities into virtually all waters in the United States.

## 5.2    Permitting Procedures

Under Section 402 of the Clean Water Act, the Environmental Protection Agency is the issuing authority for all NPDES permits in a state until such time as the state elects to take over the programs administration and obtains EPA approval of its program. As of November 1990, 18 states and territories did not have approved NPDES programs; EPA functions as the issuing authorities for permits in their jurisdictions.[70]   The 1987 amendments gave EPA the authority to approve partial state permit programs, with the proviso that the program be complete within five years of program submission. This revision should increase the number of states with NPDES programs.[71]   Where the state is the issuing authority, permitting procedures are generally comparable to the EPA procedures discussed below, with certain exceptions. For example, the states, unlike EPA, are not required to provide for an evidentiary hearing, though many do. Where the state is the issuing authority, procedures for judicial review of permit issuance are those provided under the state's administrative procedure act rather than under the Clean Water Act and the federal Administrative Procedure Act. State permit issuance is not a federal action subject to the requirements of the National Environmental Policy Act.[72]

Permits issued by states are subject to review by EPA, and a state permit may not be issued if the EPA Administrator objects within ninety days after the state's proposed issuance. EPA may issue its own permit to the discharger if EPA objects to the state permit.[73]   The administrator must state the reasons supporting the objections and must provide a statement of the limitations and conditions which would be included in the permit if it were to

---

[70] The states and territories without an approved program are:   Alaska, Arizona, District of Columbia, Florida, Guam, Idaho, Louisiana, Maine, Massachusetts, New Hampshire, New Mexico, Oklahoma, Puerto Rico, Samoa, South Dakota, Texas, Commonwealth of the Northern Marianas, and Trust Territory of the Pacific.

[71] CWA, § 402(n).

[72] *See Chesapeake Bay Foundation, Inc. v. Virginia State Water Control Bd.*, 453 F. Supp. 122 (E.D.Va. 1978).

[73] *See Champion International Corp. v. EPA*, 850 F. 2d 182, 28 ERC 1013 (4th Cir. 1988) which upheld EPA's veto of a North Carolina permit on the ground that it failed to assure compliance with water quality standards downstream in Tennessee. EPA then issued a more stringent permit.

be issued by EPA. States are entitled to a public hearing regarding the administrator's objections, and if the objections are not resolved at the hearing or otherwise, the administrator can issue the permit. EPA has the authority to withdraw its approval of a state program and take over the entire program administration if it finds that the state is not carrying out the program in accordance with the act's requirements. This authority has not been exercised.

Procedures for permit issuance are generally as follows: A permit application, on the appropriate form, must be submitted to the EPA regional administrator (or the state, if it is the issuing authority) at least 180 days in advance of the date on which a proposed discharge is to commence or the expiration of the present permit, as the case may be. Where EPA is the issuing authority, it will require for new dischargers, submission of a new source questionnaire before it will process the permit application. This questionnaire serves as the basis for an EPA determination as to whether the facility is a "new source." If the facility is determined to be a new source, the applicant will be required to prepare an environmental assessment for EPA's use in determining whether an environmental impact statement is required by the National Environmental Policy Act.[74]

After the application is filed, the district engineer of the Corps of Engineers must be given an opportunity to review the application to evaluate the impact of permit issuance upon anchorage and navigation. Other federal agencies, and specifically the Fish and Wildlife Service of the Department of the Interior and the National Marine Fisheries Service of the Department of Commerce, are provided a similar opportunity to comment on the application.

Where EPA is the issuing authority, the state in which the discharge will occur must be provided with an opportunity to review the application. Based on that review, the state is asked to certify, pursuant to Section 401 of the act, that the permitted discharge will comply with applicable provisions of Sections 301, 302, 303, 306, and 307 of the act. Since provisions in Sections 301 and 303 deal with the question of compliance with state water quality standards, the state, in effect, is asked to certify that the discharge in question will comply with all limitations necessary to meet water quality standards, treatment standards, or schedules of compliance established pursuant to any state law or regulations. In one recent case, the Court of Appeals has reversed the grant of an NPDES permit because EPA failed to consider and assure compliance with downstream state water quality standards.[75]

Although the applicable regulations would appear to require the applicant for an NPDES permit to provide EPA with the required certification, in practice EPA forwards applications received without a certification to the appropriate state and keeps the state advised throughout the permit

---

[74] CWA, § 511(c).

[75] *Oklahoma v. EPA*, 31 ERC 1741 (10th Cir. 1990).

proceedings. If a state does not either certify or deny certification within a reasonable time after the receipt of the permit application, it will be deemed to have waived the certification requirement. Because this time period starts to run on the state's receipt of an application, it is advisable for the applicant to send a copy of the application to the state rather than waiting for EPA to do so. EPA is barred from issuing any NPDES permit unless the state has either certified the permit or waived its right to certify.

In processing the application, the issuing authority makes tentative determinations as to whether a permit should be issued, and, if so, as to the required effluent limitations, schedules of compliance, monitoring requirements and so forth. These tentative determinations are organized into a draft permit, and the discharger is normally given an opportunity to review and comment on this draft. The public is given notice of the permit application proceeding and the issuing authority's preliminary determinations with respect thereto.[76]

The regulations provide for a period of not less than thirty days during which the public may submit written comments and/or request that a public hearing be held. The issuing authority is required to hold a public hearing if there is a significant degree of public interest in a proposed permit or group of permits. The public must be notified of such hearings and interested persons must be given at least thirty days in which to prepare for the hearings. Following the public hearing, the issuing authority issues a final determination regarding permit issuance after taking into account the comments received. Where the final determination is substantially unchanged from the tentative determination outlined in the original public notice, the issuing authority must forward a copy of the determination to any person who submitted written comments regarding the permit. Where the issuing authority's decision substantially changes the tentative determinations and draft permit, public notice must be given.

Within thirty days following the date of the notice of final determination, any interested person may request an evidentiary hearing or a legal review to reconsider the determination.

The granting of an evidentiary hearing or legal review stays the effective date of all contested provisions of the permit.[77] The hearing is an on-the-record quasi-judicial proceeding presided over by an administrative law judge. The decision reached on the basis of the evidentiary hearing[78] may be

---

[76] If a variance request or other effort to secure relaxation of generally applicable effluent limits is indicated, it is appropriate to submit the request at this point in the proceedings. If this is done, a stay of further action on the permit, pending disposition of the request, would be appropriate.

[77] 40 C.F.R. § 124.16(a).

[78] *Id.*, § 124.81.

appealed to the EPA administrator.[79]  Where EPA is the issuing authority, the entire permit issuance proceeding, of course, is subject to judicial review under the federal Administrative Procedure Act.  This review, however, takes place in the Court of Appeals, not the District Court.  Where the state is the issuing authority, the state administrative procedure act probably governs.

Contested provisions of the permit become effective, and a final permit is issued, upon completion of these review proceedings.  The issuance of a permit under the Clean Water Act will be deemed to fulfill the permit requirements of the Refuse Act of 1899, as well as those under the act itself, except for requirements under Section 307(a) covering discharge of toxic pollutants presenting human health risks.  It should be noted, however, that issuance of a permit does not mean that no further action will be required during the permit term.  As the permit makes clear, additional applications must be filed and processed whenever modifications to the facility or method of operation will result in changes to the discharge.  Thus, keeping permits up-to-date will often be a continuous endeavor.

### 5.3    Permit Conditions

An NPDES permit performs two basic functions in the Clean Water Act regulatory process. It establishes specific levels of performance the discharger must maintain and it requires the discharger to report failures to meet those levels to the appropriate regulatory agency.

Many conditions typically included in industrial permits are either negotiable or susceptible to legal attack.  Accordingly, proposed permit conditions should be carefully analyzed and, if inappropriate, modified, and if need be, contested.  The more significant permit conditions are discussed below.

**Monitoring and Reporting**--The monitoring requirements in an NPDES permit are critically important, especially with the emergence of biomonitoring as a requirement for some sources. The effectiveness of the permit program in assuring compliance with applicable effluent limitations, water quality standards, pretreatment standards and other requirements established pursuant to the act will depend, in major part, on the effectiveness of monitoring and data maintenance requirements included in permits pursuant to Section 308.[80] Under that section, EPA is authorized to require the owner or operator of any point source to establish and maintain specified records, make specified reports, install, use and maintain monitoring equipment and methods, take specified samples, and provide other information which EPA may reasonably require.  As with the permit program in general, the states have the opportunity to administer their own monitoring programs and, upon obtaining

---

[79] *Id.*, § 124.91.

[80] POTWs subject to the act's permit requirements must also require industrial dischargers to monitor their discharges to the POTWs.

EPA's approval of an appropriate monitoring program, the state becomes the monitoring authority for all point sources within its jurisdiction.

The enforcing authority will have the right to enter the premises of the discharger at any reasonable time, inspect the records required to be maintained, take test samples and so forth. All data obtained under Section 308 is required to be open to the public except to the extent non-disclosure is necessary to protect trade secrets. This public disclosure requirement is an essential underpinning of the act's provision for citizen enforcement actions against non-complying dischargers.

The NPDES regulations specify the manner in which effluent limitations are to be included in permits and thus imposed on permittees.[81] The monitoring requirements in various sections of Part 122 are intended to assure compliance with the limits included in permits. Under these provisions, limits are to be imposed and monitoring is to take place at the point of discharge except in limited situations where monitoring at point of discharge is infeasible. The regulations do provide the permit issuer with authority to require monitoring of internal waste streams in certain situations such as where the final discharge point is inaccessible, where wastes at the point of discharge are so diluted as to make monitoring impracticable, or where interference among pollutants at the point of discharge would prevent detection or analysis. A permittee is required to monitor, as specified in his permit, to determine (1) compliance with the limitations on amounts, concentrations or other pollutant measures specified in the permit, (2) the total volume of effluent discharged from each discharge point and (3) otherwise as required by the permit.[82]

The permit must include requirements for maintenance and proper installation of the monitoring equipment, must specify monitoring methods and frequencies adequate to provide reliable data regarding the volume of flow and quantity of pollutants discharged, and must specify the test methodology to be used in analyzing the samples taken. The regulations put the burden on the applicant, if he believes that the monitoring requirements specified in a draft permit are inadequate to yield accurate data, to request additional monitoring requirements which are sufficient to achieve an acceptable degree of accuracy. Compliance with the effluent limits set in the permit will be assessed through application of the monitoring methods which the permit provides. Thus, unless inadequate monitoring requirements are contested during the permit issuance procedures, it may be difficult to use such inadequacy as a defense in any later enforcement action.

Monitoring records, including charts from continuous monitoring devices and calibration and maintenance records, must be maintained for a minimum period of three years, and that period may be extended by request of the permit

---

[81] 40 C.F.R. §§ 122.44, 122.45.

[82] 40 C.F.R. § 122.44(i).

issuing authority at any time.[83] As the statute of limitations applicable to permit violations is the five-year limitation in 28 U.S.C. § 2462 (1988),[84] it would be wise to maintain the records for that longer five-year period.

The results of monitoring must be reported periodically to the permit issuing authority on forms provided by the authority. Frequency of reporting is governed by the terms of each individual permit and must be at least annual. In addition to the periodic reporting requirement, certain toxic discharges must be reported within twenty-four hours.[85] Failure properly to monitor and to report is a violation of the permit and any person who knowingly makes any false statement in monitoring records, monitoring reports, or compliance or non-compliance notifications is subject upon conviction to substantial fines and criminal penalties, both under the Clean Water Act and under the applicable provisions of the federal criminal code, including 18 U.S.C. Section 1001.

It is evident from the foregoing that the monitoring requirements may occupy a considerable amount of employee time, require the installation of sophisticated sampling devices, extensive analysis and testing, and detailed recordkeeping and reporting. Many companies may find it appropriate to develop additional in-house technical capability in order to meet the Section 308 requirements as imposed in the permit.

**Schedules of Compliance**--Although the act itself establishes firm deadlines for the achievement of the required levels of treatment, the issuing authority has considerable latitude to require compliance or interim steps towards compliance at earlier dates. The act also provides mechanisms to extend compliance deadlines in limited situations, as where compliance is dependent on connection to a yet-to-be constructed public treatment works or where use of innovative technology is involved. Most of the statutory bases for extensions, however, have now expired.

**Effluent Limitations**--Where a permit issues prior to the publication of effluent limitations for a particular pollutant or applicable industrial category or subcategory, the determination of the precise effluent limitations to be included in the permit are to be based on "engineering judgment," which is obviously more flexible than published rules. This situation is now most likely to arise as EPA works to promulgate limitations for toxic pollutants, or

---

[83] 40 C.F.R. § 122.41(j).

[84] *See, e.g., Chesapeake Bay Foundation v. Bethlehem Steel Corp.,* 608 F.Supp 440, 446-50 (D.Md. 1985); *Connecticut Fund for the Environment v. Job Plating Co.,* 623 F.Supp 207, 211-13 (D.Conn. 1985); *Atlantic States Legal Foundation v. Al-Tech Specialty,* 635 F.Supp 284, 287 (N.D. N.Y. 1986).

[85] 40 C.F.R. §§ 122.41(k)(6), 122.42(a). The non-compliance reporting requirements are specific and detailed and should be carefully reviewed by all permittees.

for facilities for which no specific set of limitations is wholly applicable.

Even after promulgation of limitations, the applicant may in certain cases seek modification of limits in the permit, and there is also considerable opportunity for the permitting authority to impose discharge limitations more stringent than the "base-level" effluent guidelines, where necessary to meet water quality standards, water quality related effluent limitations, the requirements of state planning processes, or other applicable limitations. Thus, there is considerable room for discussion regarding limits to be imposed in permits and a careful engineering analysis of proposed permit limits is a prerequisite to intelligent evaluation and negotiation of permit requirements. By the same token, once a permit has been issued on the basis of "Best Engineering Judgment" and it proves more stringent than the promulgated regulations require, the 1987 amendments included an "anti-backsliding" provision which made it quite difficult to relax stringent permit conditions a discharger is actually meeting.[86]

**Additional Effluent Limitations**--Until recently, NPDES permits normally specified four or five pollutants as being subject to effluent limitations; a far greater number are now included in permits as a result of EPA's toxics strategy. EPA's NPDES permit application and related regulations (Section 122.21) require extensive waste stream analysis in order to file permit applications, extensive cataloging in the application of virtually all chemicals in the waste stream, and imposition of controls on the discharge of those chemicals. Implementation of these requirements complicates the permit process and requires more extensive monitoring than was true in the past.

**Duration and Revocation**--Permits may be valid for terms of up to five years, and may be subject to revocation or modification based on a very minimal showing of "cause." A discharger's interest in connection with the permit process will generally be best served by obtaining a permit with the maximum duration and with as much specificity as is obtainable in regard to the possible grounds of revocation or modification. On the permit's expiration, the permittee, in order to obtain reissuance, must demonstrate compliance with any more stringent criteria which have been promulgated during the term of the original permit. Under EPA's rules, the *completed* permit application must be filed at least 180 days in advance of the existing permit's expiration date. Prudent practice suggests earlier filing in case the application is found incomplete in some respect.

**Other**--Depending on the precise nature of the applicant's operation, consideration might be given to bypass and upset provisions, start-up exclusions and so forth. Those who will be responsible for complying with the permits are well advised to make every reasonable effort to predict potential compliance problems and discuss them fully during the permit issuance process rather than in later enforcement proceedings.

---

[86] Clean Water Act, § 402 (o).

## 6.0    CONTROLLING NON-PROCESS-RELATED WASTE DISCHARGES

Although the system of effluent limits imposed through the NPDES permit program is an effective means of regulating waste discharges which result from normal industrial or municipal processes and which are amenable to treatment prior to discharge, this system is an inappropriate means of regulating and controlling accidental and unanticipated discharges or discharges which, by their nature, are not subject to confinement and treatment (e.g., area-wide or plant site runoff). For this latter class of discharges, the focus of regulation must be on preventing the discharge (in the case of the accidental spill) or on minimizing the volume of pollutants carried (in the case of area-wide and plant site runoff). Since accidental spills and "non-point source" discharges are responsible for a large percentage of the total pollutants introduced into the nation's waterways, the act provides a number of mechanisms, supplemental to the NPDES permit program, to control discharges which are unrelated to industrial process wastes. This system of supplemental regulatory controls is the subject of this section and the next one.

### 6.1    Controlling Non-Point Source Pollution

The primary mechanism contemplated by the 1972 act for controlling area-wide, non-point source pollution was the planning and regulatory program created by Section 208. Although the Section 208 process produced some high quality area-wide waste treatment plans, in about 1980, Congress stopped funding this development and implementation of 208 plans. Consequently, little progress has been made in controlling non-point source pollution.

The 1987 amendments made non-point sources of toxic pollutants an important aspect of water quality planning under Sections 303 and 304(l). As part of identifying water bodies which fail to attain and maintain water quality standards after compliance with technology-based standards, states must also identify those water bodies which fail to meet standards for toxic pollutants as a result of non-point sources of such pollutants. In Section 319 of the 1987 amendments, Congress authorized $400 million over four years to fund state efforts to plan control measures for non-point source controls. Additionally, the 1987 amendments added Section 320, the National Estuary Program. Under this provision, states are (among other things) to plan and to implement additional controls on point and non-point sources of pollutants to estuaries included in this program. Although state participation in this estuary program is voluntary, a number of important estuaries (e.g., Chesapeake Bay, Puget Sound) are involved, and are apparently being treated as priorities by the states involved.

### 6.2    Stormwater Discharges and Best Management Practices

The regulation of municipal and industrial stormwater discharges has been controversial since enactment of the 1972 amendments. That controversy persisted in large part because Congress failed to devise a regulatory program tailored to stormwater discharges, leaving EPA the unpleasant choice of regulating all stormwater discharges from point sources in the same fashion as process waste water from major industries, or to leave all such discharges unregulated. The first choice is unworkable because of the potentially vast number of such discharges and the high cost of treating all of them; the second choice would have left a number of major discharges of toxic and other pollutants completely unregulated, resulting in significant harm to the environment.

EPA arrived at a middle course, regulating discharges from industrial areas and municipalities above a certain size. The 1987 amendments adopted, but substantially modified, this approach. The amended act now requires that five categories of municipal or industrial stormwater discharges be regulated as NPDES discharges:

(1)     discharges which have NPDES permits issued as of February 1987.

(2)     discharges "associated with industrial activity."

(3)     discharges "from a municipal separate storm sewer system serving a population of 250,000 or more."

(4)     discharges "from a municipal separate storm sewer system serving a population of 100,000 or more but less than 250,000."

(5)     other discharges designated by the EPA administrator or the State if such discharge "contributes to a violation of a water quality standard or is a significant contributor of pollutants to waters of the United States."[87]

For discharges associated with industrial activities, NPDES permits must meet the applicable effluent limitations imposed upon the industry in question. Many industrial dischargers, of course, already have NPDES permits governing the discharge of stormwater from plant yards and other ancillary areas. These continue to be regulated under existing permits.

Stormwater discharges "associated with industrial activity" which do not currently have permits are subject to different procedures. By February 1989 (two years after enactment), the EPA was supposed to establish permit application requirements for such discharges. By February 1990 (three years after enactment), permit applications were to be filed, and by February 1991, EPA (or the State) was to issue or deny such permit. The permittee must comply with the permit "as expeditiously as practicable, but in no event later than 3 years after the date of issuance of such permit," or February 1994 if the earlier steps had been completed in a timely fashion.

Large municipal discharges, i.e., from stormwater sewer systems serving more than 250,000 people, must meet the same schedule for permit application regulations, application filing, and deadlines for permit issuance and compliance. Thus, EPA's application regulations were to be issued by February 1989, permit applications were to be filed by February 1990, EPA (or States)

---

[87] CWA, § 402(p)(2).

were to decide and issue permits by February 1991, and permittees must comply with them by February 1994.

The 1987 amendments allow the EPA administrator flexibility to issue permits for discharges from municipal storm sewers on either a system or jurisdiction-wide basis. The permit must "include a requirement to effectively prohibit non-stormwater discharges into storm sewers." The amendments impose substantive requirements on the permitted discharges. Such permits:

> shall require controls to the maximum extent practicable, including management practices, control techniques and systems, design and engineering methods, and such other provisions as the Administrator or the State determines appropriate for the control of such pollutants.[88]

Although smaller municipal storm sewer systems (i.e., serving 100,000 to 250,000 people) are subject to these same substantive permit requirements, the timetable for applications, permit decisions, and compliance is longer than for large municipal systems. Thus, EPA is supposed to issue permit regulations for these smaller dischargers by February 1991, permit applications must be filed by February 1992, permits must be granted or denied by February 1993, and compliance is required within three years of such issuance, or February 1996, if the timetable is met.

EPA at last published its final regulations concerning NPDES permits for storm water discharges in November 1990.[89] These rules address application requirements for storm water discharges associated with industrial activity and for discharges from municipal separate storm sewer systems serving a population of 100,000 or more.[90] Unlike the EPA's proposed storm water rules, the final rules require direct permit coverage for all storm water discharges associated with industrial activity, *including those that discharge through municipal separate storm sewers.*

The storm water regulations do not apply to all discharges of storm water by industries but only to storm water discharges associated with industrial activity. The regulations define "storm water discharge associated with industrial activity" to mean:

> the discharge from any conveyance which is used for collecting and conveying storm water and which is directly related to the manufacturing,

---

[88] CWA, § 402(p)(3)(B)(iii).

[89] 55 Fed. Reg. 47990 (Nov. 16, 1990).

[90] "Storm water" means storm water runoff, snow melt runoff, and surface runoff and drainage. 40 C.F.R. § 122.26(b)(13).

processing or raw materials storage areas at an industrial plant.[91]

For a majority of the categories of industries (which are identified at 40 C.F.R. § 122.26(b)(14)(i)-(x)), storm water discharges associated with industrial activity include, but are not limited to, storm water discharges from:

(1)  industrial plant yards;

(2)  immediate access roads and rail lines used or traveled by carriers of raw materials, manufactured products, waste materials, or by-products used or created by the facility;

(3)  material handling sites;

(4)  refuse sites;

(5)  sites used for the application or disposal of process waste waters (as defined at 40 CFR Part 401);

(6)  sites used for the storage and maintenance of material handling equipment;

(7)  sites used for residual treatment, storage, or disposal;

(8)  shipping and receiving areas;

(9)  manufacturing buildings;

(10) storage areas (including tank farms) for raw materials, and intermediate and finished products; and

(11) areas where industrial activity has taken place in the past and significant materials remain and are exposed to storm water.

However, for a limited number of categories of industries, storm water discharges associated with industrial activity include only storm water discharges from all the areas listed in the previous sentence:

where material handling equipment or activities, raw materials, intermediate products, final products, waste materials, by-products, or industrial machinery are exposed to storm water.[92]

The regulations therefore make a critical distinction between facilities identified at 40 C.F.R. § 122.26(b)(14)(xi) and facilities identified at 40 C.F.R. § 122.26(b)(14)(i)-(x). The former types of facilities (which include, *inter alia*, food processors, cigarette manufacturers, clothing producers, furniture makers, printers, pharmaceutical producers, and paint manufacturers) are not regarded as having storm water discharges associated with industrial activity unless the

---

[91] 40 C.F.R. § 122.26(b)(14).

[92] "Material handling activities" include the storage, loading and unloading, transportation, or conveyance of any raw material, intermediate product, finished product, by-product or waste product. 40 C.F.R. § 122.26(b)(14).

materials or activities specified above are exposed to storm water. Contrarily, storm water discharges from the latter types of facilities (which include, *inter alia*, sawmills, paper mills, chemical producers, petroleum industry facilities, and metal smelters and refiners) are considered to be associated with industrial activity *regardless* of the actual exposure of these same materials or activities to storm water.

If a facility does discharge storm water associated with its industrial activity, the facility must seek coverage under a promulgated storm water general permit, apply for a permit through a group application, or apply for an individual permit.

A discharger of storm water associated with industrial activity may apply for an NPDES permit through a notice of intent to be covered by a general permit. In the near future, EPA intends to propose and promulgate general permits that will indicate what facilities are eligible for coverage by the permits. Although, as of January 1991, EPA has not yet proposed or promulgated any general storm water discharge permits, industrial facilities should anticipate the future promulgation of such permits because obtaining coverage under a general permit should impose a lesser burden on a facility than submitting an individual or group permit application.

Facilities not eligible for coverage under a general permit are required to file either a group or individual permit application. The ability of a facility to obtain a permit under the group application procedure will depend upon whether that facility is a member of the same effluent guideline subcategory or is sufficiently similar to other members of the group to be appropriate for general permit coverage. In determining whether a group is appropriate for general permit coverage, the group applicant should use the factors set forth in 40 C.F.R. § 122.28(a)(2)(ii), the current regulations governing general permits, as a guide.

A group application consists of two parts. Part 1 of a group application requires information concerning the participants in the application and their industrial activities. After approval of Part 1 of a group application by EPA, the applicants must submit Part 2, which requires a percentage of the participants (usually 10%) to provide the detailed quantitative data that all applicants for individual permits must provide.[93]

Part 1 of a group application must be submitted to EPA by March 18, 1991. Based on information contained in Part 1, EPA will approve or deny the members in the group application within 60 days after receipt. Part 2 of the application must be submitted no later than 12 months after the date of approval of Part 1. Facilities that are rejected as members of a group will have 12 months to file individual permit applications from the date they receive notification of their rejection.[94]

---

[93] 40 C.F.R. § 122.26(c)(2).

[94] 40 C.F.R. § 122.26(e)(2).

If a facility cannot seek coverage under a general permit and cannot obtain a group permit, then it must bear the considerable burden of applying for an individual permit. To obtain an individual permit, the discharger must provide detailed information about the facility, including, *inter alia*, a topographic map of the facility and a narrative description of certain activities at the facility, such as materials and waste management practices.[95]

In addition, dischargers seeking individual permits must present quantitative data, based on samples of storm water discharges collected during storm events, from all outfalls containing a storm water discharge associated with industrial activity. The sampling must be conducted in accordance with the elaborate regulations set forth in 40 C.F.R. § 122.21(g)(3) and (7).[96] The parameters required to be tested are set forth at 40 C.F.R. § 122.26(c)(i)(E).

Because gathering the data for an individual permit application is very costly, a discharger of storm water associated with industrial activity should, if possible, seek coverage under a general permit (when promulgated) or submit a group application. If, however, an industrial facility must apply for an individual permit, the facility should begin the data collection and the field testing at an appropriately early date, given the extensive data required to be submitted. Individual permit applications must be submitted by the facility to EPA or permitting state by November 18, 1991.[97]

This permit system is the primary mechanism for regulating plant site runoff where toxic and hazardous pollutants are not involved. In addition, Section 304(e), which was added by the 1977 amendments, authorizes EPA to require permittees to adopt "Best Management Practices" to control toxic pollutants resulting from ancillary industrial activities. EPA also is authorized to prescribe regulations to control plant site runoff, spillage or leaks, and sludge or waste disposal. The legislative history of this provision indicates that Congress anticipated that EPA's regulations would specify treatment requirements, operating procedures, and other management practices by classes and categories of point source discharges.

EPA proposed sweeping regulations to implement the best management practices provisions of Section 304(e),[98] but issued final regulations of more modest scope.[99] Both the proposed and final regulations, however, attempt to

---

[95] 40 C.F.R. § 122.26(c)(i)(A)-(D).

[96] These regulations require a grab sample taken during the first thirty minutes (or as soon thereafter as practicable) of the storm water discharge. A flow-weighted composite must also be taken. 40 C.F.R. § 122.21(g)(7).

[97] 40 C.F.R. § 122.26(e)(1).

[98] 43 Fed. Reg. 39282 (September 1, 1978).

[99] 40 C.F.R. Part 125, Subpart K.

apply the BMP requirements on an across-the-board basis, instead of by categories, an administrative short-cut which may cause difficulties when EPA applies BMP requirements to particular operations.

The final regulations emphasize BMPs of a procedural nature (especially preventive maintenance and housekeeping) and BMPs requiring only minor construction. EPA stated that these regulations are the first of two or more steps; Spill Prevention, Control and Countermeasure (SPCC) plans for hazardous substances (which have been proposed but never promulgated) and possibly additional BMP provisions are scheduled as regulatory requirements in the future. EPA also writes BMPs into effluent guidelines for some industry categories. As a practical matter, RCRA and CERCLA regulations for handling hazardous wastes or releases of hazardous substances have largely taken the place of additional BMP requirements.

The existing BMP requirements are applicable to all dischargers who use, manufacture, store, handle or discharge any pollutant listed as toxic under Section 307 or as hazardous under Section 311 and for all ancillary manufacturing operations which may result in significant amounts of toxic or hazardous pollutants reaching waters of the U.S. Any BMPs required by a Section 304(e) effluent limitations guideline must be expressly incorporated into an NPDES permit, and BMPs may be so incorporated if EPA or the State agency determines this to be "necessary to carry out the provisions of the Act . . . ." These requirements appear to have been specifically contemplated by Congress when it added the BMP provisions in 1977.

In addition, the regulations require the permittee to develop a "Best Management Practices" program, which must be submitted as part of the permit application and which will be subject to all permit issuance procedures. This program must be written, must establish toxic and hazardous substances control objectives, and must establish specific BMPs to meet these objectives. The program must also address a number of points concerning ancillary activities such as materials inventory and compatibility, employee training, visual inspections, preventive maintenance, housekeeping, and security. These requirements will tend to overlap to some extent with requirements under the OSHA hazard communication standard, with some RCRA requirements, and some requirements under Title III of SARA.

## 7.0   OIL AND HAZARDOUS SUBSTANCE SPILLS

When Congress enacted the Oil Pollution Act of 1990,[100] it replaced the prior haphazard system of overlapping federal statutes and inadequately funded response mechanisms to deal with oil spills. Congress made these amendments in response to the massive Exxon Valdez oil spill in Prince William Sound in March 1989. That tragic incident, and the strong political consensus that it should never be permitted to recur, is reflected throughout the new statute, in

---

[100] Pub. L. No. 101-380, 101 Stat. 484 (1990).

its stringent regulatory requirements, harsh liability scheme, and comprehensive approach to oil pollution problems.

Until the 101st Congress and the Valdez incident, Congress had sought unsuccessfully since 1975 to enact comprehensive oil spill liability legislation. These efforts cleared committees and individual houses on several occasions, but sharp differences over federal preemption of state regulations, the role of international conventions, and the degree of regulation truly needed to prevent oil spills precluded the reconciliation of differences between the House and Senate versions of these bills. The Valdez incident sufficiently galvanized public opinion so that these differences were finally resolved after a lengthy and difficult conference. As a result of this long genesis, courts are likely to pay very close attention to the statutory text in interpreting the new statute, and to view legislative history cautiously as an aid to interpretation.

The new Act mandates a comprehensive federal oil spill response system, and establishes the Oil Spill Liability Trust Fund to provide much greater federal resources for oil spill response and cleanup, prompt and adequate compensation for those harmed by oil spills, and an effective and consistent system of assigning liability.

The new Act also significantly strengthens requirements for the proper handling, storage, and transportation of oil and for the full and prompt response in the event discharges occur. The Act made many of these regulatory changes, with potentially significant effects far beyond the oil industry, by amending section 311 of the Clean Water Act as well as many provisions of Title 46, governing navigation safety, the Deepwater Ports Act,[101] the Outer Continental Shelf Lands Act (OCSLA),[102] and the Trans-Alaska Pipeline Authorization Act (TAPAA).[103]

Because the Oil Pollution Act is a lengthy statute which is to be codified in scattered portions of the United States Code, it is helpful to outline its major parts before discussing them in detail:

Title I is a free-standing statute, establishing the strict liability standards and the billion dollar Oil Spill Liability Trust Fund to pay for oil spill responses and to compensate for damages not recovered from responsible parties. The money for the Fund is paid for through a tax imposed under sections 4611 and 9509 of the Internal Revenue Code of 1986, sections which are amended by Title IX of the Oil Pollution Act. A tax of five cents per barrel of oil is imposed on oil delivered at the refinery.

Title IV contains the regulatory standards. Subtitle A contains numerous amendments to the vessel manning, equipment, construction and operating standards contained in Title 46 of United States Code. These amendments

---

[101] 33 U.S.C. § 1501 *et seq.* (1988).

[102] 43 U.S.C. § 1331 *et seq.* (1988).

[103] 43 U.S.C. § 1651 *et seq.* (1988).

provide for the phaseout of tankers without double hulls, the use of overfill protection and tank pressure monitors, and more stringent licensing of merchant marine officers and seamen, including reviews of criminal and driving records, and drug and alcohol testing.

Subtitles B and C drastically amend section 311 of the Clean Water Act to improve federal responses to oil spills, to make spill prevention control and countermeasure (SPCC) plan requirements facing the private sector more stringent, and to impose severe penalties, much higher than allowed under prior law, for violations including spills.

Title III concerns international cooperation. It is remarkable for what it does not do: it does not require the United States to adopt any international convention concerning oil spills, and as is made abundantly clear in the legislative history, the new Act **DOES NOT PREEMPT STATE LAW**. Thus states are free to impose more stringent liability schemes and to set up their own response funds. At the time of enactment, 24 states had some form of oil spill statute, many with response funds of various kinds.

The other titles are of less immediate concern to the regulated community at large. Title II contains conforming amendments transferring money from funds under OCSLA, the Deepwater Port Act, and the Clean Water Act's oil spill funds to the new Oil Spill Liability Trust Fund. Title V concerns Prince William Sound; Title VI contains savings provisions and unrelated provisions concerning drilling offshore Louisiana and North Carolina; Title VII provides for a comprehensive federal research program; Title VIII amends TAPAA to make it consistent with the Oil Pollution Act, but TAPAA continues to govern spills suffered in bringing oil to the Trans-Alaska Pipeline System (TAPS) or through it. Spills suffered once oil is transferred to a tanker are governed by the Oil Pollution Act.

## 7.1 Liability Under the Oil Pollution Act

Under section 311 of the Clean Water Act, the owners and operators of vessels and onshore and offshore facilities from which oil is discharged to navigable waters, shorelines, or into the exclusive economic zone, are strictly responsible for the cost of conducting the cleanup of that spill and for natural resource damages suffered as a result of it. Section 311 prohibits discharges of oil in harmful quantities, which were defined to mean those which caused a sheen on the water. This sheen test meant that virtually no discharge of oil was permissible. These rules had been the law since what became section 311 of the Clean Water Act was first enacted as part of the Water Quality Improvement Act of 1970.

The Oil Pollution Act continues these rules, but eliminates some of the few defenses available under the Clean Water Act, and increases the liability limitations to levels so high they are almost meaningless. The Oil Pollution Act does not rewrite or amend the liability provisions of section 311 of the Clean Water Act; rather it establishes a separate liability scheme, explicitly modelled on section 311, and implicitly modelled on section 107 of the

Comprehensive Environmental Response, Compensation and Liability Act (CERCLA).

Section 1002(a) makes responsible parties -- owners and operators, and in the event of vessels, charterers as well -- liable for removal costs and damages. The same standard of strict liability applicable under section 311 of the Clean Water Act is applicable here.[104] This standard, the same as applied under CERCLA, is one of strict, joint and several liability as the courts have so far interpreted it.

The Conference Committee rejected House efforts to make the owners of the oil secondarily liable for cleanup costs and damages. Had this rule been adopted, it would have created the equivalent of generator liability under Superfund for oil spills. Congress' rejection of this provision is important, for its practical result would have been almost to eliminate the petroleum exclusion under CERCLA as far as generators were concerned. Instead, the Oil Pollution Act as enacted contained a definition of petroleum modified to exclude fractions of petroleum specifically designated as hazardous substances under CERCLA.[105] This modification was intended to help assure that CERCLA and the Oil Pollution Act do not overlap. The distinction may become important because the cleanup and compensation mechanisms under the two statutes have some important differences.

Defenses to liability by responsible parties under the Oil Pollution Act are limited to (1) act of God, (2) act of war, (3) act or omission of a third party, other than an employee, agent, or party in a contractual relationship with the responsible party, or (4) some combination of 1, 2, and 3. These are also defenses under section 311. Case law interpreting them under section 311, and their counterparts under CERCLA, suggests that these defenses are extremely limited. For example, predictable bad weather causing a release is not an act of God. Similarly, actions by vandals resulting in discharges is not an act of a third party amounting to a defense where security precautions were inadequate. The Oil Pollution Act does not provide one defense available under section 311: negligence on the part of the United States government.

The Oil Pollution Act, like section 311 and CERCLA § 101(10), excludes from liability discharges permitted by a federal, state, or local permit. This "federally permitted release" concept, first developed in the 1978 amendments to section 311, is extremely important in the oil pollution area because oil and grease are such common pollutants. This language places a premium on compliance with discharge and pretreatment permit terms, and on assuring that adequate bypass and upset provisions are in such permits. Otherwise, discharges in violation of a permit might be interpreted to give rise to liability under the Oil Pollution Act.

Responsible parties under the Act are liable for removal costs and damages.

---

[104] Oil Pollution Act, § 1001(17).

[105] *Id.*, § 1001(23).

Removal costs mean the costs of removing, containing, and cleaning up an oil discharge, or of mitigating or preventing a discharge or substantial threat of discharge. These costs are recoverable by federal, state, and local governments, as well as by private parties which have to incur them.

Damages are also recoverable from responsible parties. These damages include natural resource damages, loss of tax and other revenue, and increased service costs. These categories are recoverable by the governmental bodies; natural resource damages by the properly designated governmental trustee. Private parties may recover damages to real and personal property (including loss of use), lost profits or earning capacity, and loss of subsistence use of resources.

The Oil Pollution Act places limitations on liability, but these limits may be of little help to responsible parties because of the high levels at which they are set, because they can be overcome by a showing that a discharge resulted from a violation of a safety or operating standard, and because state law liability schemes may provide unlimited liability. The limits under section 1104 of the Oil Pollution Act are:

$1,200 per gross ton for tank vessels, or $10,000,000, whichever is higher, unless the vessel is less than 3,000 tons, in which case the limit is $2,000,000;

$600 per gross ton for non-tank vessels, or $500,000, whichever is greater;

$75,000,000 plus all removal costs for offshore facilities, and no limit for Outer Continental Shelf facilities;

$350,000,000 for onshore facilities and deepwater ports licensed under the Deepwater Port Act.

The limits for onshore facilities can be adjusted downward based on size, throughput, storage capacity, type of oil, discharge history, and other factors. The limit for onshore facilities may be lowered on these bases down to $8,000,000. As is true under the Clean Water Act and CERCLA, these liability limits may be avoided if the discharge resulted from gross negligence, willful misconduct, or a violation of an applicable federal safety, construction, or operating regulation. The limited defenses discussed above -- act of God, act of war, act of unrelated third party -- are also lost in the event of such negligence, misconduct, or violation.

Claim procedures under the Oil Pollution Act are different than those found in other environmental statutes. They emphasize that responsible parties are to be the primary sources of compensation, not the Oil Spill Liability Trust Fund. Under § 1014, the federal government is to designate the source or sources of an oil discharge (or threat of discharge) as soon as possible. This designation can be made because of the mandatory reporting requirements for oil discharges which remain in force under section 311 of the Clean Water Act.

A party designated as a source under § 1014 has only five days to deny such designation if it believes there is a basis to deny it. If the designation is not denied, the responsible party is to begin advertising claim procedures within 15 days of receipt of the designation and continue advertising for at least 30 days. If no designation can be made, or the designation is denied, or if a public vessel has caused the discharge, then the federal government is to advertise claim procedures under the Oil Spill Liability Trust Fund.

As was true under section 311, vessels are required by section 1016 to establish and to maintain evidence of financial responsibility (*e.g.*, an insurance policy and appropriate certificates) up to the maximum liability limitation. The sharp increase in these limits, however, makes it likely that vessels will pay far higher insurance premiums, and may have difficulty finding adequate insurance.

Where a responsible party pays claims made against it under the Oil Pollution Act, it is subrogated to all of the reimbursed party's rights against other responsible parties.[106] Section 1009 of the Act allows actions to be brought for contribution by responsible parties, and these actions may include all claims arising from the incident, including common law claims, not just those arising under the Oil Pollution Act. Such contribution claims must be initiated within three years of payment of a claim by the plaintiff.[107]

Where the Oil Spill Liability Trust Fund pays claims, it is subrogated to the claimants' rights and may bring actions against the responsible parties to recover these claims. Parties are first to present claims to responsible parties before presenting them to the Fund. If responsible parties do not act within 90 days, the claimants may then present them to the Fund.

The Fund also is to recover removal costs and natural resource damages from responsible parties. Removal and other costs must be determined to be consistent with the National Contingency Plan in order to be compensable. Removal costs include the costs of "monitoring" private cleanup efforts,[108] making this the equivalent of "oversight costs" under CERCLA. Unlike the case with CERCLA, however, the government's entitlement to "indirect costs," a large charge for government overhead in connection with cleanup and oversight efforts, is highly debatable under the Oil Pollution Act, in part because the statute contains separate authorizations to pay such administrative costs out of the Oil Spill Liability Trust Fund.

Natural resource damages are broadly defined under § 1006(d). The legislative history makes clear the broad definition is intentional and meant to follow the 1989 Court of Appeals decision in *State of Ohio v. Department of Interior*.[109] The replacement cost of the resource is to be the primary basis for determining natural resource damages. Under § 1006(d), such damages include the cost of assessing such damages, the costs of restoring, replacing,

---

[106] *Id.*, § 1015.

[107] *Id.*. § 1017 (f)(3),(4).

[108] *Id.*, § 1012(a)(1).

[109] 880 F.2d 432 (D.C. Cir. 1989).

rehabilitating, or acquiring the equivalent of the damaged resources, and any diminution in value of those resources. Restoration is the preferred alternative; restoration is to take place according to a restoration plan prepared and approved by the designated natural resource trustee. The plan is to be subjected to public comment before approval, and may function much like a record of decision or remedial investigation/feasibility study in a CERCLA cleanup.

### 7.2 Oil Spill Removal Actions

The Oil Pollution Act rewrote sections 311(c) and (d) of the Clean Water Act, provisions governing federal action to assure oil spill removals. Under these revised provisions, the federal government is required to take action to assure proper removal is conducted, either by undertaking such action with federal resources, or by monitoring state, local, or private actions. These removals are to assure the "effective and immediate removal of a discharge, and mitigation and prevention of a substantial threat of discharge."[110] Removals must be consistent with the National Contingency Plan; contractors hired to conduct such removals have immunity from damages actions brought resulting from removal actions taken consistently with federal orders or the NCP. This immunity does not extend to responsible parties conducting such a removal action.

Section 311(b) is amended to give strong enforcement powers to the on-scene coordinator or other appropriate federal official. Any responsible party who, "without sufficient cause, fails to properly carry out removal of a discharge" under a federal order, is subject to a $25,000 per day fine, or treble damages based on the costs incurred by the Oil Spill Liability Trust Fund as a result of such a refusal. This language is based on similar CERCLA provisions.[111]

### 7.3 Contingency Plan Requirements

Congress was highly critical of the unrealistic and unworkable contingency plans in place in Prince William Sound when the Valdez spill occurred. The plans overlapped; they were uncoordinated; they assumed far too small a spill, and far too quick a response time in practice. Many of these problems had been identified in drills but not corrected. As a result, a spill cleanup around the Valdez became a multi-year shore cleanup, at a cost of over two billion dollars.

Section 4202 of the Oil Pollution Act rewrites requirements governing national, area, and facility contingency plans. The National Contingency Plan is to be revised by August 1991 to reflect the many changes in the statute; area contingency plans are to be prepared or revised; and individual facility spill prevention control and countermeasure (SPCC) plan requirements must be

---

[110] § 311(c)(1).

[111] CERCLA, §§ 106(b)(1), 107(c)(3).

prepared and considerably updated.

Under section 311(j) prior to the Oil Pollution Act, facilities were to prepare SPCC plans if they stored more than 1,320 gallons of oil aboveground, or 42,000 gallons below ground.[112] Facilities subject to this requirement include those storing vegetable or mineral oils, not simply petroleum products. Thus many food processing companies are subject to these rules.

Section 311(j)(5) now requires tank vessels and offshore and onshore facilities to prepare SPCC plans, and specifies requirements for these plans. An onshore facility is required to prepare SPCC plans if it handles, transports, or stores oil, and if, "because of its location, [the facility] could reasonably be expected to cause substantial harm to the environment by discharging into or on the navigable waters, adjoining shorelines, or the exclusive economic zone."[113] Given the broad definition of navigable waters used under the Clean Water Act, a potential oil discharge to a storm sewer could be sufficient to require preparation of SPCC plans.

The SPCC plan must be a plan to respond, to the maximum extent practicable, to a worst case discharge, and to a substantial threat of such discharge, of oil or hazardous substances.[114] The plan must:

(1)   be consistent with the NCP and area contingency plans;

(2)   identify the person in charge of the facility, who must have authority to implement the plan;

(3)   require immediate communication between the person in charge and appropriate federal officials and response action contractors;

(4)   ensure by contract (or other means allowed under regulation) that adequate private personnel and equipment will be available to remove the worst case discharge to the maximum extent practicable;

(5)   require training, periodic unannounced drills, and equipment testing necessary to assure effective response actions;

(6)   be updated periodically; and

(7)   be resubmitted for approval with each significant change.[115]

The SPCC plans are to be submitted for federal approval. The language of the statute suggests all such plans must be submitted and approved in order for facilities to continue operations. The legislative history suggests that only a

---

[112] 40 C.F.R. Part 112.

[113] Clean Water Act, § 311(j)(5)(B)(iii).

[114] Clean Water Act, § 311(j)(5)(A).

[115] Clean Water Act, § 311(j)(5)(C).

fraction of these will have to be submitted and reviewed; otherwise the Coast Guard or EPA, as the case may be, would be overwhelmed with SPCC plans for small facilities.

The statute requires SPCC plans to be submitted for approval by February 1993. Without submission of such a plan, vessels and facilities are not permitted to continue to operate. Vessels and facilities submitting such plans may continue to operate for up to two years pending such approval. If the statutory time period expires without action by the regulatory agency, or if approval is denied, then the vessel or facility may not continue to store, transport, or handle oil.

These new requirements will place a premium on the early preparation or update of SPCC plans, in part because these plans must assure that a response action contractor is ready to bring adequate cleanup equipment in the event of a spill, and in part because the approval process may be slow. Although it seems unlikely that enforcement officials would in fact require facilities to shut down if regulatory delays slow plan approvals, the facility is in a better position to argue against such a shutdown if it has timely prepared and filed the needed plans, and has a reputable cleanup contractor ready.

### 7.4 Spill Reporting and Enforcement

Since 1970, Section 311(b)(5) has required that the person in charge of a facility or vessel must make an immediate report to the appropriate federal agency of discharges of harmful quantities of oil to navigable waters. In practice this means that any discharge of oil to the waters must be reported to the National Response Center, which is run by the Coast Guard. Such reports may not be used as the basis for any criminal prosecution against the person reporting, except for false statement or perjury. Is a criminal offense to *fail* to report, punishable by up to five years in jail.

The Oil Pollution Act completely revised the penalties applicable to discharges of oil, and to violations of the SPCC and other regulations. A new provision, section 311(b)(6), is added, allowing the government to seek administrative penalties of up to $125,000 for violations of regulations or for discharges. This provision is very similar to the administrative penalty provision in section 309(g), and will probably be implemented using the same procedural rules.

Under section 311(b)(7), as added by the Oil Pollution Act, much larger civil penalties may now be assessed in civil penalty actions brought in federal court. Any owner, operator, or person in charge may be fined up to $25,000 per day for a discharge, or $1,000 per barrel of oil discharged. Although the daily penalty level is consistent with that provided for violations of other provisions of the Clean Water Act, the quantity-based penalty is new, and may reach extremely high levels quickly in the event of a large spill. Civil penalties may be trebled where a discharge results from gross negligence or misconduct. The *minimum* penalty in such cases is $100,000.

New criminal penalties are provided to punish dischargers. This change was accomplished simply by making the Clean Water Act's criminal penalty provision applicable to discharges in violation of section 311(b)(3). Where such a discharge is negligent, the penalty could be a year in prison and a $25,000 fine; where the discharge was done "knowingly," the penalty could be three years in prison, and a $50,000 fine; where the discharge resulted in placing others in imminent danger of serious bodily injury or death (knowing endangerment), the prison term is fifteen years, and the fine, $250,000 for an individual, and $1,000,000 for an organization. These criminal penalties may be difficult to obtain in practice, however, because of the mandatory self-reporting in section 311(b)(5), and immunity from prosecution for compelled reports written into the statute and from the Fifth Amendment.

## 7.5 Hazardous Substance Spills

Section 311 also governs the discharge of hazardous substances. EPA was slow to implement the hazardous substances provision, and shortly after regulations were promulgated in March 1978, a court enjoined significant parts of the regulations before they became effective. Congress responded to the court's action by amending Section 311 to simplify and clarify its provisions along the lines agreed to in a compromise between EPA and the industry plaintiffs in that case.[116] The 1978 amendments were directed toward the two most significant problems identified by the court: the elements necessary to establish what was to be considered a harmful quantity and the relationship of Section 311 to the NPDES program.

Pursuant to these amendments, EPA has designated approximately 300 substances as hazardous and thus subject to the Section 311 program.[117] In addition, the agency has designated quantities of these substances that may be harmful (called a "reportable quantity").[118] Hazardous substances are placed in one of five categories: X, A, B, C, D. A harmful quantity of a category X substance is one pound, of a category A substance is 10 pounds, of a category B substance is 100 pounds, of a category C substance is 1000 pounds, and of a category D substance is 5000 pounds.[119]

The second principal feature of EPA's hazardous substance regulations is the exclusion of discharges made in compliance with an NPDES permit. Since a primary purpose of the amendments was to limit Section 311 to "classic" hazardous substance spills, the regulations specify that they are not applicable to chronic discharges of designated substances if the discharge complies with

---

[116] Pub. L. No. 95-576, 92 Stat. 2467 (1978).

[117] 40 C.F.R. Part 116.

[118] 40 C.F.R. Part 117.

[119] 40 C.F.R. § 117.3.

an NPDES permit.[120] Such discharges, of course, remain subject to regulation under the NPDES program.

Further, if an NPDES facility has intermittent, anticipated spills of hazardous substances (i.e., into plant drainage ditches), it should determine whether these discharges ought to be brought within the terms of its NPDES permit. The regulations give the facility the option of having such discharges regulated through the NPDES program or pursuant to Section 311.

Discharges of hazardous substances may also reach navigable waters through municipal sewers and publicly owned treatment works. Discharges from industrial facilities to a POTW are not covered by the regulations at present. The regulations do apply to all discharges of reportable quantities of hazardous substances to POTWs by a mobile source such as trucks unless the discharger has met certain requirements.[121]

A facility owner or operator who spills a harmful quantity of a hazardous substance must report the spill; failure to do so will subject him to criminal penalties.

The new Oil Pollution Act made spills of hazardous substances to navigable waters, even if reported, subject to criminal prosecution. Section 309(c), the Clean Water Act's criminal penalty provision, is amended to include discharges in violation of section 311(b)(3), which forbids discharges of oil and harmful quantities of hazardous substances.

New judicial civil penalties -- based on the volume of the hazardous substances discharged -- are now provided in section 311(b)(7). For every unit of reportable quantity of a hazardous substance discharged, a penalty of $1,000 may be assessed. Thus, for example, if the reportable quantity is 10 pounds and 1000 pounds are discharged, the discharger could be subjected to a $100,000 civil penalty. (Civil penalties triple if the discharge results from gross negligence or willful misconduct). Alternatively, EPA may seek the standard civil judicial penalty of $25,000 per day of violation or seek administrative civil penalties for discharges of hazardous substances.

Finally, it should be noted that the reporting requirements for spills of hazardous substances (as well as other defined wastes) have been substantially supplemented by the Comprehensive Environmental, Response, Compensation and Liability Act (also known as CERCLA or Superfund) and by the Emergency Planning and Community Right-to-Know Act, also referred to as Title III of the Superfund Amendments and Reauthorization Act (SARA) of 1986. For a fuller description of these requirements, see those chapters.

The nature of these regulations and the potential penalties thereunder place a premium on developing compliance procedures before a spill occurs. A facility should first be evaluated to determine whether it discharges, or might discharge, a reportable quantity of any hazardous substance to the waters of

---

[120] 40 C.F.R. § 117.12.

[121] 40 C.F.R. § 117.13.

the United States. If there is a risk of such a discharge, the exemptions established by the regulations should be considered in order to determine if they will be applicable to the potential discharge. If no exemption is available, it may be advisable to develop a program to prevent such discharges. Further, it is essential to implement a contingency plan capable of assuring a prompt and appropriate response in the event of a non-exempt reportable discharge.

## 8.0   ENFORCEMENT

The CWA, especially after the 1987 amendments, provides a number of enforcement options to EPA and the states, as well as a heavily-used citizen suit provision. As companies' potential exposure under these enforcement and penalty provisions can be staggering, even for infractions causing little actual harm, it is important for regulated entities to understand what their potential exposure is under the CWA's criminal, civil, and administrative penalty provisions, as well as for citizen suits.

### 8.1   Criminal Penalties

Section 309(c), the criminal penalty provisions of the CWA was substantially revised and stiffened by the 1987 amendments. The 1990 Oil Pollution Act extended these criminal penalties to spills and other violations of section 311. Under the amended Section 309(c):

-- "Negligent violations" in § 309(c)(1) are subject to criminal penalties of not less than $2,500 or more than $25,000 per day of violation, as well as up to one year's imprisonment per day of violation. Penalties and length of imprisonment are doubled for a second offense.

-- "Knowing violations" in § 309(c)(2) are subject to fines of not less than $5,000 nor more than $50,000 per day of violation and up to three years imprisonment per day of violation. As with "negligent violations," penalty levels double for second offenses.

-- Section 309(c)(3) creates a new class of offense for "knowing endangerment," where a person knowingly violates a permit or other requirement "and who knows at that time that he thereby places another person in imminent danger of death or serious bodily injury." Conviction of "knowing endangerment" requires proof of "actual awareness or actual belief" which may be shown by "circumstantial evidence, including evidence that the defendant took affirmative steps to shield himself from relevant information." The penalty for knowing endangerment is imprisonment for 15 years and a fine of up to $250,000, or in the case of an organization, a fine of not more than $1,000,000. Fines and penalties are doubled for second offenses.

-- Section 309(c)(4) strengthened criminal penalties for anyone who files false reports or who knowingly falsifies, tampers, or renders inaccurate any monitoring device or method. Violations are now punishable by a $10,000 fine and imprisonment of up to two years; penalties double for second offenses.

Because negligent violations are potentially criminal, the scope of potential criminal violations under the amended CWA is extremely broad, and reason for diligent attention to compliance.

Additionally, the degree of knowledge required to satisfy the "knowing" requirement may include many situations where a discharger is aware of a violation but continues to operate while seeking to abate the violation. A situation where a discharger has received an administrative order requiring cessation of a violation would likely meet the definition of "knowing" violation if the violation continued unabated. Also of concern are situations where a discharger is asked to accept a limitation it cannot timely meet, but to rely on the enforcement discretion of EPA, state, or local officials to protect the discharger from enforcement action while the discharger works to meet the new limitation.

The "knowing endangerment" provision is nearly identical to the similar penalty provision in RCRA. In the Clean Water Act context, knowing endangerment becomes an issue where water supplies are contaminated, where pretreatment requirements for toxics are deliberately violated, or where hazardous substances are deliberately dumped in sewers or waterways instead of being sent to a proper treatment, storage, and disposal facility (TSDF) under RCRA. Several knowing endangerment prosecutions have now been initiated for violations of pretreatment requirements, violations which allegedly endangered employees.[122]

In recent years, criminal charges have been brought repeatedly against large and small violators of the Clean Water Act. In addition to the knowing endangerment cases noted above, the United States has obtained indictments against Exxon Shipping, arising out of the Valdez spill, against Pennwalt Chemical, for negligent violations resulting in a tank failure and spills, against Ocean Spray for knowing violations of pretreatment requirements, and against a number of individuals for violations of dredge-fill requirements. Other cases have resulted in sentences of imprisonment,[123] which are becoming much more common as a result of sentencing guidelines. The statute allows the United States to proceed criminally not only against the companies involved, but also

---

[122] *United States v. Borjohn Optical Technology, Inc.*, Cr. No. 89-256 (D. Mass. Nov. 7, 1990).

[123] *See, e.g., United States v. Frezzo Bros., Inc.*, 546 F. Supp. 713 (E.D.Pa. 1982), *affirmed*, 703 F.2d 62 (3d Cir. 1983).

against "responsible corporate officers."[124] Moreover, circumstantial evidence may be used to prove violations of the knowing endangerment provision, including evidence that an officer deliberately shielded himself from knowledge of such violations.[125] Thus a "white heart, empty head" defense will not be legally sufficient.

States also provide criminal penalties for violations of their statutes implementing the Clean Water Act. Moreover, in circumstances involving violations of both the water pollution control statutes and hazardous waste statutes, defendants have been sentenced to prison under state water pollution control laws.

## 8.2 Civil Enforcement Options

Under the Clean Water Act as amended in 1987, EPA acting through the Department of Justice, has a number of civil enforcement options to address violations of the act, the implementing regulations, and NPDES and other permits. These civil enforcement options are usually found in state procedure as well.

EPA can decide to do nothing in response to a violation. There is divided authority for the proposition that EPA need not take enforcement action in response to every reported violation.[126] As a practical matter, EPA must let many infractions pass unpunished because the agency's resources are limited and because it would be inequitable to bring enforcement actions in some circumstances.

If EPA does decide to take civil enforcement action, as opposed to referring the matter for criminal prosection or initiating an administrative proceeding, the agency may and often does seek both injunctive relief and civil penalties. EPA may seek injunctive relief under either Section 504 or Section 309(b). Section 504 applies to discharges which present an imminent and substantial endangerment to the health, welfare, or livelihood of persons. (The statute specifically refers to an inability to market shellfish as a factor warranting action under Section 504.) In such circumstances EPA may seek an injunction "to immediately restrain any person causing or contributing the alleged pollution to stop the discharge . . . ." A former version of this provision was invoked by EPA to restrain the discharge of taconite tailings in

---

[124] CWA, § 309(c)(6).

[125] CWA, § 309(c)(3)(B).

[126] *Compare Dubois v. Thomas*, 820 F.2d 943 (8th Cir. 1987) and *Sierra Club v. Train*, 557 F.2d 485 (5th Cir. 1977) (no enforcement required) with *Green v. Costle*, 577 F. Supp. 1225 (W.D. Tenn. 1983).

the famous *Reserve Mining* case[127] in Minnesota, but the emergency provision has received little use since that time.

EPA normally relies upon Section 309(b) when it seeks injunctive relief. This section empowers the district courts to enter preliminary and permanent injunctions to restrain and abate violations of the statute, regulations, and permits, including state NPDES permits. If an injunction is issued and subsequently violated, not only are the criminal and civil penalty provisions of the Clean Water Act applicable, but so are the criminal and civil contempt powers of the court. Normally where a Clean Water Act case is settled through entry of a consent decree, EPA will insist on a schedule of stipulated penalties addressing any future violations of the decree. In settlement of several recent cases, EPA has obtained consent decrees requiring the discharger to undertake substantial remedial action to address the environmental problems caused by the discharge.[128]

Where EPA believes that a violation is serious enough for referral to the Department of Justice for civil enforcement action, the agency normally seeks substantial civil penalties. The 1987 amendments increased available civil penalties under section 309(d) from $10,000 per day of violation up to $25,000 per day of violation. Moreover, the amendments changed § 309(d) to set forth a number of factors for the court to weigh in assessing the appropriate amount of civil penalties to assess against a violator, including:

-- the seriousness of the violation;

-- the economic benefit (if any) resulting from the violation;

-- any history of such violations;

-- any good faith efforts to comply with applicable requirements;

-- the economic impact of the penalty on the violator; and

-- such other factors as justice may require.

---

[127] *Reserve Mining Co. v. EPA*, 514 F.2d 492 (8th Cir. 1975). The Court of Appeals modified the district court's injunction to allow the discharger additional time to comply rather than to require immediate cessation of operations. *Id.* at 538.

[128] *United States v. USX Corp.*, C.A. No. H88-558 (N.D. Ind. July 27, 1990); 55 Fed. Reg. 32319, 32320 (Aug. 8, 1990) (proposing approval of decree). Under this decree, USX is to pay a $1.6 million fine and spend up to $7.5 million to study and remedy contaminated sediments.

The statute's Polonius-like advice to the district courts about how to calculate penalties is unlikely to result in any sort of uniform penalties being assessed, but may tend to even out some of the extremes on either end of the spectrum.

The amendments did resolve one other civil penalty issue: how should process upsets be treated, particularly where the upset caused a number of pollutant parameters listed in the permit to be simultaneously exceeded? Under the amended section 309(d) "a single operational upset which leads to simultaneous violations of more than one parameter shall be treated as a single violation." Where violations of multiple parameters do not result from an identifiable operational upset, however, the government may try to argue that Congress' silence about that situation means that multiple violations have occurred.

Shortly after the 1987 amendments were enacted, the Supreme Court held in *United States v. Tull*[129] that defendants in civil penalty cases under the Clean Water Act have a constitutional right to a jury trial. The *Tull* case involved civil penalties imposed for violation of the dredge-fill provisions of Section 404. The decision clearly applies to all civil penalty proceedings brought in federal court under the Clean Water Act and other environmental statutes as well. The jury may only decide liability, however; the district judge decides the amount of penalty which is appropriate in the event a violation is found by the jury.[130]

The amounts of civil penalties paid in Clean Water Act cases increased dramatically during the 1980s. There are a significant number of federal enforcement cases where the government has collected over half a million dollars in penalties and several where the government has collected more than a million dollars. Indeed, in one case, involving noncompliance by a number of sewage treatment plants in Puerto Rico, the court assessed a penalty of more than $32,000,000.[131] Civil and criminal penalties are not deductible business expenses for federal income tax purposes, so the financial impact of these penalties on industrial dischargers can be quite severe. As EPA's emphasis on enforcement is increasing, and as the compliance dates for most standards have now passed, it is likely that civil penalties assessed in these cases will continue to increase as will the attention dischargers must pay to compliance.

### 8.3 Administrative Orders and Penalties

Section 309(a) authorizes EPA to issue administrative compliance orders to persons in violation of their permits or other Clean Water Act obligations. The order may require compliance with an interim compliance schedule or an

---

[129] 481 U.S. 412 (1987).

[130] *Id.* at 426-27.

[131] *United States v. Puerto Rico Aqueduct and Sewer Authority*, 25 ERC 1921 (D.P.R. 1987).

operation and maintenance requirement in not more than 30 days; permanent compliance is to be required in a time that EPA determines is reasonable under the circumstances. The state is to be sent copies of any such order.

The issuance of an EPA compliance order is a serious matter for a discharger, since failure to comply or at least to make good faith efforts to do so may be the basis to initiate a criminal prosecution for "knowing" violations, or to initiate a civil penalty proceeding where the claim is made that the discharger is recalcitrant or acting in bad faith.

The 1987 amendments added a new Subsection 309(g) which authorizes EPA to initiate administrative penalty proceedings against violators. The Corps of Engineers may also initiate administrative penalty proceedings for violations of dredge fill permits or permit conditions under Section 404 of the act. Likewise, under the Oil Pollution Act, the Coast Guard may initiate administrative penalty proceedings for violations of section 311.

The statute provides Class I and Class II penalties, which differ primarily with respect to (1) the limits on what penalties EPA or the Corps can impose and, (2) the procedures EPA or the Corps must follow to impose them. The upper limit on the penalty which may be imposed in a Class I proceeding is $25,000 total for the proceeding and $10,000 per violation. The defendant has the right to an informal hearing.

The upper limit on penalties in Class II proceedings is $125,000, with a $10,000 maximum penalty per day of violation. The defendant is entitled to a more elaborate hearing than in Class I penalty proceedings, a hearing before an independent administrative law judge (ALJ). In determining the amount of penalties to be imposed in the event violations are found, the ALJ (or EPA or the Corps in the case of Class I violations) is to consider the same factors the district court is required to consider in assessing civil penalties under Section 309(d).

Administrative penalty proceedings initiated by EPA, the Corps, or by states under comparable state administrative penalty schemes are a bar to citizen suits under Section 505 of the act for the same violations *if* the administrative penalty proceeding is initiated prior to notice that a citizen suit will be filed. This statutory rule is a significant departure from the prior case law rule that state administrative proceedings do *not* bar citizen suits. Although the new provision does limit citizen suits significantly, citizens may participate in the administrative proceeding.

In the event an unsuccessful defendant disagrees with EPA's (or the Corps' or Coast Guard's) penalty decision, judicial review may be obtained in district court for Class I penalties, and in the court of appeals for Class II penalties. Citizens who commented in the administrative proceeding may also seek judicial review. In order to prevail in such a judicial review, the person challenging the EPA decision must show either that EPA's decision is unsupported by substantial evidence or is an abuse of discretion. Although the statutory language is unclear, it may be read to permit the court to *increase* penalties where EPA (or the Corps) has abused its discretion to impose too low a penalty.

EPA has proposed a number of administrative penalties since passage of the 1987 amendments. The agency frequently proposes the maximum penalty, thereby shifting the burden to the defendant to show factors mitigating the violation and thus reducing the level of penalties assessed. EPA has used administrative penalties extensively in pursuing pretreatment violations. Often, EPA will bring multiple administrative proceedings to address multiple parties discharging inadequately treated wastes to a single POTW.

### 8.4    Compliance Strategy

The broad enforcement discretion enjoyed by EPA and the states, coupled with the requirement of publicly filing monitoring reports, including those showing violations, requires potential violators to take the initiative in dealing with compliance problems. In the event of a possible violation, a discharger must be prepared to spend substantial time and effort with all relevant agencies. When several parts of EPA and several different state agencies are involved, there is no assurance that they are pursuing a coherent strategy or, indeed, are even talking to each other. Thus the discharger must be prepared to keep all federal and state agencies fully informed, preferably in a way that will ensure the most favorable processing of any potential violations. In doing this, the discharger should attempt to accomplish the following three goals:

-- Convince the relevant enforcement agencies of its good faith. The EPA civil penalty policy makes it clear that "recalcitrance" is an aggravating factor and cooperation a mitigating one. Since the enforcement agencies will not, for the foreseeable future, be able to move against every violation, a discharger's good faith or bad faith will be an important factor in deciding who to move against, and, if so, how severely.

-- The discharger must attempt to deal with any major health or environmental problems caused by a potential violation in a manner that is as serious as the manner EPA or the state enforcement agency would adopt. Discharges which may create public health problems, or create unique environmental impacts, or which are likely to be the subject of adverse publicity are recognized as aggravating factors in the EPA's civil penalty policy. To the degree possible, special efforts should be made to avoid discharges of such substances and to quickly control and clean up any spill.

-- The discharger must realistically appraise not only its chances of ultimately prevailing in any enforcement litigation, but the bureaucratic constraints such as the civil penalty policy on EPA and the Department of Justice in settlement negotiations. In any settlement calculus, a discharger must understand that even a successfully defended enforcement action will likely result in substantial adverse publicity. This negative exposure is not fully overcome by a favorable verdict.

Although these guidelines are not a panacea to the problems involved in dealing with potential enforcement actions, they can reduce the uncertainty surrounding the present enforcement system.

## 8.5    Citizen Suits

Section 505 of the act provides an additional impetus to vigorous enforcement of the act's provisions.    It authorizes any person "having an interest which is or may be adversely affected" to commence civil actions either against a discharger, for violation of any effluent standard or limitation under the act, or against EPA for failure to proceed expeditiously to enforce the act's provisions.    Experience under the Clean Water Act indicates that citizen suit provisions are highly effective in increasing the number of enforcement actions brought.    While the Clean Water Act, unlike the Refuse Act, does not make provision for the payment of a "bounty" to a citizen providing information leading to successful enforcement, it does make specific provision for the payment of attorney and expert witness fees.    More importantly, the Clean Water Act plainly authorizes citizen actions, while the Refuse Act, which provides only criminal penalties, was construed by the courts not to permit citizen suits.

Since about 1985 an average of approximately 200 notices of intent to bring citizen suits against dischargers were filed with EPA each year. Giving such notice is the first step in bringing a citizens' enforcement action, and is frequently the start of settlement negotiations between the discharger and the citizens' group.    Normally in citizens' enforcement actions which are litigated, the plaintiffs use a discharger's required Discharge Monitoring Reports (DMRs) to establish the discharger's liability.    As some courts have held that dischargers are strictly liable for permit violations, intent is not a good defense. Most of the recent citizen suits have been settled on the basis of some combination of:

(1)  payment of civil penalties;

(2)  adoption of a compliance schedule;

(3)  stipulated penalties for failure to meet the schedule; and

(4)  attorney's fees and costs to plaintiffs.

Although EPA's minimal enforcement efforts in the early years of the Reagan administration were a primary cause of the recent flurry of citizens' enforcement actions, EPA's view of the enforcement action can be an important factor in settlement negotiations.    In several cases, EPA has refused to agree to settlement conditions worked out by environmentalist plaintiffs and dischargers, on the ground that the conditions were too generous to the discharger.    EPA's leverage in these negotiations is derived from its statutory right to intervene in any citizen's enforcement action.    The 1987 amendments have formalized EPA's role in reviewing consent decrees in citizen suit cases, and allow EPA 45 days to object in court.[132]

The bulk of reported citizen enforcement cases have been litigated in Connecticut, New York, New Jersey, the Chesapeake Bay area, Louisiana and California. A number of new cases are contemplated by environmental groups in most parts of the country. Frequently, national environmental groups such as the Sierra Club or Natural Resources Defense Council will work with local environmental groups such as the Connecticut Fund for the Environment or the Chesapeake Bay Foundation.

Courts ruling on motions to dismiss these citizens' suits have generally held that the members of these groups have standing--the right to file the action--and have sometimes extended standing to the groups themselves. In addition, the courts have resolved a number of other potential procedural obstacles to the citizen suits favorable to the environmentalists, holding that:

1. the five-year federal statute of limitations for civil penalties, 28 U.S.C. § 2462, governs these proceedings, and not shorter state limitations periods;

2. the citizens' suits can be used to recover civil penalties assessed by the court and payable to the federal government, as well as to obtain injunctive relief against the violator.

The primary limitations placed on citizen suits by the courts result from the Supreme Court's construction of section 505 in *Gwaltney v. Chesapeake Bay Foundation* in 1987,[133] and the Court's strict reading of notice requirements in the RCRA citizen suit provision in *Hallstrom v. Tillamook County* in 1989.[134] In *Gwaltney*, the Court held that citizen suits must allege either continuing or intermittent violations; citizen suits may not be

---

[132] CWA, § 505 (c)(3). The United States has objected to settlements which fail to provide for the payment of civil penalties to the United States. These challenges have had limited success. E.g., *Compare Friends of the Earth v. Archer Daniels Midland Co.*, 31 ERC 1779 (N.D.N.Y. 1990) (rejecting such challenge); *Sierra Club v. Electronic Controls Design, Inc.*, 31 ERC 1789 (9th Cir. 1990).

[133] 484 U.S. 49 (1987).

[134] 110 S.Ct. 304 (1989). The *Hallstrom* case requires strict compliance with the 60-day notice requirement in the RCRA citizens' suit provision, similar to section 505 of the Clean Water Act. Unless the provision is strictly adhered to, the citizens' suit may be dismissed.

maintained for wholly past violations.[135]  This limitation has not significantly impaired citizen suits because all the Court has required is a good-faith allegation of continuous or intermittent violation at the time the statutory 60-day notice is given.  Indeed, even in the *Gwaltney* case, the lower courts found on remand that there was sufficient evidence to support the claim of a continuing or intermittent violation, and affirmed a penalty of nearly $300,000.[136]  Fines of almost a million dollars were recently affirmed in another Chesapeake Bay case, which involved several years of reporting violations by a pretreater.[137]  It is evident from this record that citizens' suits can be a potent enforcement tool.

## 9.0.  PROVISIONS HAVING SPECIAL APPLICABILITY

### 9.1  Discharges to Ground Waters

One byproduct of the Clean Air Act and the Clean Water Act has been increased pressure to dispose of waste materials on or below land and the consequential increased threat of groundwater contamination.  However, aquifers are a class of water bodies which the act's definition of "waters of the United States" does not clearly include.  Thus, although the act, in Section 402(b)(1)(D), requires states, as a precondition to approval of their NPDES programs, to "control the discharge of pollutants into wells," it gives EPA no direct authority to regulate disposal of pollutants by subsurface injection.

Although EPA initially sought to regulate underground discharges pursuant to the Clean Water Act, it met with mixed results. The courts disagreed as to whether EPA had authority to regulate disposal into wells under that statute.[138]  EPA now relies on the authority of RCRA and the Safe Drinking Water Act (SDWA) to regulate such discharges and is encouraging the states to develop underground injection control programs pursuant to 40 C.F.R. Part 146.

---

[135]  484 U.S. 49, 64-67.

[136]  *Chesapeake Bay Foundation v. Gwaltney of Smithfield Ltd.*, 890 F.2d 691 (4th Cir. 1989).

[137]  *Sierra Club v. Simkins Industries, Inc.*, 617 F. Supp. 1120 (D.Md. 1985), *affirmed*, 27 E.R.C. 1881 (4th Cir. 1988).

[138]  *See United States Steel v. Train*, 556 F.2d 822 (7th Cir. 1977), and *Exxon Corp. v. Train*, 554 F.2d 1310 (5th Cir. 1977).  The Seventh Circuit has since decided that regulation of a well under the Clean Water Act is not a bar to regulation of the well under RCRA. *Inland Steel Company v. EPA*, 31 ERC 1527 (7th Cir. 1990).

Part C of the SDWA applies to injection wells. However, well injection is broadly defined as the:

> subsurface emplacement of fluids through a bored, drilled or driven well; or through a dug well, where the depth is greater than the largest surface dimension.

Thus, the state underground injection programs will have broad applicability.

EPA is also regulating the injection of hazardous wastes under the Resource Conservation and Recovery Act. Waste lagoons and ponds will continue to be regulated by EPA and the states pursuant to the hazardous waste program.

Thus, many companies which may be exempt from wastewater discharge regulation under the Clean Water Act because they did not discharge to navigable waters are subject to requirements governing wastewater discharges pursuant to the Safe Drinking Water Act and the Resource Conservation and Recovery Act.

## 9.2 Dredged or Fill Material

Section 404 of the Clean Water Act substantially affects development in areas adjacent to navigable waters. The section stringently controls dredging activity and the disposal of dredged or fill material into navigable water by granting the Corps of Engineers the authority to designate disposal areas and issue permits to discharge dredged and fill material therein, rather than making such discharges subject to the general permit program provided by Sections 301, 304, and 402 of the act. The stringency of these requirements has been reinforced by three factors:

-- Section 404 has been construed to extend to all waters of the United States,[139] including wetlands which are themselves very broadly defined in a definition upheld by the Supreme Court.[140] Accordingly, the Corps permit program under Section 404 is applicable to many dredge and fill projects which would not have required permits under prior law;

-- The Corps has construed Section 404 broadly, so as to cover not only *disposal* of dredged or fill material, as the section would seem to contemplate, but also the emplacement of dredge or fill material for development purposes and the construction of structures;[141] and

---

[139] *NRDC v. Callaway,* 392 F. Supp. 685 (D.D.C. 1975).

[140] *United States v. Riverside Bayview Homes, Inc.,* 474 U.S. 121 (1985).

[141] 33 C.F.R. § 323.2 (1).

-- Section 511(c) of the act covers only permits issued by the EPA administrator, so that Section 404 permits, unlike most other permits under the act, are subject to NEPA and possibly to the EIS requirements.

Congress extensively revised Section 404 in the 1977 amendments. The principal change was to authorize the states to establish permit programs for dredge and fill activities in non-navigable waters.[142] In order to establish such a program, a state must comply with extensive requirements prescribed by the act and must obtain EPA's approval of the program. There are also requirements for the state's operation of its program, including a requirement that a copy of each permit application and each proposed permit be sent to EPA. EPA, the Corps of Engineers, and the United States Fish and Wildlife Service have the right to comment on applications and proposed permits, and provision is made for the situation in which EPA objects to issuance of a permit.

A second change authorized the Corps of Engineers (or a state having an approved program) to issue "general" permits for specified categories of activities involving the discharge of dredge and fill materials. To issue such a permit, there must be a finding that the activities in the category are similar in nature and will have minimal adverse effects. Any activity covered by a general permit can be conducted without obtaining an individual Section 404 permit so long as the requirements and standards set forth in the general permit are complied with. The Corps expanded the scope of its general permit program to reduce the regulatory burden on a number of activities which involve incidental dredge or fill work.[143] As part of a settlement agreement with environmental groups which had challenged these regulations, the Corps changed these rules to assure that they are only applied in practice to activities which have a minimal environmental impact.[144]

Finally, Section 404(f) exempts certain dredge and fill discharges from regulation under Section 404 if specified effects on navigable waters are avoided. The activities thus excluded from the scope of Section 404 include maintenance operations, the construction of temporary sedimentation basins, temporary farm, forest and mining roads, and several types of agricultural activities.

The Corps of Engineers, through the United States Attorney for the district in which a violation occurs, has the power to bring enforcement

---

[142] It is generally thought that, if a state does establish its own program, it will not be subject to NEPA constraints in its permit issuing activities.

[143] 33 C.F.R. Parts 320-330.

[144] 49 Fed. Reg. 37482 (October 5, 1984).

actions in the name of the United States not only to collect penalties of up to $25,000 per day of violation but to compel restoration of areas which have been dredged or filled without obtaining a necessary permit, or dredged in violation of permit conditions. Under the 1987 amendments, the Corps may also bring administrative penalty proceedings under § 309(g) of the act. In civil penalty proceedings in district court, the Supreme Court has held in a case involving restoration work and penalties that a defendant in a civil penalty action has the right to a jury trial.[145] The Court's holding may cause the Corps to rely heavily on administrative proceedings because of their flexibility.

In November 1989, EPA and the Corps of Engineers executed a memorandum of understanding, under which the Corps, in exercising its authority to review permits under section 404, will strive to minimize the loss of wetlands. Under this policy initiative, known as the "no-net loss" policy, the Corps is to avoid adverse impacts in its permit decisions as much as possible. The Corps must choose the least environmentally damaging practical alternative. The adverse effects on wetlands are to be minimized as much as possible. Only as a last resort is off-site mitigation to be used.

The policy has proven quite controversial, and may be the subject of legislative amendment. Those critical of the policy contend that it protects many non-tidal wetlands of little ecological value, but at great expense to the regulated community. The oil industry did obtain a clarification of the policy in early 1990 so that it does not apply to tundra areas in Alaska, many of which will meet the technical definitions of wetlands in the summer months.

### 9.3 Ocean Discharge Criteria

Section 403(c) of the act directed EPA to promulgate guidelines for determining the effects of pollution discharges on ocean water quality and other aesthetic, recreational, and economic values of the oceans. No permit for an ocean discharge may be issued unless the permit issuing authority determines that the discharge will not cause unreasonable degradation of the environment, and permit conditions may be imposed to insure that such degradation will not occur.[146] An ocean discharge applicant may be required to submit substantial additional information about receiving waters. The intent of this provision was to assure that limitations were relaxed only in situations involving deep, fast-moving marine waters which resulted in the rapid mixing of very large quantities of water with the discharge of pollutants.

The 1981 amendments to the Clean Water Act extended the time for municipalities to apply for waivers of secondary treatment requirements for

---

[145] *United States v. Tull*, 481 U.S. 412 (1987).

[146] 40 C.F.R. Part 125, Subpart M.

ocean discharges.[147] The 1987 amendments have tightened the requirements to assure that waivers are granted only in unusual circumstances.[148] The intention of the 1987 amendments was to assure that these waivers could not be obtained where the POTWs had no (or an insufficient) pretreatment program, where the effluent volume was very large and receiving waters were shallow and not rapidly mixed, or where in combination with other sources the POTW discharge would interfere with marine waters. Recent EPA enforcement action under CERCLA against dischargers to marine POTWs suggest that relaxations of effluent limits under section 301 will be of little benefit to municipalities in the future.

### 9.4    Ocean Dumping and the Marine Protection Research and Sanctuaries Act

The Marine Protection Research and Sanctuaries Act (MPRSA)[149] was first enacted almost simultaneously with the 1972 Federal Water Pollution Control Act. Except for oil spills and ocean outfalls governed under Sections 311, 301(h) and 403 of the Clean Water Act, and several minor exceptions, the MPRSA governs all discharges of wastes to ocean waters within United States' jurisdiction or by United States' vessels or persons to the oceans anywhere.[150]

As a result of numerous amendments, no ocean dumping of industrial wastes is permitted, except in exigent circumstances, and except for sewage sludge from the New York City area, no dumping of sewage sludge is permitted either.[151]    The exemptions for New York City and its environs--created by court decision and EPA's failure to issue revised regulations--has recently been terminated by statute, effective in 1991. Recent efforts to extend the deadline have been rejected by the courts.[152]    By its terms the statute bars ocean disposal of radiological, chemical, and biological warfare agents and high level radioactive wastes.[153]    Disposal of fish wastes is permitted and is regulated under the Clean Water Act.

---

[147] Pub. L. No. 97-117, 95 Stat. 1632.

[148] CWA, § 301(h).

[149] 33 U.S.C. § 1401-14.

[150] 33 U.S.C. § 1401.   Other exceptions include marine sanitation devices under section 312 of the CWA, and emissions from marine engines, fishing wastes, oyster shells, and marine structures. MPRSA, § 1402(f).

[151] § 1412a.

[152] *United States v. Nassau County*, 733 F. Supp. 563 (E.D.N.Y.), *affirmed*, 31 ERC 1648 (2d Cir. 1990).

[153] § 1412.

Under the amended statute, the only ocean dumping activities of any significance permitted are the disposal of dredged spoil. Under the MPRSA, the Corps of Engineers is authorized to issue permits for transporting dredged materials for ocean disposal.[154] The Corps has promulgated regulations applicable to such activity,[155] which is also subject to EPA's substantive review criteria,[156] unless EPA waives the criteria.[157]

EPA is also to establish criteria for designating dump sites and then designate sites for dumping and sites where dumping will not be allowed.[158] When EPA first promulgated its comprehensive ocean dumping regulations, it had not yet done baseline and other studies necessary to determine whether its criteria could be met. Accordingly, EPA designated sites already in use on an interim basis. Environmental groups strongly objected to continued use of sites which had not undergone the requisite studies and review. Following litigation, a consent decree was entered which imposed schedules for EPA to conduct the studies and decide whether to designate 22 interim dredge spoil sites.[159] The Corps may use disposal sites for dredged spoils at locations other than those designated by EPA for disposal of other materials.[160] EPA assumed additional obligations by voluntarily adopting a policy of preparing Environmental Impact Statements (EIS) for all site designations.[161] This policy has proved to be a substantial hurdle in final site designations.

More than 140 interim dredge material sites have been designated, although not all are currently in use.[162] EPA is currently planning to delegate to its regional offices the authority for designated dump sites.

Ocean incineration is considered a type of ocean dumping and therefore requires a permit under MPRSA. Only research permits have been granted to

---

[154] MPRSA § 103, 33 U.S.C. § 1413.

[155] 33 C.F.R. Part 324.

[156] MPRSA § 103(b) and (c), 33 U.S.C. § 1413(b) and (c).

[157] MPRSA § 103(d), 33 U.S.C. § 1413(d), 40 C.F.R. Part 225.

[158] MPRSA § 102(a)(g), 33 U.S.C. § 1412(a)(g), 40 C.F.R. Part 228.4.

[159] *National Wildlife Federation v. Costle*, Civ. No. 80-0405 (D.D.C. October 1980).

[160] 40 C.F.R. § 228.4(e)(2).

[161] 39 C.F.R. 16186 (May 7, 1974), 39 Fed. Reg. 37419 (October 21, 1974), 40 C.F.R. § 228.6(b).

[162] 40 C.F.R. § 228.12.

date, and extremely strong opposition has led to the denial of the most recent application for a research permit.[163] This denial has been upheld by the district court, pending the time, if ever, when EPA issues special regulations governing ocean incineration of hazardous wastes.[164] EPA has now indefinitely deferred the issue of ocean incineration regulations, and that deferral decision has been upheld.[165]

General permits may be issued upon application, or by regulation without application, for material having minimal environmental impact which is disposed of in small quantities.[166] EPA has promulgated regulations generally authorizing ocean dumping for the purposes of burial at sea, the sinking of Navy target vessels, and disposal of vessels (subject to specified limitations).[167] Permits for ocean disposal of materials meeting EPA's discharge criteria are called "special permits" and may be issued for three-year terms.[168] Research permits can be issued for some materials with a term of eighteen months.[169]

Surveillance to determine or detect violations of the act is to be conducted by the Coast Guard and other appropriate federal agencies.[170] Violations of the act or of permits issued under it are subject to:

(1)     an administratively assessed penalty of up to $50,000 per day of violation;

(2)     injunctive relief in court;

(3)     criminal penalties of up to $50,000 and/or imprisonment of up to one year;

(4)     seizure of the offending vessel; and

---

[163] 51 Fed. Reg. 20344 (June 4, 1986).

[164] *Waste Management, Inc. v. EPA*, 669 F. Supp 536 (D.D.C. 1987).

[165] *Seaburn v. United States*, 29 ERC 1597 (D.D.C. 1989).

[166] 40 C.F.R. § 220.3(a).

[167] 40 C.F.R. § 220.3(a).

[168] 40 C.F.R. § 220.3(b).

[169] 40 C.F.R. § 220.3(e).

[170] MPRSA, § 107, 33 U.S.C. § 1417.

(5)   citizen enforcement for injunctive relief in court.[171]

In *Middlesex Sewage Authority v. National Sea Clammers*,[172] the Supreme Court has held that the act does not create a private right of action for damages for fisherman or others economically harmed by violations of the act. Presumably monetary damages could be sought under common law and admiralty law theories.[173]

### 9.5   Thermal Discharges

Although heat is defined as a pollutant by the Clean Water Act and thereby is subject to technology-based effluent limitations imposed on industrial dischargers and POTWs, Congress included special provisions for the regulation of thermal discharges, in order to avoid unnecessary control costs. If the discharger can show that the technology-based effluent limitations under Section 301 or under a new source performance standard are more stringent than necessary to assure protection and propagation of a balanced, indigenous population of shellfish, fish and wildlife in and on the body of water where the discharge is to occur, the administrator or state may adjust the effluent limitation to a less stringent level, which will still assure such protection and propagation.

This provision--Section 316--is particularly important to power plants because heat is such a significant part of their discharge and because EPA established a "no-discharge" BAT requirement for heat. Even though this effluent limitation was overturned by the courts,[174] permit issuers often initially propose no-discharge of heat as an effluent limitation under Section 402(a).

Section 316 proceedings are quite complex; EPA requires substantial amounts of scientific data. There are difficult questions regarding what is the "indigenous" population; when a population is "balanced"; and how heat will in fact affect the aquatic organisms. Nonetheless, this provision does excuse thermal dischargers from control requirements to the extent such requirements are unnecessary to protect the environment.

### 10.0   THE EPA CONSTRUCTION GRANTS PROGRAM

The stringent treatment requirements imposed on POTWs by the 1972 act made a major federal assistance program a necessity if most municipalities

---

[171] MPRSA, § 105, 33 U.S.C. § 1415.

[172] 453 U.S. 1 (1981).

[173] *Union Oil v. Oppen*, 501 F.2d 558 (9th Cir. 1974).

[174] *Appalachian Power Co. v. Train*, 545 F.2d 1351 (4th Cir. 1976).

were to be able to construct the facilities necessary to comply with the new effluent limitations. The construction grant program which the 1972 act established in response to this need is one of the largest public works programs now being funded by the federal government. The 1987 amendments converted the grant program into a revolving loan program administered by states beginning in 1990, with moneys disbursed after that time taking the form of loans, the repayment of which will fund additional construction.

Under the grant program enacted by the 1972 act, the federal share of the cost of approved treatment works was originally 75 percent, but that percentage was decreased to 55 percent in 1981, where it remained until replaced by the revolving loan program in 1990. The act and EPA's implementing regulations[175] impose substantial conditions governing factors such as the share of operating costs which industrial users must pay, the eligibility of different parts of the plant and related sewer systems and so forth. The objective is to assure that loans will fund the construction of plants which will meet applicable treatment limits in a cost-effective manner. These conditions can substantially affect the costs of POTW treatment to industrial users.

### 10.1 Revolving Loan Program

The 1987 amendments added a new title, Title VI, to the Clean Water Act, governing federal grants to states for sewage treatment plant construction. Beginning in 1990, EPA is to make capitalization grants to the states for the states to establish revolving loan programs for POTW construction. The states are to administer these loan programs pursuant to agreements with EPA. Under these agreements, states are to pay an additional 20 percent above the federal grant into the state fund.[176] There are requirements for the prompt obligation of loan moneys, and for regular auditing and accounting.

The state agency is to make loans for POTW construction through 1995 according to most of the same substantive criteria used previously to make grants, e.g., requirements to minimize infiltration and inflow, and combined sewer overflows, to encourage use of innovative technology, and to achieve at least secondary treatment levels.[177] Funds may also be lent to help with nonpoint source controls and estuarine management plans under sections 319 and 320. Loans are to be made at or below market rates for a term not longer than 20 years, and repayment is to begin within one year of project completion. The loan recipient is to establish a dedicated source of revenue to repay the loans.

---

[175] 40 C.F.R. Part 35, Subpart E.

[176] § 602(b)(2).

[177] § 602(b)(6).

If states are found not to be administering their loan programs in compliance with these requirements, then EPA can withhold future federal grant money and reallocate that state's money. States are to prepare annual plans for the use of loan moneys after public comment, as well as annual reports documenting how such funds were in fact used.

In 1990, EPA adopted implementing regulations for Title VI.[178] Under these regulations states must enter formal delegation agreements with EPA, identifying the state agency administering the loan program, the program costs, the personnel needed, the accounting system to be used, among other factors. These agreements have a five year term. Under these agreements states are to perform virtually all of the functions in loan review EPA previously performed for grants. Grantees will have the right to dispute state decision before the EPA Region.

Perhaps most noteworthy of these rules is the requirement that construction projects receiving grant assistance undergo state environmental review similar to NEPA scrutiny.[179] These regulations track many federal NEPA requirements including public participation, consideration of alternatives, and careful documentation of the decision process. This environmental review process is, according to EPA, based on sections 602(b)(6) and 511(c). Section 511 sets forth EPA's NEPA obligations for POTW construction grants and other issues under the Clean Water Act; section 603(b)(6) incorporates this provision by reference.

### 10.2   User Charges

When the 1972 act became law, Congress feared that the substantial grant assistance available to municipalities could function as an indirect subsidy to industrial users of the funded treatment works and that this subsidy would give users of POTWs an unfair competitive advantage over direct dischargers. Consequently, the act required that municipalities provide for repayment of that portion of the construction grant allocable to industrial users.

From the industrial user's viewpoint, the Industrial Cost Recovery (ICR) requirement converted the construction "grant" to the equivalent of a long-term, no-interest loan. However, ICR proved quite difficult to administer and was repealed in 1980 after a legislative moratorium on such projects had expired. Some local communities continue to assess ICR payments even though they are no longer required by federal law. Such local ICR requirements are often of questionable legality under state law.

As the cost recovery regulations defined industrial users' proportionate share of the *capital cost* of new grant-funded treatment facilities, the user charge regulations establish requirements to be met by a municipal system for

---

[178] 55 Fed. Reg. 10178 (March 10, 1990); 55 Fed. Reg. 27095 (June 29, 1990) promulgating 40 CFR § 35.3000-.3170.

[179] 40 CFR § 35.3140.

industrial sharing of the annual *operating and maintenance charges* of such facilities. Section 204 of the act requires, as a condition of federal construction grant assistance, a finding that the applicant has adopted or will adopt:

> a system of charges to assure that each recipient of waste treatment services within the applicant's jurisdiction . . . will pay its proportional share. . .of the costs of operation and maintenance (including replacement)[180] of any waste treatment services provided by the applicant.

The EPA regulations[181] elaborate on the statutory requirement for proportionate distribution of O&M costs as follows:

> A grantee's user charge system based on actual use (or estimated use) of waste water treatment services may be approved if each user (or user class) pays its proportionate share of operation and maintenance (including replacement) costs of treatment works within the grantee's service area, based on the user's proportionate contribution to the total waste water loading from all users (or user classes).
>
> To insure proportional distribution of operation and maintenance costs to each user (or user class), the user's contribution shall be based on factors such as strength, volume, and delivery flow rate characteristics.

Quantity discounts to large volume users are not acceptable. EPA's philosophy is that savings resulting from economies of scale should be apportioned to all users or user classes. This policy would not, however, appear to preclude recognition of the other efficiencies that some large volume users are able to provide to the treatment facility to which they discharge. These efficiencies may include flow equalization or other measures to control delivery flow rate. User charges may be established based on a percentage of the charge for water usage only in cases where the water charges are based on a constant cost per unit of consumption and thus may be reasonably reflective of the amount of wastewater discharged. The regulations also specifically provide that an industrial user which discharges, to a treatment works, wastewater containing toxic pollutants that cause an increase in the cost of managing the effluent or sludge from the treatment works, must pay for those increased costs. Finally, it should be noted that user charges, unlike cost recovery payments, are to be based on actual use of the facility and not

---

[180] The term "replacement" has been defined by EPA to mean "expenditures for . . . equipment . . . which are necessary to maintain . . . capacity and performance during the service life of the treatment works. . . ."

[181] 40 C.F.R. § 35-929-1.

on reserved shares, as is sometimes erroneously asserted by some municipalities.

Appendix B to EPA's regulations sets forth in more detail the guidelines for user charge computations and provides sample formulae for use in that connection. The guidelines are necessarily complex and technical. There is considerable potential for misapplication, particularly by small municipalities. A discharger which is a substantial contributor to a treatment works should thus pay close attention to the municipality's adoption of a user charge system.

As indicated above, the treatment works operator is obligated to develop a user charge mechanism, which will require each user to pay its proportionate share of the cost of waste treatment. This obligation is not fulfilled if, due to the selection of an inappropriate or defective formula or improper application of the formula selected, industrial users are required to subsidize waste treatment services performed for other users of the system. EPA or state approval of any planned construction grant or loan application could, if necessary, be contested on that basis.

The basic approach in discussions with the POTW operating entity should be to make certain that the formula adopted (1) gives recognition to economies, other than economies of scale, which may be inherent in the nature of the company's discharge (e.g., the discharge may occur at non-peak periods, it may be low in suspended solids as compared to domestic sewage) and (2) does not give excessive weight to characteristics of the company's discharge, such as BOD content, which do not result in additional treatment costs. For example, if the cost of the treatment works is primarily flow dependent, a high surcharge based on strength of effluent may well be inappropriate. Numerous other technical questions such as the following may arise and should be addressed:

-- If the industrial user pretreats its effluent so that its strength is less than that of domestic waste, shouldn't it be entitled to a cheaper rate?

-- Shouldn't an industrial user's charge be reduced if it holds its effluent for discharge at non-peak flow periods, thereby contributing to the efficiency of the treatment works?

-- If the particular type of industrial effluent makes the treatment works operate more efficiently, shouldn't that factor be recognized? (For example, iron in industrial discharges is used by some municipalities to help remove phosphorous from waste water.)

-- If an industrial user's wastes are phosphorous and nitrogen-deficient, isn't it inappropriate to require that user to pay the portion of plant operation and maintenance expense allocable to removal of those pollutants?

-- If a substantial portion of the plant capacity is for treatment of water flowing into the system during periods of rainfall due to infiltration and inflow, shouldn't costs allocable to the treatment of this wastewater be primarily allocated to residential connections which are the primary cause of this circumstance?

These and many other similar questions are commonly answered by local authorities when they develop the user charge system which will be proposed for EPA (or state) acceptance. As user charges are an increasingly important cost component of waste treatment services provided by POTWs, affected users must be alert to the proposal of ordinances establishing new user charge systems and must ask questions such as these when such proposals are made.

## 10.3   Cost Effectiveness and Eligibility

Both POTW officials and industrial dischargers which use POTWs have an immediate and substantial interest in minimizing the costs of constructing and operating such works. The POTW owner-grantee or borrower, however, may be unsophisticated in the waste treatment area (or underfunded) and need technical and other assistance to assure that their waste treatment program is cost-effective. There unfortunately have been numerous cases where plants have been designed to achieve levels of treatment beyond that required by the applicable permit limits, or with capacities in excess of that necessary to serve foreseeable needs. The procedures mandated for the development of Section 201 facilities plans, the preparation of related environmental assessments, and the conduct of value engineering studies provide both industry and concerned citizens with considerable opportunities to help municipalities avoid these wasteful practices.

The final issue which should be considered in any effort to minimize the cost of industrial participation in a loan or grant-funded POTW program is the question of whether all or only some of the elements of the POTW are eligible for federal (or state) loan or grant funding. Treatment works costs which are found to be ineligible must be fully funded by the grantee without benefit of generous state loan programs. The resulting bond costs will be correspondingly higher as localities have to raise money on the open market. Industrial users are generally called upon to pay their proportionate share of the cost of amortizing the required bonds. Thus, where a portion of the facilities is found to be ineligible, industrial users will be called upon to pay, not only the costs of the treatment works over its useful life, but also their share of the bond interest--at market rates--on that facility.

As federal and state budget deficit problems mount, it seems likely that EPA and states will subject grant and loan applications to increasingly rigorous scrutiny in order to conserve limited grant and loan funds. EPA has narrowly interpreted the act's eligibility provisions as they apply to treatment facilities designed to handle industrial wastes. Thus though the act's definition of treatment works would appear to apply to facilities which handle industrial wastes, EPA's regulations specify that allowable projects do not include "(1) costs of interceptor or collector lines constructed exclusively or almost exclusively to serve industrial users or (2) costs allocable to the treatment for control or removal of pollutants in wastewater introduced into the treatment works by industrial users, unless the applicant is required to remove such pollutants introduced from non-industrial sources." The scope of this exclusion in individual circumstances is subject to considerable interpretation and there are also considerable legal questions regarding the statutory authorization for this provision. Its application does merit careful attention in a number of situations.

### 10.4 POTW Costs to Industrial Discharges--Summary

The factors referenced above make it clear that users of POTWs are no longer insulated from the substantial costs of complying with Clean Water Act requirements. In many circumstances, POTWs can be an expensive way for an industrial discharger to meet the act's requirements. The economics of alternative on-site treatment and direct discharge should be carefully examined before making or continuing commitments to rely on a POTW as a method of compliance.

## 11.0 POLLUTION CONTROL PLANNING IN THE CURRENT REGULATORY CLIMATE

Compliance with the Clean Water Act requirements outlined above would be difficult and costly under the best of circumstances. These difficulties are compounded by inconsistencies in EPA (and state) enforcement policies, EPA's tardiness in developing standards, and the periodic congressional rewriting of statutory requirements for the construction grant program. Consequently, the questions of how the law will be interpreted and enforced are often not amenable to predictable answers. Participation in the development and revision of standards and continuing contact with officials responsible for permitting and enforcement is necessary if industrial dischargers wish to operate in a more consistent and predictable regulatory environment.

### 11.1 EPA Standards Development and Revision

The suitability and practicability of the standards and regulations which EPA promulgates under the act are dependent on EPA's thorough understanding of the processes and products to be regulated, the availability of detailed and reliable data on the applicability and limits of available treatment technology, and careful consideration of the economic and environmental impacts involved. Except for industry inputs, most standards (whether done by EPA staff or through outside contractors) tend to be based principally on technical data readily obtainable through review of existing literature. In some cases, these data are outdated, unreliable or inadequate. Thus, absent effective and technically documented participation by industry spokesmen, the standards which EPA promulgates are likely to have unanticipated effects when applied to real world conditions. Particular process or design factors may not have been considered and may be inequitable when applied to a specific plant or product.

Thus, early and active participation in the standards development and revision process, either directly or through appropriate industry organizations, is advisable. Although EPA has completed the development of most standards, the toxics strategy and development of toxics water quality standards and discharge limitations based on them will continue to require such participation, as will the periodic updating and revision of existing standards which are mandated by various provisions of the act. Such participation could properly involve the following steps, which were made especially important by the provisions of the 1987 amendments governing the fundamentally different factors (FDF) variance:

1. Assess the probability that standards (or revisions) applicable to your company's operations will be promulgated.

2. Determine the procedure which will be followed in developing the standard, the contemplated time schedule, and the areas under consideration where data available to EPA may be deficient.

3. Assess the standards development procedure to determine whether it provides for taking into account any unusual aspects of your plant process or product design. Make comments to EPA and any private contractor involved as to how the procedure could be improved.

4. Consider providing EPA and/or the appropriate private contractor any relevant technical data possessed by companies in the industry which is unpublished or otherwise not generally accessible.

5. If the time schedule permits, consider the desirability of industry sponsored research or analytical projects to fill gaps in existing data on available technology or environmental and economic impact. In this connection, consideration should be given to consulting with EPA on the structuring of the project and exploring the possibility of EPA involvement in the conduct of the project.

6. After a proposed standard is published in the *Federal Register*, the company or its spokesmen should participate in the usual comment procedure and consider the possibility of obtaining judicial review if the standard, as finally promulgated, is still unreasonable. In this connection, it should be kept in mind that if objections to standards are not timely asserted in judicial review proceedings, then they are waived. Further, it is generally wiser for a company to litigate a standard at a time when it does not stand accused of a violation.

## 11.2   Negotiation of Permit Conditions

Whether a company's authorization to discharge is in the form of an NPDES permit for direct discharge into a waterway or a contract with a municipality for use of its treatment facilities, the terms and conditions of that permit or contract may be every bit as important, in terms of impact on profits, as a major corporate contract.   Moreover, the addition of the anti-backsliding provision by the 1987 amendments make it especially important that the initial permit or contract be correct, as costly errors can be very hard to fix.

These requirements can be the subject of negotiations. Accordingly, pollution control managers should determine the areas in which the act and regulations leave room for negotiation and, based on a careful assessment of the company's long-term interests, should negotiate actively in an effort to obtain favorable permit terms and conditions.   These negotiations will be more important and much more complicated if toxic pollutants are involved.

## 11.3   Discussions With Regional Office and State Officials

No matter how good the standards are or how carefully permits are drawn, there will inevitably be situations where companies are forced to make major investment decisions which are affected by significant uncertainties in determining the applicable environmental control requirements.   In these circumstances, serious consideration should be given to obtaining advance guidance from the appropriate EPA regional office and/or state enforcement personnel--whether or not the applicable statute makes provision for obtaining such guidance. A written indication that the cognizant authority has reviewed your proposal and found it acceptable, while perhaps not legally binding, can be of great future benefit.   If the proposal is not acceptable to EPA or the state, it may be better to find that out before money has been spent.   The chances of acceptance are generally far greater when the company goes to the regulator, rather than the other way around.

## 11.4   State and Local Planning Activities

Industry would also be well advised to pay considerable attention to the substantial planning requirements which are imposed by the act on state and local governments, especially the numerous water quality planning requirements imposed by the 1987 amendments.   The state and regional water quality implementation plans, continuing planning processes and area-wide waste treatment management plans may well be as important as federal rules and regulations in determining a company's future abatement costs.   If properly carried out, these planning processes can be of immeasurable aid to business planners in predicting and planning for the future.

## 12.0   CONCLUSION

Both the implementation of and compliance with the Clean Water Act have been and remain complex, difficult, and expensive for all concerned.   The increasing focus on toxic pollutants and water quality improvement, while environmentally sound, increases the complexity of regulations, the costs of compliance, and the difficulty of monitoring.

Under these circumstances, it is obvious that the development and implementation of a workable and effective program will require the best efforts of regulators, environmentalists, and the regulated community. EPA, for its own part, must establish priorities and allow both industry and its own enforcement personnel to concentrate their attention on resolving the problems which are most significant in terms of impact on human health and the environment. It does little for the environment to spend time, money and effort identifying and monitoring pollutants which are present in inconsequential amounts and to which significant portions of the population are not exposed.

Environmentalists, for their part, must focus their attention on problems which make the most difference in protecting human health and the environment. The *NRDC* consent decree is a good example of this focus. Environmental progress is better measured by improvements in the quality of life rather than costs inflicted on industry. Industry, for its part, must participate fully in the development and revision of EPA standards, if it is to avoid wasteful and frequently unsuccessful litigation to resolve EPA mistakes and omissions. Pollution abatement costs can constitute a substantial portion of the total cost of many companies' final product. Consequently, the effectiveness with which a company plans its pollution control program may determine the extent to which the company remains competitive in its industry.

With this kind of cooperative effort there is at least some hope for achieving a regulatory environment in which a company can intelligently plan for compliance with water pollution control requirements--when the requirements established are:

(1)     predictable and understandable;

(2)     equally applicable to and equitably enforced against all companies;

(3)     technologically and economically feasible;

(4)     announced sufficiently in advance of effectiveness to permit lead time for compliance; and

(5)     constant for a reasonable period of time after final adoption.

Achievement and maintenance of a regulatory climate which facilitates cooperative and intelligent planning is the best, and perhaps the only way of achieving the pollution control objectives announced by Congress when it passed the 1972 act and repeatedly ratified by Congress since. These goals will best be met where all parties avoid unnecessary confrontations, focus on the real regulatory issues, and develop a program which reasonably and cost effectively achieves essential water quality objectives without major economic or social dislocation.

## ANNEX A -- SECTION 307 -- TOXIC POLLUTANTS

Acenaphthene
Acrolein
Acrylonitrile
Aldrin/Dieldrin
Antimony and compounds*[182]
Arsenic and compounds
Asbestos
Benzene
Benzidine
Beryllium and compounds
Cadmium and compounds
Carbon tetrachloride
Chlordane (technical mixture and metabolites)
Chlorinated benzenes (other than dichlorobenzenes)
Chlorinated ethanes (including 1,2-dichloroethane, 1,1,1-ethane and hexachloroethane)
Chlorinated naphthalene
Chlorinated phenols (other than those listed elsewhere; includes
    trichlorophenols and chlorinated cresols)
Chloroalkyl ethers (chloromethyl, chloroethyl, and mixed ethers)
Chloroform
2-chlorophenol
Chromium and compounds
Copper and compounds
Cyanides
DDT and metabolites
Dichlorobenzenes (1,2-, 1,3-, and 1,4-dichlorobenzenes)
Dichlorobenzinine
Dichloroethylenes (1,1-and 1,2-dichloroethylene)
2,4-dichlorophenol
Dichloropropane and dichloropropene
2,4-dimethylphenol
Dinitrotoluene
Diphenylhydrazine
Endosulfan and metabolites
Endrin and metabolites
Ethylbenzene
Fluoranthene

---

[182] *The term "compound" shall include organic and inorganic compounds.

Haloethers (other than those listed elsewhere; includes chlorophenylphenyl
ethers, bromophenylphenyl ether, bis (dischloroisopropyl) ether, bis-
(chloroethoxy) methane and polychlorinated diphenyl ethers)
Halomethanes (other than those listed elsewhere; includes methylenechloride
methylchloride, methylbromide, bromoform, dichlorobromomethane,
trichlorofluoromethane, dichlorodifluoromethane)
Heptachlor and metabolites
Hexachlorobutadiene
Hexachlorocyclohexane (all isomers)
Hexachlorocyclopentadiene
Isophorone
Lead and compounds
Mercury and compounds
Naphthalene
Nickel and compounds
Nitrobenzene
Nitrophenols (including 2,4-dinitrophenol, dinitrocresol)
Nitrosamines
Pentachlorophenol
Phenol
Phthalate esters
Polychlorinated biphenyls (PCBs)
Polynuclear aromatic hydrocarbons (including benzanthracenes, benzo-pyrenes,
benzofluoranthene, chrysenes, dibenzanthracenes, and indenopyrenes)
Selenium and compounds
Silver and compounds
2,3,7,8-Tetrachlorodibenzo-p-dioxin (TCDD)
Tetrachloroethylene
Thallium and compounds
Toluene
Toxaphene
Trichloroethylene
Vinyl chloride
Zinc and compounds

## ANNEX B -- INDUSTRY CATEGORIES

1. Adhesives and Sealants
2. Aluminum Forming
3. Asbestos Manufacturing
4. Auto and Other Laundries
5. Battery Manufacturing
6. Coal Mining
7. Coil Coating
8. Copper Forming
9. Electric and Electronic Components
10. Electroplating
11. Explosives Manufacturing
12. Ferroalloys
13. Foundries
14. Gum and Wood Chemicals
15. Inorganic Chemicals Manufacturing
16. Iron and Steel Manufacturing
17. Leather Tanning and Finishing
18. Mechanical Products Manufacturing
19. Nonferrous Metals Manufacturing
20. Ore Mining
21. Organic Chemicals Manufacturing
22. Pesticides
23. Petroleum Refining
24. Pharmaceutical Preparations
25. Photographic Equipment and Supplies
26. Plastic and Synthetic Materials Manufacturing
27. Plastic Processing
28. Porcelain Enamelling
29. Printing and Publishing
30. Pulp and Paperboard Mills
31. Soap and Detergent Manufacturing
32. Steam Electric Power Plants
33. Textile Mills
34. Timber Products Processing

Chapter 4


SAFE DRINKING WATER ACT


Russell V. Randle
Partner
Patton, Boggs & Blow
Washington, DC


## 1.0 OVERVIEW AND BACKGROUND

Congress enacted the Safe Drinking Water Act in 1974, and extensively amended it in 1986.[1] The 1974 amendments federalized regulation of drinking water systems, required EPA to set national standards for levels of contaminants in drinking water, created a program for states to regulate underground injection wells, and for the protection of sole source aquifers. The 1974 act dramatically expanded the federal role: prior to its enactment the federal government only had authority to enforce standards for water used on interstate carriers to prevent communicable disease. (Advisory standards for other contaminants were also set.)

In the 1974 act, Congress responded to information suggesting that chlorinated organic chemicals were contaminating major surface and underground supplies of drinking water, that widespread underground injection operations were threatening major aquifers -- notably the enormous Edwards aquifer supplying much of Texas -- and that public water supply systems were antiquated, underfunded, understaffed, and increasingly a threat to public health. Implementation of the 1974 act was very slow and action to enforce its requirements was rare. This glacial pace resulted partly from the composition of much of the regulated community: local governments providing an essential public service.

Congress intended the 1986 amendments to quicken EPA's pace in issuing standards and in implementing other provisions of the act. The amendments:

---

[1] The Safe Drinking Water Act is codified at 42 U.S.C. §§ 300f - 300j-11. The 1974 version is Pub.L.No. 93-523, 88 Stat. 1661 (1974); the 1986 amendments are Pub.L. No. 99-339, 100 Stat. 666 (1986).

(a) mandate issuance of standards for 83 specified contaminants by June 1989, with standards for 25 additional contaminants to be issued every three years thereafter;

(b) increase EPA's enforcement powers;

(c) provide increased protection for sole source aquifers and wellhead areas;

(d) regulate the presence of lead in drinking water systems.

Although EPA's implementation of the SDWA has necessarily been more vigorous since the adoption of the 1986 amendments, the agency has fallen far behind the statute's schedule for the issuance of drinking water standards. EPA has now (January 1991) proposed all but a few of the drinking water standards the statute required to be issued by June 1989 or earlier, but has promulgated only a few of them in final form. This slow pace was anticipated by the drafters of the 1986 amendments, who put statutory deadlines in the act so that environmental groups could bring citizen suits to force promulgation of standards if EPA missed the deadlines. EPA is now under court-ordered deadlines to propose and promulgate the remaining drinking water standards, but it appears unlikely that the agency will complete the job before 1993.

Despite EPA's slow pace in promulgating the drinking water standards, the SDWA standards have taken on considerable importance outside the drinking water program. Under section 121 of the Comprehensive Environmental Response Compensation and Liability Act (CERCLA),[2] the health-based goals issued with these SDWA primary drinking water standards are made the clean-up standards for superfund sites with contaminated ground water, subject to limited exceptions. Additionally, some states are adopting SDWA drinking water standards for groundwater quality in other contexts. Various Congressional proposals for groundwater protection legislation would also apply SDWA standards--developed for water delivered for human consumption--to water in the ground. As such groundwater protection legislation becomes more likely with the attraction of Western state co-sponsors, these drinking water standards have the potential to become groundwater standards for the whole country.

The drinking water program itself is receiving increased emphasis by EPA. In one recent EPA report, entitled Unfinished Business, EPA officials rated drinking water contamination, together with indoor air quality and public exposure to pesticides, as one of three major unaddressed (or underemphasized) environmental health threats. Administration budget requests for the 1991

---

[2] 42 U.S.C. § 9621.

Fiscal Year enforcement and implementation efforts have also begun to reflect this increased EPA priority.

Under the SDWA as now structured--

- Part B requires EPA to set minimum national standards to protect public health from contaminants found in drinking water. Part B governs public drinking water systems;

- Part C governs underground injection wells, and provides for state programs to regulate (or ban) such wells. Most states now have such programs. This provision is now intertwined with regulations under RCRA's land ban and "no-migration" petitions to permit the continued underground disposal of untreated hazardous waste;

- Other provisions establish procedures to protect sole source aquifers and wellhead areas;

- Lead in new water supply piping and solder is now banned; in 1988, lead in water coolers was also banned, and recall procedures provided;

- Substantial federal financial assistance is authorized, but Congress has often failed to appropriate such sums.

## 2.0 REGULATION OF PUBLIC WATER SUPPLIES

### 2.1 Status of Drinking Water Standards

The SDWA requires EPA to identify contaminants in drinking water which may have an adverse effect on people's health, and where feasible, to specify for each such contaminant a maximum contaminant level (MCL). The MCL is to be the National Primary Drinking Water Standard. These standards are to be met by "public water systems."

EPA acted very slowly to set standards under the 1974 act: only 23 contaminants or groups of contaminants had been regulated by 1986,[3] and some of these contaminants were substances for which standards had been set even prior to 1974. EPA's decision concerning the levels at which primary standards were to be set for particular contaminants have been upheld by the courts to date.[4] The 1986 amendments also ratify previously adopted standards.[5]

---

[3] 40 C.F.R. §§ 141.11 - 141.16.

[4] *Natural Resources Defense Council v. EPA*, 824 F.2d 1211 (D.C.Cir. 1987), (VOC standards); *Natural Resources Defense Council v. EPA*, 812 F.2d 721 (D.C.Cir. 1987) (fluoride standard); *Environmental Defense Fund v. EPA*, 578 F.2d 337 (D.C.Cir. 1978) (interim fluoride standard).

(continued...)

The 1986 amendments completely change the process for establishing Maximum Contaminant Level Goals (MCLGs) and National Primary Drinking Water Standards -- usually maximum contaminant levels (MCLs) -- under § 1412. The amendments also restrict EPA's discretion in determining which contaminants to regulate and by what date enforceable standards must be promulgated.

The amendments require EPA, by June 1989, to regulate 83 contaminants previously proposed for regulation.[6] The list of contaminants is set forth in Table One. Some of these contaminants had standards set for them under the prior version of the statute. The effect of their inclusion on this list is to require revisions of the standard by EPA.

TABLE ONE

### 83 Contaminants Required to be Regulated under the SDWA of 1986

*Volatile Organic Chemicals*

| | |
|---|---|
| Trichloroethylene | Benzene |
| Tetrachloroethylene | Chlorobenzene |
| Carbon tetrachloride | Dichlorobenzene |
| 1,1,1-Trichloroethane | Trichlorobenzene |
| 1,2-Dichloroethane | 1,1-Dichloroethylene |
| Vinyl chloride | trans1,2 Dichloroethylene |
| Methylene chloride | Cis-1,2-Dichloroethylene |

*Microbiology and Turbidity*

| | |
|---|---|
| Total coliforms | Viruses |
| Turbidity | Standard plate count |
| Giardia lamblia | Legionella |

*Inorganics*

| | |
|---|---|
| Arsenic | Molybdenum |
| Barium | Asbestos |
| Cadmium | Sulfate |
| Chromium | Copper |
| Lead | Vanadium |
| Mercury | Sodium |

---

[5](..continued)
§ 1412(a).

[6] EPA listed these contaminants in two advance notices of proposed rulemaking which are incorporated by reference in § 1412 of the statute.

Nitrate

Nickel

Selenium

Zinc

Silver

Thallium

Fluoride

Beryllium

Aluminum

Cyanide

Antimony

### Organics

Endrin

1,1,2-Trichloroethane

Lindane

Vydate

Methoxychlor

Simazine

Toxaphene

PAHs

2,4-D

PCBs

2,4,5-TP

Atrazine

Aldicarb

Phthalates

Chlordane

Acrylamide

Dalapon

Dibromochloropropane (DBCP)

Diquat

1,2-Dichloropropane

Endothall

Pentachlorophenol

Glyphosate

Pichloram

Carbofuran

Dinoseb

Alachlor

Ethylene dibromide (EDB)

Epichlorohydrin

Dibromomethane

Toluene

Xylene

Adipates

Hexachlorocyclopentadiene

2,3,7,8-TCDD (Dioxin)

### Radionuclides

Radium 226 & 228

Gross Alpha particle activity

Beta particle & photon
  radioactivity

Uranium

Radon

### Substitutions: (53 Fed. Reg. 1986)

Aldicarb Sulfone

Zinc

Aldicarb Sulfoxide

Silver

Ethybenzene        *replace*

Aluminum

Heptachlor

Sodium

Heptachlor Expoxide

Dibromomethane

Nitrite

Molybdenum

Styrene

Vanadium

EPA promulgated MCLGs and MCLs for nine of the listed contaminants in July 1987.[7] Standards for forty additional contaminants were due out in June 1988; standards for the final thirty-four contaminants on the list were due out by June 1989. The purpose of these deadlines is to permit environmental groups and others to use litigation to force EPA to issue standards. Prior to the amendments, the Office of Management and Budget (OMB) had blocked or greatly delayed EPA's efforts to issue standards for the listed contaminants.

These enforceable deadlines are now the basis for successful litigation by environmentalists against the agency to set new deadlines for the proposal and promulgation of the new standards.[8] Pursuant to court orders, EPA has now proposed all but a few of the standards required to be promulgated by the 1986 amendments. Under the district court's orders, promulgation of these standards should be completed by late 1992.

The agency did promulgate final standards and maximum contaminant level goals for the six turbidity and microbiological parameters in June 1989.[9] These standards for bacteriological quality and turbidity are part of the agency's rules concerning disinfection and filtration by public water systems, discussed more fully below. The effect of these rules is greatly to tighten standards related to water-borne diseases. EPA has made clear that it believes that the incidence of such disease is far higher than public health statistics currently demonstrate.

EPA proposed standards for 38 contaminants in May 1989,[10] promulgated standards for 33 of them in January 1991,[11] and reproposed standards for 5 others for promulgation in June 1991.[12] The agency proposed standards for 24 more inorganic and organic compounds in the summer of 1990, and is required by the court order to promulgate them by March 1992. Similarly, EPA is required by court order to propose standards for radionuclides by January 1991, and to promulgate them by December 1992.

The statute allows EPA to substitute up to seven of the eighty-three contaminants on the list, if regulation of the new contaminant is likely to do

---

[7] 52 Fed. Reg. 25712 (July 8, 1987).

[8] Miller v. Reilly, Civil Action No. 89-6328-E (D. Ore.)(e.g., order filed June 25, 1990).

[9] These standards are for turbidity, *Giardia lamblia* viruses, and *Legionella*, 54 Fed. Reg. 27486 (June 29, 1989), as well as for total coliforms, including fecal coliforms and *E. coli.* 54 Fed. Reg. 27544 (June 29, 1989).

[10] 54 Fed. Reg. (May 22, 1989).

[11] 54 Fed. Reg. 3526 (January 30, 1991).

[12] 54 Fed. Reg. 3600 (January 30, 1991).

more to protect public health than will regulation of the contaminant previously listed.[13] EPA has exercised its substitution option by replacing seven contaminants, all but one inorganic, with seven suspected carcinogens, all but one organic.[14] These substitutions do not change the statutory schedule for regulation: standards for the revised list of eighty-three contaminants still had to be adopted by June 1989.

EPA has proposed cutting the standard for lead contamination by a factor of ten, down to five parts per billion,[15] a move that may place a number of public water systems in violation. Unsuccessful efforts were made at the end of the 100th and 101th Congresses to legislate such a reduction in the lead standards. EPA is now required by court order to promulgate the MCL and MCLG for lead and copper by early 1991. The proposal is currently stalled in a debate over where compliance with the standards is to be measured: as the water leaves the treatment works, or as it is delivered to the customer's tap. The municipalities operating many of the treatment works argue that they can only be responsible for contamination in the parts of the system they control. Environmentalists argue that the quality of the water actually consumed is what matters to health, especially in light of disturbing new evidence about the severe adverse effects of lead on children. Regardless of the level at which it is finally set, the final standard seems certain to prove controversial, expensive, and severely to affect numerous public water systems, to say nothing of the people drinking the water.

In addition to the Congressionally-mandated list of contaminants, the 1986 amendments require EPA to devise a priority list of contaminants for regulation *after* it completes standards for the list of eighty-three. EPA is required to place contaminants on the priority list which may have an adverse effect on people's health and which are known or anticipated to occur in public water systems.[16]

EPA published this list in January 1988 and revised it in January 1991.[17] There are now seventy-seven substances or classes of substance. This priority list is reproduced at Table Two.

---

[13] § 142(b)(2)(A).

[14] 53 Fed. Reg. 1892 (Jan. 22, 1988).

[15] 53 Fed. Reg. 31356 (Aug. 18, 1988).

[16] § 1412(b)(3)(A).

[17] 55 Fed. Reg. 1470 (January 14, 1991).

## TABLE TWO

### SDWA Priority List of Drinking Water Contaminants

#### Inorganics (Total number = (14)

Aluminum
Boron
Chloramines
Chlorate
Chlorine
Chlorine dioxide
Chlorite

Cyanogen chloride
Hypochlorite ion
Manganese
Molybdenum
Strontium
Vanadium
Zinc

#### Pesticides (Total number = 19)

Asulam
Bentazon
Bromacil
Cyanazine
Cyromazine
DCPA (and its acid metabolites)
Dicamba
Ethylenethiourea
Fomesafen
Lactofen/Acifluorfen

Metalaxyl
Methomyl
Metolachlor
Metribuzin
Parathion degradation
    product (4-Nitrophenol)
Prometon
2,4,5-T
Thiodicarb
Trifluralin

#### Synthetic Organic Chemicals (Total number = 43)

Acrylonitrile
Bromobenzene
Bromochloroacetonitrile
Bromodichloromethane
Bromoform
Bromomethane
Chlorination/Chloramination
    by products (Misc.), e.g.,
    Haloacetic acids, Haloketones,
    Chloral hydrate, MX-2 [3-chloro-
    4-[dichloromethyl)-5-hydroxy-2
    (5H-furanone], N-Organochloramines
Chloroethane
Chloroform
Chloromethane
Chloropicrin
o-Chlorotoluene

p-Chlorotoluene
Dibromoacetonitrile
Dibromochloromethane
Dibromomethane
Dichloroacetonitrile
1,3-Dichlorobenzene
Dichlorodifluoromethane
1,1-Dichloroethane
2,2-Dichloropropane
1,3-Dichloropropane
1,1-Dichloropropene
2,4-Dinitrophenol
2,4-Dinitrotoluene
2,6-Dinitrotoluene
1,2-Diphenylhydrazine
Fluorotrichloromethane
Hexachlorobutadiene

## Synthetic Organic Chemicals, continued

Hexachloroethane
Isophorone
Methyl ethyl ketone
Methyl isobutyl ketone
Methyl-t-butyl ether
Naphthalene
Nitrobenzene
Ozone by-products, e.g., Aldehydes, Epoxides,
  Peroxides, Nitrosamines, Bromate, Iodate

1,1,1,2-Tetrachloroethane
1,1,2,2-Tetrachloroethane
Tetrahydrofuran
Trichloroacetonitrile
1,2,3-Trichloropropane

## Microorganisms (Total number = 1)

Cryptosporidum

EPA included in this priority list the seven contaminants it had dropped from the list of eighty-three requiring action by June 1989.

By January 1991, the statute requires EPA to promulgate MCLs and MCLGs for twenty-five of the contaminants on the priority list.[18] At that time, EPA also must update the list, and every three years thereafter, issue MCLs and MCLGs for another twenty-five contaminants.[19] Despite these statutory commands, EPA's regulatory agenda shows that EPA will not propose standards for the first twenty-five contaminants until June 1992, and will not promulgate them until December 1993. Whether this leisurely regulatory pace is allowed by the courts once the statutory deadlines have passed is open to question.

### 2.2 Procedure for Setting Maximum Contaminant Level Goals (MCLGs)

Under the SDWA as amended, the maximum contaminant level goal (MCLG) for a contaminant must be set at a level at which no known or anticipated adverse effects on the health of people occur and which allows an adequate margin of safety.[20] The MCLG is almost entirely a health-based determination. Consequently, EPA has set some MCLGs for suspected carcinogens at zero.[21] Similarly, EPA has also set the MCLGs for viral and

---

[18] § 1412 (b)(3)(C), (D).

[19] § 1412 (b)(3)(A).

[20] § 1412(b)(4).

[21] 40 C.F.R. § 141.50(a).

bacterial contamination at zero.[22]   Fortunately for public water systems, the MCLG is only a goal and not an enforceable standard.[23]

EPA sets MCLGs through an elaborate process, a process which varies depending on which of three categories of contaminants are being regulated: carcinogens, non-carcinogens, or substances for which the evidence of carcinogenicity is unclear.   For substances which EPA believes there is strong evidence of carcinogenicity (Category One), EPA sets the MCLG at zero. Category One substances are also referred to as EPA Groups A and Groups B1 and B2 substances, known and possible human carcinogens.

For substances which EPA believes are not carcinogenic, the MCLG is set based upon calculations of a "no-effect" level for chronic exposure, including a margin of safety.   This level is referred to as the Reference Dose (RfD) and is derived from the "No Observed Adverse Effect Level" (NOAEL) or "Lowest Observed Adverse Effect Level" (LOAEL), information usually developed from animal studies.   In setting the reference dose, the NOAEL is reduced by an uncertainty factor, ranging from 100 up to 1000.[24]   Uncertainty factors are employed because the data must be used to estimate a "no effect" level for a widely differing human population, based on extrapolations from animal studies.

After a reference dose is calculated, a Drinking Water Equivalent Level (DWEL) is calculated, using the reference dose to help determine the specific level in drinking water at which non-carcinogenic health effects should not occur. The DWEL is calculated assuming that a seventy kilogram adult drinks two liters of water per day.

In order finally to arrive at the MCLG for the noncarcinogenic substances, the DWEL is reduced to account for other sources of human exposure to the substance besides drinking water.   For inorganic substances, EPA believes data for dietary exposure are well-quantified by FDA studies, and will rely on such studies.   For organic contaminants, however, data on dietary and other exposures are thought inadequate.   EPA assumes that only twenty

---

[22] 54 Fed. Reg. 27527 (June 29, 1989), promulgating 40 C.F.R. § 141.52 (1989).

[23] An MCLG is, however, "enforceable" under the Comprehensive Environmental Response, Compensation, and Liability Act (CERCLA) because, in selecting remedial actions, EPA "shall require a level or standard of control which at least attains Maximum Contamination Level Goals established under the Safe Drinking Water Act ... where such goals ... are relevant and appropriate under the circumstances of the release or threatened release."   *See* Section 121(d)(2)(A) of the Superfund Amendments and Reauthorization Act of 1986, PL No. 99-499.

[24] For example, the uncertainty factor proposed with  the cyanide standard is 500; for nickel, 300; for thallium, 1000.   55 Fed. Reg. 30370, 30379.83 (July 25, 1990).

percent of such exposure results from drinking water, and so reduces the DWEL by a factor of five to arrive at the MCLG. The resulting figure is a conservative one indeed, given the conservative uncertainty and exposure assumptions underlying it.

For a third category of substances, those for which EPA believes there is equivocal evidence of carcinogenicity (Class C Substances), the DWEL is set based upon non-carcinogenic health effects. The MCLG is derived from the DWEL as explained above, but with the use of an additional uncertainty factor to account for possible carcinogenic risk. Alternatively, where data about non-carcinogenic health effects are viewed as insufficient, the MCLG is set based on an estimated lifetime risk of developing cancer from exposure to the substance in drinking water.

## 2.3 Calculation of Maximum Contaminant Levels (MCLs) and National Primary and Secondary Drinking Water Standards

The National Primary Drinking Water Regulation (NPDWR) -- usually the maximum contaminant level (MCL) -- for a contaminant *is* an enforceable standard. EPA may promulgate MCLs, which are to be set as close to the MCLG as "feasible." Under the statute, "feasible" is defined to mean the MCL which is "feasible with the use of the best technology, treatment techniques and other means." These treatment technologies must be effective "under field conditions" and take cost into consideration.[25] If it is infeasible to determine the level of contaminant, EPA is authorized to promulgate an NPDWR requiring the use of a specified treatment technique in lieu of setting an MCL.[26] EPA has not so far adopted regulations requiring the use of a specified treatment technology as opposed to establishing MCLs, although it has specified treatment technology capable of meeting MCLs so far promulgated for organic chemicals.[27]

In determining "best available technology" (BAT), EPA does not limit itself to technology which has been field-tested for each contaminant. Rather, EPA views such technologies as field-tested if the technologies themselves

---

[25] § 1412(b)(5). Granulated Activated Carbon (GAC) is explicitly defined by statute as feasible for treatment of synthetic organic chemicals. Thus, BAT must be at least as effective as GAC in controlling synthetic organic chemicals. § 1412(b)(3).

[26] § 1412(b)(7). In adding this provision, Congress addressed circumstances similar to those which arose in *Adamo Wrecking Co. v. EPA*, 434 U.S. 275 (1978). In that case the Supreme Court held that an emission limitation for asbestos had to be expressed numerically, and that specified work practices were not enforceable emission limitations.

[27] 40 C.F.R. § 141.61(b).

have been operated in the field and laboratory or pilot-scale tests show that the treatment technology will work for the particular contaminant of concern.

EPA looks first to removal efficiencies in determining what constitutes "best technology." EPA also evaluates affordability. In doing so, the agency studies affordability for large municipalities as well as national compliance costs. Finally, EPA looks at the capabilities of monitoring technologies in determining the MCL and thus the enforceable standard for the contaminant.

The enforceable standards resulting from the MCLG and MCL process are quite conservative. Because many of the regulated contaminants are rarely encountered in drinking water, these stringent limitations often have little practical impact besides forcing dramatic increases in monitoring costs. Nonetheless, the financial impacts of standards now being set for several common contaminants may be quite severe, just as the calculated health benefit may be substantial. Notable among these widely-occurring contaminants are four:

(1) the microbiological parameters, for which the MCLG is set at zero, and for which treatment operations across the country will have to be upgraded by disinfection, filtration, or alternatives to them;

(2) lead, for which both the MCL and MCLG should be dramatically reduced soon in light of disturbing new epidemiological and medical data about the effects of lead on children;

(3) radon, which is widespread in groundwater from natural sources, and which may have significant carcinogenic effects;

(4) sulfates, which are widespread and are linked to over 100,000 cases per year of intestinal disorders.

The standards for these contaminants will have widespread cost and health effects in addition to the monitoring burden they will impose on most public water systems.

The 1986 amendments did not affect the statutory requirements for National Secondary Drinking Water Regulations.[28] EPA is to promulgate such standards to protect "public welfare" from odor and aesthetic problems which may cause a substantial number of people to stop using the public water system affected.[29] These standards are advisory for the states: EPA cannot enforce them. EPA has set secondary standards for thirteen parameters, which

---

[28] §§ 1401(2), 1412(c).

[29] § 1401(2).

are set forth in Table 3. EPA has also proposed additional secondary standards for taste and odor thresholds.[30]

## TABLE 3

### National Secondary Drinking Water Standards: 40 C.F.R. § 143.3

| | |
|---|---|
| Chloride | Manganese |
| Color | Odor |
| Copper | pH |
| Corrosivity | Sulfate |
| Fluoride | Total Dissolved Solids |
| Foaming Agents | Zinc |
| Iron | |

### 2.4  Disinfection, Filtration, and Treatment Technology Requirements

The 1986 amendments required EPA to set standards for filtration and disinfection of drinking water.  EPA was required by December 1987 to promulgate NPDWRs specifying the criteria under which filtration will be required, especially for systems relying on surface waters.[31] EPA's proposal became extraordinarily controversial, attracting several thousand written comments, especially from smaller systems potentially affected by the proposal.

By June 1989, EPA also was required to set standards requiring disinfection by public water systems.[32]  The circumstances for variances are also to be spelled out in detail in the standards.[33]

In June 1989, EPA promulgated elaborate requirements for disinfection and filtration by public water systems.  These rules require systems relying on surface waters (or ground water under the direct influence of surface waters) to use disinfection and to use filtration unless stringent standards are met for microbiological contamination, turbidity, and protection of surface waters.[34] To avoid filtration requirements, source waters must have very low coliform counts and must have consistently low turbidity.  Additionally, systems seeking to avoid filtration must:

---

[30] 54 Fed. Reg. 22062 (May 22, 1989).

[31] § 1412(b)(7)(C).

[32] § 1412(b)(8).

[33] *Id.*

[34] 54 Fed. Reg. 27486 (June 29, 1989).

(1) use disinfection and provide redundant disinfection capacity or an automatic shut-off if residual disinfectant levels drop too low;

(2) must maintain disinfectant levels and operating conditions sufficient to inactivate 99.9% of Giardia lamblia cysts and 99.99% of viruses;

(3) establish and maintain an effective watershed control program to minimize contamination from Giardia lamblia cysts and viruses in source waters;

(4) verify the watershed and disinfectant programs through annual state inspections;

(5) prevent any outbreaks of waterborne disease; and

(6) comply with total coliform and trihalomethane MCLs.

Systems required to install filtration under this rule should be determined by the states by December 1991, and filtration installed by June 1993, unless an extension is granted on grounds of infeasibility.

The filtration rule also tightens operating requirements for systems which already use filtration. For all systems, operator qualifications are made more stringent.

The disinfection and filtration rule may be the most costly requirement imposed under the SDWA. EPA estimated compliance costs of the final rule at more than $3.1 billion, with annualized costs in excess of $500 million. The impacts of the rule may be most pronounced in the Northeast and New England, where a number of systems rely on surface reservoirs without filtration. New York City and Boston are two very large examples of this situation. EPA reports that these two cities are among fifteen public water systems serving more than 100,000 people each with unfiltered water. The fifteen systems together serve 16 million people. Altogether, EPA estimates there are 3000 public water systems relying on unfiltered surface waters to serve about 21 million people. The bulk of the health benefits and capital costs can be linked to the large systems; the bulk of the monitoring costs to the small systems.

EPA is in the process of developing MCLs and MCLGs for disinfectants and disinfectant byproducts. These rules should be proposed in the fall of 1991, and may have to rely heavily on work practice standards to minimize formation of undesirable byproducts. The filtration rules should help reduce formation of some of these byproducts by removing many organic materials from the water before it is treated with disinfectant.

## 2.5 The Regulated Public

Once promulgated, standards apply to "public water systems," systems which regularly supply water to fifteen or more connections or to twenty-five or more individuals at least sixty days a year.[35] This definition applies to most industrial and commercial establishments which supply water to employees and/or customers, although only residential systems are required to meet all the NPDWRs. Systems are excluded from all coverage, however, if they: only store and distribute water; obtain water from a regulated public water supply; sell no water; and are not a carrier of persons in interstate commerce.[36] Courts have upheld broad readings of the definition of public water systems.[37]

In July 1987, EPA extended the definition of "public water system" to include water systems serving nonresidential populations of more than twenty-five of the same persons more than six months per year.[38] The intention of the change is to protect people who "because of regular long-term exposure, might incur long-term risks of adverse health effects."[39] The effect of the change is to include schools, offices, and factories which have their own water supply, normally wells. These water systems may face significant compliance problems if EPA goes forward with proposals to tighten the MCL for lead.

### 2.6 Variances and Exemptions

The SDWA provides variances and exemptions for public water supply systems which cannot meet the primary drinking water standards. If a system cannot meet an MCL *despite application of the best treatment technology,*[40] it may receive a variance. Cost considerations and the nature of raw water supplies are taken into account in issuing such variances. Variances also require eventual compliance and cannot be granted if such a variance would result in an unreasonable risk to public health.[41] Eventual compliance may be illusory because EPA may specify "an indefinite time period for compliance"

---

[35] § 1401(4), 40 C.F.R. § 141.11(e).

[36] § 1411, 40 C.F.R. § 141.3.

[37] E.g. *United States v. Virgin Islands Housing Authority,* 27 ERC 2187 (D.V.I. 1988).

[38] 52 Fed. Reg. 25712, promulgating 40 C.F.R. § 141.3 definition of Community Water System.

[39] *Id.*

[40] 40 C.F.R. § 142.42(c).

[41] SDWA § 1415, 40 C.F.R. 142.40-.46.

awaiting the development of new treatment technology.[42] A variance may also be granted to a system from a treatment technology specified by a primary standard, if the nature of the system's raw water supply makes such treatment unnecessary to protect public health. Such a variance need not require eventual compliance with the standard.

If a system cannot meet an MCL for reasons other than the nature of its raw water supply or cannot install a treatment technology specified by a primary standard, it may receive an exemption. Exemptions, however, require compliance within three years and cannot be granted if they could result in an unreasonable risk to public health. Exemptions cannot be granted to new systems unless there is no reasonably available alternative source of drinking water. Special flexibility is allowed for systems that elect to comply by entering into enforceable agreements to become part of a regional public water system.[43] Small systems may receive renewable exemptions.[44]

EPA's disinfection and filtration rules forbid states to grant variances from their requirements. In explaining this decision, EPA noted that the filtration rule already provides criteria to determine which systems will be required to filter, creating the equivalent of a variance to qualifying systems. With respect to disinfection, EPA simply stated that because of "the acute nature and high risk associated with poor disinfection of surface waters, no variances are allowed."[45]

## 2.7 State Role

SDWA provides for state implementation, upon application, if a state has drinking water standards "no less stringent" than the federal standards, "adequate" enforcement procedures, and variance and exemption conditions "no less stringent" than the federal conditions.[46] These relatively lax entry requirements and the fact that virtually all states already operated a drinking water program have led all but two states to assume SDWA primacy for public water systems. States with primary enforcement authority must notify EPA upon granting a variance or exemption and must submit an annual status report on all public water supply systems within the state.[47]

---

[42] 40 C.F.R. § 142.43(e).

[43] SDWA § 1416, 40 C.F.R. §§ 142.50 - 142.57.

[44] § 1416(b)(2)(C).

[45] 54 Fed. Reg. 27513 (June 29, 1989).

[46] § 1412, 40 C.F.R. §§ 142.10 - 142.15.

[47] 40 C.F.R. § 142.15.

their deficiencies.[48] This review mechanism effectively allows correction of deficiencies only if a substantial number of deficiencies exist and allows corrective action only if an abuse of discretion is shown. Use of this review mechanism presents hard legal and political problems for EPA. These problems may explain why EPA has only taken one action to revoke variances.[49]

State variances from MCLs, however, may be a basis under CERCLA to argue that MCLs should not be used as groundwater cleanup standards at superfund sites. Under CERCLA, if a state is inconsistent, requiring MCLs to be used at superfund sites, but not for water it knows people actually drink, then it may lose arguments about appropriate cleanup standards.[50]

### 2.8 Enforcement Against Public Water Systems

The SDWA has separate enforcement provisions for public water systems regulated under Part B of the statute, and underground injection wells under Part C of the statute. Both enforcement provisions were strengthened by the 1986 amendments.

Violations of standards governing public water systems are now punishable by civil penalties of up to $25,000 per day of violation.[51] In assessing such penalties, the statute requires the court to take into account the population at risk, the "seriousness of the violation," and other "appropriate factors."[52] Unlike the situation under the prior version of the statute, EPA need not prove that the violation is "willful." Thus, negligent violations are subject to civil penalties, as is the case under other environmental statutes.

The amendments also authorize EPA to issue administrative orders requiring compliance with regulations or other requirements.[53] Failure to comply with such orders may result in civil penalties of up to $25,000 per day,[54] or administrative penalties assessed by EPA of up to $5,000, after opportunity for

---

[48] §§ 1415(d), 1416(d).

[49] 51 Fed Reg. 23468 (June 27, 1986).

[50] CERCLA, § 121(d)(4)(E).

[51] § 1414(b).

[52] *Id.*

[53] § 1414(g).

[54] § 1414(g)(3)(A).

an informal hearing in accordance with Section 554 of the Administrative Procedure Act.[55]

Federal enforcement shall be commenced in states with primary enforcement authority, if, 30 days after EPA's notice to the state, the state has not commenced "appropriate enforcement action."[56]

These strengthened enforcement provisions reflect Congress' dissatisfaction with EPA's enforcement record.[57] In order to encourage EPA to use these new tools, Congress strongly implied that EPA enforcement was mandatory whenever a violation is detected.[58] While this change may increase enforcement actions, it will not necessarily focus enforcement resources on the most serious violations, and, in fact, could lead to *pro forma* orders for all violations, both serious and minor.

The amendments also create a new section of the act which makes tampering with a public water supply a criminal offense, subject to imprisonment of up to five years and a fine of $50,000.[59] Threats or attempts to tamper can lead to imprisonment of up to three years and a fine of up to $20,000.[60]

The SDWA may be enforced by private citizens in federal district court. As under other environmental statutes, they must give sixty days prior notice to EPA, the state, and the alleged violator.[61] Although this provision has seldom, if ever, been used against public water systems, the new statutory requirements for notice to customers of violations may result in an increasing number of citizen suits being filed, suits possibly joined with private civil actions for personal injuries and damages against systems in violation of NPDWRs. Substantial damages have been awarded in personal injury actions

---

[55] § 1414(g)(3)(B).

[56] § 1414(a)(1)(B).

[57] H.R. Rep. No. 99-168, 99th Cong., 1st Sess. at 260 (1985) and S.Rep. No. 99-56, 99th Cong., 1st Sess. at 9 (1985).

[58] *Id.*

[59] § 1432(a).

[60] § 1432(b).

[61] § 1449.

alleging illness and fear of illness from contaminated water supplies.[62] Additionally, food processors relying on contaminated public water supplies may have substantial actions for damages, as well as concern about products liability cases against them.

An unusual enforcement feature of SDWA is the requirement that public water supply systems notify customers of violations of MCLs, failure to install required treatment technology, failure to conduct required monitoring, the procurement of a variance and exemption, and any violations of the compliance schedule in a variance or exemption. Notice must be given both in the news media and in customer bills. Failure to give notice is subject to a civil penalty of $25,000.[63]

The statute distinguishes between the notice required for "intermittent or infrequent" violations and for violations which "are continuous or frequent."[64] Notice of a violation of an MCL or otherwise posing a serious potential adverse health effect is required to be made within 14 days of the violation. Notice of continuous violations is required every 3 months; notice of less serious violations is required annually.

Regulations implementing the notice requirements of the 1986 amendments became effective in April 1989. These rules require written notice to customers of violations of MCLs or related requirements within 45 days; notice in a newspaper of general circulation within 14 days of the violation; and in the event of an "acute" violation, notice through the electronic media within 72 hours of the violation.[65] The regulations actually prescribe what the notice is to say about the health effects of the MCL which has been violated, at least for trichloroethylene, carbon tetrachloride, 1-2 dichloroethane, vinyl chloride, benzene, 1,1-dichloroethylene, para-dichlorobenzene, 1,1,1-trichloroethane, and lead. The language of these notices is both clear and

---

[62] *See Sterling v. Velsicol Chemical Corp.*, 24 ERC 2077 (W.D.Tenn. 1986), (awarding $21,738,465 to five plaintiffs), affirmed in part, reversed in part, 27 ERC 1985 (6th Cir. 1987).

[63] § 1414(c).

[64] *Id.*

[65] § 141.32(a) *as added by 52 Fed. Reg.* 41546 (Oct. 28, 1987).

disturbing.[66] Presumably, EPA will promulgate similar mandatory language as it adopts additional MCLs.

## 3.0 UNDERGROUND INJECTION CONTROL

The SDWA's most direct effect on industry is through regulation on underground injection to protect usable aquifers from contamination. Underground injection is the subsurface emplacement of fluid through a well or dug-hole whose depth is greater than its width. It can include emplacement through a septic tank, a cesspool, or a dry well.[67] The regulation most directly affects hazardous waste disposal, the reinjection of brine from oil and gas production, and certain mining processes. As a result of the 1984 amendments to RCRA, implemented in July and August 1988, hazardous waste injection well operations have become strictly controlled, and some types of wastes cannot, absent an exemption, be injected in such wells.

### 3.1 The Regulatory Scheme

SDWA requires EPA to publish both a list of states where underground injection control (UIC) programs would be necessary to prevent endangerment of drinking water and to issue regulations governing the approval of state UIC programs.[68] EPA listed all states as requiring UIC programs and states were

---

[66] The notice for trichloroethylene, (TCE) is typical, 40 C.F.R. § 141.32(c)(1), particularly its statement that TCE, "generally gets into drinking water by improper waste disposal." The notice states:

The United States Environmental Protection Agency (EPA) sets drinking water standards and has determined that trichloroethylene is a health concern at certain levels of exposure. This chemical is a common metal cleaning and dry cleaning fluid. It generally gets into drinking water by improper waste disposal. This chemical has been shown to cause cancer in laboratory animals such as rats and mice when the animals are exposed at high levels over their lifetimes. Chemicals that cause cancer in laboratory animals also may increase the risk of cancer in humans who are exposed at lower levels over long periods of time. EPA has set forth the enforceable drinking water standard for trichloroethylene at 0.005 parts per million (ppm) to reduce the risk of cancer or other adverse health effects which have been observed in laboratory animals. Drinking water which meets this standard is associated with little to none of this risk and should be considered safe.

[67] 40 C.F.R. §§ 144.1(g) and .3.

[68] §§ 1421(a) and 1422.

supposed to submit their applications by the end of January 1981.[69] To be approved, state programs must: prevent underground injection unless authorized by permit or rule; authorize underground injection only where the applicant demonstrates it will not endanger drinking water sources; and maintain records, reports, inspection programs, and other such provisions.[70] EPA may allow temporary permits, either to authorize existing injection until state permitting can catch up, or to authorize temporary injection when no other means of disposal is technologically or economically feasible. Approved programs must protect aquifers that are or may reasonably be expected to be sources of drinking water supply. These programs must be designed to protect such aquifers from contamination that violates an MCL or otherwise adversely affects human health.[71]

Congress imposed several constraints upon EPA's regulations, reflecting deference to state programs and a desire not to disrupt oil and gas production. EPA's regulations are supposed to reflect geological and historical differences between the states.[72] Unless absolutely necessary to protect public health, EPA may not issue regulations that would interfere with existing UIC regulation in a substantial number of states.[73] EPA is also prevented from issuing regulations that interfere with the reinjection of brine from oil and gas production or gas storage requirements or with secondary or tertiary oil or gas recovery, unless essential to protect public health.[74]

If EPA disapproves a state's application for approval of a UIC program or a state does not seek approval of a UIC program, EPA must promulgate a UIC program for the state within ninety days.[75] For the fifty-six states, territories, and the District of Columbia, as of September 1990, twenty-nine had full UIC authority, and four more had authority over some classes of wells.[76] EPA has promulgated programs for the remaining twenty-three jurisdictions, and regulates underground injection for Indian lands in all of the states.

---

[69] 40 C.F.R. § 144.1(e).

[70] § 1421(b).

[71] § 1421(d).

[72] § 1421(b)(3)(A).

[73] § 1421(b)(3)(B).

[74] § 1421(b)(2).

[75] § 1422(c).

[76] 40 C.F.R. Part 147.

## 3.2 UIC Permits

Once a UIC permit program is in existence, no underground injection may take place except as authorized by permit or rule.[77] EPA has authorized most existing injections by rule.[78] In the meantime, injection must comply with substantive and reporting requirements that are abbreviated versions of ultimate permit requirements.[79] Permit application, issuance, and appeal procedures and permit conditions are based on those of the more familiar NPDES permitting program under the Clean Water Act.[80] There are some noteworthy differences. Substantive permit requirements may be less stringent than established by EPA's regulations if the injection does not result in an increased risk of fluid movement into an underground source of drinking water,[81] and states may, subject to EPA review, classify aquifers as not being underground sources of drinking water if they meet specific criteria.[82] Permits may be issued on an area basis as well as on an individual well basis, except for hazardous waste injection.[83] Short term temporary permits may be

---

[77] 40 C.F.R. § 144.11.

[78] 40 C.F.R. § 144.21. - .28.

[79] 40 C.F.R. §§ 144.26 to 144.28.

[80] 40 C.F.R. §§ 144.31 to 144.61 and Part 124.

[81] 40 C.F.R. § 144.16.

[82] 40 C.F.R. § 144.7. *See Western Nebraska Resources Council v. EPA,* 793 F.2d 194 (8th Cir. 1986) (contesting an exemption of an underground source of drinking water). EPA, having prevailed in that litigation, has now exempted all 300 acres of the aquifer in question at the request of the applicant proposing to conduct *in situ* uranium mining, a Class III injection well operation. The aquifer contains commercially producible uranium and is not used for drinking water. The permittee is required to restore the aquifer when mining is complete, and to post financial instruments demonstrating the financial capacity to accomplish the restoration of the aquifer when mining is complete. 55 Fed. Reg. 21191 (May 23, 1990). EPA also conducted a detailed environmental assessment under NEPA before granting the exemption.

The regulations exempt a number of other aquifers, but almost all of these exemptions appear to be related to secondary and tertiary oil production.

[83] 40 C.F.R. § 144.33.

issued in emergencies, which include the loss or delay in production of oil and gas, and may be continued until a final permit is issued.[84]

### 3.3 UIC Regulatory Enforcement

The 1986 amendments greatly strengthened enforcement provisions for the UIC program. Civil penalty liability was raised to a maximum of $25,000 per day of violation.[85] In addition, EPA was given authority to issue administrative orders and assess administrative penalties of up to $10,000 per day, up to a maximum total penalty of $125,000.[86] EPA has started to use this administrative enforcement authority in cases involving the unpermitted use of dry wells for injection of wastewater containing solvents.[87] A hearing is required before assessment of an administrative penalty, but it need not afford the full process of the Administrative Procedure Act.[88]

EPA, through the Department of Justice, has brought both civil and criminal proceedings to enforce underground injection rules. In one recent case involving alleged violations of Class II requirements, the settlement involved the payment of a substantial civil penalty, and plugging of injection wells, and a cessation of injection well activities.[89] In another case, involving hazardous waste injection activities, criminal penalties including imprisonment were sought and obtained against the defendant.

Injection well operations can also be the subject of substantial civil actions for damages. In one recent case involving manufacture of salt and contamination of an aquifer with brine, the court awarded $10,000,000 in punitive damages, as well as substantial compensatory damages.[90]

---

[84] 40 C.F.R. § 144.34.

[85] § 1423(b).

[86] § 1423(c).

[87] *See In re Mistlin Honda, Inc,* Docket No. UIC AO-88-04 (Region IX, 1988).

[88] § 1423(c)(3)(A).

[89] *United States v. Pioneer Exploration Co.,* Civil Action No. CV-88-240-GF-PGH (D. Mont.)(filed Dec. 12, 1988). *See* 55 Fed. Reg. 24943 (June 19, 1990).

[90] *Miller v. Cudahy,* 656 F.Supp. 316 (D.Kan. 1987), *affirmed,* 858 F.2d 1449 (10th Cir. 1988), *cert. denied,* 109 S. Ct. 3265 (1989).

## 3.4 Well Classification

The heart of the UIC program is its classification of wells into five classes, with regulations varying according to class of well. These classes, briefly stated, are:

**Class I:** Industrial and municipal disposal wells and nuclear storage and disposal wells that inject below all underground sources of drinking water in the area; and hazardous waste injection wells other than Class IV wells.

**Class II:** Wells which inject fluid for oil or gas recovery, and for storage of liquid hydrocarbons at standard temperature and pressure.

**Class III:** Wells which inject for extraction of minerals or energy.

**Class IV:** Wells which inject hazardous waste or radioactive wastes into or above underground sources of drinking water.

**Class V:** Wells associated with certain alternative energy development and all other injection wells, including septic tanks.[91]

According to EPA, there are about 173,000 Class V shallow injection wells divided into thirty-two subcategories. The agency notes that the number could in reality be as high as a million,[92] making potential groundwater contamination from these sources as widespread as that resulting from underground storage tanks, and as important to check in due diligence investigations for property transfers. In part because of their widespread impact, EPA is formulating proposals to devise new and more elaborate regulations to govern Class V wells. The agency says it will propose such rules in the fall of 1991; they are likely to prove expensive and controversial.[93]

EPA is working to formulate new and more stringent requirements for new Class II brine wells used in secondary oil recovery.[94]

Class IV wells are now banned by section 3020(a) of RCRA. The "hammer provisions" of the 1984 RCRA amendments also impose substantial new requirements on Class I wells, including prohibition on injection of certain

---

[91] Residential septic tanks are not regulated under the SDWA.

[92] 55 Fed. Reg. 8534 (March 8, 1990).

[93] 55 Fed. Reg. 16853 (April 23, 1990).

[94] *Id.*

kinds of "California list wastes." The 1984 RCRA amendments also ban Class I wells injecting into mines, caves, and salt domes.[95]

The primary objective of injection well regulations under the SDWA -- for all classes of injection wells -- is to ensure the mechanical integrity of the injection apparatus and to prevent migration of fluids from the injection zone into underground sources of drinking water (USDWs). EPA approval of mechanical integrity requirements of this kind has been upheld against challenges by the oil industry.[96] The Court of Appeals has invalidated regulations governing high level nuclear waste disposal in part because they failed to satisfy the "no-migration" standard,[97] i.e. contamination of USDWs beyond facility boundary lines was permitted under the invalidated regulations.

### 3.5 Class I Wells

In promulgating regulations to implement provisions of the 1984 amendments to RCRA,[98] EPA has now subdivided Class I wells into non-hazardous and hazardous categories, and imposed more stringent requirements on those Class I wells injecting hazardous wastes.[99] In addition, as part of its implementation of RCRA's "land ban," EPA has promulgated rules restricting what hazardous wastes may be injected into Class I wells, subject to certain exemption procedures.[100]

### 3.5.1 Class I Wells Injecting Non-hazardous Waste

The regulations governing Class I wells implement both the SDWA and RCRA, and employ RCRA's hazardous waste definitions in 40 C.F.R. § 261.3 to determine how stringently to control such wells. Class I wells which do not inject hazardous waste are subject to the technical standards which formerly

---

[95] RCRA, § 3004(k).

[96] *See Phillips Petroleum Co. v. EPA*, 803 F.2d 545 (10th Cir. 1986).

[97] *See NRDC v. EPA*, 824 F.2d 1258 (1st Cir. 1987). The Court upheld the portion of the regulations under the Nuclear Waste Policy Act allowing contamination of underground sources of drinking water within disposal facility boundaries, but not regulation permitting such contamination outside facility boundaries.

[98] 53 Fed. Reg. 28118 (July 26, 1988) promulgating amendments to 40 C.F.R. Parts 124, 144, 146, and 148.

[99] Compare 40 C.F.R. Part 146 Subpart B (non-hazardous) with 40 C.F.R. Part 146 Subpart G, as promulgated, 53 Fed. Reg. 28148-54 (July 26, 1988).

[100] 53 Fed. Reg 28155-57 (July 26, 1988) and 53 Fed. Reg. 30918 (Aug. 16, 1988) promulgating 40 C.F.R. Part 148.

governed all Class I wells, standards set forth in Subpart B of 40 C.F.R. Part 146. These technical standards are mirrored in the Subpart G regulations for hazardous waste injection wells, but Subpart G imposes additional requirements. Thus the standards discussed below effectively apply to *all* Class I wells.

Class I wells may not be located where another known well penetrates the part of the injection zone expected to be influenced by the Class I well, if the other well could act as a conduit for wastes to escape from the injection zone.[101] Class I wells must inject below the lowest underground source of drinking water, must be cased and cemented, and must have a packer or approved fluid seal set between the injection tubing and the casing, immediately above the injection zone.[102] The mechanical integrity of the well must be determined from both construction logs and mechanical integrity testing. Also, mechanical integrity demonstrations must be repeated at least once every five years.[103] The injected wastes must be sampled and analyzed periodically, presumably to determine compatibility with the injection equipment and the injection formation.[104] In July 1988, EPA promulgated additional monitoring regulations, requiring annual monitoring of the pressure buildup in the injection zone.[105]

The injection rate of the injection fluid and the pressures maintained on both the injection fluid in the injection tubing and the annular fluid between the injection tubing and the well casing must be continuously recorded.[106] Monitoring wells must be located in underground sources of drinking water to detect fluid movement or pressure from the injection.[107] Continuous monitoring for pressure changes in the first aquifer overlying confining zone may also be required, as well as quarterly sampling of groundwater quality.[108] A maximum operating pressure for the injection tubing is to be established to

---

[101] 40 C.F.R. §§ 144.55, 146.6 and 144.7.

[102] 40 C.F.R. § 146.13.

[103] 40 C.F.R. §§ 146.13(b)(3) and .8.

[104] 40 C.F.R. § 146.13(b)(1).

[105] 40 C.F.R. § 146.13(d)(1) as added by 53 Fed. Reg. 28147 (July 26, 1988).

[106] 40 C.F.R. § 146.13(b)(2).

[107] 40 C.F.R. §§ 146.6 and .13(b)(4).

[108] 40 C.F.R. § 146.13(d)(2) as added by 53 Fed. Reg. 28147 (July 26, 1988).

prevent fractures of the injection zone of the confirming zone above it.[109] However, stimulation, e.g., controlled fracturing of the injection zone to increase its injection capacity, is allowed.[110] Pressure on the annular fluid between the injection tubing and the casing is also to be regulated.[111]

Diesel fuel is often used as an annular fluid, which should be innocuous. Pressure on the annular fluid should be maintained at a higher rate than on the injection fluid so that a leak in the injection tubing will result in a flow of innocuous annular fluid into the tubing rather than possibly hazardous injection fluid leaking out. Injection at a constant rate with constant pressures on both injection and annular fluids is indicative of a properly functioning well. Changes in any one of them may indicate a malfunction and should be investigated. Loss of annular fluid, other than the minimum amount routinely lost through the packer or seal assembly, indicates a leak in the tubing or casing. With good equipment, potential leaks of a few gallons a day can be detected, enabling prompt detection and repair of problems with the integrity of injection well. All of this is not clearly required in the Subpart B regulations, but should be, and now largely is in the Subpart G regulations governing Class I wells injecting hazardous wastes.

Class I wells must be plugged and abandoned at the end of their useful lives by specified methods to prevent migration of wastes from the injection zone.[112]

Through a regulation patterned on the RCRA financial responsibility requirements, owners of Class I wells must establish their financial ability to properly plug and abandon the wells at the end of their useful lives.[113]

### 3.5.2 Class I Wells Injecting Hazardous Wastes

In July and October 1988, EPA promulgated regulations implementing RCRA requirements as they pertain to underground injection of RCRA hazardous wastes.[114] These regulations, especially Subpart G of Part 146, impose substantial new requirements on Class I injection wells injecting RCRA hazardous wastes. These Subpart G requirements, in turn, distinguish between existing Class I hazardous waste injection wells and new ones, imposing the most stringent requirements on new wells.

---

[109] 40 C.F.R. § 146.13(a)(1).

[110] *Id.*

[111] 40 C.F.R. § 146.13(a)(3).

[112] 40 C.F.R. § 146.10.

[113] 40 C.F.R. §§ 144.60 to 144.70.

[114] 53 Fed. Reg. 28148 (July 26, 1988).

Class I wells into which hazardous wastes are injected are hazardous waste disposal facilities and therefore subject to RCRA permitting requirements. For the moment, however, the RCRA program has deferred to the UIC program and exempts UIC permitted Class I wells from RCRA permitting requirements and from interim status regulations.[115] However, UIC wells may be subject to some of the RCRA interim status and permit requirements.[116] Any related surface facilities for storage, treatment or disposal of hazardous waste, however, require RCRA permits and are subject to RCRA interim status or permit regulations.[117] Moreover, the UIC regulations subject owners and operators of Class I wells to some RCRA regulations, including waste minimization obligations.[118]

The Subpart G regulations mirror the earlier Subpart B regulations, but go much farther with respect to minimum siting criteria, the area of review, corrective action, construction, logging and sampling, operations, and post-closure care and financial responsibility. All Class I wells injecting hazardous wastes must now demonstrate that the area is "geologically suitable," with detailed requirements for both the injection and confining zones.[119] Moreover, the regulations now require that the upper layer of the confining zone be separated from the lowermost underground source of drinking water (USDW) by a buffer zone of additional strata -- at least one relatively permeable stratum and one relatively impermeable stratum.[120]

The "area of review," i.e. area around the Class I well to be reviewed for effects on USDWs, is dramatically increased in Subpart G. Under the prior rules, the area was usually defined by a quarter mile radius from the well bore.[121] The new rules increase this radius from a quarter of a mile to two miles,[122] and so increase the area of review by a factor of sixty-four, from about 1/5 of a square mile to about 12 1/2 square miles. Additionally, if the cone of influence of the injection well is greater than two miles, the area of review is increased to that greater distance.

---

[115] 40 C.F.R. §§ 264.1(d), 265.1(c)(2), and 265.430.

[116] 40 C.F.R. §§ 265.1(c)(2) and 265.430.

[117] *See* comments to 40 C.F.R. §§ 264.1(d) and 265.1(c)(2).

[118] 40 C.F.R. § 144.14.

[119] 40 C.F.R. § 146.62(b), (c).

[120] 40 C.F.R. § 146.62(d).

[121] 40 C.F.R. § 146.6(b).

[122] § 146.63.

The operator of a Class I well injecting hazardous waste must thus propose corrective action for potentially many more wells than other injection well operators. In the injection well context, corrective action normally means assurance that other wells penetrating the confining or injection zones have been adequately plugged and sealed, and will not be a way for contamination to reach USDWs. (Limitations on injection pressure are an alternative way of satisfying this requirement.) The demonstration that hazardous waste injection wells must make in this regard is far more elaborate than other injection wells must make.[123]

During construction of new hazardous waste injection wells, steps must be taken to assure that well materials are compatible with the injection wastes. Additionally, elaborate logging requirements are imposed in order to assure that geological information presented in the permit application is correct and that an accurate baseline is established.[124]

In addition to operating requirements already imposed on Class I wells prior to adoption of Subpart G, the new rules require elaborate automatic shutoffs and alarms in the event pressure is lost or certain operating parameters are exceeded.[125] In the event of such an alarm and shutdown, EPA or the state must be notified within 24 hours, and injection operations must cease until the problem is corrected.[126] Moreover, if an USDW is contaminated a notice must be placed in local newspapers.[127]

The testing, monitoring, and reporting requirements imposed under Subpart G are very similar to those previously required. In the event a generator uses its own Class I injection well, however, it must make the same waste minimization certification that other generators must on their manifests.[128] Finally, the operator of a Class I hazardous waste injection well must have a post-closure plan -- primarily concerned with monitoring -- and demonstrate financial responsibility for such post-closure care.[129]

---

[123] Compare 40 C.F.R. § 146.64 with 40 C.F.R. §§ 144.55, 146.7.

[124] 40 C.F.R. §§ 146.65, .66.

[125] 40 C.F.R. § 146.67(f)-(i).

[126] Id.

[127] 40 C.F.R. § 146.67(i)(1)(V).

[128] 40 C.F.R. § 146.70(d).

[129] 40 C.F.R. §§ 146.72, .73.

### 3.5.3 Implementation of Land Ban

The 1984 RCRA amendments contain a number of provisions directly applicable to Class I hazardous waste injection wells. The most important of these are the so called "hammer" provisions.[130] Under these provisions EPA must serially review all RCRA listed hazardous wastes to determine whether injection or other land disposal of those wastes may continue. If it fails to make the determination by the statutorily mandated schedule, injection is automatically prohibited, with no possibility of an administrative reprieve. The schedule for EPA action on injection of those wastes is somewhat different than the schedule for its action on other means of land disposal of the wastes. The schedule for EPA determination is:

(1) August 8, 1988, wastes containing free cyanides or certain heavy metals in significant concentration, PCBs in concentrations greater than 50 ppm, halogenated organic compounds in excess of 1,000 ppm, specified dioxin containing waste streams, or specified solvents, or with a pH of less than 2.0 and one-third of RCRA listed wastes;

(2) June 8, 1989, another third of RCRA listed wastes; and

(3) May 8, 1990, the final third of RCRA listed wastes.[131]

EPA has implemented these restrictions by adopting 40 C.F.R. Part 148 and amending it as it promulgated other aspects of land ban rules.[132] These rules now ban injection of wastes containing (1) dioxin; (2) more than 50 parts per million of PCBs; (3) 10,000 parts per million of halogenated organic compounds; or (4) more than one percent of certain listed solvents or solvent wastes.[133] Additionally, injection of the rest of the "California list" wastes has now been banned.[134] Injection of the so-called "first third, "second third," and "third third" wastes are now mostly banned, with the rest of the ban coming into force in 1991 and 1992, depending upon the RCRA waste code involved.[135]

---

[130] RCRA §§ 3004(f)-(g), 42 U.S.C. §§ 6924(f)-(g).

[131] With regard to when a particular RCRA listed waste is to be reviewed, see 51 FR 19300, May 28, 1986.

[132] 53 Fed. Reg. 28154 (July 26, 1988) and 53 Fed. Reg. 30918 (Aug. 16, 1988).

[133] 40 C.F.R. §§ 148.10(a), .11, .12(a).

[134] 40 C.F.R. § 148.12.

[135] 40 C.F.R. §§ 148.10, .14 to .16.

Special requirements apply to characteristic wastes, which may make injection of them easier.[136]

Operators of hazardous waste injection wells may be exempted from these prohibitions if they make an elaborate demonstration that there will be no migration of hazardous wastes into USDWs as long as the waste remains hazardous. This demonstration can rely on chemical changes -- attenuation, immobilization, transformation -- in the waste to render it non-hazardous, or upon a demonstration that the waste will not migrate into USDWs for 10,000 years.[137]

Since EPA promulgated the regulations, it has approved or proposed to approve a number of "no-migration" petitions, exempting the injection well operator from land ban requirements. These petitions are time-consuming to prepare, submit, and process, requiring a detailed geologic demonstration that hazardous wastes will not in fact migrate into underground sources of drinking water.[138] Where EPA has not completed processing prior to the effective date of land ban requirements, it has granted case-by-case extensions of these requirements, provided the applicants have been unsuccessful in obtaining alternate treatment capacity after a good-faith effort to do so.[139] There is no assurance EPA will grant no-migration petitions; some have been rejected on substantive grounds.[140] Moreover, citizen groups have filed lawsuits to challenge the grant of such no-migration petitions as a violation of the rules.

Despite substantial legal challenges by industry and environmental groups, EPA's no-migration petition regulations were upheld by the Court of Appeals, with the exception of EPA's failure to promulgate provisions concerning

---

[136] 40 C.F.R. § 148.1(d), as promulgated by 55 Fed. Reg. 22683 (June 1, 1990).

[137] 40 C.F.R. §§ 148.20 - 148.24.

[138] *See, e.g.,* 55 Fed. Reg. 2691 (Jan. 26, 1990)(National Steel petition for injection of waste pickling liquor); 55 Fed. Reg. 19032 (May 7, 1990) (LTV Steel petition).

[139] 55 Fed. Reg. 27660 (July 5, 1990)(outlining conditions for such extensions).

[140] 55 Fed. Reg. 33375 (Aug. 15, 1990) (petition withdrawn after EPA proposed to disapprove it; EPA states that applicant improperly assumed that abandoned wells into the injection zone had been or would be plugged without action by the applicant to do so).

injection into salt domes, underground mines, and caves. The court remanded those portions of the rules to EPA for further action.[141]

## 4.0 PROTECTION OF SOLE SOURCE AQUIFERS

Section 1424(e) provides that special protection may be given, either upon petition or upon EPA initiative where:

an area has an aquifer which is the sole or principal drinking water source for an area, and which if contaminated would create a significant hazard to public health.

The legislative history of the sole source aquifer (SSA) provision suggests that Congress viewed it as a way to provide interim protection to critical aquifers such as the Edwards Aquifer in Texas prior to the adoption of state UIC programs. The provision was quickly used to designate the Edwards Aquifer, the first designated under the act, and to issue implementing regulations.[142]

The legal effect of SSA designation is to bar federal financial assistance to projects which pose a threat to the aquifer, and since the addition of section 1427 by the 1986 amendments, to allow areas so designated before May 1988 to qualify for special federal planning grants to local governments for "critical aquifer protection areas".[143] Congress, however, has not appropriated money for the demonstration grant program.

The provision's use since its enactment has not been closely related to injection well programs (or the lack of them). Rather, citizens groups and local governments have been the moving force behind such petitions, petitions which are related to perceived threats to local groundwater from all sources, public and private. These groups seek SSA designation in order to obtain an authoritative determination of the value of the aquifer. They plan and often do use this determination in political struggles to block projects viewed as a threat to the aquifer, projects such as sewage treatment plants,[144] or

---

[141] *Natural Resources Defense Council v. EPA,* 907 F.2d 1146 (D.C. Cir. 1990).

[142] 40 C.F.R. §§ 149.100-.111. EPA has never adopted formal regulations governing the SSA designation process. It proposed such regulations in 1977, 42 Fed. Reg. 51620 (Sept. 29, 1977), and followed these proposed regulations until 1987, when it issued a guidance document.

[143] SDWA, §§ 1424(e), 1427; 40 C.F.R. §§ 149.1 - 149.3.

[144] 52 Fed. Reg. 37009 (Oct. 2, 1987) (Catawba Island, Ohio designation). The Catawba Island petitioners raised serious concerns about the effect of blasting for pipelaying for the sewage treatment system, and the adverse effects of leakage of sewage on the aquifer.

hazardous waste treatment installations.[145]   EPA solemnly disclaims such use of the SSA provision, a disclaimer that has had no discernible effect on such usage.

As of January 1991, there are over 50 sole source aquifers.   More than half of these designations have been made after the 1986 amendments.   One reason for this flurry of designations was the possibility of federal demonstration grants for local governments under section 1427.   Another reason is EPA's 1987 delegation of authority to Regional Administrators to make such designations.   This delegation cut as much as several years from the process of designation.   The aquifers designated to date are listed in Annex One to this Chapter, together with a map of their locations.

As is evident, the areas designated include some of the most populous in the country.   Most of New Jersey, all of Long Island, a substantial area near San Antonio, Texas, much of Montgomery County, Maryland, and the Biscayne aquifer in Florida -- near Miami -- are now included in sole source aquifer areas.   A number of less populated but well known resort areas have been designated, including Cape Cod, Nantucket, and Block Island, reflecting both the acute vulnerability of coastal groundwater and the relative ease of aquifer definition these areas present.

The formal basis for designation as a sole source aquifer is a determination that:

(a) the aquifer supplies drinking water to fifty percent or more of an area's population;

(b) if contaminated the aquifer would present a significant risk of public health.

In making these determinations, EPA has developed guidance and policies to decide boundaries of the area to be protected, and whether alternative sources of water are economically feasible.   Normally the boundaries of the area to be protected must be hydrologic or geologic:   political boundaries or arbitrarily selected lines on the map are not satisfactory to EPA.   As the geologic boundaries of an aquifer are hard to determine, the expense of presenting such information is a key obstacle facing petitioners.   The need for clear geologic definition of the aquifer is an important reason, in addition to their inherent vulnerability, that islands and peninsulas are a significant portion of the SSA's designated by date.   By the same token, because aquifer boundaries may bear little relation to population concentrations or political boundaries, some areas proposed for protection have been rejected by EPA because they failed

---

[145] 50 Fed. Reg. 9126 (March 6, 1985).

population tests for the area as EPA redefined it.[146] EPA has substantial discretion, however, in setting boundaries for SSAs: in one case, the Court of Appeals upheld a designation where seven non-contiguous aquifers were grouped together as one unit.[147]

In determining whether an aquifer supplies drinking water to more than 50 percent of an area's population, EPA must decide whether the population has readily available alternative supplies. EPA has devised an economic test to decide whether an alternative source of water is available, since it is almost always physically possible to obtain alternative water supplies. EPA's guidelines provide that for an alternative water supply to be "economically feasible" and thus available, it must not cost the typical household in the area more than 0.4 to 0.6 percent of the household's average annual household income. As alternate water sources usually require construction of elaborate treatment and distribution systems, for most areas alternate sources will not be "economically feasible". This result is not surprising if one assumes economically rational behavior by most people in choosing sources of drinking water: presumably most have already chosen the cheapest source.

The SSA program matters not only to the millions of people and thousands of businesses in these areas, but also as a forerunner of federal groundwater protection programs. Much of the United States could qualify for SSA protection under the guidelines EPA has developed for aquifer definition and economic feasibility of alternate sources of drinking water.

In addition, by June 1989, states had to adopt and submit to EPA programs to protect "wellhead" areas within the state from contaminants which may have any adverse effects on the health of persons.[148] "Wellhead Protection Area" is defined as "the surface and subsurface area surrounding a water well or wellfield, supplying a public water system, through which contaminants are reasonably likely to move toward and reach such well or wellfield".[149] The incentive for states to enter the program is financial: federal grants of up to 90 percent of the cost of developing these programs are authorized under the statute, although not necessarily funded through the appropriations process. A number of states did prepare and submit plans for EPA review, although EPA's enforcement leverage is quite limited because of the lack of federal grant money.

This program represents an important federal role in groundwater protection, traditionally an area of state concern, a role which will probably

---

[146] 49 Fed. Reg. 2945 (Jan. 24, 1984) (rejecting Milwaukee area for designation.)

[147] *Montgomery County, Maryland v. EPA*, 662 F.2d 1040 (4th Cir. 1981).

[148] § 1428(a).

[149] § 1428(e).

increase soon. In addition, full implementation necessarily involves issues of land use planning, another area of historically local concern. Finally, federal agencies would be required to bring any facilities within a wellhead protection area into compliance with the applicable state plan, unless the President determines it is not in the "paramount" interest of the United States.[150]

## 5.0 PROHIBITION ON USE OF LEAD PIPES AND LEAD IN WATER COOLERS

The 1986 amendments prohibit the use of lead solder, pipes, or flux in drinking water systems (including those in homes and buildings) by requiring "lead-free" materials.[151] "Lead free" is defined as not more than 0.2 percent lead in solders and flux and not more than 8 percent lead in pipes.[152] The ban took effect in all states in June 1988.[153] Public water systems must identify and provide notice to customers that may be affected by lead contamination of their drinking water, regardless of whether they meet the MCL for lead.[154] This notification and prohibition on future use of lead appears to have arrived none to soon. EPA studies suggest that lead-contaminated drinking water may be a significant problem in many areas of the country, and EPA has publicly stated that it intends to tighten the MCL for lead substantially. It must promulgate the lead standard early in 1991.

Congress amended the SDWA in October 1988, to provide for the recall of water coolers (fountains) with lead content higher than 8.0 percent in the piping, and 0.2 percent in any solder.[155] The recall of water coolers which fail standards is to be managed by the Consumer Products Safety Commission within one year.[156] EPA has published a list of cooler models which fail these tests.[157] After publication of this list, sales of such coolers are banned.[158]

---

[150] § 1428(h).

[151] § 1417(a)(1).

[152] § 1417(d).

[153] § 1417(b).

[154] § 1417(a)(2).

[155] Lead Contamination Control Act of 1988, Pub.L.No. 100-572.

[156] SDWA, § 1462.

[157] 55 Fed. Reg. 1772 (Jan. 18, 1990).

(continued...)

Special provisions address the problem of lead contamination in school water coolers,[159] provisions similar in concept (although less elaborate) to those in the Toxic Substances Control Act governing abatement of asbestos in schools.

## 6.0 CONCLUSION: IMPORTANCE OF SDWA

Implementation of the 1986 amendments and of RCRA's hammer provisions are drastically altering the SDWA regulatory program. That program is important not only to the public water systems and injection well operators directly regulated under the SDWA, but because drinking water standards are used in other regulatory contexts. For example, MCLGs are now to be cleanup standards in many superfund cases. In addition, proposals for federal groundwater protection legislation and similar state efforts are applying MCLGs or MCLs to groundwater over broad areas.

Other provisions concerning sole source aquifers and wellhead protection are becoming far more important, not only because of the number of people affected has increased dramatically, but because these programs may be the foundation for more elaborate federal and state groundwater protection legislation.

Given the increasingly broad applicability of SDWA programs, developments under this statute must be closely followed by environmentalists, industries, and state and local governments.

---

[158] (..continued)
§ 1463.

[159] §§ 1464, 1465.

# ANNEX ONE

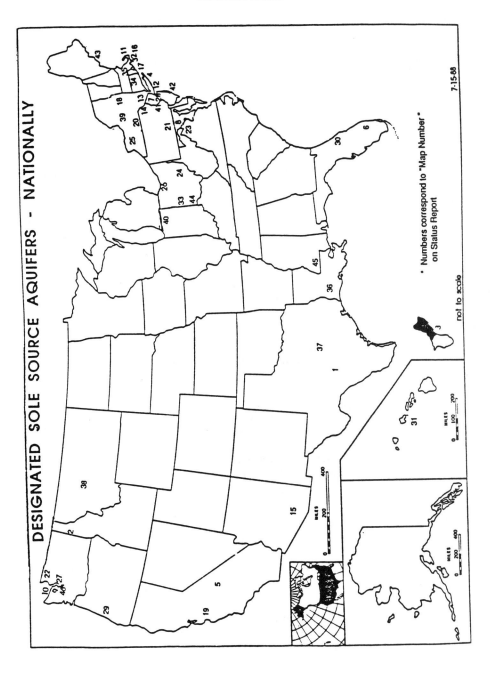

DESIGNATED SOLE SOURCE AQUIFERS - NATIONALLY

• Numbers correspond to "Map Number" on Status Report

not to scale

7-15-88

## STATUS OF 1/15/91

## DESIGNATED SOLE SOURCE AQUIFERS - NATIONALLY

| Map Number | Aquifer and/or Location | State | Citation |
|:---:|---|:---:|:---:|
| 1. | Edwards Aquifer | TX | 40 FR 58344 (02/16/75) |
| 2. | Spokane Valley Rathdrum Prairie Aquifer | WA-ID | 43 FR 5566 (02/09/78) |
| 3. | Northern Guam | Guam | 43 FR 17868 (04/26/78) |
| 4. | Nassau/Suffolk Counties Long Island | NY | 43 FR 26611 (06/21/78) |
| 5. | Fresno County | CA | 44 FR 52751 (09/10/79) |
| 6. | Biscayne Aquifer | FL | 44 FR 58797 (10/11/79) |
| 7. | Buried Valley Squifer System | NJ | 45 FR 30537 (05/08/80) |
| 8. | Maryland Piedmont Aquifer Montgomery, Frederick, Howard, Carroll Counties | MD | 45 FR 57165 (08/27/80) |
| 9. | Camano Island Aquifer | WA | 47 FR 14779 (04/06/82) |
| 10. | Whidbey Island Aquifer | WA | 47 FR 14779 (04/06/82) |
| 11. | Cape Cod Aquifer | MA | 47 FR 30282 (07/13/82) |
| 12. | Kings/Queens Counties | NY | 49 FR 2950 (01/24/84) |

| Map Number | Aquifer and/or Location | State | Citation |
|---|---|---|---|
| 13. | Ridgewood Area | NY/NJ | 49 FR 2943 (01/24/84) |
| 14. | Upper Rockaway River Basin Area | NJ | 49 FR 2946 (01/24/84) |
| 15. | Upper Santa Cruz & Ayra Altar Basin Aquifers | AZ | 49 FR 2948 (01/24/84) |
| 16. | Nantucket Island Aquifer | MA | 49 FR 2952 (01/24/84) |
| 17. | Block Island Aquifer | RI | 49 FR 2952 (01/24/84) |
| 18. | Schenectady/Niskayuna Schenectady, Saratoga and Albany Counties | NY | 50 FR 2022 (01/14/85) |
| 19. | Santa Marqarita Aquifer Scotts Valley, Santa Cruz County | CA | 50 FR 2023 (01/14/85) |
| 20. | Clinton Street-Ballpark Valley, Aquifer System Broome & Tioga Counties | NY | 50 FR 2025 (01/14/85) |
| 21. | Seven Valleys Aquifer York County | PA | 50 FR 9126 (03/06/85) |
| 22. | Cross Valley Aquifer | WA | 52 FR 18606 (05/18/87) |
| 23. | Prospect Hill Aquifer Clark County | VA | 52 FR 21733 (06/09/87) |
| 24. | Pleasant City Aquifer | OH | 52 FR 32342 (08/27/87) |
| 25. | Cattaraugus Creek-Sardinia | NY | 52 FR 36100 (09/25/87) |

| Map Number | Aquifer and/or Location | State | Citation |
|---|---|---|---|
| 26. | Bass Island Aquifer Catawba Island | OH | 52 FR 37009 (10/02/87) |
| 27. | Newberg Area Aquifer | WA | 52 FR 37215 (10/05/87) |
| 28. | Highlands Aquifer System | NY/NJ | 52 FR 37213 (10/05/87) |
| 29. | North Florance Dunal Aquifer | OR | 52 FR 37519 (10/07/87) |
| 30. | Volusia-Floridan Aquifer | FL | 52 FR 44221 (11/18/87) |
| 31. | Southern Oahu Basal Aquifer | HI | 52 FR 45496 (11/30/87) |
| 32. | Martha's Vineyard Regional Aquifer | MA | 53 FR 3451 (02/05/88) |
| 33. | Buried Valley Aquifer System (BVAS) | OH | 53 FR 15876 (05/04/88) |
| 34. | Pawcatuck Basin Aquifer System | RI/CT | 53 FR 17108 (05/13/88) |
| 35. | Hunt-Annaquatucket Pettaquamscutt Aquifer System | RI | 53 FR 19026 (05/26/88) |
| 36. | Chicot Aquifer | LA | 53 FR 20893 (06/09/88) |
| 37. | Edwards Aquifer Austin Area | TX | 53 FR 20897 (06/07/88) |
| 38. | Missoula Valley Aquifer | MT | 53 FR 20895 (06/07/88) |

| Map Number | Aquifer and/or Location | State | Citation |
|---|---|---|---|
| 39. | Cortland- Homer-Preble Aquifer System | NY | 53 FR 22045 (06/13/88) |
| 40. | St. Joseph Aquifer System (Elkhart Co) | IN | 53 FR 23682 (06/23/88) |
| 41. | N.J. Fifteen Basin Aquifer System | NJ/NY | 53 FR 23685 (06/23/88) |
| 42. | N.J. Coastal Plain Aquifer System | NJ | 53 FR 23791 (06/24/88) |
| 43. | Monhegan Island | ME | 53 FR 24496 (06/29/88) |
| 44. | OKI - Miami Buried Valley Aquifer | OH | 53 FR 25670 (07/08/88) |
| 45. | Southern Hills Aquifer System | LA/MS | 53 FR 25538 (07/07/88) |
| 46. | Cedar Valley Aquifer | WA | 53 FR 39779 (10/03/88) |
| 47. | Lewiston Basin Aquifer | WA/ID | 53 FR 38782 (10/03/88) |
| 48. | North Haven Island | ME | 54 FR 29934 (07/17/89) |
| 49. | Arbuckle- Simpson Aquifer | OK | 55 FR 39236 (09/25/89) |
| 50. | Pootatuck Aquifer | CT | 55 FR 11055 (03/26/90) |
| 51. | Plymouth- Carver Aquifer | MA | 55 FR 32137 (08/07/90) |

Chapter 5


EMERGENCY PLANNING AND
COMMUNITY RIGHT-TO-KNOW ACT
(EPCRA)[1]


J. Gordon Arbuckle, Russell V. Randle, and Paul A. J. Wilson
Patton, Boggs & Blow
Washington, D.C.


## 1.0   INTRODUCTION

The Emergency Planning and Community Right-to-Know Act of 1986 (EPCRA) was enacted as a freestanding provision of the Superfund Amendments and Reauthorization Act of 1986.[2]  A major stimulus behind the statute was the December 1984 release of methyl isocyanate from the Union Carbide plant in Bhopal, India, and the thousands of deaths which resulted.  Through EPCRA, Congress has attempted to forestall similar disasters by requiring state and local governments to develop emergency plans for responding to unanticipated environmental releases of a number of acutely toxic materials known as "extremely hazardous substances."

Beyond this the statute has established a sweeping information collection and transfer program the particular requirements of which vary depending upon which of three subsets of hazardous materials are concerned.  In general, businesses covered by EPCRA are required to notify state and local emergency planning entitles of the presence and quantities in inventory of such

---

[1] For more information on this subject, readers are referred to *SARA Title III, Law and Regulations* by the authors, listed at the back of the book.

[2] Enacted by Pub. L. No. 99-499, October 17, 1986 (Title III of the Superfund Amendments and Reauthorization Act of 1986).  EPCRA is codified at 42 U.S.C. § 11001, *et seq.*

substances at their facilities and to notify federal, state, and local authorities of planned and unplanned environmental releases of those substances.[3] The regulatory authorities receiving the information, in turn, are required to make it easily available to any interested person.[4] The EPCRA reporting obligations cannot be avoided. The statute contains a variety of enforcement mechanisms, including citizens' suits and criminal sanctions. These sanctions permit facility owners or operators to be heavily penalized for failing to comply scrupulously with the statute's requirements.[5]

Although EPCRA is still relatively new, its impact is becoming increasingly visible. EPA has begun to use the data collected through EPCRA as building blocks of a variety of other substantive regulatory programs and has undertaken a vigorous enforcement program to compel compliance. Citizens groups are also taking advantage of this information as evidenced by the increasing number of reports identifying businesses that release covered substances on a local, state, and national basis.

Contrary to earlier concerns, it appears that from an environmental perspective, at least, the benefits Congress envisioned from the statute are being realized.[6]

---

[3] See 98 Cong. Rec. S14907 (daily ed. Oct. 3, 1986), (Statement of Sen. Stafford).

[4] The breadth and detail of the information so disseminated creates a host of new challenges for the regulated industries. These range from public relations issues that might arise when the citizens of a community in which a facility is located are made aware of the quantity of "toxic chemicals" emitted annually by that facility through its Section 313 Release Inventory Report, to demands for further regulation from citizens groups and regulatory authorities, to evidence that can be used against the facility in toxic tort suits by plaintiffs' lawyers.

[5] See generally EPCRA § 325 and 326, 42 U.S.C. § 11045 and 11046.

[6] A variety of legislators had expressed concern that the potential benefits of the statute would be undone by an unmanageable avalanche of information. *See e.g.* 98 Cong. Rec. H9575 (daily ed. Oct. 3, 1986) (statement of Rep. Snyder):

> Certain facilities will have to file at least three kinds of reports for use by fire departments, local emergency planning committees, State emergency response commissions, environmental agency personnel, and the public. Despite our good intentions, we may have established a program with so many different lists of chemicals and reporting requirements that it collapses from its own weight.

## 1.1 Overview

EPCRA has three subtitles. The first, Subtitle A, establishes the framework for emergency response planning and release notification. These mechanisms are intended to respond to releases of a listed group of "extremely hazardous substances."[7]

Subtitle B requires three different sets of reports concerning two different groups of chemical substances.[8] The first two of these, imposed by Sections 311 and 312 of the Act,[9] require submission of inventory-related data on "hazardous chemicals," i.e., those substances for which a Material Safety Data Sheet (MSDS) is mandated under the hazard communication regulations of the Occupational Safety and Health Administration.[10] The third reporting requirement, under Section 313 of the Act,[11] obligates certain manufacturing sector facilities (SIC Codes 20 through 39) to file annual reports with EPA and the state in which the facility is located concerning listed "toxic chemicals". These reports provide information on the quantities of those substances at the facility, how those substances are treated or disposed of, and the annual quantity of each such toxic chemical entering each environmental medium.[12]

Subtitle C of EPCRA contains a variety of general provisions.[13] Section 325[14] creates a number of civil, criminal, and administrative penalties for

---

[7] Subtitle A is composed of EPCRA §§ 301 - 305, 42 U.S.C. §§ 11001-11005. EPA regulations implementing the emergency planning and reporting provisions are found at 40 C.F.R. Part 355; *See* 52 Fed. Reg. 13378 (April 22, 1987).

[8] Subtitle B contains EPCRA §§ 311 - 313, 42 U.S.C. §§ 11021 - 11023.

[9] 42 U.S.C. §§ 11021 (a) (1) and 11022. (a) (1), EPCRA §§311 (a) (1) and 312 (a) (1). Regulations implementing these requirements are found at 52 Fed. Reg. 38344 (Oct. 15, 1987) and are codified at 40 C.F.R. Part 370; *see* 40 C.F.R. §§ 370.21 and 370.25.

[10] 52 Fed. Reg. 31852 (August 24, 1987).

[11] 42 U.S.C. § 11023.

[12] Regulations codifying Section 313 are found at 53 Fed. Reg. 4500 (Feb. 16, 1988) and are codified at 40 C.F.R. Part 372.

[13] §§ 321 - 330, 42 U.S.C. §§ 11041 - 11050.

[14] 42 U.S.C. § 11045.

various violations of the statute's reporting requirements, and Section 326[15] authorizes similar enforcement actions to be brought by citizens as well as state and local governmental entities. Another provision (Section 322) restricts an owner's or operator's right to make trade secrecy claims in the reports required by EPCRA to the specific chemical identity of the substance.[16]

## 2.0 SUBTITLE A--EMERGENCY PLANNING AND NOTIFICATION

### 2.1 Overview

The general object of Subtitle A (EPCRA Sections 301-305) is to enable states and communities to prepare to respond to unplanned releases of certain hazardous materials. The statute also require facilities at which such substances are present to report on their release to the environment. Subtitle A mandates the creation of emergency response and emergency planning authorities--the so-called State Emergency Response Commissions (SERCs) and the Local Emergency Planning Committees (LEPCs). These entities are charged with developing and implementing the emergency response plans mandated by EPCRA. The statue also requires facilities at which specified "extremely hazardous substances" (EHSs) are present in excess of specified thresholds planning quantities (TPQs) to undertake two activities: First, these facilities must notify the SERC that those substances are present and provide their LEPC with the name of a facility representative who will participate in the yemergency planning process; second, these facilities must report releases of EHSs in excess of specified reportable quantities (RQs) (as well as releases of other substances designated under the Comprehensive Environmental Response, Compensation, and Liability Act) to designated authorities.

### 2.2 Emergency Planning

As of April 17, 1987, the governor of each state was required to have appointed a SERC comprising, insofar as possible, persons knowledgeable in the area of emergency response.[17] SERCs are given two general duties -- the

---

[15] 42 U.S.C. § 11046.

[16] § 322(a)(1)(A), 42 U.S.C. §§ 11042(a)(1)(A). Regulations implementing these requirements are found at 53 Fed. Reg. 28772 (July 29, 1988) and are codified at 40 C.F.R. Part 350.

[17] § 301(a), 42 U.S.C. §§ 11001(a).

designation of emergency planning districts[18] and the appointment, supervision, and coordination of the activities of the LEPCs within the state.[19]

By October 17, 1988, each LEPC was to have prepared an emergency plan that contains, at a minimum, consideration of the following:[20]

1. Identification of facilities subject to Subtitle A within the emergency planning district, the routes used for transporting extremely hazardous substances; and institutions such as hospitals or natural gas facilities that are subject to or which contribute to additional risk by virtue of their proximity to facilities subject to Subtitle A;

2. Methods and procedures for responding to a release of any extremely hazardous substance;

3. Designation of community and facility emergency coordinators responsible for implementing the emergency plan;

4. Procedures for the effective notification of the public and the persons designated in the emergency plan in the event of a release;

5. Means for determining if a release has occurred and the area or population likely to be affected;

6. A description of available emergency equipment and facilities and an identification of persons responsible for them;

---

[18] These districts may be existing political subdivisions of a state or may comprise multiple jurisdictions. If an emergency planning area crosses state boundaries, the SERCs of all affected states may agree to designate trans-boundary planning districts. § 301(b), 42 U.S.C. §§ 11001(b).

[19] §§ 301(a) and (c), 42 U.S.C. §§ 11001(a) and (c). At a minimum, the following groups are to be represented on LEPCs: elected state and local officials; law enforcement; civil defense; fire fighting, first aid, health, local environmental, hospital, and transportation personnel; broadcast and print media representatives; community groups; and owners and operators of facilities subject to regulation under EPCRA. § 301(c), 42 U.S.C. §§ 11001(c).

[20] § 303(a), 42 U.S.C. §§ 11003(a). SERCs are directed to review these plans at least once a year. Id.

7. Evacuation plans and alternate traffic routes;

8. Training programs and schedules for the training of emergency response of medical personnel; and

9. Methods and schedules for exercising the emergency plan.[21]

Additionally, SERCs and LEPCs were required to establish procedures for handling public requests for the information submitted to them by facilities subject to EPCRA reporting.[22]

## 2.3  Covered Facilities and Substances

A "facility"[23] at which an extremely hazardous substance[24] (EHS) is present in excess of the threshold planning quantity[25] (TPQ) set for that substance is subject to the notification requirements of Subtitle A.[26]  The TPQ represents

---

[21] §§ 303(c)(1)-(9), 42 U.S.C. §§ 11003(c)(1)-(9).

[22] §§ 301(a) and (c), 42 U.S.C. §§ 11001(a) and (c).

[23] The term "facility" is defined to mean: "all buildings, equipment, structures, and other stationary items which are located on a single site or on contiguous or adjacent sites and which are owned or operated by the same person (or by any person which controls, is controlled by, or under common control with, such person). For purposes of [emergency release notification under Section 304], the term includes motor vehicles, rolling stock, and aircraft." § 329(4), 42 U.S.C. §§ 11049(4), and 40 C.F.R. § 355.20. The term "person" is defined as, "any individual, trust, firm, joint stock company, corporation (including a government corporation), partnership, association, State, municipality, commission, political subdivision of a State, or interstate body." § 329(7), 42 U.S.C. §§ 11049(7), and 40 C.F.R. § 355.20.  The term does not include the United States;  nonetheless, many federal facilities are voluntarily complying with Title III requirements.

[24] 40 C.F.R. Part 355, Appendices A and B.  This list of EHSs and the applicable TPQs and RQs is periodically updated, most recently in February 15, 1990 at 55 Fed. Reg. 5544.

[25] § 302(a) (3), 42 U.S.C. § 11002(a) (3).

[26] Additionally a governor or SERC may designate other facilities to be subject to Subtitle A following notice and opportunity for public comment.  §

(continued...)

the amount of an EHS present at any one time at a facility, irrespective of location, number of containers, or method of storage, which gives rise to the emergency planning and notification requirements under Subtitle A. There are currently 360 listed extremely hazardous substances.[27] EPA has now proposed to list certain explosives as extremely hazardous substances in order to facilitate local emergency planning.[28] If it does so, reporting thresholds will likely be lowered significantly from the 10,000 pound limit currently in force.

EPA has adopted a one percent *de minimis* rule for EHSs present in mixtures, solutions, or formulations. Thus, EHSs present in such compounds at less than one percent concentration need not be considered when a facility owner/operator is determining whether that EHS is present in excess of the TPQ. Conversely, if an EHS is present in a concentration greater than one percent, the concentration of that EHS, in weight percent, is multiplied by the mass, in pounds, of the mixture or solution to determine the quantity of the EHS. For example, if the TPQ of an EHS is 100 pounds, and that EHS represents 20 percent of a mixture, notification is required if 500 pounds or more of that mixture is present at the facility.[29]

If an EHS is present at a facility in a quantity equal to or in excess of the TPQ, the facility owner/operator must notify the SERC that the facility is subject to Subtitle A.[30] This notification requirement is not substance-

---

[26](..continued)
302(b) (2), 42 U.S.C. § 11002(b) (2). Note that Subtitle A requirements apply to all facilities, irrespective of size, if they contain a TPQ of any listed EHS. § 302(b), 42 U.S.C. § 11002(b). *See also* 132 Cong. Rec. H9576 (daily ed., Oct. 8, 1986), statement of Rep. Snyder.

[27] 55 Fed. Reg. 35012 (Aug. 27, 1990) (advanced notice of proposed rule-making).

[28] 55 Fed. Reg. 35012 (Aug. 27, 1990). This number was reduced from 402 by court decision, *A.L. Laboratories v. EPA,* 674 F. Supp. 894 (D.D.C. 1987), and by subsequent deletions by EPA. The district court and not the Court of Appeals has jurisdiction to review challenges to such listing. *A.L. Laboratories v. EPA,* 826 F. 2d 1123 (D.C. Cir. 1987).

[29] *See* 40 C.F.R. § 355.30(e), and 52 Fed. Reg. 13392 (April 22, 1987).

[30] In general, this notification was required to be made by May 17, 1987. § 302(c), 42 U.S.C. § 11002(c), and 40 C.F.R. § 355.30(b). If, however, such notice was not provided, notification must be made within sixty days after a facility first becomes subject to the emergency planning notification requirements, *i.e.* any EHS is first present at the facility in excess of the TPQ. *Id.*

specific. Consequently, once the SERC has been advised that a facility is subject to Subtitle A, subsequent acquisition of another EHS in excess of the TPQ does not require the owner/operator to renotify the SERC.[31] Additionally, the owner/operator must designate and identify to the LPEC a facility emergency response coordinator who will participate in the local emergency planning process.[32] The LEPC must also be informed of any changes at the facility that might be relevant to its emergency planning function. Additionally, upon request by the LEPC, an owner/operator must provide any information necessary for the development or implementation of the local emergency plan.[33]

### 2.4 Emergency Reporting of Releases

Owners or operators of facilities at which "hazardous chemicals"[34] are produced, used or stored must give immediate notice of the release[35] of a reportable quantity[36] (RQ) of specific hazardous materials.[37] The substances

---

[30](..continued)
notice was not provided, notification must be made within sixty days after a facility first becomes subject to the emergency planning notification requirements, *i.e.* any EHS is first present at the facility in excess of the TPQ. *Id.*

[31] H.R. Conf. Rep. No. 962, 99th Cong., 2nd Sess. 282-283 (1986)

[32] § 303(d)(1), 42 U.S.C. §§ 11003(d)(1), and 40 C.F.R. § 355.30(c).

[33] §§ 303(d)(2) and (3), 42 U.S.C. §§ 11003(d)(2) and (3), and 40 C.F.R. § 355.30(d).

[34] Note that this requirement applies to facilities at which "hazardous chemicals" are present. This universe of materials is much broader than the EHS, and CERCLA hazardous substances to which the Subtitle A release reporting requirement itself applies. *See* discussion of "hazardous chemicals" at Section 3.2 below.

[35] The term "release" is defined as, "any spilling, leaking, pumping, pouring, emitting, emptying, discharging, injecting, escaping, leaching, dumping, or disposing into the environment (including the abandonment or discarding of barrels, containers, and other closed receptacles) of any hazardous chemical, extremely hazardous substance, or CERCLA hazardous substance." § 329(8), 42 U.S.C. §§ 11049(8), and 40 C.F.R. § 355.20.

[36] *See* 40 C.F.R. Part 302 and 40 C.F.R. Part 355, Appendices A and B.

(continued...)

for which such notification must be given are the extremely hazardous substances listed under EPCRA Section 302 and the "hazardous substances" designated under Section 102 of CERCLA. Notice need *not* be given if the release results in exposure to persons solely within the facility boundaries.[38] This reporting requirement does not apply, however, to "federally permitted" releases (as defined by Section 101(10) of CERCLA) or to "continuous" releases as defined by Section 103(f) of CERCLA.[39]

If an EHS or CERCLA hazardous substance is released in excess of the specified RQ and results in exposure beyond the facility boundary, notice must be given immediately[40] to the LEPC, SERC, and the National Response Center.[41] As a result, two different types of reporting will be necessary. Reporting to the National Response Center must conform to the CERCLA Section 103 reporting requirements codified at 40 C.F.R. Part 302. The contents of the notice given to the LPEC and SERC are specified by the

---

[37] (..continued)
§ 304, 42 U.S.C. §§ 11004, and 40 C.F.R. § 355.40.

[38] § 304(a) (4), 42 U.S.C. § 11004(a) (4), and 40 C.F.R. §355.40(a) (2).

[39] 42 U.S.C. §§ 9601(10) and 9603(f) respectively. EPA has promulgated regulations defining the reporting requirements for continuous releases. *See* 55 Fed. Reg. 30185 (July 24, 1990) (promulgating 40 C.F.R. § 302.8, § 355.40 (a)(2)(iii). EPA has proposed regulations defining federally-permitted releases. 53 Fed. Reg. 27268 (July 19, 1988). Similarly, reporting is not required for releases excluded from reporting by Section 101(22) of CERCLA.

[40] Neither the statute nor the regulations (40 C.F.R. § 355.40) define what is meant by the term "immediately". In its Final Penalty Policy for Section 304 (OSWER DIR. # 9841.2), however, EPA indicates that in some circumstances notification within one hour after the release may still be untimely. Thus as a practical matter, the term should read literally and notification be given immediately after the release unless notification will result in a delay in responding to the release. *See* 42 U.S.C. 11004(b) (2).

[41] This is not technically wholly accurate, but is prudent practice until the regulation designating all EHSs as CERCLA hazardous substances becomes effective. EPA proposed this rule on January 23, 1989. 54 Fed. Reg. 3388. Until this rule is in force, as a technical matter, releases of those EHSs that are not listed under CERCLA Section 102 need only be reported to the LEPC and SERC.

1. The chemical name or identity of any substance involved in the release;[43]

2. An indication whether the material released is a listed extremely hazardous substance;

3. The estimated quantity of the substance that was released;

4. The time and duration of the release;

5. The environmental medium or media into which the release occurred;

6. Any known or anticipated acute or chronic health effects associated with the release, and, if appropriate, advice regarding medical attention needed for exposed individuals;

7. Proper precautions to take as a result of the release, including evacuation (unless such information is readily available in the emergency plan); and

8. The identity and telephone number of the person or persons to be contacted for further information.

Additionally, as soon as practicable following the release,[44] the owner or operator must give the LEPC and SERC a written follow-up report confirming the information provided in the initial notice. The follow-up notice must also update information on actions taken to respond to and contain the release, known or anticipated health risks from exposure to the released material, and advice regarding medical attention necessary for exposed individuals.[45]

Note that if a reportable release occurs in connection to the transpor-

---

[43] "The specific chemical identity of the substance released must be provided and is not provided trade secret protection under Section 322." H.R. Conf. Rep. No. 962, 99th Cong., 2nd Sess. 285 (1986).

[44] Again, there is no formal definition of this requirement, although the Penalty Policy, *supra*, note 37, indicates that given the particular circumstances, failure to file a written follow-up within the week of the release may be deemed a violation.

[45] §§ 304(b) and (c), 42 U.S.C. §§ 11004(b) and (c), and 40 C.F.R. §§ 355.40(b)(2) and (3).

tation of an EHS or CERCLA hazardous substance the reporting differs from those governing other types of releases[46]. In this case, the owner/operator may satisfy the EPCRA reporting requirements by providing the eight items of information listed above to the 911 Operator. If no 911 Operator exists, this information may be given to the "0" Operator.[47] In this context "'transportation-related release' means a release during transportation, or storage incident to transportation, if the stored substance is moving under active shipping papers and has not reached the ultimate consignee."[48]

## 3.0   SUBTITLE B -- REPORTING REQUIREMENTS

### 3.1   Overview

Subtitle B (Sections 311-313) contains three distinct reporting provisions, the first two of which are basically complementary.   Section 311 requires facilities at which "hazardous chemicals" are present in excess of specified thresholds to submit copies of the material safety data sheets, (MSDSs),[49] or a list of the substances for which they maintain MSDSs to the SERC, LEPC, and local fire department.   This reporting requirement gives emergency planners and response entities notice of the types of hazards presented by materials at a facility.   Section 312 annually provides these authorities with additional data on these substances by requiring submission of annual and daily inventory information on the quantities of those materials and their locations at the reporting facilities.

This inventory information may be reported in either of two forms.   So-called "Tier I" reports provide the required information on hazardous chemicals grouped by hazard category, and "Tier II" reports provide the information on individual hazardous chemicals.   Tier II reports must be submitted upon request and may be submitted in lieu of the Tier I report.

---

[46] The general exemption from reporting accorded to transportation or storage incident to transportation of  materials otherwise subject to EPCRA (§ 327, 42 U.S.C. §§ 11047) does not apply in the Section 304 context.  § 304(d), 42 U.S.C. §§ 11004(d).

[47] 40 C.F.R. § 355.40(b)(4)(ii).

[48] *Id.*

[49] Under the hazard communications regulations promulgated by the Occupational Safety and Health Administration, almost every business may be required to have or to prepare a material safety data sheet (MSDS) for "hazardous chemicals."  52 Fed. Reg. 31852 (Aug. 24, 1987).

Section 313, the third reporting provision of Subtitle B, requires annual reporting to EPA and the state in which the reporting facility is located on environmental releases of listed "toxic chemicals" manufactured, processed, or otherwise used at the facility in excess of specified threshold quantities. These reports provide previously unavailable data on a large number of chemicals released into the environment by manufacturing sector facilities.

### 3.2 Section 311 -- Material Safety Data Sheets

The owner/operator of a facility required by OSHA's hazard communication regulations[50] to generate or maintain an MSDS[51] for any "hazardous chemical" must provide a copy of each MSDS or a list of the substances for which the facility has an MSDS to the LEPC, the SERC, and the fire department with jurisdiction over the facility. These submissions are required for any hazardous chemical present at the facility, as of the date the report is due, in a quantity equal to or greater than 10,000 pounds. If the hazardous chemical is also a listed EHS, however, then the reporting threshold is 500 pounds, 59 gallons, or the TPQ, whichever is less.[52] With certain significant exceptions,

---

[50] 29 C.F.R. Parts 1910, 1915, 1917, 1918, 1926, and 1928, 52 Fed.Reg. 31852 (August 24, 1987). These standards originally required chemical manufacturers and importers to obtain or develop an MSDS for each hazardous chemical they produced or imported. Additionally, all manufacturing sector employers in SIC Codes 20 through 39 were to provide, *inter alia,* information to their employees about the hazardous chemicals to which they were exposed through the use of MSDSs obtained from the chemical manufacturers or importers from whom they purchased the subject hazardous chemicals. Distributors of such substances were required to supply copies of MSDSs they received to other distributors and manufacturing sector purchasers. However, in the August 24, 1987, rulemaking, OSHA expanded the scope of the hazard communication rules to cover all employers with employees exposed to hazardous chemicals in their workplaces. The rule survived a challenge by the construction industry and is in full effect for all employers.

[51] Section 329(6) of EPCRA, 42 U.S.C. §§ 11049(6) defines the term "material safety data sheet" to have the same definition as that promulgated by OSHA in its hazard communication rules. Those rules define the term to mean "written or printed material concerning a hazardous chemical which is prepared in accordance with Paragraph (g) of this section." *See, e.g.,* 29 C.F.R. § 1910.1200(c).

[52] *See* 40 C.F.R. § 370.20(b). EPA has amended its original reporting threshold which have required reporting on all hazardous chemicals present in

(continued...)

EPCRA defines "hazardous chemical" having the meaning given it by the OSHA hazard communication regulations.[53] The OSHA rule defines the term as "any chemical which is a physical hazard or health hazard."[54] A chemical that is a "physical hazard" is one for which there is scientifically valid evidence that it is a combustible liquid, a compressed gas, explosive, flammable, an organic peroxide, an oxidizer, pyrophoric, unstable (reactive) or water-reactive."[55] A chemical that is a "health hazard" is one:

for which there is statistically significant evidence based on at least one study conducted in accordance with established scientific principles that acute or chronic health effects may occur in exposed employees. The term "health hazard" includes chemicals which are carcinogens, toxic or highly toxic agents, reproductive toxins, irritants, corrosives, sensitizers, hepatotoxins, nephrotoxins, neurotoxins, agents which act on the hematopoietic system, and agents which damage the lungs, skin, eyes, or mucous membranes....[56]

It is important to note that a wide range of materials are excluded from this definition. The OSHA Regulations (Section 1910.1200(b)) exempt the following materials:

1. Any hazardous waste as that term is defined by the Solid Waste Disposal Act, as amended (42 U.S.C. Section 6901, *et seq.*), when subject to regulation under that act;

2. Tobacco or tobacco products;

3. Wood or wood products;

4. "Articles", which are defined as manufactured items which are:

   (a) formed to a specific shape or design during manufacture;

---

[52](..continued)
quantities between zero and 10,000 pounds in the final scheduled year of Section 311 reporting and has set 10,000 pounds as the final reporting threshold.

[53] *See* §§ 329(5) and 311(e); 42 U.S.C. §§ 11049(5) and 11021(e).

[54] 29 C.F.R. § 1910.1200(c)

[55] *Id.*

[56] *Id.*

    (b) which have end use functions dependent in whole or in part upon its shape or design during end use; and

    (c) which do not release or otherwise result in exposure to a hazardous chemical under normal conditions of use.

5. Food, drugs, cosmetics, or alcoholic beverages in a retail establishment which are packaged for sale to consumers;

6. Foods, drugs, or cosmetics intended for personal consumption by employees while in the workplace;

7. Any consumer product or hazardous substance, as those terms are defined in the Consumer Product Safety Act,[57] and the Federal Hazardous Substances Act,[58] respectively, where the employer can demonstrate that such material is used in the workplace in the same manner as in normal consumer use and that such use results in an exposure which is not greater than that experienced by consumers in terms of duration and frequency; and

8. Any drug, as that term is defined in the Federal Food, Drug and Cosmetic Act,[59] when it is in its final form for direct administration to the patient.[60]

In addition, Section 311(e) of EPCRA excludes the following substances:

1. Any food, food additive, color additive, drug, or cosmetic regulated by the Food and Drug Administration;

2. Any substance present as a solid in any manufactured item to the extent exposure to the substance does not occur under normal conditions of use;

3. Any substance to the extent it is used for personal, family, or household purposes, or is present in the same form and concentration as a product packaged for distribution and use by

---

[57] 15 U.S.C. § 2051, *et seq.*

[58] 15 U.S.C. § 1261, *et seq.*

[59] 21 U.S.C. § 301, *et seq.*

[60] 29 C.F.R. § 1910.1200(b)(6).

the general public;

4. Any substance to the extent it is used in a research laboratory or a hospital or other medical facility under the direct supervision of a technically qualified individual;

5. Any substance to the extent it is used in routine agricultural operations or as a fertilizer held for sale by a retailer to the ultimate customer.[61]

These requirements are subject to several points of clarification. First, the initial Section 311 reports were due from facilities in SIC Codes 20-39 on October 17, 1987. The first such submission for facilities other than in the construction industry was due by September 24, 1988.[62] MSDS submissions were due from employers in the construction industry by April 30, 1990.

A facility owner/operator may submit a copy of the MSDS for each hazard-ous chemical present at the facility in excess of the reporting threshold to the LPEC, SERC, and local fire department. Alternatively, he may submit a list of those hazardous chemicals.[63] If the listing option is selected the list must contain the following three types of information:

1. The hazardous substances must be grouped into the five specified hazard categories;[64]

---

[61] § 311(a) (1), 42 U.S.C. § 11021(a) (1), and 40 C.F.R. § 370.21.

[62] *See* 53 Fed. Reg. 8331 (August 4, 1988). This is based on the requirement of EPCRA Section 311(d) (1) (B) that MSDS submissions are due within three months after a facility owner/operator is required to prepare or have available an MSDS under the OSHA regulations.

[63] § 311(a)(2), 42 U.S.C. § 11021(a)(2) and 40 C.F.R. § 370.21(b).

[64] EPA has compressed the 23 OSHA hazard categories into five:

(1) "Immediate (acute) health hazard" (which includes the OSHA categories "highly toxic," "toxic," "irritant," "sensitizer," and "corrosive");

(2) "Delayed (chronic) health hazard" (which includes carcinogens);

(3) "Fire hazard" (which includes the OSHA categories "flammable," "combustible liquid," "pyrophoric," and "oxidizer");

(continued...)

2. The chemical or common name of each hazardous chemical as provided on the MSDS;[65] and

3. An identification of any hazardous component of the substance as provided on the MSDS.[66]

If asked by the LEPC, an owner/operator who submitted a list rather than the MSDS themselves must submit a copy of the MSDS to the LPEC within thirty days of such request.[67]    Any person may request a copy of an MSDS from the LEPC, and if a local committee does not have the requested MSDS in its possession, it is obligated to request it from a facility owner or operator and provide it to the requester.[68]

If an owner/operator who has submitted an MSDS for a hazardous chemical receives significant new information concerning that material, he must provide a revised MSDS to the LEPC, SERC, and local fire department within three months of the discovery of such information.[69]    Similarly, within three months of the time a facility owner/operator is first required to have an MSDS available, or after a hazardous chemical requiring an MSDS first becomes present in an amount exceeding the reporting threshold, he must submit an MSDS or a listing concerning that chemical to the LEPC, SERC, and

---

[64](..continued)

(4) "Sudden release of pressure" (which includes the categories "explosive" and "compressed gas"); and

(5) "Reactive" (which includes the OSHA categories "unstable reactive," "organic peroxide," and "water reactive").

§ 311(a)(2)(A)(i), 42 U.S.C. § 11021(a)(2)(A)(i); 40 C.F.R. § 370.21(b)(1) and 40 C.F.R. § 370.2.

[65] § 311(a)(2)(A)(ii), 42 U.S.C. § 11021(a)(2)(A)(ii), and 40 C.F.R. § 370.21(b)(2).

[66] § 311(a)(2)(A)(iii), 42 U.S.C. § 11021(a)(2)(A)(iii) and 40 C.F.R. § 370.21(b)(3).

[67] § 311(c)(1), 42 U.S.C. § 11021(c)(1), 40 C.F.R. § 370.21(d).

[68] § 311(c)(2), 42 U.S.C. § 11021(c)(2), 40 C.F.R. § 370.30(a).

[69] § 311(d)(2), 42 U.S.C. § 11021(d)(2), 40 C.F.R. § 370.21(c).

local fire department.[70]

Finally, because mixtures are included within OSHA's definition of "chemical,"[71] MSDSs have been prepared for tens of thousands of products. In recognition of this fact, two options have been provided for reporting on mixtures. In the first instance, an owner/operator may submit an MSDS or make a listing entry for the mixture itself.[72] In this event to determine whether the mixture meets the reporting threshold, the total quantity of the mixture must be considered.[73] Alternatively, an MSDS or listing entry may be submitted for each element or compound in the mixture which is itself a hazardous chemical[74]. To determine the threshold quantity in this case, a *de minimis* rule applies. Thus, for each hazardous chemical that is a component of a mixture which is present at more than one percent by weight (or 0.1 percent if the chemical is a carcinogen), that weight percentage is to be multiplied by the mass (in pounds) of the total mixture to determine the quantity of the hazardous chemical present in the mixture.[75]

## 3.3 Section 312--Emergency and Hazardous Chemical Inventory Form

The "Emergency and Hazardous Chemical Inventory Forms" mandated by Section 312 of EPCRA supplement the MSDS information collected under Section 311 by providing data on the quantities of and locations of hazardous chemicals at reporting facilities. Anyone who reported under Section 311 must report under Section 312.[76] Section 312 inventory forms are submitted annually to the same entities that received MSDSs or lists under Section 311,

---

[70] § 311(d)(1)(B), 42 U.S.C. § 11021(d)(1)(B), 40 C.F.R. § 370.21(c)(2).

[71] " 'Chemical' means any element, chemical compound, or mixtures of elements and/or compounds." 29 C.F.R. § 1910.1200(c).

[72] § 311(a)(3)(B), 42 U.S.C. § 11021(a)(3)(B), 40 C.F.R. § 370.28(a)(2).

[73] 40 C.F.R. § 370.28(b)(2).

[74] § 311(a)(3)(A), 42 U.S.C. § 11021(a)(3)(A), 40 C.F.R. § 370.28(a)(1).

[75] 40 C.F.R. § 370.28(b).

[76] § 312(a)(1), 42 U.S.C. § 11022(a)(1), and 40 C.F.R. § 370.20(a).

*i.e.*, the LEPC, SERC, and local fire department.[77]   Section 312 reporting is an annual obligation: for facility owners or operators in SIC Codes 20 through 39 who were originally subject to the OSHA hazard communication regulations, the first Section 312 was due on March 1, 1988.[78]   For all other non-construction employers, the first Section 312 report was due March 1, 1989.[79] The first inventory was due for construction industry employers on March 1, 1990.   Section 312 reports are due annually on March 1 of each succeeding year.[80]   The same quantity-based reporting thresholds that apply to Section 311 also apply to Section 312 inventory reporting.[81]

Section 312 creates a reporting system that calls for two different levels of detail.  So-called Tier I information must be submitted annually,[82] although Tier II reports may be submitted in lieu of Tier I data.[83]   Upon request of the LEPC, SERC, or local fire department, an owner or operator must submit Tier II data within thirty days.[84]   The basic distinction between Tier I and Tier II reports is that the former presents information on aggregated hazardous chemical groups, and the latter on individual substances.

The statute specifies the information to be provided, and EPA has promulgated Tier I and Tier II reporting forms to collect these data.[85]   Tier I

---

[77] §§ 312(a)(1)(A)-(C), 42 U.S.C. §§ 11022(a)(1)(A)-(C), 40 C.F.R. § 370.25(a).

[78] § 312(a)(2), 42 U.S.C. § 11022(a)(2), 40 C.F.R. § 370.20(b)(2).

[79] *See* 53 Fed. Reg. 29331 (Aug. 4, 1988).

[80] § 312(a)(2), 42 U.S.C. § 11022(a)(2), 40 C.F.R. § 370.20(b)(2).  Note that EPA has established uniform reporting deadlines for all facilities under both Sections 311 and 312.  For non-manufacturing facilities, the final Section 311 deadline was set at October 17, 1990, and for Section 312 reporting at March 1, 1991. *See* 54 Fed. Reg. 30632 (July 26, 1990).

[81] § 312(b), 42 U.S.C. § 11022(b), 40 C.F.R. § 370.20(b)(2).

[82] § 312(a)(2), 42 U.S.C. § 11022(a)(2), 40 C.F.R. § 370.25(b).

[83] § 312(a)(2), 42 U.S.C. § 11022(a)(2), 40 C.F.R. § 370.25(b).

[84] § 312(e), 42 U.S.C. § 11022(e), 40 C.F.R. § 370.28(c).

[85] § 312(d)(1), 42 U.S.C. § 11022(d)(1), 40 C.F.R. § 370.40 (Tier I); and § 312(d)(2), 42 U.S.C. § 11022(d)(2), and 40 C.F.R. § 370.41 (Tier II).  EPA
(continued...)

reports call for the following three basic categories of information in aggregate terms for hazardous chemicals grouped into five health and physical hazard categories:[86]

1. An estimate, expressed in a range of weights, of the maximum amount of each category of hazardous chemicals in each of the five hazard categories present at the facility at any time during the preceding calendar year;

2. An estimate, expressed as a range, of the average daily amount of each category of hazardous chemical present during the preceding calendar year; and

3. The general location of each category of hazardous chemicals.[87]

The hazard classes are (1) immediate (acute) health hazard, (2) delayed (chronic) heath hazard, (3) fire hazard, (4) sudden release of pressure, and (5) reactive.[88]

By contrast, Tier II reports are chemical-specific. That is data are required for individual hazardous chemicals rather than for substances grouped by hazard category.[89] The data required for Tier II submissions are:

1. The chemical or common name of the hazardous chemical as given on the MSDS;

---

[85](..continued)
promulgated Tier I and Tier II reporting forms in its October 15, 1987 rulemaking (52 Fed. Reg. 38344) pursuant to its statutory mandate, § 312(g), 42 U.S.C. § 11022(g). The regulations provide, however, that an owner or operator may submit Tier I and Tier II data on state or local forms provided that such forms' contents are identical to the Federal forms. 40 C.F.R. §§ 370.40 and 370.41. EPA republished these forms with revised instructions on July 26, 1990. 54 Fed. Reg. 30632, 30646-56.

[86] These hazard categories are the same as those established for Section 311 reporting, *i.e.* fire hazard, sudden release of pressure, reactivity, immediate (acute) health hazard, and delayed (chronic) health hazard.

[87] § 312(d)(1)(B), 42 U.S.C. § 11022(d)(1)(B), and 40 C.F.R. § 370.40.

[88] 40 C.F.R. § § 370.2, 370.21(b) (1).

[89] § 312(d)(2), 42 U.S.C. § 11022(d)(2), and 40 C.F.R. § 370.41.

2. An estimate, expressed as a range, of the greatest amount of the substance present at the facility during the preceding calendar year;

3. An estimate, expressed as a range, of the average daily amount of the substance present during the preceding calendar year;

4. A brief description of the manner in which the substance is stored;

5. The location of the substance at the facility; and

6. Whether the owner or operator wishes to have the storage information withheld from public disclosure.[90]

The same provisions governing reporting on hazardous chemicals containing mixtures under Section 311 apply to inventory reporting under Section 312.[91] To the extent practicable, the method used to report on mixtures under Section 311 must be followed in Section 312 reports.[92]

---

[90] §§ 312(d)(2)(A)-(F), 42 U.S.C. §§ 11022(d)(2)(A)-(F), 40 C.F.R. § 370.41. Note that item six is an exception to EPCRA's blanket prohibition on confidentiality claims for information other than specific chemical identity. An owner or operator who wishes to have storage information withheld from public disclosure need not substantiate that request. If the owner or operator wishes to claim the specific chemical identity as a trade secret, however, he must submit the Federal Tier II form to EPA along with appropriate substantiation for that claim in accordance with the Agency's regulations implementing Sections 322 and 323. *See* 52 Fed. Reg. 38355 (Oct. 15, 1987).

[91] § 312(a)(3), 42 U.S.C. § 11022(a)(3), 40 C.F.R. § 370.28.

[92] 40 C.F.R. § 370.28(a)(2). *See also* H. R. Conf. Rep. No. 962, 99th Cong., 2nd Sess. 289 (1986). The Conference Report is particularly illuminating with regard to reporting on mixtures. It indicates, for example, that if a mixture is hazardous, although its constituents *per se* are not, an inventory form must be submitted. It also observes that if an owner or operator submits inventory data on each element or compound in the mixture, he may aggregate the amount of such element or compound present at the facility in its pure state with the amount in all mixtures at the facility as a

(continued...)

The statute explicitly makes Tier II reports publicly available. An owner or operator must respond to a request by the LPEC, SERC, or local fire department for Tier II data,[93] irrespective of the quantity of the hazardous chemical for which Tier II data are requested. The reporting thresholds do not apply in this instance.[94] In addition, any person may submit a written request to a SERC or LEPC for Tier II information. If the SERC or LEPC possess these data it must provide them. If it does not, it must request this information from the appropriate facility and supply it to the requestor for any hazardous chemical present at the facility in an amount in excess of 10,000 pounds.[95] If the SERC or LEPC receives a request for Tier II information that it does not possess on a substance present at a facility in an amount less than 10,000 pounds, the LEPC or SERC has discretion to request such information.[96]

## 3.4.    Section 313 - Toxic Chemical Release Reporting

### 3.4.1.    Reporting Threshold Issues

The final reporting provision of Subtitle B is the Toxic Chemical Release Inventory Report mandated by Section 313. These reports are to be submitted annually on July 1 to EPA and to a designated state official[97] beginning on July 1, 1988. Section 313 requires reporting on releases[98] into each environmental medium of specified "toxic chemicals" that can reasonably be anticipated to cause adverse human health effects or significant adverse effects on the

---

[92](..continued)
single inventory entry for the amount of that compound or element present at the facility. *Id.*

[93] § 312(e)(1), 42 U.S.C. § 11022(e)(1), 40 C.F.R. § 370.25(c).

[94] 40 C.F.R. § 370.20(b)(3).

[95] §§ 312(e)(3)(A) and (B), 42 U.S.C. §§ 11022(e)(3)(A) and (B), 40 C.F.R. § 370.30 (b).

[96] § 312(e)(3)(C), 42 U.S.C. § 11022(e)(3)(C), 40 C.F.R. § 370.30(b)(3). Additionally, the person making such a request must include with the request a statement of the general need for such information.

[97] § 313(a), 42 U.S.C. § 11023(a), 40 C.F.R. § 372.30(d).

[98] See note 35, *supra*.

environment.[99]    EPA promulgated the final Section 313 regulations and reporting form (the so-called "Form R") on February 16, 1988.[100]

The statute defines the criteria used to determine a facility's obligation to report. The first of these is that the facility must have ten or more full time employees.[101]   Second, the facility must be grouped in SIC codes 20-39.[102] Third, the facility must manufacture,[103] process,[104] or otherwise use[105] a toxic chemical in excess of the established reporting thresholds. The statute defines the term "manufacture" to mean: "produce, prepare, import, or compound a toxic chemical." EPA has expanded this definition to construe the term "manufacture" to mean:

---

[99] H. R. Conf. Rep. No. 962, 99th Cong., 2nd Sess. 292 (1986).

[100] 53 Fed. Reg. 4500.

[101] § 313(b)(1)(A), 42 U.S.C. § 11023(b)(1)(A), 40 C.F.R. § 372.22(a). The term "full time employee" is defined to mean "2,000 hours per year of full time equivalent employment." 40 C.F.R. § 372.3.  To determine the number of full time employees a facility has, the total number of hours worked by all employees, including contract employees, is totalled and that number is divided by 2,000. *Id.*

[102] § 313(b)(1)(A), 42 U.S.C. § 11023(b)(1)(A), 40 C.F.R. § 372.22(b). EPA interprets this requirement to relate to the primary SIC code of the facility. If the facility comprises more than one establishment, the applicability of Section 313 is based on a relative comparison of the value of products shipped and or produced at the establishments within Codes 20-39 as opposed to those grouped in other SIC codes. *Id.*; *see also* 53 Fed. Reg. 4501-4504. (Feb. 16, 1988).

[103] § 313(b)(1)(C)(i), 42 U.S.C. § 11023(b)(1)(C)(i), 40 C.F.R § 372.3.

[104] § 313(b)(1)(C)(ii), 42 U.S.C. § 11023(b)(1)(C)(ii).

[105] EPCRA does not define the term "otherwise used." EPA, however, has defined the term to mean:  "any use of a toxic chemical that is not covered by the terms "manufacture" or "process" and includes use of a toxic chemical contained in a mixture or trade name product. Relabeling or redistributing a container of a toxic chemical where no repackaging of the toxic chemical occurs does not constitute use or processing of the toxic chemical." 40 C.F.R. § 372.3.

to produce, prepare, import, or compound a toxic chemical. Manufacture also applies to a toxic chemical that is produced coincidentally during the manufacture, processing, use or disposal of another chemical or mixture of chemicals, including a toxic chemical that is separated from that other chemical or mixture of chemicals as a by-product, and a toxic chemical that remains in that other chemical or other mixture of chemicals as an impurity.

Note that while EPA expands EPCRA's definition of "manufacture" to include coincidental production of toxic chemicals, the Agency distinguishes between toxic chemicals remaining as impurities in another chemical that is processed, distributed, or used from toxic chemicals that are by-products which are either sent for disposal or processed, distributed, or used in their own right.[106] Thus, if a toxic chemical is produced coincidentally as a by-product in excess of the reporting threshold, reporting will be required. If it exists in another chemical or mixture of chemicals as an impurity, however, a *de minimis* rule applies and if it is present as an impurity at a concentration of less than one percent (or 0.1% if the toxic chemical is a carcinogen), it need not be considered for purposes of determining whether a reporting threshold has been met.[107]

The statute defines the term "process" to mean:

the preparation of a toxic chemical after its manufacture for distribution in commerce--
(I) in the same form or physical state as, or in a different form or physical state from, that in which it was received by the person so preparing such chemical, or
(II) as part of an article containing the toxic chemical.

In its definition of the term EPA added another provision to part (II) of the statutory definition which provides that: "Process also applies to the processing of a toxic chemical contained in a mixture or trade name product."[108]

"Process" means to prepare a toxic chemical after manufacture for distribution in commerce. Processing includes a variety of activities, such as blending, mixing, changing the physical state of the chemical, and incorporating the chemical into an article. A material is processed, if, after manufacture

---

[106] *See* 53 Fed. Reg. 4504-06 (Feb. 16, 1988).

[107] *Id.*, *See also*, 40 C.F.R. § 372.28.

[108] 40 C.F.R. § 372.3. *See* 53 Fed. Reg. 4505-06.

it is made part of a material or product distributed in commerce. Note that a toxic chemical is processed if it is part of a mixture or trade name product, even if it is present as an  impurity in that product. If a material containing an impurity is processed, the impurity also is being processed, and if it is a toxic chemical and is present above the reporting threshold quantity, it must be reported.[109]

A toxic chemical that is "otherwise used" is one which does not deliberately become a part of the product distributed in commerce, such as a toxic chemical used as a catalyst, solvent, or reaction terminator.  Other examples include toxic chemicals used as lubricants, refrigerants, metal working fluids, or cleaners, degreasers, or fuels.[110]

The statute sets the following threshold quantities of toxic chemicals that trigger reporting:

(1)    for a toxic chemical *used* at the facility -- 10,000 pounds (during the preceding calendar year);

(2)    for a toxic chemical *manufactured* or *processed* at a facility:
    (a) 75,000 pounds for the report that was due July 1, 1988;
    (b) 50,000 pounds for the report due July 1, 1989;  and
    (c) 25,000 pounds for the reports due July 1, 1990 and for each year thereafter.[111]

Note that while the terms "process" and "otherwise used" do not relate to the amount of toxic chemical brought on-site, the term "manufacture" does. Thus, if a toxic chemical is brought on-site via importation in excess of the applicable "manufacture" reporting threshold chemical, a Form R for that

---

[109] *Id.*

[110] *See* 53 Fed. Reg. 4505-4506.

[111] § 313(f)(1), 42 U.S.C. § 11023(f)(1), 40 C.F.R. § 372.28. Note, however, that if more than one threshold quantity applies to activities involving a toxic chemical at a facility, *i.e.*, if it is both manufactured and otherwise used, all activities at the facility involving the chemical if any  reporting threshold is exceeded must be reported. 40 C.F.R. § 372.25(c). To determine if the threshold quantity has been exceeded for a toxic chemical reused or recycled on site, one determines how much of that chemical was added to the reuse/recycle system during the preceding year. 40 C.F.R. § 372.25(e). *See also,* 53 Fed. Reg. 4508.

chemical must be filed.[112]

### 3.4.2. Reporting on Mixtures and Trade Name Products

Subject to the 1% / 0.1% *de minimis* limit, reporting is also required for toxic chemicals in trade name products that are imported, processed, or otherwise used, if the applicable reporting threshold is exceeded. Central to this requirement is the provision that reporting is required for toxic chemicals exceeding the relevant threshold for "each listed toxic chemical known to be present at the facility."[113] One has such knowledge concerning a mixture or trade name product if one knows or has been told the identity or Chemical Abstracts Service (CAS) Registry Number of a substance, and that identity or CAS number corresponds to a toxic chemical listed in 40 C.F.R. § 372.65.[114] Knowledge also results from notification by the supplier of the mixture or trade name product that the substance contains an unspecified toxic chemical listed under Section 313.[115]

There are a variety of reporting alternatives for mixtures or trade name products based upon the amount of available information. For example, if both the specific chemical identity of the toxic chemical and its specific concentration in the mixture or the trade name product aren't known, reporting may be required if the applicable threshold is exceeded.[116]

Conversely, if the specific chemical identity but neither the specific concentration nor the upper bound concentration is known and information on the composition of the chemical has not otherwise been developed, then the quantity of that chemical in the mixture or trade name product need not be

---

[112] 40 C.F.R. § 372.25(e).

[113] § 313(g)(1)(C), 42 U.S.C. § 11023(g)(1)(C).

[114] It is very important to note that EPA expects more than a perfunctory comparison of the 313 list with the CAS numbers or names of substances at a facility. In many cases the chemical name in the 313 list may not correspond with the name on an MSDS at the facility. Publications listing chemical name synonyms are readily available and EPA would expect them to be used. Thus, just because a substance does not appear to be listed in the Section 313 regulations, does not mean reporting is not required. Synonym lists and CAS number lists should be consulted.

[115] 40 C.F.R. § 372.30(a)(2). *See also,* 53 Fed. Reg. 4508-4511.

[116] 40 C.F.R. § 372.30(b)(3)(i).

considered in threshold reporting quantity calculations[117] or, if the owner or operator has been told that a mixture or trade name product contains a toxic chemical, does not know the specific chemical identity, does know specific concentration, and does not know the upper bound concentration, the presence of that chemical in the mixture or trade name product need not be considered in making this threshold quantity determination.[118]

To facilitate reporting on trade name products containing toxic chemicals, EPA has imposed supplier notification requirements.[119] These requirements apply to facility owners or operators in SIC codes 20-39 who manufacture or process products containing toxic chemicals which they sell or distribute in mixtures or trade name products to facilities subject to Section 313 reporting.[120] This notice, to be attached to an MSDS, if one is required, must contain specific information, including:

(1)　A statement that the mixture or trade name product contains a toxic chemical subject to Section 313 reporting;

(2)　The name and CAS number for each such toxic chemical and;

(3)　The percent, by weight, of each toxic chemical in the mixture or trade name product.[121]

Notification is not required if the concentration of a toxic chemical in a mixture or trade name product does not exceed the applicable *de minimis* concentration, or if it is an article,[122] food, drug, cosmetic, alcoholic

---

[117] 40 C.F.R. § 372.30(b)(3)(iii).

[118] 40 C.F.R. § 372.30(b)(3)(vi). The regulations discuss other scenarios when reporting may be required based upon the type of information that is available.

[119] 40 C.F.R. § 372.45.

[120] 40 C.F.R. § 372.45(a).

[121] 40 C.F.R. § 372.45(b).

[122] "Article" means: "a manufactured item (1) which is formed to a specific shape or design during manufacture; (2) which has end use functions dependent in whole or in part upon its shape or design during end use; and (3)
(continued...)

beverage, tobacco, or tobacco product packaged for distribution for general public, or a consumer product as defined by the Consumer Product Safety Act.[123]

The contents of supplier notifications are variable. For example, if the supplier claims the specific chemical identity of a toxic chemical in a mixture or trade name product to be a trade secret (as defined by the OSHA Hazard Communication rules (29 C.F.R. § 1910.1200)), the notice must contain a generic chemical name.[124] Similarly, if the supplier considers the specific percent-by-weight composition to be a trade secret under state law or under Section 757, comment b, of the Restatement of Torts, the notice must provide an upper bound concentration value.[125] These requirements do not apply to an owner or operator who does not know if his facility is selling or otherwise distributing a toxic chemical in a mixture or trade name products, although if he receives a supplier notification from an upstream supplier, however, he is deemed to have such knowledge.[126]

### 3.4.3. Data To Be Reported

Reports are made on EPA Form R, the Toxic Chemical Release Inventory Reporting Form,[127] which renders the following types of information for each toxic chemical subject to reporting:[128]

(1) The name, location, and principal business activities of the facility. EPA has expanded this basic statutory requirement to include the latitude and longitude of the reporting facility, the facility's Dunn & Bradstreet number, and, if applicable, the facility's parent company's Dunn &

---

[122](..continued)
which does not release a toxic chemical under normal conditions of processing or use of that item at the facility or establishments." 40 C.F.R. § 372.3. *See* 53 Fed. Reg. 4507.

[123] 40 C.F.R. § 372.45(d).

[124] 40 C.F.R. § 372.45(e).

[125] 40 C.F.R. § 372.45(f).

[126] 40 C.F.R. § 372.45(g).

[127] 53 Fed. Reg. 4500 (Feb. 16, 1988).

[128] § 313(g)(1), 42 U.S.C. § 11023(g)(1), 40 C.F.R. § 372.85. *See also*, 53 Fed. Reg. 4511-4518.

Bradstreet number, the names of technical and public contact persons, RCRA identification number, NPDES permit number, and underground injection well code. The Agency also wants reported the names of each stream or surface water body receiving toxic chemical discharges from the facility and an identification of any off-site treatment, storage, or disposal facilities and POTW to which wastes containing toxic chemicals from the facility were sent.

(2) The submission must be certified as accurate by "a senior official with management responsibility for the person or persons completing the report, regarding the accuracy and completeness of the report.[129] EPA has construed this requirement broadly, and has defined the term "senior management official" to mean:

an official with management responsibility for the person or persons completing a report, or the manager of environmental programs for the facility or establishments, or for the corporation owning or operating the facility or establishments responsible for certifying similar reports under other environmental regulatory requirements.[130]

(3) For each listed toxic chemical known to be present at the facility in excess of the applicable threshold, the report is to state the chemical name, and if applicable, CAS number of the substance and to provide the following information:[131]

(a) Whether the toxic chemical is manufactured, processed, or otherwise used at the facility and the general category of such use;

(b) An estimate, in ranges, of the maximum amount of a toxic chemical present at the facility at any time during the preceding calendar year;

---

[129] § 313(g)(1)(B), 42, U.S.C. § 11023(g)(1)(B).

[130] 40 C.F.R. § 372.3

[131] Note that the specific chemical identity can be claimed to be a trade secret in accordance with Section 322 of EPCRA. If an owner or operator wishes to make such a claim, he must supply a generic chemical name in the report, and submit a substantiation of the claim to EPA along with the report. He must also submit a non-confidential copy of the report to EPA and to the state official designated to receive the report. EPA has published a form for the submission of substantiations accompanying trade secrecy claims. *See*, 40 C.F.R. Part 350, 53 Fed. Reg. 28772 (July 29, 1988).

(c) Identification of the waste treatment or disposal method used by the facility for each waste stream containing any listed toxic chemical, a ranged estimate of the concentration of the toxic chemical in the influent to the waste treatment system,[132] and "an estimate of the treatment efficiency typically achieved by such methods for that waste stream."[133] Waste streams treated in the same manner are aggregated. For example, all the wastes going to a secondary waste water treatment system on site would be combined in the report rather than each individual waste stream being reported separately. If some waste streams containing the toxic chemical are treated separately, however, then they must be reported individually. The term "treatment efficiency" refers to the mass percent by which the subject toxic chemical is removed from the waste stream, not to overall system efficiency. Removal in this context includes destruction, chemical conversion, physical removal, or some combination thereof and;

(d) The quantity of each toxic chemical entering each environmental medium annually. This requirement includes the offsite shipment of waste, including discharges to POTWs and applies to total annual releases to environmental media, including both routine and accidental releases.[134]

Reports may be based on "reasonably available data", including monitoring and emission measurements collected pursuant to other environmental statutes, but if no such data exist, reasonable estimates may be used.[135] These estimates may be rounded to no more than two significant digits, and the basis from which they are derived, *e.g.* monitoring data, mass balance data, emission factors, or best engineering judgment must be indicated. Data on releases to

---

[132] *See,* 53 Fed. Reg. 4516-4519.

[133] § 313(g)(1)(C)(iii), 42 U.S.C. § 11023(g)(1)(C)(iii).

[134] *See,* 53 Fed. Reg. 4513.

[135] "In order to provide the information required under this section, the owner or operator of a facility may use readily available data (including monitoring data) collected pursuant to other provisions of law, or, where such data are not readily available, reasonable estimates of the amounts involved. Nothing in this section requires the monitoring or measurement of the quantities, concentration, or frequency of any toxic chemical released into the environment beyond that monitoring and measurement required under other provisions of law or regulation." § 313(g)(2), 42 U.S.C. § 11023(g)(2).

the individual environmental media must be disaggregated: for example, air emissions must be reported separately as fugitive or point source and releases to water separated by receiving stream (waste water sent to a POTW is identified as a off-site transfer).[136]

### 3. 4. 4. Exemptions from Reporting

Finally, there are several exemptions from the Section 313 reporting requirement. Two of these, the *de minimis* concentration and articles exemptions have been identified previously. Another applies to certain uses of toxic chemicals including:

-- those used as structural components of a facility;

-- products used for routine janitorial or facility maintenance (*e.g.* fertilizers and pesticides);

-- toxic chemicals used for personal purposes by employees or other persons at the facility as foods, drugs, cosmetics, or other personal items (including products within the facilities in a cafeteria, store, or infirmary);

-- products containing toxic chemicals used for maintaining motor vehicles; and

-- toxic chemicals contained in process water and noncontact cooling water or in air used as compressed air or as part of combustion.[137] Similarly, toxic chemicals that are manufactured, processed, or used in a laboratory under the supervision of a technically qualified individual need not be considered in determining whether a threshold quantity of the toxic chemical is present at the facility. This exemption, however, does not apply to specialty chemical production, pilot plant operations, or activities conducted outside the laboratory.[138]

Note that a person who owns a facility otherwise subject to Section 313 reporting, need not report if his only interest in the facility is ownership of the real estate upon which the facility is operated. This applies to owners of

---

[136] *See*, 53 Fed. Reg. 4513-4516.

[137] 40 C.F.R. § 372.38(c) (1)-(5).

[138] 40 C.F.R. §§ 372.38(d)(1)-(3).

such facilities as industrial parks.[139]  Also, if two or more persons, without any common corporate or business interests, operate separate establishments within a single facility, each such person must report separately to the extent that person is covered by the requirements of Section 313.[140]

### 3. 4. 5.  Changes to Reporting Requirements

EPCRA authorizes EPA, *sua sponte*, or upon petition, to initiate a rulemaking to add or delete substances from the list of toxic chemicals.[141]  A chemical may be added to the list if sufficient evidence supports a finding that: (1) the toxic chemical causes or may reasonably be anticipated to cause significant adverse acute human health effects; (2) it causes or can reasonably be anticipated to cause various chronic human health effects; or (3) because of its toxicity, environmental persistence, or tendency to bioaccumulate, the toxic chemical causes or can reasonably be anticipated to cause significant adverse environmental effects.[142]  A chemical may be deleted if EPA determines that

---

[139] 40 C.F.R. § 372.38 (e).

[140] 40 C.F.R. §§ 372.38(e) and (f).

[141] §§ 313(d) and (e), 42 U.S.C. §§ 11023(d) and (e).

[142] § 313(d)(2), 42 U.S.C. § 11023(d)(2).  Acute health effects are those reasonably likely to exist beyond a facility boundary as a result of continuous or frequently recurring releases.  *Id.*  In determining whether to list a particular chemical because of its propensity to cause acute human health effects, EPA is directed to consider a variety of factors, *e.g.* volume and pattern of use or release and individuals who are sensitive to that chemical.  H.R. Conf. Rep. No. 962, 99th Cong., 2nd Sess. 284 (1988).  The term "continuing or frequently recurring releases" is used to distinguish releases that are a normal part of a facility's operations from "episodic and accidental" releases that are subject to emergency reporting under Section 304.  *Id.*
The statute identifies the following chronic health effects: (1) Cancer or teratogenic, or (2) serious or irreversible -- (a) reproductive dysfunctions, (b) neurological disorders, (c) effects of heritable genetic mutations, or (d) other chronic health defects.  § 313(d)(2)(b), 42 U.S.C. § 11023(d)(2)(b). Note that although the statute speaks of such health effects in humans, EPA is not restricted in deciding whether to list a substance because of its potential to cause such effects to chemicals for which human data exists. H.R. Conf. Rep. No. 962, 99th Cong., 2nd Sess. 294 (1986).
Chemicals listed because of adverse environmental effects may not exceed twenty-five percent of the total number of toxic chemicals listed.  § 313(d)(2)(C)(iii), 42 U.S.C. § 11023(d)(2)(C)(iii).

there is insufficient evidence to establish the preceding criteria.[143]

Listing/delisting actions are fairly common. The Federal Register must be consulted to determine what modifications to the list of toxic chemicals have been made (or proposed) between the annual issues of the Code of Federal Regulations. (Specifically, rulemakings affecting 40 C.F.R. § 372.65 must be reviewed.) For example, since the 1989 edition of this text was printed, three chemicals, sodium hydroxide, non-fibrous aluminum oxide, and terephthalic acid have been removed from the Section 313 list and seventeen others, including seven ozone-depleting chemicals, have been added to the list.[144]

EPA is also authorized to modify the reporting thresholds,[145] and it may change the frequency of reporting, although it may not require that such reports be submitted more frequently than once per year.[146] Modifications to the frequency of reporting must be made by rulemaking, and substantial evidence[147] must support the finding that such a modification is consistent with the function of Section 313.[148]

The statute required EPA to develop and maintain in a computerized data base a national toxic chemical inventory based upon data submitted in Section

---

[143] § 313(d)(3), 42 U.S.C. § 11023(d)(3).

[144] 2, 3-dichloropropene, m-dinitrobenzene, p-dinitrobenzene, allyl alcohol, diethylamine, isosafrole, o-dinitrobenzene, creosote, dinitrotoluene (mixed isoners), toluenediisocyanate (mixed isomers), trichlorofluoromethane (CFC-11), dichlorodifluoromethane (CFC-12), dichlorotetrafluoroethane (CFC-114), monochloropentafluoroethane (CFC-115), bromochlorodifluoromethane (Halon 1211), bromotrifluoromethane (Halon 1301), and dibromotetrafluoroethane (Halon 2402).

[145] So long as the resulting reports cover a substantial majority of the aggregate releases of a chemical at a facility. § 313(f)(2), 42 U.S.C. § 11023(f)(2).

[146] § 313(i)(1), 42 U.S.C. § 313(i)(1).

[147] §§ 313(i)(2)(B) and (i)(6), 42 U.S.C. §§ 11023(i)(2)(B) and (i)(6).

[148] *i.e.*, "to inform persons about releases of toxic chemicals to the environment; to assist governmental agencies, researchers, and other persons in the conduct of research and data gathering; to aid in the development of appropriate regulations, guidelines, and standards; and for other similar purposes." § 313(h), 42 U.S.C. § 11023(h); H.R. Conf. Rep. No. 962, 99th Cong., 2nd Sess. 299-300 (1986).

313 reports.[149] These data are to be made available, at cost, to any person via computer telecommunications.[150] This information is maintained in the Toxic Release Inventory (TRI) database and is accessible through the National Library of Medicine's TOXNET (Toxicology Network) database.

## 4.0  SUBTITLE C -- GENERAL PROVISIONS

### 4.1  Overview

Subtitle C of EPCRA contains a number of provisions of general applicability. This section discusses four of these:  1) the procedures through which a facility owner or operator may protect the specific chemical identity of a substance for which a report is filed;  2)  information to be provided to health professionals for the diagnosis or treatment of exposed persons or for conducting sampling or epidemiological studies of exposed individuals;  3) enforcement of EPCRA's requirements by federal authorities; and  4) enforcement actions that can be brought by citizens, states, and emergency planning and response entities.

### 4.2  Trade Secrets

With the exception of Tier II information concerning the location of hazardous chemicals at a facility,[151] the only information reported under EPCRA Sections 303(d)(2) and (3), 311, 312, or 313,[152] that may be claimed as a trade secret is the specific chemical identity of the substance for which the report is filed.[153] To withhold such information, a person must make various factual

---

[149] § 313(j), 42 U.S.C. § 11023(j).

[150] *Id.*

[151] *See* text following Note 84, *supra.*

[152] Recall that the chemical identity of an extremely hazardous substance for which a release is reported under Section 304 may not be claimed to be confidential.

[153] § 322(a)(1)(A), 42 U.S.C. § 11042(a)(1)(A). The term "specific chemical identity" is defined by the EPA regulation, 53 Fed. Reg. 28772 (July 29, 1988), as: "the chemical name, Chemical Abstracts Service (CAS) Registry Number, or any other information that reveals the precise chemical designation of the substance. Where the trade name is reported in lieu of the specific chemical identity, the trade name will be treated as the specific chemical identity for

(continued...)

assertions at the time of the required reporting, which, if true, would warrant trade secret protection. These assertions must be submitted to EPA along with the information asserted to be the trade secret and a copy of the EPCRA submission being made.[154]   Each of the following items must be demonstrated in a trade secrecy substantiation:

(1) That the submitter has not disclosed the information to any other person, other than a member of an LEPC, an officer or employee of the United States or state or local government, an employee of the submitter, or another person bound by a confidentiality agreement, and that the submitter has taken reasonable measures to protect the confidentiality of such information and intends to continue to take such measures;[155]

(2) That disclosure of the information is not required  by any other federal or state law;[156]

(3) That disclosure of the information is likely to cause substantial harm to the submitter's competitive position[157]

(4) That the chemical identity is not readily discoverable through reverse engineering.[158]

---

[153](..continued)
purposes of this part. 40 C.F.R. § 350.1. *See also*, H.R. Conf. Rep. No. 962, 99th Cong., 2nd Sess. 303 (1986).

[154] § 322(a)(2), 42 U.S.C. § 11042(a)(2), 40 C.F.R. § 350.5.

[155] § 322(b)(1), 42 U.S.C. § 11042(b)(1), 40 C.F.R. §§ 350.7 and 350.27.

[156] § 322(b)(2), 42 U.S.C. § 11042(b)(2), 40 C.F.R. §§ 350.7 and 350.27.

[157] § 322(b)(3), 42 U.S.C. § 11042(b)(3), 40 C.F.R. §§ 350.7 and 350.27.

[158] § 322(b)(4), 42 U.S.C. § 11022(b)(4), 40 C.F.R. §§ 350.7 and 350.27. The meaning of the term "reverse engineering" is to be derived from *United States Steel Workers of America v. Auchter*, 763 F. 2d 728, 739-42 (3d Cir. 1985).   Further explication of these requirements is found in the EPA trade secrecy form which poses a number of questions for the trade secrecy claimant to answer. 40 C.F.R. § 350.27, 53 *Fed. Reg.* 2880 ff. (July 29, 1988).

Once a trade secrecy claim has been properly asserted, the information for which the claim is made will be treated as confidential unless and until a contrary determination is made.[159]   Impetus for such a determination can arise in two ways;  EPA, on its own initiative, may undertake a determination whether the chemical identity is subject to trade secrecy protection,[160]  or, any person may petition EPA for the release of a specific chemical identity.[161]

Generally, when EPA undertakes to determine the validity of a trade secrecy claim, the Agency has thirty days in which to decide whether the submitter presented sufficient support for its trade secrecy claim in its initial substantiation submission.[162]   If the claim is found sufficiently substantiated, EPA will notify the claimant of that finding.   The claimant has thirty days from receipt of that notice to submit supplemental information supporting the truth of the facts averred in its initial substantiation.[163]   If, after reviewing this supplemental material, EPA finds that the information submitted in support of the trade secrecy claim is true,  the person requesting disclosure of the chemical identity will be notified that this information is a trade secret. Within thirty days that person may file suit in U.S. District Court to challenge EPA's decision not to release the data.[164]

If upon review of the initial assertions, however, EPA finds them insufficient to support a trade secrecy claim, the Agency will provide notice to the claimant of its intention to release the information.   The claimant then has thirty days in which to appeal that decision to the Agency's Office of General Counsel or, upon a showing of good cause, to submit additional material in

---

[159] 40 C.F.R. § 350.9(a).

[160] 40 C.F.R. § 350.9(b).

[161] § 322(d), 42 U.S.C. § 11042(d), 40 C.F.R. § 350.15.

[162] § 322(d)(2), 42 U.S.C. § 11042(d)(2), 40 C.F.R. § 350.11.

[163] § 322(d)(3)(A), 42 U.S.C. § 11042(d)(3)(A), 40 C.F.R. § 350.11(a)(1). The sufficiency of an initial trade secrecy assertion will be determined by the degree to which those assertions support the trade secrecy factors, *i.e.*, nondisclosure and competitive injury as a result of disclosure, contained in the statute. §§322(b)(1)-(4), 42 U.S.C. §§ 11042(b)(1)-(4).   EPA has fleshed out these requirements at 40 C.F.R. § 350.13.

[164] § 322(d)(3)(B), 42 U.S.C. § 11042(d)(3)(B), 40 C.F.R. § 350.13(b)(1). EPA will rule on such petitions within nine months of their receipt.  40 C.F.R. § 350.15(e).

support of its trade secrecy claim.[165]

If the good cause standard is met, EPA will determine whether the submitter's claim meets the standards for sufficiency of substantiation.[166] If EPA finds the claim to be sufficient, it will determine whether or not the chemical identity is a trade secret.[167]

Under any circumstances, if EPA decides the information submitted in support of the trade secrecy claim is not true, and that the chemical identity is not a trade secret, the Agency will advise the claimant of this determination, and the claimant is provided with thirty days in which to appeal that determination to the EPA Office of General Counsel.[168] An adverse determination by that office is appealable by the claimant to U.S. District Court within thirty days of notification of the adverse determination.[169]

Nothing in Section 322 authorizes a person to withhold the information that EPCRA Section 323 requires to be submitted to a health professional.[170] Similarly, when the chemical identity of a hazardous chemical or extremely hazardous substance is claimed to be a trade secret, a state governor or SERC must make any adverse health effects associated with such substance publicly available.[171] In the case of a toxic chemical, the identity of which is claimed to be a trade secret, EPA must identify adverse health effects associated with chemical in the computerized data base mandated by Section 313(j) of the statute.[172]

Finally, by written request the governor of any state may ask EPA for access to any trade secrecy claims, substantiations, supplemental substantiations, and additional information submitted to the Agency. EPA must release

---

[165] § 322(d)(3)(C), 42 U.S.C. § 11042(d)(3)(C), 40 C.F.R. § 350.11(a)(2). EPA's limited definition of what constitutes "good cause" is found in 40 C.F.R. §§ 350.11(a) (2) (iii) (A)-(C).

[166] 40 C.F.R. § 350.11(a)(2)(iv).

[167] 40 C.F.R. § 350.11(a)(2)(iv)(A).

[168] 40 C.F.R. § 350.11(b)(2).

[169] 40 C.F.R. § 350.11(b)(2).

[170] § 322(e), 42 U.S.C. § 11042(e).

[171] § 322(h)(1), 42 U.S.C. § 11042(h)(1), 40 C.F.R. § 350.21. The SERC may do this by providing copies of the MSDSs available to it.

[172] §322(h)(2), 42 U.S.C. § 11042(h)(2).

this information if the state provides a level of protection for the data equivalent to that employed by EPA and makes the information available only to state employees.[173]   Note also, that a person making a trade secrecy claim may assert a confidential business information claim for the material submitted in the substantiation.  The material so claimed must be clearly delineated, and the submitter must certify that those portions of the substantiation claimed as confidential would, if disclosed, reveal the chemical identity being claimed as a trade secret or would reveal other confidential business or trade secret information.[174]

### 4.3    Section 323 -- Provision of Information to Health Professionals, Doctors, and Nurses

Notwithstanding the preceding trade secrecy provisions, under certain circumstances owners or operators of facilities subject to Sections 311, 312 and 313 must provide the chemical identities of extremely hazardous substances, hazardous chemicals, or toxic chemicals, if known.

The first such circumstance is for purposes of diagnosis or treatment by health professionals in non-emergency situations.[175]   A facility owner or operator must provide the specific chemical identity of an extremely hazardous substance, hazardous chemical, or toxic chemical, if known to him, upon receipt of a written request from a health professional that states the following:  that the health professional has a reasonable basis to suspect that the chemical identity is needed for purposes of diagnosis or treatment of an individual; that the individual or individuals being diagnosed or treated have been exposed to the chemical concerned; and that the chemical identity will assist in diagnosis or treatment.[176]   Such a request must contain a confidentiality agreement that includes a description of the procedures that will be used to maintain confidentiality and a statement that the health professional will not use the information for any purpose other than those asserted in the statement of need.  It must also contain a certification signed by the health professional stating that the statement of need is true.[177]

---

[173] § 322(g), 42 U.S.C. § 11042(g), 40 C.F.R. § 350.19.

[174] § 322(f), 42 U.S.C. § 11042(f), 40 C.F.R. § 350.7(d).

[175] § 323(a), 42 U.S.C. § 11043(a), 40 C.F.R. § 350.40(c).

[176] §§ 323(a)(1)-(3), 42 U.S.C. §§ 11043(a)(1)-(3), 40 C.F.R. § 350.40(c)(1).

[177] *Id.* and § 323(d), 42 U.S.C. § 11043(d).

Second, in the event of a medical emergency[178] the owner or operator of a facility subject to the requirements of EPCRA Sections 311, 312 and 313, must provide a copy of a material safety data sheet, an inventory form, or a toxic chemical release form, including the specific chemical identity, if known, of a hazardous chemical, extremely hazardous substance, or toxic chemical to any treating physician or nurse who requests such information, provided that:

(1) A medical emergency exists;

(2) The specific chemical identity is necessary for or will assist in emergency or first aid diagnosis or treatment; and

(3) The individual or individuals being diagnosed or treated have been exposed to the chemical concerned.[179]

This information must be supplied immediately upon request, with no written confidentiality agreement or statement of need as a precondition to such disclosure. The owner or operator may, however, require a written statement of need and confidentiality agreement as soon as circumstances permit.[180]

Third, an owner or operator subject to EPCRA Sections 311, 312, or 313 must provide the specific chemical identity, if known, of a hazardous chemical, extremely hazardous substance, or toxic chemical to any health professional who is a local government employee or who is under contract to the local government if such person submits a written request asserting one or more of the following health needs for the information:

(1) To assess exposure of persons living in a local community to the hazards of the chemical concerned;

(2) To conduct or assess sampling to determine exposure levels of various population groups;

---

[178] The term "medical emergency" is defined to mean: "any unforseen condition which a health professional would judge to require urgent and unscheduled medical attention. Such a condition is one which results in sudden and/or serious symptom(s) constituting a threat to a person's physical or psychological well-being and which requires immediate medical attention to prevent possible deterioration, disability, or death." 40 C.F.R. § 350.40(a).

[179] § 323(b), 42 U.S.C § 11043(b), 40 C.F.R. § 350.40(e).

[180] *Id.*

(3) To conduct periodic medical surveillance of exposed population groups;

(4) To provide medical treatment to exposed individuals or population groups;

(5) To conduct studies to determine the health effects of exposure;

(6) To conduct studies to aid in the identification of a chemical that may reasonable be anticipated to cause an observed health effect.[181]

The confidentiality agreement may restrict the use of the information to the stated health purposes, provide for legal remedies in the event of breach, and may not include requirements for the posting of a penalty bond.[182]

## 4.4    Section 325 - Enforcement

### 4. 4. 1. Statutory Provisions

Section 325 of EPCRA list the civil and administrative penalties EPA may use to prosecute the violations of the Act. With regard to emergency planning (Sections 302 and 303), for example, EPA may order a facility to comply with the requirements of Sections 302(c) and (d) concerning notification of state and local officials that the facility is subject to Subtitle A because it contains any of the listed extremely hazardous substances in excess of the established threshold planning quantities.[183]    Such an order is enforceable in the U.S. District Court for the district in which the facility is located, and the court may assess a penalty of up to $25,000 for each day of noncompliance.[184]

The Act establishes two classes of administrative penalties, as well as criminal penalties that may be sought against an owner or operator who fails to comply with the release reporting provisions of Section 304.[185]

EPA may assess Class I administrative penalties for violations of Section

---

[181] §§ 323(c)(2)(A)-(F), 42 U.S.C. §§ 11043(c)(2)(A)-(F), 40 C.F.R. § 350.40(d).

[182] § 323(d), 42 U.S.C. § 11043(d), 40 C.F.R. § 350.40(f).

[183] § 325(a), 42 U.S.C. § 11045(a).

[184] *Id.*

[185] § 325(b), 42 U.S.C. § 11045(b).

304 of up to $25,000 per violation following notice and opportunity for hearing.[186]

Alternatively, the Agency may bring an action in the federal district court for the district in which the facility is located to seek a penalty of up to $25,000 for each day of such violation. Second and subsequent violations may be penalized by up to $75,000 for each day of violation.[187] EPA is instructed to consider various factors in determining how large Class I penalty to assess. These include considerations of the nature and circumstances of the violation, the violator's culpability, ability to pay, history of prior violations, and economic benefit derived by the violations.[188]

EPA may also assess a Class II administrative penalty of up to $25,000 per day for violations of the reporting requirements of Section 304.[189] For second or subsequent violations, the Agency may assess a penalty of up to $75,000 per day of violation.[190] The Agency is given subpoena power in proceedings to assess Class II penalties and may thereby compel testimony and document production.[191] Class II penalty actions are to be conducted in the same manner EPA currently uses to levy penalties under Section 16 of the Toxic Substances Control Act.[192] As with Class I penalties, in lieu of an administrative proceeding, EPA may file suit in federal district court.[193]

The knowing and willful violation of the release reporting provisions of Section 304 is punishable by criminal penalties, including a fine as high as $25,000, up to two years imprisonment, or both.[194] For second and subsequent violations, the sanctions are increased to a fine of up to $50,000, as

---

[186] § 325(b)(1)(B), 42 U.S.C. § 11045(b)(1)(B).

[187] § 325(b)(3), 42 U.S.C. § 11045(b)(3).

[188] § 325(b)(1)(C), 42 U.S.C. § 11045 (b)(1)(C).

[189] § 325(b)(2), 42 U.S.C. § 11045(b)(2).

[190] *Id.*

[191] *Id.* EPA is also authorized to promulgate procedural rules governing such discovery.

[192] *Id. See* 15 U.S.C. § 2615; 40 C.F.R. § 22.01, *et seq.*

[193] § 325(b)(3), 42 U.S.C. § 11045(b)(3).

[194] Section 325(b)(4), 42 U.S.C. § 11045(b)(4).

many as five years incarceration, or both.[195]

Failure by a person other than a governmental entity to satisfy any of the requirements concerning Tier I and Tier II information under Section 312 or Toxic Chemical Release inventory reporting under Section 313, is subject to a penalty of up to $25,000 per day of violation.[196] Similarly, any person other than a governmental entity who violates any provisions of Section 311 (regarding MSDS's) or Section 323(b) (providing information in response to medical emergency), or who fails to submit information concerning specific chemical identity in a trade secrecy claim to EPA is liable for a $10,000 fine for each day such violation continues.[197] EPA may assess penalties under this subsection administratively or may bring an action in federal district court.[198]

With regard to trade secrecy claims, EPA either may assess a penalty of $25,000 or file suit in federal district court if it determines (1) that information submitted under Section 322 fails to support a trade secrecy claim regarding a specific chemical identity and (2) that the trade secret claim was frivolous.[199] Also, any person who knowingly and willfully discloses any trade secret information protected by Section 322 is subject to a fine of up to $20,000, one year's imprisonment, or both.[200]

Any health professional who has requested information from an owner or operator pursuant to Section 323 may bring an action in federal district court to compel a recalcitrant owner or operator to provide such information.[201]

A person against whom EPA has assessed an administrative penalty may file an appeal with the federal district court within thirty days after the date of EPA's order.[202] If such person fails to pay the penalty assessed against

---

[195] *Id.*

[196] §§ 325(c)(1) and (3), 42 U.S.C. §§ 11045(c)(1) and (3).

[197] §§ 325(c)(2) and (3), 42 U.S.C. §§ 11045(c)(2) and (3).

[198] § 325(c)(4), 42 U.S.C. § 11045(c)(4).

[199] § 325(d)(1), 42 U.S.C. § 11045(d)(1).

[200] § 325(d)(2), 42 U.S.C. § 11045(d)(2).

[201] § 325(e), 42 U.S.C. § 11045(e).

[202] § 325(f)(1), 42 U.S.C. § 11045(f)(1). At the same time the person appealing the order must send a copy of the notice of appeal to EPA by certified mail. EPA will thereupon file a certified copy of the record with the court. *Id.*

him, EPA may refer the matter to the Department of Justice for collection.[203]

The Agency may issue subpoenas to compel testimony and document production. Failure to comply with such subpoenas is punishable as contempt by the federal district court for the district in which the person disobeying the subpoena resides, is found, or transacts business.[204]

### 4.4.2. EPA Enforcement Policy

#### 4.4.2.A. Enforcement Policy for Section 313 of EPCRA

As it has with other statutes it enforces, e.g. the Clean Water Act and the Resource Conservation and Recovery Act, EPA has issued an internal policy document that sets out the range of options EPA may take in responding to a violation of Section 313 of EPCRA and providing a matrix for determining amounts to be sought in penalties.[205] The stated purpose of the Response Policy is: "to assure that enforcement actions for violations of section 313 and of the section 313 regulations are arrived at in a fair, uniform and consistent manner; that the enforcement response is appropriate for the violation committed: and that persons will be deterred from committing section 313 violations."[206]

To achieve these ends, the Response Policy establishes the following four enforcement alternatives, termed "levels of action:"

1. Taking no action;

2. Issuing a Notice of Noncompliance (NON);

3. Seeking administrative civil penalties; and

4. Seeking criminal sanctions under 18 U.S.C. 1001.

These four potential responses are discussed seriatim below.

---

[203] *Id.*

[204] § 325(f)(2), 42 U.S.C. § 11045(f)(2).

[205] Enforcement Response Policy for Section 313 of the Emergency Planning and Community Right-to-Know Act Also Known as Title III of the Superfund Amendments and Reauthorization Act (SARA), Office of Compliance Monitoring, Office of Pesticides and Toxic Substances, U.S. Environmental Protection Agency (Dec. 2, 1988).

[206] *Id.* at 1.

The no action alternative has a limited application. Historically, the Response Policy provided that in 1988, the first year that Form Rs were due, no action was to be taken within a thirty-day grace period (between July 1 and August 1) after the first Form Rs were due. The present application of the no action option is when a facility "is amending its submission(s) after the reporting period to reflect improved information/ procedures which were not previously available."[207]

Note that this does not suggest EPA will not seek a penalty when an owner/operator is seeking to amend a submission to add data on previously unreported toxic chemicals. EPA views this as late reporting or non-reporting. Instead, EPA will not act against an owner/operator who has upgraded his section 313 compliance program in a manner that permits the submission of more accurate data. An example of such a circumstance would be when mass balance or monitoring data are used to substitute for estimates based upon best engineering judgement.

EPA considers issuance of a Notice of Noncompliance (NON) the appropriate response when minor errors have been detected (either by EPA or by the submitter) in a timely-filed Form R. If EPA detects the error, the NON will provide thirty days for its correction. If a company realizes that it made an error in its Form R, or EPA discovers the error during an inspection, and this error is corrected within thirty days of discovery and within 180 days of the reporting date, a NON is also deemed appropriate. The policy objective of this approach is to encourage reporting facilities to audit themselves, to advise EPA of errors, and voluntarily to correct them.

The Response Policy lists a number of other circumstances in which a NON is the appropriate sanction. These include failure to submit a Form R containing trade secrets without an accompanying "sanitized" version of the report with the trade secret material deleted, failure to submit a Form R to a state, various recordkeeping violations, sending the Form R to the wrong address and late filing. The last of these provides that as of July 1, 1990, companies that submit Form Rs one to thirty days late may receive a NON, provided that the report is submitted prior to any contact by EPA and if the facility has not received a NON for late reporting during the previous five reporting periods.

Administrative civil penalties are appropriate for the following infractions:

1. Non-reporting, including failure to report for each chemical and reports submitted by a facility after being contacted about a pending inspection, after an inspection, or for purposes of determining compliance;

---

[207] *Id.* at 2.

2. Incomplete reporting;

3. Failure to respond to or comply with a NON;

4. Late reporting (for periods specified in the penalty matrix) and repeated late reporting;

5. Repeated violations that would otherwise warrant a NON; and

6. Other violations not specifically enumerated in the discussion of NONs.

While EPCRA does not itself provide criminal sanctions for violation of Section 313, it is a crime to make false or fraudulent statements to the federal government under 18 U.S.C. § 1001. Also, knowing failure to file a section 313 report may be actionable under that statute as concealment. Though EPA is unlikely to seek criminal sanctions in any but the worst case, the threat of such severe sanctions should never be forgotten.

EPA has devised a matrix that is used for determining the base penalty for each individual Section 313 violation. See Appendix A for specific details. The total penalty is determined by adding the penalty for each chemical at each facility. That is, a company's failure to report on the same two toxic chemicals at two facilities yields four violations, the penalties for which would be combined to determine a total penalty.

The penalty matrix uses a six-stage "circumstance level" on the x-axis and a three-stage "penalty adjustment level" on the y-axis. Application of this matrix to the violation at issue yields a "gravity-based penalty". Once the gravity-based penalty is determined, the Response Policy permits upward and downward adjustments to the penalty amount based upon various factors.

The circumstance level of the matrix considers the "seriousness of the violation as it relates to the accuracy and availability of the information to the community, to states, and to the government."[208]

The penalty adjustment level is based on the amount of the toxic chemical at issue in the violation that was manufactured, processed, or otherwise used by the facility and on the size of the total corporate entity in violation. Penalty Level A is a facility for which the total corporate entity (this refers to all sites taken together owned or controlled by the parent company) has sales of ten million dollars or more, or fifty employees or more and which manufactures, processes, or uses the subject toxic chemical at ten times or more the threshold level for reporting. Penalty Level B applies to a facility for which the total corporate entity has sales of ten million dollars or more or

---

[208] *Id.* at 7.

fifty or more employees and which manufactures, processes, or uses the subject toxic chemical at less than ten times the threshold for reporting. Penalty Level C applies to a facility for which the total corporate entity has sales of less than ten million dollars or fewer than fifty employees and which manufactures, processes, or uses the subject toxic chemical at less than ten times the threshold for reporting.

Once the gravity-based penalty is found, a number of factors such as whether the violation was voluntarily reported, culpability, and ability of the violator to pay and then evaluation for an upward or downward adjustment of the penalty.

### 4.4.2.B    Penalty Policy for EPCRA Sections 302, 303, 304, 311, and 312

On June 13, 1990, EPA issued its final penalty policy for enforcing EPCRA sections 302, 303, 311, 312 and Section 103 of CERCLA.[209]    Like the Section 313 Response Policy, the Enforcement Policy for EPCRA sections 302, et al., uses a matrix approach, although, because the statute specifies different penalties for Section 311 violations than for violations of EPCRA Sections 302, 303, 304, and 312 and CERCLA Section 103, two different matrices are employed (a $10,000 maximum for the former and a $25,000 maximum for the latter). Akin to the Section 313 matrix, these two matrices rank the "nature" and "extent" of the violation in ascending order on the x-axis and the "gravity" of the violation on the y-axis.    Once a base penalty is derived from the matrix using these considerations, consideration is given to the "circumstances" of the violation to select a penalty figure from the range of penalties in each cell in the matrices.    The factors on the two axes are equally weighted, and the penalties range from 100 percent of the statutory penalty to ten percent of the penalty.    Two penalty amounts are displayed in each cell of the matrices;    the lower amount is eighty percent of the upper range of the cell.

The "nature" of the violation refers to the type of violation or the requirement violated.    For EPCRA and CERCLA there are basically two types of violations -- violations of emergency response requirements and violations of emergency preparedness/right-to-know provisions.    The former refers to breaches of duties in responding to a release of a CERCLA hazardous sub-

---

[209] Final Penalty Policy for Sections 302, 303, 304, 311, and 312 of the Emergency Planning and Community Right-to-Know Act and Section 103 of the Comprehensive Environmental Response, Compensation, and Liability Act, U.S. EPA, Office of Solid Waste and Emergency Response, Office of Waste Programs Enforcement, and Office of Enforcement, OSWER Directive No, 9841.2 (June 13, 1990).    Copies of this document can be obtained from the EPA RCRA/Superfund hotline.

stance or an EPCRA extremely hazardous substance. Emergency preparedness/ right-to-know violations refer to failures to provide required information in accordance with statutory or regulatory deadlines. See Appendix B for the details of these elements and the two penalty matrices.

The "gravity" component, for purposes of emergency response violations, is based upon the amount of the substance involved in the violation. For emergency preparedness/right-to-know violations, the gravity component is based on the number and/or amount of the subject chemical(s) present at the facility in excess of the reporting threshold.

Considerations of "circumstances" apply to the potential consequences of the violation. The Penalty Policy identifies two criteria through which the potential for harm by a particular violation can be assessed. The first of these is the potential for exposure of emergency personnel, the community, and/or the environment to hazards resulting from the noncompliance. The second is the adverse effect of the noncompliance on the statutory or regulatory goals or procedures of the CERCLA 103 and EPCRA programs. As noted above, circumstance considerations are applied once the proper cell in a penalty matrix is selected. As with the Section 313 Enforcement Policy, the bare penalty can be adjusted up or down based upon a number of specified considerations. See Appendix B for the two penalty matrices and listing of the adjustment criteria.

## 4.8  Section 326 -- Civil Action

In addition to federal enforcement actions, EPCRA identifies other actions that may be brought by citizens and state and local governments.[210] In these cases, the courts are authorized to award the costs of litigation, including attorneys fees, to the prevailing or substantially prevailing party,[211] to enforce statutory requirements and impose civil penalties against facility owners or operators, and to order EPA to perform a required act of duty.[212]

At least sixty days before filing one of the listed actions against an owner or operator, the plaintiff must give notice to the Agency, the state in which the alleged violation occurred, and the alleged violator.[213] Likewise no action may

---

[210] § 326, 42 U.S.C. § 11046. Venue for such suits against facility owners or operators lies in the federal district court for the district for which the alleged violation occurred.  § 326(b) (1), 42 U.S.C. § 11046(b) (1). Venue for actions against EPA lies in the U.S. District Court for the District of Columbia. § 326(b) (2), 42 U.S.C. § 11046(b) (2).

[211] § 326(f), 42 U.S.C. § 11046(f).

[212] § 326(c), 42 U.S.C. § 11046(c).

[213] § 326(d)(1), 42 U.S.C. § 11046(d)(1).

be started against EPA, or a governor or SERC before sixty days after notice was given.[214]

Any person[215] may bring an action against a facility owner or operator for the following:[216]

1. Failure to submit a Section 304(c) emergency follow-up notice;

2. Failure to submit an MSDS or list under Section 311(a);

3. Failure to submit Tier I data on an inventory form under Section 312(a);[217]

4. Failure to submit a toxic chemical release form under Section 313(a).

Any person may file suit against EPA for failing to render a timely decision on a petition to add or delist a toxic chemical under Section 313(e) (1), or for release of the specific chemical identity of a chemical substance under Section 322(d).[218]

Any person may bring an action for failure to provide a mechanism guaranteeing public access to information submitted under the Act pursuant to Section 324(a) against a state governor, or a SERC.[219] A person may also bring an action against a governor or SERC. A person may also bring an action against a governor or SERC for failure to respond within 120 days to a request for Tier II information.[220]

---

[214] § 326(d)(2), 42 U.S.C. § 11046(d)(2).

[215] *See* Note 23, *supra*.

[216] § 326(a)(1)(A)(i)-(iv), 42 U.S.C. § 11046(a)(1)(A)(i)-(iv).

[217] § 326(a)(1)(A)(iii), 42 U.S.C. § 11046(a)(1)(A)(iii). An owner or operator is not amenable to suit under the section, if he has submitted Tier II data pursuant to § 312(d)(2).

[218] §§ 326(a)(1)(B)(i)-(vi), 42 U.S.C. §§ 11046(a)(1)(8)(i)-(vi). EPA has carried out the other provisions of the statute for which a citizens suit could have been brought against it to compel action.

[219] § 326(a)(1)(C), 42 U.S.C. § 11046(a)(1)(C).

[220] § 326(a)(1)(D), 42 U.S.C. § 11046(a)(1)(D).

A state or local government may bring suit against the owner or operator of a facility for the following:[221]

1. Failure to provide notification to an SERC pursuant to Section 302(c);

2. Failure to submit an MSDS or list under Section 311(a);

3. Failure to make information requested under Section 311(c) available;[222]

4. Failure to submit an inventory form containing Tier I data under Section 312(a).[223]

A SERC or LEPC may also sue an owner or operator for failure to provide information under Section 303(d) or for failing to submit Tier II information under Section 312(e) (1).[224]

A state may bring an action against EPA for failure to provide it with information supporting trade secrecy claims under Section 322(g).[225]

No suit, however, may be brought against an owner or operator if EPA has brought an administrative or civil action to enforce the requirement concerning which the would-be plaintiff intends to file suit.[226] The United States or a state may intervene as of right in any action under Section 326;[227] generally, a person who has a direct interest that is, or may be, adversely affected by

---

[221] §§ 326(a)(2)(A)(i)-(iv), 42 U.S.C. §§ 326(a)(2)(A)(i)-(iv).

[222] § 326(a)(2)(A)(iii), 42 U.S.C. § 11046(a)(2)(A)(iii). Section 311(c) requires an owner or operator who submitted a list of hazardous chemicals for which he maintains an MSDS to provide a copy of the MSDS for a listed hazardous chemical upon request.

[223] § 326(a)(2)(A)(iv), 42 U.S.C. § 11046(a)(2)(A)(iv). The same exemption for owners or operators who have submitted Tier II data applies in this case as in suits brought by an individual.

[224] § 326(a)(2)(B), 42 U.S.C. § 11046(a)(2)(B).

[225] §326(a)(2)(C), 42 U.S.C. § 11046(a)(2)(C).

[226] § 326(e), 42 U.S.C. § 11046(e).

[227] § 326(h)(1), 42 U.S.C. § 11046(h)(1).

the action and may be unable adequately to protect that interest may intervene as of right.[228]

In at least one case, a citizens group has successfully used the citizens suit provision to obtain monetary penalties against an alleged violator.[229] The pace of such litigation is expected to quicken in the near future.

## 5.0  COMPLIANCE ISSUES

EPCRA presents continuing challenges to facilities subject to its reporting and planning provisions.  For example, facilities subject to Subtitle A should participate actively in the planning process both as a matter of public relations and to provide the much-needed technical expertise that facility representatives can provide.  In addition, clearly written and rigorously implemented compliance plans and information management programs will be needed to keep abreast of the responsibilities imposed by the statute and to avoid or mitigate penalties associated with noncompliance.

Section 313 presents the greatest challenges to covered facilities.  For example, owners or operators must decide from a range of options what kind of data to report, *e.g.*, to estimate conservatively (which will tend to inflate values) or to monitor (which can be very expensive).  The reports filed under Section 313 can also be used to verify a facility's compliance with other release reporting requirements and with the limits established by its various permits.[230]

---

[228] § 326(h)(2), 42 U.S.C. § 11046(h)(2).  Such intervention may not be permitted if the state or EPA demonstrates that existing parties to the action will adequately protect the intervenor's interests. *Id.*

[229] *Atlantic States Legal Foundation v. ARO Corp.*, No. CIV-90-1133 (W.D.N.Y. 1990).  This case was settled by payment of penalties to EPA and the state as well as environmentally beneficial expenditures. *See* 14 *Chem. Reg. Rep. (BNA)* 1371 (Dec. 14, 1990).

[230] For example, assuming that no reporting exceptions (such as for continuous releases) apply, a facility which uses large quantities of ammonia (which is both an extremely hazardous chemical under Section 304 and a toxic chemical under Section 313) may lose tons of that chemical annually through routine fugitive emissions.  Significant problems could arise for that facility, however, if such releases are reported pursuant to Section 313 and no emergency notification has been made for those releases under Section 304. This example illustrates one of the inherent problems in the statute because

(continued...)

Additionally, because the bulk of the data in Section 313 reports concern routine releases, owners or operators will need to develop, in addition to a rigorous compliance program, both in-house and community-wide information programs to provide a context from which the release data can be viewed in perspective. Companies must also be prepared to have other uses made of the data they report. For example, Section 313 data can be used as the basis of regulatory initiatives or public health studies, as the foundation for actions to enforce existing environmental requirements, as a predicate for toxic tort actions, and as the basis for local actions to constrain or impose additional conditions on industrial operations.

Consequently, compliance with EPCRA will require not only corporate commitment to rigorous satisfaction of the specific requirements of the Act but also a sophisticated planning and community relations effort both to provide the requisite information and to anticipate and respond to the consequences of filing the mandated reports.

---

[230](..continued)
the reportable quantity for ammonia is set at 100 pounds. For a high-volume user of ammonia, therefore, this could effectively require daily emergency release reporting, which would be of questionable value.

## APPENDIX A - SECTION 313 PENALTY MATRIX

The six circumstance levels in order of decreasing seriousness:

Level 1   Non-reporting/failure to report a chemical;  falsified reporting;

Level 2   Late reporting (after 180 days);

Level 3   Failure to correct errors specified in a NON or within 30 days of being told of errors during an inspection;  serious errors found through inspection, audit, tip, complaint, or voluntary disclosure (voluntary disclosure of errors may result in reduction of penalty);

Level 4   Errors/incorrect reports voluntarily disclosed but not corrected within 30 days of discovery and 180 days of due date of report:

Level 5   Late reporting (1 - 30 days after reporting is due);  report sent to EPA but not to state and facility has not received a previous NON from EPA for this violation;  and

Level 6   Error correction not reported to state when responding to a NON/civil complaint for errors;  minor errors in report not corrected within 30 days of discovery.

---

The upward and downward penalty adjustment factors are:

1.  Voluntary disclosure;

2.  Culpability includes the violator's knowledge, his control over the situation, and the violator's attitude);

3.  History of prior violations of Section 313 (i.e. within five years of the present violation).  In the case of wholly-owned or partly-owned facilities the violation history of the parent applies to the subsidiaries and vice versa;

4.  Ability of the violator to pay and continue in business;

5.  Other factors as justice may require (such as new ownership or environmentally beneficial expenditures made in lieu of penalty).

The penalty matrix is as follows:

PENALTY MATRIX
**Penalty Adjustment Level**

| Circumstance Levels | A | B | C |
|---|---|---|---|
| 1 | $25,000 | $17,000 | $5,000 |
| 2 | $20,000 | $13,000 | $3,000 |
| 3 | $15,000 | $10,000 | $1,500 |
| 4 | $10,000 | $ 6,000 | $1,000 |
| 5 | $ 5,000 | $ 3,000 | $ 500 |
| 6 | $ 2,000 | $ 1,300 | $ 200 |

---

## APPENDIX B - PENALTY POLICY FOR SECTION 302, 303, 304, 311 AND 312

Types of violations evaluated under the "nature" component of the penalty policy are as follows:

### i. *Emergency Response Violations*:

**LEVEL 1:**

CERCLA § 103: No notification to the NRC within 2 hours after the person in charge has knowledge that a reportable quantity of a substance was released unless extenuating circumstances existed that prevented notification.

EPCRA § 304(a): No notification to the appropriate SERC(s) and LEPC(s) within 2 hours after the owner or operator had knowledge of the release unless extenuating circumstances existed that prevented notification.

EPCRA § 304(c): No written follow-up report to the appropriate SERC(s) and LEPC(s) within 2 weeks following the release unless extenuating circumstances prevented its submission.

**LEVEL 2:**

CERCLA § 103:   No notification to the NRC within 1 hour (but within 2 hours) after the person in charge had knowledge that a reportable quantity of a substance was released unless extenuating circumstances prevented the notification.

EPCRA § 304(a):   Notification to the appropriate SERC(s) and LEPC(s) within 1 hour (but within 2 hours) after the owner or operator had knowledge of the release unless extenuating circumstances prevented the notification.

EPCRA § 304(c):   No written follow-up report to the appropriate SERC(s) and LEPC(s) within 1 week (but within 2 weeks) following the release unless extenuating circumstances prevented its submission.

**LEVEL 3:**

CERCLA § 103:   No immediate notification to the NRC, i.e., although notification occurred within one hour, the facts and circumstances indicate that the notification could have been made sooner then actually made.

EPCRA § 304(a):   No immediate notification to the appropriate SERC(s) and LEPC(s), i.e., although notification occurred within one hours, the facts and circumstances of the incident indicate that the notification(s) could have been made sooner than actually made.

EPCRA § 304(c):   No written follow-up report to the appropriate SERC(s) and LEPC(s) as soon as practicable, i.e., although follow-up notification occurred within one week, the facts and circumstances of the incident indicate that the follow-up was not as soon as practicable.

### ii. Emergency Preparedness/Right-to-Know Violations:

**LEVEL 1:**

EPCRA § 302:   Respondent fails to notify the SERC that it is subject to the Act within 30 calendar days of the reporting deadline.

EPCRA § 303:    Respondent fails to notify the LEPC within 30 calendar days of reporting obligation.

Respondent fails to respond to Administrative Order for § 303(d)(3) within 30 calendar days of required response date.

Respondent submits information in response to § 303 information request, claims trade secret any chemical identity, but fails to submit trade secret substantiation to justify the claim (thereby rendering the § 303 submission substantively incomplete and potentially fraudulent).

EPCRA § 311:    Respondent fails to submit MSDS for each required hazardous chemical (or list of MSDSs) as required by § 311(a) to the SERC, LEPC, or fire department within 30 calendar days of the reporting obligation.

Respondent fails to include chemical on list submitted.

Respondent submits MSDS or list claiming chemical identity a trade secret, but fails to submit trade secret substantiation to justify the claim (thereby rendering the § 311 submission substantively incomplete and potentially fraudulent).

Respondent fails to respond to request under § 311(c) within 30 calendar days of the reporting obligation.

EPCRA § 312:    Respondent fails to submit Inventory Form to the SERC, LEPC, or fire department within 30 calendar days of reporting deadline.

Inventory form submitted fails to address each hazard category present at the facility.

Respondent fails to respond to request under § 312(e) within 30 calendar days of the reporting obligation.

Respondent submits form that claims trade secret status for chemical identification, but Respondent fails to submit trade secret substantiation to justify the claim (thereby rendering the § 312 submission substantively incomplete and potentially fraudulent).

## LEVEL 2:

EPCRA § 302:   Respondent fails to notify the SERC that it is subject to the Act within 20 (but does within 30) calendar days of reporting obligation.

EPCRA § 303:   Respondent fails to notify the LEPC within 20 (but does within 30) calendar days of reporting obligation.

Respondent fails to respond to an Administrative Order within 20 (but does within 30) calendar days of required response date.

EPCRA § 311:   Respondent fails to submit MSDS (or list of MSDSs) to the SERC, LEPC, or fire department within 20 (but does within 30) calendar days of reporting deadline.

Respondent fails to respond to request under § 311(c) within 20 (but does within 30) calendar days of the reporting obligation.

EPCRA § 312:   Respondent fails to submit Inventory Form to the SERC, LEPC, or fire department within 20 (but does within 30) calendar days of reporting deadline.

Inventory form submitted covers all hazard categories present at the facility, but fails to cover all hazardous chemical present at the facility during the preceding calendar year in amounts equal to or greater than the reporting thresholds. Respondent's failure to address all of the hazardous chemicals renders the submission incomplete(i.e., all general locations not supplied) or inaccurate(i.e., different ranges apply).

Respondent fails to respond to request under § 312(e) within 20 (but does within 30) calendar days of required response date..

EPCRA § 302:   Respondent fails to notify the SERC within 10 (but does within 20) calendar days of reporting obligation.

EPCRA § 303:   Respondent fails to notify the LEPC within 10 (but does within 20) calendar days of reporting obligation.

Respondent fails to respond to an Administrative Order within 10 (but does within 20) calendar days of required response date.

EPCRA § 311:    Respondent fails to submit MSDS (or list of MSDSs) to the SERC, LEPC, or fire department within 10 (but does within 20) calendar days of reporting obligation.

Respondent fails to respond to request under § 311(c) within 10 (but does within 20) calendar days of the reporting obligation.

EPCRA § 312:    Respondent fails to submit Inventory Form to the SERC, LEPC, or fire department within 10 (but does within 20) calendar days of reporting deadline.

Respondent submitted form addresses all hazard categories, but fails to meet the standard required by the Statute or Rule.

Respondent fails to respond to request under § 312(e) within 10 (but does within 20) calendar days of required response date.

Level 1    Substantial noncompliance because of the extent that the violation deviates from the requirements of the statute;

Level 2    Significant deviation from statutory requirements, but some requirements are met;

Level 3    Substantial compliance although there is some deviation from the requirements of the statute.

- - -

The "gravity" components of the penalty policy involve the following for Section 304 releases:

Level A    The amount released was more than ten times the RQ;

Level B    The amount released was more than five but less than or equal to ten times the RQ;

Level C   The amount released was more than five but less than or equal to five times the RQ.

For Section 311 violations, the gravity levels are:

Level A   The amount of the hazardous chemical present at the facility at any time during the reporting period was more than ten times the reporting threshold;

Level B   The amount of the hazardous chemical present at the facility at any time during the reporting period was more than five but less than or equal to ten times the reporting threshold:

Level C   The amount of the hazardous chemical present at the facility at any time during the reporting period was greater than one but less than or equal to five times the reporting threshold.

For Section 312 violations, the gravity levels are:

Level A   For non-reporting situations, the amount of any hazardous chemical not included in the report was greater than ten times the reporting threshold;

For timely reports, ten or more hazardous chemicals were required to be submitted in the report but were not included in the report;

Level B   For non-reporting situations, the amount of any hazardous chemical not included in the report was more than five but less than or equal to ten times the reporting threshold;

For timely reports, more than five but fewer than ten hazardous chemicals were required to be submitted in the report but were not included in the report;

Level C   For non-reporting situations, the amount of any hazardous chemical not included in the report was more than one but less than or equal to five times the reporting threshold;

For timely reports, five or more hazardous chemicals were required to be submitted in the report but were not included in the report;

Level C also applies to submissions in which the form addresses all hazard categories and all hazardous chemicals present in excess of the applicable threshold but which in some other manner fails to meet the reporting requirements of Section 312.

- - -

The two penalty matrices are as follows:
The base penalty matrices and penalty adjustment criteria are as follows:

TABLE I
**Base Penalty Matrices**

CERCLA § 103 and EPCRA §§ 302, 303, 304 and 312

| Extent | Level A | Gravity Level B | Level C |
|--------|---------|---------|---------|
| **Level 1:** . . . . . . | $25,000 . . . . . | $16,500. . . . . . | $8,250 |
| . . . . . | $20,000 . . . . . | $13,200. . . . . . | $6,600 |
| **Level 2:** . . . . . . | $16,500 . . . . . | $ 6,250. . . . . . | $4,500 |
| . . . . . | $13,200 . . . . . | $ 5,000. . . . . . | $3,600 |
| **Level 3:** . . . . . . | $ 8,250 . . . . . | $ 4,500. . . . . . | $2,500 |
| . . . . . | $ 6,600 . . . . . | $ 3,600. . . . . . | $2,000 |

EPCRA § 311 Violations

| Extent | Level A | Gravity Level B | Level C |
|--------|---------|---------|---------|
| **Level 1:** . . . . . . | $10,000 . . . . . | $ 6,600. . . . . . | $3,300 |
| . . . . . . | $ 8,000 . . . . . | $ 5,280. . . . . . | $2,640 |
| **Level 2:** . . . . . . . | $ 6,600 . . . . . | $ 2,500. . . . . . | $1,800 |
| . . . . . . | $ 5,280 . . . . . | $ 2,000. . . . . . | $1,440 |
| **Level 3:** . . . . . . | $ 3,300 . . . . . | $ 1,800. . . . . . | $1,000 |
| . . . . . | $ 2,640 . . . . . | $ 1,440. . . . . . | $ 800 |

1. Ability to pay and continue in business. This is a downward adjustment factor only;

2. Prior history of violation. This is an upward adjustment factor only and applies to a final order, default judgment, or consent decree entered within the previous five years. In the case of wholly-owned or partially-owned subsidiaries, the violation history of the parent is imputed to the subsidiary and vice versa. Note also that "a violation of § 313 will count as a prior violation if the § 313 violation occurred in one of the previous five years;[230]

3. Degree of culpability. This can be either an upward or downward adjustment and is based upon the violator's knowledge of the requirements and control over the violative act. There are three levels of degree of culpability:

   Level 1  The violator had prior knowledge of EPCRA and its reporting requirements shown by attendance at an EPCRA seminar or workshop or by documented contact with EPA, a SERC, or LEPC. This yields an upward adjustment of up to twenty-five percent;

   Level 2  The violator did not comply either because of lack of knowledge of the requirement, lack of management, or failure to adhere to procedures. No adjustment results;

   Level 3  The violator attempted to comply or self-reported the violation before EPA detected the violation. This decreases the penalty by up to twenty-five percent.

4. Economic benefits or savings. For EPCRA Section 304(c), 311, and 312 the economic benefit is basically the money saved in producing the requisite reports. The economic benefit of failure to provide emergency notification is negligible.

5. The final adjustment factor, "other matters as justice may require" includes reductions based upon the proposed delisting of an extremely hazardous chemical by EPA and environmentally beneficial expenditures. The former applies to chemicals proposed for delisting or delisted before or during the pendency of the enforcement action and can result in a deferral of twenty-five percent of the penalty. Environmentally

---

[230] *Id.* at 25.

beneficial expenditures involve circumstances where a violator offers to make expenditures for environmentally beneficial projects beyond that required by law.

Chapter 6


NATIONAL ENVIRONMENTAL POLICY ACT
(NEPA)


Timothy A. Vanderver, Jr., Russell V. Randle,
and John C. Martin
Patton, Boggs & Blow
Washington, D.C.


## 1.0 INTRODUCTION

The National Environmental Policy Act of 1969,[1] commonly referred to as
"NEPA," was signed into law by President Nixon on New Year's Day, 1970.
NEPA is a short, general statute: it declares a national environmental policy
and promotes consideration of environmental concerns by federal agencies.
Nonetheless, NEPA has had a pervasive effect on the federal decisionmaking
process as a result of thousands of judicial decisions construing the statute's
meaning in concrete situations.

Compliance with NEPA matters very much to private interests dependent
upon many federal permit decisions, e.g. dredge-fill permits under section 404
of the Clean Water Act, or upon federal construction grants and assistance,
e.g. federal highway money. NEPA continues to be a primary basis for
challenges to public or private development decisions, most of which can be
argued to have an environmental component. NEPA matters to environmentalists because it gives a statutory basis to force review of federal
decisions regardless of, and perhaps especially, when the federal agency
involved is not an agency with distinct environmental responsibilities.

---

[1] Pub. L. No. 91-190, 42 U.S.C. §§ 4321-4347, as amended by Pub. L. No.
95-52 (July 3, 1975) (appropriations) and Pub. L. No. 94-83 (August 9, 1975)
(delegation to States to prepare environmental impact statements in certain
limited cases).

In great measure, NEPA's importance results from the vast amount of litigation it precipitated. Consequently, a large body of NEPA case law has been developed, fleshing out and giving specific force to NEPA's general provisions. In response, even recalcitrant federal agencies have incorporated NEPA requirements into their routine procedures, and the early flood of NEPA litigation has slowed to a steady stream of challenges to whether agency decisions comply with the procedures and regulations issued by the Council on Environmental Quality (CEQ) and by the implementing agency.

## 2.0 OVERVIEW

NEPA is divided into two titles. Title I declares a national environmental policy and goals, provides a method for accomplishing those goals and includes some guidance on the fundamental question of how NEPA relates to other federal law. Title II creates the Council on Environmental Quality (CEQ) and defines its responsibilities. In turn, CEQ has promulgated regulations which guide the NEPA process.[2]

### 2.1 Policy and Goals

The national environmental policy declared in Title I of NEPA is the first ever enacted by Congress. It announces a general commitment to "use all practicable means" to conduct federal activities in a way that will promote "the general welfare" and be in "harmony" with the environment. NEPA's six related goals are set with an eye toward assuring "safe, healthful, productive and aesthetically and culturally pleasing surroundings" for all generations of Americans.

### 2.1.1 Enforceability of Title I Policy and Goals

An important practical question about the policy and goals embodied in NEPA is whether they create any enforceable "substantive rights." That is, does NEPA require that a federal agency make a particular decision in certain circumstances, or does the statute only require that the agency consider specified environmental factors in its decisionmaking process. Although there was once a split of opinion in the United States Courts of Appeals on this question, the Supreme Court has resolved that conflict.

In *Vermont Yankee Nuclear Power Corp. v. NRDC*,[3] the Court found that although "NEPA does set forth significant substantive goals for the Nation, . . . its mandate to the agencies is essentially procedural." And in *Strycker's Bay*

---

[2] 40 C.F.R. § 1500 *et seq.*

[3] 435 U.S. 519 (1978).

*Neighborhood Council v. Karlen*,[4] the Court reversed a Second Circuit decision that looked to the provisions of NEPA for the substantive standards necessary to review the merits of agency decisions. In so doing, the Court ruled that:

Once an agency has made a decision subject to NEPA's procedural requirements, the only role for a court is to insure that the agency has considered the environmental consequences; it cannot "interject itself within the area of discretion of the executive as to the choice of action to be taken."[5] Thus, the Supreme Court has held that the policy and goals set forth in Title I of NEPA create no judicially enforceable substantive rights, but impose only a procedural duty on federal agencies to consider NEPA's aims when making decisions. So, although federal agencies are bound to exercise their decisionmaking discretion in ways that are consistent with NEPA's ends, NEPA does not require agencies to make decisions promoting the preservation or protection of the environment.

The Supreme Court recently reaffirmed this fundamental aspect of NEPA case law in *Robertson v. Methow Valley Citizens Council*.[6] In that case, the Ninth Circuit Court of Appeals had reversed a Forest Service decision to grant a special use permit for construction of a ski area in a national forest. The Court of Appeals based this reversal on its view that the mitigation measures relied on in the impact statement were unforceable and thus inadequate to satisfy NEPA's procedural requirements.

The Court reversed, making clear in the process that courts are not to 0make substantive environmental decisions under NEPA by attacking the mitigation measures portion of the impact statement. According to Justice Stevens, writing for the Court:

> [I]t would not have violated NEPA if the Forest Service, after complying with the Act's procedural prerequisites, had decided that the benefits to be derived from downhill skiing at Sandy Butte justified issuance of a special use permit, notwithstanding the loss of 15 percent, 50 percent, or even 100 percent of the mule deer herd. Other statutes may impose substantive environmental obligations on federal agencies, but NEPA merely prohibits uninformed--rather than unwise--agency action.[7]

---

[4] 444 U.S. 223 (1980).

[5] 444 U.S. at 227 (citations and footnote omitted). The Court also added that "the reviewing Court may not elevate environmental concerns over other legitimate considerations in its decision-making process." Id. at 228 n.2. See also, *Baltimore Gas & Electric Co. v. NRDC*, 426 U.S. 87, 101 (1983).

[6] 109 S.Ct. 1835 (1989).

[7] 109 S.Ct. 1835, 1846 (1989).

The Court's insistence that NEPA is procedural does not leave opponents of environmentally misguided federal action without a remedy. Rather, as the court recognized, that remedy lies with other, substantive environmental statutes, and implicitly, with the political process.

Because NEPA creates no new substantive rights, NEPA's importance stems almost entirely from procedural provisions designed to insure that agencies do in fact consider the environmental consequences of federal actions before they are taken.

## 2.2 Council on Environmental Quality (CEQ)

CEQ, established under Title II of NEPA, is charged with monitoring progress toward achieving the national environmental goals as set forth in Section 101 of NEPA. The specific statutory duties of CEQ are set out in Section 204 of NEPA. CEQ is to "assist and advise the president in the preparation of the Environmental Quality Report." Issues as broad as its title implies are addressed in this annual report, and an analysis of the need for any further legislation is specifically required to be included in the report by Section 201. It is also the duty of CEQ to gather environmental information and to conduct studies on the conditions and trends in environmental quality. Moreover, CEQ is charged with developing and recommending to the president national policies and legislation to protect the environment.

Until the Reagan administration, CEQ played a prominent and controversial role in raising environmental issues such as offshore drilling, toxic substances and marine pollution. The Reagan administration gutted CEQ so that its only significant accomplishment since 1980 has been the issuance of amendments to its regulations in 1986. Under the Bush Administration, CEQ has become more active, and its budget and staff have increased. Efforts are being made to consolidate CEQ with EPA, however, in the proposed cabinet department of the environment. It remains to be seen whether CEQ will survive in its current form.

In addition to its role as advisor to the president on environmental issues, CEQ has also been afforded the duty of providing guidance to other federal agencies on compliance with NEPA. In discharging this obligation, CEQ promulgated regulations in 1979 (amended in 1986) governing the NEPA process for all federal agencies. These regulations are discussed below.

## 3.0 PROPOSED ACTIONS REQUIRING AN EIS

Section 102(2)(C) requires that an environmental impact statement (EIS) shall be "included in every recommendation or report on proposals for legislation and other major federal actions significantly affecting the quality of the human environment."

Because NEPA makes no pretense of applying its requirements to other than federal agencies, perhaps the best first step toward deciding whether an

EIS is required is to determine whether "federal" action is involved. Federal action obviously includes what is undertaken directly by the federal agencies, including operation of programs, construction of facilities, and the provision of funding to others.[8] Federal action also clearly includes a federal agency's decision on whether to grant its required permission for activities of others, such as private businesses or state or local governments. The CEQ regulations have amplified the judicial interpretation of this element. As a general matter, the regulation notes that "major Federal action" encompasses "actions which may be major and which are potentially subject to Federal control and responsibility."[9]

In addition to federal involvement, there must also be a "proposal" for action before preparation of an EIS will be required.[10] In 1976, the Sierra Club contended that Interior Secretary Kleppe was required to prepare an EIS on coal development in the Northern Great Plains region of the country. The Supreme Court carefully reviewed Interior's past and contemplated actions. It found that there was no *proposal* for regional action concerning coal development. All Interior proposals were for actions that were either local or national in scope, even though such actions affected the Northern Great Plains region. Thus, because there was no proposal for regional action, the court held that no EIS was required on coal development in the Northern Great Plains region.

The Supreme Court has also held that federal agencies are not required by Section 102(2)(C) to prepare an EIS to accompany appropriations requests, as such requests do not constitute "proposals" for legislation or for major federal action.[11] In so ruling, the court noted that the language of Section 102(2)(C) is best interpreted as applying to those recommendations or reports that actually propose programmatic actions, rather than to those that merely suggest how such actions may be funded.

---

[8] General revenue sharing has been held not to require an EIS because it is not sufficiently federal in nature. *Carolina Action v. Simon*, 389 F. Supp. 1244 (M.D.N.C. 1975), *aff'd*, 522 F.2d 295 (4th Cir., 1975). This holding is specifically supported by the CEQ regulations. 40 C.F.R. § 1508.18(a). On the other hand, block grants for more specific projects have been held to require an EIS. *See, e.g., Ely v. Velde*, 451 F.2d 1130 (4th Cir., 1971).

[9] 40 C.F.R. § 1508.18. The regulation specifically includes: projects financed, assisted, conducted, regulated or approved by federal agencies; new or revised agency rules, regulations, plans, policies or procedures; and legislative proposals. 40 C.F.R. § 1508.18(a).

[10] 427 U.S. 390 (1976).

[11] *Andrus v. Sierra Club*, 442 U.S. 347 (1979).

There are a multitude of cases on the question of whether a given federal action is "major" and/or "significantly affects" the quality of the human environment within the meaning of NEPA. Almost all of these cases, as well as the CEQ regulations, however, avoid the futile effort of trying to define the amorphous words "major" and "significantly."[12] The few cases where definition is attempted shed no more light on the issue than does the dictionary. The usual long analysis of those NEPA cases interpreting the meaning of "major" and "significantly affects" is therefore omitted here. Such an analysis yields no valid criterion for deciding whether any *other* federal action is "major" or "significantly affects" the environment.

Practically speaking, the initial decision of whether to prepare an EIS for any given proposed project lies within the sound discretion of the various federal agencies.[13] Accordingly, in the last few years, increasing attention has been given to "findings of no significant impact."[14]

### 3.1 Findings of No Significant Impact

The CEQ regulations define a "finding of no significant impact" (FONSI) as "a document prepared by a federal agency briefly presenting the reasons why

---

[12] The regulations do provide some limited guidance as to what is "significant." The term is said to require consideration of both context and intensity. "Context" means the subjects that are affected, such as society as a whole, the region, interests or the locality. It includes both short-term and long-term effects. 40 C.F.R. § 1508.27(a). "Intensity" refers to the severity of the impact. 40 C.F.R. § 1508.27(b).

[13] There has been a split in the circuits of the United States courts of appeals as to the appropriate standard to employ in reviewing an agency's "threshold decision" not to prepare an EIS for a given project. Some circuits have adopted an "arbitrary and capricious" standard, others have employed a "reasonableness" standard. See *Aertsen v. Landrieu*, 488 F.Supp. 314 (D. Mass. 1980) for a discussion of this difference of opinion. Although the level of judicial scrutiny differs in some measure as a result of choosing one standard rather than the other, it is generally true that reviewing courts will simply look for an administrative record that evidences a rational basis for the agency's determination on the issue of whether or not to prepare an EIS on a particular project.

[14] The CEQ regulations prescribe the use of the term "finding of no significant impact" for such documents. 40 C.F.R. § 1508.13. Before the promulgation of the regulations, these documents were most frequently called "negative declarations."

an action, not otherwise excluded[15] ... will not have a significant effect on the human environment and for which an environmental impact statement therefore will not be prepared."[16] The regulations further provide that a FONSI must include an environmental assessment or a summary of one.[17] Although a federal agency need not itself prepare that environmental assessment, the agency is responsible for its content, for if the environmental assessment prepared in connection with the issuance of a FONSI does not provide sufficient evidence to support the agency's finding of no significant impact, that finding will be overturned.

Thus, a FONSI can avoid the lengthy EIS process if properly substantiated. Early NEPA cases confronted many agency determinations that particular actions exerted no significant impact and these determinations were consistently overturned by reviewing courts. This has changed in recent years as agencies have become more familiar with what is legally required for a FONSI, and with the substantiation necessary to support one.

### 3.2 EIS Requirements for Special Types of Federal Action

Some particular types of federal agency actions merit special mention in connection with the EIS requirement. One is the preparation of an EIS in connection with legislation. In view of the unique nature of legislative recommendations and reports, CEQ's regulations provide for certain special features for EISs that accompany legislative proposals.[18] First, the statement may be transmitted to the Congress up to thirty days after submission of the proposal, in order to allow time for the preparation of an accurate and complete EIS. Second, a legislative EIS is to be prepared in the same manner as an ordinary draft EIS. Draft *and* final statements are required only in certain limited circumstances. Finally, comments on a legislative EIS are to be collected by the lead agency and forwarded to the Congress, together with the agency's responses to the comments.

---

[15] There are a few exemptions from the EIS requirement. Most notable are the statutory exemptions for United States Environmental Protection Agency actions under most provisions of the Clean Water Act and under all Clean Air Act provisions. 33 U.S.C. § 1371(c)(1); 15 U.S.C. § 793(c)(1). In addition, special exemptions are occasionally granted by Congress for some federal agency projects and for a few private projects that involve some federal agency action. *See, e.g.,* 15 U.S.C. § 793(d). *See also,* 40 C.F.R. § 1508.4.

[16] 40 C.F.R. § 1508.13.

[17] *Id.*

[18] 40 C.F.R. § 1506.08.

A second type of federal agency action that merits special mention in connection with EIS requirements is the agency "program." Although NEPA does not specifically require the preparation of a "programmatic" EIS, the courts have required such EISs in certain circumstances. The courts also have had considerable difficulty in deciding issues relating to the proper scope of a programmatic EIS. However, one simple way to state the EIS requirements for a program involving future developments is to say that a programmatic EIS must be prepared if institution of the program will foreclose decisions on whether to approve individual projects that would in themselves require EISs.

*Scientists' Institute for Public Information v. Atomic Energy Commission*,[19] is a leading case dealing with EIS requirements for agency programs relating to future developments. In that case, the Commission had concluded that it did not need to prepare a programmatic EIS before deciding to proceed with its liquid metal fast breeder reactor demonstration program because the environmental impact of that program would be evaluated in EISs on each demonstration plant. The court, looking to environmental effects that today's decisions on development of technology may have years hence, held that a programmatic EIS was indeed required.

The applicability of the EIS requirement to ongoing federal agency programs is demonstrated by *Minnesota Public Interest Research Group v. Butz*,[20] which held that the cumulative environmental impact of Forest Service decisions on the management of timber in a certain area required a programmatic EIS on what amounted to an ongoing, but apparently ad hoc, management plan. The applicability of the EIS requirement to ongoing federal agency programs appears to have significant potential for those--both environmentalists and private interests--who seek to change what are to them unacceptable, yet entrenched, federal agency policies and practices.

### 3.3 Procedure and Time of Required Issuance

As noted above, Section 102(2)(C) requires that an EIS be "included in every recommendation or report on proposals for major federal action significantly affecting the environment." That section also requires an agency, prior to preparing its EIS, to consult with, and obtain the comments of, any other federal agency that has either jurisdiction by law or special expertise with respect to any environmental impact involved. In addition, copies of the EIS, federal agency comments on it, and the views of appropriate state and local agencies must be made available to the president, CEQ, and the public, and must accompany the proposal through the existing agency review process.

The concept of preparing and circulating for comment a draft EIS is embodied in the CEQ regulations where EIS preparation procedures are set out. The draft is to be prepared "early enough so that it can serve . . . as an

---

[19] 481 F.2d 1079 (D.C. Cir., 1973).

[20] 498 F.2d 1314 (8th Cir., 1974).

important contribution to the decision-making process,"[21] and circulated for comment for a period not less than forty-five days.[22] The regulations also provide that, as a general rule, no agency action should occur earlier than ninety days after the draft EIS, or thirty days after the final EIS is made available to CEQ and the public.[23] For informal rulemaking, the draft EIS should normally accompany the proposed rules.[24]

The regulations state that a "proposal" exists at the stage when an agency "has a goal and is actively preparing to make a decision on one or more means of accomplishing that goal and the effects can be meaningfully evaluated."[25] The CEQ regulation goes on to note that the EIS "should" be timed so that the final EIS may be included in any recommendation or report on the proposal.[26]

In SCRAP II,[27] the Supreme Court rejected the holding of several courts of appeals that a final EIS must be prepared prior to agency hearings on an applicant's request for federal action or, at other times, before the agency actually takes a position on a proposal. The Supreme Court made it clear that "the time at which the agency must prepare the final EIS is the time at which it makes a 'recommendation or report' on a proposal." Since then, the CEQ regulations have prescribed the timing for final EISs in most circumstances.

### 3.4 Delegation

It is strongly implied, but not explicitly stated, in Section 102(2)(C), that the federal agency or the "responsible federal official" proposing to take action is charged with preparing the requisite EIS. Early in NEPA's history, several courts of appeals' decisions addressed the question of whether, and, to what extent, a federal agency can lawfully delegate responsibility for preparing an EIS. The issue divided the courts into three camps: (1) those disallowing any

---

[21] 40 C.F.R. § 1502.5.

[22] 40 C.F.R. § 1506.10(c).

[23] 40 C.F.R. § 1506.10(b).

[24] 40 C.F.R. § 1502.5(d).

[25] 40 C.F.R. § 1508.23.

[26] *Id.*

[27] *Aberdeen & Rockfish RR. Co. v. Students Challenging Regulatory Agency Procedures (SCRAP II)*, 422 U.S. 289 (1975), reaffirmed in dicta in *Kleppe v. Sierra Club*, 427 U.S. 390 (1976).

delegation of responsibility;[28] (2) those allowing some delegation, but requiring the responsible federal official to significantly and actively participate in the preparation of the EIS[29] and (3) those permitting extensive delegation of responsibility, followed only by review and adoption by the agency.[30] In August of 1975, Congress enacted Pub. L. No. 94-83, adding to Section 102(2) a new subsection that settled the delegation question with respect to state officials and agencies, but left open issues involving delegation to private consultants.

The new subsection, which is designated as Section 102(2)(D), provides that an EIS "for any major federal action funded under a program of grants to States shall not be deemed to be legally insufficient solely by reason of having been prepared by a state agency or official," if (1) the state agency or official has state-wide jurisdiction and is responsible for the action, and (2) the responsible federal official (a) furnishes guidance and participates in the preparation of the EIS, (b) independently evaluates it prior to its approval and adoption, and (c) provides early notice to, and solicits the view of, any other state or any federal land management entity on any action or alternatives thereto which may affect its responsibilities. The responsible federal official must also prepare a written assessment of the impacts on other agencies' responsibilities for incorporation into the EIS if there is any disagreement. Section 102(2)(D) goes on to state it does not relieve the federal official of responsibility for the scope, objectivity and content of an EIS or any other responsibilities under NEPA. The provisions of Section 102(2)(D) have been of primary importance in situations involving federal grants to states for highway construction.[31]

Thus, Congress rejected the *per se* no delegation rule of *Greene County* in the case of projects involving grants to states, and adopted the views expressed by those courts taking the middle course, which allowed delegation, but required significant, active participation by the responsible federal agency. The law regarding delegation to private consultants, however, remains unsettled.

---

[28] *See, e.g., Greene County Planning Board v. Federal Power Commission*, 455 F.2d 412 (2d Cir. 1972), *cert. denied*, 409 U.S. 849 (1972).

[29] *See, e.g., Life of the Land v. Brinegar*, 485 F.2d 460 (9th Cir. 1973), *cert. denied*, 416 U.S. 961 (1974).

[30] *See, e.g., Citizens Environmental Council v. Volpe*, 484 F.2d 870 (10th Cir. 1973), *cert. denied*, 461 U.S. 936 (1974).

[31] Congress enacted a special total delegation of responsibility provision for preparing an EIS to applicants under the Community Development Block Grant Program established by the Housing and Community Development Act of 1974. 42 U.S.C. § 5304(h).

## 3.5 The Lead Agency System

Projects requiring "major actions" by more than one federal agency are not uncommon. The concept of a "lead agency" to prepare or to supervise the preparation of an EIS for such an action was developed in order to satisfy the requirements of NEPA in the most efficient manner possible. CEQ's regulations incorporate that concept and require that a "lead agency" be designated to supervise the preparation of an EIS in such circumstances.[32]

Involved agencies are to determine which shall be the lead agency on the basis of five enumerated factors (listed in order of descending importance):

(i)     magnitude of agency's involvement;
(ii)    project approval/disapproval authority;
(iii)   expertise concerning the action's environmental effects;
(iv)   duration of agency's involvement; and
(v)    sequence of agency's involvement.[33]

CEQ will designate the lead agency if there is no consensual selection.[34]

## 3.6 Contents of an EIS

The broad outline of an EIS is set forth in Section 102(2)(C). The EIS must be a "detailed" statement which is issued only after consultation with other appropriate government agencies. It must address the environmental impact of the proposed action, unavoidable adverse environmental effects, alternatives, the relationship between local short-term uses of the environment and the maintenance and enhancement of long-term productivity, and irreversible and irretrievable commitments of resources. Obviously, what a particular EIS must include depends on the proposal and the facts surrounding it.

The federal courts have supplemented the statutory requirements on a case-by-case basis. Although each of the cases concerns a particular EIS and surrounding facts, the decisions make clear that: (1) the EIS must be a self-contained document written in language that is understandable to the layman, yet allows for meaningful consideration by decisionmakers and scientists;[35] and (2) it must also be responsive to opposing opinions, and of sufficient depth to permit a reasoned choice.

A fatally defective EIS is usually characterized by one or more of the following: sweeping conclusions unsupported by the facts; vagueness as to important issues; internal contradiction; disregard for local land use planning

---

[32] 40 C.F.R. § 1501.5(a).

[33] 40 C.F.R. § 1501.5(c).

[34] 40 C.F.R. § 1501.5(e) and (f).

[35] *See* 40 C.F.R. § 1502.8 (requiring "plain language").

requirements; cursory treatment of secondary and cumulative environmental impacts; failure to include sufficient information on the environmental impact of realistic and plausible alternatives, and to make an unbiased comparison of them with the proposal; and failure to include adequate (or any) mitigation measures or plans. Because the consideration of alternatives is accorded the role of "linchpin" of the EIS, it merits some further mention.

The requirement to consider alternatives embodies the simple principle that a rational decision requires a knowledge of the available choices and their ramifications. The alternative of no action must always be discussed. NEPA does not, however, require that the consideration of alternatives be a "crystal ball" inquiry.[36] Detailed discussion and consideration of alternatives that are remote or speculative are not required. Yet, an alternative may not be given short shrift because it is outside the jurisdiction of the agency or because it is contrary to existing agency policy. Simply put, the agency's consideration of alternatives must be reasonable such that a reviewing court may conclude that a proposing agency has taken a "hard look" at the decision's environmental consequences.[37]

## 4.0 CEQ's PROCEDURAL REGULATIONS

The regulations promulgated by CEQ set out procedures which may be broken down into six general stages of NEPA implementation: (i) agency guidance and categorical exclusions; (ii) the environmental assessments; (iii) the scoping process; (iv) the draft environmental impact statement; (v) the final environmental impact statement; and (vi) the agency decision and its accompanying record of decision. Any project within the purview of NEPA will proceed through these steps as required by the regulations.

The CEQ regulations require that federal agencies simplify the NEPA process by providing broad guidance concerning the degree to which projects are subject to NEPA. Agencies are to establish specific criteria for classes of action: (i) which usually require environmental impact statements; (ii) which require neither an environmental impact statement nor an environmental assessment (the "categorical exclusion"); and (iii) which normally require an environmental assessment (EA) but do not necessarily require an

---

[36] *Natural Resources Defense Council, Inc. v. Morton*, 458 F.2d 827, 837 (D.C. Cir., 1972).

[37] *See, Baltimore Gas & Electric Corp. v. NRDC*, 462 U.S. 87,97 (1983); *Vermont Yankee Nuclear Power Corp. v. NRDC*, 435 U.S. 519 (1978); *California v. Block*, 690 F.2d 753,761 (9th Cir., 1985).

environmental impact statement.[38]    The categorical exclusion generally provides the first clearly defined exemption for a federal action.    If the agency has determined by way of a regulation that the subject is one for which neither an EA nor an EIS is necessary,[39] the action may proceed, in many instances, without the necessity of complying with further NEPA requirements.    Thus, for many routine activities, such as personnel actions, agencies have specified that an EIS will not be required.

The Department of Energy has, however, recently tightened its categorical exclusion regulations to assure more projects are subject to NEPA scrutiny, in particular, NEPA scrutiny by DOE headquarters.    The perception had arisen that DOE was using the categorical exclusion practice to avoid NEPA scrutiny of important projects.    By the same token, DOE has also proposed to exempt certain remedial actions from NEPA scrutiny because the substantially the same procedural protections for the environment.

For federal actions that are neither within categorical exclusions nor within the category of actions designated by the agency as requiring an EIS, an "environmental assessment" is necessary.[40]    The purpose of an environmental assessment is to provide the basis for determining whether an environmental impact statement is necessary.[41]    The environmental assessment is a concise public document which provides sufficient evidence and analysis to determine whether to prepare an environmental impact statement.[42]    The document must include a discussion of the need for the proposal, the alternatives considered, the environmental impacts of the proposed action and

---

[38] 40 C.F.R. § 1507.3(b)(2).

[39] 40 C.F.R. § 1508.4 defines "categorical exclusion" in pertinent part to mean a category of actions which do not cumulatively have a significant effect on the human environment and which have been found to have no such effect on procedures adopted by a federal agency in implementation of these regulations (§ 1507.3) and, for which, therefore, neither an environmental assessment nor an environmental impact statement is required. 40 C.F.R. § 1508.4. The regulations permit the agency to conduct an environmental assessment even for a categorical exclusion and require that the procedures include a provision for extraordinary circumstances when an excluded subject has a significant environmental effect. *Id.*

[40] 40 C.F.R. § 1501.4(b).

[41] 40 C.F.R. § 1501.4(c).

[42] 40 C.F.R. § 1508.9(a).

alternatives, and a listing of agencies and persons consulted.[43]   While there are no limits on an environmental assessment's length, the CEQ has recommended that the length be no more than 10 to 15 pages.[44]

If the agency finds, based on the environmental assessment, that the project does not significantly affect the environment, the agency must issue a "finding of no significant impact" which briefly explains why an EIS is not necessary.[45]

Assuming that the agency determines that an EIS is necessary, it must publish a notice of intent[46] and begin the next stage mandated by CEQ regulations--the scoping process.   The scoping process is a preliminary step employed to foster participation and focus the agency's EIS.[47]   The agency must determine within the scope of the EIS the range of actions, alternatives and impacts to be considered in an EIS.[48]   The regulations specify that an agency must consider three types of actions:   (i) connected actions;[49] (ii) cumulative actions; and (iii) similar actions.[50]   Likewise, CEQ has broken down the alternatives to be considered in the scoping process into:  (i) the no action alternative; (ii) other reasonable courses of action; and (iii) mitigation measures.[51]   Finally, the regulations specify three separate categories of

---

[43] *Id.*

[44] *See Forty Most Asked Questions Concerning CEQ's National Environmental Policy Act Regulations*, 46 Fed. Reg. 18037 (March 23, 1981).

[45] 40 C.F.R. §§ 1501.4(a), 1508.3.

[46] 40 C.F.R. § 1501.7.   The "notice of intent" must (i) describe the proposed action and possible alternatives; (ii) describe the proposed scoping process; and (iii) provide the name and address of a person within the agency to contact concerning the EIS. 40 C.F.R. § 1508.22.

[47] 40 C.F.R. § 1501.7.

[48] 40 C.F.R. § 1508.25.

[49] The CEQ has specified that actions are connected if (i) they automatically trigger other actions; (ii) they cannot or will not proceed unless other actions are taken previously or simultaneously; and (iii) they are interdependent parts of a larger action and depend on the larger action for their justification. 40 C.F.R. § 1508.25(a)(1).

[50] 40 C.F.R. § 1508.25(a).

[51] 40 C.F.R. § 1508.25(b).

impacts which must be addressed in the EIS's scope: (i) direct impacts; (ii) indirect impacts; and (iii) cumulative impacts.[52]

The scoping process provides an early opportunity to influence the subject matter of the EIS. Participants wishing to influence the decision may take the opportunity to bring subjects to the agency's attention. Indeed, one might argue that without a proposal that a certain topic be considered within the scope of the EIS, the absence of the topic in the EIS may not be used to overturn the agency decision.[53] In addition to raising subjects for the EIS, affected parties may request time limits and page limits. Normally the agency is required to set such limits if requested.[54]

Once the scoping process is completed, the agency begins preparation of the EIS. First, a draft EIS is prepared. The draft EIS is prepared to disclose all major points of view on the environmental impacts of the alternatives considered. The draft EIS must "fulfill and satisfy to the fullest extent possible" the requirements of a final EIS.[55] The agency must solicit comments from various governmental entities and affected parties,[56] and the draft EIS is subject to a comment period of at least 45 days.[57]

The final environmental impact statement responds to comments on the draft EIS[58] and meets the criteria set out in Section 102(2)(C) of NEPA.[59]

---

[52] 40 C.F.R. § 1508.25(c).

[53] *See Vermont Yankee Nuclear Power Corp. v. NRDC*, 435 U.S. 519, 551-54 (1977).

[54] 40 C.F.R. § 1501.7(b); 1501.8.

[55] 40 C.F.R. § 1502.9(a).

[56] 40 C.F.R. § 1503.1(a). The provision implements NEPA § 102(2)(C) which requires consultation with and comments from various federal, state and local agencies.

[57] 40 C.F.R. § 1506.10(c).

[58] 40 C.F.R. § 1502.9(b).

[59] NEPA § 102(2)(C), 42 U.S.C. § 4332(2)(C), provides, in pertinent part, that:

all agencies of the federal government shall (C) Include in every recommendation or report on proposals for legislation and other major Federal actions significantly affecting the quality of the human environment, a detailed statement by the responsible official on--

(i) The environmental impact of the proposed action; (ii) Any adverse

(continued...)

In general, the final EIS must address (i) the environmental impact of an action; (ii) any unavoidable adverse environmental impacts of the action; (iii) alternatives to the proposed action; (iv) the relationship between short-term uses and long-term productivity; and (v) any irreversible and unretrievable commitments of resources involved in the proposed action.[60]

The regulations prescribe a format for EISs[61] and some general mechanics of the document.[62] More substantively, the regulations provide guidance as to the alternatives considered, the affected environment and environmental consequences.

The regulations require that the alternatives in an EIS be presented in a comparative form, "sharply defining the issues and providing a clear basis for choice among options."[63] The agency must: (i) "rigorously" explore and objectively evaluate all reasonable alternatives; (ii) devote substantial treatment to each alternative considered in detail; (iii) include the "no action" alternative; (iv) include reasonable alternatives outside the agency's jurisdiction; (v) identify, if possible, the agency's preferred alternative; and (vi) include appropriate mitigation measures.[64]

The CEQ has prescribed that any EIS is to "succinctly describe" the environment of affected areas. Data and analyses concerning the affected environment are to be commensurate with the importance of the impact; less important material is to be summarized, consolidated or simply referenced.[65]

---

[59](..continued)
environmental effects which cannot be avoided should the proposal be implemented; (iii) Alternatives to the proposed action; (iv) The relationship between local short-term uses of man's environment and the maintenance and enhancement of long-term productivity; and (v) Any irreversible and irretrievable commitments of resources which would be involved in the proposed action should it be implemented.

[60] NEPA § 102(2)(C), 42 U.S.C. § 4332(2)(C).

[61] 40 C.F.R. § 1502.10; see also 40 C.F.R. § 1502.11 (cover sheet requirements).

[62] 40 C.F.R. § 1502.7 dictates that an EIS should not "normally" exceed 150 pages in length. 40 C.F.R. § 1502.8 requires that the agency employ "plain language" and 40 C.F.R. § 1502.12 mandates inclusion of a summary in the EIS. There is also a requirement that preparers be listed, 40 C.F.R. § 1502.17, and directions concerning the appendix, 40 C.F.R. § 1502.18.

[63] 40 C.F.R. § 1502.14.

[64] 40 C.F.R. § 1502.14.

[65] 40 C.F.R. § 1502.15.

Discussion of the environmental consequences of an action within the EIS is to be a consolidation of the consideration of criteria within Section 102(2)(C) of NEPA.[66] The discussion must include: (i) direct effects; (ii) indirect effects; (iii) possible conflicts with land use plans and controls for the area concerned; (iv) environmental effects; (v) energy requirements and conservation potential of various alternatives and mitigation measures; (vi) resource requirements and conservation potential of alternatives and mitigation measures; (vii) urban quality, historic and cultural resources and the design of the built environment; and (viii) means to mitigate adverse environmental impacts.[67]

Beyond this direction, the environmental effects which an agency must consider are not clearly delineated in the regulations. However, the Supreme Court cast some light on the subject in *Metropolitan Edison Co. v. People Against Nuclear Energy*,[68] which confronted the argument that damage to psychological health and community well-being are among the environmental effects which must be considered in an EIS. The court held that the statute was intended to embrace only effects on the "physical environment." While human health and welfare are goals of NEPA, Congress intended to reach those ends by protecting the physical environment. Hence, the court reasoned that the terms "environmental effects" and "environmental impacts" in Section 102(2)(C) should be read to require a reasonably close causal relationship between a change in the physical environment and the effect at issue. Because the psychological health damage at issue was so attenuated from the federal action at issue, the causal relationship was not sufficiently close to bring it within the reach of NEPA. Thus in recent cases involving challenges to Air Force communications systems, courts have held that the Air Force need not consider the effects of nuclear war, as the relation between nuclear war and the proposed system was too attenuated.[69]

In 1986, CEQ modified the provisions governing instances when information on environmental consequences is lacking. Where there is incomplete or unavailable information concerning reasonably foreseeable significant environmental effects of an alternative, an agency is to disclose the lack of information.[70] If this information is essential to a reasoned choice among alternatives and the overall cost to obtain the information is not exorbitant,

---

[66] 40 C.F.R. § 1502.16.

[67] 40 C.F.R. § 1502.16.

[68] 460 U.S. 766 (1983).

[69] *No GWEN Alliance of Lane County, Inc. v. Air Force Department*, 27 ERC 1487 (9th Cir. 1988).

[70] 40 C.F.R. § 1502.22.

the agency must include the information in the EIS. If such information cannot be obtained because the cost of obtaining it would be exorbitant or the means to obtain it are not known, the agency must include in the EIS a declaration that the information is lacking. Moreover, the agency must add a statement describing the relevance of the information to evaluating foreseeable significant adverse impacts, and its evaluation of such impacts based upon theoretical approaches or research methods generally accepted in the scientific community.[71]

This 1986 regulation supplants its predecessor, which called for a "worst case analysis" in certain circumstances.[72] The original regulation spawned a great deal of litigation[73] and presented agencies with a regulatory mandate which was ambiguous at best.[74]

The Supreme Court has applied the regulation in *Robertson v. Methow Valley Citizens Council*,[75] making clear that the courts of appeals must defer to agency decisions in conformity with that regulation.

Once the EIS is finalized, an agency is to consider its contents when making its decision on the action at issue.[76] At the time of its decision, the agency is to write a "record of decision"--a concise statement of its decision discussing its choice among alternatives and the means employed to mitigate or minimize environmental harm.[77] The regulations provide that, in most

---

[71] 40 C.F.R. § 1502.22. The provision applies to "reasonably foreseeable" impacts, which includes impacts which have a catastrophic effect, even if the probability of occurrence is low, so long as the analysis is supported by credible scientific evidence, is not based on pure conjecture and is within the rule of reason.

[72] 40 C.F.R. § 1502.22 (1985).

[73] *E.g., Save our Ecosystems v. Clark*, 747 F.2d 1240 (9th Cir., 1984); *Sierra Club v. Sigler*, 695 F.2d 957, 972 (5th Cir., 1983).

[74] As a condition to proceed with an agency action, the regulation required a "worst case analysis" and its probability when information relevant to adverse impacts is important to the decision and is not known. The probability of the "worst case" was not addressed. Hence, agencies found it difficult to discern the extent to which they were required to analyze very remote environmental effects. *See* also 51 Fed. Reg. 15618, 15625 (April 25, 1986) (explaining the 1986 regulation's approach).

[75] 109 S.Ct. 1835, 1847-49 (1989).

[76] See generally, 40 C.F.R. § 1501.1.

[77] 40 C.F.R. § 1505.2.

circumstances, the decision on the action may not be taken or recorded until the later of either ninety days after notice of the draft EIS is provided, or thirty days after notice of the final EIS is provided.[78]

The Supreme Court addressed the issue of necessary supplementation to impact statements in *Marsh v. Oregon Natural Resources Council*,[79] which was decided the same day as *Robertson v. Methow Valley Citizens Council*.[80] In the *Marsh* case, the Army Corps of Engineers was carrying out a series of flood control projects on the Rogue River in Oregon over a period of years. After completion of the initial impact statement and after construction of some of the projects, new information was submitted to the Corps suggesting that the effects of the projects on sedimentation, water turbidity, and salmon would be more severe than anticipated in the first impact statement. The Corps hired an independent consultant to evaluate the significance of the data, who concluded that the new data were not as significant as the proponents of them suggested. The Corps then decided that the impacts had already been sufficiently evaluated and declined to prepare a supplemental EIS. The Court of Appeals ruled that the Corps should have prepared a supplemental impact statement.[81]

The Supreme Court reversed, holding that the Corps had acted properly. In so holding, the Supreme Court laid out guidelines for supplementation of impact statements, placing a gloss on the CEQ regulation in process. That regulation requires agencies to supplement draft or final impact statements if there "are significant new circumstances or information relevant to environmental concerns and bearing on the proposed action or its impacts."[82] If there is major federal action still to occur, and the new information is sufficient to show that the remaining action will affect the quality of the human environment in a significant manner or to a significant extent not already considered, then a supplemental impact statement must be prepared.[83]

The Court applies a deferential standard of review in this context, holding that where the agency had taken steps to evaluate the factual significance of that new information, then the courts should only reverse where the agency's decision was arbitrary and capricious. Thus a court reviewing a decision not

---

[78] 40 C.F.R. § 1506.10(b).

[79] 109 S.Ct. 1851 (1989).

[80] 109 S.Ct. 1835 (1989).

[81] *Oregon Natural Resources Council v. Army Department*, 820 F.2d 1051 (9th Cir. 1987).

[82] 40 C.F.R. § 1502.9(c) (1989).

[83] 40 C.F.R. § 1508.7 (1989).

to prepare a supplemental impact statement should defer to agency's substantive expertise on highly technical issues, provided that the court reviews the record to assure itself that the agency in fact did make a reasoned decision based on its evaluation of the significance of the new data.[84]

## 5.0 NEPA'S RELATIONSHIP WITH OTHER FEDERAL LAW

One of the most fundamental NEPA concerns is its relationship with other federal law. More specifically, the question is this: How is NEPA to be construed with other federal laws that govern federal agencies?

Although the Supreme Court has held that a *final* EIS need not be prepared until an agency makes a recommendation or report on a proposal,[85] NEPA requires all federal agencies to *consider* environmental impacts at every important stage in the decisionmaking process. This requirement is not explicitly set forth in NEPA, but it is implicit in its various provisions. It was clearly enunciated in the still definitive case, *Calvert Cliffs' Coordinating Committee v. AEC.*[86]

*Calvert Cliffs'* involved Atomic Energy Commission (AEC) rules implementing NEPA, which, in part, provided that if no party to a proceeding raised any environmental issue, environmental issues would not be considered in the decisionmaking process. In reviewing this rule, the U.S. Court of Appeals for the District of Columbia Circuit Court said, "We believe that the Commission's crabbed interpretation of NEPA makes a mockery of the Act,"[87] and proceeded to wonder out loud what possible purpose there could be in requiring an EIS to "accompany the proposal through the existing agency review process" or, indeed, in requiring EISs at all, if agencies could simply ignore their contents. The court then found that:

---

[84] 109 S.Ct. 1851, 1961 (1989).

[85] *Aberdeen & Rockfish RR. Co. v. Students Challenging Regulatory Agency Procedures (SCRAP II)*, 422 U.S. 289 (1975), reaffirmed in dicta in *Kleppe v. Sierra Club*, 427 U.S. 390 (1976).

[86] 449 F.2d 1109 (D.C. Cir., 1971), *cert. denied*, 404 U.S. 942 (1972).

[87] 449 F.2d at 1117.

NEPA require[s] the . . . agencies to *consider* environmental issues just as they consider other matters within their mandate.[88]

Thus, *Calvert Cliffs'* added NEPA's environmental impact provisions to the decisionmaking criteria set forth in other federal law.

If NEPA requires agencies to consider environmental factors when making decisions, does NEPA then expand the authority of federal agencies beyond what is granted them under other federal law? There is no case holding that NEPA gives an agency any *direct* authority not otherwise afforded it by other federal law. NEPA, however, was enacted in order to provide federal agencies with a new tool for protecting the environment, and the authority to deny agency approval of actions that would result in unacceptable environmental consequences is implicit in the requirement that agencies consider the environmental consequences of an action before deciding to proceed with it. Thus, an agency's authority does appear to be expanded under NEPA, for an agency might well decide not to proceed with a project based on environmental concerns that, but for NEPA, might be found to be beyond the agency's power to consider.

A related issue is whether when an agency believes, on the basis of an EIS or otherwise, that on balance it should grant its approval *if* certain conditions are satisfied, but the agency does not have the regular, i.e., non-NEPA based, statutory authority to impose such conditions. For example, the United States Environmental Protection Agency (EPA) once conditioned a grant to Sussex County, Delaware for the construction of a sewage-treatment facility on the County's agreement to halt all rezoning plans (thus effectively blocking major planned construction) until a comprehensive land-use plan was completed. Did NEPA grant EPA the authority to lawfully withhold its approval until this condition was satisfied? The issue was never litigated, but is open to serious questions in light of at least one recent court of appeals decision construing the relationship between the Clean Water Act's new source provisions and NEPA.[89] How far an agency can go in expanding its authority under the aegis of NEPA, then, remains an open question of considerable importance.[90]

---

[88] 449 F.2d at 1112 (emphasis supplied).

[89] *Natural Resources Defense Council v. EPA*, 822 F.2d 104 (DC Cir., 1987). EPA maintains that it has the authority under NEPA to impose non-water quality related conditions in NPDES discharge permits under the Clean Water Act, based upon the findings of the EIS, or even to deny a permit on that basis. The agency has consistently asserted this authority in administering its permitting regulations under the Clean Water Act. *See* 49 Fed. Reg. 37998, 38016-38018 (September 26, 1984).

[90] *See Note, Implementation of the Environmental Impact Statement*, 88 Yale L.J. 596 (1979).

Conflicts between NEPA and provisions of other statutes is also a fundamental concern. Posed directly, the question is: does NEPA override another federal law when the two are in irreconcilable conflict? Sections 102(1), 103, 104 and 105 of NEPA all bear on this question. Section 102 "authorizes and directs that, to the fullest extent possible: (1) the policies, regulations, and public laws of the United States shall be interpreted and administered in accordance with the policies set forth in this Act." Section 103 requires all federal agencies to recommend to the president by 1 July 1971, the changes necessary to bring their authority and policies into conformity with NEPA. Section 104 provides that nothing in Sections 102 or 103 changes the specific statutory obligations of any federal agency to comply with other laws protecting the environment, to coordinate or consult with other federal or state agencies, or to act in accordance with the recommendations or certifications of any other federal or state agency. Section 105 simply states that the policies and goals set forth in NEPA are "supplementary" to the existing authorizations of federal agencies. These are the statutory provisions upon which the Supreme Court has twice rested decisions finding that NEPA does not override another federal law when the two conflict.

At issue in *United States v. Students Challenging Regulatory Agency Procedures (SCRAP I)*[91] was a District Court decision concerning the Interstate Commerce Commission's (ICC) authorization, without first preparing an EIS, of a railroad surcharge. The District Court held that NEPA empowered it to issue an injunction against the Commission's action, notwithstanding another federal law vesting sole and exclusive power from the judiciary. Reversing that decision, the Supreme Court held that NEPA was not intended to supplant other statutes.[92]

---

[91] 412 U.S. 669 (1973).

[92] The court held that, *The statutory language, in fact, indicates that NEPA was not intended to repeal by implication any other statute.*

Thus, Section 105 specifies that "the policies and goals set forth in NEPA are supplementary to those set forth in existing authorizations of federal agencies," and . . . Section 104 instructs that the Act "shall not in any way affect the specific statutory obligations of any Federal agency . . ." Rather than providing for any wholesale overruling of prior law, Section 103 of NEPA requires all federal agencies to review their "present statutory authority, administrative regulations, and current policies and procedures for the purpose of determining whether there are any deficiencies or inconsistencies therein which prohibit full compliance with the purposes and provisions of NEPA and shall propose to the President . . . such measures as may be necessary to bring their authority and policies into conformity with the intent, purposes, and procedures set forth in NEPA . . . It would be anomalous if Congress had provided at one and the same time that Federal agencies, which have the

(continued...)

In *Flint Ridge Development Co. v. Scenic Rivers Association, et al.*,[93] the Supreme Court reiterated the holding, but this time relied entirely on Section 102. *Flint Ridge* addressed the claim of environmental organizations that an EIS was required for approval of a land development project on which an antifraud disclosure document had been filed with the Department of Housing and Urban Development pursuant to the Interstate Land Sales Full Disclosure Act. That act provides that disclosure documents automatically become effective thirty days after filing (thus allowing sales in interstate commerce), unless suspended because of inadequate disclosure. The document at issue was not found to be an inadequate disclosure, nor was it disputed that an EIS could not be prepared within the thirty day period.

The Supreme Court, relying upon the principle announced in *SCRAP I*, and the language in Section 102, stating that "to the fullest extent *possible*" (emphasis supplied) all federal agencies shall comply with NEPA's requirements, concluded:

> Section 102 recognizes . . . that where a clear and unavoidable conflict in statutory authority exists, NEPA must give way.[94]

Thus, it is clear that NEPA will not prevail when it is in irreconcilable conflict with another federal law.

The courts have developed a "functional equivalency" test to determine whether regulatory action under another environmental statute will require EPA to prepare an EIS. In cases where EPA's failure to prepare an EIS concerning regulatory action has been challenged, the courts have examined the underlying environmental statute in order to determine whether EPA performed the functional equivalent of NEPA review under the other statute. Thus the courts have concluded that most of EPA's regulatory activities under the Clean Air Act, the Federal Insecticide, Fungicide and Rodenticide Act (FIFRA), the Marine Research, Protection, and Sanctuaries Act (MPRSA), and the Resource Conservation and Recovery Act (RCRA) require EPA to perform the functional

---

[92](..continued)
primary responsibility for the implementation of NEPA, must comply with the present law and ask for any necessary new legislation, but that courts may simply ignore what we described in the previous *Arrow* case as "a clear congressional purpose to oust judicial power. . . ." 412 U.S. at 694-695 (emphasis supplied and footnote omitted).

[93] 426 U.S. 776 (1976).

[94] 426 U.S. at 788.

equivalent of NEPA review so that separate NEPA review is unnecessary.[95] Under the Clean Water Act, the issue has largely been resolved by section 511(c).

## 6.0 "INTERNATIONAL" ENVIRONMENTAL STATEMENTS

There is nothing in Section 102(2)(C) to indicate that actions having international ramifications are to be treated any differently than others subject to the EIS requirement. Indeed, there is precedent for applying the EIS requirement to international programs.[96]

Nevertheless, federal agencies with international responsibilities expressed concern that compliance with EIS requirements could interfere with foreign policy objectives. As a consequence, these agencies and CEQ developed a program designed to accommodate these concerns while meeting the objectives of NEPA. In January of 1979, President Carter approved this program and issued Executive Order No. 12114.[97]

Although Executive Order No. 12114 is not formally based on NEPA, its objective is to further the purposes of the act. It is designed to insure that federal decisionmakers are informed of pertinent environmental considerations concerning actions having effects outside the geographical boundaries of the United States, and that such considerations are taken into account when decisions are made. The order prescribes the circumstances under which its requirements are applicable and also specifies a number of procedures that must be followed. Affected agencies are further required to develop their own implementing procedures.

Because it is not feasible, from a foreign policy viewpoint, to perform environmental reviews in connection with every action that has environmental impacts outside the United States, specific types of actions are exempted from the requirements of the Order. Examples are intelligence activities, arms

---

[95] *See Alabamians for a Clean Environment v. EPA*, 26 ERC 2116, 2121-22 (N.D.A1. 1987) and cases collected therein.

[96] *See, e.g., Sierra Club v. Coleman*, 405 F. Supp. 53 (D.D.C. 1975), *rev'd and remanded on other grounds*, 578 Fed. 384 (D.C. Cir., 1978), in which an EIS was assumed to be required for preliminary construction activities by the Federal Highway Administration in connection with a highway through Panama and Colombia. *Cf. Natural Resources Defense Council v. Nuclear Regulatory Commission*, 647 Fed. 1345 (D.C. Cir., 1981), in which the court declined to require an EIS for export of a nuclear reactor to the Philippines, holding that NEPA does not impose an EIS obligation with respect to impacts felt solely outside the United States.

[97] 44 Fed. Reg. 1957 (January 9, 1979).

transfers, and disaster and emergency relief action. Finally, the order specifically does not create any right of judicial review.

In the years since its issuance, the order has had little effect. Its lack of impact has been primarily due to three factors: (1) excepted actions far outnumber the actions to which the order's prescriptions are applicable; (2) even those agency actions to which the order does apply are not judicially reviewable; and (3) the Reagan administration had little interest in enforcing its provisions.

## 7.0 APPLICANT'S ENVIRONMENTAL REPORTS

In situations where the federal action involved is federal agency approval of a non-federal party's proposal, the agency is virtually certain to require an environmental report. The required contents of such a report prepared by an applicant for a permit or other authorization will vary, but are generally spelled out by the federal agency.

In practice, the agency's environmental assessment on which a FONSI may be based is often a rehash of the applicant's environmental report. And, as a practical matter, an EIS itself is often only as good as the applicant's environmental report. Thus, it is apparent that this report is critical to the EIS process and is a document on which the applicant should spend much care and effort.

Despite this, frequent difficulties arise from flawed environmental reports. A variety of problems stem from the frequent failure of such a report to reflect a thorough knowledge and appreciation of the law of NEPA. These problems are avoidable to a great extent. In particular, two potentially serious problems can readily be avoided.

The first problem arises from a failure to write carefully, or to think all the way through, the practical or legal ramifications of an issue or position. One should understand at the outset that an applicant's environmental report must state the relevant information in an honest and straightforward manner.[98] Too often, though, a careful examination of an applicant's environmental report reveals language that is an overstatement, understatement or misstatement of the facts and conclusions. This is damaging to the applicant, for reviewing courts look to the information that was before the agency when its decisions were made, and will not themselves undertake to build a more accurate factual record supporting the agency action. Thus, the agency's decision is apt to stand or fall on the accuracy of the applicant's environmental report.

The second problem that can arise in connection with applicants' environmental reports involves the ability of those who conduct the studies and analyses and prepare parts of the report to also serve as convincing

---

[98] There are very few instances of an applicant or an environmental consultant intentionally attempting to deceive.

expert witnesses if an agency hearing or court action arises at some point. No attempt will be made here to tell an applicant how to select an environmental consultant. Yet it can be a crucial flaw, in some cases, to discover too late that one has a barely qualified or inexperienced expert witness, or one who is unconvincing or offensive in oral presentations under pressure. Thus, it may be prudent for an applicant to make a careful assessment of the qualifications and the demeanor of the environmental consultant's personnel, particularly those who will be doing the actual work and thus would be the strongly preferred expert witnesses if the need arose.

## 8.0 THE SEVEN OTHER "ACTION-FORCING" PROVISIONS

In· addition to NEPA's EIS requirements, there are seven other "action-forcing" provisions in Section 102(2). They require federal agencies to: (A) utilize an interdisciplinary approach to planning and decisionmaking; (B) insure appropriate consideration of unquantified environmental values; (E) study and develop alternatives to proposals involving unresolved conflicts over use of resources; (F) recognize the worldwide and long-range character of environmental problems; (G) make usable environmental information generally available; (H) initiate ecological information for resource-oriented projects; and (I) assist the CEQ. These sections are discussed briefly below with a view to neither ignoring, nor overstating, their individual and cumulative potential for important practical significance in the years ahead.

The seven "other" provisions of Section 102(2) are often thought of as relatively unimportant appendages to the EIS requirement. There is, however, a body of case law indicating that courts view at least some of these provisions as imposing on federal agencies duties that are both independent of, and wider in scope, than NEPA's EIS requirement. This view suggests that increased attention to these provisions could cause a significant change in the nature and extent of scientific data and information that must be compiled by the agencies in order to comply with NEPA. For, as the boundaries of environmental science continue to expand, national concern over mitigation measures and post-operational monitoring programs is likely to increase concomitantly. Thus, the extra-EIS provisions of Section 102(2) may come to play an ever more important role in the law of NEPA, serving as the legal basis for requiring agencies to secure more and better scientific data on environmental impacts both before and after federal action is taken, whether or not an EIS is required.

Section 102(2)(A) authorizes and directs all agencies to "utilize a systematic, inter-disciplinary approach" in planning and decisionmaking through an integrated use of natural and social sciences and environmental design arts. This section has been held to apply to all federal decisions that may have an impact on the environment, even those that do not themselves require the preparation of an EIS.[99]

Hence, its provisions might also be used in conjunction with the EIS requirement to produce greater court scrutiny of federal agency decisions. The result could well be judicial opinions compelling a significantly more systematic and integrated disciplinary approach to planning and decisionmaking, an approach that employs "state-of-the-art" scientific techniques.

Section 102(2)(B) directs federal agencies to "identify and develop methods and procedures . . . which will insure that presently unquantified environmental amenities and values may be given appropriate consideration in decisionmaking along with economic and technical considerations." What Section 102(2)(B) does and does not do is described very well in the *Tennessee-Tombigbee* decision:

> [Section 102(2)(B)] cannot be fairly read to command an agency to develop or define any general or specific quantification process . . . [I]t requires no more than that an agency search out, develop and follow procedures reasonably calculated to bring environmental factors to peer status with dollars and technology in their decisionmaking.[100]

Section 102(2)(B) clearly adds to the list of factors that must be considered in the agency decisionmaking process, and thus also provides an additional basis upon which to review agency action.

Section 102(2)(E)[101] requires all federal agencies to "study, develop, and describe appropriate alternatives to recommended courses of action in any proposal which involves unresolved conflicts concerning alternative uses of available resources."[102] This section, like Section 102(2)(A), has been held to impose duties on federal agencies that are independent of NEPA's EIS

---

[99] *McDowell v. Schlesinger*, 404 F. Supp. 212 (D.C. Mo. 1975).

[100] *Environmental Defense Fund, Inc. v. Corps of Engineers*, 429 F.2d 1123, 1133 (5th Cir., 1974); *see also, Hanly v. Kliendienst*, 471 F.2d 823 (2nd Cir., 1972), *cert. denied*, 412 U.S. 908 (1973).

[101] This provision was originally Section 102(2)(D). It was redesignated when NEPA was amended by Pub. L. No. 94-83 (1975).

[102] The last part of Section 102(2)(E) appears to limit its application to only those proposals which involve unresolved conflicts concerning alternative uses of available resources. It is difficult, however, to conjure up good examples of choices involving environmental impact that are clearly outside the apparent limitation.

requirements. For example, in *Trinity Episcopal School Corp. v. Romney*,[103] the Court of Appeals for the Second Circuit reversed and remanded to HUD an agency decision to proceed with a low income housing project in New York City because HUD had not fully considered alternative sites for the project. The court came to this conclusion despite the fact that HUD's decision not to prepare an EIS for the project went unchallenged.

Section 102(2)(F) requires all federal agencies to "recognize the worldwide and long-range character of environmental problems" and to lend such support as is consistent with our foreign policy to international efforts to protect the world environment. This section has received almost no attention from the federal courts. It could in the future, however, provide a basis for claims that agencies must develop and consider more scientific data and information in order to assess "long-range" effects of federal actions, such as effects on global warming from federal energy research and development projects such as production of methanol. Though not explicitly based on section 102(2)(F), at least one court has held that challenges to energy projects because of a failure to consider the impacts of global warming does state a valid NEPA claim for purpose of a motion to dismiss.[104] It may also be used to buttress efforts to develop more comprehensive policies on international environmental protection issues.

Section 102(2)(G) requires all federal agencies to "make available to States, counties, municipalities, institutions, and individuals, advice and information useful in restoring, maintaining and enhancing the quality of the environment." This section has been of extremely limited practical utility with respect to particular projects. It does not require by its own terms disclosure of information different from that obtainable under the provisions of the Freedom of Information Act. Nor does it add much, if anything, to the Administrative Procedure Act requirement that an agency be fair with public participants and disclose the basis for its decisions.

Another "action-forcing" provision that has received only limited attention to date, but which has great potential significance, is Section 102(2)(H). This section provides that all federal agencies shall "initiate and utilize ecological information in the planning and development of resource-oriented projects." The usual agency practice, evidenced in many EISs, is to make decisions simply on the best *available* information at the time. The requirement to "initiate" ecological information, then, could be used to require agencies themselves to generate additional information on particular projects before reaching a final decision to proceed.

---

[103] 523 F. 2d 88 (2d Cir., 1975), *rev'd on other grounds following remand sub nom. Strycker's Bay Neighborhood Council v. Karlen*, 444 U.S. 223 (1979).

[104] *Center for Economic Trends v. Department of Energy*, 29 E.R.C. 2111 (D.D.C. 1990).

Section 102(2)(I) simply requires federal agencies to assist the Council on Environmental Quality. At most, this section slightly strengthens the hand of CEQ (which has relatively little funding or staff) when it wants the cooperation of other federal agencies in undertaking a major examination of an environmental problem area.

## 9.0 STANDING TO SUE FOR ALLEGED VIOLATIONS OF NEPA

Standing is an issue that has received a great deal of attention from the United States Supreme Court since 1970. In general, the Court's opinions on the issue are in conflict and a lengthy analysis of them yields little of predictive value. When environmental interests are at stake, however, the Court has consistently left the door to the courthouse wide open. A brief examination of the two leading Supreme Court decisions on standing in environmental cases reveals the limits to which the Court's liberal stand on this issue goes.

*Sierra Club v. Morton*[105] involved a challenge to agency approval of construction of the Mineral King Resort in the Sequoia National Forest. The Sierra Club treated the action as a test case, seeking to establish the principle that a membership organization with a "special interest" in the environment has standing to challenge action that would adversely affect the environment. Accordingly, the Sierra Club intentionally failed to allege that it or any of its members *actually used* the Mineral King Valley for recreational purposes. Although the Court held that aesthetic or environmental harm could constitute "injury in fact" sufficient to confer standing, it denied standing in this case because the Club had not pleaded facts establishing any such injury. The mere fact that the Club had a "special interest" in protecting the environment was not sufficient to allow the Club to challenge the agency action concerned.

The other leading Supreme Court decision on standing in the environmental area is *United States v. Students Challenging Regulatory Agency Procedures (SCRAP I)*[106]. *SCRAP I* is generally considered to be among the most liberal standing cases. There, an unincorporated association of law students sued the Interstate Commerce Commission for failing to prepare an EIS before allowing railroads to collect a surcharge on freight. They claimed to be "injured in fact" by the Commission's order because they used national parks and forests, and the order would raise the price of recycled materials, thereby discouraging the use of such materials. This, in turn, would lead to increased mining operations, which would consequently harm national recreational enclaves. The government claimed that the alleged chain of causation was too attenuated to

---

[105] 405 U.S. 727 (1972).

[106] 412 U.S. 669 (1973).

confer standing on the students. The Court, however, responded in a footnote that a "trifle" of injury in fact is enough.[107]   Although subsequent cases[108] cast some doubt on whether *SCRAP I* will be followed in the future, no case has directly reversed that decision, and it remains a leading precedent in the environmental area.   Thus, when violations of NEPA are alleged, anyone who can claim at least a "trifle" of "injury in fact" has standing to sue.

---

[107] *Id.*, at 689, n. 14.

[108] *See, e.g., Simon v. Eastern Kentucky Welfare Rights Organization*, 426 U.S. 26 (1976).  The Court's decision in *Lujan v. National Wildlife Federation*, 110 S.Ct. 3177 (1990), suggests that the courts are becoming far more insistent that the membership interests affected by the challenged decision be closely connected to the government decision being contested.  In that case, the Court upheld a district court decision to dismiss a challenge to the Interior Department's public land withdrawal policies.  The district court did so on standing grounds where the interests identified in members' affidavits were not sufficiently connected to the government actions begin challenged.

Chapter 7

TOXIC SUBSTANCES CONTROL ACT
(TSCA)

Marshall Lee Miller, Esq.
Washington, D.C.

## 1.0 INTRODUCTION

The problem of toxic chemicals, including pesticides and especially hazardous wastes, is acquiring increasing importance with the public realization that thousands of carcinogenic (cancer-causing), teratogenic (birth defect-causing) and mutagenic (genetic-damaging) substances are present in our environment. Both the World Health Organization and the National Cancer Institute have estimated that between 60 and 90 percent of cancers are environmentally induced.[1] The Toxic Substances Control Act (TSCA) of 1976 provides EPA with authority to require testing of chemical substances, both new and old, entering the environment and to regulate them where necessary. This authority supplements sections of existing toxic substances laws, such as Section 112 of the Clean Air Act,[2] Section 307 of the Water Act,[3] and Section 6 of the Occupational Safety and Health Act,[4] which already provide regulatory control over toxic substances. It may also be used to regulate the development of biotechnology and genetic engineering.

---

[1] See for example, "WHO Reports on Cancer," cited in *In re Shell*, 6 ERC 2047, 2051. The term "environment," of course, encompasses a wide range of possible exposures from industrial chemicals to food and cosmic radiation.

[2] Clean Air Act, 42 U.S.C. § 1857 *et seq.*, PL 91-604 (1970).

[3] Federal Water Pollution Control Act, 33 U.S.C. § 1251 *et seq.*, Pub. L. No. 92-500 (1972).

[4] 29 U.S.C. § 651 *et seq.*, Pub. L. No. 91-596, 84 Stat. 1950 (1970).

**1.1 TSCA Overview**

When enacted in 1976, the toxic substances statute was described as the most powerful of all the environmental laws; it was the single law that could cover all areas of environmental regulation if perchance the air, water, and other statutes ceased to exist. With hindsight, we see that the act has never lived up to these billings. Putting aside the hyperbola and hoopla, how has the law worked out in practice?

The premanufacture notification procedure has been applied to thousands of new chemicals, a few of which have been withdrawn by manufacturers after being challenged by EPA for more data. It is not clear, however, that more than a handful of those few were really withdrawn because of some danger to health and the environment, rather than because the producers were reluctant to expend more resources on fledgling chemicals with uncertain financial prospects.

For would-be producers trying to determine if a chemical is new and a PMN therefore necessary, the problem is becoming increasingly more difficult. The overwhelming majority of new chemicals placed on the inventory have been put on a confidential list. Even for those items on the public list, the difficulties of terminology and concept mean that identical substances can be called different chemicals, while quite different substances can be termed the same chemical.

These inconsistencies would be of little significance, except that in the past couple of years the slumbering TSCA enforcement section has finally stirred and is levying penalties in the millions of dollars for putative technical violations, few of which are even claimed to have any effect on the environment whatsoever.

Similarly, the agency has begun reinterpreting the record and reporting requirements of TSCA Section 8 and then penalizing companies which were not prescient enough to follow these changes, which have not been made part of the official regulations, before they were announced.

On the other hand, EPA enforcement has been virtually absent from the area where it should have been strongest, namely in action against hazardous chemicals under Sections 6 and 7 of TSCA. There have been almost no actions taken under the former, except those directed by Congress itself, and no cases at all under the latter provision which covers imminent hazards to man and the environment. This compares poorly with the utilization of the comparable provisions, cancellation and suspension respectively, of FIFRA against hazardous pesticides.

Thus, after a decade and a half of desultory existence, culminating in the latest wave of majoring on minors, a critical review of TSCA is in order.

**2.0 PROBLEM OF UNREGULATED CHEMICALS**

Prior to the passage of the Toxic Substances Control Act of 1976, there was no general federal requirement that the thousands of new chemicals developed each year be tested for their potential environmental or health effects before they were introduced into commerce. An estimated two million chemical compounds have been recognized, with thousands of additional substances being developed each year.[5] While most such chemicals never reach the market, EPA calculates that approximately a thousand of these new chemicals are produced annually in commercial quantities. Of these, only a fraction are subject to mandatory testing requirements under the Pesticide Act (FIFRA) or Food, Drug and Cosmetic Act (FDCA).[6]

Recent tragic experiences illustrate the consequences of this lack of testing. In the late 1960s, there arose national concern over the widespread contamination of food, water, and soil by certain highly toxic compounds of organic mercury. By 1972 the government had authority under the Clean Air Act and the Federal Water Pollution Control Act to control direct emissions of mercury into the environment, but there was no federal authority to require testing of the effects of various mercuric compounds or to regulate the multiple uses of mercury in industrial, commercial and consumer products.

Another episode in the early 1970s involved polychlorinated biphenyls (PCBs), used in such diverse applications as printing inks and dielectric fluids. PCBs are similar to DDT, Aldrin-Dieldrin, and other chlorinated hydrocarbons in their pervasiveness and persistence in the environment and in their suspected carcinogenicity.

A host of other chemicals have also received recent public attention. A partial list includes asbestos, lead (including tetraethyl lead), arsenic, fluorocarbons (freon), nitrosamines, methyl butyl ketone, cadmium, and fluorides.

Vinyl chloride was involved in one of the most publicized episodes. In January 1975, a link was confirmed between worker exposure to vinyl chloride monomer (VCM) and a rare form of cancer, angiosarcoma of the liver. Except for the extreme rarity of this disease and the unusual number of workers in whom it was found, the carcinogenic properties of VCM might have remained undetected. Medical experts now fear that it may also result in damage to the brain and other key organs. An OSHA standard in 1975 set a permissible limit at one part per million (1 ppm) but not before three decades of workers had

---

[5] *New York Times*, July 8, 1975, estimated as high as 250,000.

[6] Only three federal statutes give the government authority to require chemical manufacturers to test their products. They are the Federal Insecticide, Fungicide and Rodenticide Act, as amended (7 U.S.C. § 135 *et seq.*), dealing with pesticides; the Federal Food, Drug and Cosmetic Act, (21 U.S.C. § 321 *et seq.*) requiring testing of drugs and food additives; and Section 211 of the Clean Air Act (42 U.S.C. § 1857 *et seq.*), providing authority to require testing of fuel additives.

been exposed to levels as high as several hundred parts per million.[7]

The incident which contributed directly to the passage of TSCA was the discovery in mid-1975 that workers in a small Virginia manufacturing plant had sustained severe neurological and reproductive damage from exposure to the chemical Kepone. Federal and state health agencies were widely criticized for failure to prevent this tragedy. The head of one agency responded, "We could accomplish a great deal if we were able to keep track of what toxic chemicals are entering our environment. Toxic substances legislation ... is therefore an important need."[8] While Kepone may not actually be a good example of this need (as a pesticide, it had long been screened and registered with EPA), the national attention engendered by such tragedies finally prodded Congress to enact the Toxic Substances Control Act.

## 3.0 THE NEED FOR A TOXIC SUBSTANCES CONTROL ACT

Prior to the passage of the Toxic Substances Control Act, significant gaps existed in the federal government's authority to test and regulate problem chemicals. The Clean Air Act, the Federal Water Pollution Control Act, and other laws dealt with chemical substances only when they entered the environment as wastes (emissions to the air or discharges into the water). In many cases, controls could not be easily fashioned or required without severe economic consequences. Toxic substances legislation, which theoretically would require testing before a chemical reached the production phase, overcame this difficulty.

Other statutes, such as the Occupational Safety and Health Act and the Consumer Product Safety Act, deal only with one phase of the chemical's existence (worker exposure or direct consumer exposure) and contain no authority to address environmental hazards. While both of these statutes are clearly needed, the life cycle of a chemical, from production to ultimate disposal, provides many opportunities for its escape into the environment and human exposure, and federal authority to deal with the overall cycle is fragmented. The Toxic Substances Control Act was designed to fill these gaps, both in regulatory powers and in authority to require that tests be conducted before the human or environmental exposure occurs.

---

[7] OSHA "Vinyl Chloride Standard," 29 C.F.R. 1910, 1017. This was upheld unanimously by the Court of Appeals in *Society of Plastics Industry v. U.S. Dept. of Labor*, 509 F. 2d 131 (2nd Cir. 1975); the Supreme Court denied certiorari, sub. nom. *Firestone Plastics Co. v. U.S. Dept. of Labor*, 95 S. Ct. 1998 (1975).

[8] Testimony of the Assistant Secretary of Labor for OSHA before a Subcommittee of the Senate Committee on Agriculture and Forestry (February 2, 1976).

## 4.0 LEGISLATIVE BACKGROUND

In 1970, the President's Council on Environmental Quality recommended that the administrator of EPA be empowered "to restrict the use or distribution of any substance which he finds is hazardous to human health or the environment."

In the 93rd Congress, both houses approved toxic substance legislation, but were unable to reach a compromise in conference due to a fundamental disagreement over whether the proposed law would require new chemicals to be registered, as with pesticides or drugs, or simply that EPA be notified of plans to manufacture. After considerable debate, on March 26, 1975, the Senate of the 94th Congress passed S.3149 favoring the latter view by a vote of 60-13.

Three separate bills were introduced in the House. The first, H.R. 7229, was reported with amendments from the Subcommittee on Commerce to the full House Commerce Committee. A more limited bill, H.R. 12336, was supported by the Ford administration and most of the chemical industry. The third bill was supported by organizations such as Ralph Nader's Health Research Group. The bill that emerged, H.R. 14032, was a compromise that the House passed on August 23, 1976, and which the Senate found acceptable.

The final version of the Toxic Substances bill was enacted and signed into law by the President on October 11, 1976. It became effective on January 1, 1977 with the exception of Section 4(f) which only took effect two years later. In practice, without implementing regulations, none of the sections had immediate force on January 1, 1977 except for Section 8(e) requiring the reporting of significant adverse effects.

The Asbestos Hazard Emergency Response Act (AHERA) was passed on October 22, 1986, thereby adding Title II to the Toxic Substances Control Act. This amendment establishes asbestos abatement programs in schools.

## 5.0 TOXIC SUBSTANCES CONTROL ACT OF 1976

The Toxic Substances Control Act (TSCA) has two main regulatory features:

First, acquisition of sufficient information by EPA to identify and evaluate potential hazards from chemical substances;

Second, regulation of the production, use, distribution, and disposal of such substances where necessary.

The principal provisions of the act are described in the following sections.

### 6.0 PREMANUFACTURE NOTIFICATION --

The premanufacture notification (PMN) provisions in Section 5 of TSCA are the heart of the legislation, and are now the principal focus of EPA enforcement. The environmental benefits of this procedure are less clear. After a decade or more of experience, we cannot confidently assert the Section 5 has kept dangerous chemicals off the market, or that it has been worth anything near the growing difficulty of compliance. No one favors repeal, but it is fair to say that the experience has not lived up to its original, over-blown expectations.

#### 6.1 Statutory Provisions

Under Section 5(a), a manufacturer must notify EPA ninety days before producing a new chemical substance, defined as any chemical not listed on a specially compiled inventory list (discussed later). Notification is also necessary even for older chemicals, already on that list, if the administrator concludes that there is a significant new use which increases human or environmental exposure.[9] In either case, EPA may extend the notification processing period once for an additional ninety days, but the reasons for requiring longer consideration may be challenged in court.[10]

Many companies may wish to notify EPA well before the ninety day period in order to forestall last-minute delays in marketing. There are disadvantages to this, however: competitors will thereby be tipped off to the company's marketing plans, and EPA has warned that PMN data submitted too far in advance may be rejected as lacking sufficient certainty of the ultimate intention to manufacture.

Within five days of receiving the notice, EPA must publish in the *Federal Register* an item identifying the chemical substance, listing its intended uses, and a description of the toxicological tests required to demonstrate that there will be no "unreasonable risk of injury to health or the environment."

If the administrator decides that the data submitted is "insufficient to permit a reasoned evaluation" and that the chemical may pose a risk to man or the environment, he may restrict or even prohibit any aspect of the chemical's production or distribution. Such an order, however, must be issued no later than forty-five days before the expiration of the notification period, meaning that the agency must respond very quickly. The manufacturer then has thirty

---

[9] TSCA §5(a). The criteria the administrator must consider for a new use determination (Significant New Use Regulation -- SNUR) include the expected production volume, increased quantity or duration of human and environmental exposure, and hazards of manufacturing and distribution.

[10] TSCA §5(c). Such a challenge is subject to the confidentiality restrictions of Section 14.

days to submit specific objections to the order.[11]

Finally, for those chemicals on the priority list for which special testing is required, the administrator is required to publish in the *Federal Register* his reason for *not* taking action to limit production and use, before the end of the notification period.[12]

By statute, Section 5 was to take effect thirty days after the publication of the inventory list, which was due in November 1977. Since this did not occur until the summer of 1979, implementation of pre-manufacturing notification was delayed for almost three years after passage of the act.

### 6.2 PMN Regulations Proposed and Reproposed

In January 1979, EPA proposed voluminous PMN regulations,[13] which required not only the submission of data specified by Congress in Section 5(d) but also extensive reporting and recordkeeping derived presumably from Section 8.

An EPA-commissioned study estimated that the cost of complying with the regulations could range from $2,500 to $41,000, depending on the testing required. At the higher level, the study predicted, 90 percent of the new chemicals would not be introduced.[14] The irony is that the original EPA estimates on PMN costs, made before passage of the act, were negligible. They assumed that companies would be required to submit information which most would have developed anyway.[15] In October 1979, EPA responded to public criticism of its voluminous regulations by issuing a new PMN proposal.[16]

---

[11] TSCA § 5(e)(1). This description, although complex, is nevertheless an oversimplification.

[12] TSCA § 5(g). This publication, however, is not a prerequisite for the production or marketing of the product.

[13] 44 Fed. Reg. 2242 (January 10, 1979).

[14] Arthur D. Little, Inc., study of PMN costs.

[15] Letter from Gary H. Baise, Director of EPA's Office of Legislation, to Senator John V. Tunney (D-Calif.), no date but approximately June 1973, reprinted in Senate Commerce Committee Report No. 93-254 on S. 426, pp. 50-51.

[16] 44 Fed. Reg. 59764. EPA claimed this revised rule would reduce mandatory PMN compliance costs to a $1,200 - $8,900 range per chemical, provided neither health questions not confidentiality was raised. Despite requests, the October reproposal again did not provide special treatment for low-volume substances of, say, less than one metric ton a year.

### 6.3 PMN Policy and Final Regulations

In November 1980, just after the presidential election, the outgoing Carter administration published a revised interim policy to be followed until final rules were promulgated.[17] With the advent of the Reagan administration, a much-simplified PMN procedure was promised that would minimize the burden on the reporting industries, but this shorter version did not prove any easier to prepare. Thus, after almost seven years, no final regulation had yet appeared. Meanwhile, companies were complying with Section 5 as best they could, given EPA's shifting attitudes.

The PMN regulations, finally issued in May 1983,[18] require that any manufacturer who intends to commence the production of a new chemical substance for a non-exempt commercial purpose first submit a "Premanufacture Notice For New Chemical Substances" which shall include extensive test data such as health and environmental effects data for the substance, as well as environmental fate data. Any information on this notice may be claimed as confidential and all proposed manufacture, processing, or use operations must be described.

### 6.4 Importing Equals Manufacturing

It should be noted that the PMN regulations are also applicable to anyone who intends to import a new chemical substance, and that only manufacturers that are incorporated, licensed or doing business in the United States may submit a notice.[19] On April 19, 1988, BASF Corp. agreed to pay a $1.28 million penalty for violating the import provisions of TSCA.[20] Previously, the largest PMN penalty had been a May 1987 assessment of $1 million against AT&T.

This rule means that an importer, or broker, or even a company that replaces the middleman and begins purchasing directly from foreign suppliers is liable for PMN violations.

### 6.5 Testing Guidelines Under Section 5

Under Section 5(e), the administrator is empowered to seek an injunction to prevent the manufacture or distribution of a substance for which data is insufficient and from which there might be an unreasonable risk. Producers naturally wished to know what data EPA would regard as sufficient, because of their concern that Section 5(e) might be used to delay production indefinitely.

---

[17] 45 Fed. Reg. 74378 (November 7, 1980).

[18] 48 Fed. Reg. 21742 (May 13, 1983); codified at 40 C.F.R. § 720.

[19] 40 C.F.R. § 720.22.

[20] BNA Chemical Regulation Reporter, April 22, 1988.

Manufacturers' concern was heightened by a provision in the proposed PMN regulation that the 90-day clock would stop on a notice found to be deficient in some respect.[21] Despite agency denials, many companies feared that this was an imaginative loophole created to extend the statutory 90/180-day notice period and thereby to convert the process into a certification program akin to FIFRA or FDA.

For that reason, in March 1979 EPA's proposed guidelines for PMN testing under Section 5,[22] rather than under Section 4 which generally authorizes TSCA's testing rules.

Each PMN submitted must contain all test data in the applicants' possession or control concerning the new substance and its possible effects on health or the environment resulting from any activity for which it may be used. This includes data concerning the new substance in a pure, technical grade or formulated form. More specifically, a full report shall include the following: health effects data, ecological effects data, physical and chemical properties data, environmental fate characteristics and monitoring data related to human exposure to and environmental release of the substance. If the data appear in published scientific literature, a standard literature citation must be included with any information submitted in this form.

## 6.6 Exemptions and Alternatives in the PMN Process

### 6.6.1 PMN Exemption: Section 5(h)(4)

The statute provides that the administrator can exempt a manufacturer of a new substance from all or part of PMN if he decides that its production, distribution, use and disposal "will not present an unreasonable risk of injury to health or the environment."[23]

In 1980, Polaroid petitioned EPA for a blanket exemption on minor changes made from time to time in the formulation of instant photographic film.[24] After similar requests from other companies, prolonged debate, and an initial rejection of the exemption by the White House's Office of Management and Budget (OMB) as (ironically) too restrictive,[25] the agency finally approved the first Section 5(h)(4) exemption in a rule published in June 1982.[26]

---

[21] 44 Fed. Reg. 2242 at 2272.

[22] 44 Fed. Reg. 16240 (March 16, 1979).

[23] TSCA § 5(h)(4).

[24] See BNA, *Chemical Regulation Reporter*, October 17, 1980, p. 913.

[25] *Ibid.*, October 23, 1981, p. 803; October 30, 1981, p. 819.

[26] 47 Fed. Reg. 24308 (June 4, 1982).

### 6.6.2 The Polymer "Exemption"

In July 1982, in response to industry petitions, EPA proposed other rules under Section 5(h)(4) which would exempt about half of all new chemicals produced in the U.S.[27] They would provide that manufacture of certain polymers, chemicals used solely at the plant site, and low volume chemicals (defined generally by the companies as 25 thousand pounds annually.)[28] For chemicals produced in volumes under one thousand kilos a year, only a brief notice was to be submitted to EPA under the polymer exemption proposal: namely, manufacturer's name, location, chemical identity, and the polymer's molecular weight. Another category of polymers, those produced in quantities of between one thousand and ten thousand kilograms annually, would have to be submitted with somewhat more information under an abbreviated 14-day PMN. Environmentalists, such as the NRDC, predictably reacted with alarm to the proposals.[29]

Since long-chain polymers were not likely to be a hazard to man and the environment. After an extended comment period and a review of approximately a thousand polymer PMNs submitted to that date, EPA was reluctant to certify that no hazard at all existed, though none so far had been found. The agency therefore deferred a fuller exemption, pending longer experience, but did allow a shortened review period of 21-days for polymers. A broader review of polymer safety is in order. Meanwhile, the careless use of the term "polymer exemption" has sometimes mislead people into believing that a more comprehensive exclusion applies. So far, it does not.

### 6.6.3 Low Volume Chemicals

In April 1985 EPA published a rule expediting PMN review for low-volume chemicals (described as 1,000 kilograms or less a year). A chemical eligible for this exemption undergoes a 21-day review, rather than a 90-day, and has fewer information requirements.[30]

---

[27] 47 Fed. Reg. 32609 (July 28, 1982).

[28] Section 26 provides that action taken for a single chemical may also be taken for a group; so, to grant a broad Section 5(h)(4) exemption, EPA must follow the rulemaking procedures of TSCA § 6(c)(2) and (3). Within five days of receipt, EPA under Section 5(d)(2) must publish in the Federal Register, subject to Section 14 provisions on confidentiality, information on the new substance and its uses. Section 5(c) allows a 90-day extension period, if necessary for good cause, subject to Section 5(e) and (f) regulatory triggers.

[29] BNA, *Chemical Regulation Reporter*, July 30, 1982, p. 555.

[30] 50 Fed. Reg. 16477 (April 26, 1985).

### 6.6.4 R & D Exemption

The manufacturer or importer of a chemical substance manufactured or imported only in small quantities[31] solely for research and development may be exempt from notification requirements if certain qualifications are met (40 CFR 720.36). Among these qualifications are that the substance be used only under the supervision of a "technically qualified individual," and that all employees of the manufacturer or importer, or persons to whom it directly distributes the chemical substance who might come in contact with it, must be notified of any health risks that might be associated with the substance. Therefore, it would be necessary for the manufacturer or importer to have in its possession or control some information concerning the possible health and environmental effects of the chemical substance. No exemption is given for any substance distributed in commerce (40 CFR 720.36(d)), although the distinction may not be a clear one.

### 6.6.5 The Test Marketing Exemption

Under TSCA § 5(h)(1) EPA may, at its discretion, grant approval of a test marketing exemption (TME), thereby granting the applicant an exemption from some of the PMN requirements if the agency finds that the manufacture, processing and distribution in commerce, use and disposal of the substance for test marketing purposes "will not present any unreasonable risk of injury to health or the environment."[32] However, EPA may impose restrictions on test marketing activities or may change the terms of or revoke an exemption if it receives new data that casts significant doubt on former findings.

### 6.7 Small Business Under the Act

Under the act, "small business" is defined quite differently in the various sections. In Section 8(a) on certain recordkeeping and reporting, the level is $30 million; in the Section 8(b) inventory reporting requirements the determinative amount is $5 million; and in Section 5's provisions on supplementary reporting, the cutoff is a minuscule $1 million.

### 6.8 Significant New Use Regulations (SNURs)

Although commonly forgotten, Section 5's PMN requirement applies not only to new chemicals but to significant new uses of existing chemicals or even an

---

[31] Small quantities means quantities of a chemical substance manufactured, imported or processed or proposed to be manufactured, imported or processed solely for research and development that are not greater than reasonably necessary for such purpose. A presumption for quantities under one thousand pounds was in the original Section 5 proposed regulations but was dropped from the final version. This was retained for Section 8(b) inventory regulations, 43 Fed. Reg. 9254-55, March 6, 1978.

[32] 40 C.F.R. § 720.38.

appreciable increase in their utilization for an existing purpose. According to Section 5(a)(2), relevant factors include:

(A)    the projected volume of manufacturing and processing of a chemical substance,

(B)    the extent to which a use changes the type of form of exposure of human beings or the environment to a chemical substance,

(C)    the extent to which a use increases the magnitude and duration of exposure of human beings or the environment to a chemical substance, and

(D)    the reasonably anticipated manner and methods of manufacturing, processing, distribution in commerce, and disposal of a chemical substance.

Determining when a use is a new one, especially for a chemical already having scores of applications, can be difficult. EPA found that drafting rules concerning a multitude of such situations was even harder than anticipated. After several unsuccessful attempts, the agency decided to issue SNURs on an ad hoc basis. Then, after a pattern perhaps developed, regulations could be prepared.

The first final SNUR, on two potassium phosphate chemicals, was issued only in September 1984. The manufacturer was required to notify EPA if the concentration of these substances in consumer products exceeded 5 percent in order to avoid eye irritation.[33] In another case, at the same time, the agency decided to use the monitoring authority of Section 8(a), rather than issue a SNUR on a chlorinated naphthalene.[34]

On July 27, 1988, EPA published in the *Federal Register*[35] amendments to the General Provisions of the Significant New Use Rules (SNURs). Once EPA determines the use of a chemical substance to be a "significant new use," persons who intend to manufacture, import or process the substance for that use must submit a SNUR to EPA at least 90 days before beginning to manufacture, import or process the substance for that use. Persons submitting a SNUR must comply with the same regulations as those submitting a PMN.

A person may begin an activity designated as a significant new use in a proposed SNUR until such SNUR is promulgated and becomes effective, at

---

[33] 49 Fed. Reg. 35011 (September 5, 1984).

[34] 49 Fed. Reg. 33649 (August 24, 1984).

[35] 53 Fed. Reg. 28354.

which time they then must stop, file a SNUR, and then wait for EPA's review of the notice before resuming the activity. Compliance with these new rules can be completed in advance if a company submits a SNUR to EPA prior to the promulgation of the final SNUR. However, should EPA's 90-day review period of the SNUR extend beyond the final promulgation date of the SNUR, the person must still cease to manufacture, import or process the chemical for the time remaining.

Provisions for an R&D exemption from the rule are identical to those for PMNs[36] as long as the manufacturer, importer or processor notifies persons who will participate in the research and development of any and all possible health effects associated with the substance.

### 6.9 Rejection of PMNs

Since the purpose of Section 5 PMN process is to screen out harmful substances before they enter commercial production, EPA has to reject certain of the PMN or SNUR submissions.[37] This is more complex than it seems, for most chemicals are potentially hazardous under some circumstances. Although that is also true of pesticides, they are generally used in more precisely defined conditions, whereas there can be no certainty how many different uses will be found for a newly-introduced chemical substance. Not surprisingly, therefore, EPA's first rejection of a PMN, in December 1979, was for failing to include specific data required under the statute.

Under Sections 5(e) and 5(f) of the act, if the administrator determines that there could be environmental risk and that the information provided is inadequate to make a "reasoned evaluation", he may prohibit chemical production.[38] If the agency decides that there is an actual indication of hazard, rather than simply insufficient evidence to rebut, Section 5(f) provides that it may prohibit, limit, or otherwise restrict production or use, as set forth in various portions of Section 6.[39] Initially, the manufacturers' withdrawal of PMNs when challenged for more data was seen as a vindication of the program. However, for many chemical manufacturers, the costs of responding to anything more than a routine challenge to a PMN is not

---

[36] 40 C.F.R. 720.36.

[37] In December 1979, EPA rejected its first PMN because of inadequate information concerning production volume, disposal methods and other essentials. The company, which EPA declined to identify, responded that it had assumed only the facts set forth in Section 5(d)(2) were needed. The reply was unconvincing because Section 5(d)(1), specifying the required data, referred directly to the information listed in Section 8(a)(2)

[38] TSCA, § 5(e).

[39] TSCA, § 5(f), esp. (f)(2) referring to TSCA §§ 6(a) and 6(a)(2)(B).

worthwhile. Thus, we cannot be confident that the number of withdrawn submissions is any indication of the value of the Section 5 program.

The first Section 5(e) notice, announced in April 1980, proposed delaying the manufacture of six new but questionable chemicals. The firm dropped its manufacturing plans shortly thereafter.[40]   In September 1980, EPA issued another order to block production of a new chemical pending development of additional information on its human health rules.[41]   That has been the pattern, and to date no manufacturer, either foreign[42] or domestic, has contested the EPA determinations as far as federal district court, as permitted in Section 5(f).[43]

It is still not clear under the law what happens next, for the statute is ambiguous; there are as yet no court decisions, and the legislative history offers two inconsistent views. Senator Warren Magnuson (D-Wash.) explained that the House-Senate compromise language here was based on procedure in the FDA law,[44] whereby the agency could determine that valid objections had merit: "If the Administrator determines that valid objections have been filed, then he is required either to seek an injunction or to dismiss the order. If he decides that the objections are not reasonable, then the proposed order becomes effective upon the expiration of the premarket notification."[45]   Rep. James T. Broyhill (R-N.C.), on the other hand, informed the House that a company objection, no matter how frivolous, blocks the effect of the administrator's order and forces him to resort to a federal district court for injunctive relief.[46]

When EPA concludes that there is significant information to classify a chemical as an unreasonable risk, it may issue a proposed order restricting manufacture, processing or distribution.   It may also directly seek an

---

[40] *Ibid.*

[41] *Ibid.*

[42] BNA, *Chemical Regulation Reporter*, October 16, 1981, p. 787.

[43] TSCA, § 5(f)(3)(B).

[44] Food, Drug, and Cosmetic Act § 701(e); see also *Pfizer v. Richardson*, 434 F.2d 536 (2nd Cir., 1970).

[45] 122 Congressional Record 16803, September 28, 1976:   see TSCA § 5(e)(2). The Senate interpretation seems more consistent with the actual language of the act and is probably the approach which EPA will adopt.

[46] *Ibid.*, H-11344.

injunction which, like the above procedure for insufficient data, is also necessary if a company challenges the prospective order.[47]


## 7.0 INVENTORY LIST: SECTION 8(b)

The inventory provisions of the act seem obvious and straight-forward, a mere appendage of the crucial section on PMN. Only recently, however, has the realization grown that this portion of TSCA is exceedingly complex and, possibly, could be one of the gravest defects of the act.

### 7.1 The Role of the Inventory

Because the notification rules apply primarily to new chemical substances, there obviously needs to be a list available of pre-existing chemicals. Under Section 8(b), EPA was therefore required to compile an inventory of chemicals manufactured or processed in the United States. This was not to cover every chemical ever produced but was statutorily limited to those substances produced within the three-year period preceding the promulgation of applicable regulations, namely since January 1, 1975.[48]

The statute required that this list be prepared and published "not later than 315 days after the effective date of this act." This November 11, 1977, deadline proved far too optimistic, for the inventory reporting regulations were not even published until late December 1977, six weeks afterward.[49] This gave chemical companies until May 1, 1978, to submit their products for inclusion in the inventory, which was finally scheduled for publication in June 1979.[50] Processors and importers had an additional 210 days to report any other chemicals, and only after that was a final revised inventory list published.[51] This process thus turned into a rather lengthy one, which

---

[47] TSCA, § 5(f). See also Enforcement, Part 11.0.

[48] TSCA § 8(b). The regulations according to Section 8(a) were supposed to have appeared 180 days after the effective date or July 1, 1977. However, they were signed on December 12, 1977 effective July 1, 1978.

[49] 42 Fed. Reg. 64572 (December 23, 1977). Regulations were first proposed on March 9, 1977 (42 Fed. Reg. 13130) and after modification, were reproposed on August 2, 1977 (42 Fed. Reg. 39182).

[50] Some manufacturers complained that EPA itself should have compiled the basic inventory list and then asked chemical companies only to fill in any gaps. This proposal was rejected as infeasible. See, e.g. Appendix A, Comment 2, 42 Fed. Reg. 64580.

[51] 42 Fed. Reg. 64572 (December 23, 1977).

consequently considerably delayed the implementation of other parts of the act, particularly premarket notification.[52]

Any substance not reported for the Inventory by August 30, 1980, or subsequently added through the PMN process, must undergo premanufacture review before it may be manufactured or imported for a commercial purpose. This applies even if a producer can demonstrate that a substance was, in fact, produced before then. The converse, however, does not hold true: From time to time, EPA has removed from the list certain substances which it claims were improperly registered as commercial products and hence "grandfathered," when in fact they were only in research and development at the time.[53]

The inventory list is also updated as new PMNs are submitted. This is available by computer or, every few years, in a multi-volume hardcopy edition.

## 7.2 Characterization of a Substance

EPA has engaged in considerable debate on whether the particular production process should affect the definition of a substance on the inventory list. Initially, the agency said it did. In the case of one common substance, sulfuric acid, EPA ruled that since the chemical on the 8(b) list was produced by a method using different raw materials, an identical chemical with identical properties produced by another method was not considered to be on the inventory list and hence was not "grandfathered." In early 1984, however, the agency reconsidered the logic of this position and reversed this stance. In November 1984, EPA made a similar decision in agreeing that petroleum produced by the synfuels process was indeed petroleum and hence no new PMN was needed.

EPA periodically updates the inventory list to include products for which notification forms have been submitted. The most recent compilation was released in 1988. Future manufacturers can therefore consult the revised list and know that no further notification to EPA is required, unless special testing under Section 4 is necessary.

## 7.3 Problems of the Inventory

While there is a mechanism for discovering if a chemical is on this list, it is complex, limited to companies filing a notice of intent to manufacture, and prone to human error by EPA officials who find the inventory list only slightly less inscrutable than scientists outside the agency. That points to the single biggest problem with the inventory: chemical nomenclature is an

---

[52] EPA published inventory reporting regulations on December 23, 1977 (42 Fed. Reg. 64572). A cumulative supplement and revised inventory was published in the Federal Register on July 29, 1980 (45 Fed. Reg. 5544), and a revised version appeared in 1988.

[53] BNA, *Chemical Regulation Reporter*, August 7, 1981, p. 428; June 18, 1982, p. 390.

arcane field, exacerbated by the fact that EPA uses a system quite different from that commonly used by most of the chemical industry, and there can be considerable ambiguity as to how the more complex substances might be characterized. (As noted above, this is most notable in the case of polymers, long strings of repeating monomers that now comprise around half of all new chemical submissions.) It can be technically difficult to determine when a chemical is the same as. or different from, an existing formulation. It is even more difficult when the vast majority of new chemicals have been placed on EPA's confidential list, where they can be checked only imperfectly. (see below) The present system is scientific nonsense and, since EPA can and does impose millions of dollars of fines for these "offenses", the system is also legally infirm. While there may be no perfect inventory system, the present TSCA inventory is badly in need of serious revision.

## 7.4 Searching the Confidential Inventory List

A manufacturer seeking to discover whether a substance requires a PMN would first search the Inventory list. Failing to find the substance, however, would not be dispositive; it might be on the confidential list, as are roughly 90% of the new entries. The manufacturer can therefore elect to prepare a full PMN, even though EPA would just send it back as unnecessary if the chemical was secretly listed. Or the company could submit to EPA a notice of "bona fide intent to manufacture" and likewise be informed whether or not the substance was on the list. Considering the growing difficulty in submitting acceptable PMNs, the latter approach would seem clearly preferred. It is not. Whereas EPA has to race the clock in reviewing PMNs, it has no time limit to respond to notices of intent, which often are accorded much lower priority. There have also been instances, although illogical, in which data requested for the intent notices was more onerous than for PMNS.

## 8.0 REPORTING REQUIREMENTS

### 8.1 Section 8(a)

There are some chemicals about which EPA has concern but not enough to warrant immediate regulations or restrictions. For these, the agency needs to gather information on use, production volume, and other aspects which could affect human exposure and the eventual need for controls. This data can be collected for a specified list of chemicals under Section 8 of TSCA.

Under Section 8(a) of TSCA, the administrator must promulgate rules under which each person who "manufactures or processes or proposes to manufacture or process a chemical substance" must keep records and make reports to the administrator as is deemed necessary for the effective enforcement of the act. The administrator may require such information as molecular structure, categories of use, amounts produced, description of by-products, disposal methods, and all existing data concerning the environment and health effects of each substance. Manufacturers and processors are persons who manufacture or process chemicals for "commercial purposes."

Section 8 generally exempts small manufacturers or processors from the provisions, although they may be subject under certain circumstances.[54]   In the case of manufacturers or processors of mixtures or small quantities of research and development chemicals, reports and records may be required to the extent "necessary for the enforcement of this Act."

## 8.2 Regulations on Section 8(a)

Rules governing Section 8(a) were to be promulgated no later than 180 days after TSCA went into effect in 1977, but in fact rules were not even proposed until February 29, 1980.[55]

The proposal required chemical manufacturers, including miners, importers, and some processors, to report production and exposure-related data on approximately 2,300 chemicals, chosen because of toxicity or exposure levels. EPA intended to use this data for preliminary risk assessment and for ranking chemicals.

The final Section 8(a) regulation, when issued in June 1982,[56] cut the reporting list down drastically from almost 2,300 to only 245 chemicals. Manufacturers must report production, release and exposure data, which will then be used to determine which chemicals deserve further testing.[57]

EPA also published concurrently a three-part proposed rule under Section 8(a), requiring processors to report on the listed 245 chemicals whenever the manufacturers' reports fail to account for use of 80 percent of the substance. The proposal added another 50 chemicals for consideration for inclusion in the final list.[58]

Subsequently, EPA has indicated an intention to use Section 8(a) to monitor suspect chemicals that are not deemed to merit regulation under Sections 4(f), 5(e), 6 or other sections.  There are also plans to follow up all PMN chemicals for several years using this procedure.[59]

On June 12, 1986, EPA issued a final inventory update[60] under Section 8(a)

---

[54] Section 8(a)(3)(A)(ii).

[55] 45 Fed. Reg. 13646.

[56] 47 Fed. Reg. 26992 (June 22, 1982).

[57] See, e.g., 49 Fed. Reg. 25856 (June 1984).

[58] 47 Fed. Reg. 26992 (June 22, 1982); BNA *Chemical Regulation Reporter*, June 25, 1982, p. 412 and 423ff; April 2, 1982, p. 3.

[59] See, e.g., *ibid.*, March 9, 1984, p. 1707.

[60] 51 Fed. Reg. 21438.

requiring manufacturers and importers of certain chemical substances in the TSCA Chemical Substances Inventory to report current data on the production, volume, plant site, and site-limited status of the substances. Four categories of substances are generally exempt: polymers, inorganic substances, micro-organisms, and naturally occurring substances. Small manufacturers and firms making less than 10,000 pounds of a subject chemical per year are also exempt. After the initial reporting, recurring reporting will be required every four years for as long as the rule is in effect.

In October 1986, EPA proposed a comprehensive assessment information rule (CAIR) under Section 8(a) which would be used by the agency to gather information for use in risk assessments and in developing regulatory strategies for 47 substances.[61] It

-- required a 100-page standardized report
-- would allow EPA to add chemicals to the CAIR list in a shorter period of time than the current procedures allow
-- would centralize data collection in the Office of Toxic Substances

## 8.3 Reporting of Health and Safety Studies: Section 8(d)

Section 8(d) requires the administrator to promulgate rules requiring any person who manufactures, processes, or distributes in commerce any chemical substance or mixture to submit to the administrator:

(1) lists of health and safety studies (A) conducted or initiated by or for such person with respect to such substance or mixture at any time, (B) known to such person, or (C) reasonably ascertainable by such person, except that the administrator may exclude certain types or categories of studies from the requirements of this subsection if the administrator finds that submission of lists of such studies are unnecessary to carry out the purposes of this act; and

(2) copies of any study contained on a list submitted pursuant to paragraph (1) or otherwise known by such person.[62]

In July 1978, EPA promulgated rules governing this subsection of TSCA,[63] requiring manufacturers, processors, or persons distributing in commerce the chemicals on the first Interagency Testing Committee priority list to submit

---

[61] 51 Fed. Reg. 35762.

[62] TSCA, § 8(d)(a) and 8(d)(2).

[63] 43 Fed. Reg. 30984 (July 18, 1978).

lists and copies of health and safety studies on those chemicals.[64]

The Manufacturing Chemists Association filed a petition requesting EPA to amend or repeal the rule in September 1978. EPA rejected the petition, with minor exceptions.[65]

A petition for review of the rule filed on September 15, 1978, by Dow Chemical Company questioned EPA's authority to obtain studies on chemicals manufactured or processed for research and development purposes, since it was claimed such chemicals are not manufactured or processed for "commercial purposes." Although the Court denied Dow's challenge of EPA's authority on August 24, 1979,[66] EPA decided that Dow has raised substantial questions on whether adequate notice and comment were provided with respect to some provisions of the rule. Therefore, the rule was revoked on January 31, 1979.[67]

The final rule, which appeared in September 1982,[68] after extensive public comment, somewhat reduced the reporting requirements set forth in the earlier rule.

First, the sweeping definitions of "known to" or in the "possession of" were replaced with a procedural definition that would better indicate when an extensive search could be considered final for purposes of the act. Companies, henceforth, need only search "the company files in which they ordinarily keep studies and records kept by employees whose assigned duty is to advise the company on health and environmental effects of chemicals."[69] This search may be limited to records developed after December 31, 1979, when the revised rule 8(d) was proposed.

However, companies which manufactured a chemical within the past ten years, even if they are not currently doing so, are obliged to submit copies of studies but need not provide lists of other known studies. This could be helpful where, say, a company's research uncovered that one of its chemicals was potentially harmful and therefore discontinued it, although other manufacturers continued production unaware.

Distributors are exempted from Section 8(d) reporting by this revised

---

[64] Two minor corrections were made to the rule shortly thereafter ((43 Fed. Reg. 36249 (August 16, 1978) and 43 Fed. Reg. 41205 (September 15, 1978)).

[65] 43 Fed. Reg. 56724 (December 4, 1978).

[66] *Dow Chemical Co. v. EPA*, 605 F.2d 673 (3rd Cir., 1979).

[67] 44 Fed. Reg. 6099.

[68] 47 Fed. Reg. 38780 (September 2, 1982) 40 C.F.R. Part 716.

[69] *Ibid.*

regulation. They do not normally conduct studies anyway, and a review of all submissions under the provisions of the Section 8(d) rule indicated none were from distributors.

Also exempted were seven types of studies that the agency had not found useful in assessing risks but which were burdensome to compile. These exceptions include studies of impurities (which, however, would presumably exempt reports on, say, hazardous dioxin impurities), published studies, and studies submitted previously to EPA or on a non-confidential basis to another federal agency.

EPA declined, however, to retreat from its previous position that research and development studies are nevertheless "for commercial purposes" and therefore reportable. Because the agency's contention had already been judicially approved, a subsequent change would have been difficult. The final rule nevertheless relied on a different argument, namely that the purpose of Section 8(d) "is to give the agency access to information from which it can assess the nature and significance of chemical hazards and risks to health or the environment whether or not the chemicals are desired commercial products."[70]

## 8.4 Reports of Health and Safety Studies

Companies routinely test their chemical products for efficiency and safety. Section 8(d) directs that EPA issue rules requiring any person manufacturing, etc., a chemical to provide the agency with copies of such health and safety studies.[71] But the rule is broader than just that. If the company has copies of, knows of, or reasonably could ascertain that other experimental reports or studies exist regardless of who performed or conducted them, it must also provide copies or lists of those reports.[72]

The administrator is given the statutory authority to exclude certain categories of studies, however, if he determines they are "unnecessary to carry out the purposes of this Act."[73]

This seemingly straightforward section has been the source of considerable controversy. One issue involved a query from a major industry-supported but independent testing lab which had important studies; since it was not a manufacturer, however, it contended it had no obligation under Section 8(d) to report them to EPA. (The information was, of course, provided to EPA in due course.)

A chemical company challenged an obligation to report studies conducted

---

[70] *Ibid.*, p. 38781.

[71] TSCA, § 8(d)(1)(A).

[72] TSCA, § 8(d)(1)(B), (C), and 8(d)(2).

[73] TSCA § 8(d)(1)(C).

for research and development on substances produced in small quantities and not offered for sale. The company contended that the statutory definition of "manufacture" under Section 8 meant "manufacture or process for commercial purposes" and that this excluded R&D.[74] The Court of Appeals held, however, that Section 8(d) included just such limited manufacture and, therefore, EPA was authorized to seek the data.[75]

In September 1982, EPA issued a final rule requiring companies to provide the agency with unpublished studies.[76] The specifically requested information on forty chemicals and chemical categories -- thirty-nine recommended for Section 4(e) testing by the eight-agency federal Interagency Testing Committee (ITC) through June 1981 (actually about 175 substances), plus asbestos added by EPA.[77]

At the same time, the agency proposed adding another sixty-five chemicals more recently recommended by the ITC.[78]

## 9.0 HAZARD REPORTING REQUIREMENTS

These Section 8 reporting obligations are becoming more important as the realization grows that the high expectations for Section 5 PMN procedures was unwarranted as a method for uncovering potential environmental hazards. Ironically, this after-the-fact uncovering of hazards undermines the principal reason for TSCA, which was to discover hazards without making workers and others the guinea pigs for several decades.

Another irony is that just as industry was adjusting to the reporting laws, EPA's office of toxic substances decided around 1987 to change its interpretation considerably and enforce this new reading with large penalties.

### 9.1 Substantial Risk Notification: Section 8(e)

The sweeping general notification requirements of TSCA have swamped EPA with data that, however inadequate, is still more than it could properly analyze and absorb. For the next few years, until comprehensive screening criteria are established, this could mean that information on potentially hazardous substances could languish unanalyzed in EPA files while some

---

[74] TSCA, § 8(f).

[75] *Dow Chemical Co. v. EPA*, 605 F.2d 673 (3rd Cir., 1979).

[76] 47 Fed. Reg. 38780 (September 2, 1982).

[77] See this Chapter, Paragraph 10.3.

[78] 47 Fed. Reg. 38800 (September 2, 1982). This process of adding to, and removing, chemicals from the list continues apace.

chemical tragedy occurs. Indeed, even if analyzed, there is no assurance that the EPA reviewers could differentiate the hazardous from the non-hazardous chemicals. The field of chemical structure analogies is much shakier than the drafters of TSCA assumed. This suggests that notification -- the key feature of the entire statute -- may require a scientific sophistication that may not be developed for many years.

If health effects cannot be confidently predicted in advance, then EPA must learn of them as soon as they are discovered. Section 8(e) places upon chemical manufacturers, etc., the responsibility for reporting any indication of adverse effect. In the words of the act, any person:

Who obtains information which reasonably supports the conclusion that such substance or mixture presents a substantial risk of injury to health or the environment shall immediately inform the administrator of such information unless such person has actual knowledge that the administrator has been adequately informed of such information.[79]

Such a reporting requirement is not unprecedented. Section 6 of FIFRA has a similar provision for "factual information regarding unreasonable, adverse effects on the environment."[80] However, FIFRA's use of the word "unreasonable" assumes, perhaps naively, that the manufacturer himself will make an adverse risk-benefit analysis and then report it. TSCA insists that any evidence of "substantial risk" must be reported. Failure to report may subject any individual or company to civil penalties and even criminal prosecution.[81]

In March 1978, after receipt of public comments, EPA issued its policy interpretation implementing Section 8(e).[82] This placed upon corporation presidents and other top officials the responsibility for ensuring that adverse information is reported.[83] The policy states, however, that:

An employing organization may relieve its individual officers and employees of any responsibility for reporting substantial-risk information directly to EPA by establishing, internally publicizing, and affirmatively implementing procedures for employee submission and corporate processing of pertinent

---

[79] TSCA, § 8(e).

[80] FIFRA, § 6(a)(2).

[81] TSCA, §§ 15[3], 16, and 17. It is interesting to note that in the first major criminal case against a company (Velsicol) for failure to disclose adverse data on the pesticides chlordane and heptachlor, the Justice Department chose to use the general federal criminal laws rather than FIFRA, § 6(a)(2).

[82] 43 Fed. Reg. 11110 (March 16, 1978), entitled "Statement of Interpretation and Enforcement Policy; Notification of Substantial Risk."

[83] This is not an empty threat. See *U.S. v. Park*, 421 US 658 (1975).

information.[84]

In defining substantial risk, the document excludes from consideration the "economic or social benefits of use, or cost of restricting use." Moreover, it takes a strongly healthy protectionist view by directing that the extent of exposure is to be given little weight in assessing human health risks, since "the mere fact the implicated chemical is in commerce constitutes sufficient evidence of exposure."[85]

## 9.2 Significant Adverse Reactions: Section 8(c)

A subsection surprisingly similar to Section 8(e) is Section 8(c). Why are both provisions necessary?

Under Section 8(c) of TSCA, any person who manufactures, etc., any chemical substance or mixture shall maintain records of "significant adverse reactions" alleged to have been caused by the chemical. Those records relating to possible health reactions of employees must be kept for thirty years, during which time they may be inspected by or submitted to anyone he designates. All other recorded allegations need be preserved for only five years.

A comparison of Section 8(c) indicates that both the standard of proof and the required response is appreciably lower than for Section 8(e).

|  | TSCA § 8(c) | TSCA § 8(e) |
|---|---|---|
| Trigger | "Significant adverse reactions" | "Substantial risk of injury" |
| Evidence | "Alleged" | "Information which reasonably supports the conclusion" |
| Response | Record and retain for 5 or 30 years | Notify EPA immediately |
| *Regulation* | 1982 | 1978 |

The proposal, published by EPA in July 1980[86] defined "significant adverse reactions" as "reactions which may indicate a tendency of a chemical substance

[84] 43 Fed. Reg. 11110, *supra*, Section II.

[85] *Ibid.*, at 11111, Section V.

[86] 45 Fed. Reg. 47008 (July 11, 1980).

or mixture to cause long-lasting irreversible damage to health or the environment." Second, all manufacturers, processors and chemical distributors -- except retailers -- were included in the rule (an estimated 580,000 firms). And third, oral as well as written allegations were required to be recorded.

The final version in September 1982[87] reflected the Reagan administration's desire for less burdensome regulations. First, the definition was changed to place more emphasis on the word "significant":

> Significant adverse reactions are reactions that may indicate a tendency of a chemical substance or mixture to cause long-lasting or irreversible damage to health or the environment.

Moreover, only previously "unknown" effects need be recorded. This borrows a concept from Section 8(e) that may be appropriate there, where the goal is to inform EPA of new hazards, but is not fitting in a section that essentially provides for a log of health problems and complaints.

Second, the requirement to record oral allegations is dropped, although realistically that is the form in which most worker complaints would be made. Third, only processors in certain SIC code industries (namely, SIC categories 28 and 2911) are covered, while manufacturers of "naturally-occurring" substances are exempted entirely. This reduces the number of affected firms by over 98 percent, to only 10,000. And fourth, while the statute gave EPA an alternative of record inspection or submission, the final regulation opted for the former, with no automatic reporting requirement.

### 9.3 New EPA Interpretation Merges Sections 8(c), 8(d), and 8(e)

In the past several years, EPA has taken a somewhat different approach to Section 8 reporting, an approach which many industry associations and companies declare is in violation of the existing regulations. Their objections have been even louder since EPA has brought enforcement actions against several companies for violations of Section 8(e), as newly interpreted. Since this area is in flux, it is better to summarize the broad outlines of EPA's new approach.

In essence, EPA seems to be merging all three sub-sections into one reporting requirement and seeks to minimize a company's discretion to make health risk judgments. That is, the trend is more and more toward characterizing as Section 8(e) cases, and hence reportable, those episodes that hitherto would have been regarded as Section 8(c) cases, which would only have to be noted in the company files. The difference is one of judgment, and increasingly EPA has stated that companies were not to be such decisions.

Section 8(d) has also been swept into the 8(e) vortex. In fact, the

---

[87] 47 Fed. Reg. 38780 (September 2, 1982); see also EPA Concept Paper on Section 8(c), July 8, 1982.

preponderance of recent 8(e) reportings have been scientific studies instead of the expected worker and customer complaints.

EPA's interpretation is under criticism and may be modified. But until then, when in doubt, utilize Section 8(e) and report even fairly trivial environmental suspicions to EPA.


## 10.0 TESTING REQUIREMENTS

### 10.1 General Testing Requirements: Section 4(a)

Section 4(a) of TSCA permits EPA to require the testing of any chemicals, both old and new, if an unreasonable risk to health or the environment is suspected.[88] Testing may also be required if a chemical will be produced in such quantities that significant human or environmental exposure could result.[89]

Mixtures are also subject to the above rules, but only when the effects cannot be determined or predicted by testing the individual chemical substances which comprise the mixture.[90] This should reduce the testing burden, particularly for small producers and formulators.

Note that not all questionable chemicals need be tested -- only those for which EPA makes a specific determination that additional data is necessary and issues a formal testing rule. This standard may prescribe the biochemical effects to be investigated, the tests to be conducted, and even the experimental protocols to be followed.[91] The statute itself, in Section 4(b), details many of the studies that may be required, including carcinogenicity, mutagenicity, teratogenicity, behavioral modification, synergism, and various degrees of toxicity. Moreover, EPA must review all testing standards at least once a year and revise them where warranted.[92]

In setting these testing standards, the EPA administrator is to consider the relative costs and availability of facilities and personnel, and the period

---

[88] TSCA, § 4(a)(1)(A).

[89] TSCA, § 4(a)(1)(B).

[90] TSCA, § 4(a)(2).

[91] This rulemaking is subject to the Administrative Procedure Act, 5 U. S. C. § 551, including requirements for a transcript.

[92] TSCA, § 4(b)(2). An earlier bill required EPA to propose test protocols within one year of enactment but this was not in the final version. See Senate Committee on Commerce, "Toxic Substance Control Act of 1973, Report on S. 426," (D.C.: G.P.O., 1973), p. 7.

within which they can reasonably be performed.[93]

A company intending to run tests on a chemical for which EPA has issued no standard under Section 4(a) but may do so in the future, can formally request from EPA testing rules for that product.[94] This could help avoid later charges that the tests were inadequate or otherwise not in conformity with EPA requirements. It would also help a company in litigation with OSHA or other parties, even if no Section 4(a) rule is ever issued.

In 1981, for example, EPA took 14 test rule actions and decided not to regulate testing on three other chemicals.[95] This was overshadowed, however, by the Reagan administration's penchant for voluntary testing over required rules, despite charges from environmental groups that it undermines TSCA.[96] In August 1984, a federal district court agreed with environmentalists and held that the voluntary system subverted the mandatory system set forth in the statute.

## 10.2  Testing Requirement

Because toxicological testing is so expensive, TSCA borrowed from the pesticide act a provision for sharing of testing costs.[97] The reimbursement period is generally five years from date of submission but may be modified by the administrator to conform to the time that was necessary to develop such data.[98] If the manufacturers cannot decide among themselves a proper allocation of costs, the administrator -- as formerly in FIFRA -- is required to adjudicate the dispute after consultation with the Attorney General and the Federal Trade Commission.[99] Sharing such data exempts subsequent producers from having to conduct or submit duplicative test results.

The agency has proposed a reimbursement rule under Section 4 which will share the cost of testing between producers in proportion to their production volume. The proposal also suggests a mechanism for adjudicating disputes on

---

[93] TSCA, § 4(b)(1).

[94] TSCA, § 4(g). EPA has sixty days to grant or deny the petition. Then, if granted, it has only seventy-five days to issue test standards; if denied, the agency must publish reasons for the denial in the Federal Register.

[95] BNA, *Chemical Regulation Reporter*, March 26, 1982, p. 1323.

[96] *Ibid.*, July 9, 1982, p. 468.

[97] FIFRA, § 3(c)(1)(D), 7 U.S.C. § 136a(C)(1)(D). This issue is discussed later, in the chapter on Pesticides.

[98] TSCA, § 4(c)(3)(B).

[99] TSCA, § 4(c).

cost claims.[100]

The equivalent section in the pesticide act has been the source of more controversy, uncertainty, and administrative inconvenience than any other issue. Except that the testing burden for notification is less than for registration of pesticides, this section is unlikely to be a greater success under TSCA than FIFRA.


### 10.3  Priority List for Chemical Testing

There are tens of thousands of potentially toxic substances. Congress recognized that if EPA tried simultaneously to regulate all of them with its limited resources, it might actually accomplish nothing. This was important, for an earlier agency attempt to keep short the first list of regulated toxic substances under Section 307 of the Clean Water Act had failed when challenged by environmentalists in court.[101]

Section 4(e) of the act therefore provided for a priority list of chemicals for testing and directed that it "may not, at any time, exceed 50."[102] The "list of 50" may contain groups of chemicals as well as individual substances. This permits considerable expansion of the list's scope, if the administrator so desires.

The procedure for preparing this list is spelled out in excruciating detail: a committee of eight members, each from a designated government agency,[103] was given until the end of September 1977 to submit a candidate slate, based on toxicity and exposure, to the EPA administrator for public comment and his final decision.[104] Within twelve months he must either initiate a rulemaking under Section 4(a) or publish the reasons why not. In other words, the burden

---

100 BNA, *Chemical Regulation Reporter*, June 11, 1982, p. 349.

101 *N.R.D.C. v. Train*, 8 ERC, 2120 (D.D.C. 1976).

102 TSCA, § 4(e)(1)(A).

103 These include EPA, OSHA, CEQ, NIOSH, NIEHS, NCI, NSF, and the Department of Commerce. Several other agencies overlooked by the statute, such as FDA, have unofficially become a part of the committee. Others include the Consumer Product Safety Commission (CPSC), and the Department of Defense and Interior. Members serve four years, may not have any financial interest, or accept employment for one year from, anyone subject to TSCA.

104 TSCA, § 4(e)(2). The priority list is supposed to be updated every six months.

of proof is on the administrator to put the item on the list.[105]

The preparation of the inventory priority list began with an initial list of approximately 3,650 chemicals compiled from nineteen scientific sources. Next, substances under the jurisdiction of other federal laws, such as pesticides and drugs, were deleted. These and other deletions led to a Master File of 1,700, which was then screened for production volume and population exposure to produce a Preliminary List of 330 chemicals which was published in July 1977. The list was in turn reduced to a candidate list of eighty.

In October 1978, twelve months after the publication of the initial priority list, EPA decided it was not yet prepared to issue rules by the statutory deadline, so it withdrew that first group of ten substances and declared that it would postpone testing rule-making until appropriate standards were developed.[106] This action was widely criticized as both illegal and unimaginative. On May 8, 1979, the National Resources Defense Council (NRDC) instituted an eventually successful suit against EPA for failure to develop testing rules on the initial ITC recommendations.[107]

The chairman of the ITC under the Reagan administration, Elizabeth Weinburger, announced in March 1982 that the committee would no longer examine broad categories of chemicals, but half of the first group listed were categories rather than individual substances.[108]

The list, it should be noted, is not a permanent one. A chemical is placed on it until designated for testing or determined to be inappropriate. There has thus been a parade of substances on and off the 4(e) list. So far, there have been several hundred substances on and off this list.

## 11.0 EPA'S ENFORCEMENT AND REGULATORY ROLE

EPA is given broad authority to take whatever regulatory measures are deemed necessary to restrict chemicals suspected of posing harm to man or the environment. The procedures are modeled basically on the pesticide act, although there are several important differences. Like FIFRA, there is a regulatory distinction between substances presenting unreasonable risks

---

[105] TSCA, § 4(e)(1))B). One observer, who believed the nine month period was too long, had earlier described the process as confirmation of Parkinson's law that work expands to fit the time. He was overly optimistic.

[106] 43 Fed. Reg. 50134 (October 26, 1978).

[107] *NRDC v. Costle*, 14 ERC 1858 (S.C.N.Y., 1980).

[108] BNA, *Chemical Regulation Reporter*, March 26, 1982, p. 1323.

(Section 6) and those severe cases which constitute an imminent hazard (Section 7).[109]

## 11.1 Section 6

TSCA borrows its definition of hazard for invoking "cancellation" directly from FIFRA: "unreasonable risk of injury to health or the environment."[110] There is, however, one small change -- the phrase is preceded by the words "presents or will present." This was added to avoid the contention that "risk" meant a certainty of harm, as had been proposed by an appellate court panel (later reversed) in a case under Section 211 of the Clean Air Act.[111]

Section 6 authority is not restricted to removing a chemical from the market. It may also include limiting the amount that can be produced, prohibiting or limiting specific uses considered most hazardous, requiring labels and warnings, mandating extensive manufacturing and monitoring records, controlling disposal, "or otherwise regulating any manner or method of commercial use of such substance or mixture." Restrictions may even be applied in some geographical areas and not in others. Quality controls in manufacturing or processing may be required if there is a potential problem of highly toxic impurities, such as TCDD in the herbicide, 2,4,5-T. The manufacturer or processor may be required to replace or repurchase products held to constitute a hazard.[112]

The regulations for implementing Section 6 rulemakings were issued in final form on December 1977.[113] These emphasized flexible procedures, rather than strict adherence to the Administrative Procedure Act, although a limited right of cross examination is provided. Subpoena authority is also available, although to be used sparingly.

Final authority to grant or deny petitions submitted under 6(e)(3)(B) of TSCA rests with the assistant administrator for toxic substances. For example, in determining whether to allow an exemption to the PCB ban, the two stan-

---

[109] Compare FIFRA, §§ 6(b) and 6(c) with TSCA, §§ 6 and 7. Note that while TSCA does not use the terms "cancellation" or "suspension," since there is no registration to cancel or suspend as under FIFRA, these are nevertheless convenient terms to use for the process in Section 6 and 7.

[110] TSCA, § 6(a).

[111] *Ethyl Corp. v. EPA*, 7 ERC 1353 (CADC, 1975): reversed en banc by 541 F.2d 1, 8 ERC 1785 (CADC, 1976); cert. denied 426 U.S. 941, 8 ERC 220 (1976). Section 112 of the Clean Air Act authorizes regulation of potentially harmful fuel additives, especially lead.

[112] TSCA, § 6(a) and (b).

[113] 40 C.F.R. Part 750, December 2, 1977.

dards enunciated in Section 6(e)(3)(B) would be applied, these standards being: (1) an unreasonable risk of injury to health or environment would not result; and (2) "good faith efforts have been made to develop a chemical substitute which does not present an unreasonable risk of injury to health or the environment . . . for such PCBs."[114]

### 11.2 PCB, CFC and Asbestos

One of the most controversial chemicals EPA has had to deal with is polychlorinated biphenyl (PCB). (These chemicals are discussed more fully in Section 12.0, below.) Congress sought to insure that EPA would confront the problem by specifically mandating action and a regulatory timetable in Section 6(e). This unusual step prodded EPA into banning some uses of PCBs in 1977 and most production and use in April 1979.[115] EPA estimated that the new more stringent standard will bring nearly a million additional pounds of PCBs under control. PCB regulation and enforcement has become so important under TSCA that a main heading in this chapter is devoted exclusively to it.

Another widely publicized chemical group is the chlorofluorocarbons (CFC). On March 17, 1978, EPA promulgated final regulations prohibiting almost all of the manufacturing, processing, and distribution of chlorofluorocarbons for those aerosol propellant uses subject to TSCA.[116]

As for asbestos, in a move that reflected the public's growing awareness and concern about the health effects of these materials used in buildings, insulation, and surfacing materials, late in 1988, the 100th Congress passed the "Asbestos Information Act" (Pub. L. No. 100-577, 15 U.S.C. 2607, enacted October 31, 1988). (Asbestos is discussed in more detail in Section 17, below.) This act requires manufacturers or processors of asbestos-containing building materials to submit to EPA a description of the product, the year of manufacture, and all other pertinent information about their product. More recently, in 1989, EPA ordered a phase out of virtually all production and use of asbestos under Section 6 and to force users to find alternatives to asbestos over the next decade.

In July 1989 EPA issued its long-awaited ban on most manufacture and distribution of asbestos products in the United States.[117] The ban is not

---

[114] 40 C.F.R. 750.21. The burden for developing such chemical substitutes does not rest entirely with the industry. In the spring of 1988, EPA issued four major documents for public comment concerning substitutes for asbestos.

[115] BNA, *Chemical Regulation Reporter*, April 20, 1979, p. 49. See also Preamble to EPA Final Rules for PCBs Manuf., April 17, 1979.

[116] 43 Fed. Reg. 55241 (November 27, 1978).

[117] 54 FR 29460, July, 12, 198

immediate but a three-staged phase out, ranging from 1990 to 1997, depending on the product and the use. The scheduled phase-out of distribution generally follows manufacture, import, and processing bans by one to two years. EPA declares that the cost of this regulation will be relatively low, because substitutes have already been developed for most of these products, or are expected to be available soon. On the other hand, the benefits also seem to be surprisingly small, a claimed saving of around 200 lives. This number equates in this country to less than one in a million, which happens to coincide with the level often defined as zero detectable effect.[118]

### 11.3  Imminent Hazards: Section 7

Although "imminent hazard" determinations have been invoked repeatedly under FIFRA (i.e., suspension), and EPA has been criticized for not using it more, the equivalent provision under TSCA, Section 7, has not once been used. It has rarely even been seriously considered as a regulatory option.

The standard for "suspension" actions under section 7 of TSCA is, as with pesticides, an "imminent hazard." This is defined more stringently than in FIFRA, however, as "a chemical substance or mixture which presents an imminent and unreasonable risk of serious or widespread injury to health or the environment."[119]

Unlike FIFRA, enforcement orders under TSCA cannot be issued solely on the agency's own authority, challengeable only before the court of appeals. Instead, if a proposed restrictive rule is contested, EPA must seek an injunction from a federal district court, which will itself determine whether there is sufficient basis for legal action. EPA may also initiate a civil suit in district court to seize an imminently hazardous chemical.[120] Judicial review of final EPA orders is limited to the circuit court of appeals, which must determine whether the agency action is supported by substantial evidence on the record as a whole.[121]

The rulemaking procedures assure manufacturers of a full range of due process safeguards, including reasonable hearing procedures, the right of cross-examination during rulemaking, and the right of appeal. EPA's authority to propose an immediately effective rule to ban or limit manufacture of an existing chemical is limited by the requirement that it first obtain a court injunction based on the same legal criteria as applied in cases of imminent hazard. Therefore, a substantial degree of proof is required, procedural safeguards afforded, and assurance provided that EPA cannot act without good

---

[118]  51 Fed. Reg. 3738 (January 23, 1986).

[119]  TSCA, § 7(f).

[120]  TSCA, § 7(a),(b); see also § 6(c),(d).

[121]  TSCA, § 19.

cause.

While the agency has used its Section 6 authority sparingly apart from the specific instance of Section 6(e) PCB regulation, it has not used Section 7 at all yet.

## 12.0  PCB REGULATION

The regulation of polychlorinated biphenyls (PCBs) is an anomaly. Nowhere else in the environmental laws is a substance banned or phased out by name.[122] Because of perennial dissatisfaction with various agency actions, Congress has discussed utilizing this device further, Thus, the PCB issue is interesting not only because of the broad public attention it has received but also as a possible regulatory precedent for future actions.

PCBs have been used as transformer fluids and dielectrics, but their darker side was not revealed until a tragic episode in Japan in 1969. Cooking oil somehow became contaminated with PCB leaking from a transformer. Whether from the PCBs themselves or from furans and other contaminants, this resulted in deaths, central nervous system damage, serious stomach and liver disorders, and possibly cancer. Immediate steps were taken in Japan to prevent this problem from recurring. No action was taken in the United States, however, until several more years and several serious incidents later.

PCBs are ubiquitous in the environment. They are stable even at high temperatures, and may not break down into non-toxic compounds for many years. PCBs sealed in a transformer may last 15, 20, or perhaps 25 years before needing replacement because of eventual leaks.

Following a large number of episodes in Michigan and elsewhere (actually due in large part to the unrelated polybrominated biphenyls, PBB, rather than PCB), Congressman John Dingell (D-Mich.) and other representatives inserted Section 6(e) into the final version of TSCA. It provided for a schedule which would first stop PCB manufacture and then gradually curtail its use. EPA, as usual, missed most of the subsequent regulatory deadlines, but did finally issue a series of regulations implementing the statute.

Section 6(e) directed EPA to phase-out PCB manufacture and use according to a statutorily-mandated timetable. After one year from the passage of the act (that is, by October 1977) no one was allowed to manufacture, process, distribute, or use any PCB except in "a totally enclosed manner"[123] which is defined in 40 CFR 761.3 as "any manner that will insure no exposure of human

---

[122] There have been occasional requirements that EPA examine specific substances -- such as asbestos, mercury, beryllium and cadmium under Clean Air Act Section 112 -- for possible eventual regulation, but a ban or phase-out was not specifically mandated.

[123] Defined in TSCA, § 6(e)(2)(C).

beings or the environment to *any* concentration of PCBs." Unless the administrator finds no unreasonable risk,[124] no one may manufacture PCBs at all after two years, nor distribute them after 2-1/2 years.[125] If needed, the administrator may utilize any other provision of TSCA or of any other federal law to regulate PCBs.[126]

At the time of the enactment, these provisions seemed to pose no problem. There was only one remaining PCB manufacturer in the United States and it intended to abandon the business. Utilities and other owners of PCB-filled electric transformers and capacitors were permitted to maintain their equipment for its working life, provided it did not leak or require major servicing.

EPA's initial regulations addressed four categories: PCB transformers (those having over 500 parts per million of PCB in the transformer fluid); PCB-contaminated "electrical equipment"[127] (having between 50 and 500 parts per million); and a category not specifically defined except by exclusion, which would be non-PCB transformers, defined as those less than 50 parts per million. The fourth category, not discussed, was railroad transformers.

Such transformers were required to be appropriately labeled, standards were set for transport of PCBs, and disposal techniques were outlined including incineration.

The statute exempted transformers and other uses that were "totally enclosed." If a transformer were not "totally enclosed," it must be banned. But how would EPA know; and did a tiny, well-contained leak of a thimbleful a year constitute a non-enclosed use requiring tens of thousands of dollars for equipment replacement? First of all, there is a problem called "sweating" -- a fancy word EPA likes for small leaks, and in March 1980, it requested comments on the extent "weeping" or "sweating" was a problem for PCB transformers. The answers the agency received were quite varied, ranging from estimates of 80-90 percent sweating to a fraction of that. EPA decided not to issue regulations, hoping the issue would just fade away.

An environmental group, the Environmental Defense Fund (EDF), brought suit against EPA's 1978 and 1979 implementing regulations[128] and persuaded

---

[124] See TSCA, § 6(e)(3)(B).

[125] TSCA, § 6(e)(3).

[126] TSCA, § 6(e)(5).

[127] 40 C.F.R. § 761.3.

[128] 43 Fed. Reg. 7150 (February 17, 1978); 44 Fed. Reg. 31542 (May 31, 1979).

the court of appeals to strike them down as "unsupported by the record."[129] Because of the broad nature of the suit, this meant that EDF won not only on the issue that prompted the suit, namely a desire for stringent inspection and maintenance of electrical equipment, but on most other issues as well. This included the 50 ppm cut-off level of PCB regulation, which was admittedly arbitrary but reflected the consensus of authorities. And that led to problem number two.

Many chemical processes involving aromatics and chlorine were found to produce small but measurable traces of PCBs as unintended by-products. This could affect up to a quarter of all American chemical operations, most of whom did not (and probably still do not) realize they were vulnerable to EPA enforcement or citizens' suits for "manufacturing" PCBs in violation of the law.

After a series of chemical and electrical industry surveys, EPA proposals,[130] and public hearings, EPA decided to issue three sets of regulations. Rule One, published in August 1982,[131] applied to electric transformers and capacitors. It prohibited PCB-filled equipment near food and feed after October 1985 (the proposed rule allowed indefinite use, subject to weekly self-inspections), authorized most other electrical equipment for the remainder of its useful life, subject to (for large transformers) a quarterly self-inspection, allowed storage for disposal of non-leaking equipment outside of qualified storage facilities, and provided for retaining three years of maintenance records.

Rule Two, issued in October 1982,[132] exempted by-product manufacture which took place entirely within closed systems or separated as designated waste for disposal by EPA-approved methods. Although originally requested by the companies, the lengthy final version was opposed because it promised an "exemption" for which few if any companies could honestly qualify. None did.

Rule Three, applying generally to the incidental by-product problem in the chemical industry, is currently in preparation.

A related question involved in protracted litigation is whether monochlorinated biphenyls are polychlorinated biphenyls. Despite linguistic and persistence arguments, EPA decided they were and brought a major enforcement action against a leading chemical company. The company challenge to the regulations was dismissed for lack of jurisdiction,[133] then pursued through a

---

[129] *Environmental Defense Fund v. EPA*, 636 F.2nd 1267, 15 ERC 1081 (CADC, 1980).

[130] See 47 Fed. Reg. 24976 (June 8, 1982).

[131] 47 Fed. Reg. 37342 (August 25, 1982).

[132] 47 Fed. Reg. 46980 (October 21, 1982).

[133] *Dow Chemical Co. v. Costle*, 484 F.Supp. 101 (D.Del. 1980).

protracted series of hearings and appeals within EPA. The agency judicial officer, Ron McCallum, ruled in July 1982, that the company had indeed violated the PCB rules and that the courts of appeals, not an enforcement proceeding, was the proper forum for a challenge to the definition of PCB.[134] Subsequently, the agent did provide for considerable different treatment for mono- and di- forms but did not exempt them from coverage under Section 6 (e).

Meanwhile, the debate continues. The definition of "totally enclosed" had to be modified, with comments obtained in September 1984. For "inadvertent generation" of PCB by-products, EPA prepared new rules in 1984 which showed an annual average of 25 ppm and a maximum concentration of 50 ppm. PCBs vented into the outside air cannot exceed 10 ppm.[135]

The transformer rule issued in 1982 exempted approximately 140,000 potentially dioxin-containing electrical transformers. But the concern has grown that this did not do enough to prevent transformer fires in heavily populated areas that could emit large quantities of dangerous fumes. Therefore, EPA prepared proposed regulations in 1984 to isolate transformers from ventilation ducts and require the removal of combustibles stored near transformers.[136] A final rule restricting the use of certain PCB transformers in commercial buildings was issued July 17, 1985.[137] The rule is a more stringent version of the electrical transformers rule published by EPA in October 1984.

The once-simple PCB issue remains a troublesome one because of this lawsuit and its consequences, because the agency was long unwilling to make decisions on incineration and on other disposal techniques, and because the problem is technically and legally more complex than anyone imagined. Meanwhile, Congress has grown impatient with the delays.

## 13.0 CONFIDENTIALITY

Since a principal function of TSCA is the collection of voluminous information on chemical substances, concern for the protection of genuine trade secrets while assuring the public's access to necessary information has been a hotly debated topic.

Section 14 provides that EPA may not release any information which is not

---

[134] BNA, *Chemical Regulation Reporter*, August 20, 1982, p. 645; see also July 30, 1982, p. 558.

[135] *Ibid.*, September 7, 1984, p. 590; *Washington Post*, July 2, 1984.

[136] *Washington Post*, April 2, 1984, October 17, 1984.

[137] 50 Fed. Reg. 29170.

exempt from mandatory disclosure under the Freedom of Information Act (FOIA).[138]   This excludes "trade secrets and commercial or financial information obtained from a person and is privileged or confidential."[139] TSCA does not prohibit the disclosure of health and safety studies nor, of course, the release of information to federal officials in the performance of their duties.  Data may also be disclosed to protect "against an unreasonable risk of injury to health or the environment" in a legal proceeding.  There is interestingly no allowance for release of information to state health authorities, despite the lessons of the Kepone tragedy, although perhaps they could qualify by being made "contractors with the United States."[140]

EPA's general regulations for dealing with FOIA requests under its various statutes were issued in September 1976.[141]   Although they tend strongly to favor disclosure, EPA had relatively few business secrets in its files, so industry has had few objections for far to these procedures.  The exception is pesticides regulation, which for several years has been entangled by litigation over release of data.[142]

Some chemical industry representatives have complained that existing laws are not sufficiently protective of confidential business information.   The president of the Manufacturing Chemists Association, for example, has expressed concern that as long as the trade secret exemption under the FOIA remains permissive, "there is no assurance that privately developed information submitted to the government in confidence will not be disclosed."[143]

EPA modified some portions of the original March 1977 inventory reporting proposal[144] to assuage certain industry fears, such as deleting the

---

[138] TSCA, § 14(a).

[139] Administrative Procedure Act § 2, 5 U.S.C. § 552(b)(4).

[140] TSCA § 14(b) and (a); see also 40 C.F.R. § 2.301(h), 43 Fed. Reg. 2637 (January 18, 1978).

[141] 41 Fed. Reg. 36902 (September 1, 1976).

[142] *Mobay Chemical Corp. v. Train*, F.Supp., 8 ERC 1227 (D.C.W. Mich. 1975); dismissed per curiam U.S., January 8, 1979.

[143] Letter from former MCA President William J. Driver to Sen. James Abourezk (D-S.D.), January 18, 1978, quoted in BNA *Environment Reporter*, 1978, p. 1468.

[144] 42 Fed. Reg. 13130 (March 9, 1977).

requirements that a toxicological bibliography be submitted.[145] The agency has also established a task force to establish computer security precautions to protect information submitted or stored on magnetic tape.[146]

Polaroid Corporation challenged the adequacy of protection provided for chemical trade secrets which the company was required to furnish EPA under the reporting regulations. In June 1978, a U.S. district judge denied the request that Polaroid be excused from reporting the information, but also issued an injunction ordering EPA not to disclose the information outside the agency.[147]

Then on September 8, 1978, EPA issued amendments to its confidential business information regulations[148] providing substantial protection for TSCA confidential information and providing for notice to affected businesses before confidential information is disclosed outside EPA.[149] Polaroid withdrew its suit and the Court order was vacated. The problem of confidentiality nevertheless will continue to be a sensitive issue for the foreseeable future.

EPA has consistently insisted that requests for confidentiality be accompanied by an explanation as to why it is needed. Merely calling something a trade secret does not make it so. Although the first policy issued by the Reagan administration on Section 5 provided that under PMN a manufacturer could withhold data as confidential without providing a rationale,[150] Congress is monitoring this area very closely and has threatened to pass legislation restricting the scope of confidentiality if companies abuse the privilege.[151]

---

[145] 42 Fed. Reg. 39182, 39188 (August 2, 1977), reproposing 40 C.F.R. 710.7(e).

[146] See, e.g., 42 Fed. Reg. 53804, 53805 (October 3, 1977), 43 Fed. Reg. 1836 (January 12, 1978).

[147] *Polaroid Corp. v. Costle*, No. 78-11335 (D.Mass. 1978).

[148] 40 C.F.R. Part 2, 43 C.F.R. 3997, September 8, 1978.

[149] This provision for notification to the company was already set forth in Section 14(c) of the statute.

[150] BNA, *Chemical Regulation Reporter*, February 7, 1982, p. 443.

[151] See, e.g., reports in *ibid.*, August 3, 1984, p. 483. The head of EPA's toxics office, John Moore, requested that companies claim less data as confidential to ease the evaluation by his staff. *Ibid.*, April 6, 1984, p. 3.

## 14.0 TSCA ENFORCEMENT

EPA has recently announced a stricter enforcement policy through stiffer penalties. For example, in the summer of 1985, six chemical manufacturers were fined a total of $6.9 million for allegedly failing to notify the agency prior to making new chemicals.

At around the same time, Chemical Waste Management, Inc. was required to pay a $2.5 million fine (originally proposed as $6.8 million) for violations of TSCA Section 6 regulations governing processing, storage, distribution, recordkeeping, marking, and disposal requirements for PCBs.

On March 1, 1985, EPA proposed to fine Union Carbide Corporation $3.9 million for its alleged delay of Section 8(e) reporting safety data on diethyl sulfate, the second largest fine then proposed by EPA. Four months later, Diamond Shamrock Corporation agreed to pay $800,000 in penalties after it was charged with illegally disposing of wastes contaminated with PCBs.

The first enforcement cases under Section 13 chemical import certification requirements and Section 4 chemical testing requirements were announced by EPA on October 3, 1985.

## 15.0 CITIZEN ENFORCEMENT AND LEGAL FEES

Private citizens are allowed, even encouraged, to participate in TSCA administrative and judicial proceedings.[152] Section 21 provides that any person may petition the administrator to take action on rules under Sections 4-8, excepting imminent hazard determinations under Section 7; the administrator then has 90 days either to grant or deny the petition. If he denies the petition, a citizen may initiate civil action in a federal district court.[153]

The section has been used by the Service Employees International Union requesting asbestos standards for schools (granted), a company wishing to leave PCB-contaminated soil in a mine shaft (denied), and an association wishing to delete the inventory designation of inorganic glass as mixtures (denied).[154] Despite its name, it has been little used by ordinary citizens.

Citizens may also file suit under Section 20 to compel the administrator to

---

[152] The citizen participation sections were missing in whole or part from earlier versions of TSCA. For example, H.R. 5356 of 1973 had neither section, while the Senate bill (S.426) had a citizens suit provision (§19) but only an oblique reference to citizen petitions (§24a). See House Report 93-360 (1973) and Senate Report 93-254 (1973).

[153] TSCA, §21.

[154] EPA Office of Toxic Substances, *Bulletin*, March 1984; *ibid.*, May 1984; 49 Fed. Reg. 36844 (September 20, 1984).

perform any non-discretionary duty, or against anyone, including the government, alleged to be in violation of any rules issued under Sections 4-6. The plaintiff, however, must give EPA the traditional 60 days notice before he may commence his litigation.[155]

The exclusion of Section 7 from both the citizens petition and citizens suit sections of TSCA is particularly striking, considering that under the pesticide act the comparable imminent hazard area has been a prime focus of activity by environmental groups.

Attorney and witness fees may be awarded by the courts to persons litigating under TSCA. There is no requirement that the person's legal position has prevailed, or that such an award be limited to so-called public interest groups, although that is surely its main concern. The statutory test is simply that costs and reasonable fees may be granted "if the court determines that such an award is appropriate."[156]

## 16.0    BIOTECHNOLOGY: TOXIC REGULATION

The field of biotechnology promises great advances in human well being, such as the creation of wondrous new substances, and curing cancer and other diseases. However, it also holds the threat of creating destructive new plagues and organisms  and poses untold moral dilemmas which the human race has never before had to confront.   Because genetic engineering is so new, still being developed, and little understood, it has been surrounded by controversy over both its safeness and who should regulate it.

On June 18, 1986, President Reagan signed the Coordinated Framework for Regulation of Biotechnology, which sets out specific agency roles and statutory authority and ensures the industry's environmental safety and economic viability.   Legislation has also been proposed recently in Congress to set up a regulatory structure for reviewing the safety of genetically engineered products under TSCA. However, the Biotechnology Science Coordination Act (HR 4452) was criticized by industry for defining genetically engineered organisms too narrowly.   The bill was also criticized for not giving EPA enough discretion to regulate genetically engineered products on a case-by-case basis.   EPA's ability to regulate biotechnology under TSCA has also been questioned.

Despite the efforts to regulate biotechnology, there are some who are dissatisfied that the efforts have not regulated the biotechnology industry enough. Jeremy Rifkin, who heads the environmental group called Foundation for Economic Trends, is one of the most determined opponents.   In fact, he believes that biotechnology should be banned altogether.  Although most of his attention has focused on biotechnology developments and efforts in the pesti-

---

[155] TSCA, §20.

[156] TSCA, §19(d).

cides field (see the chapter on Pesticides) he has also fought the biotechnology industry in all other areas, including toxics.

For example, on September 2, 1986, Rifkin filed suit in the U.S. District Court for the District of Columbia against the Department of Defense (DOD) to enjoin the U.S. military from testing, developing and producing toxic biological warfare materials until the military prepares environmental impact statements. The foundation first sued DOD in November 1984 to prohibit the military from building a proposed biological warfare testing facility in Utah. An injunction was granted in May 1985 and is still in effect.

A landmark case decided in 1980, which Rifkin lost and which should be mentioned here, is *Diamond v. Chakrobatry*[157] in which the Supreme Court ruled in June 1980 that genetically altered organisms may be patented. Now when individuals and firms put time and money into biotechnology research, they can be assured of earning economic rewards. Rifkin's foundation has filed a "friend of the court" brief supporting the U.S. Attorney General's office in its contention that the federal patent laws should not cover such organisms.

## 17.0 ASBESTOS AMENDMENT: AHERA

On October 22, 1986, President Reagan signed into law a measure, Public Law 99-519, amending the Toxic Substances Control Act by adding a new Title II, the Asbestos Hazard Emergency Response Act of 1986. It required school systems to identify and abate asbestos hazards in school buildings. (Previously, school districts were required to inspect facilities for asbestos and inform teachers and parents of the inspection results, but were not required to take any abatement action.)

EPA is required to issue regulations defining what response actions must be taken in school buildings containing friable (i.e., crumbling) asbestos. Furthermore, before April 1987 EPA had to propose regulations prescribing proper asbestos inspection procedures, standards for asbestos abatement, procedures for periodic re-inspection of buildings with encapsulated or remaining asbestos, and the establishment of a model contractor accreditation program for the states.

The final EPA regulations, issued October 30, 1987.[158] outlined the responsibility of each local education agency to conduct specified inspections for asbestos-containing material (ACM) and, if found, to conduct sampling and analysis procedures the results of which should comprise a written assessment as defined in §763.88 of the regulations. Note that nowhere does the law require the removal of ACM. Any hazard may be remedied by one of several different methods, including "encapsulation" (wrapping or binding), enclosure

---

[157] 100 S.Ct. 2204, 447 U.S. 303.

[158] 40 C.F.R. §763.80-99 and Appendices A, B and D to Subpart E.

(walling off the hazard), or of course by removal itself, which though more costly may be cheaper in the long run. Political pressures within the school community have naturally tended to make removal the preferred option. The amendment also includes regulations for response actions, operations and maintenance, training, management plans and recordkeeping.[159]

These federal regulations may be waived in a given state if this state implements its own asbestos inspection and management requirements that are at least as stringent as those in Subpart E of the Regulations.[160]

Under AHERA, EPA distributes loan and grant money to financially needy schools to help pay for abatement costs. This amendment to the Toxic Substance Control Act establishes an Asbestos Trust Fund where funds received from schools that receive loans are to be deposited. Under the previous law, funds were simply returned to the U.S. Treasury.

AHERA has created a large market for asbestos contractors but poor work training and other deficiencies, including one of the rare cases of an EPA inspector being bribed, have plagued the field, so careful security of a prospective contractor's record should be undertaken before one is hired.

At this time the abatement provisions affect only schools, at a cost of around $3 billion; however, there has been considerable support in Congress to include commercial buildings in the future, at a cost of over $50 billion, and several bills have been introduced which have a chance of enactment in a future session.

In cases where the asbestos is not crumbling or threatening to disperse into the environment, many experts believe that the asbestos is best left in place but monitored closely with a self-inspection system, since attempted removal could pose more risk (as well as being enormously expensive) than leaving the material in place. Moreover, there is considerable scientific doubt that the type of asbestos present in most schools, and in most commercial buildings, is the type that poses the most risk of adverse health effects. In other words, the billions of dollars spent on asbestos remediation may have been largely wasted.

## 18.0   RELATIONSHIP OF TSCA TO OTHER LAWS

TSCA was enacted to fill gaps left by other laws, but Congress was also concerned that it not lead to jurisdictional conflicts with other agencies or even between different divisions of EPA. There was no wish to see a repetition of the bitter OSHA-EPA dispute of 1973 over pesticide re-entry standards. Consequently, Section 9 of TSCA sets forth in some detail the coordination procedures to be followed when two health regulatory laws

---

[159] 40 C.F.R. §763.90-94.

[160] 40 C.F.R. 763.98.

overlap.

Under Section 9, the EPA administrator may ask another agency to undertake regulation of a substance that presents an "unreasonable risk" which may be prevented by the other agency. The receiving agency must then take whatever regulatory measures it deems necessary, or reply in the *Federal Register* with a "detailed statement" why no action is warranted. There the matter rests, whether EPA is in accord with the decision or not. (A citizen suit against the second agency is nevertheless possible.) EPA cannot thereafter bring an enforcement action of its own under Sections 6 or 7 concerning that hazard.[161]

EPA issued its first referral on June 26, 1985, when it referred regulatory control over 4,4,-methylene-dianiline to OSHA because of its exclusively workplace-related risks. (Earlier, in the same year, EPA had attempted to refer the regulation of asbestos to OSHA, but rescinded that decision after much controversy, especially criticism from Congress that reflected a low opinion of OSHA's capabilities.)

For other laws administered under EPA, the administrator is given the flexibility to apply them where they would be most useful or to rely on the provisions of TSCA. He is not relieved of the procedural or substantive requirements in those other laws, however, if he chooses to rely on them.[162]

Finally, Congress added a special provision concerning OSHA, stating the Environmental Protection Agency's exercise of authority under TSCA did not constitute a preemption of OSHA jurisdiction under OSH Act Section 4.[163]

## 18.1 Existing Toxic Substance Laws

The term "toxic substance" has become so identified with this new act that one often forgets there is considerable legislation dealing with chemical substances already on the books. In one sense, almost all of the recent environmental laws have in fact been directed at toxic substances.

One generally excludes from the term "toxic substances" the six original air pollutants regulated by EPA under Sections 108-110 of the Clean Air Act: carbon monoxide, hydrocarbons, photochemical oxidant, sulfur dioxide, nitrogen oxides, and particulate matter. In sufficient concentrations most of these substances can be immediately deadly and all have serious long-term effects on health. They tend, however, to be the ubiquitous products of combustion, the

---

[161] TSCA, §9(a). EPA could try to circumvent this bar by first initiating an enforcement action and then sending the notification to the other agency under Section 9(a)(3).

[162] TSCA, §9(b). At least theoretically, the application of the doctrine to all laws "administered in whole or in part by the Administration" also includes the Food, Drug, and Cosmetic Act. See the chapter on Pesticides.

[163] TSCA, §9(c); OSH Act, §4(b)(1).

waste products of an industrial society, and their control necessitates a general national policy that cuts across many diverse industries. Similarly, a number of the substances controlled under the water pollution laws are usually excluded from the definition, including suspended soil particles and decaying organic products which adversely affect the biological oxygen demand (BOD) of the water.

## 18.2   Clean Air Act

Section 112 of the Clean Air Act, entitled "National Emission Standards for Hazardous Air Pollutants" (NESHAP), is specifically directed toward toxic substances.   Although this provision has so far been used only for a few substances, such as asbestos, mercury, beryllium, and vinyl chloride, it now bids to develop into one of the most important parts of the act.

One reason for its infrequent use has been its deliberate omission of economic or technical feasibility in standard setting; the only relevant factor for the administrator is "the level which in his judgment provides an ample margin of safety to protect the public health from such pollutants."[164]  EPA tacitly ignored this unusual provision in the vinyl chloride deliberations,[165] and this had some support in the legislative history. However, the D.C. Court of appeals has held *en banc* that economic considerations may not be applied to standard setting under this section.[166]

Only slightly over a half dozen substances have been regulated by EPA under Section 112.   Congress has been irritated that this section has been so little used over the past decade and a half.   In the Clean Air Amendments of 1990, Congress finally mandated that many more chemicals should be examined and regulated under this provision.

## 18.3   Water Pollution Act

Another key law is Section 307 of the Federal Water Pollution Control Act entitled "Toxic and Pre-Treatment Effluent Standards."[167]   This provides specifically for the listing and setting of standards with an "ample margin of safety" for hazardous chemicals discharged into the nation's waterways.   In September 1973, EPA listed nine chemicals, mostly pesticides, on this list,

---

[164] Clean Air Act, §112(b)(1)(B).

[165] EPA, "Proposed Standard for Vinyl Chloride," December 16, 1975.

[166] The original Clean Air bill considered by Congress has two toxic substances sections -- the present one for extreme hazards and a milder version allowing economic considerations for the less serious toxic pollutants. The House-Senate Conference Committee in 1970 dropped the latter section from the final bill without giving any reason.

[167] Federal Water Pollution Control Act §307, 33 U.S.C. §1317.

including DDT, Aldrin-Dieldrin, PCBs, Toxaphene, and cadmium and mercury compounds.[168] Effluent standards for these substances do not apply to all industries but only to about two dozen broad categories such as non-ferrous metal smelters, textile manufacturers, and agricultural fertilizer manufacturing.[169] By the consent decree between EPA and the Natural Resources Defense Counsel in June 1976, a total of sixty-five substances comprising approximately 160 individual chemicals was added to the Section 307 list.[170] This decree was subsequently written into the 1977 amendments to the Clean Water Act.[171]

Under Section 311 entitled "Oil and Hazardous Substance Liability," EPA is to regulate "spills" of hazardous substances into the nation's waterways and coastal zones. The administrator is required to list those elements and compounds which should be designated "hazardous substances."

The administrator also has emergency authority under Section 504 of the Clean Water Act to seek to enjoin any person from discharging any pollutants which are "presenting an imminent and substantial endangerment to health or welfare."[172] This section has rarely been invoked by EPA, despite numerous situations for which it would be appropriate.

### 18.4 Occupational Safety and Health Administration

The Occupational Safety and Health Act, although not usually regarded as a toxic substance act, is potentially the most important statute in the field.[173] Although limited to occupational situations, the act covers 80 million workers, many of whom have much greater exposure to highly toxic chemicals than they are ever likely to encounter in the general environment.

---

[168] 38 Fed. Reg. 24342 (September 7, 1975). The rules of practice under §307 were amended by 41 Fed. Reg. 1765 (January 12, 1976).

[169] For more detailed information, see the chapter on Water Pollution Control.

[170] *NRDC v. Train*, 8 ERC 2120, (D.D.C. 1976); see also *NRDC v. Train*, 510 F.2d 692 (D.C. Cir., 1974).

[171] PL 95-217. There has been some dispute about the degree to which Congress incorporated the consent decree into the amendments. Rep. Ray Roberts (D-Tex.) insisted that it didn't, or at least modified it considerably; Sen. Edmund Muskie (D-Me.) said that it did. The latter view is preferred.

[172] Federal Water Pollution Control Act §504, 33 U.S.C. §1364.

[173] 29 U.S.C. §651 *et seq.*, Pub. L. 91-596, 84 Stat. 1590.

Section 6 of the act[174] requires OSHA to set strict health standards at a level "which most adequately assures, to the extent feasible, on the basis of the best available evidence, that *no* employee will suffer material impairment of health or functional capacity even if such employee has regular exposure to the hazard dealt with by such standard for the period of his working life.[175] This act, if fully implemented, could have a tremendous effect.

## 18.5   Consumer Product Safety Commission

The Consumer Product Safety Act and related statutes such as the Hazardous Substances Act administered by the Consumer Product Safety Commission (CPSC) also confer jurisdiction over certain forms of toxic substances. One should note, however, that "hazardous substances" as used in this act includes devices and equipment, and thus is much broader than the term toxic substances. Furthermore, the CPSC may address only human safety questions derived from the use of consumer products, and thus it has no authority over environmental problems.

In the past, the CPSC has exhibited little activity in the chemical area, except for limited involvement in cases concerning two spray can propellants, vinyl chloride and freon, and a fumbled effort on asbestos hair dryers. Because of budget and staff cuts, this disfavored agency is unlikely to be a more important factor in the next few years.

## 19.0   PROPOSED FEDERAL CANCER POLICY

The proposed Federal Cancer Policy was initiated by OSHA in October 1977 and coordinated with the four health regulatory agencies -- OSHA, EPA, FDA, and CPSC.   A coherent, consistent federal policy could help control dangerous carcinogenic chemicals.  Unfortunately, these interagency discussions were  delayed by the Supreme Court's decision in the *Benzene* case, placed on hold by the Reagan administration, and are currently pending.

The three goals hoped to be reached through OSHA's Federal Cancer Policy are:

First, to avoid repetitive scientific debate at OSHA hearings and ad hoc decisions on health standards involving carcinogens,

Second, to streamline OSHA's ponderous standard setting process by "prefabricating" the essential elements of several alternative versions, and

Third, ultimately to harmonize the policies of the four health regulatory agencies.   The regulatory requirements, derived from the cancer principles, spell out monitoring and medical tests in rigorous detail and set a goal of reducing levels of "confirmed" carcinogens to near zero.

---

[174] OSH Act §6, 29 U.S.C. §655.

[175] OSH Act §6, 29 U.S.C. §6(b)(5).

## 19.1   Scientific Principles of the Cancer Policy

The policy takes a hardline regulatory approach to carcinogens, namely that exposure should be reduced to zero, or as close to zero as is feasible. If safer alternative chemicals are available, they should be substituted.

The leading scientific policy conclusions in the proposal are as follows:

(1)   A carcinogen is defined as a substance or condition which increases the incidence of generally irreversible benign or malignant tumors, reduces the latency period, or produces unusual tumors in animals or man.

(2)   The results of cancer tests on animals, particularly rodents and other animals, are relevant to human exposure. ("Any substance which is shown to cause tumors in animals should be considered carcinogenic and, therefore, a potential cancer hazard for man.")

(3)   A threshold or "no effect" level may theoretically exist for carcinogens but this has not been conclusively demonstrated; and, even so, it would have to be determined separately for each substance. Therefore, the only safe level is zero.

(4)   Most carcinogens are neither species-specific nor organ-specific.

(5)   A substance may be termed a confirmed carcinogen after replicated tests in only one species. ("If carcinogens are not species-specific, it logically follows that the demonstration of carcinogenic effect in more than one species is not absolutely necessary for finding of carcinogenicity.") Note that EPA has recently commented that under some circumstances even replication should be waived as unnecessary.

(6)   In evaluating test data, no distinction will be made between benign and malignant tumors. ("The Agency proposes to place as much weight on an experiment in which only benign tumors are observed, as upon experiments in which both malignant and benign tumors are induced.")

(7)   Positive test results (i.e., indicators that a substance is carcinogenic) outweigh negative findings.

(8)   Chemical structural similarity of a suspect chemical to a known carcinogen may be a guide for testing priority but is itself insufficient to classify the former as a carcinogen.

(9)   Induced tumors appearing in animals at the point of application, or due to physical rather than chemical effect, may be disregarded.

(10) The administration of high doses is a methodological device necessary for finding gross effects in small test samples. "Consequently, a substance that will induce cancer in experimental animals at any dose level, no matter how high or low, should be treated with great caution."

(11) The Ames test or other in vitro experiments using non-mammalian species are not an appropriate basis for regulatory action, but positive results plus carcinogenicity in one mammalian species may be.

(12) Human epidemiological studies are generally an insensitive indicator of carcinogenicity, unless the study is exhaustively controlled or the particular cancer is quite unusual (e.g., angiosarcoma from vinyl chloride).


## 20.0  CONCLUSION

The Toxic Substances Control Act got off to a slow start, due in part to the delay in filling top EPA positions. The ponderous pace did not accelerate thereafter, and for most of its history TSCA has been essentially an information-gathering act. Recently the law has shifted to a much more active mode, not as long expected in legal proceedings under Sections 6 and 7 against hazardous substances, but in multi-million dollar fines against purported PMN violations. This has succeeded for the first time in getting industry's attention on TSCA, but unfortunately it has not had a clear relationship to protecting the environment and public health.

Chapter 8


FEDERAL REGULATION OF PESTICIDES


Marshall Lee Miller, Esq.
Washington, D.C.


## 1.0 BACKGROUND TO THE FEDERAL REGULATION OF PESTICIDES

The benefits of pesticides, herbicides, rodenticides, and other economic poisons are well known. They have done much to spare us from the ravages of disease, crop infestations, noxious animals, and choking weeds. Over the past several decades, however, beginning with Rachel Carson's *Silent Spring* in 1962, [1] there has been a growing awareness of the hazards as well as the benefits of these chemicals, which may be harmful to man and the balance of nature. The ability to balance these often conflicting effects is hampered by our lack of understanding of adverse side effects, a problem which will become increasingly acute during the next few years as the EPA attempts to conduct accelerated reviews of hundreds of chemicals registered earlier under less strict standards.

### 1.1 Overview

Public concern regarding pesticides was a principal cause of the rise of the environmental movement in the U.S. in the late sixties and early seventies and therefore was a major reason for the creation of the EPA. While public attention since then has often shifted to various other environmental media, the pesticide issue - with its implications for the safety of food supply and of people in the agricultural area - is still central to the public's notion of environmental protection. Indeed, interest in this topic is often an accurate barometer of public distrust in the official environmental agencies. For that reason, the recent renewed interest in pesticides, on matters ranging from the Alar apple episode to the sweeping provisions in California's (unsuccessful but hotly-contested) Proposition 128, is a signal of alarm. The public perceptions may be due to a time lag, for the situation in pesticide regulation is not worse

---

[1] Rachel Carson, *Silent Spring* (New York, 1962).

now than in the past, and it is certainly far better than it was in the early 1980s. But this could mean increased media and environmental organizations' attention to pesticides in the coming few years.

## 1.2 Early Efforts at Pesticide Regulations

Although chemical pesticides have been subject to some degree of federal control since the Insecticide Act of 1910, [2] the relatively insignificant usage of pesticides before World War II made regulation a matter of low priority. This act was primarily concerned with protecting consumers from ineffective products or deceptive labeling, and it contained neither a federal registration requirement nor any significant safety standards. The war enormously stimulated the development and use of pesticides. The resulting benefits to health and farm production made pesticides a necessity and transformed the agricultural chemical industry into an influential sector of the economy. In 1947 Congress responded to the situation by enacting the more comprehensive Federal Insecticide, Fungicide, and Rodenticide Act (FIFRA).[3] It required that pesticides distributed in interstate commerce be registered with the United States Department of Agriculture (USDA) and contained a rudimentary labeling provision. This act, like its predecessor, was more concerned with product safety, but the statute did declare pesticides "misbranded" if they were necessarily harmful to man, animals, or vegetation (except weeds) even when properly used. [4]

Three major defects in the new law soon became evident. First, the registration process was largely an empty formality since the Secretary of Agriculture could not refuse registration even to a chemical he deemed highly dangerous. He could register "under protest," but this had no legal effect on the registrant's ability to manufacture or distribute the product. Second, there was no regulatory control over the use of a pesticide contrary to its label, as long as the label itself complied with the statutory requirements. Third, the Secretary's only remedy against a hazardous product was a legal action for misbranding or adulteration, and--this was crucial--the difficult burden of proof was on the government. The statute nevertheless remained unchanged for fifteen years. Pesticides were not then a matter of public concern and the Department of Agriculture (USDA) was under little pressure to tighten regulatory control. Only a handful of registrations under protest were made

---

[2] 36 Stat. 331 (1910).

[3] 61 Stat. 190 (1947). The present act is still known by this name, although there have been major changes, especially in 1972, in the law since then. For convenience, we will refer to the pre-1972 version as the "Old FIFRA."

[4] Old FIFRA (pre-1972) § 2(z)(2)(d). See H. Rep. 313 (80th Cong., 1st Sess.). 1947 U.S. Code Cong. Serv. 1200, 1201.

during that period, and virtually all these actions involved minor companies with ineffective products. The one notable lawsuit involving a fraudulently ineffective product was lost by the USDA at the district court level and mooted by the court of appeals. [5] In 1964 the USDA persuaded Congress to remedy two of these three defects: the registration system was revised to permit the Secretary to refuse to register a new product or to cancel an existing registration, and the burden of proof for safety and effectiveness was placed on the registrant. [6] These changes considerably strengthened the act but made little difference in practice. The Pesticide Registration Division, a section of USDA's Agricultural Research Service, was understaffed--in 1966 the only toxicologist on the staff was the division's director--and the division was buried deep in a bureaucracy primarily concerned with promoting agriculture and facilitating the registration of pesticides. The cancellation procedure was seldom if ever used, [7] and there was still no legal sanction against a consumer's applying the chemical for a delisted use. The growth of the environmental movement in the late 1960s, with its concern about the widespread use of agricultural chemicals, overwhelmed the meager resources of the Pesticide Division. Environmental groups filed a barrage of law suits demanding the cancellation or suspension of a host of major pesticides such as DDT, Aldrin-Dieldrin, and the herbicide 2, 4, 5 - T. This demanding situation required a new approach to pesticide regulations.

## 1.3 Pesticide Regulation Transferred to the Environmental Protection Agency

On December 2, 1970, President Richard Nixon signed Reorganization Order No. 3 [8] creating the Environmental Protection Agency (EPA) and assigned to it the functions and many of the personnel previously under Interior, Agriculture, and other government departments. EPA inherited from USDA not only the Pesticides Division but also the environmental law suits against the Secretary of Agriculture. Thus, within the first two or three months the new agency was compelled to make a number of tough regulatory decisions. The EPA's outlook was considerably influenced by judicial decisions in several of the cases it had inherited from USDA or, concerning pesticide residues, from the Food and Drug Administration (FDA) of the Department of Health, Education,

---

[5] *Victrylite Candle Co. v. Brannan*, 201 F.2d 206 (D.C. Cir., 1952).

[6] Act of May 12, 1964, Pub. L. No. 88-30S, 78 Stat. 190. There were other, less significant, amendments in 1959 (73 Stat. 286) and 1961 (75 Stat. 18, 42).

[7] Instead, a Pesticide Registration Notice would be sent ordering the removal of one or more listed uses from the registration.

[8] Reorganization Order No. 3 of 1970, §2(a)(1), 1970 U.S. Code Cong. Ad. News 2996, 2998, 91st Cong. 2nd Sess.

and Welfare (HEW), now the Department of Health and Human Services (HHS). These court decisions consistently held that the responsible federal agencies had not sufficiently examined the health and environmental problems associated with pesticide use. These helped to shape, indeed force, EPA's pesticide policy during its formative period. [9]

## 2.0 OVERVIEW OF THE FEDERAL INSECTICIDE, FUNGICIDE AND RODENTICIDE ACT (FIFRA) AND AMENDMENTS

### 2.1 Background to FIFRA and the 1972 FEPCA

The Federal Insecticide, Fungicide, and Rodenticide Act (FIFRA)[10], as amended by the Federal Environmental Pesticide Control Act (FEPCA) of October 1972 and the FIFRA amendments of 1975, 1978, 1980, and 1988, [11] is a complex statute. Terms sometimes have a meaning different from, or even directly contrary to, normal English usage. For example, the term "suspension" really means an immediate ban on a pesticide, while the harsher-sounding term "cancellation" indicates only the initiation of administrative proceedings which can drag on for years. The repeated amending of FIFRA reflects congressional, industry, and environmentalist concern about the federal control of pesticide distribution, sale, and use. The amendments to FIFRA in 1972, known as the Federal Environmental Pesticides Control Act (FEPCA),[12] amounted to a virtual rewriting of the law. FEPCA, not the 1947 FIFRA, is the contemporary pesticide law. They were considered necessary to (1) strengthen the enforcement provisions of FIFRA, (2) shift the legal emphasis from labeling and efficacy to health and environment, (3) provide for greater flexibility in controlling dangerous chemicals, (4) extend the scope of federal law to cover intrastate registrations and the specific uses of a given pesticide, and (5) streamline the administrative appeals process. EPA was given expanded authority over field use of pesticides, and several categories of registration were created which give EPA more flexibility in fashioning appropriate control over pesticides.

---

[9] These cases will be discussed in a later section.

[10] 7U.S.C. § 135, *et seq.*

[11] Pub. L. No. 96-516, 86 Stat. 973, October 1972; Pub. L. No. 94-140, November 28, 1975; Pub. L. No. 95-396, 92 Stat. 819, September 30, 1978; Pub. L. No. 96-539, 94 Stat. 3194; December 17, 1980.

[12] Pub. L. No. 92-516, 86 Stat. 973, October 21, 1972.

## 2.2 The Subsequent FIFRA Amendments

The 1975 amendments are significant not for what they actually changed but because of the motivations that prompted them. These amendments were viewed by many as, at best, unnecessary and, at worst, a further encumbrance upon an already complicated administrative procedure. EPA was required to consult with the Department of Agriculture and Agricultural Committees of Congress before issuing proposed or final standards regarding pesticides. EPA also got the authority to require that farmers take exams before being certified as applicators. The 1978 amendments reflected the near-collapse of EPA's pesticide registration program. EPA was given the authority to conditionally register a pesticide pending study of the product's safety and was authorized to perform generic reviews without requiring compensation for use of a company's data.

The 1980 amendments provided for a two-house veto over EPA rules and regulations, and they required the Administrator to obtain Scientific Advisory Review (SAR) of suspension actions after they were initiated. The 1988 legislation provided for accelerated review of pre-1970 registrations and removed most of the indemnification requirements for canceled pesticides.

## 3.0 PESTICIDE REGISTRATION

### 3.1 Pesticide Registration Procedures

All new pesticide products used in the United States, with minor exceptions, must first be registered with EPA. This involves the submittal of the complete formula, a proposed label, and "full description of the tests made and the results thereof upon which the claims are based." The Administrator must approve the registration if the following conditions are met:

(A)    its composition is such as to warrant the proposed claim for it;

(B)    its labeling and other materials required to be submitted comply with the requirements of this act;

(C)    it will perform its intended function without unreasonable adverse effects on the environment; and

(D)    when used in accordance with widespread and commonly recognized practice it will not generally cause unreasonable adverse effects on the environment.

The operative phrase in the above criteria is "unreasonable adverse effects on the environment", which was added to the act in 1972. This phrase is defined elsewhere in FIFRA as meaning "any unreasonable risk to man or the environment, taking into account the economic, social, and environmental costs and benefits of the use of the pesticide." [13]This controversial expression, which appears also in the cancellation-suspension section of the act,[14] disturbed some environmentalists who feared that the word "unreasonable" plus the consideration of social and economic factors would undermine the effectiveness of the cancellation procedure, but experience to date has not indicated that this is really a problem.The registration is not valid for all uses of a particular chemical. Each registration specifies the crops and insects on which it may be applied, and each use must be supported by research data on safety and efficacy. Registrations are for a five-year period, after which they automatically expire unless an interested party petitions for renewal and, if requested by EPA, provides additional data indicating the safety of the product. [15] For the past few years, pre-EPA registrations have been coming up for renewal under much stricter standards than when originally issued. The agricultural chemical companies have justifiably complained that the increased burden of registration is discouraging the development of new pesticides, but there seems no responsible alternative.

### 3.2 Trade Secrets

The issue in FIFRA that has generated more controversy than any other over the past decade has involved the treatment of trade secrets in the data submitted to EPA for registration. [16] The judicial protection of commercial trade secrets has gradually eroded during the past few years. Many so-called trade secrets were in fact widely known throughout the industry and did not merit confidential status. Section 10 of FIFRA, added in the 1972 amendments, provides that trade secrets should not be released but, if the Administrator proposes to release them, he should provide notice to the company to enable it to seek a declaratory judgment in the appropriate district court.It is, of course, desirable that scientists and others outside industry and government should be able to conduct tests on the effects of various pesticides. In one case debated by the Agency for several years, a professor needed to know the chemical composition of a particular pesticide to conduct certain medical experiments. The question of whether EPA or a court should furnish this information to a bona fide researcher, with or without appropriate safeguards to preserve confidentiality, was resolved in the experimenter's favor after an

---

13 FIFRA § 2(bb), 7 U.S.C. § U.S.C. § 136(bb). The 1975 amendments, as will be discussed, added the specific requirement that decisions also include consideration of their impact on various aspects of the agricultural economy.

14 FIFRA § 6, 7 U.S.C. § 136d.

15 FIFRA § 6(a), 7 U.S.C. § 136d(a).

16 FIFRA § 10, 7 U.S.C. § 136h. Trade secrets are also becoming a source of contention in the implementation of the Toxic Substances Control Act.

investigation revealed that the chemical composition in fact was not a trade secret within the industry. [17]Section 10 provides that "when necessary to carry out the provisions of this act, information relating to formulas of products acquired by authorization of this act may be revealed to any federal agency consulted and may be revealed at a public hearing or in findings of fact issued by the Administrator." [18] Consequently, if the public interest requires, a registrant must assume that the formula for his product can be made available, although in practice this may not occur very often.Because of the controversy surrounding the disclosure of trade secrets, Congress amended FIFRA in 1975 and 1978. The 1975 amendments [19] cleaned up an ambiguity created by the 1972 amendments by specifying that the new use restrictions applied only to data submitted on or after January 1, 1970. The definition of trade secrets was left to the Administrator.EPA took the position that the 1972 and 1975 amendments restricted use and disclosure of only a narrow range of data, such as formulas and manufacturing processes, but not hazard and efficacy data. However, the industry challenged this view with some initial success. [20] In 1978, Congress again amended Section 10 to limit trade secrets protection to formulas and manufacturing processes, thus reflecting EPA's position. This was a significant change and has spawned a host of litigation in recent years.[21] In *Ruckelshaus v. Monsanto*, [22] the Supreme Court held almost unanimously (7-1/2 to 1/2) that while a company did have a property right to the data under state law, the key question was whether it had a reasonable expectation that it would not be disclosed or used by other companies, albeit with adequate compensation. This expectation, the Court found, could only be for the period between the 1972 FIFRA amendments and the 1978 amendments, when the

---

[17] The reverse situation, where a chemical company sought an administrative subpoena of the testing files of two university researchers on pesticides, was raised in *Dow Chemical Co. v. Allen*, 672 F.2d. 1262, 17 ERC 1013 (7th Cir., 1982). The request was rejected as unduly burdensome and not particularly probative, since the EPA had not relied on their data in studies still uncompleted.

[18] FIFRA § 10(b), 7 U.S.C. § 136h(b). Note that state agencies are not mentioned.

[19] Pub. L. No. 94-140, 89 Stat. 75 (1975).

[20] *Mobay Chemical Corp. v. Costle*, 447 F.Supp 811, 12 ERC 1228 (W.D. Mo. 1978), appeal dismissed 439 U.S. 320, reh. denied 440 U.S. 940 (1979); *Chevron Chemical Co. v. Costle*, 443 F.Supp 1024 (N.D. Cal. 1978).

[21] Pub. L. No. 95-396, 92 Stat. 812.

[22] 104 S. Ct. 2862, 21 ERC 1062 (1984).

interim change in Section 10 of the act first promised strict confidentiality. [23] For this period, compensation is available through the federal Tucker Act, and probably through the statutory arbitration process too.

### 3.3 "Featherbedding" or "Me-Too" Registrants

The second most contested provision in FEPCA, after the question of indemnities, was the issue of "featherbedding" on registration. The original version in the House stated that "data submitted in support of an application shall not, without permission of the applicant, be considered by the Administrator in the support of any other application for registration." [24] Supporters of the provision, basically the larger manufacturers, claimed that it prevented one company from "free-loading" on the expensive scientific data produced by another company; environmentalists dubbed this the "mice extermination amendment" for requiring subsequent registrants to needlessly duplicate the laboratory experiments of the first registrant.The groups finally found an acceptable compromise allowing subsequent registrants to reimburse the initial registrant for reliance on its data, adding to the above language the words: "unless such other applicant shall first offer to pay reasonable compensation for producing the test data to be relied upon." The section provides that disputes over the amount of compensation should be decided by the Administrator, but the 1975 amendments deleted the unfortunate clause which ensured that the original registrant should have nothing to lose by appealing to a district court, since "in no event shall the amount of payment determined by the court be less than that determined by the Administrator." The 1978 amendments removed the unwelcome task from the Administrator entirely by providing for mediation by the Federal Mediation & Conciliation Service. [25] The 1975 amendments also pushed back the effective date of the compensation provision from October 1972, the date of the enactment of the FEPCA amendments, to January 1, 1970. [26]The data compensation provision has created many problems in the registration process. Pesticide manufacturers brought several lawsuits to determine the breadth of this provision, the proper use of the data, and the amount of compensation that a manufacturer is

---

[23] 28 U.S.C. §1491.

[24] FIFRA, § 3(C)(1)(D), 9 U.S.C. § 136a(C)(1)(D).

[25] Pub. L. No. 95-396 § 2(2), 92 Stat. 819.

[26] Pub. L. No. 94-140, §12, amending FIFRA §3(c)(1)(D). The 1972 amendments had not actually specified an effective date but most authorities assumed it was the date of enactment.

entitled to for use of its data. [27] In the case *In re Ciba-Geigy Corp. v. Farmland Industries, Inc.,* [28] EPA set out criteria to be applied in determining what constitutes reasonable compensation under Section 3(c). Plaintiff Ciba-Geigy claimed that it was entitled to $8.11 million in compensation from Farmland Industries for the latter's use of test data to register three pesticides. The defendant argued that it should pay only a proportional share of the actual cost of producing the data based on its share of the market for the products, approximately $49,000. The plaintiff contended that reasonable compensation should be based on the standards used in licensing technical knowledge: an amount equal to the cost of reproducing the data plus a royalty on gross sales for three years. The administrative law judge hearing the case ruled that the latter, cost-royalty formula was closer to Congress' intent to avoid unnecessary testing costs. He concluded that the reasonable compensation provision was not intended to provide reward for research and development as the plaintiff's formula would do. The fairest compensatory formula, according to the judge, was using the data producer's cost adjusted for inflation and the defendant's market share two or three years after initial registration. Although no reward for research and development was created, this compensation formula does create an incentive to research because the benefits gained from decreased costs of subsequent registrants outweighs the disadvantages of decreasing the original data producer's projects.In 1984, the United States Supreme Court ruled in *Ruckelshaus v. Monsanto Co.* [29] that pesticide health and safety data was property under Missouri law and thus was protected under the Fifth Amendment of the Constitution. However, the Court overruled a lower court in finding that data submitted prior to 1972 and after 1978 was not a "taking" since the registrant had no expectation of confidentiality. For the period between the 1972 and 1978 amendments, the Supreme Court decided there was sufficient ambiguity to warrant a claim. The remedy was not to find FIFRA unconstitutional, however, as the lower court had done, but to allow a claim against the government for compensation under the Tucker Act, 28 U.S.C. Section 1491.

## 3.4 Essentiality in Registration

Another registration change strongly supported by the pesticide industry was a prohibition against EPA refusing to register a substance because it served no useful or necessary purpose. This is not the same as efficacy,

---

[27] See *Amchem Products Inc. v. GAF Corp.,* 594 F.2d 470 (5th Cir., 1979), reh. den. 602 F.2d 724 (5th Cir. 1979); *Mobay Chemical v. EPA,* 447 F.Supp. 811, 12 ERC 1572 (W.D. Mo., 1975), 439 U.S. 320, 12 ERC 1581 (per curiam) (1979).

[28] Initial Decision, FIFRA Comp. Dockets Nos. 33, 34 and 41 (August 19, 1980).

[29] *Ruckelshaus v. Monsanto Co.,* 104 S.Ct. 2862 (1984).

above, nor was this a dispute as to whether, under both the old and new FIFRA, a registration application must demonstrate that a product would "perform its intended function." The agricultural chemical companies, however, were apprehensive that EPA might refuse to register a new product because an old one satisfactorily performed its intended function. These fears have hitherto proved groundless; EPA's best interest, and that of the public, lies in having as much duplication of pesticides as reasonably possible, since the existence of a similar but safer chemical facilitates the removal of a hazardous pesticide from the market.

### 3.5 Intrastate Registrations

Under the old FIFRA[30] federal authority did not extend to intrastate use and shipment of pesticides with state registrations. This meant that federal authority could be avoided simply by having manufacturing plants in the principal agricultural states. The FEPCA amendments broadened the registration requirement to include any person in any state who sells or distributes pesticides. The states do retain some authority under Section 24 "to regulate the sale or use of any pesticide or device in the state, but only if and to the extent the regulation does not permit any sale or use prohibited by this Act." States, furthermore, cannot have labeling and packaging requirements different from those required by the act -- a measure which was popular among some chemical manufacturers who feared that each state might have different labeling requirements. It also seems to exclude a feature common to several of the other environmental laws whereby states may impose stricter requirements than the federal ones on pesticide use within their jurisdiction. Finally, the section gives a state the authority, subject to certification by EPA, to register pesticides for limited local use in treating sudden and limited pest infestations, without the time and administrative burden required by a full EPA certification. The fears of pesticide manufacturers that the states would impose more stringent labeling requirements were justified in spite of the FEPCA amendments. California imposed additional data requirements under its restricted-use registration. In *National Agricultural Chemicals Association v. Rominger,*[31] a federal district court declined to issue a preliminary injunction against the state's regulations on the grounds that there was no congressional mandate to occupy the field when Section 24 was enacted, thus there was no federal preemption of restricted-use registrations.[32]

---

[30] Old FIFRA § 4(a).

[31] 500 F. Supp 465, 15 ERC 1039 (E.D. Cal. 1980).

[32] The court also dismissed challenges to two other provisions of the California laws for lack of ripeness. These challenges were claims that the statute improperly allowed the state to set residue tolerances different from

(continued...)

## 3.6 Conditional Registration

The near-collapse of EPA's pesticide registration process prompted creation of a system of *conditional* registration or reregistration. This could be applied when certain data on a product's safety had either not yet been supplied to EPA or had not yet been analyzed to ensure, according to FIFRA Section 3(a)(5)(D), that "it will perform its intended function without unreasonable adverse effects on the environment." Three kinds of conditional registrations are authorized by Section 6 of the 1978 law which amends FIFRA Section 3(c) with a new section, entitled "Registration Under Special Circumstances": pesticides identical or very similar to currently registered products; new uses to existing pesticide registrations; and pesticides containing active ingredients not contained in any currently registered pesticide for which data need be obtained for registration. These conditional registrations must be conducted on a case-by-case basis, with the last type of conditional registration further limited both by duration and by the requirement that the "use of the pesticide is in the public interest." Conditional registration is prohibited if a Notice of Rebuttable Presumption Against Registration (RPAR) has been issued for the pesticide, and the proposed new use involves use on a minor food or feed crop for which there is an effective registered pesticide not subject to a RPAR proceeding. Cancellation of conditional registrations must be followed by a public hearing, if requested, within seventy-five days of the request, but must be limited to the issue of whether the registrant has fulfilled its conditions for the registration. [33] EPA published final regulations implementing conditional registration on May 11, 1979. [34]

## 3.7 Streamlining of Registration

EPA's reregistration of pesticides, required every five years, has always been plagued by both a slow regulatory pace and the feeling that much of the safety data underlying the registrations was inadequate by contemporary scientific standards. The 1988 amendments added an entire section, which will be renumbered as FIFRA Section 4, covering this topic. [35] This section provided that the data submitted in support of registrations before EPA's creation in 1970 would no longer be considered adequate for reregistration,

---

[32] (..continued)
EPA tolerances and that certain labeling requirements for insecticides were improperly imposed.

[33] § 12 of 1978 act, amending FIFRA § 6.

[34] 44 Fed. Reg. 27932 (May 11, 1979).

[35] Section 102 of the 1988 amendments, redesignated as Section 4 of FIFRA by Section 801(q) of the 1988 law.

unless the applicant bears the burden of proof otherwise. [36]The new section set a 48-month timetable for the completion of the studies needed for reregistration. These deadlines are to parallel the time requirements currently in FIFRA Section 3(c)(2)(B), entitled "Additional Data to Support Existing Registration." These timetables are to be virtually absolute; they may be extended only in such extraordinary circumstances as a major animal loss, the unintentional loss of laboratory results, or the destruction of laboratory equipment and facilities. After the Administrator's review is completed, he may ask for additional data to support the reregistration, declare the pesticide canceled or suspended. Otherwise, he is to approve the reregistration. Under the previous version of FIFRA, no consequences were set for failure of a registrant to provide compensation to the original provider of any data relied upon, or share in the payments. The 1988 amendments specified that the Administrator, in such a case, must issue a notice of intent to suspend that registrant's registration.

The reregistration continues to lag, despite years of criticism from Congress and environmentalists, and one can safely anticipate these complaints will persist for years to come.

### 3.8 Registration of "Me-Too" Pesticides

For those pesticides which are identical or very similar to other registered products, akin to generic drugs, the 1988 amendments provide that EPA should expedite approvals of these registrations. [37] To assist this process, the Administrator is to utilize up to $2 million of the fees collected (see below). [38]

### 3.9 Registration Fees

A one-time registration fee per active ingredient is authorized by the 1988 amendments. [39] In addition, registrants must pay an annual fee through 1997 to supplement EPA's pesticide reregistration budget. The legislation emphasizes, however, that no other fee can be imposed by EPA other than the above. Moreover, the Administrator is empowered to reduce or waive the fees for minor use pesticides where their availability would otherwise be in question. He is to report annually to Congress on the application of this authority.

---

[36] The actual cut-off date is given as January 1, 1970; the EPA was not created until December 2, 1970.

[37] FIFRA, Section 3(c) (3).

[38] FIFRA, Section 4(k) (3).

[39] FIFRA, Section 4(i).

### 3.10 Generic Pesticide Review

EPA has long complained that registration, and especially reregistration reviews, should be conducted for entire classes of chemicals rather than being limited to examining each particular registration as it comes up for five-year renewal. This authority has always existed under FIFRA, but a district court decision in 1975[40] on compensation for data made this so complicated that the plan was dropped pending a legislative solution.

The amendment that finally emerged under this label in Section 4 of the 1978 act, however, is considerably different in scope: "No applicant for registration of a pesticide who proposes to purchase a registered pesticide from another producer in order to formulate such purchased pesticide into an end-use product shall be required to (i) submit or cite data pertaining to the safety of such purchased product; or (ii) offer to pay reasonable compensation ... for the use of any such data."[41]

### 3.11 Efficacy

The requirements for test data on a pesticide's efficacy are now made discretionary for EPA. This does not change the present practice very much, because efficacy information has been increasingly less important over the past few years. But the provision is interesting because it marks a complete reversal from the original purpose of federal pesticide legislation earlier in this century, which was to protect farmers from "snake oil" pesticide claims.

## 4.0 CONTROL OVER PESTICIDE USAGE

### 4.1 Statutory Basis for Control over Pesticide Usage

Until the 1972 FEPCA reforms, the government had no control over the actual use of a pesticide once it had left a manufacturer or distributor properly labeled. Thus, for example, a chemical which would be perfectly safe for use on a dry field might be environmentally hazardous if applied in a marshy area, and a chemical acceptable for use on one crop might leave dangerous residues on another. EPA's only recourse (other than occasional subtle hints to the producer) was to cancel the entire registration--obviously too unwieldy a weapon to constitute a normal means of enforcement. A second problem was that a potential chemical might be too dangerous for general use but could be used safely by trained personnel. There was, however, no legal mechanism for limiting its use only to qualified individuals. Because of these problems, both environmentalists and the industry agreed that

---

[40] *Mobay Chemical Corp. v. Train*, 392 F. Supp. 1342, 8 ERC 1227 (W.D. Mo. 1975).

[41] 1978 act, amending FIFRA § 3(c)(2).

EPA should be given more flexibility than merely the choice between canceling or approving a pesticide. Congress therefore provided for the classification of pesticides into general and restricted categories, with the latter group available only to Certified Applicators. There are several categories of applicators, including private applicators and commercial applicators, who use or supervise the application of pesticides on property other than their own. A pesticide label permitting use only "under the direct supervision of a Certified Applicator" means of course that the chemical is to be applied under the instructions and control of a Certified Applicator who, however, curiously is not required to be physically present when and where the pesticide is applied. The additional flexibility of the certification program was a principal reason the agro-chemical industry eventually supported the 1972 amendments to FIFRA, but some environmentalists were concerned that the program might become a farce, especially when administered by certain states. Certification standards are prescribed by EPA, but any state desiring to establish its own certification program may do so if the Administrator determines that it satisfies the guidelines and statutory criteria. The efficacy of the entire certification program, however, has become questionable as a result of the 1975 amendments to FIFRA. The amendments considerably relaxed the procedures for certification by forbidding EPA to demand any examinations of an applicant's knowledge. [42] Some states may license anyone who applies, but EPA requirements for periodic reporting and inspection provide some degree of control. There would be no objection to every farmer becoming a Certified Applicator if he so desired, provided that they were seriously willing to undergo training. Finally, since 1972 it has been unlawful either "to make available for use, or to use, any registered pesticide classified for restricted use for some or all purposes other than in accordance with" the registration and applicable regulations. Stiff penalties for violations of these restrictions include fines up to $25,000 and imprisonment for up to a year.

### 4.2 Experimental Use Permits

FIFRA provides for experimental use permits for registered pesticides.[43] The purpose of this seemingly innocuous section is to permit a registration applicant to conduct tests and "accumulate information necessary to register a pesticide under Section 3." [44] This provision, however, has already been used in at least one successful effort to evade a FIFRA cancellation-suspension order. Under strong political pressure from Western sheep interests and their congressional spokesmen, EPA granted a Section 5 permit for the limited use

---

[42] Pub. L. No. 94-140 § 5, amending FIFRA § 4(a)(1).

[43] FIFRA § 5, 7 U.S.C. § 136c. The 1975 amendments added a specific provision for agricultural research agencies, public or private.

[44] FIFRA § 5(a), 7 U.S.C. § 136c(a).

of certain banned predacides and devices including the "coyote getter." On July 18, 1979, EPA issued final regulations under which a state may develop its own experimental permits program. [45] A state, by submitting a plan which meets the requirements of EPA's regulations, may receive authorization to issue experimental use permits to potential registrants under 24(c) of FIFRA (restricted use registration), agricultural or educational research agencies, and certified applicators for use of a restricted use pesticide.Permits cannot be issued by a state for a pesticide containing ingredients subject to an EPA cancellation or suspension order, or a notice of intent to cancel or suspend or which are not found in any EPA registered product. [46] The regulations also contain strict limitations on the production and use of a pesticide. Periodic reports must be submitted by the permittee to the state detailing the progress of the research or restricted use. In addition, permits cannot be issued for more than three years.

## 4.3 Self-Certification of Private Applicators

The clearest illustration of Congress' altered view toward FIFRA is their treatment of the certification program which had been a major reason for the enactment of the FIFRA overhaul in 1972. The amendments provided that the pesticides which might be too harmful to the applicators or to the environment if indiscriminately used could continue to be applied by farmers and pesticide operators who had received special training in avoiding these problems.The program had run into resistance from the beginning from farmers who resented the requirement that they be trained to use chemicals on their own property. The changed law does not remove the examination requirement from commercial applicators, who apply pesticides to property other than their own.[47]

It does create an exemption, however, which covers not only the farmer who is applying pesticides to his own land but also his employees. And it must be remembered that the hazards are not necessarily limited to the applicator; organophosphates, which are nerve gases, may be highly toxic to the applicators, may be highly toxic to the applicators, but many other substances if improperly used may run off to threaten neighboring farms or the environment in general. The amended law does not seem to recognize this latter problem. The 1975 amendments also removed the authority of the Administrator to require, under state plans submitted for his approval, that farmers take exams before being certified. In other words, EPA may require a training program but may not require any examination to determine if the

---

[45] 44 Fed. Reg. at 41783 (July 18, 1978); 40 C.F.R. § 172.20.

[46] 44 Fed. Reg. at 41788. States may, however, issue permits for products containing ingredients subject to the Rebuttable Presumption Against Review process (RPAR).

[47] See the definition of commercial applicator in FIFRA § 2(e).

information has been learned. [48] In the opinion of the House Agriculture Committee, "The farmer would be more aware of the dangers of restricted use pesticides if each time he makes a purchase he is given a self-certification form to read and sign." One wonders if a similar arrangement for airline pilot certification would be considered acceptable. [49]

### 4.4 Greater State Authority

Several sections of the 1978 amendments reflect Congress' intent to give the states greater responsibility in regulating pesticides. This includes not only training and cooperative agreements, but also increasing federal delegation over such matters as intra-state registrations and enforcement. The EPA Administrator, however, retains overall supervisory responsibility and ultimate veto authority. Because some states, such as California, have promulgated stringent guidelines for pesticide regulations, there has been proposed legislation to limit state authority under Section 24 to gather data about a pesticide for state registration. [50] Pesticide manufacturers have complained for several years that state registration procedures, which may require additional studies and data gathering, are time-consuming and costly. There have been no changes in Section 24 yet; however, Congress may limit the regulatory authority of the states in future legislation.

### 4.5 Two-House Congressional Veto Over EPA Regulations

The 1980 amendments amended Section 25(a) to provide a two-house congressional veto over EPA rules or regulations. [51] Under the amendments, the Administrator is required to submit to each house of Congress new FIFRA regulations. If Congress adopts a concurrent resolution disapproving the new regulation within ninety days of its promulgation it will not become effective. However, if neither house disapproves the regulation after sixty days and the

---

[48] States may themselves require an examination of certified applicators but, under the amended FIFRA, EPA could not make this a prerequisite for state plan approval. See Pub. L. 94-140 § 5, amending FIFRA § 4, 7 U.S.C. 136b. See also Senate Report No. 94-452, pp. 7-8.

[49] House Report No. 94-497, p. 9.

[50] See "Hearings Before the House Agricultural Committee, Federal Insecticide, Fungicide, and Rodenticide Act Amendments," H.R. 5203, Serial No. 97-R, (1982).

[51] Pub. L. No. 96-539, 94 Stat. 3194, 3195 amending 7 U.S.C. § 136w(4).

appropriate committee of neither house has reported out a disapproving regulation, the regulation becomes effective. [52]

## 5.0 REMOVAL OF PESTICIDES FROM THE MARKET

FIFRA is not merely concerned with the registration, or reregistration, of pesticides coming on the market. It also has mechanisms for taking action against products considered to pose a risk to man and the environment.

### 5.1 Cancellation

While the registration process may be the heart of FIFRA, cancellation represents the cutting edge of the law and attracts the most public attention. Cancellation is used to initiate review of a substance suspected of posing a "substantial question of safety" to man or the environment. [53] Contrary to public assumptions, during the pendency of the proceedings the product may be freely manufactured and shipped in commerce. A cancellation order, although final if not challenged within thirty days, usually leads to a public hearing or scientific review committee, or both, and can be quite protracted; this can last a matter of months or years. A recommended decision from the agency hearing examiner (now called the administrative law judge) goes to the Administrator or to his delegated representative, the chief agency judicial officer, for a final determination on the cancellation. If the decision is upheld, the product would be banned from shipment or use in the United States. [54]

There are several quite different types of action covered under the single term "cancellation". [55] First, there is a cancellation when EPA believes a substance is a highly probable threat to man or the environment but for which

---

[52] The constitutionality of congressional vetoes of administrative rules is unsettled. The Supreme Court in 1983 held that one-house vetoes are unconstitutional, and since then legislation has had to be revised to conform to the legislative mode: *both* houses must pass legislation which is then presented to the president for his approval or disapproval. *Immigration & Naturalization Service v. Chadha*, 462 U.S. 919, 103 S.Ct. 2764 (1983), affirming 64 F.d 408 (9th Cir., 1980).

[53] *EDF v. Ruckelshaus*, 439 F.2d 584, 591-92, 2 ERC 1114, 1119 (D.C. Cir., 1971).

[54] The scientific review committee and other features of this process will be discussed later in more detail.

[55] The cancellation-suspension section of the old act was § 4(c); it is § 6 of the post-1972 FIFRA.

there is not yet sufficient evidence to warrant immediate suspension. This is the usual meaning. Second, there can be a cancellation when scientific tests indicate some cause for concern, and a public hearing or scientific advisory committee is desired to explore the issue more thoroughly. And third, there could be a cancellation issued in response to a citizens' suit to enable both critics and defenders of the pesticide to present their arguments. These distinctions, although not found in the statute, are nevertheless quite important. State authorities, for example, often recommend that farmers cease using a canceled product which they thought had been declared unsafe, although EPA may have considered the action in category two or three above. Conversely, there were occasions when EPA wanted to communicate its great concern over the continued use of a product without resorting to the more immediate and drastic remedy of suspension.This problem is not resolved completely by the amended FIFRA, but two levels of action are distinguished:

The Administrator may issue a notice of his intent either (1) to cancel its registration or to change its classification together with the reasons (including the factual basis) for his action, or (2) to hold a hearing to determine whether or not its registration should be canceled or its classification changed. [56] This revision of the law may not have solved EPA's communications problem with local officials, but it does provide a basis for a distinction which EPA sometimes needed to make.

## 5.2 Suspension

A suspension order, despite its misleading name, is an immediate ban on the production and distribution of a pesticide. It is mandated when a product constitutes an "imminent hazard" to man or the environment, and may be invoked at any stage of the cancellation proceeding, or even before a cancellation procedure has been initiated. According to the 18th of March Statement, a seminal 1971 EPA pronouncement, "an imminent hazard may be declared at any point in the chain of events which may ultimately result in harm to the public." [57] A suspension order must be accompanied by a cancellation order if one is not then outstanding.

### 5.2.1 Ordinary Suspension

The purpose of an ordinary suspension is to prevent an imminent hazard during the time required for cancellation or change in classification proceedings. An ordinary suspension proceeding is initiated when the Administrator issues notice to the registrant that he is suspending use of the

---

[56] FIFRA § 6(b), 7 U.S.C. § 136d(b). Note that the administrator himself may request a hearing, a power which he did not have under the old FIFRA, although in fact he assumed this authority in his August 1971 cancellation order on 2,4,5-T.

[57] See EPA's March 18, 1971, Statement, p. 6.

pesticide and includes the requisite findings as to imminent hazard. The registrant may request an expedited hearing within five days of receipt of the Administrator's notice. If no hearing is requested, the suspension order can take effect immediately thereafter and the order is not reviewable by a court. The original notion was that suspension procedurally "resembles . . . the judicial proceedings on a contested motion for a preliminary injunction,"[58] and that it remains in effect until the cancellation hearing is completed and a final decision is issued by the Administrator. [59] This connotation of temporariness does not actually accord with reality but has been the consistent theme of judicial decisions since the agency's inception. According to this view, the function of a suspension order is not to reach a definitive decision on the registration of a pesticide but to grant temporary, interim relief. [60] The Circuit Court of Appeals for the District of Columbia has repeatedly stated this view: "The function of the suspension decision is to make a preliminary assessment of evidence and probabilities, not an ultimate resolution of difficult issues," [61] and "the suspension order thus operates to afford interim relief during the course of the lengthy administrative proceedings." [62] The court of appeals has specifically noted that "imminent hazard" does not refer only to the danger of an immediate disaster: "We must caution against any approach to the term 'imminent hazard' used in the statute, that restricts it to a concept of crises." [63] In another case, the court declared that the Secretary of Agriculture: has concluded that the most important element of an "imminent hazard to the public" is a serious threat to public health, that a hazard may be "imminent" even if its impact will not be apparent for many years, and that the "public" protected by the suspension provision includes fish and wildlife. These interpretations all seem consistent with the statutory language and purpose.[64]

---

[58] *EDF v. EPA*, 465 F. 2d 538, 4 ERC 1523, 1530 (D.C. Cir., 1972).

[59] *Nor-Am v. Hardin*, 435 F. 2d 1151, 2 ERC 1016 (7th Cir., 1970), *cert. denied* 402 U.S. 935 (1971).

[60] See, *In re Shell Chemical*, Opinion of the Administrator, pp. 8-11, 6 ERC 2047 at 2050 (1974).

[61] *EDF v. EPA, supra*, 465 F. 2d at 537, 4 ERC at 1529.

[62] *EDF v. Ruckelshaus, supra*, 439 F. 2d at 589, 2 ERC at 1115.

[63] *EDF v. EPA, supra*, 465 F. 2d at 540, 4 ERC at 1531.

[64] *EDF v. Ruckelshaus, supra*, 439 F.2d at 597, 2 ERC at 1121-22.

### 5.2.2 Emergency Suspension

The emergency suspension is the strongest environmental action EPA can take under FIFRA and immediately halts all uses, sales, and distribution of the pesticide. [65] An emergency suspension differs from an ordinary suspension in that the registrant is not given notice or the opportunity for an expedited hearing prior to the suspension order taking effect. The registrant is, however, entitled to an expedited hearing to determine the propriety of the emergency suspension. The Administrator can only use this procedure when he determines that an emergency exists which does not allow him to hold a hearing before suspending use of a pesticide. This authority has only rarely been invoked. EPA first used the emergency suspension procedure in 1979 when it suspended the sale and use of 2,4,5-T and Silvex for specified uses. EPA issued the suspension orders based on its judgment that exposure to the pesticides created an immediate and unreasonable risk to human health. EPA's action was reviewed by a Michigan district court in *Dow Chemical Co. v. Blum,*[66] where the plaintiffs petitioned for judicial review of EPA's decision and a stay of the emergency suspension orders. In upholding EPA's order, the court analogized the emergency suspension order to a temporary restraining order and defined the term emergency as a "substantial likelihood that serious harm will be experienced during the three or four months required in any realistic projection of the administrative suspension process." [67]The court held that this standard required the Administrator to examine five factors: (1) the seriousness of the threatened harm; (2) the immediacy of the threatened harm; (3) the probability that the threatened harm would result; (4) the benefits to the public of the continued use of the pesticides in question during the suspension process; and (5) the nature and extent of the information before the Administrator at the time he makes his decision. The court also held that an emergency suspension order may be overturned only if it was arbitrary, capricious, or an abuse of discretion or if it was not "issued in accordance with the procedures established by law." [68]

---

[65] Its counterpart in the Toxic Substances Control Act, TSCA, is Section 7, but that provision has remained virtually unused over the past decade.

[66] 469 F. Supp. 892, 13 ERC 1129 (E.D. Mich., 1979).

[67] *Ibid.* at 902, 13 ERC at 1135.

[68] *Ibid.* The court stated that it arrived at its decision to uphold EPA's order "with great reluctance" and would not have ordered the emergency suspension on the basis of the information before EPA, but was not empowered to substitute its judgment for that of EPA's. 469 F. Supp. at 907, 13 ERC at 1140.

## 5.3 Disposal and Recall

An important question following a cancellation or suspension action is whether to recall those products already in commerce. [69] "Misbranded" pesticides may be confiscated, and on several occasions EPA has ordered manufacturers to recall a pesticide when the hazard so warranted, but for both practical and administrative reasons cancellation-suspension orders have generally provided that banned pesticides may be used until supplies are exhausted, without being subject to recall. [70] It may seem inconsistent to ban a substance as an imminent hazard and yet allow quantities already on the market to be sold, but repeated challenges by environmentalist groups have been unsuccessful. [71] This policy was thought necessary, for example, in the mercury pesticides case when EPA scientists concluded that the recall of certain mercuric compounds would result in a concentration more harmful to the environment than permitting the remaining supplies to be thinly spread around the country. In the DDT case the Administrator decided that his final cancellation order would not go into effect for six months to ensure the availability of adequate supplies of alternative pesticides (namely, organophosphates which can be very hazardous to untrained applicators) and to allow time for training and educational programs to prevent misuse of the new chemicals. EPA promulgated regulations for the storage and disposal of pesticides in May 1974. [72] These detailed the appropriate conditions for incinerations, soil injection, and other means of disposal, established procedures for shipment back to the manufacturers or to the federal government, directed that transportation costs should be borne by the owner of the pesticide, and provided standards for storage. The regulations devote considerable attention to the disposal problem of pesticide containers, which have caused a significant proportion of accidental poisonings.

## 5.4 Compensation for Canceled Pesticides

Section 15 provides financial compensation to registrants and applicators owning quantities of pesticides who are unable to use them because of cancellation or suspension. This section was the most controversial in the

---

[69] FIFRA §§ 19 and 25, 7 U.S.C. §§ 136q and 136w. See also the previous discussion of indemnities.

[70] Compare the recall authority of the Consumer Product Safety Commission under Section 15 of its Hazardous Substance Act, 15 U.S.C. §1274, Pub. L. No. 91-113, which makes recall almost mandatory. The Consumer Product Safety Act, Section 15, on the other hand, provides several options, 15 U.S.C. 2064, Pub. L. No. 92-573.

[71] See, e.g., *EDF v. EPA* 510 F. 2d 1292, 7 ERC 1689 (D.C. Cir., 1975).

[72] 39 Fed. Reg. 15236, (May 1, 1974), 40 C.F.R. § 165.

entire act; the amendment's industry supporters threatened to block passage of the entire 1972 legislation if this section were not attached. Public interest groups complained that it would force taxpayers to indemnify manufacturers for inadequate testing and would encourage the production of unsafe chemicals.[73] To the extent that this provision was intended not so much for indemnification as to deter EPA cancellations,[74] it served to undermine the purposes of this act. As a partial compromise, a clause was added to bar indemnification to any person who "had knowledge of facts which, in themselves, would have shown that such pesticide did not meet the requirements" for registration and continued thereafter to produce such pesticide without giving notice of such facts to the Administrator. If properly applied, even under the most expedited agency procedures, that saving clause could have disqualified registrants and manufacturers from compensation in virtually all cancellation and suspension actions. Under this provision, the EPA has paid out $20 million to manufacturers of the two pesticides, 2,4,5-T and ethylene dibromide (EDB). An additional $40 million indemnification is estimated for a third canceled pesticide, dinoseb. These sums come directly from the budget of EPA's Pesticide Office, which last year totaled only $40 million, and thus would require that the agency cut back on other activities.[75] This indemnities provision is now generally regarded as a mistake. In the 1988 legislation on FIFRA, the House and Senate both voted to remove the section, except for the indemnification of end users (i.e., farmers and applicators), so chemical manufacturers would no longer be covered. [76] Farmers and other users would still be eligible for compensation through the federal government's regular Judgment Fund. [77] This reflects the philosophy of an earlier congressional prohibition, contained in the Appropriations Bill for fiscal year 1988, which provided that any sums should be paid from the general U.S. Treasury, not from EPA's budget, so the agency would not be penalized for taking measures it deemed proper. [78]

---

[73] FIFRA § 15, Pub. L. No. 92-516.

[74] See section 4.1 "Indemnities" in this chapter.

[75] *Washington Post*, September 15, 1988.

[76] See the fuller discussion of the, FIFRA Amendments of 1988, *infra*.

[77] Section 501 of the 1988 amendments.

[78] FY 1988 Continuing Appropriation Act, Pub. L. No. 100-202.

## 5.5 Balancing Test in FIFRA

The balancing of risks versus benefits is mandated by FIFRA, and its importance warrants a separate discussion. There are some who feel that certain types of pesticides, particularly carcinogens, should be forbidden *per se* as done under the Delaney Amendment to the Food, Drug, and Cosmetics Act.[79] FIFRA does not require this inflexibility, although the courts have cautioned that the law "places a heavy burden on any administrative officer to explain the basis for his decision to permit the continued use of a chemical known to produce cancer in experimental animals." [80] The balancing that is applied during the registration process and, more formally, during the cancellation proceedings is to determine whether there are "unreasonable adverse effects on the environment", taking into consideration the "economic, social, and environmental costs and benefits of the use of any pesticide." In a suspension proceeding, however, the FIFRA does not require a balancing of environmental risks and benefits. It has nevertheless been EPA's policy since its inception to conduct such an analysis, although in practice the benefits would obviously need to be considerable to balance a finding of "imminent hazard." One Administrator noted that "the Agency traditionally has considered benefits as well as risks . . . and, in his opinion, should continue to do so." [81]

## 5.6 Requirements of Consultation by EPA with USDA

Congress decided in the 1975 amendments to require that EPA engage in formal consultation with USDA and with the Agriculture Committees of the House and Senate before issuing proposals or final standards regarding pesticides. This amended Section 6(b) of the FIFRA to provide that EPA should give 60 days' notice to the Secretary of Agriculture before a notice is made public. The Secretary then must respond within 30 days, and these comments, along with the response of the EPA Administrator, are published in the *Federal Register*. [82] These consultations, however, are not required in the event of an imminent hazard to human health for which a suspension order under Section 6(c) is warranted. At the same time that the Administrator provides a copy of any proposed regulations to the Secretary of Agriculture,

---

[79] FDCA § 409(c)(3)(A), 21 U.S.C. § 348(c)(3)(A). The relationship between the FIFRA and the FDCA will be discussed later in more detail.

[80] *EDF v. Ruckelshaus, supra*, 439 F. 2d at 596, 2 ERC at 1121.

[81] *In re Shell Chemical, supra.*, p. 11, 6 ERC at 2050-51, upheld unanimously by the D.C. Court of Appeals in *EDF v. EPA*, 510 F. 2d 1292, 7 ERC 1689 (April 4, 1975).

[82] These time deadlines may be by agreement between the administrator and the secretary, Pub. L. No. 94-140, § 1.

he is also required to provide copies to the respective House and Senate Agricultural Committees. The practical impact of this requirement is that Congress is provided an opportunity to communicate displeasure to the Administrator before a proposal is issued without necessarily having to subject these comments to scrutiny in the public record. [83]

## 5.7 Economic Impact On Agriculture Statement

The 1975 amendments also reflected the increasing trend in government toward requiring impact statements before regulations can be issued. Congress, borrowing from the environmental impact statement process[84] and the economic impact statement requirements, [85] mandated that the Administrator, when deciding to issue a proposal, "shall include among those factors to be taken into account the impact of the action proposed in such notice on production and prices of agricultural commodities, retail food prices, and otherwise on the agricultural economy." [86] The necessity for this legal provision is questionable since the balancing of risks and benefits is at the heart of FIFRA. No one at EPA or anywhere else has contended that the agricultural benefits of pesticides should not be taken into consideration in this balancing equation. In fact, although the courts have stated that EPA legally need not consider benefits in suspension actions involving an imminent hazard to human health and the environment, EPA from the beginning has always made the agricultural factor an essential element in its determinations. [87] The committees themselves were vague about the actual need for this legislation. (The Senate stated, "The Committee concurs in the House position that EPA has not always given adequate consideration to agriculture in its decisions. This concern was also expressed by many witnesses appearing before the Committee.") [88]

---

[83] EPA has often required that congressional communications after the issuance of a proposal be placed on the public record; and where this was not done, as in the DDT proceedings, environmental groups successfully sued to ensure that these contacts and written comments were made public.

[84] National Environmental Policy Act, § 102(2)(c), U.S.C. §§ 4321 *et seq.*, (1969); see also 36 Fed. Reg. 7724 (1971) and 38 Fed. Reg. 20549 (1973).

[85] Presidential Executive Order No. 11821, November 29, 1974.

[86] Pub. L. No. 94-104, § 1, amending FIFRA § 6(b), 7 U.S.C. § 136d.

[87] See the discussion of this in paragraph 2.6 of this chapter.

[88] Senate Report No. 94-452, p. 9.

## 5.8 Scientific Advisory Committees

Because the Scientific Advisory Committees play such an important role in the cancellation-suspension process, they deserve special attention in this section.

According to the old FIFRA, prior to 1972, a registrant challenging a cancellation order could request either a public hearing or a scientific advisory committee; and in practice, cases involving several registrants usually resulted in both. EPA was also strongly dissatisfied with the vague and often contradictory reports of the advisory committees.In the 1972 amendments to FIFRA, the advisory committee was transformed into an adjunct of the hearing process, resolving those scientific questions which the administrative law judge or the parties determined were essential to the final decision by the Administrator. The amendments streamlined the process so that Committee deliberations could proceed simultaneously with the administrative hearings, thereby saving time and making them a part of the fact-finding and evaluation system, rather than in a separate proceeding with long delays and divisions of responsibility. By meeting outside of the public hearing, the scientists can also avoid being subject to cross examination and other legal burdens they consider unappealing. The advisory process, however, was again made more formalistic by the 1975 amendments. The use of a scientific advisory committee was mandated both for cancellation actions (where they are usually requested anyway) and for any general pesticide regulations.[89] The amendments required that the Administrator submit proposed and final regulations to a specially constituted scientific advisory panel, separate from the regular Scientific Advisory Committees, at the same time that he provides copies to the Secretary of Agriculture and to the two agricultural committees of Congress. The advisory committee then has 30 days in which to respond. Membership on this committee is prescribed in unusual detail. The Administrator can select seven members from a group of twelve nominees, six nominated by the National Science Foundation, and six by the National Institutes of Health. [90] In 1980, Section 25(d) was amended to allow the chairman of a Scientific Advisory Committee to create temporary subpanels on specific projects. [91] Section 25(d) was also amended to require the Administrator to submit any decision to suspend the registration of a pesticide to a scientific advisory panel (SAP) for its comment. [92] The amendment does not alter the Administrator's authority to issue a suspension notice prior to the

---

[89] Pub. L. No. 94-140, § 7, amending FIFRA § 25. A more detailed analysis of the 1975 changes appears in 5.0.

[90] Pub. L. No. 94-140, § 7, amending FIFRA § 25(d), 7 U.S.C. § 136w.

[91] Pub. L. No. 96-539, 94 Stat. 3195.

[92] *Id.*

SAP review, it only requires him to obtain SAP review after the suspension is initiated. The 1980 amendments also require the Administrator to issue written procedures for independent peer review of the design, protocol and conduct of major studies conducted under FIFRA. [93] One might question the value of ever more advisory committees when, as EPA Administrator Russell Train pointed out years ago, "EPA is already awash in scientific advisory panels." [94]

## 5.9 The Scope of the Administrator's Flexibility

The EPA Administrator renders the final agency judgment on administrative actions and appeals.[95] Since issues reach him only after passing through a series of committees, lower level enforcement officials, and administrative law judges, the question is how much discretion he has to come to a decision at variance with those rendered below?

### 5.9.1 Concerning the Scientific Advisory Committee

In emphasizing the Administrator's regulatory flexibility, the courts have rejected the contention that he must "rubber stamp" the findings of the Scientific Advisory Committee or the administrative law judge. This is illustrated by *Dow Chemical v. Ruckelshaus* [96] concerning the herbicide 2,4,5-T. In 1970 the USDA suspended some uses of the chemical and canceled others because of the high risk that it, or a dioxin contaminant known as TCDD, had proved a potent teratogen in laboratory tests. Most of these uses were not challenged, but Dow did contest the cancellation on rice. A Scientific Advisory Committee convoked by EPA concluded that the "confused aggregate of observations indicated registrations should be maintained" but that there remained serious questions needing further extensive research. The Administrator reviewed the report in considerable detail and concluded that a "substantial question of safety" existed sufficient to justify an administrative hearing; in the meantime, the cancellation was maintained. [97] Dow appealed, but the Court of Appeals for the Eighth Circuit held that the Administrator was not compelled to follow the recommendations of the advisory committee if

---

[93] No. 96-1020, 96th Cong., 2d Sess. (1980) p. 4.

[94] Statement of EPA Administrator Russell Train to the Senate Agricultural Committee, reprinted in Senate Report No. 94-452, p. 18.

[95] In practice, most appeals to the Administrator are handled and decided by the Chief Judicial Officer, in the office of the Administrator.

[96] 477 F.2d 1317, 5 ERC 1244 (8th Cir., 1973).

[97] The deficiencies in the advisory report, which was poorly reasoned and internally inconsistent, contributed to the agency's skepticism towards this system of information collection and analysis.

--and this is, of course, crucial--he had a justifiable basis for doing other-wise. [98]

### 5.9.2 Concerning the Administrative Law Judge

The Administrator is also not bound by findings of the administrative law judges. This conclusion follows the general principle of administrative law that a hearing examiner's decision should be accorded only the deference it merits. As the Supreme Court said long ago in *Universal Camera*, "we do not require that the examiner's findings be given more weight than in reason and in light of judicial experience they deserve." [99] Only if the decision-maker arbitrarily and capriciously ignored the findings of an examiner, or if the credibility of witnesses was crucial to the case--a situation that rarely exists in an administrative hearing--would a different conclusion be indicated.

## 6.0 ADMINISTRATIVE AND JUDICIAL APPEALS

### 6.1 Standing for Registration, Appeals and Subpoenas

FIFRA originally assumed that only registrants would be interested in the continuation of a product's registration or the setting of public hearings and scientific advisory committees. It was increasingly evident, however, that this unintended exclusion of both users and environmentalists needed revision. Whereas a registrant, when faced with cancellation, might prefer not to contest those minor categories of use which it regarded as financially insignificant, a user might regard them as essential for the protection of his crops. The law was therefore amended by FEPCA to allow not only registrants but any "other interested person with the concurrence of the registrant" to request continuation of the registration. [100] While this amendment remedies the problem of legal standing, it does not provide the resources and data which users, particularly small farmers or organizations, would need to

---

[98] This case is better remembered for its unconscionable delay of the administrative process. Dow appealed first to a district court in Arkansas and obtained an injunction against further EPA action on 2,4,5-T, although the statute explicitly excluded district courts from jurisdiction. The Eighth Circuit reversed, noting that the court below lacked jurisdiction and that in any case Dow was not entitled to an injunction during a period when "the cancellation orders have no effect on Dow's right to ship and market its product until the administration cancellation process has been completed." *Ibid.*, at 1326, 5 ERC at 1250.

[99] *Universal Camera Corp. v. NLRB*, 340 U.S. 474 (1951).

[100] FIFRA § 6(a)(1), 7 U.S.C. § 136d(a)(1). See also *McGill v. EPA*, 593 F. 2d 631, 13 ERC 1156 (5th Cir., 1979).

support a renewal application. [101] Another problem of standing relates to the right of environmental and consumer groups to utilize the administrative procedures under cancellation-suspension. The act does not specifically give citizens' groups the right to request a public hearing, but the Administrator himself is now empowered to call a hearing which he might do at the request of such a group. Furthermore, as already discussed, all interested parties may request consent of the administrative law judge to refer scientific questions to a special committee of the National Academy of Sciences for determination, a right which did not exist before.The issue of standing came up in *Environmental Defense Fund v. Costle* [102] when the D.C. Circuit upheld EPA's denial of standing for an environmental group which requested a Section 6(d) cancellation hearing for the continued use of chlorobenzilate in four states. The Environmental Defense Fund (EDF) requested the hearing after the Administrator issued a Notice of Intent to Cancel the registration of chlorobenzilate for all uses other than citrus spraying in four states. The Administrator denied the hearing holding that FIFRA was not structured for the purpose of entertaining objections by persons having no real interest in stopping the cancellation from going into effect, but who object to the agency's refusal to propose actions. [103] The D.C. Circuit upheld the Administrator's decision that EDF was not an "adversely affected" party under Section 6(d), stating that a 6(d) hearing may be used only to stop a cancellation proceeding, not initiate one. The proper procedure for EDF in seeking review of EPA's decision to retain the registration for citrus users was to challenge the notice provisions permitting the limited use in district court under Section 16(a) of FIFRA. [104]

---

[101] A good example is the Aldrin-Dieldrin suspension proceeding, in which the registrant was almost solely interested in the use for crops, while the USDA had to join the proceeding to insure that other registrations were properly represented. This USDA action under the new FIFRA, however, was necessary not because the users now lacked legal standing, but presumably because they lacked adequate resources. *In re Shell Chemical, supra.*, 6 ERC 2047.

[102] 631 F.2d 922, 15 ERC 1217 (D.C. Cir., 1980), *cert. denied* 449 U.S. 1112.

[103] Final Decision, FIFRA Docket No. 411 (August 20, 1979) at 12-22.

[104] 631 F. 2d at 935, 15 ERC at 1229. This case is also noteworthy for its treatment of judicial review under Section 16(b): See discussion of Judicial Review in 4.2.

## 6.2 Judicial Appeals

Under the old version of FIFRA, [105] appeals from decisions of the Administrator went to the United States court of appeals. According to Section 16 of the amended FIFRA, however, appeals under some circumstances may go to a federal district court. [106] Other appeals go to the court of appeals.This change provoked considerable controversy in EPA during the legislative process. The rationale for change was that courts of appeals are not designed to develop a record if none existed from the proceeding below. It thus seemed logical that in those instances where a record was developed, after public hearing or otherwise, the appeal should be to the court of appeals, whereas in cases where there was no record for the court to review the matter should go to a district court for findings of fact. Section 16 has been the focus of two courts of appeals decisions which reached contrary holdings on the issue of whether the federal courts or the courts of appeals have jurisdiction to review the denial of a request for a FIFRA Section 6(d) hearing on a notice of cancellation. In *Environmental Defense Fund v. Costle*, [107] the D.C. Circuit Court held that if an administrative record exists in support of a denial of a hearing request, jurisdiction lies exclusively with the courts of appeals. In *AMVAC Chemical Corp. v. EPA*, [108] a divided Ninth Circuit rejected the D.C. Circuit's analysis and held that a denial of a hearing was a procedural action and not an "order" following a "public hearing" within the meaning of Section 16(b). Hence, the Court held that judicial review of hearing request denials lies in the district courts.

## 7.0 LITIGATION ISSUES

The litigation over FIFRA for the last decade has shifted from being concerned with product safety to focusing on data confidentiality and the financial compensation for its use by other companies. That does not necessarily mean that safety is ignored nor that all sides have reached consensus on what constitutes a health risk, but that the environmental safety issue is now contested more at the staff level within EPA's Pesticide Office than at the Administrator's level or in the courts. (There is also, admittedly, much less federal regulatory activity, namely cancellations and suspensions,

---

[105] Old FIFRA § 4(d).

[106] FIFRA § 16(a)-(c), 7 U.S.C. § 136n(a)-(c).

[107] 631 F. 2d 922, 15 ERC 1217 (D.C. Cir., 1980) *cert. denied* 449 U.S. 1112. This case is also important for its treatment of standing, discussed in the previous subsection.

[108] 653 F. 2d 1260, 15 ERC 1467 (9th Cir., 1980) as amended February 5, 1981, *reh. denied*, April 10, 1981.

than there once was.) The pesticide industry has focused instead on allocating the tremendously expensive costs of developing and registering the few products that survive the testing process and can be marketed. But for that reason, the judicial doctrines set forth in EPA's first half dozen years remain the basis for pesticide regulation.

## 7.1 Basic Cases

The early cases, originating in the period before EPA's creation, generally resulted in court determinations that the responsible federal agency had not sufficiently examined the health and environmental problems.A leading case in this respect is the 1970 court of appeals decision by Judge Bazelon in *Environmental Defense Fund v. Hardin,* [109] which not only gave legal standing to environmental groups under the FIFRA but also determined that the Secretary of Agriculture's failure to take prompt action on a request for suspension of the registration of DDT was tantamount to a denial of suspension and therefore was suitable for judicial review.[110] That same year the Seventh Circuit Court of Appeals held *en banc* in *Nor-Am v. Hardin*[111] that a pesticide registrant could not enjoin a suspension order by the Secretary of Agriculture, since the administrative remedies, namely the full cancellation proceedings, had not been exhausted: "The emergency suspension becomes final only if unopposed or affirmed in whole or in part, by subsequent decisions based upon a full and formal consideration."[112] An underlying reason for the court's action, which reversed a three-judge court of appeals panel in the same circuit, [113] was the realization that the suspension procedure, which had been designed to deal with imminent hazards to the public, could effectively be short-circuited by injunctions. In the court's view, therefore, a suspension decision is only equivalent to a temporary injunction which shall hold until the full cancellation proceedings are completed. [114] One of the most important of

---

[109] 428 F. 2d 1083, 1 ERC 1347 (D.C. Cir., 1970).

[110] As there was no administrative record underlying the Secretary's inaction, however, the court remanded the issue to the Department of Agriculture "to provide the court with a record necessary for meaningful appellate review."

[111] 435 F. 2d 1151, 2 ERC 1016 (7th Cir., en banc, 1970).

[112] *Ibid.*, at 1157, 2 ERC at 1019.

[113] 435 F. 2d 1133, 1 ERC 1460 (7th Cir., 1970).

[114] 435 F. 2d at 1160-1161.

the earlier cases was *EDF v. Ruckelshaus*. [115] The court in another opinion by Judge Bazelon found that the Secretary of Agriculture failed to take prompt action on a request for the interim suspension of DDT registration but that the Secretary's findings of fact, such as the risk of cancer and its toxic effect on certain animals, implicitly constituted a finding of "substantial question concerning the safety of DDT" which the court declared warranted a cancellation decision. The suspension issue was remanded once again for further consideration. The decision is worthy of attention on two additional points. First, Judge Bazelon made the sweeping statement that "the FIFRA requires the Secretary to issue notices and thereby initiate the administrative process whenever there is a substantial question about the safety of the registered pesticide, . . . The statutory scheme contemplates that these questions will be explored in the full light of a public hearing and not resolved behind the closed doors of the secretary." [116] Second, the court approved the findings of the secretary that a hazard may be "imminent" even if its effect would not become realized for many years, as is the case with most carcinogens, and that the "public" protected by the suspension provision includes fish and wildlife in the environment as well as narrow threat to human health. *Wellford v. Ruckelshaus*, [117] another case inherited by EPA from USDA, involved a partial remand of the Secretary of Agriculture's decision concerning suspension and cancellation of certain uses of the herbicide 2,4,5-T for use around the home, in aquatic areas, and on food crops. This case is primarily important for its articulation of certain procedural ground. It agreed with the contention that suspension is only "a matter of interim relief," and stated that the criteria for suspension during an administrative process involved the Secretary's first determining "what harm, if any, is likely to flow from the use of the product during the course of administrative proceedings. He must consider both the magnitude of the anticipated harm and the likelihood that it would occur. On the basis of that factual determination, he must decide whether anticipated harm amounts to an 'imminent hazard to the public.' "

---

[115] *EDF v. Ruckelshaus*, 439 F.2d 584, 2 ERC 1114 (D.C. Cir., 1971). This was a sequel to the earlier *EDF v. Hardin* case, supra, but the name of the administrator of EPA was substituted for the Secretary of Agriculture since the authority of USDA had been transferred to the EPA the month before.

[116] *Ibid.*, at 594, 2 ERC at 1119. Because there may be a "substantial question of safety" about most pesticides, administrative necessity has forced EPA to interpret this as requiring cancellation of only the most harmful chemicals.

[117] 439 F. 2d 598, 2 ERC 1123 (D.C. Cir., 1971).

## 7.2 Label Restrictions: Theory and Practice

One of the most interesting pesticide cases, *In re Stearns,* [118] raised the question whether a chemical could be banned that was too toxic to be safely used around the home but which nevertheless was labeled properly with cautionary statements and symbols such as the skull and crossbones. "Stearn's Electric Paste," a phosphorous rat and roach killer, was so potent that even a small portion of a tube could kill a child and a larger dose would be fatal to an adult. There was no known antidote. An incomplete survey of state health officials indicated several dozen deaths and many serious accidents, most involving young children. Because of this hazard and the existence of safer substitutes, the USDA canceled the registration of the paste in May 1969, before the creation of EPA, and a USDA Judicial Officer upheld this action in January 1971 by relying on the provision in the old FIFRA that "the term misbranded shall apply. . .to any economic poison. . .if the labeling accompanying it does not contain directions for use which are necessary and, if complied with, adequate for the protection of the public." [119] A year and a half later, however, the Seventh Circuit Court of Appeals concluded that the statutory test for misbranding was whether a product was safe when used in conformity with the label directions, not whether abuse or misuse was inevitable. The court was impressed with the conspicuous "poison" markings and contended that "disregard of such a simple warning would constitute gross negligence." [120] The hazard of young children left the court unmoved: "such tragedies are a common occurrence in today's complex society and must be appraised as discompassionately as possible." The cancellation order was set aside. The issue was confronted more decisively by the Eighth Circuit a year later in another Lindane case, *Southern National v. EPA.* [121] The registrants challenged a proposed EPA label reading in part, "Not for use or sale to drug stores, supermarkets, or hardware stores or other establishments that sell insecticides to consumers. Not for sale to or use in food handling, processing or serving establishments." In EPA's opinion, acceptance of such a label would avoid the necessity of canceling the entire registration. The court questioned whether EPA was within the scope of its powers under the (old) FIFRA in placing the burden on the manufacturer to discourage distribution to homes, but nevertheless sustained the agency action in all respects. EPA's policy

---

[118] 2 ERC 1364 (Opinion of Judicial Officer, USDA, 1971); *Stearns Electric Paste Company v. EPA*, 461 F. 2d 293, 4 ERC 1164 (7th Cir., 1972).

[119] Old FIFRA § 2(z)2(c).

[120] *Stearns Electric Paste, supra.*, 461 F.2d at 310, 4 ERC at 1175.

[121] 470 F. 2d 194, 4 ERC 1881 (8th Cir., 1972). This case was decided about a month after the enactment of the new FIFRA on October 21, 1972, but that law was not applied here.

position, under both the old and new FIFRA, is that if there are safer alternatives to a product which arguably constitutes a substantial question of safety, the hazardous product should be removed from the market. [122]

## 8.0 EXPORTS AND IMPORTS

Section 17 of FIFRA, in addition to maintaining the provision that imports should be subject to the same requirements of testing and registration as domestic products, also retained the controversial provision excluding U.S. exports from coverage under the act, other than for certain record keeping requirements. [123] There were two reasons for this. First, the agricultural chemical producers, seeing the market for some of their products such as the chlorinated hydrocarbons drying up in this country, wished to continue exporting the products abroad. They argued that foreign producers would not be stopped from manufacturing these chemicals and they wished to continue to compete, as well as to keep in operation profitable product lines.A secondary but more compelling reason was that cancellation decisions made in the United States are based upon a risk-benefit analysis that might have little relevance to conditions abroad. For example, DDT is neither needed nor, because of insect resistance, very useful for the control of malaria in the United States. However, the situation in, say, Ceylon, may be quite different (although resistance is becoming an increasing problem there as well) and should be considered separately. One objection to this approach is that persistent pesticides may be distributed by oceans and the atmosphere in a world-wide circulation pattern that does not stop at national boundaries. A second problem is that there is no requirement that foreign purchasers relying on EPA registration as proof of a product's safety be notified of cancellation-suspension proceedings. Only after a final agency decision--which may take years--is the State Department legally required to inform foreign governments. The 1978 amendments did add a requirement that such exports be labeled that they are "not registered for use in the U.S." [124] In 1980, EPA issued a final policy statement on labeling requirements. [125] Under the 1978 amendments, pesticides which are manufactured for export must have bilingual labeling

---

[122] See *In re King Paint*, 2 ERC 1819 (Opinion of EPA Judicial Officer, 1971).

[123] FIFRA § 8, 17(c), 7 U.S.C. § 1360(c). The old FIFRA provisions on exports is § 3(a)(5)(b); FIFRA § 8, 7 U.S.C. § 136 f.

[124] FIFRA § 17(a)(2), 7 U.S.C. § 1360(e)(f). See also 44 Fed. Reg. 4358 (January 19, 1979).

[125] 45 Fed. Reg. 50274 (July 28, 1980).

which identifies the product and protects the persons who come into contact with it. If the pesticide is not registered for use in the United States, the exporter must obtain a statement from the foreign purchaser acknowledging its unregistered status. [126] The policy statement implements these new requirements by requiring exported products to bear labels containing an EPA establishment number, a use classification statement, the identity of the producer, as well as information about whether the pesticide is registered for use in the United States. In the case of highly toxic pesticides, a skull and crossbones must appear and the word "poison" along with a statement of practical treatment written bilingually. [127] The policy statement also requires that a foreign purchaser of an unregistered pesticide sign a statement showing that he understands that the pesticide is not registered for use in the United States. The exporter must receive the acknowledgment before the product is released for shipment and submit it to EPA within seven days of receipt. EPA then transmits the acknowledgments to the appropriate foreign officials via the State Department. The acknowledgement procedure applies only to the first annual shipment of an unregistered pesticide to a producer; subsequent shipments of the product to the same producer need not comply with the acknowledgment process. [128]

During the farm bill debates in autumn 1990, there was strong pressure for much stricter controls on the export of American pesticides which have been banned in the United States or have been rejected or never approved for registration. There are only two in the first category, the related pesticides termiticides heptachlor and chloradane; reportedly, there are around eight chemicals currently in the second category.

## 9.0 AMENDMENTS TO FIFRA

### 9.1 Need for FIFRA Renewal

The authorization for FIFRA under the 1972 act was limited to three years.[129] Congress was therefore provided the opportunity in 1975 and periodically thereafter to review the strengths and shortcomings of the 1972 legislation, even though some portions of that law were not scheduled to go into effect

---

[126] Pub. L. No. 95-396, 92 Stat 833; codified at 7 U.S.C. § 136(o).

[127] 45 Fed. Reg. at 50274, 50278 (July 28, 1980).

[128] *Ibid.*, at 50276-77.

[129] FIFRA § 27. Actually the term for the act was less than three years since the act finally went into effect in October 1972 and the authorization expired June 30, 1975.

until four years after enactment. [130] This review, however, also provided a chance to redress the balance for those, both within and without Congress, who believed that EPA had been given too much authority. [131]

## 9.2  1975 Amendments to FIFRA

Congress' 1975 amendments to the FIFRA are significant not for what they actually changed but because of the motivations that prompted them.  The amendments themselves were viewed by many as, at best, unnecessary and, at worst, a further encumbrance upon an already complicated administrative procedure.  They did, however, indicate a strong desire on the part of Congress--or at least the respective agriculture committees of the House and Senate--to restrict EPA's authority to regulate pesticides.  The situation was summarized by an editorial in a Washington, D.C., newspaper head-line, "Trying to Hogtie the EPA." [132]

## 9.3  1978 Amendments to FIFRA

The 1978 amendments made changes in a number of areas.  Studies showing pesticide efficacy were made optional, relieving EPA of the chore of determining whether a pesticide actually worked for the purposes claimed.  The data compensation provisions of the Act were made even more complex, although the EPA Administrator was removed from his role as arbitrator of the financial settlement.

## 9.4  1980 Amendments to FIFRA

FIFRA was amended again in 1980, but the amendments made only minor changes in Section 25 of the act, to provide for a two-house congressional veto of EPA rules and regulations, and some additional tampering with the Scientific Advisory Committee.

## 9.5  1988 Amendments to FIFRA

FIFRA was amended again in 1988. [133] The amendments were notable mostly for what they did not contain, namely the hotly-debated provisions sought by environmentalists for protection of the nation's groundwater supplies from contamination by pesticides.  The bill also lacked the section sought by

---

[130] One such example is EPA's authority under § 27 to require that a pesticide be registered for use only by a certified applicator.

[131] House Report No. 94-497, "Extension and Amendment of the FIFRA, as Amended," September 19, 1975, for H.R. 8841, p. 5.

[132] *The Washington Star*, October 8, 1975.

[133] The 1988 amendments to FIFRA were signed into law by President Reagan on October 25, 1988.

the grocery manufacturers to preempt stricter state standards like those under California's Proposition 65 right-to-know law. The legislation did correct a long-standing flaw in the act involving compensation for canceled pesticides and streamlined the pesticide reregistration process, but imposed a substantial fee.

## 10.0 PESTICIDE REGULATION UNDER OTHER FEDERAL STATUTES

Pesticides are not regulated solely under the FIFRA. They may also involve regulatory authority under the Food, Drug and Cosmetic Act (FDCA), under the statutes of several other federal agencies, and under other environmental laws administered by EPA.

### 10.1 Pesticides Under the Food, Drug & Cosmetics Act

One important function of EPA regarding pesticides is not derived from the FIFRA--the setting of tolerances for pesticide residues in food. This authority, originally granted to the Food and Drug Administration under the Food, Drug and Cosmetic Act, [134] was transferred to EPA by the 1970 Reorganization Plan establishing the agency and, more specifically, by subsequent detailed memos of agreement between EPA and FDA. The reorganization plan provided that EPA should set tolerances and "monitor compliance", while the Secretary of HEW would continue to enforce compliance. The amendments to FIFRA in 1972 also invested EPA with authority to prevent misuse of registered pesticides. Under Section 408 of the FDCA, the Administrator issues regulations exempting any pesticides for which a tolerance is unnecessary to protect the public health. Otherwise, he "shall promulgate regulations establishing tolerances with respect to . . . pesticide chemicals which are not generally recognized among experts . . . as safe for use . . . to the extent necessary to protect the public health." Pesticide residues are present in most meats, fruits, and vegetables whether or not chemicals are applied to them. DDT, for example, is detectable in most foods, even in mothers' milk. Before registration of a pesticide, a residue tolerance must be set for the maximum level at which that chemical can be safely ingested. Tolerances are usually set at two orders of magnitude (one-hundredth) below the level at which the pesticide has demonstrated an effect on experimental animals. [135] Some particularly hazardous chemicals are set at "zero residue", but this is causing an increasing problem as the detection capability of analytical equipment is improved. EPA's pesticide jurisdiction is

---

[134] FDCA § 408, 21 U.S.C. § 346a, *et seq.*

[135] This is an oversimplification. The tolerance margin depends on the particular effects of the chemical.

supposed to cover only residues resulting from a chemical's use as a pesticide but not exposure resulting from, say, dust blowing from a factory (this may be covered by EPA's Clean Air Act) or a truck carrying the chemicals. In two major cases involving HCB (hexachlorobenzene) contamination of cattle in Louisiana and sheep in the Rocky Mountains, the HCB was blown from open trucks onto pasture land while being transported from one point to another. EPA assumed responsibility for these cases because the tolerance problems regarding health are really the same whether the chemical entered the food as a result of agricultural use or for some other reason, and FDA was only too glad to oblige. The question of whether DDT was a food "additive" in fish within the meaning of the FDCA was raised again in *U.S. v. Ewing Bros.* [136] The Seventh Circuit explained that prior to the Delaney Amendment, which banned all additives "found to induce cancer when ingested by man or animal", the term did not cover substances present in the raw product and unchanged by processing, but after 1958 the definition was expanded so a single tolerance could cover both raw and processed foods. Since DDT was an additive and EPA had not issued a tolerance, DDT was theoretically a food adulterant and contaminated items were liable to seizure. [137] This could mean, however, that most foods could be seized as adulterated, including the Great Lakes fish at issue in *Ewing*. Realizing this in 1969, the FDA had established an interim action level of 5 ppm DDT in fish, thereby excluding all but the most contaminated samples. [138] This procedure was approved by the Seventh Circuit Court of Appeals in *U.S. v. Goodman,* [139] which held that the Commissioner of FDA had "specific statutory authority in the Act empowering him to refrain from prosecuting minor violations", [140] and that this permitted him to set and enforce action levels in lieu of totally prohibiting the distribution of any food containing DDT at any level.

---

[136] 502 F.2d 715, 6 ERC 2073 (7th Cir., 1974).

[137] Under FDCA § 402(a)(2)(C), 21 U.S.C. § 342(a)(2)(C), this affects only a substance that "is not generally recognized among experts . . . as having been adequately shown . . . to be safe under the conditions of its intended use . . . ." See FDCA § 201(s), 21 U.S.C. § 321(s). Without a tolerance, "the presence of the DDT causes fish to be adulterated without any proof that it is actually unfit as food." 6 ERC 2073, 2077.

[138] Action levels and enforcement, unlike tolerance setting, remain a prerogative of FDA under Section 306 of the FDCA, 21 U.S.C. § 336.

[139] 486 F.2d 847, 5 ERC 1969 (7th Cir., 1973).

[140] *Ibid.,* at 855, 5 ERC at 1974; FDCA §306, 21 U.S.C. §336, *U.S. v. 1500 Cases,* 245 F.2d 208, 210-11 (7th Cir., 1956); *U.S. v. 484 Bags,* 423 F.2d 839, 841 (5th Cir., 1970).

## 10.2 Clean Air Act of 1970

Pesticides in the air may be regulated under Section 112 of the Clean Air Act pertaining to hazardous air pollutants. A hazardous pollutant is defined as one for which "no ambient air quality standard is applicable and which in the judgment of the Administrator may cause, or contribute to, an increase in mortality or an increase in severe irreversible, or incapacitating reversible illness." [141] EPA publishes a list of hazardous air pollutants from time to time and, once a pollutant is listed, proposed regulations establishing stationary source emission standards must be issued unless the substance is conclusively shown to be safe. This section has so far not been applied to pesticides but could acquire more significance in the future.

## 10.3 Federal Water Pollution Control Act of 1972

The Federal Water Pollution Control Act as amended in 1972 has at least three provisions applicable to pesticides. Under Section 301, pesticide manufacturers and formulators, like all other industrial enterprises, must apply for discharge permits if they release effluent into any body of water. These point sources of pollution must apply the "best practicable control technology" by 1977 and by 1983 must use "the best available control technology."[142] Hazardous and ubiquitous pesticides may be controlled under Section 307 governing "toxic substances." [143] Within one year of the listing of a chemical as a "toxic substance," the special discharge standards set for it must be achieved. There was originally some dispute whether pesticides should properly be regulated under this section because, unless they are part of a discharge from an industrial concern, they generally derive from non-point sources such as runoff from fields and therefore could be controlled under a third provision, Section 208, which is largely under the jurisdiction of the states. [144] EPA's principal function under Section 208 is to identify and oversee problems of agricultural pollution, regulated at the state and local level. By 1977, according to the statute, state authorities were to have formulated control programs for the protection of water quality, pesticides and other agricultural pollutants such as feed-lots.

---

[141] Clean Air Act, § 112(a)(1), 42 U.S.C. § 1857c-7(a)(1) (1970).

[142] FWPCA § 301, 33 U.S.C. § 1311.

[143] FWPCA § 307, 33 U.S.C. § 1317. The criteria for this list is given in 38 Fed. Reg. 18044 (1973).

[144] EPA, however, has not followed this reasoning. The present § 307 list of 299 toxic pollutants contains many of the major pesticides. See *NRDC v. Train* (D.C. Cir., 1976) 8 ERC 2120.

The reportedly serious problem of pesticide contamination of groundwater has been hotly debated. Legislation to address this issue was considered in the 1988 amendments to FIFRA but deferred to allow the passage of the other portions of that bill.

In January 1991, EPA issued regulations requiring operators of 80,000 drinking water systems to monitor for the presence of 60 contaminants, including a number of pesticides, and remove those in excess of permitted levels.

## 10.4 Solid Waste Disposal Acts

The EPA had very limited authority under Section 204 of the Solid Waste Disposal Act (SWDA), as amended by the Resource Recovery Act of 1970,[145] to conduct research, training, demonstrations and other activities regarding pesticide storage and disposal.[146] Enactment of the Resource Conservation and Recovery Act (RCRA) in October 1976 gave EPA an important tool for controlling the disposal of pesticides, particularly the waste from pesticide manufacture.

## 10.5 Occupational Safety and Health Act

The EPA and the Department of Labor share somewhat overlapping authority under FIFRA and the Occupational Safety and Health Act (OSHA) for the protection of agricultural workers from pesticide hazards. This produced a heated inter-agency conflict during the first half of 1973, although the FIFRA and its legislative history clearly indicated that EPA had primary responsibility for promulgating re-entry and other protective standards in this area, and that OSHA specifically yielded to existing standards by other federal agencies.[147] The question was finally settled by the White House in EPA's favor after a court had enjoined Labor's own proposed standards.[148]

Since then, the two agencies have cooperated on development of the federal cancer policy in the late 1970s, which grew out of EPA's suspension of the

---

[145] 42 U.S.C. § 3251 *et seq.*, 79 Stat. 997 (1965), 84 Stat. 1227 (1970); RCRA § 204, 42 U.S.C. § 3253.

[146] RCRA § 212, 42 U.S.C. 3241. See also RCRA § 209, 42 U.S.C. § 3254c.

[147] OSHA § 6, 29 U.S.C. § 655.

[148] *Florida Peach Growers Assn. v. Dept. of Labor*, 489 F. 2d 120, (5th Cir., 1974).

pesticides aldrin and dieldrin. Most recently, in 1990, they concluded a memorandum of understanding (MOU) to facilitate joint enforcement of their laws.

## 10.6 Federal Hazardous Substances Act

The Federal Hazardous Substances Act of 1970 regulates hazardous substances in interstate commerce. However, pesticides subject to the FIFRA and the FDCA have been specifically exempted by regulation [149] from the definition of the term "hazardous substance." This statute is administered by the Consumer Product Safety Commission (CPSC) which also administers the Poison Prevention Packaging Control Act of 1970, designed to protect children from pesticides and other harmful substances. It is not yet clear how EPA and the CPSC will divide their overlapping authority in this area. EPA might welcome the involvement of CPSC in this limited portion of the pesticide area to the extent that its own hands are tied by the Court of Appeals decision in the *Stearns Paste* case. [150]

## 10.7 Federal Pesticide Monitoring Programs

The FDA and USDA assist EPA in monitoring pesticide residues in food. The FDA conducts frequent spot checks and an annual Market Basket Survey in which pesticide residues are analyzed in a representative sampling of grocery items. The FDA's Poison Control Center also compiles current statistics on chemical poisoning. The USDA's Animal and Plant Health Inspection Service conducts spot checks on pesticides in meats and poultry based on samples taken at slaughter houses throughout the country.The Department of Interior samples pesticide residues in fish and performs experiments to determine the effects of pesticides which may be introduced into the aquatic environment. The Geological Survey Division of Interior also conducts periodic nationwide water sampling for pesticides and other contaminants. The National Oceanic Atmospheric Administration (NOAA) under the Department of Commerce monitors aquatic areas for pesticide levels, and the Department of Transportation's Office of Hazardous Substances records accidents involving pesticides in shipment and distribution.

## 10.8 National Environmental Policy Act

The EPA is also not bound by the National Environmental Policy Act (NEPA) to file environmental impact statements on its pesticide decisions, since the procedures under the FIFRA are an adequate substitute. Although the

---

[149] 16 C.F.R. § 1500 3(b)(4)(ii).

[150] *U.S. v. Stearns Electric Paste, supra.*

strict language of NEPA states that *all* agencies of the federal government should file impact statements, this law was enacted before EPA existed, and courts almost unanimously have found that there is little logic in requiring an agency whose sole function is protection of environment to file a statement obliging it to take into consideration environmental factors. [151] Courts nevertheless hesitated to grant a blanket exemption to EPA, preferring to stress that EPA actions are mandated by a given statute, although this justification has not exempted certain non-environmental agencies; or they have noted that Environmental Protection Agency procedures for articulating its position and providing for public comment were an adequate substitute for the same procedures under NEPA. [152]

## 11.0 BIOTECHNOLOGY

In May 1986, EPA authorized the first permits for the release of a genetically engineered pesticide to a professor from the University of California at Berkeley. The genetically altered bacteria strain, known as "ice-minus" or "Frostban," was developed by the university and licensed by Advanced Genetic Sciences Inc. (AGS). Designed to retard frost formation on plants which costs billions of dollars in damage each year, the bacterial material will be applied to potato seeds before planting and sprayed on young plants. [153] On September 4, 1986, EPA also gave its approval for AGS to conduct outdoor tests on Frostban, pending agency review of a test site, reinstating two permits which EPA suspended in March 1986. EPA had alleged that the company violated the federal permit process when it injected Frostban into trees on the open roof of its Oakland, California, facility in February 1985. After much dispute over statutory jurisdiction over biotechnology products, President Reagan signed on June 18, 1986 a Coordinated Framework for Regulation of Biotechnology, which maps out federal agency jurisdiction over biotechnology products. In general, the EPA is to regulate pesticides and new organisms planned for release from the laboratory into the field, the Agriculture Department will handle products that may be plant pests or cause disease in animals and the FDA will deal with human drugs, foods and food additives.

In 1990 the White House task force on biotechnology, under the direction

---

[151] For example, *Essex Chemical Corp. v. Ruckelshaus*, 486 F.2d 427, 5 ERC 1820 (D.C. Cir., 1973), *Portland Cement Assn. v. Ruckelshaus*, 486 F.2d at 375, 5 ERC 1593 (D.C. Cir., 1973).

[152] *EDF v. EPA*, 489 F.2d at 1257, 6 ERC at 1119.

[153] *Foundation on Economic Trends v. Heckler*, 756 F.2d 143. (D.C.C.A. 1985).

of Vice President Dan Quayle, issued a policy declaration that biotech products should be treated as all other substances, without regard to their biological origin. [154]

---

[154] This policy statement is discussed in more detail in the TSCA chapter of this book.

Chapter 9


OCCUPATIONAL SAFETY AND HEALTH ACT[1]


Robert D. Moran
Attorney At Law
Washington, DC


## 1.0 INTRODUCTION

The Occupational Safety and Health Act[2] was enacted by Congress on December 29, 1970 and went into effect on April 28, 1971. It remains today exactly the same as it was at that time. Only one amendment to the law was made during its first twenty years. That change, adopted as a part of the federal deficit-reduction package in late 1990, boosted the maximum penalty limits by a factor of seven and imposed a $5,000 *minimum* penalty for each willful violation.

The law was enacted in an effort to reduce workplace injuries and illnesses by establishing standards that would enhance safe and healthful working conditions in places of employment throughout the United States.

The declared congressional purpose and policy of the act is "to assure so far as possible every working man and woman in the nation safe and healthful working conditions and to preserve our human resources."[3]


## 2.0 DIFFERENCES BETWEEN OSHA AND EPA

The OSH Act is administered and enforced by the Occupational Safety and Health Administration (OSHA), a U.S. Department of Labor agency that was created by the Secretary of Labor. *See*, n. 19, *infra*. The EPA, on the other hand, was created by an Act of Congress.

---

[1] For more information on this subject, readers are referred to the *OSHA Handbook* by the author, listed at the back of the book.

[2] P.L. 91-596, 84 Stat. 1590, 29 U.S.C. § 651 *et seq.*

[3] Section 2(b), 29 U.S.C. § 651(b).

Both agencies have a mandate to reduce exposures to toxic substances but EPA's jurisdiction extends over land, sea and air. OSHA is limited to conditions that exist *in* the workplace. Within the workplace, however, OSHA's jurisdiction covers safety as well as health. EPA does not regulate safety.

Both agencies frequently regulate the same substances in a different manner but those regulations are not necessarily in conflict because they apply in different places.

Finally, OSHA is much more enforcement oriented than EPA. It emphasizes its regulations by the numerous enforcement initiatives it undertakes each year. EPA, on the other hand, tends more towards information and education to emphasize its regulations, although it can and does conduct enforcement proceedings as well.

Both agencies have had a substantial impact upon employers who must comply with both OSHA and EPA rules and regulations. The EPA regulates employers under a number of different statutes but OSHA regulates employers under only one law, the Occupational Safety and Health Act of 1970.

## 3.0 COVERAGE

The provisions of the law apply to every employer engaged in a business affecting commerce who has employees. The Bureau of Labor Statistics estimated that 4.2 million establishments employing some 57 million employees were subject to coverage in 1971. Those numbers have grown over the years as the working population has expanded. The law applies in all 50 states, the District of Columbia, Puerto Rico, the Virgin Islands, American Samoa, Guam, and other U.S. territories.[4] Federal and state employees are specifically excluded from coverage, but the act permits the adoption of measures extending substantially similar requirements to them.[5]

The act also specifically excludes from coverage persons covered under other existing occupational safety and health laws (such as the Federal Coal Mine Health and Safety Act) and under Section 274 of the Atomic Energy Act of 1954 as amended.[6]

---

[4] Section 4(a), 29 U.S.C. § 653(a).

[5] Section 3(5), 29 U.S.C. § 652(5), excludes federal, state and local agencies from the definition of the term "employer." However, other sections of the Act authorize the federal and state governments to adopt occupational safety and health programs for the benefit of their employees. Sections 18 and 19, 29 U.S.C. §§ 667 and 668.

[6] Section 4(b)(1), 29 U.S.C. § 653(b)(1). That exclusion has been the subject of considerable litigation. *See* the discussion in *U.S. Air, Inc. v.*

*(continued...)*

## 4.0 DUTIES OF EMPLOYERS AND EMPLOYEES

In general, the duty of each *employer* under the act is to furnish each of his employees a place of employment, free from recognized hazards that are causing, or likely to cause death or serious physical harm,[7] and to comply with the occupational safety and health standards promulgated under the act.[8] The duty of each *employee* is to comply with the occupational safety and health standards, and all rules, regulations and orders issued pursuant to the act which are applicable to his own actions and conduct.[9] Employers who fail to comply with those obligations can be penalized by the government but there is no government sanction against noncomplying employees.[10]

### 4.1 The General Duty Clause

Congress intended that the act would be principally enforced through specific standards that would tell employers what they must do to achieve a safe and healthful working environment. However, Congress added § 5(a)(1), the so-called "general duty clause," in order to fill gaps that might exist in the standards. It was not expected to be cited very much and was intended to only cover hazardous conditions that are obvious and admitted by all concerned, but for which no specific standard then existed.

Although it appears that more employers have been cited under the general duty clause than Congress contemplated, the courts have curtailed its use to some extent by imposing a number of requirements that must be proved before a general duty clause violation can be established.[11] As a result, it is not

---

[6](..continued)
*OSAHRC*, 689 F. 2d 1191 (4th Cir. 1982), and *Inspection of Norfolk Dredging Co.*, 783 F.2d 1526 (11th Cir. 1986).

[7] Section 5(a)(1), 29 U.S.C. § 654(a)(1).

[8] Section 5(a)(2), 29 U.S.C. § 654(a)(2).

[9] Section 5(b), 29 U.S.C. § 654(b).

[10] *Atlantic & Gulf Stevedores v. OSAHRC*, 534 F.2d 541 (3d Cir. 1976).

[11] The leading case on general duty clause enforcement is *National Realty and Construction Company v. OSAHRC*, 489 F.2d 1257 (D.C. Cir., 1973). The rule of that case has been followed innumerable times. *See*, for example, *Secretary of Labor v. Cerro Metal Products Division*, 12 BNA OSHC 1821 (1986), and cases cited therein.

enough to simply show that a workplace hazard existed that caused death or serious physical harm to an employee. The proof which the Secretary of Labor must produce includes identification of particular measures that the employer should have had in effect at the time the hazardous condition was present, that such measures would be effective in counteracting the hazard, and that it would be feasible to put such measures into effect. In the words of the court:

"...the Secretary [of Labor] must be constrained to specify the particular steps a cited employer should have taken to avoid citation, and to demonstrate the feasibility and likely utility of those measures.[12]

## 4.2 Occupational Safety and Health Standards

Shortly after the law went into effect, the Secretary of Labor, under the authority Congress delegated to him, adopted thousands of occupational safety and health standards.[13] In subsequent years, additional standards have been added. Some standards have been revised while others have been revoked. The Secretary's authority to adopt standards is a continuing one. Thus, new standards can be adopted in the future.

Job safety and health standards generally consist of rules for avoidance of hazards which have been proven by research and experience to be harmful to personal safety and health. The standards supposedly constitute an extensive compilation of wisdom. They sometimes apply to all employees. An example would be fire protection standards. A great many standards, however, apply only to workers while engaged in specific types of work--such as driving a truck or handling compressed gases.

Two of the many thousands of occupational safety and health standards are listed below in order to demonstrate the form of such standards:

Example number one. "Aisles and passageways shall be kept clear and in good repair, with no obstruction across or in aisles that could create a hazard."[14]

Example number two. "Employees working in areas where there is a possible danger of head injury from impact, or from falling or flying objects, or from electrical shock and burns, shall be protected by protective helmets."[15]

---

[12] *National Realty, supra*, 489 F.2d at 1268.

[13] 36 Federal Register 10466 *et seq.*, May 29, 1971. All OSHA standards are now codified in Title 29 of the Code of Federal Regulations (C.F.R.).

[14] 29 C.F.R. § 1910.23(b).

[15] 29 C.F.R. § 1926.100(a).

Two other occupational and health standards (the noise and hazard communication standards) are discussed in sections 12.0 and 13.0 below.

It is the obligation of all employers and employees to familiarize themselves with those standards which apply to them and to observe them at all times.[16]

## 5.0 ADOPTION OF STANDARDS

The act provided the Secretary of Labor with authority to adopt standards in three different ways. That authority appears in sections 6(a), 6(b) and 6(c) of the act.[17] He made use of all of that authority in the past but today the section 6(a) authority no longer exists and the section 6(c) authority has been so circumscribed by court decision that it has virtually fallen into disuse. Each of those three provisions is discussed below.

### 5.1 Section 6(a) Standards

This authority no longer exists but is still important because, during the time it existed, it was the basis for adopting most of the standards that are in effect today. It was limited to the adoption as OSHA standards of certain "national consensus standards" and "established Federal standards" that were in effect on December 29, 1970, the act's enactment date. Both of those kinds of "standards" are defined in the law itself.[18] No notice-and-comment rulemaking procedures were required for standards adopted under Section 6(a). The reason for that unusual leeway was to permit OSHA[19] to get so-called "start-up" standards on the books as quickly as possible. To prevent the abuse of such power, however, the authority to adopt Section 6(a) standards was restricted to so-called "consensus" and "established federal" standards and the

---

[16] 29 U.S.C. § 654.

[17] 29 U.S.C. §§ 655(a), (b) and (c).

[18] *See* 29 U.S.C. §§ 652(9) and 652(10).

[19] The acronym "OSHA" is used herein to mean "Occupational Safety and Health Administration," an agency of the United States Department of Labor. The Act delegated rulemaking and enforcement authority to the Secretary of Labor but the Secretary then created OSHA, to be headed by an Assistant Secretary, and redelegated his statutory authority to that official. *See* 29 C.F.R. §§ 1910.2(b) and 1910.4.

power to adopt them as OSHA standards lasted for only two years.[20] It expired on April 28, 1973. However, the Secretary made considerable use of that authority during the two year period it existed and the vast majority of OSHA standards that are currently in effect were adopted under Section 6(a), 29 U.S.C. § 655(a).

### 5.2. Section 6(b) Standards

This is the authority for the adoption of all OSHA standards promulgated after April 28, 1973, except emergency temporary standards authorized by Section 6(c). It requires that advance notice of the intent to promulgate a standard must be published in the Federal Register, and that the public must be given an opportunity to comment on the proposal as well as request a hearing thereon, before the proposal can be adopted as an OSHA standard. Section 6(b), 29 U.S.C. § 655(b), is one of the act's most detailed provisions and it has been the subject of considerable litigation.[21] Any OSHA standard that is adopted today must be promulgated under Section 6(b) if it is to remain in effect for longer than six months.

### 5.3 Section 6(c) Standards

This authority is very limited and rarely used. It permits the adoption of "emergency temporary standards" in those situations where the Secretary makes a satisfactory finding that (a) a "grave danger" exists as a result of employee exposure to toxic substances, harmful physical agents or "new hazards" *and* (b) an emergency standard is necessary to protect employees from such danger.[22] No notice-and-comment rulemaking is required but a Section 6(c) standard, 29 U.S.C. § 655(c), will automatically expire six months after adoption unless, prior thereto, it is promulgated under Section 6(b) procedures.

### 5.4 Variances from Standards

The Secretary, upon an employer application therefor, is authorized to grant temporary variances from standards in order to give the employer sufficient

---

[20] For a good discussion of the Secretary's Section 6(a) authority and its limitations, *see Diebold, Inc. v. Marshall*, 585 F.2d 1327 (6th Cir. 1978).

[21] Two Supreme Court cases contain detailed discussion of section 6(b): *Industrial Union Department v. American Petroleum Institute*, 448 U.S. 607 (1980), and *American Textile Manufacturers Institute v. Donovan*, 452 U.S. 490 (1981).

[22] The difficulty of establishing the existence of those conditions is demonstrated by two decisions that invalidated OSHA attempts to adopt emergency temporary standards: *Florida Peach Growers Association v. Department of Labor*, 489 F.2d 120 (5th Cir. 1974), and *Asbestos Information Association v. OSHA*, 727 F.2d 415 (5th Cir. 1984).

time to come into compliance if he can show a need and a protective plan of action.[23] Variances may be granted without time limits if the Secretary finds that an employer is using safety measures that are as safe as those required in a standard. Affected employees must be given notice of each such application and an opportunity to participate in the variance-issuance process.[24]

## 6.0 RECORDKEEPING REQUIREMENTS

In order to accurately describe the nature of the occupational safety and health problem, the act requires each employer to maintain an accurate record of work-related deaths, injuries and illnesses. Minor injuries requiring only first aid treatment need not be recorded, but a record must be made if it involves medical treatment, loss of consciousness, restriction of work or motion, or transfer to another job.

The act states that those records are to be made available to the Department of Labor and to the Department of Health and Human Services, either of which may require periodic reports thereon.[25] However, there are judicial decisions holding that such records need not be disclosed in the absence of compulsory process.[26] Employers are also required by the act to maintain whatever additional records the Secretary may prescribe for enforcement purposes or for developing information regarding the causes and prevention of occupational accidents and illnesses,[27] to maintain accurate records of employee exposures to potentially toxic materials or harmful physical agents that are required to be monitored or measured by OSHA standards,[28] and to promptly advise any employee who has had such exposure

---

[23] 29 U.S.C. § 655(b)(6).

[24] 29 U.S.C. §§ 655(b)(6) and 655(d).

[25] Section 8(c)(2), 29 U.S.C. § 657(c)(2). *See* also § 24(a), 29 U.S.C. § 673(a).

[26] *See Secretary v. Taft Broadcasting Co.*, 12 BNA OSHC 1264 (1985), *affirmed sub nom McLaughlin v. Kings Island Division, Taft Broadcasting Co.*, 849 F.2d 990 (6th Cir. 1988).

[27] Section 8(c)(1), 29 U.S.C. § 657 (c)(1). The recordkeeping regulations are in Part 1904 of Title 29 C.F.R. *See* 29 C.F.R. § 1904.1 *et seq.*

[28] Section 6(b)(7), 29 U.S.C. § 655(b)(7). Such requirements are included in various OSHA standards. *See*, for example, 29 C.F.R. § 1910.1001(m), the recordkeeping requirements of the asbestos standard.

of the same as well as the corrective action being undertaken.[29]   The Secretary of Labor, in cooperation with the Secretary of Health and Human Services, is authorized by the act to issue regulations in this area which shall provide employees or their representatives with an opportunity to observe such monitoring or measuring, to have access to the records thereof and to all records that indicate their own exposure to toxic materials or harmful physical agents.[30]

The act also authorizes the Secretary to adopt regulations requiring employers to conduct their own periodic inspections and to keep their employees informed of their protections and obligations under the law through posting of notices or other appropriate means.   The information which employers may be required to give their employees may also include the provisions of applicable standards.[31]

## 7.0 STATE PARTICIPATION

The act encourages the states to assume the fullest responsibility for the administration and enforcement of their occupational safety and health laws by providing them with monetary grants to help them adopt and enforce OSHA standards within their own borders.[32]   A specific disclaimer of federal pre-emption is included in order to permit any state agency or court to assert jurisdiction under state law over any occupational safety or health issue with respect to which no federal standard is in effect.[33]

Any state may assume responsibility for the development and enforcement of occupational safety and health standards under the act if such state submits an approved plan for so doing to the Secretary of Labor.[34]   The Secretary may approve such a plan under the following conditions:

1. An agency of the state must be designated or created to carry out the plan.

---

[29] Section 8(c)(3), 29 U.S.C. § 657(c)(3).

[30] *Id.* The implementing regulation is 29 C.F.R. § 1910.20.

[31] Section 8(c)(1), 29 U.S.C. § 657(c)(1). For an example of that, see the OSHA lead standard, 29 C.F.R. § 1910.1025. It includes a requirement that the employer shall assure that each employee is informed of "[t]he content of this standard and its appendices." 29 C.F.R. § 1910.1025(l)(1)(v).

[32] Section 2(b)(11), 29 U.S.C. § 651(b)(11).

[33] Section 18(a), 29 U.S.C. § 667(a).

[34] Section 18(b), 29 U.S.C. § 667(b).

2. Standards (and enforcement thereof) must be provided which create safe and healthful employment at least as effective as that otherwise provided for under the act.

3. There must be adequate provisions for rights of entry and inspection of workplaces.

4. Enforcement capacity must be demonstrated.

5. Adequate funds for administration must be assured.

6. Effective and comprehensive job safety and health programs for all public employees within the state will be established to the extent permitted by the particular state's law.

7. The state, and employers within the state, will make such reports as may be required by the Secretary of Labor.[35]

The Secretary is obligated to make a continuing evaluation of the manner in which each state plan is being carried out and to withdraw his approval thereof whenever there is a failure to comply substantially with any provision thereof.[36]

In accordance with those provisions, twenty-one states and two territories currently administer and enforce the act.[37] For all intents and purposes, employers in these states are only subject to their state OSHA agency. The federal OSHA people play virtually no role at all there. Those jurisdictions currently have the authority to inspect private employers, cite them, adjudicate contested enforcement actions and adopt binding occupational safety and health standards and regulations. For the most part, OSHA itself does not do any of this in these places. There are a few additional states where only state and local government agencies are within the state's OSHA authority. In all of the remaining states and territories, the state government plays no part in OSHA administration or enforcement except to provide consultative services upon request.

---

[35] Section 18(c), 29 U.S.C. § 667(c).

[36] Section 18(f), 29 U.S.C. § 667 (f).

[37] Alaska, Arizona, California, Hawaii, Indiana, Iowa, Kentucky, Maryland, Michigan, Minnesota, Nevada, New Mexico, North Carolina, Oregon, Puerto Rico, South Carolina, Tennessee, Utah, Vermont, Virgin Islands, Virginia, Washington and Wyoming.

## 8.0 ENFORCEMENT

Employer compliance with OSHA standards, the recordkeeping requirements and the act's general duty clause is enforced by means of on-site inspection of worksites by a force of approximately 2,500 state and federal OSHA inspectors who are stationed at more than a hundred different locations around the country.

The act authorizes those inspectors to enter without delay, and at any reasonable times, any establishment covered by the act to inspect the premises and all pertinent conditions, structures, machines, apparatus, devices, equipment, and materials therein, and to question privately any employer, owner, operator, agent or employee.[38]  However, if the employer does not voluntarily consent to such an inspection, it cannot be conducted unless OSHA obtains a warrant authorizing it.[39]  OSHA is also authorized to issue subpoenas to aid its inspections.[40]

The act permits the employer and a representative authorized by his employees to accompany the inspector during the physical inspection of any workplace for the purpose of aiding such inspection.[41]

The Secretary of Health and Human Services is also authorized to make inspections and question employers and employees in order to carry out those functions assigned to that agency under the act.[42]  For additional discussion of that authority, see section 11.0 below.

### 8.1 Citations and Proposed Penalties

Where an employer is believed to be in violation of the act as a result of an OSHA inspection, he is issued a written citation describing the specific nature of the violation.  The citations must fix a reasonable time for abatement of the violation, and each citation (or copies thereof) must be prominently posted by the employer at or near each place where a violation referred to in the citation occurred.  Notices, in lieu of citations, may be issued for *de minimis* violations which have no direct or immediate relationship

---

[38] Sections 8(a) and (f), 29 U.S.C. §§ 657(a) and (f).

[39] *Marshall v. Barlow, Inc.*, 436 U.S. 307 (1978).

[40] Section 8(b), 29 U.S.C. § 657(b).

[41] Section 8(e), 29 U.S.C. § 657(e).

[42] Section 20(b), 29 U.S.C. § 669(b). This authority has been used in the past for the purposes of conducting a so-called "health hazard evaluation" as set forth in section 20(a)(6), 29 U.S.C. § 669(a)(6).  *See Establishment Inspection of Keokuk Steel Castings*, 493 F. Supp. 842 (S.D. Iowa 1980), and *General Motors Corp. v. NIOSH*, 636 F.2d 163 (6th Cir. 1980).

to safety or health.[43] If OSHA believes that the cited violation should be penalized, it must notify the employer by certified mail of the penalty which it proposes to assess. The employer then has 15 working days within which to notify OSHA that he wishes to contest the citation or proposed assessment of penalty or both.[44]

If a cited employer fails to notify OSHA within such time that he intends to contest the citation or proposed assessment of penalty, the citation and the assessment shall be final, provided no employee files an objection to the time the citation allowed the employer to abate the cited violation (see "Abatement," in section 8.3 below).

If the employer notifies OSHA within such time that he does wish to contest, OSHA must certify the matter to the Occupational Safety and Health Review Commission and the Commission shall afford an opportunity for a hearing.[45] The Commission has the power to affirm, modify or vacate any contested citation or proposed penalty. Orders of the Commission are final 30 days after issuance. Review of Commission orders may be obtained in the United States Court of Appeals.[46]

## 8.2 The Occupational Safety and Health Review Commission (OSHRC)

The act created OSHRC as an independent agency of the federal government and gave it only one function--to hear and decide contested OSHA citations and penalty proposals.[47] The Commission is a two-tiered court system. At the lower level, it has a number of administrative law judges (ALJs) who hear cases and issue rulings. The ALJ decisions can be reviewed and changed by the 3-member presidentially-appointed Commission. Commission decisions can be appealed to the United States Courts of Appeal.[48]

---

[43] Section 9(a) and (b), 29 U.S.C. §§ 658(a) and (b).

[44] Sections 10(a) and (c), 29 U.S.C. 659(a) and (c). It is OSHA's current practice to use a single document that contains both the citation and the notification of proposed penalty. In OSHA's early days, the citation and proposed penalty were contained on separate documents.

[45] Section 10(c), 29 U.S.C. § 659(c).

[46] Sections 11(a) and (b), 29 U.S.C. §§ 660(a) and (b).

[47] Sections 2(b)(3) and 12, 29 U.S.C. §§ 651(b)(3) and 661.

[48] *See* n. 46, *supra*. It should be noted that an ALJ decision that is not ordered to be reviewed by the members of the Commission within 30 days of its issuance will thereby automatically become a decision of the Commission. It can then be appealed to the appropriate Court of Appeals in exactly the same manner.

The act provides that those who contest OSHA citations and penalty proposals are entitled to a fair and impartial hearing and decision on the contested matters. They receive just that from the Commission. Its record over the first twenty years of its existence is one of impeccable fairness and impartiality between employers and OSHA. The Commission has fully sustained the OSHA charges in approximately one-fourth of its cases and has fully sustained the contesting employer in approximately one-third of its cases. In the remaining cases, some issues were decided in the employer's favor and others in OSHA's favor.

Perhaps more important than the results of its decisions is the fact that *all* of its decisions are in writing and contain detailed reasons why a particular disposition is being made.

At the hearings conducted by Commission ALJs, the burden of proof is on OSHA to prove the validity of all citations that the employer has contested. When OSHA doesn't carry that burden--and it often doesn't--the citation will be vacated.

No matter how much adverse evidence OSHA presents to a Commission ALJ about an employer, the Commission will not impose any sanction or penalty greater than that set forth in the contested OSHA citation and penalty proposal. In other words, the "maximum sentence" an employer can receive in an OSHA enforcement proceeding is that listed upon the citation and penalty proposal he received after the OSHA inspection. If the cited employer does not contest, that is exactly what he will receive.

When an employer *does* contest, the Commission is empowered to impose:

1. The *same* sanction he would have received if he did not contest.
2. Something *less than* that.
3. No sanction at all.

The employer who contests an OSHA citation may walk away scot-free as many employers have done and he may even be partially reimbursed for the fees and expenses he incurred in contesting the citation.[49]

### 8.3 Abatement

Each OSHA citation must prescribe a reasonable time for elimination or abatement of the condition constituting the alleged hazard.[50] However, that time limit does not begin to run until a final order of the Review Commission, if the citation is contested by the employer in good faith and not solely for

---

[49] *See* the Equal Access to Justice Act, 5 U.S.C. § 504, which among other things, authorizes reimbursement of the fees and expenses incurred by small businesses in defending against unjustified OSHA citations.

[50] Section 9(a), 29 U.S.C. § 658(a).

delay or avoidance of penalties.[51]

Employees (or representatives of employees) also have the right to object to the period of time fixed in the citation for the abatement of a violation if, within 15 days after a citation is issued, an employee files a notice of contest with OSHA alleging that an unreasonable time was allowed for abatement. Review procedures similar to those discussed above apply when such a notice is filed.[52]

A "failure-to-abate" violation of the act exists in those situations where the time for correction of a violation has been established, either as a result of a previously uncontested citation, or the settlement or final adjudication of a prior contested citation; but the employer fails to abate within such time. In such a case, OSHA will notify the employer by certified mail of such failure and of the proposed penalty. Such notice and assessment shall be final unless the employer contests the same by filing a notice of contest with OSHA within 15 working days.[53] A failure-to-abate notification is essentially the same as a citation (but higher penalties are authorized) and an employer who contests it receives the same kind of hearing and adjudication discussed above.

Where an employer is under an abatement order for any reason and can establish that, despite a good faith effort to comply with the abatement requirements, abatement has not been completed because of factors beyond his reasonable control, OSHA can grant an extension. If it doesn't, the employer is entitled to a hearing before the Review Commission, which can issue an order affirming or modifying the abatement requirement.[54]

## 8.4 Penalties

Except in those rare instances where OSHA doesn't seek a monetary penalty, citations and failure-to-abate notices are accompanied by *proposed* penalties. If left uncontested, those proposals become fines and must be paid. If contested, however, the penalty proposals have no force or effect. The Review Commission will, after a hearing, decide what penalty, if any, will be assessed. The amount of penalty authorized depends upon the nature of the violation.

Willful or repeated violations may incur fines of up to $70,000 for each violation, while serious or nonserious violations may incur fines up to $7,000

---

[51] Section 10(b) and 17(d), 29 U.S.C. §§ 659(b) and 666(d).

[52] Section 10(c), 29 U.S.C. § 659(c).

[53] Section 10(b), 29 U.S.C. § 659(b).

[54] Section 10(c), 29 U.S.C. § 659(c). The procedures for invoking this process are set forth in 29 C.F.R. § 2200.37.

for each violation.[55] Any employer who fails to correct a violation for which a citation has been previously issued within the time period prescribed therein, may be penalized up to $7,000 for each day the violation exists.[56]

The act also authorizes criminal penalties. A willful first violation by an employer which results in the death of any employee is punishable by a fine of up to $10,000 or imprisonment for up to six months. A second or subsequent conviction carries a penalty of up to $20,000 and up to one year in prison.

Similar penalties are also included in the act for false official statements, for failure to observe the record-keeping, posting, and other requirements of the law, and for giving unauthorized advance notice of any inspections to be conducted under the act.[57]

A state or local district attorney can also bring charges of murder, assault, battery and similar charges against an employer for acts that cause death, injury or illness to an employee. See, for example, *New York v. Pymm*, an October 25, 1989 decision of the Appellate Division, New York Supreme Court, reported at 14 BNA OSHC 1297 (1989). Cases of that kind began to appear with some regularity in the late eighties and early nineties.

## 9.0 IMMINENT DANGERS

Any condition or practice in any place of employment that causes a danger to exist which could reasonably be expected to cause death or serious physical harm immediately or before the imminence of such danger can be eliminated through normal enforcement procedures, may be restrained by order of a United States District Court upon petition of the Secretary of Labor. If the Secretary arbitrarily or capriciously fails to seek action to abate an imminent danger of such kind, a mandamus action to compel him to act may be maintained in the U.S. District Court by any employee who may be injured by reason of such failure. An OSHA inspector who concludes that imminent danger conditions or practices exist in any place of employment is obligated to inform the affected employees and employers of the danger and tell them that he is recommending to the Secretary of Labor that injunctive relief be sought.[58]

---

[55] Sections 17(a), (b) and (c), 29 U.S.C. §§666(a), (b) and (c). *See* also n. 56, *infra*.

[56] Section 17(d), 29 U.S.C. § 666(d). The maximum penalty levels were increased by seven times and a $5,000 *minimum* penalty for a willful violation was imposed by the federal deficit reduction package that Congress adopted in October 1990. *See* Congressional Record for October 26, 1990 at page H-12612.

[57] Sections 17(e), (f), (g) and (i), 29 U.S.C. §§ 666 (e), (f), (g) and (h).

[58] Section 13, 29 U.S.C. § 662.

## 10.0 PROTECTION AGAINST HARASSMENT

No person may discharge or in any manner discriminate against any employee because he causes OSHA to inspect his employer's business, exercises any right under the act, files a complaint or other proceeding, or because he testifies or is about to testify in any proceeding under the act. Any employee who believes that he has been discharged or otherwise discriminated against in violation of this provision may, within 30 days of such action, file a complaint with OSHA. The Secretary is authorized to investigate the matter and to bring action in the U.S. District Court for appropriate relief. The Secretary must notify the complainant of his action on the complaint within 90 days of its receipt.[59]

For a fuller discussion of this provision, see *Marshall v. Whirlpool Corporation*,[60] and the Supreme Court decision that affirmed the result reached in that case, *Whirlpool Corporation v. Marshall.*[61]

## 11.0 NATIONAL INSTITUTE FOR OCCUPATIONAL SAFETY AND HEALTH (NIOSH)

A continuing program of research in the field of occupational safety and health, including the psychological factors involved, and the development of innovative methods, techniques and approaches for dealing with occupational safety and health problems is the responsibility of NIOSH, an organization created by the act as a part of the Department of Health and Human Services.

NIOSH is authorized to conduct such research and experimental programs as are necessary for the development of criteria for new and improved occupational safety and health standards and, on the basis of such research and experimentation, recommend new or improved OSHA standards to the Secretary of Labor. NIOSH may also require employers to measure, record and make reports on the exposure of employees to potentially toxic substances or harmful physical agents which might endanger their safety or health. The agency is authorized to establish programs for medical examinations and tests as may be necessary to determine the incidence of occupational illness, the susceptibility of employees to such illnesses, to conduct such special research experiments and demonstrations as are necessary to explore new problems, including those created by new technology in occupational safety and health, which may require ameliorative action beyond that which is otherwise provided in the operating provisions of the act, and to conduct research into the

---

[59] Section 11(c), 29 U.S.C. § 660(c).

[60] 593 F.2d 715 (6th Cir. 1979)

[61] 445 U.S. 1 (1980).

motivational and behavioral factors relating to the field of occupational safety and health.

A part of this program is the publication annually of a list of all known toxic substances and the concentrations at which toxicity is known to occur, and industry-wide studies on chronic or low-level exposure to a broad variety of industrial materials, processes, and stresses on the potential for illness, disease or loss of functional capacity in aging adults.

Upon the written request of any employer or authorized representative of employees, NIOSH is authorized to conduct on-site investigations in order to make determinations on whether any substance normally found in the place of employment has potentially toxic effects. That process, which has been used many times, is known as a "health hazard evaluation." The determinations made by NIOSH as the result of such an evaluation are printed in a report which is then submitted to both the employer and the affected employees as soon as possible. NIOSH has also made it a practice to submit such reports to OSHA. Resulting OSHA inspections and citations sometimes follow.

Information obtained by the Departments of Labor and HHS under the research provisions of the law is to be disseminated to employers and employees and organizations thereof.[62]

## 12.0 NOISE EXPOSURE STANDARDS

Before OSHA came into existence in 1971, the Labor Department had adopted a limit upon workplace noise under the Walsh-Healey Act. It applied only to certain businesses with federal government contracts. That regulation was converted into an OSHA standard in May 1971 under the Secretary's section 6(a) standards-making power.[63] It has not been changed since that time and continues to be in effect to this day.

The standard states as follows:

§ 1910.95 Occupational noise exposure.

(a) Protection against the effects of noise exposure shall be provided when the sound levels exceed those shown in Table G-16[64] when

---

[62] Sections 20 and 22, 29 U.S.C. §§ 669 and 671.

[63] That OSHA standard is codified as 29 C.F.R. §§ 1910.95(a) and (b) but its coverage does not extend to construction industry employers. They are covered under a similar but separate noise exposure standard, 29 C.F.R. § 1926.52.

[64] Table G-16 lists the "permissible noise exposure" for an 8-hour work shift as an average of 90dBA (decibels, when measured on the "A" scale of a

(continued...)

measured on the A scale of a standard sound level meter at slow response.

\*\*\*

(b)(1) When employees are subjected to sound exceeding those listed in Table G-16, feasible administrative or engineering controls shall be utilized. If such controls fail to reduce sound levels within the levels of Table G-16, personal protective equipment shall be provided and used to reduce sound levels within the levels of the table.

### 12.1 Enforcement of Noise Limits

A major OSHA effort to obtain compliance with those noise limits was undertaken soon after the agency came into existence. More than 2,000 noise citations were issued against various employers in 1975 alone. OSHA soon learned, however, that reducing workplace noise requires more than the adoption of regulatory limitations. In many business operations the technology does not exist[65] and in others, the cost of compliance would be so prohibitive that survival of the business would be jeopardized.

The framers of the noise standard contemplated those problems by inclusion in its text of the condition that controlling noise by engineering devices must be "feasible" before it would be required and that, if it was not feasible, the hearing of the employees who worked in noisy areas would be protected by ear plugs or ear muffs.

The OSH Review Commission and the courts implemented those conditions by ruling that an OSHA noise citation would not be affirmed unless the Secretary could prove that: (1) appropriate controls existed, (2) implementing those controls at the cited workplace would be both technologically and economically feasible, and (3) the benefits employees would receive by implementation of the controls was worth the money they would cost the cited employer when such cost and benefits were compared to the costs and benefits of personal ear protective devices.[66]

---

[64](..continued)
sound level meter at slow response). It permits higher levels for shorter work shifts as follows: 92 for 6 hours, 95 for 4 hours, 97 for 3 hours, 100 for 2 hours and 115 for 15 minutes.

[65] The engines of jet planes, forge hammers, jackhammers and a number of other machines produce noise levels well above the 90dBA limit. So far as is known, the functions performed by those machines could not be accomplished by any significantly less noisy alternative.

[66] There are numerous judicial decisions that so hold, including *Secretary of Labor v. Continental Can Co.*, 4 BNA OSHC 1541 (1976), *Turner Company v. Secretary of Labor*, 561 F.2d 82 (7th Cir. 1977), *RMI Company v.*

(continued...)

OSHA has been frequently unable to meet that standard of proof. As a result, the number of noise citations issued has decreased in recent years.

### 12.2 Hearing Conservation

OSHA regulators proposed a 5dBA reduction in the standard's 8-hour, 90dBA exposure limit in 1974[67] but it ran into a buzz-saw of opposition not only from business and industry but also from economic advisors to the Nixon, Ford and Carter White House who were concerned about its inflationary impact. The proposed reduction was abandoned in 1981. Instead of further pursuing lower noise limits, OSHA adopted in 1981 a wide ranging "hearing conservation standard."[68] That standard focused on the protection of employees from the effects of noise rather than the reduction of noise at its source. It went into effect in 1983.

The text of the hearing conservation standard, as well as helpful guidance on its implementation, appears in 29 C.F.R. §§ 1910.95(c) through 1910.95(p) and in 5 mandatory and 4 non-mandatory appendices thereto. It applies to all employers who have "information" that they have employees who are exposed to excessive noise levels[69] except those engaged in the construction industry, agriculture, and in oil and gas well drilling and servicing operations.

It should be noted that the obligation to reduce noise by engineering and administrative controls is triggered by employee exposure to a 90 dBA noise

---

[66](..continued)
*Secretary of Labor*, 594 F.2d 566 (6th Cir. 1979), *Secretary of Labor v. Castle & Cooke Foods*, 5 BNA OSHC 1435 (1977), affirmed *sub nom Donovan v. Castle & Cooke Foods*, 692 F.2d 641 (9th Cir. 1982), and *Secretary of Labor v. The Sherwin-Williams Company*, 11 BNA OSHC 2105 (1984).

[67] 39 Federal Register 37774 (1974).

[68] The then-existing noise standard included a one-sentence hearing conservation requirement, 29 C.F.R. § 1910.95(b)(3). OSHA's attempt to interpret and enforce it in such a manner that it would require employers to adopt particular hearing conservation measures ran aground when § 1910.5(b)(3) was held to be unenforceably vague. *Knopp Forge Co. v. Secretary of Labor*, 657 F.2d 119 (7th Cir. 1981).

[69] The exact wording of this triggering provision of the standard appears in 29 C.F.R. § 1910.95(d)(1) and states as follows:

"When information indicates that any employee's exposure may equal or exceed an 8-hour time-weighted average of 85 decibels, the employer shall develop and implement a monitoring program." The word "monitoring" means that the employer must conduct measurements to determine workplace noise levels.

level while the employers hearing conservation requirements are keyed to an 85 dBA noise level.[70]

The requirements of the hearing conservation standard are rather substantial. It requires employers to determine which employees are exposed to or above an "action level" of 85 db measured as an 8-hour time-weighted average (TWA).[71] Such employees must have hearing protectors made available to them,[72] be notified of the amount of sound they are exposed to and provided with an audiometric test to determine their hearing level.[73] At least annually thereafter, the employer must provide the exposed employee with an additional test to determine whether the employee has suffered an average loss of hearing of 10 db, known as a standard threshold shift, or "STS."[74] If there has been an STS, the employer must take follow-up measures to prevent the employee from reaching the material impairment stage. These measures include fitting the employee with hearing protectors, providing training, and requiring the employee to use the protectors.[75] The protectors must reduce the employee's exposure to an 8-hour TWA of 85 db or below.[76]

---

[70] Other differences in the two standards result from the equipment used to measure noise and the authorized quantification measure. Sections 1910.95(a) and (b) noise must be determined by a *sound level meter*. For the hearing conservation standard, noise can be measured by a *dosimeter*. Noise is measured in dB (decibels) for the latter and in dBA for the former. *See* n. 64, *supra*.

[71] 29 C.F.R. 1910.95(d).

[72] *Id.* at 1910.95(i)(1).

[73] *Id.* at 1910.95(e),(g)(1).

[74] *Id.* at § 1910.95(g)(6). Hearing loss is measured by an audiometer. Audiometers produce pure tones at specific frequencies (e.g., 250, 500, 1000, 2000, 3000, 4000, 6000, and 8000 Hz) and at specific sound levels. The record of a given individual's hearing sensitivity is called an audiogram. An audiogram shows hearing threshold level measured in decibels as a function of frequency in hertz. It indicates how intense or loud a sound at a given frequency must be before it can be perceived. Thus under the standard, follow up measures are required whenever the quietest sound an employer can hear at 2000, 3000 and 4000 hz is an average 10 db louder than it was when the baseline audiometric test was performed.

[75] *Id.* at 1910.95(g)(8).

[76] *Id.* at 1910.95(j)(3).

In addition, the employer must institute a training program on audiometric testing, hearing protectors, and effects of noise on hearing for all employees who are exposed to noise at or above an 8-hour TWA of 85 db.[77] The employer must also retain records of employee exposure measurements and audiometric tests.[78]

Those are the principal requirements but there are many others.

The hearing conservation standard appears to represent an expansion of the scope of the OSH Act itself. The act is limited to controlling *workplace conditions* that constitute hazards to employees while they are *at work*. Some of the duties imposed upon employers by the standard, however, depend upon an employee's physical condition (his hearing acuity) irrespective of the source of that condition. The validity of the standard was challenged on those grounds shortly after it took effect in 1983. A 3-judge panel of the United States Court of Appeals for the Fourth Circuit agreed with the challenger and vacated the standard but, a year later, that ruling was reversed by the entire Fourth Circuit.[79]

## 13.0 HAZARD COMMUNICATION STANDARD

The OSHA hazard communication standard (HCS)[80] is probably the most significant job safety and health regulatory action ever adopted. Its purpose is to alert workers to the existence of potentially dangerous substances in the workplace and the proper means and methods to protect themselves against them. Numerous states and some local governments have enacted substantially similar provisions. They are popularly known as "Right-to-Know" laws.

HCS is completely different from ordinary OSHA standards which obligate an employer to prevent (or minimize) workplace hazards through such means and methods as mandatory limitations upon noise levels and airborne contaminants, or guarding requirements for machinery and elevated workstations. The HCS does not impose mandatory limitations or requirements to abate hazardous

---

[77] *Id.* at 1910.95(k).

[78] *Id.* at 1910.95(m).

[79] *Forging Industry Association v. Secretary of Labor*, 748 F.2d 210 (4th Cir. 1984), and *Forging Industry Association v. Secretary of Labor*, 773 F.2d 1436 (4th Cir. 1985), en banc.

[80] The standard is codified at five different places in the Code of Federal Regulations. The text of each of the five is identical. Therefore, the subsections and appendix references will be the same no matter which CFR text is consulted. The five places in TItle 29, C.F.R, where the standard appears are: §§ 1910.1200, 1915.99, 1917.28, 1918.90 and 1926.59.

conditions. It requires rather that *information* be developed, obtained and provided. That is also true of state and local Right-to-Know laws.

HCS requires the communication of information on "hazardous chemicals" that are present in the workplace. There are few, if any, jobs today that don't involve such substances. They are present everywhere. Household cleaning materials, photocopy equipment, paint, white-out fluid, medicines, even drinking soda. Those may seem innocuous to some but, under HCS, they are "hazardous chemicals."

The OSHA standard went into effect for manufacturers in 1985 and, two years later, it was applied to all other employers. It requires each employer to adopt its own written hazard communication program, keep a material safety data sheet (MSDS) for each product containing a hazardous chemical that is on its premises, provide its employees with training and education on those chemical hazards, and make sure that proper warning labels are in place.

It doesn't matter what the employee does or where the employee works. Office workers, retail employees and persons who are not normally considered to be exposed to chemicals must receive the same protection as those who work with dangerous explosives and deadly chemicals.

### 13.1 The Material Safety Data Sheet

An MSDS is essentially a technical bulletin, usually 2 to 4 pages in length, that contains information about a hazardous chemical or a product containing one or more hazardous chemicals, such as its composition, its chemical and physical characteristics, its health and safety hazards, and the precautions for safe handling and use.[81]

The MSDS is the centerpiece of the Hazard Communication Standard. Labels are keyed to it and the employee training and information requirements are based upon it. The MSDS serves as the primary vehicle for transmitting detailed hazard information to *both* employers and employees.

Each company that is required to prepare an MSDS or have one available is also obligated to submit a copy to the local fire department, emergency planning committee and the State emergency response commission. A list of the chemicals for which MSDSs exist may be submitted as an alternative. The foregoing requirements are not part of HCS, however. They are imposed by a

---

[81] An MSDS must be prepared or obtained by each manufacturer, distributor or importer for every product that contains a hazardous chemical. A copy must be provided to each purchaser of the product. The HCS does not include a list of all chemicals for which an MSDS must be prepared. It requires, rather, that manufacturers must conduct a "hazard determination" of their products to see if they contain any hazardous chemicals. Para. "(d)" of the standard.

statute administered by the Environmental Protection Agency.[82]

### 13.2 Written Hazard Communication Program

Employers must develop, implement, and maintain at the workplace a written, comprehensive hazard communication program that includes provisions for container labeling, collection and availability of material safety data sheets, and an employee training program. Para. "(e)" of the standard. It also must contain a list of the hazardous chemicals in each work area, the means the employer will use to inform employees of the hazards of non-routine tasks (for example, the cleaning of reactor vessels), and the hazards associated with chemicals in unlabeled pipes. If the workplace has multiple employers on-site (for example, a construction site), HCS requires those employers to ensure that information regarding hazards and protective measures be made available to the other employers on-site, where appropriate.

The written program does not have to be lengthy or complicated, but it must be readily available to employees and their designated representatives, and be provided to OSHA and NIOSH representatives when they request it.

### 13.3 Labels and Other Forms of Warning

Chemical manufacturers, importers, and distributors must ensure that containers of hazardous chemicals leaving the workplace are labeled, tagged or marked with the identity, appropriate hazard warnings, and the name and address of the manufacturer or other responsible party. Each container that does *not* leave the workplace must be labeled, tagged or marked with the identity of hazardous chemicals contained herein, and must show hazard warnings appropriate for employee protection. Para. "(f)" of the standard.

The hazard warning can be any type of message, words, pictures, or symbols that convey the hazards of the chemical(s) in the container. Labels must be legible, in English (plus other languages, if desired), and prominently displayed.

There are several exceptions to the requirement for in-plant individual container labels:

o  Employers can post signs or placards that convey the hazard information if there are a number of stationary containers within a work area that have similar contents and hazards.

o  Employers can substitute various types of standard operating procedures, process sheets, batch tickets, blend tickets, and similar written materials for container labels on stationary process equipment if they

---

[82] The Emergency Planning and Community Right-to-Know Act (EPCRA), passed in 1986 as part of the Superfund Amendments and Reauthorization Act (SARA). The reporting requirements appear in 42 U.S.C. § 11021 *et seq.* and the implementing regulations appear in 40 C.F.R. Part 370.

contain the same information and are readily available to employees in the work area.

o Employers are not required to label portable containers into which hazardous chemicals are transferred from labeled containers and that are intended only for the immediate use of the employee who makes the transfer.

o Employers are not required to label pipes or piping systems.


## 13.4 Employee Information and Training

Employers must establish a training and information program for employees exposed to hazardous chemicals in their work area at the time of initial assignment and whenever a new hazard is introduced into their work area. Para. "(h)" of the standard.

At a minimum, the information that employees must be given includes the following:

o The existence of the hazard communication standard and the requirements of the standard.

o The components of the hazard communication program in the employees' workplace.

o Operations in work areas where hazardous chemicals are present.

o Where the employer will keep the written hazard evaluation procedures, communications program, list of hazardous chemicals, and the required MSDS forms.

The employee training plan must consist of the following elements:

o How the hazard communication program is implemented in that workplace, how to read and interpret information on labels and the MSDS, and how employees can obtain and use the available hazard information.

o The hazards of the chemicals in the work area. (The hazards may be discussed by individual chemical or by hazard categories such as flammability).

o Measures employees can take to protect themselves from the hazards.

o  Specific procedures put into effect by the employer to provide protection such as engineering controls, work practices, and the use of personal protective equipment (PPE).

o  Methods and observations--such as visual appearance or smell--workers can use to detect the presence of a hazardous chemical to which they may be exposed.

## 14.0  OSHA's ERGONOMIC GUIDELINES

An OSHA effort to reduce the incidence of carpel tunnel syndrome and related cumulative trauma disorders (CTDs) among employees crystallized in late 1990 with its publication of ergonomic guidelines for the meatpacking industry.  The agency has announced that similar guidelines for all employers will soon follow and that:  "Ergonomics will be the major OSHA issue of the 1990."

Prior to issuance of he guidelines, OSHA had cited numerous employers under the general duty clause, 29 U.S.C. § 654 (a)(1), because of employee CTDs.  That practice is due to continue in the future.

The guidelines have not been adopted under required rulemaking procedures and are therefore not enforceable standards, rules or regulations.[83]  Nor are they an interpretation of the general duty clause.[84]  They are simply suggestions made by OSHA that employers can either accept in full or in part or even totally reject.  Whether OSHA will attempt to impose any kind of sanction against those employers who totally ignore the guidelines remain to be seen.

### 14.1  Substantive Provisions

The substantive provisions of OSHA's ergonomic guidelines are complex, extensive, pervasive and are likely to prove very expensive for employers.  Although the ergonomics guidelines, covering all employers have not yet been published, they are virtually certain to contain the same provisions that have been written into the ergonomic settlement agreements that OSHA negotiated with Chrysler, IBP and a number of other employers that received § 5 (a)(1)

---

[83] The OSH Review Commission has consistently held that guidelines for implementing the Act "do not have the force and effect of law." *Secretary v. FMC Corporation,* 5 BNA OSHC 1707, 1710 (1977).  Pronouncements by the Secretary "that have not been promulgated as rules or regulations have *no binding legal effect* on either the Secretary or the Commission." *Secretary v. Bristol Meyers Co.,* 7 BNA OSHC 1039 (n.1)(1978), emphasis added.

[84] The meatpacking guidelines include the disclaimer that:  "Failure to implement these guidelines is not a violation of the General Duty Clause."

citations in recent years based upon employee CTD. Similar provisions were contained in the ergonomic guidelines for meatpacking plants that OSHA issued on August 30, 1990.

Here is a list of 14 things that the guidelines are expected to tell employers to do:

1. Adopt a *written* ergonomic program for each workplace that includes goals and timetables for reducing CTD by both medical treatment and changes in the way the work is done. The focus of the program must be "to make the job fit the person not to force the person to fit the job." The program must be regularly reviewed by top management with the results of that review committed writing.

2. Reduce or eliminate the following:
   (a) faulty workstation layout;
   (b) improper work methods;
   (c) improper tools, including those that vibrate too much;
   (d) job design problems like work flow, line speed, material handling, worker's posture, amount of force required, lifting methods, repetition rate and work/rest regimens.

3. Conduct periodic surveys of all jobs in order to identify the matters listed in No. 2 above.

4. Conduct an annual survey of employees to determine the extent of their symptoms or complaints of CTD.

5. Hire ergonomic professionals. Invest them with responsibility and sufficient resources to analyze all jobs and recommend changes.

6. Hire health care providers. Give them sufficient authority and resources to rectify all reports of CTD complaints and symptoms.

7. Establish safety and health committees and empower them to order needed changes.

8. Monitor "CTD trends" by periodic review of sign-in logs at the company's health care facility, the OSHA-200 logs, workers' compensation claims, and individual employee medical records.

9. Educate and train employees on ergonomic hazards, CTDs and how to avoid them. Encourage them to report their early signs and symptoms of CTD and suggest changes in the way the work is done. Require that all employee reports, complaints and suggestions be investigated by management and the results thereof reported back to

the employee. Involve employees in all aspects of the company's ergonomic program. Provide for a suitable "break-in" period prior to employee assignment to production jobs.

10. Commit adequate resources to accomplish the goals of the ergonomic program, and require rigorous adherence by management to sound medical practice recommendations.

11. Establish a medical monitoring program that includes adequate medical treatment for CTDs, light duty assignments, medical removal of employees who have CTD, and sufficient rest periods for employees.

12. Require that accomplishment of ergonomic goals receive the same management commitment and priority as production, and that the job performance of all managers be assessed accordingly.

13. Require that all scheduled and contemplated business expansion and changes in physical plant, materials and equipment be reevaluated to ensure that they will contribute to the goals of the ergonomic program.

14. Keep detailed records on all of the matters mentioned above and record all CTD conditions on the OSHA-200 Form as occupational illnesses.

## 14.2 Coverage

OSHA's efforts to stamp out CTDs will not be confined to manufacturing and construction jobs where the vast majority of its inspection activity has been concentrated in the past. The office, retail, and service industry environment will receive its share of attention as the result of a growing concern that hazardous repetitive motion is required to operate copiers, computers, word processors, laser scanners and similar types of equipment.

Employers who want to avoid OSHA citations for "ergonomic hazards" will be well advised to adopt their own written ergonomic program now -- if they have not already done so. There have been a number of reports that OSHA inspectors will leave employers with existing ergonomic programs alone and concentrate their efforts in this field on those employers with no written plans for addressing ergonomics and CTDs.

Chapter 10

ASBESTOS

Daniel M. Steinway
Partner
Anderson, Kill, Olick & Oshinsky
Washington, DC

## 1.0 ASBESTOS: A CLOSELY REGULATED SUBSTANCE

Asbestos is currently the subject of one of the major environmental issues in the U.S. because the material was so widely used in building construction up to the mid-1970s.

Asbestos is a naturally occurring mineral. Because of its properties of incombustibility, noise absorption, and resistance to electrical current, corrosive and bacterial attack, asbestos was used in a large number of building products intended for fireproofing, acoustical sound-proofing, and heating and cooling system insulation.

Exposure to airborne asbestos fibers during the manufacturing process has been known to present hazards requiring special care. Recently, however, there have been potential health concerns raised regarding exposure to these materials by occupants of buildings where building materials containing asbestos have been installed, and various studies are now underway to determine its health effects in such installations.

Asbestos fibers are small enough to penetrate deeply into the lungs if they become airborne, and have been associated with three major forms of disease in humans:

(1) **Asbestosis,** a scarring of the inner tissue of the lung which stiffens the tissues and interferes with oxygen exchange. It de-creases the lung volume and increases resistance in the lung to the passage of air. Asbestosis generally has a latency period of at least 15 to 20 years and can become progressively worse with time.

(2) **Lung cancer,** a malignant tumor of the lungs. It generally has a latency period of 20 to 30 years.

(3) **Mesothelioma,** a cancer of the mesothelium or pleural linings of the lungs. It generally has a latency period of 30 to 40 years.

The U.S. Environmental Protection Agency (EPA) has instituted a number of regulatory actions under various statutory authorities regarding asbestos materials. In 1973, EPA banned the use of asbestos-containing sprayed-on or trowelled-on friable material for all but decorative pur-poses. EPA has subsequently called for a "phased-in" ban for asbestos materials under the Toxic Substances Control Act (TSCA).

Asbestos concerns have resulted in extensive litigation with literally thousands of lawsuits filed. Typically, these suits involve claims for per-sonal injuries, property damage, costs of removal or insurance coverage.

In response, the federal, state and local governments have been focusing ever-increasing attention on the presence of asbestos-containing materials in buildings. As a result, a maze of overlapping statutes, ordinances and regulations have been adopted governing the use, handling, treatment, removal and disposal of asbestos-containing materials. The federal government has specifically established several regulatory programs in the EPA, the U.S. Occupational Safety and Health Administration (OSHA) and the Department of Transportation (DOT). In addition, many states have enacted laws to regulate hazardous substances generally and in some cases asbestos specifically. This chapter will briefly describe the current asbestos regulatory programs at both the federal and state levels.

## 2.0 EPA REGULATION OF ASBESTOS

EPA currently regulates asbestos under several federal environ-mental statutes:

o Under the **Clean Air Act,** Congress created a comprehensive, programmatic and regulatory system aimed at reducing and, when feasible, eliminating air pollution. Pursuant to the National Emission Standard for Hazardous Air Pollutants (NESHAP) program, EPA has promulgated regulations specifically addressing asbestos emissions[1] from manufacturing operations, building demolition/renovation operations, and waste disposal.

The NESHAP standard does not set a numerical threshold for asbestos fiber emissions; instead, it requires persons conducting asbestos-related activities, such as demolition and renovation operations, to notify EPA and to follow certain procedures relating to the stripping and removing of asbestos materials, and to adopt specific work practices to prevent the release of asbestos fibers

---

[1] 40 C.F.R. Part 61, Subpart M.

into the air. Persons involved in these activities must deposit all asbestos-containing material at a waste disposal site meeting specified guidelines.

o Under the **Clean Water Act**, EPA has set specific effluent limits for discharges of asbestos fibers into navigable waters by facilities such as asbestos roofing and floor tile manufacturers.[2] EPA also has set performance and pretreatment standards for those facilities which discharge asbestos fibers to public sewer systems.[3]

o Under **TSCA**, EPA has promulgated regulations requiring all persons who manufacture, import or process asbestos to meet certain reporting requirements.[4] Pursuant to section 6 of TSCA, EPA has, by regulatory action, phased-out and/or banned nearly all uses of asbestos in new products over the next seven years.[5] Exemptions from this ban may be granted on a case-by-case basis. Other EPA regulation of asbestos under TSCA pertaining to schools and other buildings is discussed below.

o EPA has not listed asbestos-containing material as hazardous waste under the **Resource Conservation and Recovery Act (RCRA)**; however, asbestos wastes are treated as solid wastes for purposes of RCRA regulation, and EPA has listed asbestos as a hazardous substance covered by the **Comprehensive Environmental Response, Compensation and Liability Act (CERCLA/Superfund)**.[6]

## 3.0 ASBESTOS HAZARD EMERGENCY RESPONSE ACT OF 1986 (AHERA)

Because of the potential for serious health hazards associated with asbestos, Congress amended TSCA in 1986 by adding a new title III, The Asbestos Hazard Emergency Response Act of 1986 or "AHERA."[7] AHERA requires the EPA to establish a comprehensive regulatory framework of

---

[2] 40 C.F.R. Part 427.

[3] 40 C.F.R. Part 427.

[4] 40 C.F.R. § 263.60.

[5] See 54 Fed. Reg. 29,461 (July 12, 1989).

[6] See 40 C.F.R. § 302.4.

[7] Pub. L. No. 99-579 (1986).

inspection, management, planning, operations and maintenance activities, and appropriate abatement responses for controlling asbestos-containing materials in schools. Under AHERA, EPA promulgated its "AHERA-in-Schools Rule" on October 17, 1987. The 1988 AHERA amendments provided additional time for local educational agencies to submit asbestos management plans to the state governors and to begin the implementation of these plans.

AHERA also required that EPA conduct a study, discussed below, to determine the extent of danger to human health posed by asbestos in public and commercial buildings and the means to respond to such danger. This study has now been submitted to Congress.

### 3.1 Asbestos In Schools and the Asbestos School Hazard Abatement Act

AHERA requires school systems to identify and abate asbestos hazards in school buildings. Previously, school districts were required to inspect school facilities for asbestos-containing materials and to inform teachers and parents of the inspection results, but they were not required to take any abatement action.

Under the current law, EPA distributes loan and grant money to financially needy schools to help pay for abatement costs. The 1984 Asbestos School Hazard Abatement Act establishes an "Asbestos Trust Fund" where funds appropriated for schools' use in the loan program are to be deposited.[8]

At the present time, AHERA's abatement provisions affect only schools, but there has been considerable attention directed toward possible regulation of public and commercial buildings in the future.

### 3.2 Asbestos in Public and Commercial Buildings

In February 1988, as required by AHERA, EPA sent Congress a study on asbestos-containing materials in public buildings. This report recommended a four-part program to address existing asbestos hazards in public and commercial buildings. The recommended program would:

(1)   increase the availability of accredited asbestos inspectors and abatement professionals,

(2)   develop procedures for dealing with thermal system insulation,

(3)   improve the enforcement of existing asbestos regulations, and

(4)   assess the effectiveness of the AHERA school program.

EPA at the present time does not recommend a regulatory program

---

[8] 20 U.S.C. §§ 4011 *et seq.*

modeled on AHERA for public and commercial buildings. Possible future activities in Congress are discussed below.

## 4.0 STATE REGULATORY ACTIVITIES

Forty-three states have enacted some form of asbestos-related legislation. In contrast to AHERA, which applies only to schools, state asbestos laws generally apply to all types of buildings.

The scope and/or status of individual state laws can vary from the federal laws, and from each other, in many areas, including:

o State accreditation plans, required by AHERA, for the training and certification of inspectors, abatement project designers, contractors, workers and others involved in the federal asbestos-in-school program.

o Performance standards and disposal methods.

o Accreditation and certification of asbestos contractors through approved training courses.

o Asbestos control measures required for issuance of building permits for demolition or renovation, or as a condition of license renewal (e.g., for state-licensed hospitals), condominium conversion, etc.

o The liability of abatement project contractors, including fines for improper removal.

### 4.1 National Implications of California's Proposition 65

In California, Proposition 65, the Safe Drinking Water and Toxics Enforcement Act of 1986, was adopted to protect citizens and drinking water from exposure to toxic chemicals. Toxic chemicals covered by Proposition 65 include those chemicals and materials such as asbestos which are known to cause cancer or to be associated with reproductive toxicity, and which have been specifically listed by the Governor as required under the law. The first list of 29 chemicals was published in February 1987 and included asbestos.

Several broad regulatory programs are established under Proposition 65, including a prohibition against knowingly discharging or releasing toxic chemicals into the water or onto land where the chemical will pass into the drinking water. Another prohibition is against knowingly and intentionally exposing any individual to a chemical known to cause can-cer, such as asbestos, without first giving a clear and reasonable warning of this exposure.[9]

---

[9] Cal. Health & Safety Code § 25249.6.

Legislation similar to Proposition 65 has been introduced in more than 20 states but as of this writing, none has passed yet.

## 5.0 OSHA REGULATIONS

Several regulatory actions have previously been taken by OSHA. OSHA also has recently proposed certain new regulatory requirements for asbestos.

### 5.1 OSHA Asbestos Standard

OSHA's asbestos regulations, which took effect on July 21, 1986, established a permissible exposure limit (PEL) of 0.2 fibers per cubic centimeter for employees who may be exposed to asbestos containing material (ACM) in the workplace.

OSHA's regulations governing asbestos in the workplace are contained in the general industry standards[10] and construction stan-dards.[11] Both standards require the employer to ensure that no employee "is exposed to an airborne concentration of asbestos in excess of 0.2 fibers per cubic centimeter of air as an eight (8)-hour time-weighted average (TWA)."[12] These standards also establish an "action level" defined as an airborne concentration of asbestos "of 0.1 fiber per cubic centimeter of air calculated as an eight (8)-hour time weighted average."[13] Under both regulations, if employees are exposed at or above the action level, the employer must initiate specific compliance activities i.e., air monitoring, employee training and medical surveillance.

This exposure limit was challenged by the Asbestos Information Association/North America and several other industrial and labor organizations,[14] but the U.S. Court of Appeals for the District of Columbia Circuit upheld the exposure limit. Even though the Circuit Court upheld the exposure limit, it directed OSHA to re-examine certain other aspects of its regulations. Specifically, the Court directed OSHA to:

o   determine whether a 0.1 fiber per cubic centimeter permissible

---

[10] 29 C.F.R. § 1910.1001.

[11] 29 C.F.R. § 1926.58.

[12] 29 C.F.R. 1910.1001(c) (general industry); 29 C.F.R. 1926.58(c) (construction industry).

[13] 29 C.F.R. 1910.1001(b) (general industry); 29 C.F.R. 1926.58(b) (construction industry).

[14] *Building and Construction Trades Department, AFL-CIO v. Secretary of Labor* (C.A. No 86-1359) (February 2, 1988); *AFL-CIO v. Department of Labor* (C.A. No. 86-1360) (February 2, 1988).

exposure limit is feasible for the automotive brake and repair industry,

o review its respirator policy and re-examine more vigorous measures to reduce smoking-related asbestos risks among workers,

o clarify that a construction industry employer must monitor air when a change in workplace conditions could result in exposure to asbestos above the permissible limit,

o consider whether bilingual warnings or universal warning signals are necessary,

o clarify the small-scale, short-duration exception under the present asbestos regulations, and

o decide whether to require all construction industry employers to file reports prior to undertaking an asbestos abatement project.

In response to the court's directions, OSHA has issued a new short-term exposure limit (STEL) for asbestos exposures.[15] The STEL for asbestos is one (1) fiber per cubic centimeter averaged over a sampling period of 30 minutes. OSHA also expanded the ban on smoking in the workplace during asbestos removal operations, and suggested that employers use warning signs with universal symbols, graphics, or foreign languages. OSHA has recently proposed new asbestos regulations which, among other things, reduce the PEL to 0.1 fibers per cubic centimeter and eliminate the existing action level standard, clarify the use of glove-bagging operations, require oversight of all construction operations by a competent person, and impose a project reporting requirement.[16]

## 5.2 OSHA Federal Hazard Communication Standard

OSHA has promulgated a revised federal hazard communication standard which would cover all employers with employees exposed to hazardous chemicals including asbestos in the workplace.[17] This standard requires both manufacturing and non-manufacturing employers to establish hazard communication programs that provide information about these chemicals. This information must be conveyed by means of labels (or other forms of warning) on containers, the preparation and distribution of material safety data sheets,

---

[15] 53 Fed. Reg. 35,610 (September 14, 1988).

[16] 55 Fed. Reg. 29,712 (July 20, 1990).

[17] 52 Fed. Reg. 31,852 (August 24, 1987).

and the development and implementation of employee training programs.[18]

### 5.3 Use of Respirators

Whenever feasible engineering controls and work practices are not sufficient to reduce employee exposures to or below the PEL limit, employers must continue to utilize these practices and, additionally, provide for the use of respiratory protection equipment.[19] Employers also must provide respirator equipment in emergency cases.[20] The OSHA regulations impose specific respirator requirements depending on the levels of airborne asbestos fibers.[21] Under its asbestos regulations, OSHA also has promulgated regulations clarifying the use of certain types of respirators.[22]

### 6.0 DOT REGULATIONS

DOT regulates the transport of asbestos in accordance with the provisions of the Hazardous Materials Transportation Act of 1975 (HMTA).[23] Pursuant to its authority under HMTA, DOT has designated asbestos as a hazardous material for purposes of transportation and has prescribed requirements for shipping papers, packaging, marking, labeling and transport vehicle placarding applicable to the shipment and transportation of asbestos materials.[24] In accordance with these requirements, commercial asbestos must be transported in (1) rigid, leak-tight packagings, (2) bags or other non-rigid packagings in closed freight containers, motor vehicles, or rail cars that are loaded by and for the exclusive use of the consignor and unloaded by the consignor, or (3) bags or other nonrigid packagings which are dust and sift-proof in strong outside fiberboard or wooden boxes.[25] Specific regulations have been promulgated for the transport of asbestos materials by highway. Under these

---

[18] 29 C.F.R. § 1910.1200.

[19] See 29 C.F.R. § 1910.1001(g) (general industry); 29 C.F.R. § 1926.58(h) (construction industry).

[20] *Id.*

[21] *Id.*

[22] 52 Fed. Reg. 17,752 (May 12, 1987).

[23] 49 U.S.C. § 1801 *et seq.*

[24] 49 C.F.R. § 172.101.

[25] 49 C.F.R. § 173.1090.

regulations, asbestos must be loaded, handled and unloaded in a manner that will minimize occupational exposure to airborne asbestos particles released incident to transportation, and any asbestos contamination of transport vehicles removed.[26]

## 7.0 FUTURE ACTIONS

The Asbestos Information Act of 1988 (Pub.L. 100-577), was enacted during the waning moments of the 100th Congress. This new law requires asbestos product manufacturers to provide EPA with information on the years of manufacture, types and classes, and other identifying charac-teristics of their asbestos products. The future impacts of this new law are uncertain.

In addition, the Congress passed a number of environmental laws affecting asbestos in the waning moments of the 101st Congress. For example, the Congress specifically designated asbestos as a hazardous air pollutant for purposes of regulation under the Clean Air Act Amendments of 1990. The Congress also passed the Sanitary Food Transportation Act of 1990, which prohibits the transportation of asbestos in motor vehicles or rail vehicles that were used to transport food and other consumer products. Under this new law, DOT is required to issue new regulations prohibiting the use of motor or rail vehicles for other purposes if these vehicles provide transportation for asbestos wastes, extremely hazardous substances, or refuse. Finally, the Asbestos School Hazard Abatement Reauthorization Act of 1989 extends AHERA training and accreditation requirements to contractors involved in asbestos projects in public and commercial buildings. It also requires EPA to issue an advisory notice to all local educational agencies and state governors on the risks associated with "in-place management of asbestos-containing building materials and removals" and methods to "promote the least burdensome response actions necessary to protect human health, safety, and the environment."

Pending Congressional response to the asbestos issue in public and commercial buildings includes ongoing discussion of several legislative initiatives relating to asbestos-containing materials. Attention was initially focused on legislation introduced by former Vermont Senator Robert Stafford. This proposal would have required EPA to set standards for the identification and abatement of hazardous asbestos-containing materials in federal and commercial buildings. It also would have directed EPA to promulgate regulations relating to inspection, response actions, operations and maintenance, periodic surveillance, transportation and disposal of asbestos-containing materials in these buildings.

A second proposal, introduced in the House of Representatives by former New Jersey Representative James Florio, would have required inspections and

---

[26] 49 C.F.R. § 177.844

management plans for all public buildings. Chances for passage of either of these proposals is quite remote at the present time.

Finally, in the near future, EPA is expected to finalize certain changes to the current requirements regarding asbestos contained in the National Emission Standard for Hazardous Air Pollutants (NESHAP) under the Clean Air Act. Most of these changes would relate to asbestos notification, work practice and disposal requirements, including project specific work practices for approved facilities, and various recordkeeping requirements. These proposed changes will make both the landfill owner/operator and the generator liable for violations under the NESHAP requirements. In addition, in an effort to signal improved enforcement of the NESHAP regulations, EPA has announced a more stringent civil penalty policy for violations of these regulations. EPA has stressed that separate penalties will be imposed for each specific violation of NESHAP requirements. Current law authorizes EPA to impose civil penalties of up to $25,000 per day for non-compliance.

## 8.0 CONCLUSION

The ever-expanding regulation of asbestos materials has broad implications for the employers, workers, and owners and occupiers of buildings containing or suspected of containing asbestos materials. Generally speaking, given building industry practices prior to the mid-1970s, buildings constructed prior to that point in time are likely to contain asbestos fireproofing and insulating materials. Asbestos may also be found in wall-board and wall finishes, floor tiles, ceiling tiles and other building components.

A facility survey for the presence of asbestos-containing material may be a worthwhile endeavor. However, to avoid potential liability, asbestos inspection testing, analysis and abatement activities are best conducted with the assistance of environmental consultants and legal counsel qualified to address properly the technical and legal/regulatory compliance issues.

Chapter 11


RESOURCE CONSERVATION AND RECOVERY ACT
(RCRA)


David R. Case
General Counsel
Hazardous Waste Treatment Council
Washington, D.C.


## 1.0 OVERVIEW

The United States has embarked upon the most ambitious regulatory program for the management of hazardous waste of any country in the world. In less than a decade, the adage "out of sight, out of mind" has given way to a comprehensive national program that seeks to encourage waste reduction and advanced treatment and disposal of hazardous wastes. Congress has enacted as national policy the mandate that hazardous waste will be treated, stored, and disposed of so as to minimize the present and future threat to human health and the environment.[1] EPA and the states have sought to implement this mandate in complex regulations issued under the Resource Conservation and Recovery Act of 1976 (RCRA), as significantly amended by the Hazardous and Solid Waste Amendments of 1984.[2] Over 500,000 companies and individuals in the United States who generate over 172 million metric tons of hazardous waste each year must comply with the RCRA regulatory program.

RCRA is a regulatory statute designed to provide "cradle-to-grave" control of hazardous waste by imposing management requirements on generators and transporters of hazardous wastes and upon owners and operators of treatment, storage and disposal (TSD) facilities. RCRA applies mainly to active facilities,

---

[1] Resource Conservation and Recovery Act, 42 U.S.C. §§ 6901 *et seq.* (1982 & Supp. III 1985). Citations throughout this chapter are to sections of the act, rather than to the U.S. Code. *See* national policy in § 1003(b).

[2] Pub. L. No. 94-550, 90 Stat. 2796 (1976), as amended, Pub. L. No. 96-482, 94 Stat. 2334 (1980); Hazardous and Solid Waste Amendments of 1984, Pub. L. No. 98-616, 98 Stat. 3221.

and does not address the equally serious problem of abandoned and inactive sites. Congress established remedies and allocated responsibilities for correcting problems at those sites in the Comprehensive Environmental Response, Compensation, and Liability Act of 1980, commonly known as Superfund,[3] which is discussed in detail in another chapter.

RCRA has been amended several times since its enactment, most importantly by the Hazardous and Solid Waste Amendments of 1984 (HSWA). The 1984 HSWA mandated far-reaching changes to the RCRA program, such as waste minimization and a national land disposal ban program, discussed below. RCRA is currently divided into ten subtitles, A through J. The most significant of these is Subtitle C, which establishes the national hazardous waste management program. Subtitle C, which encompasses Sections 3001-3020, establishes the following basic structure for the RCRA program. *See* Table 1. Section 3001 requires EPA to promulgate regulations which identify specific hazardous wastes, either by listing them or identifying characteristics which render them hazardous. Persons managing such waste are required to notify the U.S. Environmental Protection Agency of their hazardous waste activities.[4]

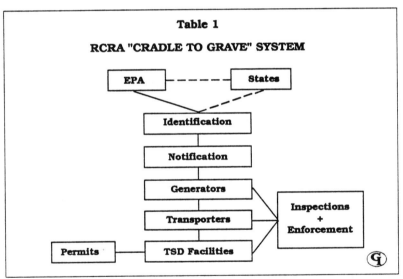

**Table 1**

**RCRA "CRADLE TO GRAVE" SYSTEM**

Persons who generate or produce these wastes (generators) must comply with a set of standards authorized by RCRA Section 3002. These include handling wastes properly and preparing manifests to track the shipment of the waste to treatment, recycling or disposal facilities. Persons who transport hazardous waste (transporters) are required by Section 3003 to comply with another set of regulations dealing with manifests, labeling and the delivery of

---

[3] 42 U.S.C. §§ 9601 *et seq.*

[4] Section 3010(a).

hazardous waste shipments to designated TSD facilities. Transporters must also comply with the U.S. Department of Transportation (DOT) requirements relating to containers, labeling, placarding of vehicles, and spill response.

Section 3004 requires TSD facilities to comply with performance standards, including statutory minimum technology requirements, groundwater monitoring, and a phased-in ban on the land disposal of untreated hazardous wastes. Section 3005 requires owners and operators of TSD facilities to obtain permits which set forth the conditions under which they may operate. Section 3005(e) establishes the "interim status" provision for existing TSD facilities which allows them to remain in operation until a site-specific permit is issued. Owners and operators of interim status TSD facilities must file a timely application for a RCRA permit under Section 3005(a) in order to qualify, and comply with interim status standards in the regulations. The 1984 HSWA sets a timetable for EPA and states to process and issue final RCRA permits.

Section 3006 of RCRA authorizes states to assume responsibility for carrying out the RCRA program, in lieu of the federal program. The state must administer and enforce a program which is consistent with and equivalent to the federal program. States can adopt more stringent requirements, but the state program may be no less stringent than the federal program. Sections 3007 and 3008 authorize site inspections and federal enforcement of RCRA and its implementing regulations.

Other provisions of Subtitle C include provisions for compiling a state-by-state hazardous waste site inventory; monitoring and enforcement authority against previous owners of TSD facilities; EPA regulation of recycled oil; and controls on the export of hazardous waste.[5]

The amendments made by the 1984 HSWA are extensive. They significantly expand both the scope of coverage and the detailed requirements of RCRA. For example, they require EPA to more fully regulate an estimated 200,000 companies that produce only small quantities of hazardous waste (less than 1,000 kilograms per month). An entirely new regulatory program was created in Subtitle I ("eye") for underground storage tanks containing hazardous substances or petroleum, which affects hundreds of thousands of facilities for the first time.[6] The numerous constraints imposed on those who treat, store or dispose of wastes in landfills, including restrictions on the disposal of liquid wastes and other common hazardous wastes, are technically complex. For example, companies using unlined surface impoundments were required to retrofit with double liners and leachate collection systems.

The 1984 HSWA contain many so-called "hammer provisions" that required EPA to implement new requirements by a deadline or a congressionally formulated standard automatically went into effect. For example, if EPA had

---

[5] Sections 3012, 3013, 3014, 3017.

[6] Sections 9001-9010. The underground storage tank program is discussed in a separate chapter.

not promulgated the land disposal restriction regulations for all RCRA hazardous wastes by the statutory deadline of May 1990, the "hammer" would have fallen and the unrestricted wastes would have been prohibited from land disposal by operation of statute. There are 72 major provisions in the 1984 HSWA, by EPA's count, and these new requirements are having a substantial impact on every U.S. business that produces hazardous waste.

These major provisions of the Subtitle C program and the impact of the 1984 amendments are discussed in detail below, as are the requirements of other important subtitles of RCRA.

## 2.0 POLICY GOALS AND OBJECTIVES OF RCRA

Subtitle A of RCRA declares that, as a matter of national policy, the generation of hazardous waste is to be reduced or eliminated as expeditiously as possible, and land disposal should be the least favored method for managing hazardous wastes. In addition, all waste that is generated must be handled so as to minimize the present and future threat to human health and the environment.[7]

Subtitle A also includes a series of objectives designed to achieve these goals, including in the first instance proper management of hazardous waste, minimization of the generation and land disposal of hazardous waste, prohibition of open dumping, encouragement of state assumption of RCRA programs, encouragement of research and development activities in the waste management area, and promotion of recovery, recycling, and treatment as alternatives to land disposal.[8] These national goals and objectives set by RCRA give direction to EPA's regulatory efforts.

## 3.0 DEFINITION OF SOLID AND HAZARDOUS WASTE

The starting point for determining the full scope of RCRA's coverage is the broad definition of "solid waste" in the statute. Section 1004(27) states that:

The term "solid waste" means *any garbage, refuse, sludge* from a waste treatment plant, water supply treatment plant or air pollution control facility *and other discarded material, including solid, liquid, semisolid, or contained gaseous materials* resulting from industrial, commercial, mining and agriculture activities and from community activities but does not include solid or dissolved material in domestic sewage, or solid or dissolved materials in irrigation return flows or

---

[7] RCRA, Sections 1003(b), 1002(b).

[8] RCRA, Section 1003(a).

industrial discharges which are point sources subject to permits under section 402 of the Federal Water Pollution Control Act, as amended, or source, special nuclear, or byproduct material as defined by the Atomic Energy Act of 1954, as amended (68 Stat. 923). (Emphasis supplied.)

The statute therefore applies to potentially any waste regardless of its physical form. EPA has further defined "solid waste" by regulation, as discussed below.

The Subtitle C regulatory program of RCRA then covers those solid wastes categorized as hazardous. As defined in Section 1004(5), the term "hazardous waste" means a solid waste, or combination of solid wastes, which because of its quantity, concentration, or physical, chemical, or infectious characteristics may--

(A) cause, or significantly contribute to an increase in mortality or an increase in serious irreversible, or incapacitating reversible illness; or

(B) pose a substantial present or potential hazard to human health or the environment when improperly treated, stored, transported, or disposed of, or otherwise managed.

These general statutory definitions have been greatly amplified and explained by EPA regulations implementing RCRA, the first set of which was issued on May 19, 1980.[9] These regulations are discussed in the following section which describes the RCRA Subtitle C program in detail.

## 4.0 SUBTITLE C: HAZARDOUS WASTE MANAGEMENT PROGRAM

### 4.1 Identification of Hazardous Wastes Under the Implementing Regulations[10]

EPA has defined solid waste to include any discarded material, provided a regulatory exclusion or specific variance granted by EPA or an authorized state does not apply.[11] "Discarded material" is in turn defined as any material that is abandoned, recycled, or "inherently waste-like."[12] A material is abandoned if it is disposed of, burned or incinerated, or accumulated, stored

---

[9] 45 Fed. Reg. 33066.

[10] For a more comprehensive description of the regulatory provisions of RCRA, the reader is referred to Hall, *et al., RCRA/Hazardous Wastes Handbook* (Government Institutes, 8th ed. 1990).

[11] 40 C.F.R. § 261.2(a). *See* 50 Fed. Reg. 664 (January 4, 1985). The list of regulatory exemptions appears at § 261.4(a) and is very limited.

[12] 40 C.F.R. § 261.2(a)(2).

or treated prior to or in lieu of abandonment. A material is inherently waste-like if EPA so defines it by regulation.[13]

A material can be a solid waste if it is recycled in a manner constituting disposal, by burning for energy recovery, by reclamation, or by speculative accumulation. Materials that are not solid wastes when recycled are materials that are directly used or reused as ingredients or feedstocks in production processes, or as effective substitutes for commercial products, or that are recycled in a closed-loop production process.[14]

These interlocking definitions result in EPA regulating a universe of materials that may not commonly be understood to be "wastes" for a particular industry or company. In particular, materials that are reclaimed or recycled, rather than disposed of, may still be considered solid wastes and therefore hazardous wastes subject to RCRA regulation.

Once a material is found to be a solid waste, the next question is whether it is a "hazardous waste." EPA's regulations automatically exempt certain solid wastes from being considered hazardous wastes. Generally these regulatory exemptions include:

(1)     household waste;

(2)     agricultural wastes which are returned to the ground as fertilizer;

(3)     mining overburden returned to the mine site;

(4)     utility wastes from coal combustion;

(5)     oil and natural gas exploration drilling waste;

(6)     wastes from the extraction, beneficiation, and processing of ores and minerals, including coal;

(7)     cement kiln dust wastes;

(8)     arsenical-treated wood wastes generated by end users of such wood;

---

[13] 40 C.F.R. § 261.2(d). EPA has designated dioxin wastes as inherently waste-like.

[14] EPA has proposed amendments to the definition of solid waste to exclude certain in-process recycled secondary materials that are part of a continuous production or manufacturing process. 53 Fed. Reg. 519 (January 8, 1988). This action was taken in response to the court decision in *American Mining Congress v. EPA*, 824 F.2d 1177 (D.C. Cir. 1987).

(9)    certain chromium-bearing wastes.[15]

EPA has also provided some limited regulatory exemptions under narrowly defined circumstances, such as for hazardous waste that is generated in a product or raw material storage tank, transport vehicle, pipeline or manufacturing process unit prior to removal for disposal. EPA has also adopted a conditional exemption for waste samples collected for testing to determine their characteristics or composition, or to conduct treatability tests.[16]

If a solid waste does not qualify for an exemption, it will be deemed a hazardous waste if it is listed by EPA in 40 C.F.R. Part 261, Subpart D, or if it exhibits any of the four hazardous waste characteristics identified in 40 C.F.R. Part 261, Subpart C.

### 4.1.1  Hazardous Waste Lists

EPA has established three hazardous wastes lists. EPA has assigned a hazardous waste number to each listed waste which can be used to identify the waste on biennial reports and other documents, and for purposes of the land disposal ban program. The first list contains hazardous wastes from *nonspecific* sources (e.g., spent nonhalogenated solvents, such as toluene or methyl ethyl ketone produced by an industrial source).[17] The hazardous wastes on this nonspecific source list are assigned an "F" number (e.g. F001-F005 are various spent solvents). The second list identifies hazardous wastes from specific sources (e.g., bottom sediment sludge from the treatment of wastewaters by the wood preserving industry).[18] The hazardous wastes on the specific source list have a "K" number (e.g., K048 - K052 are certain petroleum refining wastes). The first two hazardous waste lists are largely self-explanatory. A company need only compare its solid waste stream to those lists to determine if it manages a hazardous waste.

The third list sets forth commercial chemical products, including off-specification species, containers, and spill residues, which, when discarded,

---

[15]  40 C.F.R. § 261.4(b), 45 Fed. Reg. 33120, 45 Fed. Reg. 72037 (October 30, 1980), 45 Fed. Reg. 76620 (November 19, 1980), 45 Fed. Reg. 78531 (November 25, 1980).

[16]  40 C.F.R. § 261.4(d), 46 Fed. Reg. 47429 (September 25, 1981), 53 Fed. Reg. 27290 (July 19, 1988).

[17]  40 C.F.R. § 261.31.

[18]  40 C.F.R. § 261.32.

must be treated as hazardous wastes.[19] This hazardous waste list actually consists of two distinct sublists. One sublist sets forth chemicals deemed acute hazardous wastes when discarded (40 C.F.R. 261.33(e)). These have a "P" number and are subject to move rigorous management requirements (e.g. P076 is nitric oxide). A second list contains "U" listed chemicals which are deemed toxic and, therefore, hazardous when discarded (40 C.F.R. 261.33(f)), and which are regulated like other listed hazardous wastes (e.g., U002 is acetone).

Hazardous waste regulation under the commercial chemical list can be triggered when a company decides to reduce inventory or otherwise discards a listed commercial chemical product in its pure form. Another situation that may trigger regulation is an accidental spill of the chemical.[20] If a listed commercial chemical is spilled, the spilled chemical and any contaminated material, i.e., dirt and other residue, are likely to be discarded and thus become a hazardous waste. Therefore, even companies that generally do not discard or intend to discard any of the commercial chemical products on the list must be prepared to comply with the RCRA hazardous waste regulations in the event of an accidental spill.[21] This may involve, as discussed below, obtaining an EPA identification number and complying, at a minimum, with applicable generator standards. For disposal of small amounts of chemicals or spill materials, the company may qualify as a conditionally exempt "small quantity generator."[22]

Since the RCRA program became effective in 1980, many companies have filed "delisting petitions" with EPA to remove wastes generated at their facilities from the RCRA hazardous waste lists at 40 C.F.R. Part 261. The granting of a delisting petition exempts the waste generated at a particular facility from the RCRA hazardous waste program. A company seeking a delisting must demonstrate that its particular waste does not contain the hazardous constituents for which EPA listed the waste, or any other constituents that could cause the waste to be hazardous.[23]

For example, a company seeking to delist a waste which would otherwise be included under F006 (wastewater treatment sludge from electroplating operations) must show that the concentrations of chromium, nickel, and cyanide for which the waste was listed are below levels of regulatory concern, and also that no other heavy metals or other constituents are present that

---

[19] 40 C.F.R. § 261.33.

[20] 40 C.F.R. § 261.33(d).

[21] *See* 45 Fed. Reg. 76629 (November 19, 1980).

[22] 40 C.F.R. § 261.5. Alternatively, a small spill may qualify as a *de minimis* loss exempt from the definition of hazardous waste in § 261.3(a)(2)(iv)(D).

[23] 40 C.F.R. § 260.22.

may cause the waste to be hazardous. EPA must act on a delisting petition within two years of receiving a complete petition.

### 4.1.2 Hazardous Waste Characteristics

If a waste is not listed as hazardous, the waste is still covered by RCRA if it exhibits one of four hazardous waste characteristics: ignitability, corrosivity, reactivity, or toxicity.[24]

The hazardous waste characteristic of ignitability was established to identify solid wastes capable during routine handling of causing a fire or exacerbating a fire once started.[25] A solid waste is deemed to exhibit the characteristic of ignitability if it meets with one of the following four descriptions. First, if it is a liquid, other than an aqueous solution containing less than 24 percent alcohol by volume, with a flash point of less than 140 degrees Fahrenheit (60°C). Second, if it is a nonliquid which under normal conditions can cause fire through friction, absorption of moisture, or spontaneous chemical changes, and burns so vigorously when ignited that it creates a hazard. Third, if it is an ignitable compressed gas as defined by the DOT regulations at 49 C.F.R. 173.300. Finally, a waste exhibits ignitability if it is an oxidizer as defined by the DOT regulations at 49 C.F.R. 173.151. An ignitable hazardous waste has the EPA number of D001.

The hazardous waste characteristic of corrosivity was established because EPA believed that wastes capable of corroding metal could escape their containers and liberate other wastes.[26] In addition, wastes with a pH at either the high or low end of the scale can harm human tissue and aquatic life and may react dangerously with other wastes. Therefore, EPA determined that any solid waste is deemed to exhibit the characteristic of corrosivity if it is (1) aqueous and has a pH of less than or equal to 2.0 or greater than or equal to 12.5, or (2) a liquid and corrodes steel at a rate greater than 6.35 millimeters (.250 inches) per year under specified testing procedures. A waste that exhibits the hazardous characteristic of corrosivity has EPA number D002.

EPA established the hazardous waste characteristic of reactivity to regulate wastes that are extremely unstable and have a tendency to react violently or explode during management.[27] The regulation lists a number of situations where this may happen which warrant specific consideration (e.g., when the waste is mixed with water, when heated, etc.). Since suitable test protocols for measuring reactivity are unavailable, EPA has promulgated a narrative

---

[24] 40 C.F.R. § 261.3, § 261.20.

[25] 40 C.F.R. § 261.21.

[26] 41 C.F.R. § 261.22.

[27] 41 C.F.R. § 261.23.

definition of the reactivity characteristic that must be used. A waste that exhibits reactivity has EPA number D003.

The toxicity characteristic is designed to identify wastes that are likely to leach hazardous concentrations of specific toxic constituents into groundwater under mismanagement conditions.[28] This characteristic is determined based on a mandatory testing procedure which extracts the toxic constituents from a solid waste in a manner which EPA believes simulates the leaching action which occurs in landfills.[29] A solid waste exhibits the characteristic of toxicity if, using the test methods prescribed by EPA, the extract from a representative sample of the waste contains contaminants at levels of regulatory concern. The test method is called the Toxicity Characteristic Leaching Procedure, or TCLP. It replaces the Extraction Procedure (EP) Toxicity Characteristic that was initially promulgated by EPA in 1980. The TCLP tests for 25 organic chemicals, 8 inorganics, and 6 insecticides/ herbicides. The levels that trigger the toxicity characteristic reflect health-based concentration thresholds and a factor for dilution/attenuation that was developed using modeling of the subsurface fate and transport of contaminants. These hazardous wastes are given EPA numbers D004-D043, depending on the toxic contaminant that causes the waste to be hazardous.

### 4.1.3 Mixtures of Hazardous Wastes and Solid Wastes

Anyone concerned with hazardous waste management must be aware of the "mixture rule." Under this EPA rule, a mixture of a listed hazardous wastes and a solid waste must also be considered a hazardous waste, unless the mixture qualifies for an exemption.[30] The exemptions apply if, for example, (1) the listed hazardous waste in the mixture was listed solely because it exhibits a hazardous characteristic and the mixture does not exhibit that characteristic; or (2) the mixture consists of wastewater and certain specified hazardous wastes in dilute concentrations, the discharge of which is subject to regulation under the Clean Water Act, or (3) the mixture consists of a discarded commercial chemical product resulting from *de minimis* losses during manufacturing operations. On the other hand, a mixture of a characteristic hazardous waste and a solid waste will be deemed hazardous only if the entire mixture continues to exhibit a hazardous characteristic.

Note that these exemptions apply only when the hazardous waste becomes mixed with other wastes as part of the normal production or waste management process, not when wastes are intentionally mixed to achieve dilution. Such mixing constitutes treatment and requires a permit.

---

[28] 40 C.F.R. § 261.24, as amended, 55 Fed. Reg. 11862 (March 29, 1990).

[29] 40 C.F.R. Part 261, Appendix II.

[30] 40 C.F.R. § 261.3(a)(2).

### 4.1.4 Derived-from Hazardous Wastes

Of equal importance is EPA's so-called "derived-from rule." Under this rule, a waste that is generated from the treatment, storage, or disposal of a hazardous waste (e.g. ash, leachate, or emission control dust) is also a hazardous waste, unless exempted.[31] If the waste is derived from a listed hazardous waste, it is considered a hazardous waste until delisting procedures are followed. If the waste is derived from a characteristic hazardous waste, it is not hazardous if it does not exhibit that characteristic. Materials that are reclaimed from solid wastes for beneficial use are no longer wastes, unless the reclaimed material is burned as a fuel or used in a manner constituting disposal (i.e., applied to the ground).

### 4.1.5 Used, Reused, Recycled or Reclaimed Hazardous Wastes

EPA has defined the term "solid waste" to extend coverage to many recycling and reclamation activities.[32] This aspect of the solid waste definition is complex. Conceptually, it requires consideration of two things-- the manner of recycling, and the secondary material being recycled.

The recycling activities that are regulated are (1) use in a manner constituting disposal (e.g. land application), (2) burning for energy recovery, (3) reclamation, and (4) speculative accumulation. Secondary materials that are solid wastes when recycled include spent materials, listed and characteristic sludges, listed and characteristic byproducts, commercial chemical products, and scrap metal. These materials are all solid wastes when recycled with two exceptions. Sludges and by-products that are hazardous only by characteristic are not solid wastes when they are reclaimed. Commercial chemical products are not solid wastes when they are either reclaimed or speculatively accumulated.[33]

Materials are not solid wastes when they are directly used or reused as ingredients in an industrial process to make a product, provided the material is not being reclaimed. A material is also not a solid waste when used as an effective substitute for a commercial product, unless the material is burned as a fuel or applied to the land. Finally, a material is not a waste if it is returned to the original process from which it is generated as a substitute for a raw material feedstock, again provided it is not first reclaimed. These provisions reflect EPA's concern to avoid extending RCRA regulation to production, as distinct from waste management activities.

---

[31] 40 C.F.R. § 261.3(b).

[32] 40 C.F.R. § 261.2(c).

[33] *Id.* The definition of "sludge" is in § 260.10 and the definitions of "by-product," "scrap metal," "recycled," "reclaimed," and "accumulated speculatively" are found in § 261.1(c). These definitions are critically important to understanding the scope of RCRA's coverage of recycling activities.

Generally speaking, hazardous wastes destined for recycling are subject to the Part 262 and 263 regulations for generators and transporters, and to the storage facility requirements in Parts 264 and 265.[34]

### 4.2 Notification of Hazardous Waste Management Activities

RCRA Section 3010(a) requires that any person who manages a hazardous waste (i.e., generators, transporters, and owners or operators of TSD facilities) must file a notification with EPA within 90 days after regulations are promulgated identifying the waste as hazardous. EPA has published Form 8700-12 as the Section 3010(a) notification form. The reporting company must identify itself, its location, and the EPA identification numbers for the listed and characteristic hazardous wastes it manages. It is important to remember that notifications are required to be filed for each site (e.g., plant) at which hazardous waste is managed.

Persons managing hazardous wastes under EPA's initial RCRA regulatory program should have filed the Section 3010(a) notification form not later than August 18, 1980.[35] Failure to file makes the transport, treatment, storage or disposal of the hazardous wastes unlawful. Companies that failed to file due to excusable oversight may request that EPA exercise its enforcement discretion and permit continued operation if in the public interest.[36]

Persons who produce, market or burn hazardous waste-derived fuels were required to file a notification by February 8, 1985. These notifications also identified the location and description of the facility, the hazadous wastes involved, and a description of the fuel production or burning activity carried out at the facility.

### 4.3 Generators of Hazardous Waste

Generators play a crucial role in the overall RCRA hazardous waste regulatory scheme. The failure of a generator to properly identify and initiate the management of a hazardous waste may mean that the waste never enters the "cradle to grave" hazardous waste program. Thus the requirements imposed on generators under RCRA Section 3002 and EPA's implementing regulations at 40 C.F.R. Part 262 are of key concern.

EPA's regulations define the term "generator" as "any person, by site, whose act or process produces hazardous waste identified or listed in Part 261 of this chapter or whose act first causes hazardous waste to become subject to

---

[34] 40 C.F.R. § 261.6 Certain exemptions are also set forth in the regulation.

[35] 45 Fed. Reg. 33066 (May 19, 1980).

[36] 45 Fed. Reg. 76632 (November 19, 1980).

regulation."[37]   This definition refers explicitly to the particular site of generation.   A corporation with several plants must evaluate and comply with the generator requirements individually for the site of each facility.

A generator is initially required to determine whether any of its solid waste is a "hazardous waste" under the criteria described above.[38]   The records of any test results, waste analyses, or determinations that a waste is hazardous must be kept for at least three years from the date the waste was last sent to a TSD facility.   Most generators retain such records indefinitely.   The generator must then obtain an EPA Identification Number before any hazardous waste can be transported, treated, stored or disposed of, and only transporters and TSD facilities that have obtained their EPA Identification Numbers can be used.[39]

The generator has the responsibility for preparing the Uniform Hazardous Waste Manifest, a control and transport document that accompanies the hazardous waste at all times.[40]   The generator must specify the name and EPA Identification Numbers of each authorized transporter and the TSD facility or other designated facility that will receive the waste, describe the waste as required by DOT regulations, certify that it is properly packaged and labeled, and sign the manifest certifications by hand.

In the new era of RCRA, companies must develop new management strategies and new technologies to reduce the volume, quantity, and toxicity of hazardous wastes.   As an action-forcing mechanism, Congress now requires all generators to certify on manifests that:

I have a program in place to reduce the volume and toxicity of waste generated to the degree I have determined to be economically practicable and I have selected the method of treatment, storage or disposal currently available to me which minimizes the present and future threat to human health and the environment.

A sufficient number of copies of the manifest must be prepared so that all parties listed on the manifest as handling the hazardous waste will be provided with a copy, and a final copy can also be returned to the generator by the TSD facility.   A copy of the final signed manifest must be kept for at least

---

[37] 40 C.F.R. § 260.10(a)(26).

[38] 40 C.F.R. § 262.11.

[39] 40 C.F.R. § 262.12(c).

[40] 40 C.F.R. §§ 262.20 - 262.23.  *See* the Uniform Manifest and instructions, 40 C.F.R. Part 262, Appendix.

three years, although most generators retain copies for a much longer period.[41]

If the manifest is not received back by the generator in a timely or properly executed manner, he must file an "exception report" with EPA or the state. The regulations specifically provide that a generator must contact the transporter and/or the TSD facility to determine what happened to the manifest and the hazardous waste. If, after 45 days from shipping the waste, the generator has not received a manifest with the proper signatures back from the TSD facility, the generator must submit an exception report which consists of (1) a copy of the manifest for which the generator does not have confirmation of delivery; and (2) a cover letter which describes the efforts taken to locate the waste or manifest and the result of those efforts.[42]

A generator, in addition, must properly prepare the waste for transportation off-site. EPA has adopted the DOT regulations issued under the Hazardous Materials Transportation Act, 49 USC §§ 1802 *et seq.*, with respect to the packaging, labeling, marking, and placarding of hazardous waste shipments.[43] In addition to the DOT regulations, EPA requires that any container of 110 gallons or less must be specifically marked with the generator's name, address, manifest document number, and the words:

> Hazardous Waste--Federal law prohibits improper disposal. If found contact the nearest police or public safety authority or the United States Environmental Protection Agency.[44]

A generator is allowed to accumulate his own hazardous wastes on site without a RCRA permit for storage in two related circumstances. First, the generator can accumulate up to 55 gallons of hazardous wastes at or near the point of generation in "satellite accumulation areas."[45] The containers must be properly marked and maintained in good condition, and the waste must be moved into storage once the 55-gallon limit is reached. Second, a generator is also allowed to store hazardous waste on-site prior to shipment for a period of

---

[41] 40 C.F.R. § 262.40.

[42] 40 C.F.R. § 262.42.

[43] 40 C.F.R. § 262.31.

[44] 40 C.F.R. § 262.32.

[45] 40 C.F.R. § 262.34.

up to 90 days in tanks or containers, provided certain standards are met.[46] The generator must comply with the Part 265 interim status standards for containers and tanks (e.g., secondary containment structures) and the requirements for personnel training, contingency planning, and emergency preparedness and response.

A generator must file biennial reports with EPA or an authorized state (some states require annual reports). The biennial report is filed on March 1 of even numbered years for the preceding calendar year, and must include (1) the name, address and EPA identification number of the generator, (2) the EPA identification number for each transporter used, (3) name, address and identification number of each TSD facility to which wastes were sent, and (4) waste identification information including the DOT hazard class, EPA hazardous waste identification number, and the quantity of the wastes.[47] EPA has devised Form 8700-13A for this purpose. The 1984 HSWA requires that the reports now also include information on the "waste minimization" efforts undertaken to reduce the volume and toxicity of the hazardous wastes, and the results actually achieved in comparison with previous years. As a recordkeeping requirement, the generator must maintain copies of the biennial reports (and any exception reports filed) for at least three years.

As a practical matter, in view of the liability imposed by Superfund, discussed in the Superfund Chapter, generators should seriously consider maintaining RCRA waste determinations, test results, manifests and reports for substantially longer than the minimum three-year period.

Special rules have been issued for persons who export or import hazardous wastes.[48] A generator who intends to export his hazardous waste to a foreign country must first notify EPA in writing at least four weeks before the initial shipment in each calendar year. He must then require the foreign consignee to confirm delivery of the waste, such as by returning a signed manifest. If the generator does not receive a manifest signed by the transporter stating the date and place of departure from the U.S. within 45 days, or written confirmation of receipt from the foreign consignee within 90 days, an exception report must be filed. Annual reports of all exports must be submitted to EPA. A person who imports hazardous waste into the U.S. must initiate the manifest procedures as the generator.

### 4.3.1 Small Generators

As directed by the 1984 HSWA, EPA has promulgated special regulations for small quantity generators that produce hazardous wastes in a total monthly

---

[46] 40 C.F.R. § 262.34(a). A small quantity generator can store wastes for a longer time period, as discussed below. *See* 40 C.F.R. § 262.34(d)-(f).

[47] 40 C.F.R. § 262.41.

[48] 40 C.F.R. § 262.50.

quantity of less than 1,000 kilograms (2,200 pounds).[49] The regulations vary somewhat from the standards that currently apply to hazardous wastes of larger quantity generators. For example, small quantity generators of between 100 kg and 1000 kg may store up to 1,000 kilograms (13,200 pounds) of hazardous waste on site for up to 180 days without a permit. If the waste must be shipped over 200 miles, the waste may be stored for up to 270 days.

Besides using the Uniform Manifest, small quantity generators must have their waste treated, stored (except short-term storage on site) and disposed of at an interim status or permitted TSD facility, and no longer at a state or municipally licensed landfill. The manifest contains a modified certification of waste minimization for such generators. In almost all other respects, however, small quantity generators of between 100 kg and 1000 kg per month are regulated the same as large generators.

Very small generators of less than 100 kilograms per month are still conditionally exempt from RCRA, but they are subject to certain minimum standards.[50]

### 4.4 Transporters of Hazardous Wastes

A transporter is any person engaged in the off-site transportation of hazardous waste by air, rail, highway or water.[51] Off-site transportation includes both interstate and intrastate commerce.[52] Thus, the reach of RCRA includes not only shippers and common carriers of hazardous wastes, but also the company that occasionally transports hazardous wastes on its own trucks solely within its home state.

Anyone who moves a hazardous waste that is required to be manifested off the site where it is generated, or the site where it is being treated, stored and disposed of, will be subject to the transporter standards. The only persons not covered are generators or operators of TSD facilities who engage in on-site transportation of their hazardous waste. Once a generator or a TSD facility operator moves its hazardous waste off-site--which can be any distance along a public road--he is then considered a transporter and must comply with the regulations.[53]

---

[49] 40 C.F.R. § 261.5, § 262.34(d)-(f).

[50] 40 C.F.R. § 261.5.

[51] 40 C.F.R. § 260.10(a).

[52] Section 3003.

[53] *See* the definition of "on-site" in § 260.10(a), which by implication defines transportation off-site as any distance along, as opposed to simply going across, a public or private right-of-way.

EPA has promulgated standards for all transporters of hazardous wastes at 40 C.F.R. Part 263. These standards are closely coordinated with the standards issued by the U.S. Department of Transportation under the Hazardous Materials Transportation Act for the shipment of hazardous materials.[54] For the most part, EPA's regulations incorporate and require compliance with the DOT provisions on labeling, marking, placarding, using proper containers, and reporting spills. Of course, all transporters must obtain an EPA Identification Number prior to transporting any hazardous waste, and they may only accept hazardous waste which is accompanied by a manifest signed by the generator.[55] The transporter himself must sign and date the manifest acknowledging acceptance of the waste and return one copy to the generator before leaving the generator's property.

At all times the transporter must keep the manifest with the hazardous waste. When the transporter delivers the waste to another transporter or to the designated TSD facility, he must (1) date the manifest and obtain the signature of the next transporter or the TSD facility operator, (2) retain one copy of the manifest for his own records, and (3) give the remaining copies to the person receiving the waste.[56] If the transporter is unable to deliver the waste in accordance with the manifest, he must contact the generator for further instructions and revise the manifest accordingly.[57] The transporter must keep the executed copy of the manifest for a period of three years.[58]

The transporter may hold a hazardous waste for up to ten days at a transfer facility without being required to obtain a RCRA storage permit.[59] A transfer facility generally includes a loading dock, storage area, and similar areas where shipments of hazardous wastes are held during the normal course of transportation.

Transporters of hazardous wastes may become subject to the Part 262 requirements for generators if, for example, the transporter mixes hazardous wastes of different DOT descriptions by placing them into a single container,

---

[54] 49 U.S.C. §§ 1801, *et seq.*, 49 C.F.R. Parts 171-179.

[55] 40 C.F.R. § 263.11, § 263.20.

[56] 40 C.F.R. § 263.20. Special requirements apply to rail or water transporters of hazardous waste, and those who transport hazardous waste outside of the United States. 40 C.F.R. § 263.20(e), (f) and (g), § 263.22(b), (c) and (d).

[57] 40 C.F.R. § 263.21(b).

[58] 40 C.F.R. § 263.22.

[59] 40 C.F.R. § 263.12.

or if he imports hazardous waste from a foreign country.[60]  Also, a hazardous waste that accumulates in a transport vehicle or vessel will trigger the generator standards when the waste is removed.

If an accidental spill or other discharge of a hazardous waste occurs during transportation, the transporter is responsible for its clean up.[61]  The transporter must take immediate response action to protect human health and the environment.  Such action includes treatment or containment of the spill and notification of local police and fire departments.  DOT's discharge reporting requirements are incorporated into the RCRA regulations.[62]  They identify the situations in which telephone reporting of the discharge to the National Response Center and the filing of a written report are required.  That telephone number is 800/424-8802 or 202/426-2675.  Transporters are subject to both DOT and EPA enforcement.[63]

The 1984 HSWA affected transporters in minor respects.  For example, EPA has established requirements for the transportation of hazardous waste-derived fuels.[64]  In addition, railroads are shielded from the RCRA "citizen suit" and "imminent hazard" enforcement provisions (discussed below) if the railroad merely transports the hazardous waste under a sole contractual agreement and exercises due care.

### 4.5  Statutory and Regulatory Requirements for Treatment, Storage, and Disposal (TSD) Facilities

The term "TSD" is commonly used to refer to the three management activities that are regulated under RCRA Section 3004, and which thus require a permit under RCRA Section 3005.  These activities are treatment, storage and disposal of hazardous wastes.  Section 3004 directed EPA to establish a comprehensive set of regulations governing all aspects of TSD facilities, from location to design, operation, and closure.  The regulations adopted include both standards of general applicability to all TSD facilities and specific requirements for particular types of facilities.[65]

In 1984, Congress added a number of important provisions to Section 3004. These establish, among other things, a ban on the disposal of liquids in

---

[60]  40 C.F.R. § 263.10(c).

[61]  40 C.F.R. § 263.30.

[62]  *See* 49 C.F.R. § 171.15 and § 171.16.

[63]  45 Fed. Reg. 51645 (August 4, 1980).

[64]  40 C.F.R. § 266.33, discussed below.

[65]  *See* 40 C.F.R. Parts 264 and 265, discussed infra.

landfills, minimum technological requirements (i.e., double liners) for surface impoundments and landfills, corrective action for continuing releases at permitted TSD facilities, and controls on the marketing and burning of hazardous wastes used as fuels. Congress directed EPA to make a number of regulatory decisions under Section 3004 in short order. The most significant provisions set a strict timetable under which EPA must implement a land disposal ban of all untreated hazardous wastes, and establish treatment standards for the wastes. The requirements of the current standards and the impact of the new amendments are discussed below.

First of all, certain basic definitions must be understood. A facility will be regulated as a "treatment facility" if the operator utilizes any method, technique, or process designed to change the physical, chemical, or biological character or composition of any hazardous waste so as to neutralize such waste, to recover energy or material resources from the waste, to render the waste nonhazardous or less hazardous, safer to transport, store or dispose of, or amenable for recovery, amenable for storage, or reduced in volume.[66] There is very little that can be done to a hazardous waste that would not qualify as treatment. A "storage facility" is defined as one which engages in the holding of hazardous waste for a temporary period, at the end of which the hazardous waste is treated, disposed of, or stored elsewhere.[67]

A "disposal facility" is one at which hazardous waste is intentionally placed into or on any land or water, and at which waste will remain after closure.[68] The term "facility" is separately defined to include "all contiguous land, and structures, other appurtenances, and improvements on the land."[69] Clarification of the foregoing definitions can be sought during the permitting process.

A number of different types of TSD facilities and hazardous waste activities are currently exempted from EPA regulation altogether. The list presently contains the following exclusions:[70]

(1)   Facilities that dispose of hazardous waste by means of ocean disposal pursuant to a permit issued under the Marine Protection, Research, and Sanctuaries Act (except as provided in a RCRA permit-by-rule).

---

[66] 40 C.F.R. § 260.10(a)

[67] *Id.*

[68] *Id.*

[69] *Id.*

[70] *See* 40 C.F.R. § 264.1 and § 265.1(c).

(2)    The disposal of hazardous waste by underground injection pursuant to a permit issued under the Safe Drinking Water Act (except as provided in a RCRA permit-by-rule).

(3) A Publicly Owned Treatment Works (POTW) that treats or stores hazardous wastes which are delivered to the POTW by a transport vehicle or vessel or through a pipe.

(4)    TSD facilities that operate under a state hazardous waste program authorized pursuant to RCRA Section 3006, and which are therefore subject to regulation under the state program.

(5)    Facilities authorized by a state to manage industrial or municipal solid waste, if the only hazardous waste handled by such a facility is otherwise excluded from regulation pursuant to the special requirements for conditionally exempt small quantity generators of less than 100 kilograms.

(6)    A facility that is subject to the special exemptions for certain recyclable materials, except as provided in Part 266.

(7)    Temporary on-site accumulation of hazardous waste by generators in compliance with 40 C.F.R. § 262.34.

(8)    Farmers who dispose of waste pesticides from their own use in compliance with 40 C.F.R. § 262.51.

(9)    Owners or operators of a "totally enclosed treatment facility."

(10)    Owners and operators of "elementary neutralization units" as defined in the regulations and "wastewater treatment units," as defined in the regulations.

(11)    Persons taking immediate action to treat and contain spills.

(12)    Transporters storing manifested wastes in approved containers at a transfer facility for 10 days or less.

(13)    The act of adding absorbent material to hazardous waste in a container to reduce the amount of free liquids in the container, if the materials are added when wastes are first placed in the container.

The regulations should be consulted for the precise scope of these exemptions.

### 4.5.1 Standards of General Applicability

As discussed more fully in the permits section below, two categories of TSD facilities currently exist --interim status facilities and permitted facilities. Interim status facilities are those that are currently operating without final RCRA permits based upon a legislative decision to allow continued operation of existing facilities until RCRA permits can be issued. These facilities had to meet a three-part statutory test:

(1)     in existence on November 19, 1980, or the effective date of statutory or regulatory changes that render the facility subject to the need for a RCRA permit,

(2)     notify EPA pursuant to RCRA Section 3010(a) of its hazardous waste management activities, and

(3)     file a preliminary permit application.[71]

A facility's interim status ends when the facility receives a final RCRA permit. This in turn is based upon technical standards issued by EPA, or a state with an approved program, which are incorporated into the permit. As discussed in the next section on permits, the 1984 HSWA specify timetables for issuance of final permits to all interim status TSD facilities. All other TSD facilities must obtain an individual RCRA permit before commencing construction.

Separate standards have been issued for interim status facilities[72] and permitted facilities.[73] Both the interim and permanent status regulations for TSD facilities include standards of general applicability (e.g., personnel training, security, financial responsibility), as well as specific design and operating standards for each different type of TSD facility (e.g., storage tanks, landfills, incinerators). The standards of general applicability are discussed first. An operator of a TSD facility is required to obtain an EPA identification number.[74] The operator must also obtain or conduct a detailed chemical and physical analysis of a representative sample of a hazardous waste before the waste is treated, stored, or disposed of at the facility.[75] This is to ensure that the operator has sufficient knowledge of the particular waste being handled to be able to properly manage it. The facility's waste analysis plan

---

[71] Section 3005(e).

[72] 40 C.F.R. Part 265.

[73] 40 C.F.R. Part 264.

[74] 40 C.F.R. § 265.11, § 264.11.

[75] 40 C.F.R. § 265.13, § 264.13.

(WAP) deals with such matters as representation samples, frequency of testing and compliance with land disposal verifications.

Operators must install a security system to prevent unknowing entry, and to minimize the potential for unauthorized entry, of people or livestock to the active portion of the TSD facility.[76] This may be either a 24-hour surveillance system or a barrier around the facility and a means to control entry, and posted "Danger" signs. Operators are required to prepare and implement an inspection plan specifically tailored to the circumstances at their facility.[77] Permitted facilities located in areas prone to seismic activity or floodplains are subject to location standards designed to reduce the additional risks.[78]

TSD facility personnel are required to be properly trained in the areas to which they are assigned, thus reducing the chances that a mistake due to lack of knowledge of the regulatory requirements might lead to an environmental accident. The training may be by formal classroom instruction or on-the-job training. Facility personnel must be given the training within six months of their employment, and must take part in an annual review thereafter. The program must be directed by a person trained in hazardous waste management procedures.[79] Personnel training should focus on emergency preparations and response procedures.

Special precautions must be taken to prevent accidental ignition or reaction of ignitable, reactive or incompatible wastes. While many of the handling requirements are largely common sense practices, specific restrictions on the mixing of such wastes are included in the regulations. Compliance with the regulations concerning safe management of ignitable, reactive or incompatible wastes must be documented.[80]

Regulations for preparedness and prevention are intended to minimize the possibility or consequences of an explosion, spill, or fire at a TSD facility.[81] Facilities must have, unless unnecessary due to the nature of the wastes handled, the following equipment:

(1)    an internal alarm or communications system,

---

[76] 40 C.F.R. § 265.14, § 264.14.

[77] 40 C.F.R. § 265.15, § 264.15.

[78] 40 C.F.R. § 265.18(b), § 264.17(c), § 264.18(a).

[79] 40 C.F.R. § 265.16, § 264.16.

[80] 40 C.F.R. § 265.17, § 264.17.

[81] *See generally* 40 C.F.R. § 265.30-.49, § 264.30-.49.

(2)     a device capable of summoning emergency
        assistance from local agencies,

(3)     fire and spill control equipment, and

(4)     decontamination equipment.


Operators are required to have a contingency plan for the facility designed to minimize hazards to human health and the environment in the event of an actual explosion, fire, or unplanned release of hazardous wastes.[82]     All required equipment must be regularly tested and maintained.   Adequate aisle space to allow unobstructed movement of emergency personnel and equipment must also be maintained.   Arrangements must be made with local police, fire departments, and hospitals to familiarize them with the facility's layout and hazardous wastes.   The TSD facility must also be covered by liability insurance or other financial instruments for claims arising out of injuries to persons or property that result from hazardous waste management operations.[83]

Important recordkeeping requirements apply to TSD facilities.[84]   Upon receipt of a manifested shipment of hazardous waste, the operator of a TSD facility must immediately sign, date, and give to the transporter a copy of the manifest prepared by the generator. Within 30 days, the operator must return a completed copy of the manifest to the generator, and retain a copy of all manifests at the facility for at least three years from the date of delivery. All TSD facilities must maintain a complete operating record until closure.[85] The operating record must include, among other things, a description and the quantity of each hazardous waste received and the method and date of its treatment, storage and disposal, the location of each waste within the facility, results of waste analyses, trial tests and inspections.

There are also basic reports which the TSD facility operator is obligated to file with the EPA regional administrator or an authorized state. These include a biennial report of waste management activities for the previous calendar year,[86] an "unmanifested waste" report which the operator must file within 15 days of accepting any hazardous waste that is not accompanied by a

---

[82] *See generally* 40 C.F.R. § 265.50-.56, § 264.50-.56.

[83] 40 C.F.R. § 265.143(e), § 264.143(f).

[84] *See generally* 40 C.F.R. § 265.71-.72, § 264.71-.72.

[85] 40 C.F.R. § 265.73, §264.73.

[86] 40 C.F.R. § 265.75, § 264.75.

manifest,[87] and certain specialized reports, e.g. an incident report in the event of a hazardous waste release, fire, or explosion.

There are general closure requirements applicable to all TSD facilities, and additional requirements for each specific type of facility.[88] "Closure" is the period after which hazardous wastes are no longer accepted by a TSD facility and during which the operator completes treatment, storage or disposal operations. "Post-closure" is the 30-year period after closure when operators of *land disposal* facilities only must perform certain monitoring and maintenance activities. Generally, the TSD facility must have a detailed written closure plan and schedule, and a cost estimate for closure. The plan must be approved by EPA or the state. It must be amended when any changes in waste management operations affect its terms, and the cost estimate must be adjusted annually for inflation. The closure plan must be followed when the TSD facility ceases operations at the covered unit(s). Post-closure care must continue for 30 years after the date of completing closure, and includes groundwater monitoring and the maintenance of monitoring and waste containment systems.

Financial responsibility requirements have been established to ensure that funds for closure and post-closure care are adequate and available.[89] TSD facilities must use one of the specified financial instruments, such as a corporate guarantee, to provide the closure and post-closure funds.

### 4.5.2 Standards for Specific Types of TSD Facilities

The standards discussed above are generally applicable to all TSD facilities, from the small drum storage area to the most complex commercial landfill or incinerator. EPA has also promulgated specific design, construction, and operating standards for each different type of TSD facility regulated under RCRA. These include: (1) containers, (2) tanks, (3) surface impoundments, (4) waste piles, (5) land treatment units, (6) landfills, (7) incinerators, (8) thermal treatment units, (9) chemical, physical, and biological treatment units, (10) underground injection wells, and (11) "miscellaneous units."[90] In the years ahead, additional classes of facilities may also be addressed by distinct sets of standards such as these.

---

[87] 40 C.F.R. § 265.76, § 264.76.

[88] *See generally* 40 C.F.R. § 265.110-.120, § 264.110-.120.

[89] *See generally* 40 C.F.R. § 265.140-.151, § 264.140-.151.

[90] 40 C.F.R. 265, Subparts J-R, 264, Subparts J-X.

Discussion of the detailed regulatory requirements for all of these types of facilities is beyond the scope of this chapter.[91] The following is an overview of the more significant standards that apply to containers and tanks, surface impoundments and landfills, and incinerators and industrial furnaces used for hazardous waste burning.

A container is any portable device for storing or handling hazardous waste, including drums, pails and boxes. Tank systems are stationary devices constructed primarily of non-earthen materials which provide structural support, and any ancillary piping.[92] The RCRA standards for containers and tanks are basically good housekeeping practices.[93] For example, drums must be maintained in good condition and be handled to avoid ruptures or leaks. Containers must always be kept closed, except when adding waste. Tank systems must be constructed of suitable materials and operated so as to contain the hazardous waste during the tank's intended useful life. Tanks must be operated using controls and practices to prevent overflows and spills. Container storage areas must be inspected at least weekly, and tank systems at least daily, for leaks, corrosion, and other problems. More importantly, almost all container and tank storage areas must be constructed or retrofitted with a secondary containment system to collect spills and accumulated rainfall. Generally, a containment system consists of a diked or bermed concrete (impervious) base with sufficient capacity to collect spillage, and a sump or other method for removing collected liquids. For tanks, the operator can use a lined or diked concrete containment facility, a vault system, or double-walled tanks. Tanks without secondary containment must undergo a structural integrity assessment by a professional engineer.

A surface impoundment is any natural or man-made excavation or diked area designed to hold hazardous wastes containing free liquids, such as pits, ponds, or lagoons. A landfill is a disposal facility where hazardous waste is placed in or on the land.[94] The most important performance standards for these land-based facilities are the "minimum technology requirements" (MTRs) enacted in the 1984 HSWA. All new, replacement, and expansion units at surface impoundments and landfills must have double liners, leachate collection systems, leak detection, and groundwater monitoring systems.[95] In addition,

---

[91] These requirements are discussed in detail in chapter 7 of the *RCRA/Hazardous Waste Handbook* (Government Institutes, 8th ed. 1990).

[92] 40 C.F.R. § 260.10.

[93] *See generally* 40 C.F.R. § 265.170-265.199, § 264.170-264.200.

[94] 40 C.F.R. § 260.10.

[95] *See generally* 40 C.F.R. § 265.220-265.230, § 265.300-265.316, § 264.220-264.231, § 264.300-264.317.

existing impoundments had to be retrofitted to meet MTR by November 1988, or undergo closure. The MTR regulations are highly technical and complex, and should be carefully consulted. The groundwater monitoring requirements, for example, call for an extensive scheme for detecting leachate plumes and instituting correction action when necessary.[96]

Incinerators use controlled flame combustion to destroy hazardous wastes. Recently, industrial furnaces and boilers are increasingly being used to burn hazardous wastes as fuels and for destruction. The RCRA standards for these TSD facilities have become more stringent, in large part as a result of the 1984 HSWA.[97] Basically, an incinerator must conduct a detailed waste analysis and trial burn for waste feeds it intends to handle to establish steady state conditions and demonstrate sufficient destruction of hazardous constituents in the waste. The incinerator must achieve a destruction and removal efficiency (DRE) rate of at least 99.99% for the principal organic hazardous constituents designated by EPA for each waste feed. Emission standards are also applied. The incinerator must have continuous monitoring and automatic controls to shut off the waste feed when operating requirements are exceeded.

EPA has also promulgated standards for industrial furnaces and boilers that burn hazardous wastes.[98] Based on Congress' direction in the 1984 HSWA, EPA now requires all persons who produce, distribute, market or burn hazardous wastes as fuel to notify EPA. The invoice or bill of sale for the fuel must bear the legend: Warning -- This Fuel Contains Hazardous Waste (followed by a list of the hazardous wastes). Such fuels cannot be burned except in qualified utility boilers and industrial furnaces, such as cement kilns. Generators, transporters, marketers and burners of hazardous waste fuels are subject to storage standards for containers and tanks, and to other specific RCRA standards. The owners and operators of boilers and industrial furnaces must comply with detailed technical standards similar to incineration standards, including emission controls, and obtain RCRA permits.

### 4.5.3 The Land Disposal Ban Program

Perhaps the most significant provision of the 1984 HSWA are the prohibitions on the land disposal of hazardous wastes. These prohibitions are intended to minimize the country's reliance on land disposal of untreated hazardous wastes, and to encourage or require advanced treatment and recycling of wastes. Congress began by banning the disposal of bulk or non-containerized liquid hazardous wastes, and hazardous wastes containing free liquids, in landfills. EPA has also promulgated regulations that minimize

---

[96] *See generally* 40 C.F.R. § 265.90-265.94, § 264.90-264.101.

[97] *See generally* 40 C.F.R. § 265.340-265.352, § 264.340-264.351; 40 C.F.R. § 266.30-266.35.

[98] Section 3004 (q)-(s); 40 C.F.R. 266, Subpart D.

disposal of containerized liquid hazardous wastes in landfills. In order to discourage the use of absorbent materials (e.g., "kitty litter") to reduce free liquids in containerized wastes, EPA's regulations prohibit the landfilling of liquids that have been absorbed in materials that biodegrade or that release liquids when depressed during routine landfill operations.

Next, Congress required EPA to determine whether to ban, in whole or in part, the disposal of all RCRA hazardous wastes in land disposal facilities. These include landfills, surface impoundments, waste piles, injection wells, salt domes, and the like. At the same time, EPA must establish treatment standards for each restricted waste based on the Best Demonstrated Available Technologies (BDAT). If the restricted waste is first treated to BDAT levels, the treated waste or residue can then be land disposed. In effect, the so-called "land ban" program is really a waste pretreatment program.

Congress set forth a phased program for EPA to implement the land disposal restrictions. First, EPA has banned the land disposal of dioxin and solvent containing hazardous wastes effective November 1986, unless the wastes are pretreated.[99] EPA set BDAT treatment levels based on incineration, and based on chemical/physical treatment for dilute solvent wastewaters.

Second, EPA has banned the land disposal of certain hazardous wastes (which California had already banned) effective July 1987, unless the wastes are pretreated. The "California list" includes liquid hazardous wastes, including free liquids associated with any sludge, containing (1) free cyanides greater than 100 mg/1; (2) specified concentrations of heavy metals (arsenic, cadmium, chromium, lead, mercury, nickel, selenium and thallium); (3) acids below a pH of 2; (4) more than 50 ppm PCBs; and (5) solid or liquid hazardous wastes containing halogenated organic compounds at concentrations greater than 1000 ppm.[100]

Third, EPA published a ranking of all other hazardous wastes based on their intrinsic hazard and volume, with a schedule for determining whether to ban the land disposal of such wastes one third at a time.[101] EPA restricted the land disposal of the first-third of the highest priority hazardous wastes on the ranking list in August 1988. EPA set BDAT treatment levels for many of the F and K listed wastes in the first-third. EPA extended the ban to the second-third of the ranked hazardous wastes in June 1989. Finally, EPA imposed the land ban restrictions on the third-third wastes, including all characteristic

---

[99] 40 C.F.R. Part 268. The dioxin containing wastes are those chlorinated dioxins, -dibenzofurans, and -phenols listed as F020, F021, F022, F023, F026, F027 and F028. The solvent wastes are those listed as F001, F002, F003, F004 and F005 at 40 C.F.R. 261.31. *See generally* Section 3004(d)-(m).

[100] Disposal by deep well injection is subject to special provisions and a different schedule for implementing the ban.

[101] The ranking and schedule are published at 40 C.F.R. 268.

hazardous wastes, in May 1990. In this rule, EPA determined that it had legal authority to establish treatment standards below the characteristic level for the ignitable, corrosive, reactive and toxic wastes. Newly listed or identified wastes will be brought under the program in the future.

Congress wanted to promote treatment of hazardous wastes in lieu of or prior to land disposal. Therefore at the same time EPA promulgated these land disposal restrictions, it also promulgated regulations specifying the methods or levels of treatment that substantially diminish the toxicity or reduce the likelihood of migration of the waste from land disposal facilities. As indicated, the treatment standards are based on the levels that can be achieved by the best demonstrated technologies.[102] In most instances, the treatment standards are expressed as concentrations of constituents in the treated waste. Any treatment technology that meets the concentration-based standard can then be used. A company that treats its hazardous waste in accordance with these pretreatment standards will not have the treated waste or residue subject to the land disposal ban.

EPA has limited authority to grant up to a two year extension of the ban deadlines for specific hazardous wastes if adequate alternative treatment, recovery, or disposal capacity is not currently available. EPA has granted national capacity variances for a few types of wastes subject to the land disposal restrictions. EPA can also grant a one-year extension, renewable only once, to a company that demonstrates on a case-by-case basis that a binding contractual commitment has been made to construct or otherwise provide alternative treatment, recovery, or disposal capacity, but due to circumstances beyond its control the alternative capacity cannot reasonably be made available by the ban deadline.

Finally, land disposal facilities may submit petitions to EPA which demonstrate, to a reasonable degree of certainty, that there will be no migration of hazardous constituents from the disposal unit or injection well for as long as the waste remains hazardous. EPA has granted a number of these so-called "no migration" petitions for deep injection wells.

### 4.5.4 1984 Amendments Relevant to Used Oil

In the 1984 HSWA, Congress also directed EPA to decide whether to identify used automobile and truck crankcase oil as hazardous waste. After first proposing to list used oil as a hazardous waste in November 1984, EPA decided not to list used oil that is recycled, and to defer a decision on used

---

[102] EPA's decision to use technology-based standards, rather than risk-based standards, was upheld by the courts. *Hazardous Waste Treatment Council v. EPA*, 886 F.2d 355 (1989).

oil that is disposed of.[103] EPA's decision was based on the concern that calling recycled oil a "hazardous waste" would stigmatize it, and thereby discourage recycling. On review of this decision, a court ruled that Congress did not allow EPA to base a listing decision on a concern for "stigma," only on the statutory factors in RCRA Section 3001 relating to the hazardous properties of the waste. If EPA finally decides to list at least certain used oil as hazardous waste, companies that generate, transport, store, treat or dispose of such used oil will likely become subject to the RCRA hazardous waste regulations, as modified by any regulations EPA may promulgate specifically for used oil.

Congress also directed EPA to establish a special regulatory scheme for companies that generate and transport used oil that is listed as a hazardous waste and is recycled.[104] These used oil recycling standards may not include a manifest requirement or any recordkeeping and reporting (except records of agreements for delivery of used oil) for generators that send used oil to qualified recycling facilities. EPA is to promulgate special standards for recycling facilities, which are then deemed to have a RCRA permit if they comply with such standards.

### 4.6  Permits

RCRA requires every owner or operator of a TSD facility to obtain a permit.[105] A TSD facility that was in existence on November 19, 1980, or on the date of any statutory or regulatory change that makes the facility subject to RCRA, need only notify EPA of its hazardous waste management activity and file a Part A application to obtain interim status and continue operations.[106] An interim status TSD facility will be issued a site-specific permit in due course. A new TSD facility, or an existing facility that fails to qualify for interim status, must obtain a full RCRA permit before commencing construction, however.

A Part A application is a short form containing certain basic information about the facility, such as name, location, nature of business, regulated

---

[103] *See* Section 3014(b). EPA proposed the listing of used oil from motor vehicles and industrial manufacturing processes based on a determination that this used oil typically and frequently contains hazardous contaminants at levels of regulatory concern. 50 Fed. Reg. 49258 (November 29, 1985). The final decision was published at 51 Fed. Reg. 41900, (November 19, 1986).

[104] Section 3014(c)-(d).

[105] Section 3005.

[106] Section 3005(e). *See* the interim status standards for TSD facilities in 40 C.F.R. Part 265, discussed above.

activities, and a topographic map of the facility site.[107]  A Part B application requirequires substantially more comprehensive and detailed information that demonstrates compliance with the applicable technical standards for TSD facilities.[108]  The Part B application may consist of several volumes of material or more, including all the written plans and procedures required by the TSD facility regulations.

The final RCRA permit will govern the application of these standards to the particular facility.  New facilities must submit Part A and B applications simultaneously; existing facilities that already filed their Part A applications to gain interim status must submit their Part B applications in accordance with statutory deadlines established by Congress, or earlier if requested by EPA or a state.[109]

Permit applications are requested and final permits are issued by states authorized under RCRA to administer their own programs, and by the EPA regional administrator in other states.  In the 1984 HSWA, Congress has taken steps to accelerate the permitting of interim status TSD facilities.  Congress has provided that interim status for any existing land disposal facility automatically terminated on November 8, 1985, unless the operator submitted a Part B application for a final permit and a certification that the facility was in compliance with groundwater monitoring and financial responsibility requirements.  EPA, or an authorized state, were directed to issue issue final permits for land disposal facilities by November 1988.  Similarly, final permits for interim status incinerators were mandated by November 1989, and for all other interim status TSD facilities by November 1992.  If EPA or the state fails to meet these deadlines, the TSD facility can continue operations provided a timely Part B application was filed.

After a complete RCRA permit application is filed, the rules in 40 C.F.R. Part 124 establish the procedures for processing the application and issuing the permit.  These include preparation of draft permits, public comment and hearing, and the issuance of final decisions.  Permit issuance must be based on a determination that the TSD facility will comply with all requirements of RCRA.

HSWA provides that permits for land disposal facilities, storage facilities, incinerators and other treatment facilities can be issued only for a fixed term not to exceed ten years.[110]  While permits may be reviewed and modified at any time during their terms, permits for land disposal facilities must be reviewed every five years.  At such time, the terms of a permit may be

---

[107] 40 C.F.R. § 270.13.

[108] *See generally* 40 C.F.R. § 270.13-270.21.

[109] Section 3005(c).

[110] Section 3005(c)(3).

modified to ensure that the permit continues to incorporate the standards then applicable to land disposal facilities.

Congress also imposed new and stringent corrective action requirements on TSD facilities. All RCRA permits must now require the owner or operator of a TSD facility to take corrective action for all releases of hazardous waste and constituents from solid waste management units at the facility regardless of when the waste was placed in the unit, or whether the unit is currently active.[111] Note that a solid waste management unit can be any tank, lagoon, waste pile, or other unit where any solid waste was placed, and from which hazardous constituents are being released. RCRA permits must contain schedules of compliance for any required corrective action and assurances of financial responsibility for completing such action. If necessary, the operator of the TSD facility may have to take corrective action beyond the facility boundary. This type of authority for cleanup is analogous to Superfund, and will have a very substantial impact on many TSD facilities that need RCRA permits to continue operations.

### 4.7 State Hazardous Waste Programs

States are authorized by RCRA to develop and carry out their own hazardous waste programs in lieu of the federal program administered by EPA.[112] To obtain EPA approval, the state program must be "equivalent" to the federal program; must be "consistent" with the federal program and other authorized state programs; and must provide adequate enforcement of compliance with the requirements of RCRA Subtitle C.

Ordinarily, states have at least one year to make regulatory changes consistent with the federal program, and two years if statutory changes are necessary. Congress believed the 1984 HSWA provisions were important to implement quickly, however. Therefore, EPA regulations that implement the 1984 HSWA take effect in authorized states on the same day that they take effect under the federal program. EPA is responsible for implementing HSWA provisions until the state takes over authority. The states can then apply for final authorization for the new requirement after promulgating an equivalent regulation.

This dual administration of the RCRA program means that joint permitting is often necessary, with EPA imposing the HSWA provisions and the state taking responsibility for the rest of the permitting.

### 4.8 Inspection and Enforcement

RCRA provides that any officer, employee or representative of EPA or a state with an authorized hazardous waste program may inspect the premises and records of any person who generates, stores, treats, transports, disposes

---

[111] Section 3004(u)-(v).

[112] Section 3006; *see generally* 40 C.F.R. Part 271.

of, or otherwise handles hazardous waste.[113] EPA's inspection authority extends to persons or sites that have handled hazardous wastes in the past but no longer do so. The owner/operator must provide government officials access to records and property relating to the wastes for inspection purposes. Copying and sampling are authorized.

In the 1984 HSWA, Congress has directed EPA and authorized states to improve and regularize RCRA inspections. EPA and the states must now conduct inspections of all privately-operated TSD facilities at least once every two years. Federally-operated TSD facilities must be inspected on an annual basis. Similarly, EPA must conduct annual inspections of TSD facilities which are operated by a state or local government to ensure compliance with the requirements of RCRA.[114]

All organizations should have an established policy and procedure for handling RCRA inspections, including consideration of whether or not a search warrant should be required.

### 4.8.1 Civil and Criminal Actions

EPA can bring several types of enforcement actions under RCRA. These include administrative orders and civil and criminal penalties.[115] Whenever EPA determines that any person is violating Subtitle C of RCRA (including any regulation or permit issued thereunder), it may either issue an order requiring compliance immediately or within a specified time period, or seek injunctive relief against the alleged violator through a civil action filed in a U.S. District Court. Any person who violates any requirement of Subtitle C is liable for a civil penalty of up to $25,000 for each day of violation, regardless of whether the person had been served with a compliance order. A person subject to RCRA cannot rely on EPA to tell him when he is in violation, then take the required corrective action, and thus avoid a penalty. Failure to comply with an administrative order may also result in suspension or revocation of a permit.

RCRA also imposes criminal penalties of up to $50,000, two years imprisonment, or both for persons who "knowingly" commit certain violations. The 1984 HSWA significantly expand the list of these criminal violations.

---

[113] Section 3007. EPA's inspection activities under RCRA Section 3007 are subject to the Fourth Amendment's protection against unreasonable searches or seizures, which the Supreme Court has applied in holding that a warrant is generally required for an inspection by an administrative agency. *Marshall v. Barlow's, Inc.*, 436 U.S. 307 (1978) involving the inspection provisions of the Occupational Safety and Health Act.

[114] Section 3007(c)-(e).

[115] Section 3008.

Fines and imprisonment can be imposed on generators for knowingly allowing hazardous waste to be transported to an unpermitted facility, for knowing violations of federal interim status standards or counterpart state requirements, for knowing material omissions or the knowing failure to file reports required under RCRA by generators, transporters, and TSD facility operators, and knowing transport of hazardous waste without a manifest.

The statute also creates a crime of "knowing endangerment." The purpose of this sanction is to provide more substantial felony penalties for any person who commits the acts described above and "who knows at that time that he thereby places another person in imminent danger of death or serious bodily injury." Upon conviction, an individual faces a fine of up to $250,000 and/or up to fifteen years' imprisonment. An organizational defendant is subject to a maximum fine of $1 million. All of this is part of the message from Congress to EPA and the Justice Department that more rigorous enforcement of the nation's hazardous wastes laws is the federal policy.

### 4.8.2 Citizen Suits

Citizen suits are envisioned by Congress and many others as a key enforcement tool for environmental protection. The RCRA citizen suit provision allows any person to bring a civil action against any alleged violator of the RCRA's requirements, or against the EPA administrator for a failure to perform a nondiscretionary duty. Any person may also petition the EPA administrator for promulgation, amendment, or repeal of any regulation. Courts are authorized to award costs including attorneys' fees to a substantially prevailing party.[116]

The 1984 HSWA substantially enhanced the role accorded to these suits. The citizen suit provision has been expanded to authorize suits in cases where past or present management or disposal of hazardous wastes has contributed to a situation that may present an imminent or substantial endangerment. However, citizen suits are prohibited (1) with respect to the siting and permitting of hazardous waste facilities; (2) where EPA is prosecuting an action under RCRA or Superfund; (3) while EPA or the state is engaged in a removal action under Superfund or has incurred costs to engage in a remedial action; or (4) where the responsible party is conducting a removal or remedial action pursuant to an order obtained from EPA. Affected parties may be allowed to intervene in ongoing suits. Plaintiffs must notify EPA, the state, and affected parties ninety days prior to commencement of a citizen suit.

### 4.8.3 Imminent Hazard Actions

In addition, EPA is authorized to bring suits to restrain an imminent and substantial endangerment to health or the environment.[117] EPA has construed

---

[116] Section 7002.

[117] Section 7003.

"imminent and substantial endangerment" to mean posing a "risk of harm" or "potential harm" but not requiring proof of actual harm.[118] This interpretation was upheld in *United States v. Vertac Chemical Corp.*,[119] the first published decision interpreting RCRA Section 7003. In issuing a preliminary injunction to contain the migration of dioxin from landfills into a creek, the court held that under the endangerment provisions of RCRA harm need only be threatened rather than actually occurring.

In response to conflicting federal court decisions, Congress reworded the "imminent hazard" provision in 1984 to clarify that actions which took place prior to the enactment of RCRA are covered by this provision. Thus a non-negligent generator whose wastes are no longer being deposited at a particular site may still be ordered to abate the hazard resulting from the leaking of previously deposited wastes.

The 1984 HSWA also require EPA to provide for public notice and comment, and the opportunity for a public meeting in the affected area, prior to entering into a settlement or covenant not to sue in an imminent hazard action.

## 5.0  STATE SOLID WASTE PROGRAMS UNDER SUBTITLE D

Regulation of non-hazardous waste is the responsibility of the states pursuant to Subtitle D of RCRA. The federal involvement is limited to establishing minimum criteria that prescribe the best practicable controls and monitoring requirements for solid waste disposal facilities.

In the 1984 HSWA, Congress directed EPA to revise the criteria for facilities receiving hazardous waste from households or from small generators to enable detection of groundwater contamination, provide for corrective action as necessary, and facility siting.[120] Compliance with the minimum requirements determines whether a facility is classified as an "open dump" or not. Disposal of solid waste in "open dumps" (i.e., those facilities not meeting the criteria) is prohibited. Existing dumps were allowed to make modifications that will permit them to meet the requirements, and it is the state's responsibility to ensure that such upgrading occurs or the open dumps are closed.

EPA was not given any enforcement authority, however, for the ban on open dumps. EPA's enforcement authority under RCRA only covers hazardous wastes. EPA cannot take action against a person disposing of non-hazardous

---

[118] Memorandum, January 25, 1980, from Douglas MacMillan, Acting Director of EPA's Hazardous Waste Enforcement Task Force, to Regional Enforcement Division Directors and others.

[119] 489 F. Supp. 870 (E.D. Ark. 1980).

[120] Section 4010.

wastes in an open dump or against the state for failing to close open dumps, other than terminating certain grant funds available to the state under RCRA. Recognizing this problem, Congress has asked EPA to make recommendations on the need for additional enforcement authorities.[121]

RCRA also envisions that the state, with the help of federal grant funds, will develop regional solid waste management plans. The program is patterned on Section 208 of the Clean Water Act and relies upon a comprehensive regional planning approach to solving solid waste problems. The state is responsible for identifying appropriate management areas, developing regional plans through the use of local and regional authorities, compiling inventories and closing or upgrading existing open dumps, and generally assessing the need for additional solid waste disposal capacity in the area.

Of particular significance is a requirement that states not have any bans on the importation of waste for storage, treatment or disposal, or have requirements that are substantially dissimilar from other disposal practices that would discourage the free movement of wastes across state lines. Although enforcement of this requirement may be difficult, in light of the limited enforcement authority available to EPA, it does evidence a congressional policy for a national approach to solid waste disposal.

## 6.0   OTHER FEDERAL RESPONSIBILITIES

Subtitle E of RCRA gives the Department of Commerce (DOC) responsibility for developing standards for substituting secondary materials for virgin materials, developing markets for recovered materials, and for the promotion of resource recovery technology generally.

The authorities given to DOC are similar to those assigned to EPA in other sections of the act, specifically Subtitle H on Research, Development, Demonstrations and Information. Nevertheless, DOC has not received sufficient funding to support a major role.

Subtitle F of RCRA requires that all federal agencies and instrumentalities comply with all federal, state, interstate, and local requirements stemming from RCRA, unless exempted by the president. It also requires the federal government to institute a procurement policy that encourages the purchase of recoverable materials which, because of their performance, can be substituted for virgin material at a reasonable price.

## 7.0   RESEARCH, DEVELOPMENT, DEMONSTRATION, AND INFORMATION

In cooperation with federal, state, and interstate authorities, private agencies and institutions and individuals, EPA is directed to conduct, encourage

---

121 *Id.*

and promote the coordination of research, investigations, experiments, training, demonstrations, surveys, public education programs and studies. These R & D efforts can relate to the protection of health; planning, financing and operation of waste management systems including resource recovery; improvements in methodology of waste disposal and resource recovery; reduction of the amount of waste generated, and methods for remedying damages by earlier or existing landfills; and methods for rendering landfills safe for purposes of construction and other uses.

EPA was also directed to carry out a number of special studies including the following subjects: small-scale and low technology approaches to resource recovery; front-end separation for materials recovery; mining waste; sludge; and airport landfills.

## 8.0 MEDICAL WASTE

Congress has added a new Subtitle J to RCRA with the enactment of the Medical Waste Tracking Act of 1988. In response to the problem of hypodermic needles and other medical wastes washing up on Atlantic Coast beaches, Congress directed EPA to set up a demonstration program for tracking the shipment and disposal of medical wastes in a selected number of states. The states directed to participate are New York, New Jersey, Connecticut, the states contiguous to the Great Lakes, and any state that petitions EPA to be included in the demonstration program.

EPA promulgated regulations listing the types of medical wastes to be tracked under the program. These wastes include:

1. Cultures and stocks of infectious agents and associated biologicals;

2. Pathological wastes, including tissues, organs, and body parts;

3. Waste human blood and blood products;

4. Hypodermic needles, syringes, scapel blades, and broken glassware;

5. Contaminated animal carcasses and parts;

6. Wastes from surgery or autopsy that were in contact with infectious agents;

7. Laboratory wastes that were in contact with infectious agents;

8. Dialysis wastes;

9. Discarded medical equipment that was in contact with infectious agents;

10.     Biological wastes; and

11.     Such other medical waste material as EPA finds poses a threat to human health or the environment.

At the same time, EPA promulgated regulations establishing a demonstration program for the tracking of the listed medical waste. The program provides for tracking the transportation of the waste from the generator to the disposal facility. The generator is required to segregate wastes where practicable, and to use appropriate labels and containers. Medical waste that is incinerated need not be tracked after incineration, but the generator who conducts on-site incineration must report the types and volumes of wastes incinerated during the demonstration program.

EPA and states are authorized to conduct inspections and take enforcement actions under the program. Congress has also made clear that all federal facilities in a demonstration state must comply with all federal, state, interstate and local requirements, including permitting and reporting, that pertain to medical wastes.

At the conclusion of the program, EPA must submit a report to Congress summarizing the results and making recommendations for adequate control of medical waste shipments and disposal. Interim reports are also required.


## 9.0 CONCLUSION

As the foregoing discussion amply demonstrates, the RCRA program is complex. The 1984 HSWA has added many new requirements which represent a challenge to the will and imagination of the regulated community. Industry has been challenged to find new ways to minimize, treat and dispose of hazardous waste. This will include the use of treatment and destruction technologies such as microbiological degradation, solvent extraction, freeze crystalization, wet air oxidation, pyrolysis, and other advanced and emerging technologies. Never has the incentive been greater to reuse or reclaim wastes, or to search out new products, processes, and raw materials that do not result in the generation of hazardous waste in the first place.

Chapter 12

UNDERGROUND STORAGE TANKS

Mary Elizabeth Bosco and Russell V. Randle
Patton Boggs & Blow
Washington, D.C.

## 1.0 INTRODUCTION

Subtitle I of the Resource Conservation and Recovery Act (RCRA), 42 U.S.C. §§ 6991 *et seq.*, requires the Environmental Protection Agency (EPA) to develop a comprehensive regulatory program for "underground storage tank" (UST) systems. EPA has promulgated regulations imposing technical standards for tank performance and management, including closure and site cleanup, and establishing financial responsibility standards for tank owners.[1]

This chapter explains the statutory and regulatory requirements governing underground storage tanks, enforcement of those requirements, and the relationship of the UST regulations to other environmental laws.

## 2.0 OVERVIEW

The Hazardous and Solid Waste Amendments of 1984 extended and strengthened RCRA's provisions concerning the regulation of underground storage tanks. The amendments added Subtitle I, which provides for the development and implementation by EPA of a regulatory program for underground storage tanks and for identifying and remedying releases from these systems.

Subtitle I contains several major provisions for the regulation of UST systems. Section 9002 requires the system owners to notify their designated state agencies of the existence of their UST systems and any intent to install a new underground tank. Section 9003 requires EPA to promulgate regulations applicable to all owners and operators of UST systems, which at a minimum, are to include the following requirements:

---

[1] 53 Fed. Reg. 37082-37213 (Sept. 13, 1988), promulgated at 40 C.F.R. §§ 280 *et seq.* The financial responsibility regulations were published at 53 Fed. Reg. 43320-43370 (Oct. 26, 1988).

(1)    standards for design, construction and installation of new tanks;

(2)    standards for maintenance of a leak detection system and associated record-keeping;

(3)    standards for the reporting of releases from regulated tanks;

(4)    corrective action for confirmed releases;

(5)    and closure of existing tanks.

Additionally, Section 9003(h), as amended by the 1986 Superfund Amendments and Reauthorization Act (SARA), gives EPA (and states pursuant to cooperative agreements with EPA) the authority to clean up petroleum releases from UST systems or to require the owner or operator to do so. Finally, Section 9006 of Subtitle I authorizes EPA to issue administrative orders or to initiate civil actions in federal district court to enforce compliance with the Subtitle I regulations.

## 3.0   SUMMARY OF THE REGULATIONS

In response to Subtitle I's direction to regulate underground tanks, EPA adopted standards for new tanks and for the upgrading of existing tanks, and imposed certain operation and maintenance requirements on tanks currently in use. The final UST regulations further establish a schedule for use of release detection systems on all new and existing tanks and set forth specific procedures for reporting and investigating suspected releases and for proper cleanup. Finally, both temporary and final closure of UST systems are governed by EPA's regulations. Failure to comply with these regulations subjects the responsible party to civil penalties of up to $10,000 per tank for each day of violation.[2]

EPA estimates that there are over 700,000 UST facilities with about two million tanks and that the annual costs of compliance with the final rules over the ten-year upgrade period will be $3.6 billion. Because of the large number of systems involved and the high compliance costs, EPA must rely on the states to a certain extent to enforce the UST regulations. To receive EPA approval, a state UST program must regulate the same aspects of tank performance and operation as the federal regulations and must be no less stringent than the corresponding federal requirements.[3]

Because of the variety and number of tank systems subject to regulation, EPA is imposing general performance standards and relying on industry performance codes for more detailed guidelines. Thus, the regulations authorize installation of four general tank types, but leave to the implementing agency's discretion the approval of alternative tank designs.

---

[2] RCRA § 9006(d), 42 U.S.C. § 6991e(d).

[3] RCRA § 9004, 42 U.S.C. § 6991c. As of November 1990, EPA had approved two state UST programs.

New tanks must be equipped with spill and overfill protection devices and their proper installation must be certified to the implementing agency. The regulations require all systems to be upgraded within 10 years of their effective date (December 1998) or closed.

The general operating requirements imposed on existing tanks involve monitoring substance transfers to prevent overfills and spills, regular maintenance of corrosion prevention devices, and procedures for repair and replacement.

All existing tanks must have a functioning release detection system within the schedule established by EPA. EPA has established general performance parameters for release detection devices, but with certain exceptions, has left to the discretion of the tank owner/operator the choice of the specific type of release detection system to be used with the tank. The agency must be notified within 24 hours of any suspected release. A step-by-step procedure for investigation and confirmation of the release, as well as for conducting and documenting corrective action, is detailed in the final regulations.

Finally, even tanks which are closed temporarily are subject to the regulations' requirements. Tanks permanently taken out of service must be emptied, cleaned, and either removed from the ground or filled with an inert solid material. A more detailed summary of the final UST regulations follows and addresses these general topics:

A. Systems and substances covered by the UST regulations;
B. New tank standards;
C. Upgrading existing systems;
D. General operating requirements;
E. Release detection standards;
F. Release investigation;
G. Corrective action;
H. Tank closure;
I.  Financial Responsibility; and
J.  Enforcement.

This chapter concludes with a discussion of the relationship of the UST regulations to other environmental laws.

## 4.0 EPA's UST REGULATIONS

### 4.1. Systems and Substances Covered

#### 4.1.1. Substances Subject to the Regulations
RCRA defines an underground storage tank as:

> Any one or combination of tanks (including underground pipes connected thereto) which is used to contain an accumulation of regulated substances, and the volume of which (including the volume of the underground pipes connected thereto) is 10 percent or more beneath the surface of the ground.[4]

The final UST regulations adopt this definition, and apply generally to any underground storage tank containing a "regulated substance."[5] A "regulated substance" is (i) any substance defined in Section 101(14) of the Comprehensive Environmental Response, Compensation and Liability Act (CERCLA), except for substances regulated under RCRA Subtitle C -- hazardous wastes -- and (ii) petroleum, including crude oil or any fraction thereof that is liquid at standard conditions of temperature and pressure (60 degrees Fahrenheit and 14.7 pounds per square inch absolute).[6] The UST regulations also are applicable to underground tanks storing used oil.

#### 4.1.2. Systems Subject. to the Regulations
RCRA expressly excludes the following systems from the definition of underground storage tank:

(a) Farm or residential tanks of 1,100 gallons or less capacity used to store motor fuel for noncommercial purposes;

(b) tanks storing heating oil for use on the premises where stored;[7]

(c) septic tanks;

(d) pipeline facilities regulated under the National Gas Pipeline Safety Act of 1968, the Hazardous Liquid Pipeline Safety Act of 1979, or comparable state laws;

---

[4] RCRA § 9001(l), 42 U.S.C. § 6991(l).

[5] 40 C.F.R. § 280.12.

[6] 40 C.F.R. § 280.12.

[7] In a July 1990 report to Congress, EPA recommended continued exclusion from regulation for these first two tank categories. It should be noted, however, that at least 20 states regulate heating oil tanks to some extent, and approximately 10 states regulate noncommercial fuel tanks.

(e) surface impoundments, pits, ponds or lagoons;

(f) storm water or wastewater collection systems;

(g) liquid traps or associated gathering lines directly related to oil or gas production and gathering operations; and

(h) storage tanks situated in underground areas such as basements, mine shafts or tunnels, if situated upon or above the floor surface.[8]

EPA's final UST regulations add six more tank types to the list of tanks excluded from Subtitle I regulation. These are:

(a) UST systems containing hazardous wastes identified under RCRA Subtitle C or a mixture of such hazardous wastes and other regulated substances;

(b) wastewater treatment tanks that are part of a wastewater treatment facility regulated under the Clean Water Act;

(c) equipment or machinery containing regulated substances for operational purposes such as hydraulic lift tanks and electrical equipment tanks (*i.e.*, hydraulic elevators and automotive lifts);

(d) UST systems with capacities of 110 gallons or less;

(e) UST systems containing a *de minimis* concentration of regulated substances;[9] and

(f) emergency spill and overflow containment UST systems emptied "expeditiously" after use.[10]

Finally, EPA has determined to defer regulation of five other categories of UST systems: wastewater treatment tank systems not covered by the Clean Water Act; systems containing radioactive material subject to the Atomic Energy Act of 1954; systems which are part of emergency generator systems at nuclear power generation facilities regulated by the Nuclear Regulatory Commission; airport hydrant fuel distribution systems; and UST systems with field-constructed tanks.[11] While currently exempt from the technical tank standards, corrective action, and financial responsibility regulations, these

---

[8] RCRA §§ 9001(1)(A) - (I), 42 U.S.C. §§ 6991(1)(A)-(I).

[9] The regulations do not define "*de minimis* concentrations." The preamble to the final regulations states that the implementing agencies will determine on a "case-by-case" basis if tanks that hold very low concentrations of regulated substances are excluded under the *de minimis* rationale. 53 Fed. Reg. 37,106 (Sept. 23, 1988).

[10] 40 C.F.R. § 280.10(b).

[11] 40 C.F.R. § 280.10(c).

tanks are subject to the "interim prohibition," which establishes general standards for the installation of new tanks.

The statutory interim prohibition generally proscribes installation of any new tank system unless the system being installed (i) will prevent releases due to corrosion or structural failure for the life of the UST system; (ii) is cathodically protected against corrosion, constructed of noncorrodible material, steel clad with noncorrodible material, or designed so as to prevent the release or threatened release of any stored substance; and (iii) is constructed or lined with material that is compatible with the stored substance.[12]

## 4.2 New Tank Standards

### 4.2.1. Notification Requirements

Owners bringing new tanks into use must provide notice to the designated state or local agency at least 30 days prior to bringing the tank into use.[13] As part of the notification process, owners of new UST systems must certify that installation of the new tank was performed in accordance with the regulations. The certification also must include assurances that new steel tanks comply with the cathodic protection requirements, that all tanks meet the release detection requirements, and that the owner meets the financial responsibility requirements.[14] Further, the person installing the tank must certify on the notification form that the installation was performed

---

[12] 40 C.F.R. § 280.11(a). The regulations do, however, authorize installation of steel UST systems without corrosion protection at those sites determined by a "corrosion expert" not to be corrosive enough to cause the tank to have a release due to corrosion during its operating life. 40 C.F.R. § 280.11(b). A corrosion expert must be certified by the National Association of Corrosion Engineers or must be a registered professional engineer who has certification or licensing that includes education and experience in corrosion control of buried or submerged metal piping systems and metal tanks. 40 C.F.R. § 280.12.

[13] 40 C.F.R. § 280.22(a). Owners and operators of USTs that were in the ground on or after May 8, 1986 (unless taken out of operation before January 1, 1974) were required to give notice of the tank's operation by May 8, 1986. RCRA § 9002(a), 42 U.S.C. § 6991a(a).

[14] 40 C.F.R. § 280.22(e). Failure to notify or the submission of false information as part of the notification process subjects the owner to a civil penalty of up to $10,000 for each tank for which notification was not given or for which false information was submitted. RCRA § 9005, 42 U.S.C. § 6991e(d).

pursuant to the regulations.[15]

Finally, sellers of tanks must notify their purchasers of the owner notification obligations.[16] This obligation applies to a person selling property on which an underground tank is located.

### 4.2.2. New Tank Performance Standards

Section 9003(c) of RCRA requires EPA to establish technical tank performance standards. Accordingly, EPA's UST regulations set general performance standards for new tanks and rely heavily for detailed technical standards on industry performance codes established by nationally recognized associations or independent testing laboratories.

Each new tank generally "must be properly designed and constructed, and any portion underground that routinely contains product must be protected from corrosion, in accordance with a code of practice developed by nationally recognized association or independent testing laboratory."[17] The various industry codes which may be followed in order to comply with the individual technical performance requirements are noted in the regulations.

EPA specifically has authorized installation of four general types of new tanks: (1) tanks constructed of fiberglass-reinforced plastic;[18] (2) tanks constructed of steel and cathodically protected;[19] (3) tanks constructed of steel-fiberglass-reinforced-plastic composite;[20] and (4) metal tanks installed at sites determined by a corrosion expert not to be corrosive enough to cause

---

[15] 40 C.F.R. § 280.22(f).

[16] 40 C.F.R. § 280.22(g).

[17] 40 C.F.R. § 280.20(a).

[18] The industry codes cited with approval in the regulations for fiberglass-reinforced plastic tanks are: Underwriters Laboratories Standard 1316; Underwriters Laboratories of Canada CAN4-S615-M83; or American Society of Testing and Materials Standard D4021-86, "Standard Specification for Glass-Fiber-Reinforced Polyester Underground Petroleum Storage Tanks."

[19] The following standards and codes may be used to comply with this requirement: Steel Tank Institute, "Specification for STI-13 System of External Corrosion Protection for Underground Steel Storage Tanks;" Underwriters Laboratories of Canada Nos. CAN4-S603-M85, CAN4-G03.1-M85, CAN4-S631-M84; Underwriters Laboratories Standard 58; and National Association of Corrosion Engineers Standard RP-02-85.

[20] The listed codes applicable to this requirement are: Underwriters Laboratories Standard 1746; and the Association for Composite Tanks ACT-100.

the tank to have a release due to corrosion during its operating life.[21] Cathodic protection must be achieved in the following manner:

(i)    the tank is coated with a suitable dielectric material;

(ii)   field-installed cathodic protection systems are designed by corrosion experts;

(iii)  impressed current systems allow determination of current operating status; and

(iv)  cathodic protection systems are operated and maintained in accordance with the regulations.[22]

Additionally, other tank designs are permitted in cases where the implementing agency determines that the alternate design, construction and corrosion protection are no less protective of human health and the environment than the tank types expressly authorized by the regulations.[23]

Similarly, piping that routinely contains regulated substances and is in contact with the ground must be designed, constructed and protected from corrosion in accordance with industry codes.[24] Authorized piping systems are those constructed of fiberglass-reinforced plastic; cathodically-protected steel; and metal if installed in sites presenting no threat of corrosion. Alternate piping systems may also be used if approved by the agency.[25]

Finally, new tanks are to be equipped with spill and overfill prevention equipment. Unless an alternate system is approved by the agency, or the UST system is filled by transfers of no more than 25 gallons at a time, all new systems must have:

(a) spill prevention equipment that will prevent product release to the environment when the hose is detached from the fill pipe; and

(b) overfill protection equipment that will either shut off the flow to the tank at 95 percent capacity or alert the operator through an alarm

---

[21] 40 C.F.R. § 280.20(a)(1)-(4).

[22] 40 C.F.R. § 280.20(a)(2).

[23] 40 C.F.R. § 280.20(a)(5). The regulations' preamble lists as an example steel tanks surrounded by high-density polyethylene jackets, which have received agency approval at the state and local level. 53 Fed. Reg. 37,126-127 (Sept. 23, 1988).

[24] 40 C.F.R. § 280.20(b).

[25] 40 C.F.R. § 280.20(b)(4).

or flow shut-down when the tank reaches 90 percent capacity.[26]

### 4.2.3. Installation of New Tanks

EPA's proposed regulations had set forth nine specific performance criteria for new tank installation, including requirements for backfill material and piping layout design.[27] The final regulations do away with this approach and instead require that the installation be accomplished in accordance with acode of practice developed by a nationally recognized association or testing laboratory[28] and in accordance with the manufacturer's instructions. The installation also must be certified by a properly qualified individual.[29]

### 4.3  Upgrading Existing UST Systems

Within 10 years of the effective date of the regulations (December 22, 1988), all existing systems must meet either the new tank performance standards or specific upgrade requirements, or they must be closed down.[30]

A steel tank must be upgraded by internal lining, cathodic protection, or internal lining combined with cathodic protection.[31] This requirement includes the tank's piping. All tanks also must be upgraded to meet the spill and overfill prevention requirements imposed on new tanks within the 10-year period.[32]

Finally, all tanks must be equipped with release detection systems in accordance with a schedule established by the final regulations.

---

[26] 40 C.F.R. § 280.20(c).

[27] 52 Fed. Reg. 12,699 (April 17, 1987).

[28] The codes listed in the regulations are: American Petroleum Institute Publication 1615, "Installation of Underground Petroleum Storage Systems;" Petroleum Equipment Institute Publication RP100, "Recommended Practices for Installation of Underground Liquid Storage Systems;" and American National Standards Institute Standard B31.3, "Petroleum Refinery Piping," and Standard B31.4, "Liquid Petroleum Transportation Piping System."

[29] 40 C.F.R. §§ 280.20(d) and (e).

[30] 40 C.F.R. § 280.21(a).

[31] 40 C.F.R. § 280.21(c).

[32] 40 C.F.R. § 280.21(d).

## 4.4   General Operating Requirements For All UST Systems

The final regulations impose general operation and maintenance requirements on existing systems in four main areas: spill and overfill control, corrosion protection, tank repair, and record-keeping.

### 4.4.1.  Spill and Overfill Control

Pending compliance with the upgrade requirements, all tank owners and operators "must ensure that releases due to spilling or overfilling do not occur."[33]  To meet this requirement, the owner/operator must ensure prior to transfer that the available tank volume exceeds the volume of product to be transferred and must "constantly" monitor the transfer operation.[34] Monitoring may be accomplished through electronic or mechanical means and does not require the physical presence of an attendant.[35]

### 4.4.2  Operation, Maintenance and Testing of Existing
   Corrosion Protection

In general, all steel UST systems with corrosion protection must be operated and maintained continuously to provide corrosion protection to the metal components of the tank and piping that routinely contain regulated substances and are in contact with the ground.[36]  Cathodic protection systems must be tested by a qualified cathodic protection inspector within six months of installation and at least every three years thereafter.[37]  UST systems with impressed current cathodic protection systems must also be inspected every 60

---

[33]  40 C.F.R. § 280.30(a).

[34]  40 C.F.R. § 280.30.

[35]  In the preamble to the final rule, EPA stated that although the agency "recognizes" that tank owners and operators may attempt through contract to transfer responsibility for proper delivery techniques to the transport carrier, the final rule makes the owner and operator responsible for any damage caused by spills.  53 Fed. Reg. 37,135 (Sept. 23, 1988).

[36]  40 C.F.R. § 280.31.

[37]  40 C.F.R. § 280.31(b).

days to ensure proper operation of the equipment. Records of the inspections must be maintained.[38]

### 4.2.3. Substance Compatibility

As a result of EPA's determination that existing industry practices generally are adequate to ensure compatibility of the tank and piping with the stored material, the final regulations contain only the general requirement that an UST system be made or lined with a material compatible with the substance stored.[39]

### 4.4.4 Repairs to Existing Systems

While the proposed regulations had permitted only one repair during the operational life of the tank, EPA's final rule does not limit the number of authorized repairs. The general requirements imposed upon repairs of existing tanks are that the repairs must prevent releases due to structural failure or corrosion for the system's operating life and must be conducted in accordance with nationally recognized industry codes.[40] More specifically, if repairs are made to fiberglass-reinforced tanks, they must be made by the manufacturer's authorized representative.[41] Where pipes are found to be leaking, they *must* be replaced if metal, but may be repaired if fiberglass.[42] Repaired tanks and piping must be tested or monitored within 30 days of completion of the repair. Again, records of the repair must be maintained for the life of the system.[43]

### 4.4.5. Record-keeping Requirements

Tank owners and operators must maintain a specific set of records. These records either must be maintained on site or at a readily available alternate site and must be provided to the implementing agency for inspection upon the agency's request.[44] Although specific record-keeping requirements

---

[38] 40 C.F.R. §§ 280.31(c) and 280.31(d).

[39] 52 Fed. Reg. 12,709 (April 17, 1987); 40 C.F.R. § 280.32.

[40] 40 C.F.R. 280.33(a).

[41] 40 C.F.R. 280.33(b).

[42] 40 C.F.R. § 280.33(b).

[43] 40 C.F.R. §§ 280.33(d) and 280.33(f).

[44] 40 C.F.R. § 280.34(c).

are discussed within the sections of this chapter dealing with the corresponding technical requirement, a checklist of the required records is provided below:

1. A corrosion expert's analysis of the site corrosion potential if corrosion protection equipment is not used;

2. Documents evidencing operation of any corrosion protection equipment, including testing or inspection results;

3. Documentation of all system repairs;

4. Documents relating to release detection systems, including written performance claims, monitoring results, and maintenance or repair records; and

5. Permanent closure records.[45]

The statute provides limited protection for records considered by the owner/operator to contain confidential business information. To maintain the confidentiality of information subject to the Trade Secrets Act, 18 U.S.C. § 1905,[46] the person submitting the information to the agency must mark the information as proprietary and separate it from the other non-confidential material being submitted.[47] Otherwise the information might be released pursuant to the Freedom of Information Act[48] without notifying the submitter of the information request and allowing a chance to object to the release.[49]

---

[45] 40 C.F.R. § 280.34(b).

[46] The Trade Secrets Act imposes criminal sanctions on any Government employee who improperly discloses documents relating to "trade secrets, processes, operations, style of work or apparatus, or to the identity, confidential statistical data, amount or source of any income, profits, losses, or expenditures" of any person or business entity. *Id.*

[47] RCRA § 9001(b), 42 U.S.C. § 6991(b).

[48] 5 U.S.C. § 552.

[49] The objection to such release would normally be based on exemption (b)(4) of the Freedom of Information Act. 5 U.S.C. § 552(b)(4). *See* Liebman & Stone, *Testimonial Privileges,* pp. 539-49 §§ 9.24-26 (Shepards 1983).

**4.5 Release Detection**

The requirement for release detection for existing tanks is based on the age of the tank. The UST regulations set forth general release detection standards, as well as specific requirements based upon whether the system contains petroleum or hazardous substances.[50] When monthly testing is performed, a single release detection method may be used. When less frequent testing is performed, it must be backed up with monthly inventory control.

**4.5.1. Schedule for Compliance with Release Detection Requirements**

The schedule for phase-in of release detection is as follows:

| | | |
|---|---|---|
| 1. | Tanks installed before 1965 (or date unknown) | Release detection for tanks and suction piping by 1989; release detection for all pressurized piping by 1990 |
| 2. | 1965 - 1969 | 1990 |
| 3. | 1970 - 1974 | Release detection for pressurized piping by 1990; for tanks and suction piping by 1991 |
| 4. | 1975 - 1979 | Release detection for pressurized piping by 1990; for tanks and suction piping by 1992 |

---

[50] EPA intends to enforce the release detection requirements in the following manner: registered tank owner/operators will receive a letter from EPA requesting written evidence that the required release detection equipment has been installed and that any required tests have been performed; those owner/operators failing to respond to EPA's initial letter will receive a second letter from the agency; those owner/operators not responding to the second letter will be targeted for enforcement.

5.  1980 - 1988                    Release detection for pressurized piping by 1990; for tanks and suction piping by 1993.[51]

The general release detection requirements for all UST systems are that: (1) the system must be able to detect a release from any portion of the tank and the connected underground piping; (2) the system must be installed, operated and maintained in accordance with the manufacturer's instructions; and (3) the system must meet the performance requirements set forth in the regulations for petroleum-containing tanks and hazardous substance-containing tanks.[52]

### 4.5.2.  Release Detection for Petroleum UST Systems

With three exceptions, tanks containing petroleum must be monitored at least every 30 days using one of the following methods: (1) automatic tank gauging; (2) vapor monitoring; (3) groundwater monitoring; (4) interstitial monitoring; or (5) any other method that is capable of detecting a two-tenths of a gallon per hour leak rate or a release of 150 gallons within a month, with a probability of detection of ninety-five percent and a probability of false alarm of 5 percent or less.[53]

The first exception to this general rule is that tanks with capacities of 550 gallons or less may use weekly tank gauging.[54] Additionally, systems that now meet the new tank performance standards and use a monthly inventory control system or manual tank gauging may use tank tightness testing at least every 5 years for the 10-year upgrade period or 10 years after installation or upgrade, whichever is later.[55] Tank systems that do not meet the new tank performance standards may use a combination of monthly inventory controls

---

[51] The compliance date for each group of UST systems is December 22nd of the listed calendar year. Existing systems that cannot meet the dates for release detection must be closed.

[52] 40 C.F.R. § 280.40(a).

[53] 40 C.F.R. § 280.41(a). However, EPA has extended the compliance date for pressurized piping to meet the probability detection percentages to September 22, 1991. 56 Fed. Reg. 24 (Jan. 2, 1991).

[54] 40 C.F.R. § 280.41(a)(3).

[55] 40 C.F.R. § 280.41(a)(1).

and annual tank tightness testing for the upgrade period, at which time the tank must meet the new performance standards or be closed.[56]

Piping for petroleum UST systems also must be equipped with release detection devices. The regulations divide the type of devices according to whether pressurized or suction piping is used. Underground piping that conveys regulated substances under pressure must be equipped with an automatic line leak detector and have an annual line tightness test or monthly monitoring.[57] Generally, suction piping must have either a line tightness test conducted at least every 3 years, or use a monthly monitoring method.[58]

### 4.5.3. Requirements for Hazardous Substance UST Systems

All existing UST systems that contain hazardous substances must meet the requirements for petroleum UST systems set forth above. Additionally, by ten years after the effective date of the final regulations, all existing hazardous substance systems must meet specific requirements for secondary containment systems, double-walled tanks, and external liners.[59]

Briefly, secondary containment systems must be designed, constructed and installed in order to contain regulated substances released from the tank system until they are detected and removed and to prevent the release of regulated substances to the environment at any time during the operational life of the system. Secondary containment systems must be checked for evidence of release at least every 30 days.[60]

Double-walled tanks must be designed, constructed, and installed to contain a release from any portion of the inner tank within the outer wall,

---

[56] 40 C.F.R. § 280.41(a)(2).

[57] 40 C.F.R. § 280.41(b)(1).

[58] 40 C.F.R. § 280.41(b)(2). Suction piping, however, is exempt from release detection requirements if it is designed and constructed to meet the following standards: (i) the below-grade piping operates at less than atmospheric pressure; (ii) the below-grade piping is sloped so that the contents of the pipe will drain back into the storage area if the suction is released; (iii) only one check valve is included in each suction line; (iv) the check valve is located directly below and as close as practical to the suction pump; and (v) a method is provided that allows compliance with these requirements to be readily determined.

[59] 40 C.F.R. § 280.42(a).

[60] 40 C.F.R. § 280.42(b)(1).

and to detect the failure of the inner wall.[61]

External liners must be designed, constructed, and installed to contain 100 percent of the capacity of the largest tank within its boundary, to prevent interference by groundwater or precipitation with the ability of the tank to contain or detect a release of regulated substances, and to surround the tank completely.[62]

Finally, underground piping that is part of a hazardous substance UST system must be equipped with secondary containment that satisfies the requirements outlined above, and any piping that conveys regulated substances under pressure must be equipped with an automatic line leak detector.[63]

### 4.5.4. Methods of Release Detection

While the regulations impose general requirements for release detection systems, they also set forth standards for the specific types of release detection methods chosen by the tank owner and operator to comply with the general outlines of the regulations. These release detection methods are inventory control, manual tank gauging, tank tightness testing, automatic tank gauging, groundwater monitoring, and interstitial monitoring.

When *inventory control* is the method of release detection employed, it must be conducted on a monthly basis so as to be able to detect a release of at least 1 percent of the flow-through plus 130 gallons in accordance with the following: inventory volume measurements for regulated substance inputs, withdrawals, and the amount still remaining in the tank must be recorded each operating day; the measuring equipment must be capable of measuring the level of product over the full range of the tank's height to the nearest one-eighth of an inch; substance inputs must be reconciled with delivery receipts before and after each delivery; deliveries must be made through a drop tube that extends to within one foot of the tank bottom; product dispensing must be metered and recorded within the local standards for meter calibration or an accuracy of six cubic inches for every five gallons of product withdrawn; and the measurement of any water level in the bottom of the tank must be made to the nearest one-eighth of an inch at least once a month.[64]

*Manual tank gauging* may only be used as the sole method of release detection for tanks holding 550 gallons of product or less.[65] If used, it must

---

[61] 40 C.F.R. § 280.42(b)(2).

[62] 40 C.F.R. § 280.42(b)(3).

[63] 40 C.F.R. § 280.42(d).

[64] 40 C.F.R. § 280.43(a).

[65] 40 C.F.R. § 280.43(b)(5).

meet the following requirements: the tank liquid level measurements must be taken at the beginning and ending of a period of at least 36 hours during which no liquid is added or removed from the tank; level measurements must be based on an average of two consecutive stick readings at both the beginning and ending of the period; the equipment used must be capable of measuring the level of product over the full range of the tank's height to the nearest one-eighth of an inch; and variations between the beginning and ending measurements which exceed the standards set forth in the regulations must be treated as leaks.[66]

Where *tank tightness testing* is used, it must be capable of detection of a one-tenth of a gallon per hour leak rate from any portion of the tank that routinely contains product, while accounting for the effects of thermal expansion or contraction of the product, vapor pockets, tank deformation, evaporation or condensation, and the location of the water table.[67]

*Automatic tank gauging* may be used if the automatic product level monitor test can detect a two-tenth of a gallon per hour leak rate from any portion of the tank that routinely contains product and if it is used in conjunction with inventory control.[68]

*Vapor monitoring* may only be used if: the materials used as backfill at the site are sufficiently porous to allow diffusion of vapors from releases into the excavation area; the stored regulated substance is sufficiently volatile to result in a vapor level that is readily detectable by the monitoring device; the measurement of vapors by the monitoring device is not rendered inoperative by groundwater, rainfall or soil moisture so that a release could go undetected for more than 30 days; the level of background contamination in the excavation area will not interfere with the release detection; the vapor monitors are designed and operated to allow the threshold level to be preset specifically for the type of regulated substance stored in the tank system; the excavation area is specifically assessed prior to installation of the system to assure that the system can comply with the above five requirements; and the monitoring wells are clearly marked and secured.[69]

---

[66] 40 C.F.R. § 280.43(b).

[67] 40 C.F.R. § 280.43(c).

[68] 40 C.F.R. § 280.43(d).

[69] 40 C.F.R. § 280.43(e).

If *groundwater monitoring* is used, it must meet the following requirements: the regulated substance stored in the tank must be immiscible in water and have a specific gravity of less than one; the groundwater must never be more than 20 feet from the ground surface and the hydraulic conductivity of the soils between the UST system and the monitoring well or device cannot be less than .01 cm/sec; the monitoring well casing must be designed to prevent migration of natural soils or filter pack into the well and to allow entry of regulated substance on the water table into the well under both high and low groundwater conditions; the monitoring wells must be sealed from the ground surface to the top of the filter pack; the monitoring wells must intercept the excavation zone or must be as close to it as is technically feasible; the continuous monitoring devices used must be able to detect the presence of at least one-eighth of an inch of free product on top of the groundwater in the monitoring wells; the site must be assessed to ensure compliance with these requirements; and the monitoring wells must be clearly marked and secured.[70]

If *interstitial monitoring* is used, it must be designed, constructed and installed to detect a leak from any portion of the tank. For double-walled UST systems, the sampling or testing method must be able to detect a release through the inner wall and any portion of the tank that routinely contains product. For systems using a secondary barrier within the excavation zone, the sampling method must be able to detect a release between the system and the secondary barrier, and the barrier must be sufficiently thick and impermeable to direct a release to the monitoring point, yet installed so as not to interfere with proper operation of any cathodic protection systems.[71]

Finally, any other type of release detection method or combination of methods may be used so long as the implementing agency approves.[72]

### 4.5.5. Additional Requirements for Piping

The regulations also set forth specific requirements for certain methods of release detection for piping. First, if either vapor monitoring, groundwater monitoring, or interstitial monitoring are used for release detection from pipes,

---

[70] 40 C.F.R. § 280.43(f).

[71] 40 C.F.R. § 280.43(g).

[72] 40 C.F.R. § 280.43(h). The standard for approval of such alternate methods is that the owner or operator must be able to demonstrate to the agency that the method is capable of detecting a release before it migrates beyond the excavation area and is a method as effective as any of the methods described above. In comparing methods, the agency is to consider the size of the release that the method can detect and the frequency and reliability with which it can be detected. *Id.*

the monitoring system must meet the requirements for tank systems set forth above.[73]  Automatic line leak detectors, which are methods which alert the operator to the presence of a leak by restricting or shutting off the flow of regulated substances or triggering an alarm, may be used only if they detect leaks of three gallons per hour at 10 pounds per square inch line pressure within one hour.  Additionally, an annual test of the operation of the leak detector must be conducted.[74]  A periodic line tightness testing of piping can be conducted only if it is capable of detecting a one-tenth of a gallon per hour leak rate at one and one-half times the operating pressure.[75]

Finally, system owners and operators must maintain records demonstrating compliance with all the applicable release detection requirements.  These records are to include written performance claims, the results of any sampling, testing or monitoring, and written documentation of all calibration, maintenance and repair of release detection equipment.[76]

### 4.6  Release Reporting, Investigation, and Confirmation

Owners and operators of UST systems must report to the implementing agency within 24 hours if any of the following conditions are found:

(a) the discovery of released regulated substances at the site or in the surrounding area;

(b) unusual operating conditions (such as sudden loss of product from the UST system, or an unexplained presence of water in the tank); and

(c) monitoring results from a release detection method that indicate that a release may have occurred.[77]

Following the initial reporting of the suspected release, owners and operators must immediately investigate and confirm all suspected releases

---

[73] 40 C.F.R. § 280.44(c).

[74] 40 C.F.R. § 280.44(a).

[75] 40 C.F.R. § 280.44(b).

[76] 40 C.F.R. § 280.45.

[77] 40 C.F.R. § 280.50.  Monitoring results indicating a leak do not have to be reported where the monitoring device itself is found to be defective, or in the case of inventory control, a second month of data does not confirm the initial result. *Id.*

within a seven-day period.[78]   Unless another procedure is approved by the implementing agency, the tank owner/operator must comply with this requirement by first conducting a system test to determine whether a leak exists in that portion of the tank or piping that routinely contains product.   If a leak is found, the owner/operator must repair, replace or upgrade the system, and additionally begin corrective action if the test results indicate that a release to the environment has occurred.

If the test results do not indicate that a leak exists, and if environmental contamination is not the basis for suspecting a release, further investigation is not required.   However, if the basis for suspecting a release is environmental contamination, then a site check also must be conducted.   Again, if the test results of the site check indicate that a release has occurred, corrective action must be undertaken.[79]   These site testing and confirmation steps also may be required by the implementing agency where off-site impacts have been observed by a third party.[80]

EPA also requires that specific procedures for reporting and cleanup of spills and overfills be followed.   Spills and overfills must be reported to the implementing agency within 24 hours.[81]   Additionally, the owner or operator must undertake an immediate cleanup and containment action.   The following spills and overfills are subject to these requirements:

(a) a spill or overfill of petroleum that results in a release exceeding 25 gallons or that causes a sheen on nearby surface water; and

(b) a spill or overfill of a hazardous substance that results in a release to the environment that equals or exceeds the reportable quantity for that substance under CERCLA.[82]   If the spill or overfill is less than these quantities, the owner and operator still must contain and immediately clean up the release.   If cleanup cannot be accomplished within 24 hours, the owner or operator immediately must notify the implementing agency.

---

[78] 40 C.F.R. § 280.52.

[79] 40 C.F.R. § 280.52(b).

[80] 40 C.F.R. § 280.51.

[81] 40 C.F.R. § 280.53(a).

[82] *See* 40 C.F.R. Part 302.   In addition to the UST reporting requirements, releases equaling or exceeding the CERCLA reportable quantity must be reported immediately to the National Response Center pursuant to Sections 102 and 103 of CERCLA, 42 U.S.C. §§ 9602 and 9603, and to the appropriate state and local authorities under Title III of the Superfund Amendments and Reauthorization Act of 1986.

## 4.7 Corrective Action

Upon confirmation of a release, tank owners and operators must perform certain actions within 24 hours. They must report to the applicable agency the confirmed release and take immediate action to prevent any further release. Additionally, they must identify and mitigate fire, explosion, and vapor hazards.[83]

Next, unless directed to do otherwise by the implementing agency, the owners and operators must perform abatement measures. These consist of removing as much of the regulated substance from the system as is necessary to prevent further release to the environment; performing a visual inspection of any above-ground releases or exposed underground releases and preventing further migration into surrounding soils and groundwater; continuing to monitor and mitigate any additional fire and safety hazards; remediation of hazards posed by contaminated soils that are excavated or exposed as a result of release confirmation or site investigation; measuring for the presence of a release where contamination is most likely to be present at the site, unless the presence and source of the release have been confirmed; and investigation to determine the possible presence of free product.[84] A report summarizing these initial abatement steps must be submitted to the implementing agency within 20 days after release confirmation.[85]

Where the owner/operator has identified free product, free product removal must be conducted immediately and in a manner that "minimizes the spread of contamination into previously uncontaminated zones by using recovery and disposal techniques appropriate to the hydrogeologic conditions at the site," and a report must be submitted to the implementing agency within 45 days as to the type of free product recovery system being used.[86] Additionally, where evidence exists that groundwater has been affected by the release, an investigation for soil and groundwater cleanup must be conducted and the results must be submitted to the agency as soon as practicable.[87]

---

[83] 40 C.F.R. § 280.61.

[84] 40 C.F.R. § 280.62(a).

[85] 40 C.F.R. § 280.62(b). Additionally, within 45 days of release confirmation, owners and operators must submit to the implementing agency all information assembled about the site and the nature of the release, including data on the nature and estimated quantity of release, data concerning possible receptors of the release, results of any site checks performed, and results of any free product investigations. 40 C.F.R. § 280.63.

[86] 40 C.F.R. § 280.64.

[87] 40 C.F.R. § 280.65.

Finally, a corrective action plan may be required by the implementing agency. The regulations provide for public comment on the corrective action plan proposed by the site owner/operator.[88]

It should be noted that the release detection and corrective action regulations refer to the obligations of "owners *and* operators." The preamble to the final regulations makes clear that the corrective action requirements are imposed upon all owners and operators of UST systems.[89] Thus, upon a suspected release, in cases where the owner of the tank differs from the operator, both the owner and the operator must coordinate their efforts to ensure compliance with the regulations as both parties may be held liable if the release detection and site correction regulations are violated.

### 4.8. System Closure

Both temporary closure of UST systems and permanent closure are regulated. During periods of temporary closure, owners and operators must continue operation of corrosion protection and any release detection methods employed.[90] When the system is temporarily closed for three months or more, the following is required: the vent lines must be open and functioning, and all other lines, pumps, manways and ancillary equipment must be tapped and secured. Systems closed for more than 12 months must be permanently closed, unless the implementing agency provides an extension.[91]

When a "change-in-service" (continued use of an UST system to store a nonregulated substance) occurs, the agency must be notified, the tank must be emptied and cleaned, and a site assessment must be conducted.[92]

To close a tank permanently, the tank must be emptied and cleaned by removing all liquids and accumulated sludges. The tank must be either removed from the ground or filled with an inert solid material. The implementing agency must be notified of the intent to close permanently at least 30 days prior to beginning the process.[93] The state implementing agency most likely will request to monitor the tank closure.

---

[88] 40 C.F.R. §§ 280.66 and 280.67.

[89] 53 Fed. Reg. 37,175 (Sept. 23, 1988).

[90] 40 C.F.R. § 280.70.

[91] 40 C.F.R. § 280.70(c).

[92] 40 C.F.R. § 280.71(c).

[93] 40 C.F.R. § 280.71(b).

## 4.9 Financial Responsibility Requirements

Effective January 24, 1989, petroleum system tank owners and operators must demonstrate financial responsibility capability in accordance with a phased-in schedule. These standards apply to current owners and operators (including municipalities) of all petroleum underground storage tanks, except for those tanks excluded or deferred from EPA's final technical performance regulations, and those tanks taken out of service before the compliance dates established by the financial responsibility regulations.[94]

If the owner and operator of a covered UST system are separate persons or entities, only one must demonstrate financial responsibility. However, both parties are liable for noncompliance.[95]

### 4.9.1 Dates for Compliance

Tank owners and operators must comply with the financial responsibility criteria according to the following schedules:

(a) January 24, 1989: Petroleum marketing firms[96] owning 1000 or more USTs and all other UST owners reporting a tangible net worth of $20 million or more;

(b) October 26, 1989: Petroleum marketing firms owning 100-999 USTs;

(c) April 26, 1991: Petroleum marketing firms owning 13-99 USTs at more than one facility;

(d) October 26, 1991: All petroleum UST owners not described in paragraphs (a), (b) and (c) above.[97]

---

[94] 53 Fed. Reg. 43,327 (Oct. 26, 1988).

[95] 40 C.F.R. § 280.90(e). In this connection, the preamble to the final financial responsibility regulations notes that parent corporations generally are not subject to the regulations as a result of their subsidiaries' operation of an UST system, but that a parent corporation may be held liable for a subsidiary's noncompliance in "appropriate circumstances." 53 Fed. Reg. 43,326 (Oct. 26, 1988).

[96] A petroleum marketing firm is one which owns a petroleum marketing facility, which is a facility at which petroleum is produced or refined or from which petroleum is sold or transferred to other petroleum marketers or to the public. 40 C.F.R. §§ 280.92(i) and (j).

[97] 40 C.F.R. § 280.91, *see also* 55 Fed. Reg. 27,837 (July 6, 1990).

In mid-1990, EPA extended by one year the original financial responsibility compliance dates for the smaller "category c" and "category d" tank owners and operators.[98] EPA was reacting to both testimony before Congress and a General Accounting Office report[99] documenting the difficulty small businesses were experiencing in obtaining insurance for their underground tanks. The GAO report estimated that over one-half of the "category d" owner/operators would be unable to obtain insurance by the original October 26, 1990 deadline.[100]

### 4.9.2 Amounts of and Mechanisms for Demonstrating Financial Responsibility

Petroleum tank owners and operators must demonstrate adequate financial responsibility both on a per-occurrence and annual aggregate basis. Again, the amount of required coverage depends on the number of tanks and size of the owner.

Owners and operators of USTs located at petroleum marketing facilities, or that handle an average of more than 10,000 gallons of petroleum per month based on the average from the previous calendar year, must demonstrate financial responsibility for taking corrective action and for compensating third parties for bodily injury and property damaged caused by accidental releases in the amount of $1 million per occurrence. All other UST owners and operators are subject to a $500,000 per occurrence amount.[101]

The annual aggregate amounts are based on the number of single containment units owned. Owners and operators of 1 to 100 petroleum USTs must demonstrate financial responsibility in the annual aggregate amount of $1 million. Owners and operators of 101 or more tanks are subject to a $2 million showing of financial responsibility.[102]

The requisite level of financial responsibility may be shown by use of any one or a combination of the following mechanisms: a guarantee or surety bond (the form of which has been approved by the state attorney general's office); insurance or risk retention group coverage, a letter of credit, a trust fund, or a state-required mechanism in states without approved programs.[103]

---

[98] 55 Fed. Reg. 27,837 (July 6, 1990).

[99] GAO No. RCED-90-167FS, "Owners' Ability to Comply With EPA's Financial Responsibility Requirements" (July, 1990).

[100] *Id.*

[101] 40 C.F.R. § 280.93(a).

[102] 40 C.F.R. § 280.93(b).

[103] 40 C.F.R. §§ 280.94-103.

The regulations contain detailed standards and conditions for the use of each of these instruments. Additionally, owners or operators meeting stringent net worth and financial test requirements may act as self-insurers.[104] Records evidencing compliance with these requirements must be maintained by the tank owner or operator.[105]

An owner or operator may only be released from the financial responsibility requirements upon either proper closure of the tank or completion of corrective action.[106]

## 4.10 Enforcement

RCRA Section 9006 authorizes EPA to issue administrative orders to any person deemed to be in violation of any requirement of Subtitle I or the UST regulations, or to commence a civil action against the owner or operator in the United States district court in which the violation occurred.[107] Failure to comply with an administrative order subjects the recipient of the order to fines of up to $25,000 per day for each day of continued noncompliance. A person may challenge an order under Section 9006 by requesting, within 30 days of service of the order, a public hearing.[108]

In addition to compliance orders, EPA, subject to certain conditions, may undertake corrective action with respect to the release of petroleum into the environment from an underground storage tank if such action is necessary to protect human health and the environment.[109] Such corrective action may

---

104 40 C.F.R. § 280.95.

105 40 C.F.R. § 280.107.

106 40 C.F.R. § 280.109. Owners and operators filing as debtors under Chapter 11 of the Bankruptcy Code must notify the Director of the implementing agency by certified mail within 10 days after commencement of the proceeding. 40 C.F.R. § 280.110.

107 RCRA § 9006, 42 U.S.C. § 6991e(a). In August of 1990, EPA proposed the use of RCRA Section 3008(h) administrative hearing procedures (found at 40 C.F.R. Part 24) for Subtitle I orders involving corrective action, but no penalties. 55 Fed. Reg. 33,430 (Aug. 15, 1990). These procedures are relatively streamlined, involving only abbreviated hearings, with no cross-examination of witnesses.

108 RCRA § 9006(b), 42 U.S.C. § 6991e(b).

109 42 U.S.C. § 6991b(h)(2). The response program applies to releases which contain petroleum. Accordingly, petroleum-hazardous substance mixtures are subject to Section 9003(h) corrective action authority. *See* 53 Fed. Reg. 37116 (Sept. 23, 1988).

only be performed by EPA if one or more of the following circumstances exist: (1) within 90 days (or a shorter period if such is necessary to protect human health and the environment), no person can be located who is the owner or operator of the leaking tank, subject to the corrective action regulations, and capable of carrying out the necessary corrective action properly; (2) the situation is such that prompt action is required to protect human health and the environment; (3) the costs of the required corrective action exceeds the amount of coverage called for by the financial responsibility regulations; or (4) the tank owner or operator has failed to comply with prior compliance orders.[110] In undertaking the cleanup action, EPA or states under cooperative agreements will use funds from the Leaking Underground Storage Tank Trust Fund, which is being financed by taxes on motor fuels.[111] The tank owner or operator is liable to EPA for reimbursement to the fund for the costs of such corrective action,[112] but in assessing such costs, the agency may take into account the amount of financial responsibility required to be kept by the tank owner or operator.[113]

## 5.0 RELATIONSHIP TO OTHER LAWS

### 5.1 RCRA

Pursuant to RCRA Subtitle C, EPA has promulgated regulations for tanks containing hazardous wastes. Because the final UST regulations to not apply to hazardous substances regulated under Subtitle C, or USTs containing mixtures of these regulated substances and otherwise covered substances,[114] no overlap exists between these two sets of regulations. Thus, an interesting question arises as to application of the UST regulations at sites containing above-ground tanks, underground tanks containing hazardous wastes, and

---

110 RCRA § 9003; 42 U.S.C. § 6991b(h)(2).

111 RCRA § 9003; 42 U.S.C. § 6991b(h)(i).

112 Subtitle I provides that the standard of liability shall be the same as that in Section 311 of the Federal Water Pollution Control Act. 42 U.S.C. § 6991b(h)(6). The defenses to liability available under Section 311 are: (1) an act of God; (2) an act of war; (3) negligence on the part of the United States Government; and (4) an act or omission of a third party. 33 U.S.C. § 1321(f)(1). It is also important to note that Subtitle I excludes from the definition of owner any person who holds only an indicia of ownership primarily to protect a security interest in a tank. RCRA § 9003; 42 U.S.C. § 6991b(h)(a).

113 RCRA § 9003; 42 U.S.C. § 6991b(h)(6).

114 40 C.F.R. § 280.10(b)(1).

underground tanks subject to the regulations set forth above. EPA arguably may apply different sets of cleanup standards, for example, to different tanks located at the same site.[115]

In contrast, as EPA to date has not established regulations for the storage of used oil under Section 3014 of RCRA, the UST regulations specifically apply to UST systems containing used oil until such time as EPA promulgates used oil management regulations.

## 5.2 CERCLA

Another possible area of overlap is between the UST regulations and CERCLA, which makes owners, operators, transporters and generators liable for the cleanup of hazardous substances released to the environment.[116] CERCLA specifically excludes petroleum from its reach,[117] leaving the RCRA Subtitle I provisions as the primary federal authority for compelling the cleanup of releases of petroleum to the environment from the underground tanks. However, several recent suits have sought to retain CERCLA cleanup authority for petroleum releases, arguing that because gasoline, for example, contains hazardous substances like benzene, toulene and lead, it should remain covered by the CERCLA cleanup provisions. The Ninth Circuit Court of Appeals has rejected this argument, holding that releases of gasoline are indeed exempt from the CERCLA liability provisions.[118]

## 5.3 State Laws

As stated in Section 3.0, to receive EPA approval for primary enforcement of UST regulations, a state UST program needs to regulate the same general aspects of tank performance as do the federal regulations, and be no less stringent than federal requirements.[119] Accordingly, many of the state UST programs vary somewhat from the federal requirements (*see*, e.g., Section

---

115 As of the fall of 1990, there was legislation pending before Congress to add to RCRA Subtitle I a new section dealing with above-ground tanks. (H.R. 3735, "Pollution and Prevention and Recycling Act.") The draft bill, which did not get further than the House Committee on Energy and Commerce during the 1990 session, contains provisions for regulating above-ground tanks similar to the Subtitle I provisions regulating underground storage tanks.

116 CERCLA § 107(a); 42 U.S.C. § 9607(a).

117 CERCLA § 101(4); 41 U.S.C. § 9601(14).

118 *Wilshire Westwood Associates v. Atlantic Richfield Corp.*, 881 F.2d 801 (9th Cir. 1989).

119 RCRA § 9004; 42 U.S.C. § 69916.

4.1.2) and so must be consulted prior to undertaking any action relating to a new or existing tank. While a discussion of each state's individual requirements as to USTs is beyond the scope of this chapter, these requirements are covered by the Government Institute's handbooks on individual state environmental laws.

## Chapter 13

## COMPREHENSIVE ENVIRONMENTAL RESPONSE, COMPENSATION, AND LIABILITY ACT (CERCLA OR SUPERFUND)

Richard G. Stoll, Esq.
Freedman, Levy, Kroll & Simonds
Washington, D.C.

## 1.0 INTRODUCTION

### 1.1 CERCLA's Basic Purposes

In 1980, Congress enacted the Comprehensive Environmental, Response, Compensation, and Liability Act, usually referred to as "CERCLA" or "Superfund."[1] CERCLA's most basic purposes are to provide funding and enforcement authority for cleaning up the thousands of hazardous "waste sites" created in the U.S. in the past and for responding to hazardous substance spills.

With respect to hazardous waste, CERCLA joins the Resource Conservation and Recovery Act (RCRA) to provide "wrap-around" coverage. Generally, while RCRA establishes a cradle-to-grave regulatory program for present hazardous waste activities, CERCLA establishes a comprehensive response program for past hazardous waste activities.

Many CERCLA provisions (discussed below) go beyond the old waste-site cleanup program. Thousands of business establishments, for instance, are subject to reporting requirements for spills and other kinds of environmental "releases." The overwhelming emphasis of CERCLA, however, is on old waste sites.

### 1.2 CERCLA/"SARA" Terminology Confusion

In 1986, Congress enacted significant revisions to CERCLA through the Superfund Amendments and Reauthorization Act (or "SARA").[2] The all-encompassing nature of the amendments and the high visibility of the cleanup program have created a rash of "SARA" programs and articles.

---

[1] 42 U.S.C. §§ 9601 *et seq.*

[2] Pub. L. No. 99-499, October 17, 1986.

This has contributed to confusion as to whether "SARA" is now the appropriate name of the statute. It is not. SARA simply made CERCLA bigger and more complex. Throughout this chapter, the basic 1980 statute--as amended in 1986 by SARA--will be referred to by its proper name "CERCLA."

## 2.0 KEY CONCEPTS AND DEFINITIONS

CERCLA's scope is far broader than any of the other federal environmental statutes. While the Clean Air Act deals with air and the Clean Water Act deals with water, CERCLA covers *all* environmental media: air, surface water, groundwater, and soil. Moreover, unlike the specific media statutes, CERCLA can apply directly to any type of industrial, commercial, or even non-commercial facility regardless of whether there are specific regulations affecting that type of facility and regardless of how that facility might impact on the environment (i.e., through stacks, pipes, impoundments, etc.)

Events that may trigger CERCLA response or liability would be the *release* or "threat of" release into the *environment* of a *hazardous substance* or *pollutant or contaminant*. CERCLA defines each of these terms quite broadly.

### 2.1 CERCLA "Hazardous Substance" Defined

Under CERCLA § 101(14) a "hazardous substance" is any substance EPA has designated for special consideration under the Clean Air Act (CAA), Clean Water Act (CWA), or TSCA (Toxic Substances Control Act), and any "hazardous waste" under RCRA. Moreover, EPA must designate additional substances as hazardous which "may" present substantial danger to health and the environment.[3] EPA maintains and updates a list of all such "hazardous substances" in 40 C.F.R. part 302. As of this writing, there are a total of 724 hazardous substances and 1500 radionuclides on the list. Congress has excluded only two basic types of substances from the definition of "hazardous substances": (1) petroleum and (2) natural gas (and synthetic gas usable for fuel).[4]

### 2.2 CERCLA "Pollutant or Contaminant" Defined

Under CERCLA § 101(33) a "pollutant or contaminant" can be *any other* substance not on the list of hazardous substances which "will or may reasonably be anticipated to cause" any type of adverse effects in organisms

---

[3] § 102(a).

[4] § 101(14), last sentence.

and/or their offspring. Again, petroleum and natural gas are excluded.[5]

## 2.3 Consequences of "Hazardous Substance"/"Pollutant or Contaminant" Distinction

Combining the definitions of "hazardous substance" and "pollutant or contaminant," it appears that any substance EPA might ever want to address is covered by CERCLA authority. One might in fact wonder why Congress even bothered to distinguish between "hazardous substances" and "pollutants or contaminants."

There are at least two fundamental consequences of this distinction. First, while EPA can respond to either type of substance, private parties may be liable for cleanup costs and natural resources damages only to the extent "hazardous substances" are involved. Second, private parties are liable for reporting certain "releases" only to the extent "hazardous substances" are involved. With respect to most other major provisions of CERCLA, however, the distinction has no real consequence.

## 2.4 Comparison of CERCLA Substances to RCRA Wastes

By comparing how substances trigger jurisdiction under CERCLA to the RCRA hazardous waste program, one can see the extreme breadth of CERCLA jurisdiction. To trigger RCRA jurisdiction a substance must first be a *waste*. Under CERCLA, the issue of whether a substance is a waste or a product (or something else) is simply irrelevant.

Second, the concept of "hazardousness" is much broader under CERCLA. At least under RCRA a waste must either be "listed" or meet one of the hazardous "characteristics" to trigger jurisdiction. In either case, the RCRA determination is based on concentrations of toxic constituents in some numerical threshold amount. Under CERCLA, however, EPA says that a substance that contains *any* amount of a listed "hazardous substance" will trigger jurisdiction. EPA's position has been upheld by the courts thus far.[6]

It is very common for the uninitiated to be confused on this. Environmental lawyers frequently hear from their clients: "But our waste has always tested out as non-hazardous. How can EPA bug me about this stuff?" Again, the fact that a waste is proven "non-hazardous" under RCRA does not defeat CERCLA jurisdiction in EPA's view.

Because of this common confusion, at least one eastern EPA regional office includes the following diagram in all of its CERCLA "information requests" to private parties:

---

[5] § 101(33).

[6] *Amoco Oil Co. v. Borden*, 889 F.2d 664 (5th Cir. 1989); *U.S. v. Carolawn Co.*, 21 Env't Rep. Cas. (BNA) 2124 (D.S.C. 1984).

## 2.5 EPA's Interpretation of the "Petroleum Exclusion"

At many waste sites, some or all of the substances of concern may be petroleum products or wastes. One issue that frequently arises is whether such substances may trigger CERCLA response authority and/or liability in light of the "petroleum exclusion" mentioned above. CERCLA specifies that the petroleum exclusion protects: "petroleum, including crude oil or any fraction thereof which is not otherwise specifically listed or designated as a hazardous substance" through other CERCLA provisions.[7]

Two major questions of interpretation have been created by this exclusion. First, all petroleum naturally contains some substances (benzene, toluene, xylene) which are "otherwise specifically listed" as a hazardous substance through other CERCLA provisions. Does this mean in effect that *no* petroleum qualifies for the exclusion?

Second (assuming that the resolution of the first issue does not render the exclusion a nullity), oil found at waste sites may for various reasons (mixing, use) sometimes be contaminated with other hazardous substances not indigenous to petroleum. Does all waste oil--no matter how contaminated with other substances--qualify for the exclusion so long as it may still basically be characterized as petroleum?

In a major legal memorandum in 1987, EPA answered both questions in the negative.[8] EPA ruled that the presence of hazardous substances indigenous to petroleum (benzene, toluene, etc.) would not defeat the protection of the petroleum exclusion. EPA also ruled, however, that even though a material contains petroleum, it will lose the protection of the petroleum exclusion if the material also is found to contain substances which are "not normally found in refined petroleum fractions or present at levels which exceed those normally found in such fractions."[9] Courts have agreed with EPA's construction of the

---

[7] § 101(14).

[8] Memorandum on "Scope of the CERCLA Petroleum Exclusion Under Section 101(14) and 104(a)(2)," by Francis S. Blake, (then) EPA General Counsel, July 31, 1987.

[9] *Id.*

petroleum exclusion.[10]

Under this interpretation, then, the issue of whether a waste oil is a hazardous substance will depend upon EPA's ability to prove at a specific site that a particular party's waste oil contained levels of hazardous substances beyond those normally found in petroleum. The nature of EPA's burden has yet to be clarified by the courts.

### 2.6 CERCLA "Release" Defined

A "release" is defined extremely broadly so that any way a substance can enter the environment is covered ("spilling, leaking, pumping," etc.).[11] Congress has for policy or political reasons excluded four types of activities from the definition, however: (1) workplace exposures (covered by OSHA); (2) vehicular engine exhausts; (3) certain radioactive contamination covered by other statutes; and (4) the "normal" application of fertilizer.[12]

There is also a "federally permitted release" concept, keyed to eleven types of releases specifically allowed under other environmental statutes (CAA, CWA, etc.).[13] For instance, any release in compliance with an NPDES permit under the CWA is a "federally permitted release."[14]

The "federally permitted release" versus other kinds of "releases" distinction is analogous to the "hazardous substance" versus "pollutant or contaminant" distinction discussed above. That is, EPA has full response and cleanup authority with respect to federally permitted releases; but private parties neither have liability for such releases, nor are they obligated to report them.[15]

---

[10] See, *Wilshire Westwood Assoc. v. Atlantic Richfield Corp.*, 881 F.2d 801 (9th Cir 1989); *State of Washington v. Time Oil Co.*, 15 CWLR 1261 (W.D. Wash. 1988).

[11] § 101(22).

[12] § 101(22).

[13] § 101(10)(A).

[14] § 101(10)(A).

[15] §§ 107(j), 103(b)(2).

## 2.7 CERCLA "Environment" Defined

Finally, "environment" is defined almost as broadly as possible.[16] It includes all navigable and other surface waters, groundwaters, drinking water supplies, land surface or subsurface strata, and ambient air within the U.S. jurisdiction. Perhaps the only limitation of note would be that "indoor" air is not included, as EPA's Clean Air Act regulations have always defined "ambient" air to exclude indoor air.[17]

# 3.0 MOVING WASTE SITES THROUGH THE CLEANUP PROCESS

## 3.1 Fundamental Prerequisites

Under Section 104(a)(1), whenever there is a "release" or "substantial threat" of a release into the "environment" of any (1) hazardous substance or (2) pollutant or contaminant under circumstances where the pollutant or contaminant "may" present an imminent and substantial danger, EPA is authorized to undertake "removal" and/or "remedial" action. Both these terms are defined in CERCLA Section 101.

### 3.1.1 Removal or Remedial Action

A "removal" is a short-term, limited response to a more manageable problem while a "remedy" is a longer term, more permanent and expensive solution for a more complex problem. For instance, EPA may respond to a tank truck spill on the beltway by siphoning all spilled materials and digging up and hauling away a few inches of contaminated soil so that there is no contamination left at the site. This would be a "removal." Or EPA may enter a site where a few dozen drums of old waste are stored and haul them away. Again, this would be a "removal." On the other hand, an old landfill covering 60 acres with waste 100 feet deep may require a 4-year construction program and a 30-year groundwater pumping and treating program. This would be a "remedy."

At some sites, both a "removal" and a "remedy" might be appropriate. For instance, as a preliminary stage toward a final "remedy" at an old landfill, it may be necessary to step in and "remove" a bunch of old drums quickly to avoid fires or explosions, or prevent extra leaking that would only make the final remedy more difficult.

### 3.1.2 State Contract or Cooperative Agreement

There are two basic prerequisites to undertaking a remedial action. First, CERCLA precludes EPA from taking its own remedial action at a site unless EPA has first entered into a "contract or cooperative agreement" with the

---

[16] § 101(8).

[17] 40 C.F.R. § 50.1(e).

state in which the site is located. This agreement must obligate the state to undertake several measures,[18] the most important of which is that the state agrees to finance 10 percent of the remedy (or 50 percent in the case of a state-operated site). (Important note: This 10 or 50 percent "state share" requirement does not apply where liable parties perform remedial actions with their own funds. This option will be discussed at length in the "settlements" section which follows.)

### 3.1.3 National Priorities List

Second, under EPA regulations, only those sites listed on the "National Priorities List" (NPL) will be eligible for fund-financed remedial action.[19] It is thus important to understand what the NPL is and how sites may be placed on it.

Since the 1980 CERCLA, Section 105(8) has required EPA to develop "criteria" for determining priorities among sites for purposes of taking remedial actions and to develop and maintain a "list" of such "national priorities" when such sites have been examined under these criteria.

As part of its National Contingency Plan (NCP) regulations, (see section 4.0 below) EPA has set forth a structured program for evaluating sites and placing some of them on the NPL. Generally, from among the over 33,000 sites reported to EPA which might need remedial action, EPA has established a "winnowing down" process. *Any* site which comes to EPA's attention will receive a "preliminary assessment" (often an "armchair" review of data) to determine if further attention is currently needed.

Sites not "discarded" at this stage will next receive a physical "site inspection." After such an inspection many sites will become candidates for a more thorough evaluation and "scoring" under the "hazard ranking system" (HRS).[20] Under the HRS (also known as the "MITRE model") pertinent data about a site are evaluated and "scored." A site may be given various scores for waste volume, waste toxicity, distance to population, distance to underground drinking water, etc. Under current EPA policy, any site that receives a score of 28.50 or above will be included on the NPL. As of October 1, 1990, there were 1,187 sites on the NPL.

### 3.2 Steps in the Remedial Process for NPL Sites

As will be described more fully below, providing a "remedy" for an NPL site can be a massive and complex legal/scientific/ engineering/construction undertaking. For each site there must be a distinct "pipeline" of activities,

---

[18] See § 104(c)(3).

[19] 40 C.F.R. § 300.425(b)(1).

[20] 40 C.F.R. § 300.425(c)(1).

and it would be impossible to initiate work at all sites at once. The following generally describes EPA's approach to sites once they are on the NPL.

### 3.2.1 Superfund Comprehensive Accomplishments Plan (SCAP)

EPA does not have the resources to process cleanup activities for all NPL sites at once. It accordingly develops a plan for each fiscal year called the "Superfund Comprehensive Accomplishments Plan" or "SCAP." The SCAP shows for each fiscal quarter which stage of the cleanup process (if any) is scheduled for each NPL site. The SCAP, which can be obtained under the Freedom of Information Act, may provide useful planning intelligence to parties who suspect they may be involved with a particular site.

### 3.2.2 Studies and Remedy Selection

EPA may select a cleanup remedy at a site from a great variety of options, and the costs of these options may vary widely. This is a process in which EPA determines "how clean is clean" and "how expensive is expensive."

For this crucial process, there are basically two stages: (1) the performance of a "Remedial Investigation/Feasibility Study" (RI/FS), following the preparation of a "Work Plan" for the RI/FS; and (2) EPA's selection of the remedy with a "Record of Decision" (ROD).

In the last two or three years, a new trend of segregating each site cleanup into several "operable units" ("OU's") has further complicated this process. See Section 3.2.7 below for more detail. For each OU at a site, there will be a separate RI/FS and ROD. Thus, at some sites there is now a complex and cumbersome matrix of activities at which various OU's may be producing several different RI/FS's proceeding along different time tracks.

### 3.2.3 Remedial Investigation/Feasibility Study (RI/FS)

The "Remedial Investigation" and "Feasibility Study" are two studies which are almost always performed together. The RI will attempt to characterize with precision the conditions at a site (or portion of a site where there are multiple OU's). The RI will identify the source and extent of contamination, the pathways of possible migration or releases to the environment, and the extent of potential human or other environmental exposure to contamination. The RI will present data on these matters in sufficient detail to develop and evaluate remedial alternatives.

Based upon the RI information, the FS will present a series of specific engineering or construction alternatives for cleaning up a site. For each major alternative presented, there will be a detailed analysis of the costs, effects, engineering feasibility, and environmental impact.

The RI/FS study process is a major effort which often takes more than a year. Early in the CERCLA program, RI/FS costs tended to be in the $500,000 to $1,000,000 range. Consistent with all other CERCLA costs, they are rising dramatically. An RI/FS in the $2 to $3 million range is not uncommon, and some have reached $5 million. In fact, at one western site, an RI/FS for only one of six OU's is projected to cost over $5 million.

One recent EPA practice, now that RI/FSs have become such a major project, is to require a "work plan" to precede an RI/FS. The work plan sets forth in detail such things as the proposed type of groundwater and soil sampling (number and parameters to be tested), the location and depths of monitoring wells, the timing for accomplishing certain tasks, and generally the degree to which the site will be studied and how alternatives will be developed.

The degree to which various study requirements are written into or excluded from the work plan will largely determine the cost of the RI/FS. The work plan will also directly affect the scope of the RI/FS, and may accordingly affect the scope of remedial options presented.

### 3.2.4 Record of Decision (ROD)

Once the RI/FS has presented EPA with the detailed cost/effectiveness estimates of several cleanup options, EPA must select the appropriate option in light of the requirements of new CERCLA § 121 (discussed in section 4.3 below.) In some RI/FSs, as many as ten to fifteen alternatives may be presented, ranging from a "no action" alternative (costing perhaps nothing) to a "total exhumation and incineration" alternative costing a billion dollars. Under the 1980 CERCLA, the more likely candidates were somewhere in between; under the 1986 CERCLA the more likely candidates will almost certainly be on the high side.

### 3.2.5 Public Participation in Records of Decision

EPA prepares and publishes a proposed "Record of Decision" (ROD) in which it announces and explains its tentative selection from among the RI/FS options. EPA will then provide an opportunity for written comments and the opportunity for an informal hearing.

Under the 1986 amendments, this process will be much more formal and elaborate than in the past. Under new CERCLA § 117, EPA must abide by detailed "public participation" requirements at each site. Moreover, to assure that the "public" will "participate" (even if they had otherwise not been so inclined) EPA can at each site now give "Supergrants" of $50,000 and even more to *anyone* to "facilitate" public participation.

Moreover, new CERCLA § 121(f) requires EPA to go to extraordinary lengths to assure "State involvement" in the ROD process. When all is said and done, EPA's final ROD selection is certain to have been accomplished only after jumping extensive and arduous procedural hurdles.

Finally, EPA will issue a ROD document in which it responds to the public comments and further explains the basis for its final decision.

### 3.2.6 Design and Construction

At the ROD stage, the remedial alternative which EPA selects will be presented in fairly basic and conceptual terms and the costs will be only estimates. It is at the "design" stage that the detailed engineering plans are developed, site specifications are calculated, and all site-specific factors are incorporated into the general remedial concept. These detailed plans and specifications usually take 9-12 months to prepare and can cost in the low millions.

Finally, once design is complete, a construction contract or contracts may be awarded for the actual remedial work. These "constructions" are often complex, multi-phase projects involving many discrete tasks and different types of subcontractors over time.

In addition to the capital costs of the initial construction, there is often a long-term (20-30 years) "operation and maintenance" ("O&M") phase which is an integral part of the project. For instance, after some waste has been removed, the site has been capped, and slurry walls have been erected during "construction," there may be a 30-year program of groundwater pumping and treating in the "O&M" phase. The costs of this phase can be considerable.

### 3.2.7 Emergence of "Operable Units"

At many sites--particularly the larger ones--another major overlay to the cleanup process has emerged in the last year or two. This is the concept of segregating an overall site remedy into several "operable units" or "OU's."

For each OU at a site, there may be a separate work plan, RI/FS, ROD (with public participation), design, and construction phase. EPA personnel have justified the OU approach on the grounds that a complex site can be divided into a number of smaller, more manageable problems which can be subject to more precise focus and analysis.

EPA personnel also argue that this approach allows them to set priorities among potential problems at a site so that more urgent ones--and/or those for which data are more readily available--may receive a quicker response than others.

Another obvious reason EPA has begun dividing cleanups into OU's is that EPA feels the need to answer political critics. Many in Congress and the press have chastised EPA's CERCLA policies for being too heavy on paper studies and too light on bulldozers. With the OU segregation, EPA can have bulldozers chugging along at the same time it initiates more paper studies at a site.

As an example of the way EPA can subdivide a large site into OU's, EPA has thus far designated the following as separate OU's at one large western landfill: (1) surface water; (2) landfill solids; (3) landfill gas; (4) soils; (5) deep groundwater; and (6) shallow groundwater and subsurface liquids.

It remains to be seen whether this balkanization process will prove wise. Undoubtedly, *some* actual cleanup work will begin more quickly at more sites and Congressional and/or bureaucratic bean counters will be happier.

In the long run, however, the process may result in more confusion, duplication, overlap, and less cost-effective cleanups. At some sites, EPA and private parties are already experiencing additional delays and confusion simply trying to define the precise scope of "what's in" and "what's out" of a particular OU. Moreover, at some sites, remedial work that is undertaken before related and follow up studies are finished might prove either unnecessary or counterproductive.

## 4.0 "HOW CLEAN IS CLEAN": DETERMINING THE APPROPRIATE EXTENT OF THE REMEDY AT A SITE

### 4.1 Overview and Introduction

One of the most chronically difficult and important CERCLA issues has been how to determine the "appropriate extent of the remedy" at a particular site. Among CERCLA *cognoscenti,* this is known as the "how clean is clean" issue.

For instance, should all waste and contaminated soil at a landfill be completely excavated? If so, should the soil be disposed offsite or incinerated? Or should the waste and contaminated soil be "contained" in place to prevent further migration? If so, by which of many alternative containment methods? Should the nearby groundwater that now has X parts per billion (ppb) of a hazardous substance be treated down to Y ppb or even zero ppb?

The answers to these questions could, up to a point, present different results in the degree of health and environmental protection at any site and will definitely present extremely different results in terms of cleanup costs. One remedial option may cost $20 million and provide X level of protection; another may cost $40 million and provide 3X level of protection; while another may cost $400 million and still provide 3X level of protection.

Obviously, from the private liable party's perspective, the answer to "how clean is clean" can make all the difference in the world to the most fundamental question: "how much do I *pay*"? CERCLA's "how much do I pay" policy has developed in five basic stages, from: (1) the 1980 statute which gave EPA almost total discretion to make rational decisions on a site-by-site basis; to (2) 1982 EPA regulations which preserved most of this discretion; to (3) 1985 EPA regulations with many new ambiguous provisions but with an overall thrust towards more expensive cleanups; to (4) the 1986 CERCLA amendments which point toward even more expensive cleanups; to (5) 1990 EPA regulations with extremely detailed provisions. Some might compare the growth of this statutory and regulatory framework to the growth of the plant named Audrey II in "The Little Shop of Horrors."

### 4.2 Site-Specific Decisionmaking

Before examining these statutory and regulatory provisions, there is one "bottom line" reality that must be kept in mind. Despite all the detailed direction from Congress and EPA, there is still a tremendous amount of discretion left with EPA decisionmakers on a site-by-site basis to determine precisely what remedy will ultimately be employed. Thus far, no matter how much additional "guidance" EPA headquarters supplies through memos or regulations, this great degree of site-by-site discretion has not been curtailed and does not seem likely to be in the foreseeable future.

Thus, parties interested in the ultimate remedy selection at a particular site may have the opportunity to become very influential to the outcome so long as they understand the statutory and regulatory framework. Parties pursuing remedial settlements (part 6 below) may be able to negotiate with EPA on how clean is clean issues, and all parties will have the opportunity to influence the decision on the record through the public participation requirements (part 3.2.5 above).

### 4.3 Selection of Remedial Action: General Principles

In the 1986 "SARA" amendments, Congress added Section 121 to CERCLA. This Section sets forth in great detail the fundamental principles EPA must follow in determining the appropriate remedies at each site.

Also in the 1986 amendments, Congress directed EPA to flesh out these details through revisions to the "National Contingency Plan" ("NCP"). Ever since 1980, CERCLA has required EPA to issue regulations known as the NCP. The NCP is designed to provide the basic blueprint for the entire CERCLA response program, and in particular for EPA's "how clean is clean" decisionmaking.

On March 8, 1990, EPA issued major NCP revisions as required by the 1986 SARA amendments.[21] These NCP amendments set forth EPA's key interpretations of the various CERCLA § 121 requirements and reflect the latest detailed spins on EPA's ever-evolving cleanup policies. These revisions will hereafter be referred to as the "1990 NCP."

### 4.3.1. CERCLA Section 121(a)

This subsection states the basic rule that all CERCLA response actions--whether fund-financed under Section 104 or privately performed under Section 106--must assure compliance with the NCP cleanup standards. This subsection also provides that remedial actions are to be "cost-effective." In evaluating cost-effectiveness, EPA must consider the "total short- and long-term costs" for the entire period during which such activities will be required.

### 4.3.2 CERCLA - Section 121(b)

This subsection states two basic principles that are to govern the selection of remedies at all sites:

(1) *"Treatment" is strongly preferred over "disposal" or "leaving in place" options.* Treatment which "permanently and significantly reduces" the hazardous substances involved is to be "preferred" over other remedies and EPA must select remedies that utilize "permanent solutions" and alternative treatment technologies "to the maximum extent practicable."

---

[21] 55 Fed. Reg. 8666, March 8, 1990.

(2) *Offsite disposal is clearly disfavored.* Offsite transport and disposal of untreated waste is the "least favored" alternative where "practicable" treatment technologies are available.

### 4.3.3. CERCLA - Section 121(c)

This subsection requires the following whenever the remedy will result in "*any* hazardous substances, pollutants, or contaminants remaining at the site" (emphasis added):

(1) EPA must review the site at least each five years to assure that health and the environment are still being protected;

(2) EPA must take additional action at such sites any time in the future when warranted; and

(3) EPA must report to Congress on all such sites and the results of all reviews and/or actions.

### 4.3.4 Offsite Disposal

Paragraph Section 121(d)(3) gives real life to the general statement in Section 121(b)(1) that offsite transport and disposal is the "least favored alternative." It provides that any offsite disposal facility, to be qualified to accept waste from a CERCLA site, must meet two requirements:

(1) The waste management "unit" which will accept such waste is not releasing *any* hazardous waste constituent into the groundwater, surface water, or soil; *and*

(2) All *other* units at the facility are "being controlled" by an approved RCRA "corrective action" program.

### 4.3.5 1990 NCP Provisions

EPA has issued and amended the NCP in various stages. With the 1990 NCP, the revisions were so sweeping and comprehensive that EPA essentially rewrote and recodified the whole thing with a new numbering system. All hazardous substance response is now covered by Subpart E in 40 C.F.R. part 300. The key provisions dealing with remedy selection in Subpart E are codified at 40 C.F.R. § 300.430.

In proposing NCP revisions to accommodate the various new requirements from CERCLA § 121, EPA noted a "combination of mandates" from CERCLA which create "dynamic tensions" in remedy selection policies.[22] Among the most tension-producing statutory mandates are the requirements to select cost-effective remedies and yet "prefer" treatment technologies.

---

[22] 53 Fed. Reg. 51422, December 21, 1988.

EPA made clear that CERCLA's "overarching mandate" is to protect health and the environment, and said that cost-effectiveness considerations cannot be used to justify a nonprotective remedy. EPA nevertheless emphasized that cost must play a significant role in the remedy selection process, and that EPA must "select protective remedies whose costs are proportionate to their overall effectiveness."[23]

EPA accordingly set up a system for evaluating "trade-offs" among various remedial options which maximizes case-by-case discretion using site-specific factors. EPA has established nine criteria that are to be utilized at each site in this process.

As EPA finally issued these nine criteria in the 1990 NCP, they are divided into three groups: "threshold," "primary balancing" and "modifying":

**Threshold:**
(1) Overall protection of human health and the environment;
(2) Compliance with ARARs (see part 4.4 below);
**Primary Balancing:**
(3) Long-term effectiveness and permanence;
(4) Reduction of toxicity, mobility, or volume through treatment;
(5) Short-term effectiveness;
(6) Implementability;
(7) Cost;
**Modifying:**
(8) State acceptance; and
(9) Community acceptance.[24]

Generally, these threshold criteria are absolute requirements (although there is a statutory process for formally waiving ARARs in narrowly-drawn circumstance, see part 4.5 below). The primary balancing criteria, on the other hand, may allow for "trade-offs" based on cost-effectiveness.

The 1990 NCP provides that primary balancing criteria (3), (4) and (5) listed above are to be evaluated to determine "overall effectiveness" of proposed alternatives. Then this "overall effectiveness" is to be compared against costs to "ensure" that the remedy is cost-effective. The rule states that to be cost-effective, the costs must be "proportional" to overall effectiveness.[25]

The 1990 NCP also makes the two modifying criteria the least important of the nine. While the threshold requirements are *musts*, and the balancing

---

[23] *Id.*

[24] 40 C.F.R. §§ 300.430(e)(a)(iii) and 300.430(f).

[25] 40 C.F.R. § 300.430(f)(1)(ii)(D).

criteria *must* be balanced, the regulation simply requires that the modifying criteria be "considered."[26]

## 4.4 Degree of Cleanup: "Applicable" or "Relevant and Appropriate" Requirements ("ARARs")

As noted above, "ARAR" compliance is one of the two basic "threshold" requirements that all remedies must meet. CERCLA § 121 mandates attainment of ARARs but provides little guidance on how to determine ARARs at a given site. On the other hand, the 1990 NCP contains quite detailed ARAR guidance. When all is said and done, however, the 1990 NCP still leaves an abundance of discretion for site-by-site decisionmaking.

### 4.4.1 Background on Rationale for ARARs

Over the years, Congress and state legislatures have enacted a number of federal and state environmental laws addressing various types of pollution and various types of environmental media (Clean Air Act, Clean Water Act, RCRA, etc.). Under these laws, agencies have established many standards and criteria that are legally enforceable against certain types of facilities in certain situations.

For instance, there are hundreds of "BAT" standards under the Clean Water Act. A particular BAT standard specifies the amounts of certain types of pollutants a particular type of facility (*e.g.*, electroplaters) may discharge through a point source to a navigable water. There are also thousands of ambient "water quality standards" under the Clean Water Act. A water quality standard defines concentrations of acceptable surface water quality for certain types of uses (fishing, swimming) and is implemented through a permit (NPDES) system for point source discharges to the navigable waters.

Similarly, there are emissions standards under the Clean Air Act that govern particular types of facilities. There are standards under the Safe Drinking Water Act that must be met by municipal water systems. There are also all sorts of standards under RCRA for those who (since 1980) have been engaging in hazardous waste treatment, storage and disposal.

For the most part, these regulatory standards were conceived and designed to be enforced against particular types of facilities engaging in particular types of ongoing activities. (*E.g.*, a chemical plant discharging pollutants to a river; a landfill accepting hazardous waste.) As they have been promulgated, they are usually limited in jurisdictional scope to the type of activities they have been designed to regulate. That is, they are only legally "applicable" to a specific universe of facilities and activities.

Unlike the approach of the Clean Air Act, Clean Water Act, and other basic environmental statutes, Congress has never required EPA to issue pollution control standards to govern CERCLA sites. Rather, Congress has in effect directed that EPA "borrow" standards from other federal and state laws on a

---

[26] 40 C.F.R. § 300.430(f)(1)(ii)(E).

site-by-site basis through the ARAR approach.

The basic policy set by Congress is that EPA should apply standards from such other laws to CERCLA cleanups in either of two circumstances: (1) where such an other law is legally "applicable"; or (2) where such an other law while not legally applicable is both "relevant and appropriate." This may look simple, but in practice it has proven difficult. Congress gave EPA no real guidance for determining just when a particular requirement my be "applicable" or "relevant and appropriate," and EPA has been struggling with these concepts for years.

### 4.4.2 CERCLA Section 121(d)

Paragraph § 121(d)(2) sets forth the basic requirement that site cleanups must attain standards (from other federal/state environmental programs) that are "applicable" or "relevant and appropriate" under the circumstances. It is important to note that this "ARAR" requirement applies when "*any*" hazardous substance, pollutant or contaminant will remain onsite.[27] Thus, in light of the five-year review procedures of Section 121(c) discussed above, even sites that meet all the requirements of paragraph (d) must still be reviewed each five years (unless by operation of paragraph (d) *all* hazardous substances, pollutants, and contaminants are removed).

Paragraph Section 121(d)(2) provides that if certain types of federal or state requirements are "legally applicable" to the substance or pollutant or contaminant "concerned," or are "relevant and appropriate" under the circumstances, then the remedial action shall require that each substance of concern "at least attain" such requirement. The types of federal/state requirements subject to this ARAR standard are specified in Section 121(d)(2)(A) as follows:

(i)   Any standard, requirement, criteria, or limitation under any Federal environmental law, including, but not limited to, the Toxic Substances Control Act, the Safe Drinking Water Act, the Clean Air Act, the Clean Water Act, the Marine Protection, Research and Sanctuaries Act, or the Solid Waste Disposal Act [RCRA]; or

(ii)  Any promulgated standard, requirement, criteria, or limitation under a State environmental or facility citing law that is more stringent than any Federal standard, requirement, criteria, or limitation, including each such State standard, requirement, criteria, or limitation contained in a program approved, authorized or delegated by the Administrator under a statute cited in sub-paragraph (A), and that has been identified to the President by the State in a timely manner.

---

[27] § 121(d)(2)(A), first sentence.

With respect to federal requirements, the paragraph does not nail down precisely which are "applicable" or "relevant or appropriate" in which circumstances; that interpretation is left to the NCP. It is important to note, however, that the statute here significantly expands upon EPA's pre-1986 practices by requiring adherence to *state* requirements and to federal *criteria* (not just standards).

### 4.4.3 The 1990 NCP

#### 4.4.3.1. Section 300.400(g)(1) "Applicable"

This subsection provides that Federal and/or state requirements are "applicable" to a release or remedial action when, based on an "objective determination," the requirement *specifically addresses* a hazardous substance, pollutant, contaminant, remedial action, location or other circumstance found at a CERCLA site. The intent here is to describe those requirements which, as a matter of basic statutory/regulatory jurisdiction, would apply to an activity or situation regardless of whether a CERCLA remediation were being conducted.

For instance, assume that under the Clean Water Act, there are "in stream" ambient water quality standards (WQS) designated for a portion of a river near a waste site. Assume further that as part of a remedy, there will be a "point source" discharge (*e.g.*, through a pipe) into the river.

Under the Clean Water Act, whenever one engages in a point source discharge, he must comply with the WQS for the receiving stream. In this situation, the WQS would be an "applicable" requirement for the remedy.

In contrast, assume there will be no point source discharge associated with the remedy. There will be, however, some "runoff" and/or transport of contaminants through the soil and groundwater to the river. Under the Clean Water Act, there is no requirement that runoff and/or soil/groundwater transport achieve compliance with WQS. In this situation, the WQS will not be "applicable", although they may be "relevant and appropriate" (see below).

Determining whether a requirement is "applicable" is not necessarily a simple analysis. While it is usually more straightforward and objective than a "relevant and appropriate" analysis, reasonable minds may (and often do) differ in various situations about whether a requirement is applicable. The RCRA "land ban" discussion appearing in section 4.4.4 below demonstrates this point.

#### 4.4.3.2 Section 300.400(g)(2) "Relevant and Appropriate"

This subsection provides that if a requirement is not "applicable," it must be *both* relevant and appropriate to a remedial action in order to be an ARAR. EPA has specified the following facts for determining the relevance and appropriateness of the requirement:

(i)    the purpose of the requirement and the purpose of the CERCLA action;

(ii)     the medium regulated or affected by the requirement and the medium contaminated or affected at the CERCLA site;

(iii)    the substances regulated by the requirement and the substances found at the CERCLA site;

(iv)     the actions or activities regulated by the requirement and the remedial action contemplated at the CERCLA site;

(v)      any variances, waivers, or exemptions of the requirement and their availability for the circumstances at the CERCLA site;

(vi)     the type of place regulated and the type of place affected by the release or CERCLA action;

(vii)    the type and size of structure or facility regulated and the type and size of structure or facility affected by the release or contemplated by the CERCLA action;

(viii)   any consideration of use or potential use of affected resources in the requirement and the use or potential use of the affected resource at the CERCLA site.

### 4.4.3.3 Removal/Remedial and On-Site/Off-Site Distinctions

It is important at this point to distinguish between complying with ARARs in the removal context and complying with ARARs in the remedial context. While CERCLA is silent on this point, the NCP provides that *on-site* removals must comply with ARARs only to the greatest extent practicable.[28]  EPA recognizes that, unlike remedial actions, removal actions are quick responses to immediate problems.  By their nature, then, removal actions preclude the use of the drawn-out response selection process that is characteristic of ARARs. Further, remedial actions are often geared toward a cleanup level that is beyond the scope of a removal action; in this light, removals cannot be expected to comply with all the ARARs that a remedial action could.

As noted above, however, this limitation on compliance with ARARs applies only to *on-site* removal actions.  *Off-site* removal and remedial actions must comply with legally applicable requirements.

---

[28] 40 C.F.R. § 300.410(i)

### 4.4.4 The RCRA Land Disposal Restrictions as ARARs

Congress added the "land disposal restrictions" ("LDRs") program to RCRA in 1984.[29] EPA has issued LDR regulations in several phases since 1986. Codified at 40 C.F.R. part 268, the LDR rules are often referred to as the "land ban."

Many observers originally thought the LDR program applied only to current waste generation at manufacturing facilities. But LDRs may also apply to many site "cleanup" activities, including CERCLA remedies and removals.

Applying LDRs to these cleanups can have dramatic and unfortunate effects. As described above, cost-effectiveness is generally an important consideration in selecting CERCLA remedies on a site-specific basis. LDRs, however, are nationally applicable and are based on the best technology. The effect at many sites will be that LDRs could require far more than necessary to protect health and the environment and will often dramatically increase cleanup costs. For instance, LDRs will often call for incineration of contaminated soil.

Most basically, one will trigger LDRs in the waste site cleanup context if: (a) the party will be managing a RCRA hazardous waste, *and* (b) the party (and/or someone else) will be *placing* the waste (or its treatment residue) on the *land*.

### 4.4.4.1 Managing A RCRA Hazardous Waste

LDRs often come into play in CERCLA cleanups for two basic reasons:

a. *Retroactivity*. The fact that a material was generated, transported, and disposed before RCRA was enacted or effective is irrelevant. If a material is going to be "managed" now in any way, and is a solid waste, and fits within any of the hazardous waste lists or characteristics, it is for all purposes a RCRA hazardous waste and potentially subject to LDRs.[30]

b. *The "Midas Touch" of Listed Wastes*. For listed hazardous wastes, there is a virtually boundless taint for materials they touch in any way. Three harsh rules work to infect treatment residues, ponds, tanks, sludges, soil, leachate, groundwater and other media with the taint of listed hazardous waste: (i) "derived from," (ii) "mixture," and (iii) "contained in."

---

[29] 42 U.S.C. §§ 6924(d)-(m).

[30] See, *Chemical Waste Management v. EPA*, 869 F.2d 1526, 1535-37 (D.C. Cir. 1989).

Very generally, under the "derived from" rule residues from the treatment of listed hazardous wastes will be deemed hazardous wastes.[31] Under the "mixture rule," any mixture of a solid waste and a listed hazardous waste will be deemed a hazardous waste.[32] And under the "contained in" rule, any material (such as soil or groundwater) that contains a listed hazardous waste will be deemed a hazardous waste so long as the presence of the waste can still be detected.[33] Thus, "old" materials, and materials that don't look very much like traditional wastes, may often be deemed hazardous wastes that trigger LDRs.

### 4.4.4.2. Placement On Land

Once one has determined he must manage a RCRA hazardous waste at his facility, that does not necessarily mean LDRs will be triggered. The remaining basic issue is whether there will be "placement" of that waste and/or its treatment residue onto or into the land.

When waste is sent off-site from a site cleanup, it is generally easy to determine whether placement will occur. When waste is being managed on-site, however, complicated issues of "placement" arise. EPA has given guidance along the following lines:[34]

a. First, determine the "area of contamination" (AOC) for the waste at issue. An AOC is defined by the boundary of "contiguous contamination." Contamination in such an area must be "continuous," but may nevertheless contain various types and concentrations of hazardous materials. EPA's guidance gives the following examples of areas which qualify as AOC's:

(i) A waste source (waste pit, landfill, waste pile) and the surrounding contaminated soil.

(ii) A waste source, and the sediments in a stream contaminated by the source, where the contamination is continuous from the source to the sediments. The AOC

---

[31] 40 C.F.R. § 261.3(c).

[32] 40 C.F.R. § 261.3(a)(2)(iv).

[33] 53 Fed. Reg. 31148 (August 17, 1988); EPA OSW Directive 9347.3-05FS, July, 1989 ("Superfund LDR Guide #5).

[34] The EPA guidance on "AOCs" and "placement" appears in three fundamental EPA sources: 53 Fed. Reg. 51443-45, December 21, 1988; EPA OSW Directive 9347.3-05FS (Superfund LDR Guide #5); and 55 Fed. Reg. 8758-63, March 8, 1990.

does not, however, include any contaminated surface or groundwater that may be associated with the land-based waste source.

    (iii)    Several lagoons separated only by dikes, where the dikes are contaminated and the lagoons share a common liner.

b.    Then, determine whether wastes will be moved out of the AOC. If wastes will stay within the AOC, then generally there will be no placement. EPA's guidance gives examples of when placement will occur and will not occur:

    (i)   Placement *will* occur when wastes are:
        (a)   Consolidated from different AOCs into a single AOC;
        (b)   Moved outside of an AOC (for treatment or storage, for example) and returned to the same or a different AOC; or
        (c)   Excavated from an AOC, placed in a separate unit, such as an incinerator or tank that is within the AOC, and redeposited into the same AOC.

    (ii)   Placement *will not* occur when wastes are:
        (a)   Treated *in situ;*
        (b)   Capped in place;
        (c)   Consolidated within the AOC; or
        (d)   Processed within the AOC (but not in a separate unit, such as a tank) to improve structural stability (e.g., for capping or to support heavy machinery). Normal earthmoving and grading operations within an AOC are included within this type of processing.

### 4.4.4.3 Complying with LDRs: Special Issues for Soil and Debris

For each waste code, EPA sets a "treatment standard" that it has determined represents the "best demonstrated available technology" ("BDAT"). Depending upon the general type and "treatability" of the waste, EPA may set BDAT standards based on incineration or other thermal combustion, alkaline chlorination, chemical precipitation, carbon adsorption, chemical oxidation, thermal recovery, stabilization, vitrification, others, and combinations of these and others.

Sometimes EPA sets a BDAT numeric concentration level that a waste code must be treated to. Such a standard will be based on EPA's determination of the performance of one of the specified technologies, but people are free to use other technologies if they can achieve the same numeric standard.[35] Other times EPA specifies a particular BDAT technology or alternate

---

[35] 40 C.F.R. §§ 268.41, 268.43.

technologies that a waste code must use.[36]

One may often find that more than one waste code applies to a particular material, particularly when dealing with soil and debris. EPA generally takes the following positions: where several different concentration levels are concerned, the most stringent for each constituent of concern must be met; where several different technologies are specified, all must be used unless a "treatability variance" is given[37]

Most LDR standards (including the requirement to meet BDAT) became effective by August 8, 1990. In some situations, however, EPA has extended BDAT deadlines out as far as May 8, 1992.[38]

With respect to BDAT deadlines, EPA has been consistently more flexible with respect to "soil and debris" and most of the extensions to May 8, 1992 involve soil and debris. It is consequently important to understand what EPA means by these terms. One *cannot* assume that just because waste is "in the ground," it is soil and debris. In fact, many types of sludges, stillbottoms, and other materials may have been placed in or on dirt, and yet the waste would still be generally intact in its "as generated form" even years later.

EPA has defined soil and debris as follows:

a. *Soil.* Materials that are primarily of geological origin such as sand, silt, loam, or clay, that are indigenous to the natural geologic environment at or near the site. (In many cases, soil is mixed with liquids, sludges, and/or debris.)

b. *Debris.* Materials that are primarily non-geologic in origin, such as grass, trees, stumps, and man-made materials such as concrete, clothing, partially buried whole or empty drums, capacitors, and other synthetic manu-factured materials, such as liners. (Debris does not include synthetic organic chemicals, but may include materials contaminated with these chemicals.)[39]

EPA has recognized that there may often be close questions where soil and/or debris have been mixed with sludges or other wastes in their "as generated" matrix. EPA has not issued guidance on this issue (and does not plan to). Rather, EPA says that it "will determine on a case-by-case basis

---

[36] 40 C.F.R. § 268.42.

[37] 55 Fed. Reg. 22530, June 1, 1990.

[38] See Appendix VII, 55 Fed. Reg. 22715 *et. seq.*, June 1, 1990.

[39] EPA OSW Directive 9347.3-01FS, July 1989 ("Superfund LDR Guide #1").

whether all or portions of such mixtures should be considered" soil and/or debris.[40]

On June 1, 1990, EPA created a new category of debris and granted a two-year BDAT extension (to May 8, 1992) for this category. EPA generally refers to this new category as "inorganic solid debris."[41] To qualify, the debris must meet all of the following three requirements:

(a)  It must be a nonfriable inorganic solid that is incapable of passing through a 9.5mm standard sieve and that requires crushing, grinding, or cutting in mechanical sizing equipment prior to stabilization; *and*

(b)  It must be one of the following types of materials:
    (i)   metal slag
    (ii)  glassified slag
    (iii) glass
    (iv) concrete (including stabilized hazardous wastes)
    (v)  masonry and refractory bricks
    (vi) metal cans, containers, drums, or tanks
    (vii) metal nuts, bolts, pipes, pumps, valves appliances, or industrial equipment
    (viii) scrap metal; *and*

(c)  It must be contaminated with waste codes D004 through D011 (inorganics).[42]

### 4.5 Exceptions to the ARAR Rules

CERCLA Section 121(d)(4) allows EPA to waive compliance with ARARs in six circumstances. It is important to note that Section 121(d)(4) does not provide any exception to the basic requirement that all remedies be sufficient to protect health and the environment. These six exceptions are as follows:

(A)  The selected action is only part of a total remedial action that will comply with the ARAR requirements when completed;

(B)  Compliance with the ARAR requirements would present greater health/environmental risks than alternative options;

---

[40]  54 Fed. Reg. 48489, November 22, 1989.

[41]  55 Fed. Reg. 22650, June 1, 1990.

[42]  New 40 C.F.R. § 268.2(g), 55 Fed. Reg. 22686, June 1, 1990.

(C) Compliance with the ARAR requirements is "technically impracticable from an engineering perspective";

(D) The selected remedy will attain a "standard of performance" which is "equivalent" to an ARAR required standard through use of another "method or approach";

(E) With respect to a state requirement, the state has not demonstrated consistent application of the requirement in similar circumstances; and

(F) Where the remedy is to be Fund-financed (as opposed to private-party financed), meeting the ARAR standard would not provide "balance" between the need for cleanup at the site in question considering the amount of Fund resources that must be utilized at other sites in need of cleanup.[43]

### 4.6 Permits and Enforcement

This subsection[44] provides a significant cut to potential red-tape delays for CERCLA cleanups. It provides that no "Federal, State, or local permit" shall be required for any portion of a CERCLA remedial action that is conducted on the site of the facility being cleaned up. Under RCRA, for instance, any "treatment" of hazardous waste normally requires a permit under Section 3005 before such treatment can begin. A RCRA permit normally takes from 1-to-2 years to process. As there is "treatment" of hazardous waste involved in many CERCLA cleanups, this provision is quite significant in assisting the program.

### 4.7 State Involvement

This subsection[45] contains detailed requirements for assuring "substantial and meaningful involvement" by each state in all phases of the selection of the remedy at all sites within the state. Working in tandem with the general "public participation" provisions of new Section 119 (which even include the authority for federal "technical assistance" *grants* of $50,000 or more to citizens groups at each site), EPA's determination of remedy process for each site is virtually guaranteed to be protracted and arduous.

### 4.8 Consequences of Trend Toward RCRA/CERCLA Merger

From the perspective of one who is interested in assuring health and environmental protection, but who also hates to see billions of dollars wasted

---

[43] § 121(d)(4).

[44] § 121(e).

[45] § 121(f).

on excessive cleanup efforts, there may be significant concerns with the trend toward presuming that RCRA requirements should be lifted and imported wholesale into CERCLA cleanups. This trend can have either or both of the following unfortunate results: (a) impose cleanup costs at old sites that have no reasonable relationship to the risks presented by the site; and/or (b) weaken RCRA requirements for current and new sites that often should not as a preventative matter be weakened.

It should be remembered that CERCLA is designed as a *response* program to deal with messes that have already been created. Usually, the activities that created the mess were legal and non-negligent at the time they took place. Because no one knew when these activities took place that a cleanup would be required in the future, the cleanup costs were not built into the pricing or other economic assumptions involved in these activities.

CERCLA presumably calls for cost-effective responses, to be decided on a site-by-site basis, which assure that health and the environment be protected at that site. Now that people with past associations with a site are saddled with retroactive liability, however, it may be inappropriate to *go beyond* what is actually necessary to protect health and the environment at that site. The costs of doing so cannot be built in to the transactions associated with the disposal, as those transactions took place years ago. Moreover, there is no regulatory/enforcement virtue to imposing "uniform" standards here, as CERCLA does not govern present waste management activities.

RCRA is designed as a *regulatory* program for current and new sites to prevent messes from occurring in the future. It requires issuance of nationally applicable standards which will be preventative in nature. There are great regulatory/enforcement benefits to uniform national standards, as it would be wholly unwieldy to try to prescribe current conduct throughout the country based upon case-by-case factors. The costs of complying with RCRA may be built in to the transaction costs associated with today's hazardous waste management practices.

Moreover, as RCRA standards are nationally uniform and designed to protect health and the environment on a national basis, they must by definition be more rigorous than necessary to protect health and the environment at many locations. As a preventative measure for future activities and where the costs can be built in, this may be a laudable policy. To impose RCRA standards at old sites will, however, often impose great costs where health and the environment could be fully protected for much less cost.

# 5.0 LIABILITY OF RESPONSIBLE PARTIES AND FINANCING OPTIONS FOR REMEDIAL ACTIONS

## 5.1 Basic Scheme

It is obvious that the site planning, investigation, study, remedy selection, design, construction, and operation and maintenance processes all cost money--sometimes very significant sums. Where does this money come from?

CERCLA authorizes EPA to draw upon two basic types of resources to pay for waste site remedies: (1) from the "Superfund"--the federal trust fund discussed in section 10.0 below; and (2) under the liability scheme of CERCLA, from the pockets of "responsible parties" with certain types of relationships to the site. Responsible parties' liabilities cover not only the actual construction costs, but also the investigation, RI/FS, and design costs. The types of parties who may be liable for site remedial costs are specified in CERCLA Section 107(a) as follows:

(1) present and past "owners or operators" of the site;

(2) parties who transported wastes to the site ("transporters"); and

(3) parties (usually referred to as "generators") who arranged for wastes to be disposed or treated, either directly with an owner/operator or indirectly with a transporter.

To illustrate, assume that a commercial landfill accepted hazardous wastes for disposal from 1960 to 1970, during which time the landfill was owned and operated by company A. In 1975, five years after the landfill was totally closed, company B bought the property on which the landfill is located.

Assume further that during the landfill's operation, companies C, D, E and F were in the hauling business and transported hazardous wastes from manufacturing plants to the landfill for disposal. Assume finally that during these years, companies G through Z were in various manufacturing businesses (aircraft, auto, chemical, computers, oil, steel, etc.), produced ("generated") hazardous waste as a byproduct of their manufacturing, and had individually arranged with transporter C, D, E and/or F to have their waste disposed.

Now, in 1988, the landfill is a NPL site and EPA has determined through the RI/FS and ROD process that a $500 million cleanup is necessary. Under CERCLA, as interpreted by numerous court decisions, any of parties A through Z may be liable for some or all of the $500 million. This liability has the following characteristics:

(1) it is *retroactive*, because parties are liable for acts or omissions occurring well before the date of CERCLA's enactment (1980);[46]

(2) it is *strict*, because it is irrelevant that a generator selected a licensed hauler to take waste to a licensed landfill, that all

---

[46] *Amland Properties Corp. v. Aluminum Co. of America*, 711 F.Supp. 784 (D.N.J. 1989); *Kelley v. Thomas Solvent Co.*, 714 F. Supp. 1439 (W.D. Mich. 1989).

legal requirements at the time were fully met, and/or that a party used all due care;[47]

(3)  it may in appropriate cases be *joint and several*, because one party out of many may be held liable for more than his/her "share" under any fair allocation, and may in fact be held liable for the entire site cleanup.[48]

It is important to note that this liability scheme applies not only to cleanup costs, but also to "natural resource damages." EPA and the States may assert claims for the damages that hazardous substance releases (including waste sites) have caused to federal or state-owned natural resources. These claims are to be defined and assessed under regulations which have been issued by the Department of the Interior.[49]

"Natural resources" are those flora, fauna, groundwater, surface water, etc., which are managed by the federal or state governments. At most waste sites, before all is said and done, liable parties can expect EPA to append these claims to the cleanup costs EPA seeks to recover. At some sites, these damage claims have risen to levels on a par or even exceeding the cleanup costs. In fact, at one western site, the natural resource damage claim was for $1.6 billion.

The 1986 CERCLA amendments make few significant changes to the basic liability scheme. They exempt from the definition of "owner or operator," however, a unit of state or local government which acquired ownership involuntarily (through tax delinquencies, abandonments, etc.).[50]

And the 1986 amendments contain a limited defense for owners of facilities who acquire them after all disposal has taken place.[51] Essentially, a "subsequent" owner seeking to avail himself of such a defense must show that after all reasonable efforts consistent with "good commercial practice in an effort to minimize liability," he still did not know "and had no reason to

---

[47] *Dedham Water Co. v. Cumberland Farms Dairy, Inc.*, 889 F.2d 1146 (1st Cir. 1989); *U.S. v. Monsanto Co.*, 858 F.2d 160 (4th Cir. 1988).

[48] *U.S. v. R.W. Meyer, Inc.*, 889 F.2d 1497 (6th Cir. 1989); *U.S. v. Monsanto Co.*, 858 F.2d 160 (4th Cir. 1988).

[49] See 40 C.F.R. §§ 300.72-74.

[50] § 101(20)(d).

[51] § 101(35).

know" that disposal took place on the property.[52] This is commonly referred to as the "innocent landowner" defense.

## 5.2 Private Right of Action for Response Cost Recovery

Although parties A through Z are jointly and severally liable for response costs, EPA generally will not pursue claims against all potentially responsible parties in a CERCLA action. Rather, EPA may pursue only one or a few parties who are most able to pay and/or have the highest volume of waste at site. Recovering a share of response costs from the remaining liable parties (and proving who is responsible for what portion) is left up to the party or parties targeted by EPA.

In addition to the contribution rights discussed in Section 7.2 below, CERCLA establishes a private right of action for this type of response cost recovery in Section 107(a). This section provides that parties may be liable not only for governmental costs, but also for "any other necessary costs of response incurred *by any other person* consistent with the NCP."

What is "consistent with the NCP" has been the subject of a number of conflicting interpretations over the years,[53] but EPA recently included in its 1990 NCP a series of provisions intended to end the confusion.[54] Not surprisingly, cleanups performed in compliance with an EPA order or consent decree under CERCLA will automatically be considered "consistent with the NCP."[55] However, for "voluntary" CERCLA cleanups and cleanups performed pursuant to other authorities (RCRA, state laws), there is no automatic consistency.

For these non-CERCLA decree cleanups, the 1990 NCP makes a procedural/substantive split. A party must achieve "substantial compliance" with the NCP's numerous procedural requirements for its cleanup to be considered consistent. "Immaterial and insubstantial deviations" from the procedural requirements will not make a cleanup inconsistent with the NCP.[56] In terms of substantive requirements, a party must perform a remedial action that is a "CERCLA-quality cleanup" (CQC) in order to achieve NCP consistency.

EPA has stated that to achieve CQC status, a cleanup must meet the following tests:

---

[52] *Id.*

[53] Compare, *General Electric Co. v. Litton Business Systems*, 30 Env't Rep. Cas. (BNA) 1335 (W.D. Mo. 1989), with *Amland Properties Corp. v. Aluminum Company of America*, 711 F. Supp. 784 (D.N.J. 1989).

[54] 40 C.F.R. § 300.700, 55 Fed. Reg. 8858, March 8, 1990.

[55] 40 C.F.R. § 300.700(c)(3)(iii).

[56] 40 C.F.R. § 300.700(c)(4).

a. The cleanup must:
   (i) be protective of human health and the environment,

   (ii) utilize permanent solutions and alternative treatment technologies to the maximum extent practicable, and

   (iii) be cost effective;

b. The cleanup must attain all ARARs; and

c. Meaningful public participation must be provided in the process.[57]

As of this writing, it is too early to tell whether these 1990 NCP provisions on "consistency" will put an end to the extremely inconsistent judicial rulings on the issue. As EPA's definition of CQC is itself highly subjective, one can envision a new round of conflicting judicial opinions on just what this term means.

## 5.3 Effect on Real Estate and Business Transactions

The fact that CERCLA liability can be so all-encompassing and pervasive--coupled with the fact that CERCLA cleanups are becoming incredibly expensive--is dramatically affecting the manner in which companies engage in business and real estate transactions. For instance, assume Company A desires to buy a manufacturing facility located on 300 acres from Company B. Company A knows that if it becomes the owner of the property, it may be liable for any CERCLA cleanups on the property even if the waste disposal creating the problem was all done long ago.

Company A (if it has intelligent management) will accordingly spend a great deal of time and effort learning all it can about the condition of the soil and groundwater and past disposal practices at the facility so it can assess the potential for CERCLA cleanup liabilities. Company A and B might also devote a good deal of effort negotiating over contract terms respecting how any CERCLA liabilities might be allocated.

For another example, assume Company C wants to buy all the stock of Company D, and Company D operates 10 manufacturing facilities. Company C would need a thorough assessment of the property conditions of all 10 facilities, as in the first example. But in this example Company C (if it has intelligent management) will also need a thorough historical assessment of the *off-site* disposal practices of each of the 10 facilities because Company C will be assuming all the "generator" liability of Company D. As each of the 10

---

[57] 55 Fed. Reg. 8793, March 8, 1990.

facilities may have sent waste in the past to 10 different disposal facilities (or more), Company C may inherit generator liability for 100 CERCLA sites (or more) through the transaction.

Such "transaction" issues are bound to be more pervasive in the 1990's. Corporate environmental and legal experts are devoting more and more of their time to such matters.

# 6.0 "SETTLEMENTS" WITH PRIVATE RESPONSIBLE PARTIES

## 6.1 Background

In accomplishing a cleanup (or any phase of a cleanup) EPA may utilize a combination of funding options. EPA may perform remedial work with Superfund dollars, and then sue responsible parties for reimbursement under the "cost recovery" authority of CERCLA Section 107, or EPA may issue an administrative order (or initiate litigation) seeking to compel responsible parties to perform remedial work with their own funds under the "abatement" authority of CERCLA § 106.

Or EPA may seek through negotiations to persuade responsible parties to perform and/or pay for any or all stages of the remedial action at a site. This performance and/or payment would be in discharge of some or all of the parties' potential liabilities under Sections 106 and/or 107 of CERCLA.

EPA's policy has generally been to attempt to seek such "private party settlements" at any site where it appears there are parties willing and able to undertake or pay for such a cleanup. This "settlement" policy is grounded in large part on the fact that there are limitations on EPA's resources to perform cleanups and yet there are a tremendous number of current and future NPL sites. Accordingly, the national cleanup program can be greatly expedited if private parties can clean up some sites with their own management and resources at the same time EPA leads the cleanup at other sites (presumably where there are no financially sound responsible parties or where the parties involved are unable to agree to a cleanup).

At a particular site, different phases of a remedy might be handled by EPA or by the parties. For instance, at one site, EPA may fund and perform the entire remedy from RI/FS work plan through construction, then seek reimbursement through cost recovery. At another site, EPA may perform the RI/FS but the responsible parties may agree to fund and carry out the design and construction. At another, the parties may agree to perform the RI/FS but not the design and construction. At another, the parties may fund and perform the entire remedy. Add to this matrix the "OU" overlap (described in part 3.2.7 above) and the options approach infinity.

In analyzing "settlement" policies for waste sites, it is important to understand that at many sites, hundreds of parties may have contributed to the site problem over a period of years. And sites vary in the degree to which solvent responsible parties can be found. Today's problem sites were generally caused by activities carried on years or even decades ago; records (if they ever existed) can get lost, witnesses can lose their memories or die, and companies can go out of business or go bankrupt. Moreover, at many sites, there may be dozens or hundreds of "solvent" parties who are identified. They may be willing to consider settlements in many different degrees, ranging from "peace at any price" types to "over my dead body" types.

## 6.2 Key Settlement Issues and EPA's Basic Policy

In EPA's implementation of CERCLA before the 1986 amendments, many issues developed regarding the degree to which EPA would enter into "settlements" with parties for site cleanups. EPA's positions on several key issues evolved in three basic stages: (1) in reaction to vicious congressional criticism about the alleged "sell out" nature of some early settlements, an extremely rigid "all or nothing" approach in late 1982 and early 1983 which made multiple party settlements virtually impossible; (2) a "draft memo" dated December 12, 1983 which took a slightly more flexible approach on certain issues; (3) a formally issued "Settlement Policy" in the *Federal Register* on February 5, 1985[58] which took an even more flexible approach.

EPA's "evolution" on the most basic of these issues will first be described. Then Congress' response in the 1986 amendments will be explained.

It is important to note that even after the 1986 CERCLA amendments, the February 5, 1985 "Settlement Policy" is still cited by EPA as being the fundamental source of its current policies. Thus the following discussion--while it may appear "historic"--is very relevant to today's settlement practices.

### 6.2.1 No More 80 Percent Threshold

As a prime manifestation of the "all or nothing" approach, EPA officials had stated they would entertain settlements only for 100 percent of a site's cleanup costs. To illustrate, assume the following: at a site with 100 solvent parties, 5 of them contributed 50 percent of the waste. These five offer to "settle" their liabilities by paying 75 percent of the cleanup costs and leaving it up to EPA to collect the extra 25 percent from the remaining 95 parties. Under the early EPA policy, this offer would be automatically rejected.

By late 1983, EPA modified this policy by stating in a memo that it would at least "consider" settlement offers for less than 100 percent-- but in no event would it entertain offers which accounted for less than 80 percent of a site's cleanup costs.

The 1985 Settlement Policy contained no such arbitrary threshold. Rather, it directed the regional offices to negotiate whenever there is an offer for a "substantial proportion" of the cleanup costs.

### 6.2.2 Use of Superfund Dollars for the "Orphan" Share

At many sites, numerous parties may have contributed wastes over the years. The facts may often reveal that some significant portion of the wastes

---

[58] 50 Fed. Reg. 5034.

is attributable to parties who are now insolvent, unknown, dead, might-as-well-be dead, or otherwise judgment-proof. This portion is known as the "orphan share" of waste at the site.

A long-standing issue has been whether the government would use Superfund dollars to pay for the orphan share when reaching settlements with solvent parties willing to pay their own shares. In 1983, EPA unequivocally stated that it would not allow Superfund dollars to be used in this fashion. The 1985 Settlement Policy stated that Superfund dollars may be used to cover the orphan share.

### 6.2.3. Willingness to Accept *De Minimis* Contributors' Cash-Outs

At many multiple-party sites, some parties may account for extremely small portions of the total waste contributed. For instance, the following scenario is not unusual. There are 400 identified generators at a site. There is a ranking of the volume of waste by each of the 400. In terms of volume of waste contributed, the "top 20" parties contributed 60% in the aggregate, the next 20 contributed 30% in the aggregate, and the next 360 contributed the remaining 10%. None of the 360 contributed more than 1% of the waste to the site.

Parties who find themselves in the last category have often wanted to settle by making an early cash payment to EPA and thereby avoid extensive and costly negotiations and litigation with the EPA or many other parties. EPA has in the past refused to recognize such types of *de minimis* cash-outs. The 1985 Settlement Policy acknowledged this procedure as an option, but hardly encouraged EPA personnel to pursue it.

### 6.2.4 "Releases" from Liability

The degree to which EPA will enter into releases from liability, or "covenants not to sue," with respect to potential future liabilities has been an extremely controversial and difficult issue. On the one hand, EPA recognizes that a more complete release produces a stronger inducement for responsible parties to settle. This is because generally, when a party seeks to settle a matter, it is willing to trade the uncertainties of litigation for payment of a sum certain. Under a system in which a party can consider its "settlement" check only as a down payment to precede unspecified future installments, there will naturally be a reluctance to settle.

On the other hand, EPA may be uncertain whether a particular long-term remedy for a site will perform as predicted. If contrary to expectations, the site is still in need of further cleanup after a remedy is performed, EPA has expressed a wish to keep responsible parties "on the hook" for these costs.

After a great deal of vacillation, EPA finally provided some guidance on this difficult issue in the 1985 Settlement Policy. The most basic position could be summarized as follows: "The better the remedy, the better the release." As the Settlement Policy articulated this general "sliding-scale" approach, "The [EPA] regions will have the flexibility to negotiate releases that are relatively expansive or relatively stringent, depending upon the degree of confidence that the Agency has in the remedy."[59]

The Settlement Policy presents two examples of how EPA might have "confidence." First, with respect to remediation of groundwater contamination, EPA would regard an agreement to meet a "health based performance standard" as preferable to an agreement simply to install and apply a particular treatment technology. Second, a remedy that involved treatment of waste (such as burning in an industrial furnace) would be preferable to a remedy that involved land disposal.[60]

### 6.2.5 Reopeners

Regardless of how "expansive" EPA regions may wish to be in using this sliding-scale approach, the Settlement Policy imposes several significant limitations. For instance, it prescribes that "at a minimum" all settlement agreements must include a "re-opener" clause allowing the government to "modify" the agreement whenever the site conditions may in the future present an "imminent and substantial endangerment" because: (1) previously unknown conditions are discovered, or (2) additional scientific information becomes available about the conditions known at the time of the agreement.[61]

### 6.3 Settlements: The 1986 Amendments

The 1986 amendments add a new section 122 to CERCLA, entitled "Settlements." This section contains rather lengthy and detailed provisions relating to many of the same issues EPA addressed in its 1985 settlement policy.

In general, CERCLA Section 122 gives EPA discretion to enter into settlements under certain circumstances and with certain conditions, but it does not *require* EPA to enter into any type of settlement at any site. In fact, section 122 specifies that EPA's decision not to undertake settlement negotiations at a site is "not subject to judicial review."[62]

With respect to the "80 percent threshold" issue, there is no requirement in § 122 for *any* particular threshold. Presumably, EPA has the authority to enter into agreements with parties representing any portion of the total site cleanup costs. In fact, there is a paragraph entitled "mixed funding" which specifically authorizes EPA to agree to cover "certain [unspecified percentages] costs" of remedial actions responsible parties have agreed to perform.[63]

---

[59] 50 Fed. Reg. at 5039.

[60] *Id.*

[61] 50 Fed. Reg. at 5040.

[62] § 122(a), last sentence.

[63] § 122(a)(1).

By 1988, EPA had begun using this mixed funding authority in several settlements and had shown a willingness to accept less than 100% from the settling parties in several situations. While EPA appears to be nearing a "50% deal" at one east coast site, the general informal rule still seems to be in the range of 80%.

With respect to the "orphan share" issue, nothing in Section 122 (or any other section of CERCLA) precludes EPA from deciding that a certain portion of the site cleanup costs should be covered by Superfund dollars to account for "orphans." In practice, EPA may agree to certain mixed funding settlements which will quite possibly have the effect of the Superfund covering the orphan share. EPA has a great reluctance to concede explicitly, however, that it is doing this.

The 1986 amendments contain a new restriction on responsible party performance of RI/FS work. By way of background, EPA's policy of encouraging private party RI/FS work greatly distressed environmental groups and the State of New Jersey. They argued that this would be akin to a "fox guarding the chicken coop," because--apparently in their view--the parties would assure that a cheap and ineffective remedy would be selected and EPA would be powerless to do anything about it.

In reaction to this criticism, one close-to-final version of the House Bill actually prohibited EPA from allowing responsible parties to perform the RI/FS at a site. The 1986 amendments reflect a compromise on the issue.

Under the compromise, EPA can agree to allow responsible parties to perform an RI/FS, but only where:

(1)   EPA determines that the parties are "qualified" to do so;

(2)   EPA contracts with a "qualified person" to "oversee" and "review" the conduct of the RI/FS; and

(3)   The responsible parties agree to reimburse EPA for the costs of this extra oversight.[64]

The effect of this compromise is that parties who perform an RI/FS now not only pay their own consultants but also pay EPA's consultants to consult with the parties' consultants. At one large western landfill where RI/FS negotiations are underway, current estimates peg the RI/FS consulting costs at about $5 million and the "consultants to the consultants" cost at $2 million.

With respect to the "release" issue, the 1986 amendments specifically authorize EPA to enter into "covenants not to sue" when settling with parties. In one passage, Congress has directed EPA to "be guided by the principle that a more complete covenant not to sue shall be provided for a more permanent

---

[64] § 104(a)(1).

remedy."[65] This is very much like the EPA Settlement Policy's "sliding scale" approach. In addition, Congress has specified "factors" that EPA must consider in deciding whether and to what extent to grant a covenant not to sue.[66] In general, these factors point strongly towards the idea that a more permanent remedy will result in a more complete release.

Similar to EPA's most recent policy statements, Congress has specified that covenants not to sue must generally be subject to "reopeners" for conditions unknown at the time of the agreement.[67] There are four exceptions to this "re-opener" requirement, however:

(1)  In the case of *de minimis* settlements covered by Section 122(g) (discussed below);

(2)  In the case of any other settlement, when warranted by "extraordinary circumstances" after considering numerous factors including "strength of evidence," "ability to pay," "litigative risks," "inequities," and when there are "all reasonable assurances" that health and the environment will be protected in the future;[68]

(3)  Where (a) EPA has rejected a remedial alternative that does not contemplate offsite disposal, and (b) EPA requires offsite disposal, and (c) the offsite disposal facility meets numerous specified requirements of RCRA[69]; or

(4)  Where there is a treatment/destruction remedy which is so complete that there are no longer any "current or currently foreseeable future" risks from the substances treated or the byproducts of such treatment.[70]

Thus far, there have been only a few completed *de minimis* settlements, and the completed ones have generally avoided "reopeners." EPA has not used the

---

[65]  § 122(c)(1).

[66]  § 122(f)(4).

[67]  § 122(f)(6).

[68]  § 122(f).

[69]  § 122(f)(2)(A). This is Congress's response to the "secondary site" release issue discussed above.

[70]  § 122(f)(2)(B).

second or fourth exceptions noted above as of this writing, and has used the third at one New England site.

At many sites EPA has begun utilizing a new "special notice procedure" authorized by Section 122(e) of the 1986 amendments. This is a procedure EPA may (but is under no obligation to) use. If EPA decides to trigger this procedure, it is directed to provide all identified parties, "in advance," with the following information, "to the extent it is available":

(1)   the names and addresses of potentially responsible parties;

(2)   the volume and nature of substances contributed by each potentially responsible party; and

(3)   a "ranking by volume" of the substances at the facility.[71]

This new subsection also allows but does not require EPA to prepare a "nonbinding preliminary allocation of responsibility" (commonly referred to as "NBAR") for the responsible parties' use in trying to allocate cleanup costs among themselves. This NBAR may be based upon any weighing of any factors which EPA may consider relevant, including volume, toxicity, mobility, strength of evidence, ability to pay, litigative risks, and "inequities."[72]

An NBAR at a site (if one is ever done) is really nothing more than an "initial cut" that the parties can accept, use as a "starting point," or totally reject. Congress has made clear that NBARs cannot be admissible in evidence and are non-reviewable in court.[73]   Moreover, they shall "not constitute an apportionment or other statement on the divisibility of harm or causation."[74]

The statute says that EPA can in its discretion reject any offer based upon an NBAR, even if "substantial," and such rejection shall not be judicially reviewable.[75]   Perhaps the only thing that is real about an NBAR is that whenever EPA performs one, EPA will charge the responsible parties for the costs.[76]

Finally, with respect to the *de minimis* issue, § 122(g) provides explicit authority for EPA to allow "buy outs" in certain circumstances.   This new

---

[71]  § 122(e).

[72]  § 122(e)(3)(A).

[73]  § 122(e)(3)(C).

[74]  *Id.*

[75]  § 122(e)(3)(E).

[76]  § 122(e)(3)(D).

subsection says that EPA "shall as promptly as possible reach a final settlement" with a responsible party under certain conditions as follows:

(1) where "practicable and in the public interest, as determined by EPA;"

(2) for non-owners of the facility, where *both* the volume *and* the *toxicity* contributed by the party are "minimal in comparison to other hazardous substances at the facility;"

(3) for site owners, where the owner did not "conduct or permit" the generation or placement of any hazardous substance at the facility *and* did not "contribute" to the release or threat of release "through any act or omission.[77]

## 6.4 Benefits to Responsible Parties of Settling and/or Performing Cleanup Work

It has been very popular for government and industry leaders to make speeches and write papers extolling the great virtues of settlements. There are undeniably many real or potential benefits to responsible parties in entering into such settlements. The most prominent are as follows:

a. When parties do not agree to a settlement, they will most likely be drawn into protracted litigation (either in a Section 106 case to force a cleanup or a Section 107 case for cost recovery). The transaction costs of this litigation can be much higher than the transaction costs of negotiation. (It used to be said, in fact, that litigation transaction costs could exceed the costs of cleaning up the site in question. Congress seems to have taken care of that embarrassment to lawyers, however, by driving cleanup costs sky high in the 1986 amendments.)

b. When a party enters into a settlement, it has (at least temporarily) a relatively ascertainable exposure and can plan (at least temporarily) its future accordingly. If a party chooses to defer the ascertainment of its exposure to the lengthy litigation process, its potential exposure is much more uncertain and could easily be worse. Perhaps unfortunately, under the case law, there are few grounds upon which a party who is clearly linked to a site can hope to "win" in CERCLA litigation.

---

[77] § 122(g).

c. Under certain circumstances, a party choosing to litigate rather than negotiate may find itself subject to treble damages. See CERCLA Section 107(c)(3). Under the 1986 amendments, that party may also be subject to fines of up to $25,000 per day. See CERCLA Section 106(b).

d. Since the responsible parties are probably going to end up paying for the remedial action sooner or later in light of EPA's cost recovery authority, the parties should have an interest in controlling the remedial costs. This control can be best effectuated when the parties are performing their own studies and cleanups.

e. With the red tape of government contracting procedures, it may often cost the government significantly more to perform a project than it would for private industry to perform exactly the same project.

f. Private parties will naturally have the incentive to manage a project carefully when their own money is involved--as contrasted to government project managers who, despite all good intentions, usually cannot be expected to be as cautious with money that is not theirs.

g. Consultants hired by the government have a natural propensity to propose a gold-plated work plan for a gold-plated RI/FS in hopes that the study will lead to the need for more study or that the remedy will be extensive and gold-plated enough to require the consultants' continued services. Private parties, whose own money is directly on the line, can more effectively control consultants' appetites in this regard when the parties are paying and managing the consultants directly.

## 6.5 Disadvantages and Drawbacks

Despite all the popular notions of joining the crowd and feeling groovy with settlements, there may in some situations be definite disadvantages and drawbacks in doing so:

a. Usually the government's "releases" from future liabilities aren't all that great. As there is a thirst in Congress for ever-expanding and costly cleanup remedies, and as sites must be "reviewed" every five years for further action under CERCLA, a settlor definitely cannot rest assured that his "settling" dollars today are the only dollars he will ultimately pay for the site.

b. When parties agree to perform the work, the expectations as to the costs they will pay may receive a severe electric prod of reality before it's all over. When you're doing *study*-type work (RI/FS, design), EPA personnel often show an amazing propensity to review and nit-pick your work in great detail at every minor stage along the way. EPA may require you to re-do things, expand things, go in new directions, etc. At one site in the midwest, this process has resulted in an RI/FS that is now 300% over originally-bid costs, and there are several months of this torture left to go. Similarly, when parties are performing *work*-type work, the contractors' and consultants' original estimates have a way of proving to be quite optimistic.

c. When one is actually performing work, one may be liable or subject to suit for new hazardous waste problems caused by the cleanup work itself.

d. If a certain company gets a reputation as an easy settlor, that company may elevate itself on governmental lists of target parties for future site negotiations, as the government will naturally seek to hit people it believes it can get the best deal from.

e. While parties are likely to face aggregate governmental demands for 100 cents on the dollar (or something very close) for an "upfront" settlement, they may have rational hopes that in ultimate cost recovery litigation EPA would settle for much less. EPA is authorized by CERCLA § 122(h)(1) to settle such cost recovery suits without all the restraints running through the rest of Section 122.

f. Parties might rationally and in good faith believe that certain legal defenses or *bona fide* arguments for equitable allocations that were rejected by EPA or a gang of other settling parties (see Section 6.6 immediately below) might fare much better in the judicial system.

## 6.6 Special Problems for Individual Parties At Multi-Party Sites

At a multi-party site the government will rarely consider a separate settlement with a single party or small group of parties. Rather, the government normally will only entertain a group offer representing all or a substantial portion of the cleanup costs. While one may sympathize with EPA's resource concerns, EPA's policies can produce unfair and unfortunate results for individual parties in certain situations.

Here are two examples. The theme of both is that an individual party acting in totally good faith may have his fate twisted adversely by other parties over whom he has no control.

First, some parties at multi-party sites tend to form gangs. These gangs are often led by those parties with the greatest potential liability and without whom no overall settlement would be possible.

To illustrate the problem, assume members of such a gang sent large volumes of unquestionably hazardous material to a site while an individual party (X) sent large volumes of water mixed with small quantities of other materials. There are substantial reasons to believe in good faith these other materials are neither legally nor actually hazardous.

Even though X believes there is a strong possibility that he would ultimately be held to have no liability at the site, X may be willing to pay $100,000 to settle the matter to avoid future transaction costs and show his good citizenship. In fact, any neutral observer with knowledge of all the facts *and* 30 bishops would all agree that in fairness $100,000 would be extremely generous on X's behalf.

Once a gang decides what is a "fair" allocation formula at a site, however, an individual party's only real choice is either to capitulate or refuse. The gang may ridicule X's $100,000 offer and demand that X pay $800,000.

If X refuses, he is immediately taunted by the gang, accused of "hiding in the weeds," and has a big red "R" (for "Recalcitrant") painted on his forehead. The gang might rough up the Recalcitrant through third-party actions in court and will often mount a slander campaign against the Recalcitrant. Part of the slander campaign will be to put pressure on EPA to impose penalties and/or treble damages on the Recalcitrant.

Second, there may be situations where an individual party who clearly has some significant liability for a site cleanup is unable to settle because of other parties. Assume there are 300 parties at a site including party Y. Y believes (and 30 bishops would agree) that under any equitable allocation, considering all the factors, he should fairly pay 10% of the site cleanup costs. But to show abundant caution and good faith, Y announces he is willing to pay up to 30% of the costs.

Yet for various reasons, the remaining 299 parties cannot agree among themselves on a method to allocate the remaining 70%. In this situation Y--who was willing to pay 3 times his 30-bishop share--cannot obtain a settlement with EPA.

## 6.7 Current EPA Settlement Policies

### 6.7.1 Introduction

It is impossible to describe the up-to-date details of the Federal Government's CERCLA "settlement policies" at any given moment. First, the policies are constantly evolving. When you finally begin to digest one, another one always seems to be coming along.

Second, these "guidance" notices often contain quite general and/or vague directions and leave many interesting questions unanswered. Third--perhaps a logical follow-up from the first and second factors--there is a great deal of diversity within the Federal Government on how to address and resolve many settlement issues. If you posed the same settlement question to four different EPA officials, you might get four different answers.

### 6.7.2 Development of EPA Guidelines under Section 122

Since the enactment of Section 122 in late 1986, EPA has been engaging in the laudable practice of issuing "guidelines" on various settlement issues in the *Federal Register*. It is important to note that EPA continues to maintain that its *basic* settlement policy is contained in its February 1985 Settlement Policy. EPA and DOJ officials continually state that Section 122 is nothing more than a ratification of the EPA 1985 Settlement Policy. And in each of the "guidelines" EPA has issued thus far (see below) EPA still refers to the February 1985 document as its basic "Settlement Policy."

### 6.7.2.1 Guidelines for Preparing Nonbinding Preliminary Allocations of Responsibility (NBARs)

One of the most difficult problems in negotiating CERCLA settlements has been the problem of deciding how numerous responsible parties are to allocate the cleanup costs among themselves. As noted above, there is "joint and several" liability under the statute. EPA's traditional position has been that since each party is therefore liable for 100% of the cleanup costs, EPA simply would not get involved in trying to allocate among various parties. Whenever parties approached EPA and said that they wanted guidance on how to divvy up the costs, EPA would say--in effect--"we want a check for X dollars. We simply don't care how you divide it up and we don't want to get involved."

During the legislative deliberations leading up to the 1986 amendment, there were those who believed that EPA should be required to perform some sort of allocation function. The belief was that if EPA would simply tell all of the parties at a site how much EPA thought they owed, negotiations would proceed much more smoothly and more settlements would be accomplished. EPA fought these proposals viciously, arguing that it should remain up to the parties to decide among themselves how to allocate liability.

The result, as explained above, was the NBAR compromise. EPA has now developed its "NBAR" guidelines and issued them in the *Federal Register*.[78]

The NBAR Guidelines stress that NBAR's "will not be routine."[79] Again, EPA has stressed that its "general policy" is that "PRP's should work out among themselves questions of how much each will pay toward settlement at a site."

The Guidelines reflect a very stingy view of EPA's mixed funding and

---

[78] 52 Fed. Reg. 19919, May 28, 1987.

[79] 52 Fed. Reg. 19919, col. 1.

orphan share opportunities. The NBAR Guidelines state that NBARs will allocate *100 percent* of the costs among PRP's. "The discretion to prepare an NBAR does not change the goal of the February 1985 settlement policy, to achieve 100 percent of cleanup or costs in settlement."[80]

The Guidelines make waste *volume* the primary focus of all the allocation factors,[81] even though CERCLA specifies ten factors (toxicity, inequities, mobility, etc.) and does not specify that volume is to be pre-eminent.[82] A recent federal Court of Appeals decision, however, calls into severe question the appropriateness of using volume as the basis to allocate cleanup costs.[83]

The Guidelines touch also on the extremely difficult issue of allocation among the three basic tiers of parties: generators, transporters, and owner/operators. They provide that "a commercial owner/operator that managed waste badly should receive a higher allocation than a passive, noncommercial landowner." Among successive owners, the Guidelines provide that where all other factors are equal, allocation may be based on the "relative length of time each owned and/or operated the site."

### 6.7.2.2 Guidelines for *De Minimis* Party Settlements[84]

These Guidelines deal with *de minimis* waste contributors and not with *de minimis* landowners. This issue will be dealt with in subsequent guidance. The *De Minimis* Guidelines stress EPA's desire to deal with all *de minimis* parties at a given site in a comprehensive settlement with one settlement agreement.

Apparently, the Guidelines preclude the possibility that a *de minimis* settlement can be achieved if every party at the site would qualify as a *de minimis* contributor. Like the NBAR guidelines, the Guidelines take a stingy approach to the possibility of orphan shares.

The Guidelines strongly discourage *de minimis* settlements with "expansive" covenants not-to-sue unless and until an RI/FS and ROD have been completed at a site.[85] And, like the NBAR guidance mentioned above, the Guidelines focus almost entirely on *volume* as the method of allocation.

---

[80] 52 Fed. Reg. 19919, col. 2.

[81] 52 Fed. Reg. 19920, col. 1.

[82] CERCLA Section 122(e)(3).

[83] *U.S. v. Monsanto*, 858 F.2d 160, 172-173 (4th Cir. 1988).

[84] 52 Fed. Reg. 24333 *et seq.* (June 30, 1987).

[85] 52 Fed. Reg. 24337, col. 1.

### 6.7.2.3 Guidelines on Covenants Not to Sue[86]

The Covenant Guidelines go beyond the 1986 amendments in one important respect. EPA's February 1985 Settlement Policy called for "reopeners" for both (1) subsequent discovery of unknown conditions and (2) development of new information which indicates the cleanup remedy is no longer adequate. The 1986 amendments require only that the first type of reopener be included in covenants not to sue. EPA's Guidelines, however, require that both types be included.[87] EPA has also made clear, however, that additional information will not allow a settled matter to be reopened except in cases where health and the environment would no longer be protected.

The Covenant Guidelines provide that a covenant not to sue can take effect well before completion of all treating and pumping associated with a cleanup remedy. This is significant, as pumping and treating programs often last decades.

### 6.7.2.4 Guidelines on Notice Letters, Negotiations, and Information Exchanges[88]

As discussed above, the 1986 amendments included a new *optional* settlement mode for EPA called the "Special Notice Procedures."[89] Under this procedure, when EPA triggers a negotiation period, there are specific deadlines for offers and acceptances and there is a 120-day moratorium on EPA-performed study and cleanup work (except for emergencies). The purpose of the moratorium is to give potentially settling parties a brief but true opportunity to take control of their own work and be assured that they won't simply take over work EPA has already started.

EPA refers to notices triggering the negotiations and moratorium contemplated by Section 122(e) as "Special Notices." There is another kind of notice under Section 104(a), with which EPA puts parties on notice of their potential liability, but does not trigger any negotiating deadlines or moratoria. EPA refers to these as "general notices."

The February 23, 1988 guidance addresses both "special" and "general" notices; the type of information EPA will generally be willing to release along with each kind of notice; and policies on EPA information requests.

The guidance encourages Regions to release certain information to PRPs "as soon as reasonably possible." Such information includes the names and addresses of other PRPs, the volume and nature of substances contributed by

---

[86] 52 Fed. Reg. 28038 *et seq.* (July 27, 1987).

[87] 52 Fed. Reg. 28038, col. 3.

[88] 53 Fed. Reg. 5298 *et seq.* (February 23, 1988).

[89] § 122(e).

each PRP, and a volumetric ranking of substances at the facility.[90]

Because of the severe time constraints under the "special" notice procedures, the Regions are to issue a general notice letter to PRPs before finally issuing a special notice letter. This is *not* always done in practice, however. General notice letters should "preferably" be sent out as soon as the site has been *proposed* for the NPL. This guidance is most definitely not followed at many sites in practice.

### 6.7.2.5 Guidelines on Mixed Funding.[91]

In its new Mixed Funding Guidance, EPA identifies and explains three separate types of acceptable "mixed funding" scenarios:

(i)     PRPs fund and perform an entire cleanup and EPA agrees to reimburse them for a certain percentage from Superfund dollars;

(ii)    EPA funds and performs an entire cleanup and PRPs pay the agency for a portion of the costs; and

(iii)   EPA funds and performs a part of a response action while PRPs fund and perform another part.

On the "orphan" issue, there is waffling. EPA quotes language from the 1986 amendments Conference Report acknowledging that EPA should be able to use "monies from the Fund on behalf of parties who are unknown, insolvent, similarly unavailable, or refuse to settle." Nevertheless, EPA says it "will not approve mixed funding simply on the basis that a share of wastes at a site may be attributable to an unknown or financially non-viable party."

EPA gives examples of the "best candidates" for mixed funding as follows:

--      The settling PRPs offer a "substantial portion" of the costs. "Substantial" is defined as "predominant," so presumably EPA is talking about a > 50% threshold.

--      The government has a strong case against financially viable non-settling PRPs, from whom the Fund portion may be recovered.

EPA gives examples of "poor candidates" for mixed funding as follows:

---

[90]  *Id.*

[91]  53 Fed. Reg. 8279 *et seq.* (March 14, 1988).

-- The case against the would-be settling parties is strong, and thus the potential for successful litigation is high;

-- The potential Fund portion is "large."

## 7.0 JUDICIAL ISSUES

### 7.1 Judicial Review of Remedies

One long-standing issue has been the appropriate time a court may "judicially review" the selection of a remedy. For instance, EPA may have gone through the RI/FS-ROD process described above and, from options A through E, selected option C (which will cost $100 million).

A group of responsible parties (who will in all likelihood have to pay for the cleanup through EPA's "cost recovery" authority) may believe that EPA should have selected option B which would cost $50 million. An environmental group may believe that EPA should have selected option E which would cost $200 million.

Either group may therefore wish to challenge EPA's remedy in court. And of course, they would want to do so *before* EPA took all the time and spent all the money to complete the remedy, for after that has been done, the practical chances for obtaining meaningful judicial relief would probably evaporate.

EPA has always maintained, however, that courts should not be allowed to review EPA's remedial decisions in separate litigation, but only in connection with cases initiated by EPA to force parties to perform a remedy (under CERCLA Section 106) or to recover costs for the amount it has expended (under CERCLA Section 107). The 1980 CERCLA was silent on this issue, but the courts rather unanimously agreed with EPA's position.

The 1986 amendments now address this issue explicitly, and basically adopt EPA's long-standing position. New Section 113(h) provides that EPA's removal or remedial decisions may be judicially reviewed only at the following times:

(1) in a Section 107 cost recovery or contribution action;

(2) in an action to enforce (or recover penalties under) a Section 106 order;

(3) in an action for "reimbursement" under Section 106(b)(2);

(4) in a "citizens suit" (under new section 310) alleging that a removal or remedy taken was in "violation of the Act," but such an action may not be brought with regard to a removal "where a remedial action is to be undertaken at a site;" and

(5) a lawsuit in which EPA seeks to compel cleanup under Section 106.

### 7.2 Contribution Rights of Liable Parties; Protection for Settlers

As noted earlier, many courts have held that there is "joint and several" liability under CERCLA. Fewer courts have addressed the corollary issue of whether a party sued by EPA may turn around and sue another party (or group of parties) for "contribution." The few courts to address it have generally held that contribution rights exist,[92] and Congress ratified this point in the 1986 amendments.[93]

Congress also addressed and resolved an important dispute over the *timing* of contribution actions and the *effect of settlements* on potential future contribution actions. Before explaining the new statutory provisions, it may be useful to set forth examples to illustrate the import of these issues in a waste site setting.

Assume EPA spends $100 million to clean up a site, and has identified 100 responsible parties at the site. In seeking cost recovery, it decides to sue only five parties with the largest relative volume at the site.

Assuming that these five parties may be "jointly and severally" liable for the $100 million, can they nevertheless seek "contribution" from some or all of the other 95 parties? If so, *when?*

EPA maintained through much of the CERCLA legislative debates that while contribution rights should exist, parties sued by EPA should be *precluded* from joining other parties to the litigation until *after* EPA had concluded its litigation against the few parties it selected for suit. Others maintained that sued parties should have the right to bring in other parties at any time.

Congress resolved this issue in the 1986 amendments by providing that a party may seek contribution from any other party *during or following* EPA's litigation. Congress also made clear that this does not preclude a contribution suit even where no EPA suit has been filed.[94]

Alternatively, assume that at the site in question EPA reached a settlement with 90 of the parties to pay $60 million, with the understanding that EPA would press litigation against the other 10 parties for the remaining $40 million. What if the 10 sued parties (non-settlors) believe that the 90 settlors got "too good a deal," and under any fair scheme, the 10 non-settlors believe they should be liable for no more than $10 million (not $40 million). Could those non-settlors bring the 90 settlors *back in* to the litigation by way of "contribution" claims or any other theories?

Congress resolved this issue in the 1986 amendments by providing that a

---

[92] *E.g., Chemical Waste Management, Inc. v. Armstrong World Industries, Inc.*, 669 F. Supp. 1285 (E.D. Pa. 1987); *Colorado v. Asarco, Inc.*, 608 F. Supp. 1484 (D. Colo. 1985).

[93] § 113(f).

[94] § 113(f)(1).

party who has "resolved its liability" to EPA *or* a State in "an administrative or judicially approved settlement" shall *not* be liable for contribution claims by others for matters addressed in the settlement.[95] This principle is repeated twice (in different contexts) in the "settlement" section of CERCLA.[96]

### 7.3 CERCLA Statute of Limitations

By apparent oversight, the 1980 CERCLA specified no statute of limitations with respect to EPA cost recovery actions. This could cause (and was in fact causing) great consternation in the business community. For instance, what if EPA spent $20 million to clean up a site and a company believes that EPA might seek to recover part or all of those costs against the company. The company has honest and valid reasons for wanting to know how long it must wait to find out for sure whether EPA is going to sue. When 2, 3, or 6 years go by, can the company finally commit funds to capital expansion that it was otherwise reserving for the potential litigation? Or can it finally stop noting the potential liability in its SEC statements?

The 1986 amendments provide answers, although with respect to remedial actions, companies may have a long wait. The amendments basically provide that EPA must bring a cost recovery suit for *removal* actions within 3 years after "completion of the removal."

For *remedial* actions, it should be recalled that EPA may incur costs over a period of several years. In an effort to compromise the interests of (1) providing certainty to parties as to whether suit will *ever* be brought and (2) making the whole process more manageable, Congress provided as follows:

(1) EPA must bring "an initial action" within 6 years after initiation of physical on-site construction;

(2) During this "initial action" courts are to enter declaratory judgments respecting parties' liability for response costs that will be binding on "subsequent" cost recovery claims at the site; and

(3) A "subsequent" action or actions for "further" response costs may be brought "at any time during the response action, but must be commenced no later than 3 years after the date of completion of all response action."[97]

---

[95] § 113(f)(2).

[96] See § 122(g)(5) relating to *de minimis* settlements; § 122(h)(4) relating to cost recovery settlements.

[97] § 113(g)(2).

## 8.0  RELEASE REPORTING AND EMERGENCY RESPONSE

### 8.1  Reporting of Releases

To have a workable system for tracking "releases" so that any necessary responses can be timely, CERCLA has established an elaborate system for reporting. The basic statutory scheme is that under CERCLA § 102, EPA is to establish "reportable quantities" for all hazardous substances.[98]

Under CERCLA § 103, any person in charge of any facility, as soon as he has knowledge of any release (except a "federally permitted" release) of a hazardous substance in excess of the "reportable quantities" established under § 102, must immediately *notify* the National Response Center (NRC) of the release. There are civil and criminal penalties for failure to comply.[99]

EPA's regulations for this release reporting program are contained in 40 C.F.R. part 302. This part contains the lengthy list of hazardous substances in alphabetical order. For each substance, a table indicates the Chemical Abstracts Service Registry Number (CASRN), any common "regulatory synonyms," and the designated "quantity." If a particular substance also happens to be a RCRA listed waste, the table sets forth the appropriate RCRA waste code.[100]

For instance, if a plant was handling bromine cyanide, the appropriate plant personnel could consult the table in part 302 and obtain the following information. For purposes of ascertaining the correctness of the terminology, they would see that the CASRN is 506683 and that the common regulatory synonym is "cyanogen bromide." If they have a RCRA spill of this substance, they can see by cross-referencing that the RCRA waste code is U246.

Most importantly, they can see that the "reportable quantity" for this substance is 1,000 pounds, or 454 kilograms. Thus, if and when 1,000 pounds of this substance are "released" to the "environment" within any 24-hour time period (see part 3.0 above for a discussion of the breadth of these terms), the plant's reporting requirements may be triggered.

The basic notification requirement is set forth in Section 302.6. Whenever a release exceeds the relevant reportable quantity in any 24-hour period, the person in charge of the facility shall immediately notify the National Response Center in Washington, D.C. at (800) 424-8802 (in D.C., call 426-2675).

What if in a 24-hour period, a plant released 1,500 pounds of a *mixture*, 900

---

[98] As noted in Section 2.0, CERCLA § 101(14) broadly defines "hazardous substance" to include hundreds of substances already designated under the CAA, CWA, RCRA, etc. CERCLA § 102(a) also authorizes EPA to designate additional substances as hazardous.

[99] § 103(b).

[100] See 40 C.F.R. § 302.4.

pounds of which were bromine cyanide and 600 pounds of which were a substance which is not on the hazardous substance list? Because the release did not involve bromine cyanide in its "reportable quantity" of 1,000 pounds, the release need not be reported. EPA's regulations specify that releases of "mixtures and solutions" trigger the requirement to notify only where "a component hazardous substance of the mixture or solution is released in a quantity equal to or greater than its reportable quantity."[101]

What if certain solids are released in an amount exceeding the reportable quantity, but particle sizes are large enough to be unlikely to present risks? EPA's regulations address this issue by exempting releases of solid particles of the following metals so long as the "mean diameter" of the particles released is larger than 100 micrometers (00.004 inches): antimony, arsenic, beryllium, cadmium, chromium, copper, lead, nickel, selenium, silver, thallium, and zinc.[102]

### 8.2    Exceptions: Pesticide Products and "Continuous" Releases

As noted in Section 2.6 above, there is no obligation to report "federally permitted" releases. Two additional important exemptions are provided by law. First, CERCLA reporting requirements do not apply to the application of a pesticide product registered under FIFRA or to the handling and storage of such a product by an agricultural producer.[103]

Second, under CERCLA Section 103(f)(2), releases that are "continuous and stable in quantity and rate" do not have to be reported on a per-occurrence basis. Instead, such releases are subject to the "reduced" reporting requirements set forth in new 40 C.F.R. 302.8,[104] which EPA promulgated in 1990.

Section 302.8 requires that the following notices be given in a continuous release situation: (1) an initial telephone notification to the NRC of a facility's intent to report the release as continuous; (2) within 30 days of the telephone notification, a written report to the appropriate EPA Regional Office, establishing the basis for treating the release as continuous and stable in quantity and rate; and (3) a written follow-up (verification) report to the same EPA regional office within 30 days of the first anniversary of filing the initial written report.

After that, the only reporting required is written notification of changes in the source or composition of the release or other changes in the information submitted in the initial report. Facilities must give *immediate* telephone notifications, however, whenever there is any "statistically significant increase"

---

[101] 40 C.F.R. § 302.6(b).

[102] 40 C.F.R. § 302.6(c).

[103] 40 C.F.R. § 302.7(c).

[104] Effective September 24, 1990. See 55 Fed. Reg. 30166, July 24, 1990.

(SSI) in the release (as explained below).

To qualify a hazardous substance release as "continuous," a facility must show that there is a pattern of continuity that is predictable in terms of timing. EPA defines a "continuous" release as one that occurs "without interruption or abatement or that is routine, anticipated, and intermittent during normal operations or treatment processes".[105] In order for a release to qualify as "stable in quantity and rate," it must be shown that the release is predictable and regular in quantity and rate; releases do not need to be uniform in quantity and rate to be considered stable.[106]

Provided that a release is continuous and stable in quantity and rate, federal officials do not have to be notified each time the release occurs to decide whether a response is needed. However, the NRC must be notified by telephone each time there is an SSI. EPA defines an SSI as "any release of a hazardous substance that exceeds the upper bound of the reported normal range."[107] The normal range includes the range of releases occurring over any 24-hour period under normal operating conditions during the preceeding year. EPA considered using statistical tests for determining precisely when an SSI occurs, but opted to use the less cumbersome "normal range" rule-of-thumb, under the assumption that the empirical release data needed to perform such statistical tests is often not available to site managers. EPA believes that the establishment of a normal range of releases provides an acceptable approach to identifying SSIs.[108]

## 8.3 Reportable Quantities

In several rulemaking phases over the last few years, EPA has published reportable quantities. There are currently 724 hazardous substances under CERCLA plus 1500 radionuclides.[109] In a May 24, 1989 rulemaking,[110] EPA established reportable quantities for all radionuclides. On August 14, 1989, EPA published its most recent reportable quantity adjustments,[111] bringing the number of reportable quantities established for hazardous substances to 706. EPA still needs to establish levels for 18. *Warning*: this does *not* mean there

---

[105] 55 Fed. Reg. at 30169.

[106] 55 Fed. Reg. at 30177.

[107] 55 Fed. Reg. at 30177.

[108] 55 Fed. Reg. 30178.

[109] 40 C.F.R. § 302.4.

[110] 54 Fed. Reg. 22538.

[111] 54 Fed. Reg. 33418.

are no reporting requirements for these 18 substances. By operation of CERCLA Section 102(b), there is a statutorily-imposed reportable quantity of *one pound* until EPA takes regulatory action on a particular substance.

### 8.4 Emergency Response

There may be many old sites which will never make it to the NPL and for which, if any response is necessary, a (relatively) inexpensive "removal" will suffice to protect health and the environment. Moreover, there may be current "releases" from existing facilities which may warrant a "removal." There is actually very little in CERCLA to restrain EPA's discretion in dealing with these non-NPL removal situations. Compared to the complex detail of new § 121 explained above, EPA is simply directed to take such actions as may be "necessary to protect the public health or welfare or the environment."[112]

One significant restriction in the 1980 CERCLA to these "non-remedial" responses, however, was that EPA could not spend more than $1,000,000 or continue a response for more than six months unless there was a true "emergency" situation. The 1986 amendments have raised these numbers to $2,000,000 and 12 months, respectively.[113]

### 9.0 FACILITATION OF TOXIC TORT SUITS

Each time Congress has addressed CERCLA authorization or reauthorization, there have been massive proposals put forward for "Victims Compensation" schemes. These proposals have taken the form of administrative claims mechanisms and/or a new federal "cause of action" in tort. The main thrust behind these proposals has been to make it easier for people who claim they have been made sick (or will become sick), or have otherwise allegedly been adversely affected by hazardous substances, to recover damages. The main assumption behind these proposals is that the current state tort law system is inadequate to provide this recovery.

In the 1980 CERCLA, all victims compensation proposals were defeated. CERCLA has, however, indirectly assisted in the development of toxic tort suits.

For every NPL site, as described in section 4.0 above, EPA develops a tremendous amount of information through the RI/FS-ROD process and through identification of responsible parties. This is usually public information or may easily become public through judicial discovery and/or the Freedom of Information Act.

This information can be extremely helpful to plaintiffs' attorneys in finding out who put what waste at a site in what volumes and what the site

---

[112] § 104(a)(1).

[113] § 104(c)(1).

conditions are. From this information, which might otherwise have taken years to develop, they can simply file their complaints. Many toxic tort suits being filed today are really "tag-ons" to the work EPA is doing at CERCLA sites.

In the 1986 amendments, virtually all "victims compensation" proposals were again defeated. This time, however, there is one new "statute of limitations" provision which is likely to promote more toxic tort suits in a direct manner; and there are major new data-gathering provisions which appear designed to promote more toxic tort suits in an indirect manner.

One common complaint about the tort system is that some states have "date of exposure" rules in their statutes of limitations. For instance, if the law said that all tort claims must be filed no later than three years from the date of exposure, practically all claims for cancer and genetic defects could be barred because such adverse effects may not even manifest themselves for 15 to 20 years after exposure. (Actually very few states still have such restrictive statutes.)

Congress took care of this problem with a bang in the 1986 amendments, and enacted (if constitutional) a new nationally applicable statute of limitations for toxic torts which goes well beyond even what most "modern" state laws provide.

Section 203 of the amendments adds a new § 309 to CERCLA. This new Section 309 applies to all personal injury or property damage tort suits related to alleged exposure to hazardous substances (or even "pollutants or contaminants").

It requires that a state statute of limitations for such actions can not begin to run until "the date the plaintiff knew (or reasonably should have known)" that the injury/damages "were caused or contributed to" by certain hazardous substances or pollutants or contaminants. This new statute of limitations could extend the period for filing suits for a particular alleged injury *indefinitely*, as science and environmental politics may always develop over the years to provide new theories on which to base allegations.

Moreover, the 1986 CERCLA amendments provide a continuous mother-lode of free data and information for plaintiffs' attorneys. Section 110 of the amendments adds dozens of new requirements to existing CERCLA § 104(i) (which was originally designed to find out what sort of links could be made between waste sites and disease but which was never aggressively implemented).

This new information includes not only detailed generic data about many substances commonly found at waste sites, including each substance's potential health effects, but also site-specific "health assessments" at each facility on the NPL. Thus, while the current CERCLA materially assists plaintiffs in developing their case as to which parties to name and what type of exposure might be created, the new CERCLA will materially assist plaintiffs in building the toxicological/scientific portions of their cases.

## 10.0 FUNDING

The 1980 CERCLA was designed to derive 1.6 billion over five years from special industry taxes (87.5 percent) and general revenues (12.5 percent). The special industry taxes were largely on the petrochemical industry, with a combination of a tax on crude oil and on certain organic and inorganic chemical "feedstocks."

The 1986 amendments are designed to raise $9 billion over five years from the following sources[114]:

| Source | Billions $ |
|---|---|
| Domestic crude oil | 1.250 |
| Imported crude oil | 1.500 |
| Chemical "feedstocks" | 1.400 |
| "Environmental tax | 2.500 |
| General revenues | 1.250 |
| Interest and cost recovery | .600 |
| Fuel tax (for UST program) | .500 |
| | 9.000 |

The "environmental tax" listed above represents a major victory for the petrochemical industry, which has campaigned for years to "spread the base" of Superfund taxes. The argument has been that at most CERCLA waste sites, all basic manufacturing is well-represented on the list of responsible parties (auto, aircraft, electronics, etc.). This tax, while too complicated to explain here, applies to a broad segment of large American manufacturing corporations.

Although the Superfund program had been on the agenda for legislative reauthorization in 1991, Congress recently extended the taxing authority under the program "without modification" through December, 1995.[115] The extension was passed due to a widespread concern that Superfund would run out of money before Congress could complete a full-blown reauthorization. Having given itself this breathing room, Congress will probably make no significant changes to the Superfund program for another three years.

---

[114] SARA Title V.

[115] Pub. L. No. 101-508, November 5, 1990.

Chapter 14


AIR POLLUTION CONTROL

Russell V. Randle & Mary Elizabeth Bosco
Partners
Patton, Boggs & Blow

## 1.0 INTRODUCTION

The federal Clean Air Act was enacted in 1970, heavily amended in 1977, and overhauled and greatly expanded in 1990.[1] The law was radical when passed and has remained continuously controversial since. The 1970 statute federalized air pollution control regulation, made health protection the basis for much of that regulation, made clear that automotive and other industries would have to close or to meet then-technically infeasible emission standards, and created a pervasive and expensive regulatory system. The 1977 amendments added special provisions for areas with air cleaner than national standards, the Prevention of the Significant Deterioration (PSD) in Subtitle C of Title I. The 1977 amendments also added the nonattainment provisions of Subtitle D, addressing areas which had failed to meet deadlines to achieve national ambient air quality standards (NAAQSs).

The 1990 amendments built on this foundation, adding comprehensive provisions to regulate emissions of toxic air pollutants (section 112), acid rain (Title IV), and substances thought to threaten the ozone layer (Title VI). Additionally, the 1990 amendments added an elaborate permit program (Title V), and greatly strengthened enforcement provisions (section 113) and requirements for nonattainment areas, mobile source emissions, and automotive fuels.

The act largely prevented air pollution problems from getting worse than in the early 1970s, a substantial and little-noted achievement. But EPA's program prior to the 1990 amendments failed to bring large areas of the country, including most of the nation's large cities, into compliance with basic health standards, in part because of lack of political will, in part because for

---

[1] The 1990 amendments have not been codified at this writing. The pre-1990 version was codified at 42 U.S.C. §§ 7401-7626. The 1970 version of the Act was Pub. L. No. 91-604; the 1977 amendments were Pub. L. No. 95-95. Congress had enacted prior air pollution control legislation in 1963, 1965, and 1967, legislation which was modest in scope and quite limited in effect.

some areas the problems of nonattainment are insoluble in the time frames set by Congress in the 1970 and 1977 versions of the act. Similarly, EPA's program failed to address emissions of toxic air pollutants and widespread acid rain problems in a systematic and coherent fashion.

The 1990 amendments seek to address these difficult problems by making drastic revisions to the act, and by adding numerous additional titles and programs to it. The resulting statute and programs it mandates rival the tax code in complexity. These programs are estimated to cost American industry and consumers in excess of $25 billion per year in addition to current environmental expenditures. There are few, if any, sectors of the economy which will not be affected by the amendments and new programs required by them. Congress has now armed EPA with very broad authority to carry out the act's purposes and programs. Whether those programs will actually improve air quality and do so at a reasonable cost remains to be seen. Implementation of these new programs will be much of EPA's work for the 1990s and on into the 21st century.

## 2.0 OVERVIEW

Understanding the Clean Air Act is more akin to interpreting a geological formation than to an exercise in abstract logic. The 1970 act had three titles: Title I dealt with stationary sources, e.g. factories, Title II dealt with mobile sources such as cars and airplanes, and Title III set forth definitions, provided for citizens suits, and set standards for judicial review. The 1977 amendments kept this structure while rewriting portions of Titles II and III. The amendments to Title I, governing stationary sources, were the most extensive, and to those unfamiliar with the act before the amendments, nearly impenetrable.

The 1990 amendments overhauled the nonattainment provisions in subtitle D of Title I, created an elaborate new technology-based control program for toxic air pollutants in a rewritten section 112, added a new Title IV to address acid precipitation and the powerplant emissions thought to be the primary source of it, replaced the prior atmospheric protection provisions in Subtitle B of Title I with a new Title VI mandating the phase-out of chlorofluorocarbons (CFCs) thought to threaten the ozone layer, and greatly strengthened enforcement powers by rewriting section 113.

Most of this chapter will focus on stationary source requirements. The key regulatory distinctions made among stationary sources are these:

-- is the source new (or modified) or is it an existing source? In general, more stringent requirements are imposed on new or modified sources.
-- is the source located in an area with air quality better than national standards require (a PSD area) or worse (nonattainment area)?

As a result of regulatory evolution, almost every stationary source faces (or may soon face) emission standards based in part on the capabilities of emission control technology (technology-based standards) and in part based on ambient air quality in the area.

In order to make these distinctions clear, this chapter is laid out as follows:

-- section 3 explains the process by which EPA sets National Ambient Air Quality Standards (NAAQS);

-- section 4 explains the State Implementation Plan (SIP) process through which the states (subject to EPA approval) require existing stationary sources to reduce emissions in order for the state to comply with NAAQS;

-- section 5 explains the New Source Performance Standard (NSPS) provisions. These are federally-formulated, technology-based emission standards for new or modified stationary sources in various industry categories, as well as special requirements for solid waste combustion;

-- section 6 explains the Prevention of Significant Deterioration (PSD) program, which imposes technology-based requirements more stringent than NSPS and air quality-based emission limitations more stringent than NAAQS on new or modified sources locating in areas where air is of better quality than NAAQS require;

-- section 7 explains the nonattainment area program as it applies to new or modified stationary sources located in areas where air is worse than NAAQS require. This program imposes technology-based standards more stringent than NSPS as well as additional air quality requirements referred to as offsets. The program also requires existing sources to use Reasonably Available Control Technology (RACT). These requirements became far more stringent as a result of the 1990 amendments;

-- section 8 reviews the section 112 program for National Emission Standards for Hazardous Air Pollutants (NESHAPs) which imposes stringent technology-based standards on both new and existing stationary sources emitting any of 189 listed air pollutants, or categories of pollutants;

-- section 9 addresses Title IV's acid precipitation provisions, and the requirements they impose on fossil-fuel fired powerplants;

-- section 10 addresses Title V's new permit program for stationary sources and the obligations it imposes on sources and states;

-- section 11 addresses Title II's mobile source and fuels provisions, drastically revamped by the 1990 amendments;

-- section 12 addresses Title VI, a new title requiring the curtailment and eventual phase-out of certain chlorfluorocarbons (CFCs) and other substances thought to threaten the ozone layer;

-- section 13 addresses enforcement, and the many new tools and powers granted EPA as a result of the 1990 amendments. Section 13 also addresses citizen suits, EPA's information-gathering authority, and judicial review of EPA's rules.

# 3.0 ESTABLISHMENT OF AIR QUALITY STANDARDS

## 3.1 Air Quality Criteria

Section 108 of the act requires that EPA publish and periodically revise a list of pollutants which it determines "may reasonably be anticipated to endanger" public health or welfare, and which are emitted from numerous or diverse stationary or mobile sources. Such "listing" of a pollutant sets in motion the process for establishing ambient air quality standards for it.[2] EPA must compile and publish a criteria document for each pollutant before setting an air quality standard for it. The criteria are scientific compendia of all available studies documenting the health effects of that pollutant at various concentrations in the ambient air.

## 3.2 National Ambient Air Quality Standards

Section 109 of the act requires EPA to establish National Ambient Air Quality Standards (NAAQS) for each pollutant covered by a criteria document under Section 108. The agency must establish a primary and secondary NAAQS for each criteria pollutant. The "primary" NAAQS for a pollutant must specify the level of air quality that, based on the criteria "and allowing an adequate margin of safety," will protect the public health.[3] The secondary NAAQS must specify the level of air quality that protects the public welfare from any known or anticipated adverse effects associated with the presence of that pollutant in the ambient air.[4] Secondary NAAQS have had very little effect as they are most frequently set at the same level as primary standards.[5]

---

[2] EPA considers the initial decision to list a pollutant to be discretionary. However, flexibility was diminished by the court decision in *NRDC v. Train*, 411 F.Supp. 864, (S.D.N.Y.), aff'd 545 F.2d 320 (2d Cir. 1976) which required the administration to list lead as a pollutant once he had conceded that it met the two substantive tests quoted above.

[3] CAA § 109(b)(1).

[4] CAA § 109(b)(2).

[5] Theoretically, secondary standards should have dealt with problems such as acid rain and ozone damage to crops, which they have demonstrably failed to do. The act expansively defines the components of public welfare

(continued...)

Two points concerning the primary standards are important. First, the language and history of the act make it clear that the standards are to be set at levels which protect not only the normal healthy majority of the population, but even especially sensitive persons with pre-existing illnesses or conditions that pollution might exacerbate, although not cause, as long as these people belong to an identifiable subgroup of the population (such as infants or heart disease patients). The second, and perhaps more significant point, is that the primary NAAQS are to be established using health protection as the sole test. Cost, technical feasibility or any factor other than public health cannot be considered in setting the standards.[6]

There are currently NAAQSs for sulfur dioxide ($SO_2$), particulate matter smaller than 10 microns in size (PM10), carbon monoxide (CO), ozone ($O_3$), nitrogen oxides (NOx), and lead (Pb).[7] Most of these standards were adopted in 1971. The lead standard was added in 1978 as a result of a court order; the ozone rule was relaxed by 50% in 1979 as a result of enormous political pressure and a weak data base.[8] The particulate standard has been changed from one measuring total suspended particulates (TSP) to one measuring particulates ten microns in size or smaller (PM10). The PM10 standard was

---

[5](..continued)
that must be considered in setting the secondary standard. Section 302(h) requires such standards to protect against harm to "soil, water, crops, vegetation, man-made materials, animals, wildlife, weather, visibility, and climate, damage to and deterioration of property, and hazards to transportation, as well as effects on economic values and on personal comfort and well-being." In short, secondary standards must protect against any type of adverse effect, even if it could not be scientifically shown to affect man's physiological well-being in any medical sense.

[6] *NRDC v. EPA*, 902 F.2d 962, 973 (D.C. Cir. 1990); *American Petroleum Institute v. Costle*, 665 F.2d 1176 (D.C. Cir.), *cert denied*, 455 U.S. 1034 (1981); *Lead Industries Ass'n, Inc. v. EPA*, 647 F.2d 1 (D.C. Cir. 1980), *cert denied*, 449 U.S. 1042 (1981).

[7] 40 C.F.R. Part 50.

[8] As part of its efforts to control ozone, EPA adopted a NAAQS for hydrocarbons (HC) in 1971. Hydrocarbons are a precursor of ozone, but not necessarily harmful in themselves. EPA revoked the HC NAAQS in 1983, 48 Fed. Reg. 628 (Jan. 5, 1983), but these substances, now usually referred to as Volatile Organic Compounds (VOCs) remain strictly regulated under many state implementation plans (SIPs).

adopted in 1987,[9] but earlier TSP standards will remain in force until new emission limitations are formulated to replace the old TSP limitations. A PM10 limitation had been debated in EPA for a decade or more before it was adopted, even though there was widespread agreement early in the process than fine particulates posed the greatest hazard, passing through the body's natural defenses and penetrating deep into the lungs. The slow pace of this change suggests the complexity of decisions about NAAQS and the enormous stakes -- health and financial -- that turn upon such decisions. These stakes are increased by the nonattainment provisions of Subtitle D, which make the level of additional effort required depend in large part upon the numerical concentrations of pollutants detected in a nonattainment area. Changes in the underlying ambient air quality standard will now probably be made even more slowly, because of the large consequences resulting from changes.

Section 109(d) requires review of all NAAQS for their adequacy every five years. EPA has so far elected, despite these lengthy reviews and some disturbing new health effects studies, not to change any of the NOx, ozone, or $SO_2$ standards. Environmentalists have challenged, so far unsuccessfully, EPA's decision not to revise the $SO_2$ standards or the averaging time used to determine compliance.[10] Averaging times are critical to compliance monitoring and determining the stringency of standards: for statistical reasons related to process variability a standard measured on a three-hour basis is more stringent than one measured over a longer time, if the concentration is identical in both the three-hour and longer standards.

The NAAQS establish ceilings for individual pollutant concentrations that should not be exceeded anywhere in the United States. They, therefore, determine the degree of control that will be imposed on existing sources and the restrictions on location of new sources, depending on whether air quality is better or worse than the NAAQS in the particular area where the source is or will be located.

Despite their critical importance to the scheme of the Clean Air Act, NAAQSs are not directly enforceable. They are the controlling force behind the development and implementation of emission limitations and other controls pursuant to other sections of the statute. It is those requirements that are actually enforced against polluters, rather than the NAAQS itself.

---

[9] This standard was upheld in *NRDC v. EPA*, 902 F.2d 962 (D.C. Cir. 1990).

[10] *Environmental Defense Fund v. EPA*, 845 F.2d 1088 (D.C. Cir. 1988) (EPA must reconsider $SO_2$ standard and state its decision, but Court will not set standard); *Natural Resources Defense Council v. EPA*, 870 F.2d 892 (2nd Cir. 1989) (change in averaging times upheld on procedural grounds).

## 3.3 Air Quality Control Regions

Section 107 of the act requires that the country be divided into air quality control regions (AQCRs), interstate or intrastate areas which because of common meteorological, industrial and socioeconomic factors, should be treated as a single unit for air pollution control purposes. EPA and its predecessor agency have designated 247 such regions.[11] The purpose of these hybrid interstate or intrastate AQCRs is to help coordinate control efforts across jurisdictional lines.

The 1977 amendments in section 107(d) reduced the significance of AQCRs by requiring the states to identify, and EPA to designate formally, areas of the country which meet NAAQS, do not meet NAAQS, or for which there are insufficient data. It did not require this effort to be geared to the AQCRs, and county boundaries have now become the accustomed accounting unit instead. This reduction in the size of areas designated as nonattainment tempers the impact of nonattainment area sanctions when compared with use of larger AQCRs for this purpose.

The 1990 amendments expanded the geographic scope of many ozone nonattainment areas to include the entire standard metropolitan statistical area (SMSA) or consolidated metropolitan statistical area (CMSA), not just single counties. This change will become especially important if nonattainment area sanctions should be applied, as many more sources may be affected.

As explained below in the nonattainment and PSD sections, classification of an area as attainment or nonattainment for a pollutant very largely determines what actions the state and EPA must take to regulate air pollution from existing and new emission sources.

## 4.0 STATE IMPLEMENTATION PLANS (SIPs)

### 4.1 SIP Content

The primary regulatory mechanism for stationary source emissions is the state implementation plan or SIP provided for in section 110. The SIP is the mechanism through which emission controls are imposed by the states on stationary sources in order to meet NAAQSs. Where a state fails to devise a SIP adequate to meet NAAQSs, section 110 makes clear that EPA is to impose such emission limitations and take other necessary steps. Under section 110 and 179 as amended in 1990, EPA must take action to impose a Federal Implementation Plan (FIP) within two years after the date a state should have done so if the state fails to act, or submits an inadequate SIP. Sanctions are also required, including the cutoff of federal highway money and the imposition of more stringent standards for new or modified sources in these areas.

The states now have SIPs, and almost all states have had them since 1972. The 1990 amendments require many changes in current SIPs, and set detailed

---

[11] 40 C.F.R. Part 81.

schedules for making, reviewing, and approving these changes. The timing of these changes depends very largely on the nonattainment provisions discussed below, with different revisions due at different dates. EPA must determine whether the submissions are complete within 60 days of submission, and act to approve, disapprove, or partially approve the SIP within one year of the completeness determination.[12] EPA approval of a state plan makes its provisions enforceable by the federal government, the state, and by citizen suit.[13]

Under the 1990 amendments, section 110(a)(2) has been revised to require that an acceptable SIP contain detailed provisions addressing the following:

(a) enforceable emission limitations and control measures;

(b) monitoring devices and their operation;

(c) enforcement of emission limits and monitoring requirements, as well as review of new and modified sources for compliance with new source performance standards (NSPS), prevention of significant deterioration (PSD), and nonattainment area requirements;

(d) avoidance of interference with other states attainment with air quality standards and PSD requirements;

(e) a demonstration of adequate state legal authority to operate and enforce the program, adequate resources, and sufficient personnel;

(f) requirements for adequate operations & maintenance (O&M), periodic emission reporting by sources, and periodic compliance reporting by sources;

(g) emergency authority similar to that granted EPA under section 303 of the Clean Air Act;

(h) compliance with nonattainment provisions of the act;

(i) compliance with PSD provisions of the act;

(j) a permit program for major stationary sources, including requirements that permit fees be paid.

---

[12] EPA's minimum requirements for approvable state plans are set forth in 40 C.F.R. Part 51.

[13] See 40 C.F.R. Part 52.

These plan requirements are to adopted by the states after adequate notice to the public and opportunity to comment upon the revised plans. As discussed below, the most important change is the requirement that all major stationary sources obtain permits and pay permit fees.

The act originally required that the SIP attain the primary standards "as expeditiously as practicable," but in no event later than three years from the date of plan approval, with the possibility of a single two year extension under § 110(e). The 1990 amendments greatly extended attainment dates for nonattainment areas. Under Subtitle D, the nonattainment provisions, these dates now depend on the pollutant involved and the amount the area's pollution exceeds numerical standards.

The Clean Air Act, then as now, requires SIPs to provide for attainment of the secondary standards within a "reasonable time." The term "reasonable time" is not defined in the act and states can consider technological and economic problems in deciding on an appropriate date for achievement.[14]

Although the provisions of Section 110 in the 1970 act were relatively simple and straightforward, the development and adoption of effective emission controls involved complex technical, economic and political decisions, and many states failed to submit SIPs that could be approved in their entirety. Beyond that, a large number of plans failed to achieve the NAAQS for one or more pollutants in some regions of the state. Congress has now dramatically revised the nonattainment provisions to address these issues in detail. The nonattainment provisions are discussed separately below.

### 4.2 Role of Technology and Economics

Industry challenges to the first SIPs raised the question whether EPA, in determining whether to approve a state SIP, must consider the technological and economic feasibility of the measures in the plan. EPA took the position that this choice had been left to the states by Congress and that EPA's only job was to determine whether the states had provided an adequate measure of air pollution control. Moreover, the statutory requirement that primary NAAQS be achieved within three years overrode any considerations based on cost or availability of technology; sources could always be shut down. Section 116 gave a state the right to adopt any requirements it wanted even if it had more stringent requirements than necessary to achieve the NAAQS. Consequently, if the plan when properly enforced would result in achievement of the NAAQSs, EPA would approve it regardless of any misgivings it might have regarding the technological or economic feasibility of the particular

---

[14] EPA by regulation indicated that, where controls were reasonably available, a "reasonable time" for achievement of the secondary standards for sulfur oxides and particulates would be three years, unless the state could show that good cause exists for choosing a later date. 40 C.F.R. 51.13(b)(1) and (2).

approach chosen by the state. EPA, however, conceded the possibility of a limited review of such issues in federal enforcement actions.

The Supreme Court ultimately upheld EPA.[15] The Court read the act to necessitate a review of each state-submitted SIP only to determine whether it meets the requirements explicit in Section 110, i.e., that it include specific measures and ensure the attainment and maintenance of the NAAQS. The opinion noted that challenges concerning technological and economic feasibility could be made at the state level through administrative and judicial channels, and suggested that a source might obtain some review on its particular feasibility problems should the SIP be enforced against it in federal district court. The Court chose specifically not to decide what consideration EPA must give to technological or economic feasibility when it itself promulgates SIP measures.

The Court recognized in *Union Electric* that Congress had chosen a deliberate strategy of "technology-forcing" in the Clean Air Act: a policy of forcing emitters to invent and install the necessary control technology or to close. This policy has been highly controversial but did help force development of workable sulfur oxide control technology -- "scrubbers" -- for the electric power industry,[16] technology which may be the foundation for acid rain control efforts over the next several decades.

EPA has encouraged states to choose the most cost-effective means to meet emission requirements by the use of "emissions trading."[17] That policy, also called the "bubble" policy, allows a source which is subject to several SIP emission limits at the same facility to achieve different reductions at various emission points (higher than required in some cases and lower than required in others) as long as the total emissions from the plant are no higher than they would have been if the facility met all of the requirements originally imposed. In other words, the entire plant is treated as if encased in a "bubble," with only the total emissions from the "bubble" as a whole considered important. As discussed below, EPA has encouraged analogous approaches to implementing the "new source review" provisions of the 1977 Clean Air Act amendments. The 1990 amendments impose many new requirements on emissions trading, especially in nonattainment areas.

### 4.3 Use of Dispersion Techniques and Intermittent Control Systems

One of the major debates under the 1970 act concerned whether SIPs might rely on techniques other than continuous emission reduction to

---

[15] *Union Electric Company v. EPA*, 427 U.S. 246 (1976).

[16] Note, *Forcing Technology: The Clean Air Act Experience*, 88 Yale L.J. 1713, 1722-30 (1979).

[17] 51 FR 43814 (Dec. 4, 1986).

demonstrate attainment of the NAAQS. To some extent, any air quality management program relies upon the natural dispersion capacities of the meteorology and topography of the area being managed. However, many sources, particularly isolated facilities, proposed to go beyond that inevitable reliance by monitoring meteorological conditions and curtailing operations and emissions intermittently, as needed to meet the NAAQS without relying on technology or other means of achieving continuous emission control. A related approach was to rely upon tall stacks to disperse emissions.

The courts uniformly held that dispersion dependent techniques such as intermittent control systems and tall stacks are impermissible to attain NAAQS under section 110 of the act unless all available constant emission controls are first applied.[18]

Congress ratified these decisions in 1977 by adding section 123 to the act, generally forbidding intermittent control systems or dispersion techniques.[19] Sources are entitled to have their emission limitations calculated on the basis of the lower of actual stack height or the "Good Engineering Practice" stack height -- most often 2 1/2 times the height of the source.

EPA regulations implementing section 123 have been reviewed twice by the Court of Appeals, which largely upheld the revised regulations early in 1988.[20] The regulations, put simply, allow sources to calculate emission limitations under SIPs using stack heights 65 meters high or 2 1/2 times building height, whichever is higher, and in special circumstances to use a greater height where based on a complex air quality modeling demonstration.[21] Although most aspects of the substantive regulations were upheld, the court struck down EPA's "grandfathering" of many plants from section 123's requirements, a decision which potentially could require many power plants' emission limitations to be recalculated and tightened. Many of the affected powerplants will now

---

[18] *Natural Resources Defense Council v. Train*, 489 F.2d 390, (5th Cir. 1974), *reversed in part on other grounds*, 421 U.S. 60 (1975); *Big Rivers Electric Cooperative v. Train*, 523 F.2d 16, 20-22 (6th Cir. 1975), *cert. denied*, 425 U.S. 934 (1976); *Kennecott Copper Corp. v. Train*, 526 F.2d 1149 (9th Cir. 1975), *cert. denied*, 425 U.S. 935 (1976); *Kennecott Copper Corp. v. Costle*, 572 F.2d 1349 (9th Cir. 1978).

[19] Two limited exceptions were made, one for nonferrous smelters meeting the special requirements of section 119 for extension until 1987, and the other for fuel-burning sources ordered to burn coal in strictly limited cases.

[20] *Natural Resources Defense Council v. EPA*, 838 F.2d 1224 (D.C. Cir. 1988); *Sierra Club v. EPA*, 719 F.2d 436 (D.C. Cir. 1983), *cert. denied*, 468 U.S. 1204 (1984).

[21] 40 C.F.R. § 51.

have to cut back emissions under the acid rain control program under Title IV,[22] discussed below.

## 4.4 Transportation Control Plans

It was clear to Congress in 1970 that the standards for automobile related pollutants (HC, CO, oxidants, and $NO_2$) could not be met everywhere on schedule by the use of conventional control approaches. It therefore required SIPs to include such "transportation controls" as were needed to achieve the standards on schedule.

The courts eventually required EPA to implement these provisions, and the agency began promulgating Transportation Control Plans (TCPs) in late 1973 at the onset of the first serious energy crisis. TCPs included the following types of measures; exclusive bus and bicycle lanes; bridge tolls; area-wide computer systems to identify and bring together potential car-poolers; surcharges on parking spaces in urban areas to force people for economic reasons to look for alternative means of transportation; state inspection and maintenance systems; requirements that older cars be retrofitted with devices to reduce emissions; requirements for improvements of mass transit systems; and finally, where achievement of the standards could not be reliably predicted, gas rationing to whatever extent necessary to reduce vehicle miles traveled in the problem areas.[23]

The TCPs created enormous controversy, and it soon became clear that the states and the general public were not ready to support such pervasive measures. Congress reacted to the public mood and, in connection with energy legislation,[24] adopted provisions of law that deferred any EPA regulations regarding parking management. It also revoked EPA's authority to impose

---

[22] These stack height controversies may continue in any acid rain control program. Some environmentalists contend that raising stacks above about 200 feet enhances the long-range transport of sulfur and nitrogen oxides and promotes formation of acid rain. At least one set of commentators has suggested lowering stacks as a possible way to deal with acid rain, although section 123 as currently written may not permit that strategy. *See* Ackerman & Hassler, *Beyond the New Deal: Coal and the Clean Air Act*, 89 Yale L.J. 1466, 1531, 1534 (1980); *See* Randle & Smith, *Comment on Beyond the New Deal*, 90 Yale L.J. 1398, 1410 (1981) for a critique of this suggestion.

[23] A good example of a comprehensive TCP is the one first proposed for Boston, 38 FR 30960, 8 November 1973. This plan contains virtually every measure which EPA believed feasible to reduce car use. Other TCPs contained these types of measures plus gas rationing.

[24] The "Energy Supply and Environmental Coordination Act of 1974," Pub.L.No. 93-319, 22 June 1974.

parking surcharges. Since that time, EPA has not stressed any air pollution control measures that would affect the free use of automobiles.

The 1990 amendments amend section 108(f) to list a variety of transportation control measures which will be required in the worst nonattainment areas for ozone and carbon monoxide. These measures, however, are to be imposed after many other efforts are exhausted, reflecting the political sensitivity of such controls.

### 4.5 Variances

Historically, the grant of a variance was the chief regulatory means by which states postponed the requirement that a source comply with applicable requirements.

EPA took the position that such a variance could be approved as a simple revision to the implementation plan as long as it would not interfere with timely attainment of the NAAQS. If interference with the standards was shown the source had to proceed under section 110(f) of the act, which involved a lengthy formal hearing process.

The Natural Resources Defense Council challenged this approach, claiming that *all* variances to regulations included in a SIP required approval under section 110(f). After seven United States courts of appeals arrived at three different views on the legality of EPA's interpretation, the Supreme Court heard the case and decided for EPA.[25]

Major noncomplying sources that cannot meet this test for a SIP revision and cannot meet the standards are handled through enforcement actions, either federal actions under section 113 of the act or by the states. The 1977 and 1990 amendments place significant restraints on EPA's administrative handling of non-complying sources. EPA's preferred approach to the problem is to seek a federal court order, either litigated or on consent, which provides the source with the time it actually needs for compliance but exacts penalties -- often substantial penalties--for the noncompliance. Courts have assessed substantial penalties for failure to meet compliance schedules set forth in consent decrees.[26]

With adoption of the permit program in Title V of the 1990 amendments, most changes in source requirements will be addressed through that permit program rather than the SIP revision process. That change will probably make it far easier to make appropriate source-by-source adjustments.

---

[25] *Train v. NRDC,* 421 U.S. 60 (1975).

[26] *United States v. Borden, Inc.,* No. 83-357 (W.D.N.Y. March 11, 1987) (assessing $545,000 penalty).

## 5.0  NEW SOURCE PERFORMANCE STANDARDS (NSPSs)

The Clean Air Act requires states to develop a program for new or modified stationary sources of emissions[27] to assure that the nationally applicable, technology-based emission limitations developed for new or modified sources are enforced.  Prior to approval of such state programs, EPA enforces such limitations.

Section 111 authorizes the administrator to identify those sources which "...contribute significantly to air pollution which causes or contributes to the endangerment of the public health or welfare."  He is then to set emission standards applicable to new sources of the types identified, as well as to modifications of existing sources of that type.  The standards must reflect the "degree of emission reduction achievable" through the best technology the administrator determines has been "adequately demonstrated," considering costs and "nonair quality health and environmental imparts and energy requirements."

The NSPS apply to any new facility or modification of an existing facility that commences construction after the date of *proposal* of the NSPS.  As originally conceived, the NSPS provision had two purposes.  First, it reflected the congressional view that new plants should bear a special control burden because they had the greatest flexibility to incorporate the latest, most effective pollution control technology.  Second, it expressed a policy of requiring the same degree of control on all technologically similar new sources, regardless of where they were located, thereby preventing some states from adopting more lenient air pollution requirements than other states and creating "pollution havens" as a means of attracting industry.  The NSPS were also said to conserve air resources for future growth.

With the development of the programs to prevent significant deterioration and for nonattainment areas, the purposes of NSPS have changed substantially.  In many cases, NSPS may be only a point of departure for determining BACT or LAER for a new source -- although NSPS will always apply a ceiling on emissions in those determinations.

EPA is required to list all major stationary source categories for which NSPS had not been established and then set NSPS for those categories.  As of January 1991, EPA has adopted NSPS for 65 source categories.  For those categories which EPA had identified as needing NSPS to be set, but for which EPA has not yet done so, EPA is to complete rulemaking for all such categories in six years, according to a schedule added to section 111(f) by the 1990 amendments.  The 1990 amendments also require NSPSs to be reviewed on a eight year schedule to be established by EPA, and revised if appropriate.  Detailed review is mandatory if EPA determines that emission limitations and

---

[27] § 111(c).

percentage reductions better than those required by the NSPS are now achieved in practice.[28]

The most controversial amendment to Section 111 in the 1977 amendments required EPA to set NSPS for fossil-fuel burning sources, such as electric utility plants, that would require the standard to include a percentage reduction requirement as well as an absolute emission level.[29] This provision was repealed by the 1990 amendments which may again allow low sulfur coal again to be used as a compliance strategy.[30] This repeal resulted from the adoption of the acid rain provisions in Title IV, which will impose stringent and widespread limitations on sulfur dioxide emissions from both existing and new powerplants.

Section 111 includes authority for EPA to set NSPS as design, equipment, work practice or operational standards where numerical emission limitations would be infeasible. EPA must allow alternative control methods if they are equally effective, and must revise the NSPS to numerical limits if it becomes feasible to do so.

### 5.1 Municipal Incinerators and Other Special Sources

A little-noticed but potentially important part of Section 111 is subsection (d), which requires the states to regulate emissions from *existing* sources in any source category for which EPA sets an NSPS for new and modified sources. This requirement applies only to pollutants not covered by NAAQS or by air toxics requirements under section 112. So far the pollutants addressed include sulfuric acid mist and fluorides. Most states which have such sources have developed standards for those pollutants under control technology guidelines established by EPA. EPA must approve each state's standards or establish its own substitute standards -- an approach patterned on the SIPs. To date, the industry categories affected by this program have been phosphate fertilizer, aluminum reduction, sulfuric acid, and kraft pulp mills.

Prior to enactment of the 1990 amendments, EPA proposed controversial standards for new and existing municipal incinerators under section 111(d), in order to address the rapid increase in the number of incinerators expected in the next decade. These proposed standards include requirements for

---

[28] § 111(b)(1)(B).

[29] This provision effectively required flue gas desulfurization (scrubbers) or other technology to be installed in all cases, and forbade compliance simply by the use of untreated low sulfur fuels as in the past. The requirement was intended to discourage sources from switching to low-sulfur Western coals from high-sulfur Eastern and Midwestern coals and made use of the high-sulfur coal desirable.

[30] § 111(a)(1). Revised regulations are due in November 1993, to assure that emissions do not increase from the affected plants.

separation of certain waste streams from municipal garbage, effectively imposing recycling requirements on many municipalities for the first time. Some waste streams, e.g. batteries, are the source of toxic air pollutants such as nickel, cadmium, and mercury in the emissions from municipal incinerators. At this writing, the controversy over these proposed standards, especially the imposition of recycling requirements under the Clean Air Act, has not been resolved.

In the 1990 amendments, Congress added section 129 to the act specifically to address emissions from solid waste combustion, both municipal and industrial. This provision is a hybrid between section 111 NSPS requirements and section 112 toxic air pollutant requirements. By November 1991, EPA is to promulgate standards for new and existing solid waste incineration units, including municipal solid waste (MSW) units, burning 250 or more tons of waste per day.[31] These standards are to be set pursuant to section 111, including 111(d), as well as the new requirements of section 129. This rulemaking is to build on the current EPA proposal, as long as it is modified to take into account the changes in section 129. Standards must also be promulgated for smaller MSW and medical waste incinerators in November 1992; commercial and industrial waste incinerator standards are due in November 1994.

Congress has specified the pollutants to be controlled by these new standards: total and fine particulate matter, sulfur dioxide, hydrogen chloride, nitrogen oxides, carbon monoxide, lead, cadmium, mercury, dioxins and dibenzofurans.[32] The language imposing emission standards is a blend between sections 111 and 112:

> [Emission standards] shall reflect the maximum degree of reduction of emissions of [listed] air pollutants . . . taking into consideration the cost of achieving such emission reduction, and any non-air quality health and environmental impacts and energy requirements, determine[d to be] achievable for new or existing units in each category.[33]

Emission standards for new units must be at least as stringent as that achieved by the best similar controlled unit; emission standards for existing units must be at least as stringent as the best performing 12% of existing units, or the best five existing units if the source category has fewer than thirty units in it.

Section 129(a)(3) expressly allows EPA to include "methods and technologies for removal or destruction of pollutants before, during or after

---

[31] § 129(a)(1)(A)-(D). These provisions set the schedule discussed above.

[32] § 129(a)(4).

[33] § 129(a)(2).

combustion," language which appears to ratify recycling requirements as part of these standards. Additionally, siting requirements are required as part of these standards in order to reduce health and environmental risks. These siting standards may be redundant with PSD requirements, however, at least for units burning more than fifty tons per day.[34]

Section 129(d) imposes operator training requirements on incinerators, requiring EPA to develop a training program by November 1992, and making it unlawful to operate without certified operators after November 15, 1993. The operating conditions at incinerators can make a very large difference to emissions. This mandatory training requirement is quite unusual in the Clean Air Act. Another variation from normal practice is making the permit term last up to twelve years, instead of the usual five.[35] Permit conditions, however, are to be reviewed every five years.

## 6.0 PREVENTION OF SIGNIFICANT DETERIORATION (PSD)

### 6.1 Evolution

The 1970 Clean Air Act contained no special measures to protect air quality that was *cleaner* than the national standards required, and EPA originally took the position that it had no authority to require such measures. The Sierra Club had challenged that determination, arguing that the statement of purpose in section 101(b) indicated the act was to "protect and enhance" the quality of the nation's air resources, a statement that required measures to protect the air in pristine areas. The legislative history of the 1970 act contained statements by Administration officials to the effect that such language already imposed a "nondegradation" policy, a position EPA repudiated in 1972. In litigation which reached the Supreme Court, the Sierra Club won its case when the Court divided 4 to 4.[36] This had the effect of affirming the lower court decisions, holding not only that EPA had such authority but also was required to issue implementing regulations.

Because neither the Supreme Court nor Court of Appeals issued opinions, and because the District Court issued a short opinion in an emergency context, EPA had very little guidance about the required contents of its nondegradation

---

[34] Section 169(1) is modified to reduce the threshold for PSD review to municipal incinerators capable of charging more than 50 tons per day.

[35] § 129(e).

[36] In *Sierra Club v. Ruckelshaus*, 344 F. Supp. 253 (D.D.C. 1972), *affirmed sub nom. Fri v. Sierra Club*, 412 U.S. 541 (1973), the District Court enjoined EPA from approving portions of state implementation plans that did not provide for prevention of any significant deterioration of air quality in those regions that have air cleaner than the secondary ambient air quality standards.

policy. The Agency elected to use a zoning approach, which proved a wise political decision. These regulations allowed state and local governments to determine what degradation would be "significant" in terms of local conditions. They provided for three types of areas with certain "increments" of additional pollution allowed in each. Class I areas had increments of permissible deterioration so low as to effectively preclude any substantial growth. The increments for Class II areas were designed to allow moderate, well-controlled growth. (All areas in the country were initially classified as Class II.) The Class III areas allowed additional pollution up to the secondary standard. The only pollutants covered by the regulations were $SO_2$ and particulate matter. The court of appeals upheld the regulations.[37]

The 1977 amendments built on this approach but substantially modified it. The basic concepts of PSD are two: (1) all new or modified sources larger than certain thresholds must use best available control technology (BACT) which is at least as stringent as NSPS requirements for the source category; and (2) such new or modified sources undergo a rigorous air quality review designed to meet tightened air quality standards. EPA promulgated elaborate regulations which were upheld in large part in 1979.[38] EPA promulgated revised regulations in August 1980, which have been the subject of litigation and settlement talks since. It is unclear when, if ever, this controversy over the PSD regulations will be concluded, though a number of changes to the regulations have been promulgated as a result of the settlement talks.

## 6.2 Best Available Control Technology Requirements

The PSD program is administered primarily through review of new sources and modifications to existing sources. Each state implementation plan must have provisions that require review of such sources. Where they do not, EPA administers a permit system, established in 40 C.F.R. Section 52.21. A source must undergo new source review if it falls in one of 28 specifically designated industrial categories and has the "potential to emit" more than 100 tons per year of any pollutant regulated by the Clean Air Act, not just $SO_2$ or particulates. (The amount is 250 tons of sources outside the twenty-eight specific categories.) "Potential to emit" means the maximum design capacity of the source after application of pollution controls.[39] For a modification to undergo review, it must be modification of an existing major stationary source

---

[37] *Sierra Club v. EPA,* 540 F.2d 1114 (D.C. Cir. 1976), *cert. denied,* 430 U.S. 959 (1977).

[38] *Alabama Power Co. v. Costle,* 636 F.2d 323 (D.C. Cir. 1979); *Citizens to Save Spencer County v. EPA,* 600 F.2d 844 (D.C. Cir. 1979).

[39] EPA is revising this definition as a result of the decision in *Wisconsin Electric Power Co. v. EPA,* 893 F.2d 901 (7th Cir. 1990).

which creates a "significant net increase," as defined by EPA, in emissions of a pollutant regulated under the Clean Air Act.

In determining the "source" to which the regulations apply, EPA will examine the largest grouping of pollutant-emitting activities located on contiguous or adjacent properties which are under the control of the same person and within the same *SIC* code major group.[40] The definition of source is important because new source review applies only to a net increase in emissions from the source. If emissions can be reduced at other locations within the source to levels below 100 tons, new source review may be avoided. Thus, the larger the number of emitting activities which constitute the source, the greater the possibilities for avoiding review.

One requirement a source must meet in order to obtain a PSD permit is to show that it will use "Best Available Control Technology" or BACT to reduce emissions for each pollutant emitted by the source which is regulated under the Clean Air Act. Section 169(3) defines BACT as the

> maximum degree of [emission] reduction ... which the permitting authority, on a case-by-case basis, taking into account energy, environmental, and economic impacts and other costs, determines is achievable for such facility ....

These BACT limitations must be at least as stringent as those required by applicable requirements for NSPS or NESHAPs (discussed in section 8.0 below.) Because of the slow pace of NSPS revision, the BACT provision gives EPA or the state the ability to tighten emission control requirements by incorporating more recent control technology developments. As some NSPS requirements have not been revised since the early 1970s, this authority may result in significantly more stringent emission control requirements than NSPSs alone would require. In recent years, EPA has tightened BACT standards further by its so-called "top-down" policy. Under this policy, EPA routinely proposes the best control technology for a new or modified source, obliterating the distinction between BACT and Lowest Achievable Emissions Rate (LAER) under the nonattainment provisions.

### 6.3 PSD Increments and Air Quality Requirements

The PSD provisions contain elaborate air quality requirements in addition to those imposed by the need to comply with NAAQSs. The stringency of these air quality requirements is determined by the zoning classification of the area in which the new or modified source is located.

An air quality "increment" is a numerically defined amount of air quality degradation, a fraction of the NAAQS. Section 163 statutorily defines the increments for particulate matter and $SO_2$ in micrograms per cubic meter for

---

[40] 40 C.F.R. § 52.21(b)(6).

various time frames.[41] The statute sets forth separate increments for Class I, II, and III areas. EPA, as required by court order, added annual $NO_2$ increments,[42] and as a result of a subsequent court order must consider adding short term $NO_2$ increments,[43] an unusual result because there is no short-term NAAQS for $NO_2$.

The 1977 amendments used EPA's three-class zoning system, but tightened applicable increments significantly. Section 162 defines all national parks and national wilderness areas above a certain size (5,000 - 6,000 acres depending on the type of park) as Class I areas which cannot be redesignated.[44] The increments applicable to Class I areas are quite small, and may restrict the location of large power plants or other industrial facilities close to such Class I areas.

Section 162(b) designates the rest of the United States as Class II, for which the increments are larger than Class I. The intent of the Class II increments is, as with EPA's Class II areas, to permit moderate well-controlled growth.

The PSD provisions include a Class III designation which has the most expansive increments, increments which are still lower than NAAQS. The intent of Class III was to allow states, if they desired, to promote vigorous industrial development. Elaborate procedures are set forth for states or Indian tribes to redesignate areas to different Classes. To date, however, no state or Indian tribe has chosen to redesignate any area as Class III. Certain federal lands cannot be redesignated as Class III areas.

A new source seeking a PSD permit must demonstrate not only that it will use BACT and not violate any NAAQS, but also that its emissions will not result in air quality degradation greater than the amount of increment available. This demonstration is expensive and time consuming because the applicant must present one year of continuous air quality monitoring data, and base its demonstrations on that data.[45]

---

[41] EPA is now authorized by § 166(f), as added by the 1990 amendments, to substitute PM10 increments for the prior statutory TSP increments in sections 163(b) and 165(d).

[42] 53 Fed. Reg. 40656 (Oct. 17, 1988).

[43] *Environmental Defense Fund v. EPA,* 898 F.2d 183 (D.C. Cir. 1990).

[44] Sections 162(a) and 164(a) were changed by the 1990 amendments to provide that changes in the boundaries of Class I areas, e.g. national parks, subsequent to the 1977 amendments are to be reflected in the boundaries of these areas for PSD purposes.

[45] § 166(e).

The increment is measured from a baseline concentration which is determined as part of the process of reviewing the first PSD permit for an area. (Section 169(4) defines baseline concentration.) An applicant's installation may not exceed the amount of increment left in the area in which it is locating at the time the PSD application is submitted. There is no assurance, however, that any applicant will be allowed by the permitting authority to consume the entire amount of the remaining increment.

Public hearings are required to be held on permit applications. In addition to the quantitative analysis required to show how much of the applicable increment is consumed, the applicant must also submit information about: (1) the air quality effects projected for the area as a result of growth associated with the facility, (2) effects on vegetation, and (3) effects on visibility.

It should be evident from this discussion that the PSD program effectively tightens the air quality standards faced by major stationary sources of particulates, sulfur dioxide, and now nitrogen oxides. Section 166(a) requires EPA to adopt increments or other measures for hydrocarbons, carbon monoxide, and ozone, and to have done so by August 1979. Judging by the experience with nitrogen oxides, EPA may be forced to adopt some increment program for these pollutants, as well as lead, even though there is serious question whether such a program would work for these other parameters.

### 6.4 Visibility Protection

Congress in 1977 also set in motion, under section 169A, a program designed for "the prevention of any future, and the remedying of any existing, impairment of visibility" in Class I areas from man-made air pollution. The inclusion of the section in the Clean Air Act is somewhat anomalous, for if the secondary air quality standards and the PSD program really did the job they are theoretically supposed to do, there would be no need for such a provision. In addition, only very limited regulatory steps are required under this provision. EPA is now in the process of taking at least some of those limited steps in response to a court order.

The 1990 amendments added section 169B, requiring, among other things, that a Visibility Transport Commission be established to address impairment of visibility in the Grand Canyon area,[46] and providing that such commissions may be established elsewhere to address impairment of visibility in Class I areas. EPA must act on Commission recommendations within nine months and require appropriate SIP revisions to address visibility problems.

### 7.0 NONATTAINMENT AREAS

The act provides that new or modified sources located in areas where air is worse than NAAQS require -- "nonattainment areas" -- must meet special technology-based and air quality based requirements in addition to NSPSs.

---

[46] § 169B(f).

These requirements are referred to as Lowest Achievable Emission Rate (LAER) and offsets, and are to be imposed through a permit program, required since the 1977 amendments. Also under the 1977 amendments, existing stationary sources in nonattainment areas must use "reasonably available control technology." The 1990 amendments greatly strengthened the RACT requirements and the offset obligations, and made the threshold for the application of these LAER and RACT requirements far smaller than EPA had under the 1977 amendments.

The 1990 amendments completely overhauled the nonattainment area provisions, but built on the concepts which had been developed by EPA under the 1977 amendments, specifically the offset policy, the LAER concept, and application of sanctions to nonattainment areas which fail to meet statutory goals. The deadlines for attainment were made specific to the pollutants involved, and in the case of ozone, carbon monoxide, and particulate matter, also dependent on the severity of the nonattainment problem. Thus in the Los Angeles area, for example, the deadline for attainment with the ozone standard has now been extended until the year 2010. This is the longest extension under the amendments, and the only one for twenty years.

By adopting these graduated deadlines, based on the severity of the nonattainment problem in a particular area, Congress has sought to recognize the different degrees of difficulty different regions face in meeting the act's standards. The tradeoff for these longer deadlines are increasingly severe requirements imposed on stationary and mobile sources in the nonattainment areas with the longest deadlines, and obligations to make reasonable further progress, expressed in terms of numerical reductions in emissions.

### 7.1 Evolution of Nonattainment Area Provisions, LAER and Offsets

Section 110(a)(2)(D) as enacted in 1970 required SIPs to include a program for preconstruction review of new or modified stationary sources to ensure that such sources would not interfere with attainment or maintenance of NAAQS. After the date for achievement of the ambient standards under the original 1970 statute passed, it became difficult to justify allowing construction of any new facilities in light of this mandate; any new facility emitting a pollutant for which NAAQS were violated would obviously "interfere" with attainment. To prevent a "no growth" situation in such areas, EPA issued its "offset ruling" in late 1976, interpreting this section to allow growth under certain conditions.

The primary condition imposed on the construction of a new source was that a reduction in emissions (an offset) be obtained from existing sources, whether owned by the applicant or not, which would not otherwise have occurred and which would provide a more than one-for-one counterbalance to the emissions from the new or modified facility. The offset policy also required the source to install the Best Available Control Technology (BACT), and to certify that other sources of air pollution under common ownership in the same state also met applicable legal requirements.

The 1977 amendments adopted the EPA offset policy (with some changes) as a starting point, until states adopted revised SIP provisions incorporating a preconstruction review program as set forth in Section 172. The program required by section 172 for nonattainment areas required permits for all new or modified "sources" with the potential (design capacity after application of emission controls) to emit one hundred tons or more per year of the non-attainment pollutant were precursors of the nonattainment pollutant. A source was "modified" if its emissions increased by more than a specified de minimis amount. EPA eventually defined "source" under the nonattainment area provisions the same way it does under the PSD provision, to include the entire plant, not just individual pieces of equipment, a definition the Supreme Court upheld in *Chevron Inc. v. NRDC.*[47]

The 1990 amendments made the source definition depend in part on the type of nonattainment area in which the source was located. The worse the nonattainment problem, the lower the tonnage threshold at which a source is to be considered major for the purposes of LAER requirements and offsets. In the "extreme" nonattainment areas, the threshold is ten tons, not 100 as under prior law.

A source or modification classified as "major" for new source review purposes must undergo procedural review designed to determine its compati-bility with NAAQS attainment. These sources must be controlled to a level reflecting the Lowest Achievable Emission Rate (LAER), which is a defined term meaning the most stringent emission standard in any SIP (unless it is shown to be unachievable) or the lowest emissions any source in the same category has achieved in practice. Moreover, a new source cannot receive a permit unless other sources owned or operated by the applicant in the state are meeting all applicable emission limits or at least meeting all compliance schedule steps. Finally, the new or modified source must provide "offsets" to its emissions.

As explained below in connection with the different types of nonattainment areas, offset requirements will force new and modified sources to reduce emissions by more than one to one ratio with new emissions. The worse the nonattainment area, the greater the offset required.[48] Moreover, emission reductions required by the Clean Air Act and its implementing regulations cannot be used for offset purposes; offsets are to be granted only for efforts

---

[47] 467 U.S. 837 (1984).

[48] Additionally, § 173(b) as revised by the 1990 amendments forbids the practice of offsetting new emissions against a "growth allowance" provided under a SIP for areas which are in nonattainment status and have SIPs which are no longer approved. This change may raise questions about so-called "banked" emission credits, whereby a source shuts down emissions in one year and reserves the right to emit or sell such emission rights in later years.

going beyond that required for compliance.[49] In some circumstances, "internal" offsets, i.e. offsets within the same source or group of commonly controlled sources are permitted. Likewise, in limited circumstances, offsets with upwind nonattainment areas may be used.[50]

## 7.2 Classification of Nonattainment Areas

The 1990 amendments will require EPA and the states to review the attainment status of all areas of the country, and to decide how each nonattainment area should be classified for regulatory purposes. The amendments to section 107 set forth the detailed process by which this review and reclassification is to occur. They also impose conditions on moving from nonattainment status to attainment, conditions intended to keep areas which may not stay in attainment from moving into that status without assurances that acceptable air quality will be maintained.

By operation of law, current nonattainment designations remain in force until changed by EPA.[51] EPA cannot change a nonattainment designation to the unclassifiable category under the 1990 amendments either.[52] Instead, in order to change the classification of a nonattainment area to attainment, EPA must determine not only that air quality in the area meets NAAQS, but also that the state has a fully approved SIP, that the improvements in air quality result from permanent and enforceable emission reductions, and that an air quality maintenance plan is in place under section 175A as added by the 1990 amendments.[53] A maintenance plan must assure attainment for ten years. Until it is approved by EPA, the area remains in nonattainment status.

For ozone and carbon monoxide, states must submit lists by March 15, 1991 of the attainment and nonattainment status of the areas in their boundaries.[54] EPA must promulgate the list of nonattainment areas by July 15, 1991, making changes it deems appropriate. The boundaries of ozone and carbon monoxide nonattainment areas are extended to include the entire standard (or consolidated) metropolitan statistical area (SMSA or CSMA) affected, if the nonattainment problem is classified as "serious," "severe," or "extreme," the three most stringent nonattainment area designations.

---

[49] § 173(c)(2).

[50] § 172(c)(1)

[51] § 107(d)(1)(C).

[52] § 107(d)(3)(F).

[53] § 107(d)(3)(E).

[54] §107(d)(4)(A).

For particulate matter, where the NAAQS had changed in 1987 from one addressing total suspended particulates (TSP) to particulate matter smaller than 10 microns in size (PM10), the statute takes a different approach.[55] At the time EPA had issued the PM10 standard, it split air quality control regions into different Groups areas, depending on EPA's estimate of the severity of the PM10 problem. Under the 1990 amendments, areas EPA had classified as having a high likelihood of violating the PM10 standard (Group I areas) are now classified as nonattainment for the PM10 standard. So are areas for which violations had been measured before 1989. All other areas are initially classified as attainment for PM10.

Area designations and redesignations are not subject to judicial review until final action is taken by EPA on SIP revisions.[56] In general, nonattainment areas have five years from designation in which to comply, which is extendable by EPA by up to five more years.[57] This time may be further extended twice, each time for a year, where there is an approved SIP, and the exceedances have been minimal. These general requirements are largely superseded, however, by the pollutant-specific time frames now included by the 1990 amendments. The general requirements will be important if additional NAAQSs are promulgated, or revised.

## 7.3 Pollutant-Specific Nonattainment Area Requirements

The 1990 amendments set forth nonattainment requirements based in part upon the pollutant involved, and in part upon the degree by which the NAAQS is exceeded by that pollutant. These requirements become more stringent the more intractable the nonattainment problem. Usually, each more stringent level includes the measures required of the step below it, and adds additional requirements for the area in exchange for more time for the area to comply.

For each of the nonattainment steps, there are separate definitions of source, definitions under which the threshold grows smaller as the nonattainment problems worsen. Likewise, offset ratios become more stringent as problems worsen, and additional restrictions on offsets are imposed. Where automobiles are a source of the nonattainment problem, as is the case for ozone and carbon monoxide, Inspection and Maintenance (I&M) requirements become more stringent, and special requirements are imposed for the use of clean fuels and the reduction of vehicle traffic.

---

[55] § 107(d)(4)(B).

[56] § 172(a)(1)(C).

[57] § 172(a)(2).

### 7.3.1 Ozone Nonattainment Requirements

The 1990 amendments added the most detailed nonattainment area requirements for ozone, which affects over 100 nonattainment areas.[58] Ozone is a problem resulting in large part from emissions of volatile organic compounds from cars and trucks, from industrial operations such as painting, coating, and degreasing, from some natural sources, and from handling petroleum. Ozone is also thought to result in part from nitrogen oxide (NOx) emissions. Consequently, the ozone nonattainment provisions focus in part on stationary sources, and in part on vehicle requirements.

Section 181(a) classifies ozone nonattainment areas based on the "design value" ozone levels, those calculated by EPA based on monitoring data. These levels and the appropriate classifications are:

| | |
|---|---|
| .121 to .138 parts per million (ppm) | **Marginal,** with a compliance date of November 1993; |
| .138 to .160 ppm | **Moderate,** with a compliance date of November 1996; |
| .160 to .180 ppm | **Serious,** with a compliance date of November 1999; |
| .180 to .189 ppm | **Severe (I),** with a compliance date of November 2005; |
| .190 to .280 ppm | **Severe (II),** with a compliance date of November 2007; and |
| .280 and up | **Extreme,** with a compliance date of November 2010. |

At the time of initial classification under the 1990 amendments, and for 90 days thereafter, EPA has the discretion to vary the design value by plus or minus five percent.[59] This revision in design value is to be based on the number of exceedances, the amount of transport of ozone from other areas, and the mix of sources and pollutants in that area. Though EPA's decision may be discretionary and unreviewable by the courts, that discretion may be sorely tested because of the substantial and expensive differences that a change in classification can make to a nonattainment area.

If a nonattainment area fails to meet the deadline by one exceedance in the prior year, and if the state has met its commitments under the SIP for that nonattainment area, then EPA may grant a one year extension in the

---

[58] Subpart 2, Subtitle D, §§ 181-185B.

[59] § 181(a)(4). Section 185A provides that for areas which have had no violations from January 1987 to December 1989, the applicability of the Subpart 2 ozone nonattainment provisions is suspended for a year in order to determine if the so-called "transitional" area comes into compliance.

attainment date.[60]   That one year extension may be extended by one additional year if the same conditions, i.e. one exceedance, are met.

If a nonattainment area fails to meet the deadline by more than six months, and does not qualify for the one year extension, then the area is moved either to the next higher classification, or, if monitoring data are worse than the values addressed by the next level, to whatever higher level is appropriate.[61]

Marginal areas are those for which design values are between the NAAQS (.120 ppm) for ozone and .138 ppm.   These are the most common nonattainment areas, are thought to be closest to having their air quality problems solved, have the shortest deadlines and the least burdensome requirements.  There are thought to be 41 marginal nonattainment areas.[62]

States including marginal nonattainment areas in their boundaries must submit SIP revisions requiring that:

(1) existing sources must use Reasonably Available Control Technology as defined by EPA's control technology guidelines (CTGs) in effect in November 1990.[63] This requirement legislates EPA's guidance documents as substantive standards for existing sources of VOC emissions.  This SIP revision is due six months after EPA classifies the area, so that if deadlines are met, submission should be made in January 1992.

(2) vehicle inspection and maintenance (I&M) programs must be continued.[64] These programs are to be updated with new EPA guidance, and by November 1992, states must submit SIP revisions upgrading I&M programs in accord with EPA guidance.

---

[60] § 181(a)(5).

[61] § 181(b)(2).  For severe areas, there are special restrictions which apply, but they are not moved to the extreme category.

[62] Figures concerning the number of nonattainment areas are taken from H.R. Rep. No. 490, Part 1, 101st Cong., 2d Sess. 230-231 (1990).  These in turn are based on EPA data for the three year period 1986-88.  Thus some changes based on 1989 data may change the number of nonattainment areas in each ozone classification.  EPA's exercise of judgment concerning design values may also change these figures.

[63] § 182(a)(2)(A).

[64] § 182(a)(2)(B).

(3) the permit program for major and modified sources of VOCs must be upgraded in accord with EPA guidance, and appropriate SIP revisions submitted by November 1992.[65]

Several requirements are imposed which will have an important effect on offset requirements. First, the offset ratio for marginal nonattainment areas is to be *at least* 1.1 to 1.0 for volatile organic compounds.[66] States must also submit a "comprehensive, accurate, [and] current inventory of actual emissions from all sources" for the nonattainment area.[67] This inventory is to be updated every three years until the area is redesignated as an attainment area.[68] The SIP is also to be revised to require annual emissions reports by sources of VOCs and nitrogen oxides; the first such statement will be due in November 1993.[69] This emission inventory requirement seems innocuous but is important because of the variety of state practice and poor data on such sources currently available. Permits have sometimes been used for the inventory, but permits are usually for maximum rather than actual operating conditions. Offset arrangements which traded paper emission reductions, e.g. reduction in maximum emissions, for real emission increases, will become much harder to make once the inventory requirement is in place.

Moderate nonattainment areas are those with ozone design values of .138 to .160. There are thought to be 38 moderate ozone nonattainment areas. The compliance date is November 1996. These areas must implement the same measures as those required of marginal nonattainment areas. However, states with moderate nonattainment areas must also submit SIP revisions requiring the following:

(1) a cut in the baseline emissions inventory of fifteen percent by November 1996. These reductions must be made in both VOC and NOx

---

[65] § 182(a)(2)(C).

[66] § 182(a)(7).

[67] § 181(a)(1).

[68] § 182(a)(3)(A).

[69] § 182(a)(3)(B). The state may waive this requirement for sources emitting less than 25 tons per year of these pollutants. Nitrogen oxides are included because they too can be a precursor of ozone, although the chemical transformation is extremely complicated.

emissions,[70] and they must be made in annual increments. There are restrictions on what emission reductions may be counted towards the fifteen percent goal; reductions from certain measures required prior to the 1990 amendments may not be counted towards the fifteen percent.

(2) all existing sources of VOC emissions must comply with RACT, including numerous new control technology guidelines EPA is to issue under the 1990 amendments.[71] The state is to submit the SIP revision in November 1992; compliance by all VOC sources is required no later than May 31, 1995.

(3) gasoline vapor recovery devices must be installed by owners or operators of gasoline dispensing systems selling more than 10,000 gallons a month.[72]

The offset ratio is increased to 1.15 to 1.0 for sources of VOCs.

Serious nonattainment areas are defined as those with ozone design values between .160 to .180 ppm. There are thought to be 18 such areas, including the Washington, D.C. area. The compliance date is November 1999. Serious areas must take the same steps as required of the moderate nonattainment areas. In addition, the following requirements apply:

(1) Monitoring for these areas must be upgraded for ozone, VOCs, and NOx, according to guidance due from EPA in April 1992.

(2) The state must demonstrate "reasonable further progress" in a SIP revision made in November 1994.[73] For these areas, this means a twenty-four percent cut in emissions from those shown in the baseline emissions inventory.[74] Like the moderate areas, a fifteen percent cut

---

[70] § 182(b)(1)(A). EPA has the discretion not to require the NOx reductions where such reductions will not contribute to attainment. The definition of "reasonable further progress," one of the general statutory requirements for nonattainment areas under § 171(1), is also changed to mean "annual incremental reductions in emissions of the relevant air pollutant."

[71] § 182(b)(2).

[72] § 182(b)(3).

[73] § 182(c)(2).

[74] These reductions need not be made for NOx if EPA determines that such reductions will not help move the area towards attainment. Additionally,

(continued...)

must be accomplished by 1996; the remaining nine percent cut must be made by 1999.

(3) The I&M program must be drastically upgraded,[75] requiring annual testing, the denial of vehicle registration for cars failing the test, an inspection of vehicle diagnostic systems, and a requirement that no waivers be granted for repairs until repair costs reach $450, excluding parts covered by warranty, as most emission control parts must be warranted for eight years. These state programs must be functioning by November 1992.

(4) Clean fuel vehicle programs must be required by a SIP revision due in April 1994,[76] and implemented in model year 1998. These requirements apply to fleets of vehicles, and require the use of alternative fuels, including methanol and ethanol, with very low polluting characteristics.

(5) Transportation control measures will be required if vehicle use and congestion in 1996 is greater than the state used in its SIP to demonstrate attainment with the ozone NAAQS.[77] Every three years thereafter, the state must either demonstrate that vehicle use has not increased above projections or begin imposing transportation control measures.

(6) Stringent additional control requirements must be included in the SIP, to become effective without further action by the state if the area fails to meet its attainment deadline, or any applicable milestone.[78]

The offset ratio in serious nonattainment areas is 1.2 to 1.0,[79] and the threshold for major stationary source is reduced to one emitting 50 tons or

---

[74](..continued)
EPA is to issue guidance under which NOx control may be substituted for VOC controls in some circumstances.

[75] § 182(c)(3).

[76] § 182(c)(4).

[77] § 182(c)(5).

[78] § 182(c)(9).

[79] § 182(c)(10).

more per year of VOCs or NOx.[80]    Additionally, severe restrictions are imposed on sources which seek to avoid LAER requirements by netting emission increases and decreases to remain below threshold requirements.[81]

"Severe" nonattainment areas are those with ozone design levels between .180 and .280 ppm.    There are thought to be eight such areas: Baltimore, Chicago, Houston, Milwaukee, Muskegon, New York, Philadelphia, and San Diego.    The compliance date for Chicago, Houston, and New York, those in the "Severe (II)" category, will be November 2007; the other five, which are in the "Severe (I)" category, have until November 2005.    These projections assume that data for 1989 and 1990 do not change the standing of the cities between categories.

Severe areas must take the same steps as those taken by the serious nonattainment areas.    In addition, by November 1992, states are to adopt enforceable transportation control measures to offset emissions from increases in vehicle use.[82]    Likewise, states are to adopt measures requiring employers with more than 100 employees to increase average passenger occupancy in commuting trips by twenty-five percent.[83]

Perhaps most important, the economic measures required by section 185 become effective if the area fails to meet its attainment deadline.    Among other things, major VOC sources must pay a penalty of $5000 per ton of VOC emitted by the source, for every ton over 80% of the baseline amount.    This $5000 figure is adjusted for inflation, beginning in 1990.    States are to submit a SIP revision including these economic measures by December 2000.

The offset ratio for severe areas is increased to 1.3 to 1.0,[84] and the threshold for major stationary sources is decreased to twenty-five tons per year.

There is only one ozone nonattainment area classified as "extreme," and that is Los Angeles.    The threshold for the extreme area is a design value of .280 ppm.  Los Angeles must take the same steps as those imposed on severe nonattainment areas.  Additionally, by November 1998, boilers emitting more than twenty-five tons per year of NOx must burn natural gas, methanol, or ethanol, or use advanced control technologies.    Restrictions may be placed on

---

[80] § 182(c)(1).    The requirements for stationary sources in ozone nonattainment areas apply both to sources of NOx and VOCs in serious, severe, and extreme nonattainment areas, though EPA has far more discretion to waive or adjust the NOx requirements. § 182(f).

[81] §§ 182(c)(6)-(8).

[82] § 182(d)(1)(A).

[83] § 182(d)(1)(B).

[84] § 182(d)(2).

the use of certain types of vehicles during rush hours. These restrictions, of course, are in addition to the panoply of control measures already available for use in severe nonattainment areas.

The threshold for major stationary sources is reduced to ten tons per year, and the offset ratio is increased to 1.5 to 1.0.[85]

In the event serious, severe, or extreme ozone nonattainment areas fail to meet milestones, section 182(g) provides that the state must elect which of three consequences the area will suffer. The area may be reclassified into a higher category with those more stringent requirements, or the specific SIP contingency measures provided for failure to meet milestones will be activated, or an economic incentive program, including emission fees, marketable permits, and fees to reduce vehicle miles travelled and the use of ozone-forming products, will come into force. The economic incentive program must have been adopted in advance in accordance with EPA guidance.

Congress recognized that ozone transport across areas posed difficult compliance problems for many nonattainment areas, especially in the Northeast. Consequently, nonattainment areas which can demonstrate that nonattainment results from such transport are exempt from certain kinds of sanctions. Additionally, in section 184 Congress established an ozone transport region in the Northeast,[86] and imposed additional controls on nonattainment areas in these states, including enhanced I&M, application of CTGs to all sources of VOCs, and refueling controls. Congress also established an Interstate Transport Commission which may recommend additional control measures in this region. EPA must act on the Commission's recommendations within nine months, and if appropriate require SIP revisions to address the problems found by the Commission.

### 7.3.2 Ozone-Control Standards

Section 183 complements the detailed ozone nonattainment area requirements of section 182 in several ways. First, it requires EPA to issue additional control technology guidelines for stationary sources of VOCs and to update old ones.[87] Additionally, standards are to be set by the Coast Guard by November 1992 for VOC emissions from tankers and unloading operations.[88]

---

[85] § 182(e)(1).

[86] This region includes Connecticut, Delaware, Maine, Maryland, Massachusetts, New Hampshire, New Jersey, New York, Pennsylvania, Rhode Island, Vermont, the District of Columbia and Virginia suburbs around it.

[87] § 183(a)-(c).

[88] § 183(f). Similarly, under section 328 as added by the 1990 amendments, EPA is to set nonattainment standards for VOC emissions from plat-
(continued...)

Section 183(e) also requires EPA to embark on an ambitious regulatory program to require reformulation of many consumer and commercial products to reduce the formation of ozone from their use. By November 1993, EPA is to study and report to Congress about VOC emissions from consumer and commercial products to determine how much they contribute to ozone problems and how to regulate them. In making regulations for these products, EPA is to consider:

(1) benefits, uses and commercial demand for the product;

(2) the health and safety functions (if any) served by the product;

(3) how reactive, i.e. how prone to ozone formation are emissions of the product;

(4) the cost-effectiveness of controls; and

(5) available alternatives for the product, the costs, health, and environmental impacts of the substitutes.

In November 1993, EPA is to list categories of these products causing more than 80 percent of the VOC emissions from such products, and to publish an eight-year schedule for issuance of regulations addressing such products. Regulations are to be issued in four phases, one phase every two years.

The rules are to require the application of the best available controls, a term defined to mean:

the degree of emission reduction that [EPA] determines, on the basis of technological and economic feasibility, health, environmental, and energy impacts, is achievable through the application of the most effective equipment, measures, processes, methods, systems, or techniques, including chemical reformulation, product or feedstock substitution, repackaging, directions for use, consumption, storage, or disposal.[89]

These rules apply to manufacturers, processors, wholesalers, and importers, but not to retailers or consumers.

The definition of best available controls gives EPA considerable discretion. These discretionary powers are strengthened by language allowing EPA to prohibit or control the manufacture or sale of any consumer or commercial

---

[88](..continued)
forms offshore states with Atlantic and Pacific shorelines, taking back such authority from the Secretary of Interior.

[89] § 183(e)(1).

product which results in the emission of VOCs into the ambient air, as well as permission to use registration, labeling, self-monitoring and reporting, limitations and economic incentives. Further language in section 183(e)(8) does suggest that restrictions on the size, shape and labeling requirements are disfavored, but not if EPA finds such controls "useful."

### 7.3.3. Carbon Monoxide Nonattainment Area Provisions

Sections 186 and 187 address carbon monoxide nonattainment areas. Carbon monoxide problems primarily result from automotive exhausts, not stationary sources. Though these areas overlap with ozone nonattainment areas, the CO nonattainment provisions focus predominantly on automotive and transportation problems, and do not include the elaborate stationary source control requirements of the ozone provisions.

There are thought to be fifty-two CO nonattainment areas, forty-seven of which are thought to be in the moderate class, and five of which, including the Los Angeles and New York City areas, are thought to be in the serious class.[90] Section 186(a) divides them between moderate nonattainment areas, with CO design values between 9.1 and 16.4 ppm, and serious nonattainment areas, with value of 16.5 ppm and up. Moderate areas have a compliance deadline of December 1995; serious areas must comply by December 2000. As under the ozone nonattainment provisions, EPA has the discretion to adjust the design values by five percent within 90 days of initial classification of the area. Two one-year extensions of the deadline are possible if the state has met all its obligations under the SIP and the exceedances are minimal. However, if a moderate CO nonattainment area does not meet the 1995 deadline and does not qualify for an extension, it is to be reclassified as a serious nonattainment area.

The SIP revisions required of moderate areas are relatively few. These states must supply a comprehensive, current, and accurate inventory of emissions by November 1992.[91] Moderate areas with a design value of 12.7 ppm or more must also forecast vehicle miles travelled (VMT) and other measures of traffic congestion and car use. Specific transportation control measures must be included in the SIP so that if the forecast is too low or if the attainment deadline is not achieved, the measures will become effective without further action by the state. Finally, for moderate areas with a design value greater than 12.7 ppm, an enhanced I&M program is required by November 1992, following the requirements for serious ozone nonattainment areas.

---

[90] H.R. Rep. No. 490, 101st Cong., 2d Sess. 258-59. These data are from 1987 and 1988.

[91] § 187(a).

In addition to fulfilling the requirements for moderate areas, the five serious CO nonattainment areas must impose transportation control measures by November 1992 to reduce vehicle miles travelled and revise the SIP to require an increase in the oxygen content of gasoline sold in the area during the high CO emissions season.[92] For serious areas with major stationary sources of CO significantly contributing to the nonattainment problem, SIP revisions addressing major stationary sources are required.[93] The threshold for such CO sources is fifty tons per year.

Serious CO nonattainment areas are to meet milestones for CO reductions, beginning in 1995. If they fail to meet them, then the economic sanctions and transportation controls provided for severe ozone nonattainment areas must be imposed. If a serious CO nonattainment area misses the attainment deadline of December 2000, a SIP revision is required, mandating CO reductions of five percent a year.[94]

### 7.3.4. Nonattainment Area Requirements for Particulate Matter

EPA's adoption of the PM10 standard in 1987, and resulting uncertainties about the correct classification of areas, led Congress to adopt separate PM10 nonattainment area requirements. All PM10 nonattainment areas are initially classified as "moderate." With limited exceptions, these moderate areas have a compliance date of December 1994.[95] This compliance date may be extended for two one-year periods provided the state has met its obligations under the SIP and the exceedances are minimal.[96]

EPA is to determine by December 1991 which areas should be classified as serious for PM10 nonattainment, areas which cannot realistically be expected to meet the December 1994 compliance deadline. For these areas compliance is required "as expeditiously as practicable" and no later than December 2001.[97] Those serious areas which cannot meet the 2001 deadline may qualify for one five-year extension provided the state has met its SIP commitments and imposes the most stringent particulate control measures achieved in practice in

---

[92] § 187(b).

[93] § 187(c).

[94] § 187(g).

[95] § 188(a)-(c).

[96] § 188(d).

[97] § 188(c).

any state.[98] Waivers may be granted for certain sources where the nonattainment problems arise from natural sources or from foreign countries.[99]

By June 1992, moderate areas must submit SIP revisions requiring permits for new and modified sources of particulate matter and precursors of PM10.[100] Additionally, reasonably available control measures (RACM) must be implemented by December 10, 1993. Attainment must be demonstrated or a demonstration must be made that attainment is impracticable by that date.

Serious PM10 nonattainment areas must take these steps, but must require the application of best available control measures (BACM) instead of RACM.[101] BACM must be implemented four years from date the area is classified as a serious PM10 nonattainment area.

EPA must issue guidance for Reasonably Available Control Measures and Best Available Control Measures by April 1992.[102] These measures are to address urban fugitive dust, residential wood combustion (including curtailments), and agricultural and forestry burning practices, as well as other sources of particulates.

### 7.3.5. Nonattainment Area Requirements for SO$_2$, Lead, and NO$_2$

For nonattainment areas involving SO$_2$, lead, or NO$_2$, the 1990 amendments have relatively simple requirements.[103] SIP revisions are due 18 months after EPA designates nonattainment areas, which should be January 1993 if EPA meets its schedule. These SIP revisions must demonstrate that the area will be in compliance for the pollutant in question as soon as possible, and not later than November 1995 for areas which were previously nonattainment areas. For nonattainment areas involving these pollutants designated after enactment of the 1990 amendments, compliance is required five years after designation.

---

[98] § 188(e).

[99] § 188(f). Areas along the Mexican border are experiencing severe air quality problems from industrialization along the Mexican side of the border and from the relatively lax controls imposed by Mexico on industrial and automotive sources of air pollution. Section 179B has been added to the nonattainment provisions to address problems arising from emissions in foreign countries. Additionally, a special program with Mexico is mandated by section 815 of the 1990 amendments.

[100] § 189(a).

[101] § 189(b).

[102] § 190.

[103] §§ 191-192.

For sulfur dioxide nonattainment areas without fully approved SIPs, a construction moratorium is imposed on new or modified sources of $SO_2$ until the SIP includes appropriate permit requirements for new and modified sources under section 172(c)(5) or under sections 191 and 192.[104]

### 7.4 Nonattainment Area Sanctions

Under the prior versions of the Clean Air Act, there has been considerable uncertainty about the consequences of a state's failure to submit an adequate SIP or adequately to implement such a SIP, or to bring nonattainment areas into timely compliance. Under the 1977 amendments, a construction moratorium and cutoffs of certain kinds of federal grant money were provided as sanctions against states which failed to bring nonattainment areas into timely compliance.

The 1990 amendments added section 179, detailing the sanctions to be imposed in the event a state fails to meet an attainment deadline or milestone, or to submit an approvable SIP or maintenance plan.[105] States must correct inadequate SIPs within eighteen months of a finding of inadequacy or disapproval by EPA. If states fail to do so, EPA must either withhold federal highway money[106] or increase the offset ratio to 2.0 to 1.0 or more.[107] If the deficiencies are not corrected within twenty-four months, then both the highway money sanction and the increased offset ratio apply. Additionally, EPA must develop Federal Implementation Plan (FIP) requirements if SIP deficiencies are not corrected within twenty-four months of a nonattainment finding or notice of disapproval.[108]

### 8.0 AIR TOXICS PROVISIONS

The 1990 amendments completely revised section 112 of the Clean Air Act, which had provided for national emission standards for hazardous air pollutants (NESHAPS).

---

[104] § 110(n)(3).

[105] § 179(a).

[106] § 179(b)(1). There are a long list of conditions on the kinds of projects for which highway money can or cannot be withheld. Simply stated, projects which have safety and air quality benefits, e.g. bus lanes, bike lanes, public transit, are not meant to be covered by the fund cutoff.

[107] § 179(b)(2).

[108] § 110(c).

Under the 1970 version of section 112, these standards were supposed to be national in scope and to protect against pollutants which "may reasonably be anticipated to result in an increase in mortality, or an increase in serious irreversible, or incapacitating reversible illness." Under this provision, EPA regulated emissions of arsenic, asbestos, beryllium, mercury, radionuclides, benzene, and vinyl chloride.

The 1970 version of section 112 required that emission standards for hazardous air pollutants be set with "an ample margin of safety." This statutory language created a dilemma for EPA, which accepts the contention that for some substances thought to be carcinogenic, there is no safe level of exposure. Under this logic, EPA would have set zero emission limitations for many compounds, emitted in trace quantities from many sources. That result would require the shutdown of much of American industry, including the steel and electric power industries, which emit small quantities of toxic air pollutants.

EPA sought to escape this dilemma by treating section 112 as requiring the application of best available control technology for the listed hazardous air pollutants. This approach, however, was rejected by the court of appeals, which sought instead to give EPA discretion to set emission standards based on risk levels higher than zero emissions.[109] The resulting standard-setting process proved cumbersome at best.

Congress scrapped the existing section 112 program because it regulated far too few toxic air pollutants, and did not provide a workable statutory mandate to regulate those few actually addressed in a consistent and understandable manner. Data about toxic air pollutant emissions gathered under section 313 of the Emergency Planning and Community Right-to-Know Act (EPCRA) lent considerable force to environmentalists' contentions that most emissions of air toxics were unregulated.

Section 112 as rewritten establishes an elaborate program to regulate emissions of a list of 189 toxic air pollutants through technology-based standards and, if necessary, additional health-based standards. The resulting program resembles that established under the Clean Water Act for the regulation of toxic or priority water pollutants in the 1977 amendments, but also has many unique features, reflecting experience under the Clean Air and Clean Water Acts since 1977, as well as vigorous political compromise in order to achieve enactment.

The program established by section 112 may prove one of the costliest environmental commitments made by Congress, because of its pervasive nature and the aggressive controls mandated by the new statutory language. Section 112 now provides:

---

[109] *Natural Resources Defense Council v. EPA,* 824 F.2d 1146 (D.C. Cir. 1987) *(en banc).*

(1) detailed requirements for determining what sources are regulated and according to what schedule;

(2) a precise list of 189 toxic pollutants and compounds, with provisions to add or delete substances based on new data;

(3) a detailed schedule for the implementation of the new control requirements;

(4) aggressive, technology-based standards to be set on an industry-by-industry basis, together with a system of credits for early emission reductions;

(5) preservation of the few standards established under the previous version of section 112;

(6) numerous industry-specific provisions recognizing special circumstances facing electric utilities, coke ovens, publicly-owned treatment works (POTWs), oil and gas wells, sources addressed by standards under the Resource Conservation and Recovery Act, and emitters of mercury, hydrogen sulfide, hydrofluoric acid, and radionuclides;

(7) special permitting provisions and requirements for state programs;

(8) special provisions to address source modifications and the use of work practice standards;

(9) provisions for further tightening emission standards where needed to reduce residual risks to acceptable levels;

(10) provisions for diffuse or "area sources" of toxic air pollutants; and

(11) an elaborate program to prevent, reduce, and respond to accidental releases of toxic air pollutants and extremely hazardous substances.

## 8.1 Sources And Industries Subject to Section 112

Section 112 defines the stationary sources subject to its requirements to be "major" and "area" sources. A "major source" means a stationary source[110] which emits or has the potential to emit 10 tons or more of any hazardous air

---

[110] Or groups of stationary sources within a contiguous area under common control. § 112(a)(1).

pollutant.  Alternatively, a major source is one which emits or has the potential to emit more than 25 tons per year of any combination of hazardous air pollutants.[111]  As the list of hazardous air pollutants in section 112(b) contains 189 substances and compounds, and includes many substances in common industrial usage, especially volatile organic compounds of various kinds, there are a great many stationary sources now defined as major sources of toxic air pollutants.

In setting standards for major sources, EPA is allowed to distinguish between new and existing major sources, and to set less stringent technology-based standards for existing sources than for new sources.[112]  New sources are defined as those for which construction *or reconstruction* is commenced after the proposal of emission standards applicable to the source.[113]  Existing sources are all the rest of the major sources.[114]

Congress recognized in passing section 112 that many hazardous air pollutants are emitted largely by diffuse sources, all with small volumes of emissions, but which collectively amount to a large percentage of the hazardous air pollutants emitted.  Consequently, EPA is to regulate "area sources," defined to mean any stationary source of hazardous air pollutants other than a major source, excluding vehicles.[115]  EPA is allowed to regulate area sources under the same technology-based standards it uses to regulate major sources.  There is, however, a separate program for regulating area sources that is to be much different than that for major stationary sources; EPA is also given far more flexibility in establishing the program.[116]

## 8.2 Defining Hazardous Air Pollutants

Section 112(b)(1) as now written incorporates a list of 189 substances, or classes of substance, and defines them as hazardous air pollutants for the purposes of regulation under section 112.  Most of these are quite specifically defined, complete with Chemical Abstract Service (CAS) number.  For some of these pollutants, however, the law defines them more broadly as an element and its compounds, e.g. arsenic compounds, or by source (coke oven emissions), or by physical characteristics (e.g. fine mineral fibers) or class of chemical

---

[111] *Id.*

[112] § 112(d)(3).

[113] § 112(a)(4).

[114] § 112(a)(10).

[115] § 112(a)(2).

[116] § 112(k).

substance (e.g. polycyclic organic matter). The enacted list is reprinted as appendix A to this chapter.

Unless otherwise specified, the listing of a chemical without a CAS number and its compounds includes any unique chemical substance that contains the named chemical (i.e. antimony, arsenic, etc.) as part of that chemical's infrastructure. Fine mineral fibers are defined to include emissions from facilities manufacturing or processing glass, rock or slag fibers (or other mineral derived fibers) of average diameter of 1 micrometer or less. Polycyclic organic matter includes organic compounds with more than one benzene ring, and which have a boiling point greater than that of water.

One important effect of this new statutory list occurs under section 101(14)(E) of the Comprehensive Environmental Response, Compensation, and Liability Act (CERCLA) or superfund. By operation of § 101(14), listing under § 112 automatically lists these hazardous air pollutants as hazardous substances under CERCLA, thereby subjecting releases of them in excess of reportable quantities to release reporting to the National Response Center and to response action and liability under CERCLA. Though many of these substances are already listed hazardous substances under CERCLA, many others are not. Persons responsible for CERCLA compliance at their installations will need to reexamine their compliance programs in light of the new list, especially release reporting obligations.

Section 112(b)(2) harmonizes this list with other categories of air pollutants under the Clean Air Act. Criteria pollutants under section 108 may not be listed, though precursors of such pollutants, e.g. various volatile organic compounds as a precursor of ozone, may be listed. Special provision is made for lead, which is both a criteria pollutant and listed, together with compounds, under section 112(b)(1). Section 112(b)(7) requires that elemental lead be regulated as a criteria pollutant under section 108; lead compounds of various kinds are left for regulation under section 112(b)(1). Similarly, no substance regulated under Title VI, relating to ozone protection, may be regulated under section 112(b)(1) *solely* due to its adverse environmental effects. Section 112(b)(6) excludes pollutants listed under section 112 from regulation under the PSD provisions of Subpart C of Title I. As a practical matter, the technology-based standards of the revised section 112(d) and the residual risk provisions of section 112(f) will provide the same or greater protection to the environment as would have the application of PSD require-ments to these substances, and probably do so more quickly.

A petition process is established under section 112(b)(3) under which persons may seek to add or delete substances from the list. Petitioners may also seek -- for some categories where there is no CAS number (primarily various metallic elements and compounds) -- removal of unique chemical substances which contain the listed element or fit that class of compound.[117]

These petitions may be filed beginning in April 1991, and EPA has 18 months in which to act upon them. Addition of a pollutant to the list is mandatory if it is shown that the substance is an air pollutant and:

> that emissions, ambient concentrations, bioaccumulation or deposition of the substance are known to cause or may reasonably be anticipated to cause adverse effects to human health or adverse environmental effects.[118]

A pollutant must be deleted if two conditions are met. First, there must be adequate data about the health and environmental effects of the substance on which to base a determination, and second, those data must show that the

> emissions, ambient concentrations, bioaccumulation or deposition of the substance may not reasonably be anticipated to cause any adverse effects to human health or adverse environmental effects.[119]

For delisting petitions addressing unique substances in categories for which there is no CAS number, e.g. arsenic and compounds, the filing of such a petition by November 15, 1991, will affect EPA's issuance of emission standards. EPA may not promulgate emission standards affecting any source categories emitting that substance until the delisting petition is resolved.[120] There are thus strong incentives to file such petitions where appropriate grounds exist to argue for delisting.

Petitioners seeking listing or delisting will bear a heavy burden of proof. Nonetheless, experience under the listing and delisting provisions of section 313 of the Emergency Planning and Community Right-to-Know Act[121] suggests

---

[117] No such partial delistings are allowed for fine mineral fibers, coke oven emissions, or polycyclic organic matter. This leaves cyanide compounds, glycol ethers, and radionuclides in addition to the listed metals and compounds for which delisting of unique compounds may be sought.

[118] § 112(b)(3)(B).

[119] § 112(b)(3)(C).

[120] § 112(b)(4).

[121] See the chapter in this book on the Emergency Planning and Community Right-to-Know Act, summarizing some recent delisting action under section 313.

that the list of hazardous air pollutants under section 112 will change much more often than the list of criteria pollutants under section 108.

### 8.3 Implementation Schedule

By November 15, 1991, EPA must publish the list of source categories and subcategories it intends to regulate under section 112. EPA is required to list *all* categories and subcategories of major sources of listed hazardous air pollutants.[122] To the extent possible the lists of source categories are to be consistent with source categories established for NSPS and PSD purposes, though they will have to reach smaller sources because of differences in source definition between section 112 and these other provisions. EPA may also list categories of sources previously regulated under section 112.

Once a source category is listed, EPA must establish emission standards for that source category. Section 112(e) lays out detailed scheduling requirements for the establishment of these standards. By November 15, 1992, standards for forty source categories must be promulgated. Standards for coke oven batteries, for which there are numerous special provisions in section 112, are due on December 31, 1992; those for publicly-owned treatment works (POTWs), for which there are also special provisions, are due in November 1995.[123] Standards for twenty-five percent of the source categories must be promulgated by November 15, 1994; standards for twenty-five percent more by November 1997; and the balance by November 2000.[124] If EPA later adds source categories to the November 1991 list, standards for those additional categories are due out by November 2000, or two years after such listing, whichever is later.[125] This lengthy time schedule shows that the section 112 will occupy EPA's rulemaking resources for the balance of this century and beyond.

By November 1992, EPA is to publish its schedule showing which standards will be established at what time. The schedule is not subject to judicial review, though a failure to include a source category on it is subject to such review.[126] EPA is supposed to set the schedule after consideration of health effects of the pollutants, quantities of emissions and locations of the sources, and the efficiency of grouping various categories and subcategories

---

[122] § 112(c)(1).

[123] §§ 112(e)(1)(B), 112(e)(5).

[124] § 112(e)(1).

[125] § 112(c)(5).

[126] § 112(e)(3),(4).

together.[127] The point of such scheduling is obviously to promulgate the standards with the greatest health and environmental benefits first.

Specific scheduling provisions are made for some pollutants and industry categories. Section 112(c)(6) mandates listing of source categories emitting alkylated lead compounds, polycyclic organic matter, hexachlorobenzene, mercury, PCBs, furans, and dioxin by November 1995.[128] These source category lists must include at least 90 percent of the aggregate emissions of these pollutants. Emission standards for these source categories are to be promulgated by November 2000. Separate source categories are to be established for research facilities and for styrene emissions from boat manufacturing.[129]

Provision is made to delete source categories, either where the listing is based solely on emissions of a substance which has been deleted under section 112(b)(3), or where certain health-based criteria are met.[130] For carcinogenic pollutants, a category may be delisted if no source in the category emits enough of the pollutant to cause a lifetime risk of cancer to the most exposed individual of more than one in one million. For hazardous pollutants which are not carcinogenic, delisting may also be granted. Here the criteria for delisting require a showing that no source in the category will emit enough of the pollutant to exceed a level adequate to protect human health with an ample margin of safety, and that no adverse environmental effect will result. These criteria reflect some of the pre-1990 language of the statute and implementing regulations. The stringency of these criteria will make delisting of categories difficult. Experience with the *NRDC* toxics consent decree under the Clean Water Act suggests that some delisting of categories may nonetheless occur.

### 8.4 Technology-Based Emission Standards

The most important aspect of section 112 is the program of technology-based standards required by section 112(d). EPA is to set such standards for each source category or subcategory listed pursuant to section 112(c) according to the schedule it publishes under section 112(e).

These emission standards, according to section 112(d)(2):

> shall require the maximum degree of reduction of hazardous air pollutants . . . (including a prohibition on such emissions where achievable) that the Administrator, taking into consideration the cost of

---

[127] § 112(e)(2).

[128] § 112(c)(6).

[129] §§ 112(c)(7),(8).

[130] § 112(c)(9).

achieving such emission reduction, and any nonair quality health and environmental impacts and energy requirements, determines is achievable for new or existing sources in the category or subcategory. . . .

The acronym used for this standard in debates over the 1990 amendments is maximum available control technology (MACT). In establishing MACT standards, EPA is to consider not only emission control technology which removes pollutants at the point of emission, but "measures, processes, methods, systems or techniques which:"

(A) reduce or eliminate emissions through process changes, materials substitutions or other changes;

(B) enclose processes to eliminate emissions; or

(C) are design, equipment, work practice, or operational standards, including operator training and certification.[131]

This statutory language gives EPA broad discretion to require almost any reasonable measure, and many measures industry may consider unreasonable, to help reduce emissions of hazardous air pollutants. The language echoes the zero discharge goal in the Clean Water Act, as elimination of emissions of hazardous air pollutants is *required* where that goal is practical.

Section 112(h) does place limitations on the circumstances under which EPA may impose design, equipment, work practice, or operational standards. Similar language was added to the earlier version of section 112 by the 1977 amendments. Under the Clean Air Act there is a pronounced preference for performance standards, i.e. setting an enforceable numerical standard and leaving to the emitter the choice of technology or other means by which the standard is to be met. Nonetheless, there are circumstances where a different form of standards, including work practice standards, are necessary. These standards may be imposed where EPA determines that numerical emission standards are infeasible to set, and work practice, design, and operational standards can be set consistently with sections 112(d) and (f).[132] If EPA resorts to such standards, they must include operational and maintenance requirements. Moreover, EPA must permit a source to demonstrate and use

---

[131] § 112(e)(2).

[132] The statute defines infeasibility for these purposes to mean that the pollutant cannot be emitted through normal conveyances, or such conveyances would be inconsistent with other law, or the application of measurement technology or methods is impractical because of technical or economic limits. § 112(h)(2).

alternate means to achieve the emission reductions which would be achieved by work practice standards.[133]

EPA is expressly allowed to distinguish between new and existing sources in setting emission standards for hazardous air pollutants. The statutory language is quite precise though in practice determining its meaning will sometimes prove quite difficult. For new sources, the emission standard must be at least as stringent as the emission control that is achieved in practice by the best controlled similar source, as determined by EPA.[134] This language is very close to the definition of Lowest Achievable Emission Rate or LAER contained in section 171(3), part of the nonattainment area provisions of subtitle D.

For existing sources, the standard may be less stringent. Here the determination of the minimum permissible standard under section 112(d)(3) is more complex. For source categories or subcategories with less than 30 sources, the emission standard for existing sources must be at least as stringent as the average emission limitation achieved by the five best performing sources for which EPA has or reasonably could obtain emission data.[135] Where the source category or subcategory has 30 or more sources, the emission standard for existing sources must be at least as stringent as the best performing twelve percent of existing sources for which EPA has data. For these larger source categories, there is intricate language in section 112(d)(3)(A) to exclude certain source data from the calculation. This language seems intended to exclude sources which have very recently reached high levels of emission reduction as a result of the nonattainment provisions and LAER requirements.

EPA has considerable experience in setting technology-based standards and the courts in interpreting them. Moreover, the precision of the statutory language should make establishment of standards under the revised section 112 easier and faster than was true in the two previous decades. These standards become effective upon promulgation,[136] distinguishing them from new source performance standards, which become effective upon proposal.

Section 112 provides for the revision of these standards every eight years,[137] a provision which will not have much effect until the next century. Of greater importance in setting such standards is section 112(e)(7), which provides that no standard or other requirement under section 112 is to be

---

[133] § 112(h)(3).

[134] § 112(d)(3).

[135] § 112(d)(3)(B).

[136] § 112(e)(10).

[137] § 112(e)(6).

interpreted, construed or applied to diminish or replace more stringent emission limitations imposed under other portions of the Clean Air Act or state law. Thus other emission standards place a floor under hazardous emission standards.

Special requirements are imposed on coke oven batteries in order to account for that source category's unique problems.[138]  Likewise, under section 112(e)(9), EPA is now permitted to defer to Nuclear Regulatory Commission regulations under the Atomic Energy Act for sources of radionuclides. This deference, however, is not automatic: if EPA does so, it must consult with the NRC and conduct a formal rulemaking proceeding to determine whether the NRC standard protects the public health with an ample margin of safety. Moreover, the states are free under section 112(e)(9) to impose stricter standards on radionuclide emissions.

The savings provision also affects sources of radionuclides. Section 112(q)(1) preserves standards for hazardous air pollutants promulgated prior to enactment of the 1990 amendments. These include standards for asbestos, arsenic, mercury, beryllium, vinyl chloride, benzene, and radionuclides. The radionuclide standard was promulgated in December 1989,[139] and has been the subject of numerous court challenges and petitions for reconsideration. The savings provision addresses various industry categories affected by the radionuclide rule, keeping the old statute in force as to some, suspending it as to others.[140]

## 8.5 Compliance Schedules and Credits for Early Emission Reductions

After emission standards for a source category are promulgated, new sources, including sources which are being reconstructed, must undergo preconstruction review and demonstrate that they will comply with the emission standards before they may proceed with construction and operation of the source.[141] This determination is made by EPA, until such time as the affected state has an approved permit program under title V. If construction of a new source begins after emission standards are proposed, but before promulgation, then the new source will have three years in which to come into compliance with the final standard if it is more stringent than that proposed.[142] Otherwise, compliance is immediately required.

---

[138] § 112(e)(8).

[139] 54 Fed. Reg. 51654 (December 15, 1989).

[140] § 112(q)(2)-(4).

[141] § 112(i)(1).

[142] § 112(i)(2).

Compliance with emission standards is required of existing sources within three years of promulgation.[143] A permit may, if necessary, grant another year for an existing source to come into compliance. Sources of mining waste subject to these requirements may obtain an additional three years for the waste to dry out and be covered.

Congress and the Administration wanted to encourage early reductions of hazardous air pollutant emissions. Given the long implementation schedule provided in § 112, there would be disincentives for early reductions unless the statute provided some means to recognize these reductions and give credit for them against the emission limits ultimately promulgated.

Section 112(i)(5) is the mechanism provided to reward early emissions reductions. This provision requires EPA or a state with an approved permit program to set an alternate emission limitation for a source which achieves a 90 percent reduction in emissions of a hazardous air pollutant prior to the time the emission standard is proposed.[144] Additionally, if a source makes an enforceable commitment to achieve this 90 percent reduction before proposal of the standard, and achieves the reduction before 1994, it may use this alternate standard, even if the emission standard for the category is proposed before actual achievement of the 90 percent reduction.[145] The baseline from which this 90 percent is calculated consists of "actual and verifiable emissions" for calendar 1987 or some later year.[146]

Sources which use this alternate standard for early reductions may continue to achieve this 90 percent standard for six years after the compliance date for the standard set under section 112(d). As existing sources have three years after emission standards under section 112(d) are promulgated in which to comply, an existing source using this alternate standard may continue to use the alternate standard for up to nine years after promulgation of emission standards under section 112(d).

An existing source has two incentives to use an alternate standard: (1) greater flexibility in choosing the means to achieve the standard and (2) long-term stability in the standard once it is met. Greater flexibility will probably result in lower compliance costs to meet the 90 percent requirement than use of the same means EPA relied on in developing the final standard for the source category. The long-term stability in requirements encourages early investment in control technology because costs can be spread over a number of

---

[143] § 112(i)(3).

[144] § 112(i)(5)(A). A reduction of 95% is required if the hazardous air pollutant is in particulate form.

[145] § 112(i)(5)(B).

[146] § 112(i)(5)(C).

years with some confidence that if the equipment works, EPA will not require changes in control requirements and expensive replacement of controls.[147]

## 8.6 "Hammers," Permits, Modifications and Offsets.

### 8.6.1 "Hammers" and Alternate Emission Limits by Permit

Section 112(j) is similar to so-called "hammer" provisions under RCRA, under which certain specified events would occur unless EPA issued timely standards. Section 112(j) seeks to assure that even if EPA does not promulgate emission standards for hazardous air pollutants in a timely manner, major sources of these emissions will nonetheless have to timely apply for permits governing such emissions. Because permit applications take months to prepare, the effect of this provision will be to require major sources to begin preparing permit applications at the time EPA is supposed to promulgate standards, whether or not EPA in fact promulgates final standards on time.

After April 1994, and after a state permit program is approved, if EPA fails to promulgate emission standards for a category of major sources of hazardous air pollutants, those sources are nonetheless required to submit applications for permits governing hazardous air pollutant emissions within 18 months after EPA's statutory deadline to promulgate the emission standards.[148] Submission of such a permit application satisfies the source's legal requirement to obtain a permit until the state acts on the permit application. EPA is to publish a standardized permit application form by April 1992 to allow such applications to be made. The effect of this provision may be felt as soon as late 1992, when EPA is supposed to promulgate the first round of emission standards under section 112(d).

The state is to set permit requirements on a case-by-case basis to be equivalent to what it believes EPA would have set if EPA had promulgated a timely standard.[149] Stated differently, the state is to make a case-by-case determination of maximum available control technology. When EPA subsequently

---

[147] Compliance schedules may also be slowed down for sources which have complied with best available control technology requirements under section 169(3) of the PSD provisions, or LAER requirements under section 171(3) of the nonattainment area provisions, and did so prior to proposal of standards for the same pollutant or pollutant stream under section 112. A source subject to such double regulation, i.e. BACT or LAER on the one hand and MACT on the other, has five years from the time of installation of the other equipment in order to comply with the new section 112 requirements. § 112(i)(6).

[148] § 112(j)(2).

[149] § 112(j)(5).

promulgates the national standard, the source's limitation is to be adjusted as appropriate when the permit is renewed.

Existing sources have three years in which to comply with emission limitations set under such state permit programs; new sources must comply immediately.

### 8.6.2 State Programs

Section 112(l) provides that states may develop programs under section 112 and be delegated federal enforcement authority. This provision seems redundant with the permit program under Title V, but its actual function may to be to encourage states to focus on the accidental release provision in section 112(r), and use federal grant money to fund that program and related state work under the Emergency Planning and Community Right-to-Know Act (EPCRA).

Under section 112(l) states may develop hazardous air pollutant programs at least as stringent as federal requirements. These programs may also address the accidental release provisions in 112(r) *and* may include program elements addressing extremely hazardous substances under EPCRA. These programs, including the EPCRA portions, may qualify for federal grants under section 112(l)(4).

EPA has 180 days to approve or disapprove state programs submitted under section 112(l). Approval is to be granted if the state's authority is adequate to implement the program as to all sources, adequate resources are available, and the schedule for implementation is reasonably expeditious.

### 8.6.3 New Source Review, Modifications and Offsets

Under the new source performance standards in section 111, a modification of an existing source triggers the application of such new source performance standards. The statutory language defining modification for NSPS purposes has no de minimis cutoff, and has been the source of some confusion in the NSPS and PSD programs.[150]

Section 112(g) addresses the new source and modification issue in the hazardous air pollution context. After the effective date of a state permit program under Title V, no construction or reconstruction of a source of hazardous air pollutants may be conducted unless the state determines that the new source will comply with maximum available control technology requirements.[151] These are to be determined on a case-by-case basis if no emission standards have been promulgated for that source category by EPA.

Similarly, a physical change in, or change in the method of operation of a major source, which results in more than a "de minimis increase of actual

---

[150] *See, e.g., Wisconsin Electric Power Co. v. EPA,* 893 F.2d 901 (7th Cir. 1990).

[151] § 112(g)(3).

emissions of a hazardous air pollutant" constitutes a modification.[152]   A modification occurring after the effective date of a state permit program under Title V will require the application of maximum available control technology, again determined on a case-by-case basis if EPA has not promulgated standards.

A major source may keep changes in its operations from constituting a modification if it offsets emission increases with decreases in emissions from elsewhere in the source.   Moreover, inter-pollutant trading is permitted if the pollutant being reduced is more dangerous than the one for which emissions are increasing.[153]   EPA is to publish guidance about such emission trades by April 1992.   That guidance must provide that carcinogens are traded for carcinogens; only like health risks may be traded, even if different pollutants may be traded against each other.

### 8.7 Residual Risk Provisions

One of the dilemmas posed by the hazardous air pollutants issue is the considerable risk the emission of some pollutants may pose even after the application of the best or maximum available control technology.   This "residual risk," as it was sometimes referred to in the debate leading to the 1990 amendments proved one of the hardest issues for Congress to resolve. Ultimately, Congress chose to write a residual risk provision into the statute, section 112(f), but to provide ample opportunity for Congress to change the provision, and ample time in which to implement it.

Section 112(f)(1) requires EPA, in November 1996, to submit an elaborate report to Congress about:

(A) methods to determine the remaining risk after application of technology-based standards;

(B) the public health significance of these risks, the technological means to reduce them and cost of such reductions; and

(C) the actual human health effects on people living near such sources, the uncertainties in the risk assessment methodology, negative effects of the control efforts, and so forth.

The report is to be prepared in consultation with the Surgeon General and subject to public comment before submission to Congress.

The key aspect of the EPA report are legislative recommendations to

---

[152] § 112(g)(1).

[153] § 112(g)(1)(A).

reduce the remaining risk.[154]   Congress must act on these recommendations. Otherwise, EPA is to promulgate additional standards for each category and subcategory of sources for which technology-based standards are set under section 112(d), if these additional standards are needed either to provide an ample margin of safety in protecting public health or to prevent an adverse environmental effect.   For carcinogens, action is to be required if the individual most exposed to the source suffers an increase in lifetime risk of cancer of more than one in a million.

The 1996 EPA report is to be preceded in April 1993 by a National Academy of Sciences report concerning the validity of risk assessment techniques used to assess the carcinogenic risk posed by sources of hazardous air pollution, and improvements in the methodology.   EPA is either to publish revised guidelines for carcinogenic risk assessment following the NAS recommendations or explaining in detail any departures from the NAS recommendations.   EPA's revised risk assessment guidelines are subject to judicial review.   No standards under section 112(f) may be set until EPA publishes its revised guidelines.

The residual risk standards are to be promulgated eight years after promulgation of the technology-based standards under section 112(d).[155]   For the first 40 categories of sources, for which standards are required in November 1992, promulgation of residual risk standards is to take place in nine years, November 2001.

The residual risk standards are effective on promulgation.[156]   No additional time for compliance is provided for new sources.   For existing sources, the standards do not apply for 90 days, and EPA may grant a waiver for up to two years in which the existing source is to come into compliance with the residual risk standard.[157]   For existing sources which have obtained alternate emission limitations for early emission reductions under section 112(i), the residual risk provisions override the alternate emission limitation and require additional controls.[158]

### 8.8  Area Sources

A large quantity of hazardous air pollutants are emitted not from large industrial sources, but from small, often dispersed sources which are not effectively or economically regulated by the same means as major sources.   For

---

[154] § 112(f)(1)(D).

[155] § 112(f)(2)(C).

[156] § 112(f)(3).

[157] § 112(f)(4).

[158] § 112(i)(5)(E).

example, millions of people are exposed to benzene and other hazardous air pollutants when they pump their own gasoline, simply because benzene, xylene, and toluene are components in gasoline.

Section 112 defines all sources of hazardous air pollutants besides vehicles and major sources as "area sources." While the administrator must list for regulation under section 112(d) all categories and subcategories of area sources "warranting regulation under this section," area sources may alternatively be subject to a separate statutory regime under section 112(k). The objective of section 112(k) is to reduce cancers attributable to area sources in urban areas by 75 percent. EPA is to conduct a research program to characterize such sources, their emissions, and the fate of such emissions, and to report the results in November 1993.[159]

In November 1995, EPA is to formulate and submit to Congress a national strategy to control emissions of hazardous air pollutants from area sources in urban areas.[160] The strategy is to identify at least 30 hazardous air pollutants which result from area sources and pose the greatest public health threat in the most urban areas. The administrator must assure that source categories emitting 90 percent or more of each of the 30 identified hazardous air pollutants are subject to technology-based standards under section 112(d).

Section 112(k)(3)(C) is the key regulatory component of the strategy. The strategy is to include a schedule of specific actions to substantially reduce public health risks posed by the release of hazardous air pollutants. EPA is to take these actions under the Clean Air Act and other laws, including the Toxic Substances Control Act (TSCA), the Resource Conservation and Recovery Act (RCRA), and the Federal Insecticide, Fungicide, and Rodenticide Act (FIFRA), as well as state laws. The strategy is supposed to achieve a 75 percent reduction in cancer attributable to emissions from area sources.

The strategy is to be implemented by November 1999. This deadline is not entirely consistent with section 112(c)(3), which requires regulations governing these area source categories to be promulgated not later than November 2000.

As discussed, EPA may set technology-based and residual risk standards for area sources under sections 112(d)(3) and 112(f), or it may set alternate standards under section 112(d)(5). Under (d)(5), EPA may:

> promulgate standards or requirements for [area sources] which provide for the use of generally available control technologies or management practices by such sources to reduce emissions of hazardous air pollutants.

The term "generally available control technologies" suggests a more lenient control requirement for area sources than for major sources, which are subject

---

[159] § 112(k)(2).

[160] § 112(k)(3).

to MACT requirements. Section 112(f)(5) provides that EPA need not subject area sources regulated under the alternate provisions of 112(d)(5) to residual risk standards.

### 8.9 Prevention and Control of Accidental Releases

Although the Emergency Planning and Community Right-to-Know Act (EPCRA) already provides an elaborate program of state and local emergency planning to reduce risks posed by releases of extremely hazardous substances (EHSs), Congress added section 112(r) to the 1990 amendments to try to reduce such risks further. Section 112(r) may have the earliest, and most widespread effect of any portion of section 112.

Section 112(r)(1) creates a general duty, similar to the general duty clause of the OSHA statute, to prevent accidental releases of EHSs and of additional substances listed under section 112(r)(3), so-called "regulated substances," and to minimize the effects of such accidental releases. This general duty is enforceable by EPA, but is not a basis for citizen suits or tort actions against sources by private citizens.

Accidental releases mean unanticipated emissions of regulated substances or EHSs into the ambient air from a stationary source.[161] Regulated substances mean those 100 substances listed by EPA under 112(r)(3), the accidental release of which is known to cause death, serious injury, or serious effects on human health or the environment. In choosing the initial list of 100 regulated substances, EPA is to consider the list of extremely hazardous substances under EPCRA, but must include 16 substances specified in section 112(r)(3), including relatively common substances such as ammonia and chlorine, as well as methyl isocyanate, infamous from the Bhopal disaster. Sensibly enough, EPA is to include those substances it believes pose the greatest risks when accidental releases occur. Other factors EPA must consider are the severity of adverse effects, the likelihood of accidental releases, and the potential magnitude of human exposure.[162] Threshold quantities of such substances may be established by EPA, and presumably will be established in order to focus on the riskiest sources.[163] Criteria pollutants listed under section 108, and substances regulated under Title VI and its ozone protection provisions, are not to be listed under section 112(r)(3). The list may be revised on petition and must be revised by EPA every five years.

Section 112(r)(7) is the key regulatory component in this accident prevention program. This provision grants EPA broad authority to promulgate:

---

[161] § 112(r)(2)(A).

[162] § 112(r)(4).

[163] § 112(r)(5).

release prevention, detection, and correction requirements, including monitoring, reporting, training, vapor recovery, secondary containment, and other design, equipment, work practice and operational requirements.[164]

By November 1993, EPA is to promulgate "reasonable regulations and appropriate guidance" to prevent, detect, and require responses to releases of regulated substances. The regulations are to address training, maintenance and monitoring, and address storage of these substances as well as handling.

Owners and operators of affected sources have three years -- until November 1996 -- in which to come into compliance with these rules. Owners and operators of sources which have more than a threshold quantity of a regulated substance at their installation must prepare a risk management plan to prevent, detect, and respond to accidental releases. These plans have elaborate requirements and are similar to the spill prevention, control and countermeasure (SPCC) plan requirements imposed upon sources storing oil by section 311(j)(5) of the Clean Water Act.

Under section 112(r)(7)(B)(ii), the risk management plan must include:

(I) a hazard assessment of the effects of the worst case accidental release, including estimates of potential quantities of regulated substances released, downwind exposures, and previous release history of the source;

(II) a prevention program including safety precautions and maintenance, monitoring and employee training measures to be used at the source; and

(III) a response program stating the specific actions to be taken in response to an accidental release, including measures to protect health and the environment, contact with state and local agencies, and employee training.

These plans must be submitted to EPA before the effective date of the regulations (November 1996). They are also to be submitted to the appropriate state and local agencies (probably the State Emergency Response Commission and Local Emergency Planning Committee), as well as the new Chemical Safety and Hazard Investigation Board. EPA is to set up an auditing program to review the plans and require appropriate revisions. The plans are to be publicly available, both from EPA and the source itself.

EPA's regulations under section 112(r)(7) are to be consistent if possible with standards set by the American Society of Mechanical Engineers (ASME), the American National Standards Institute (ANSI), and the American Society of

---

[164] § 112(r)(7)(A).

Testing Materials (ASTM). EPA is also to coordinate with the Occupational Safety and Health Administration and with the Nuclear Regulatory Commission in order to avoid duplicating requirements already in place.

For enforcement purposes, these regulations are to be treated as if they were standards under section 112(d). After the effective date of the regulation, it will be a violation of § 112(d) to violate these regulations. The enforcement consequences are severe. EPA is given additional emergency order authority under section 112(r)(9) to act where there is an imminent and substantial endangerment to health or the environment because of an actual or threatened accidental release. EPA is to issue guidance by April 1991 harmonizing this new emergency order authority with that it has under CERCLA, the Clean Water Act, RCRA, the Safe Drinking Water Act, and other provisions of the Clean Air Act.

Section 112(r)(6) establishes the Chemical Safety and Hazard Investigation Board, similar in concept to the National Transportation Safety Board. The Board is to be an independent entity tasked with investigating accidental releases resulting in death, serious injury or substantial property damage, issuing reports of its investigations and recommendations to reduce risks, and establishing reporting rules for such releases to supplement current rules.[165]

The Board is to make recommendations to EPA by April 1992 for hazard assessments to reduce the risks of accidental releases of extremely hazardous substances.[166] Within 180 days, EPA is to initiate rulemaking to implement the Board's recommendations, or explain why it disagrees.[167] The Board is also to make recommendations to EPA and the Department of Labor in November 1992 for regulations governing risk management plans, accident prevention rules, and mitigation measures for releases. EPA and the Labor Department are to act on the recommendations within 180 days. These rules are to apply to sources handling more than a threshold quantity of a regulated substance.

## 9.0 TITLE IV OF THE CLEAN AIR ACT AMENDMENTS OF 1990: ACID RAIN

### 9.1. Acid Rain Control Prior to the 1990 Amendments

Since the early 1970s, scientific research has shown the widespread incidence of unusually acidic rainfall and snowfall over most of the United States east of the Mississippi River, and in some areas to the west. Rainfall is usually slightly acidic (pH 5.5) as a result of naturally occurring carbon

---

[165] § 112(r)(6)(c)(iii).

[166] § 112(r)(6)(H).

[167] § 112(r)(6)(I).

dioxide which produces carbonic acid. Repeated surveys of rainfall acidities east of the Mississippi have shown large areas where rainfall is significantly more acidic, with a pH of 4.5 or less.[168] In isolated cases rainfall acidity with a pH as low as 2.0 has been detected, a measurement so acidic that the rainfall itself might be classified as a characteristic RCRA hazardous waste.

The full extent of the damage caused by acid precipitation and associated dry deposition of acidic materials is still being assessed, but is believed to include not only the widely-reported effects on fish and lakes in New York, New England, and Canada, but widespread damage to forest growth, to building materials, paints, soil fertility, and crops, among other effects. Perhaps as important as the widespread physical damage and adverse effects on fish and wildlife is the exposure of more than 100 million people in the eastern half of the country to significant levels of sulfate particles, also referred to as acid aerosols.

The occurrence of this acid precipitation and aerosol problem is believed to be linked to the emissions of sulfur oxides and nitrogen oxides, largely from burning coal. The precise linkage between such emissions and resultant acid precipitation problems is not fully understood, but it appears to be linked much more to the quantity of these emissions than to their concentration. A complicating factor is the widespread use of tall smokestacks (up to 1000 feet high) by power plants and smelters. These stacks inject emissions at a higher level in the atmosphere, thus allowing winds to carry pollutants further and allowing a longer time for any mixing and chemical reactions to occur.

Since before 1980, environmentalists and others have argued that effective acid deposition controls require dramatic, region-wide reductions in sulfur and nitrogen oxide emissions, reductions of 50 percent or more. The National Commission on Air Quality, which submitted its report to Congress in early 1981, agreed with this approach and recommended significant reductions in such emissions from 1980 levels by 1990.[169]

The Reagan administration instead argued that additional research was needed. Many millions of dollars of research on acid precipitation were conducted. This research commitment was extended to include five billion dollars of work over five years on "clean coal technologies." This commitment was made in an agreement reached with Canada in 1985. This commitment was

---

[168] pH is a measure of acidity with 0 being the most acidic, 7 being neutral, and 14 being the most basic. This scale is logarithmic. Thus a pH of 4.0 is ten times more acidic than a pH of 5.0

[169] *To Breathe Clean Air,* p. 65 § 97 (1981). In 1980, Congress authorized a 10-year study under the National Acid Precipitation Assessment Program (NAPAP) to determine the causes and effects of acid deposition. The NAPAP study results were published in 1990 and have been subject to much controversy. Environmentalists charge that the report improperly minimizes the effects of acid rain.

not fully funded, however, and acid rain remains a dispute between the U.S. and Canada.

As a result of the controversy over both the causes and effects of acid precipitation, prior to the 1990 amendments, EPA was ill-equipped to deal with acid deposition and aerosols in that the existing Clean Air Act provisions were aimed at individual plants, and did not focus on area-wide or total emission reduction levels.

In contrast, the 1990 amendments are keyed to establishing a total national limit for sulfur dioxide and oxides of nitrogen emissions. The acid rain provisions of the 1990 amendments are designed to reduce sulfur dioxide emissions by at least 10 million tons per year from a 1980 baseline and provide a national cap on sulfur dioxide emissions beginning in the year 2000. Title IV further requires a reduction in the emissions of oxides of nitrogen by approximately two million tons per year. The amendments institute an emissions allowance system, which permits the trading and transfer of emissions among affected units. The amendments establish a permit and penalty scheme to enforce the emission limitations.

### 9.2 Phase I Sulfur Dioxide Reductions

Beginning in 1995, "affected units," that is, the 111 fossil fuel-fired public utility units listed in section 404, are prohibited from emitting sulfur dioxide in excess of the annual tonnage limitations, or allowances, established in section 404 and allocated to each unit by EPA (the "Phase I limitations").[170] To achieve the Phase II limitations which become effective in the year 2000, EPA is to propose by 1991 a second set of allowances, based on a 1985 baseline for each plant, determined by the average annual fossil fuel consumed by the unit.[171] Each unit will receive an allowance allocation from EPA each year; the total annual emissions from all plants cannot exceed 8.90 million tons of $SO_2$ after 2000.

An allowance may not be used prior to the calendar year for which is its issued, and once issued, it replaces any previously issued sulfur dioxide emission limitation promulgated under the Clean Air Act for the particular unit. The 1990 amendments allow the owners or operators of affected units to transfer sulfur dioxide allowances to other owner/operators of affected units holding allowances, so long as the allowance transfer is recorded with EPA.

---

[170] Section 404 contains a list of 111 power plants.

[171] Generally, the 1985 baseline is to be calculated by averaging the quantity of millions of British Thermal Units ("mmBtu") consumed in fuel during calendar years 1985, 1986, and 1987, as recorded by the Department of Energy on Form 767. Certain units with an emission rate of 1.0 lbs/mmBtu or less may opt for a different baseline computation formula, and a different base calculation is provided for utilities for which no form 767 is available.

Owners or operators may also reassign one unit's allowance to another unit that they control, upon application to and approval by EPA. Unused allowances may be carried forward and added to allowances allocated for subsequent years; conversely, excess emissions are deducted from the unit's subsequent year's allowances. EPA therefore is to establish regulations which permit the tracking of all allowances issued, traded, reassigned or deferred.

Owners/operators of affected units may apply to EPA for a two-year extension from the Phase I emissions limitation applicable to their unit, provided that the owner/operator holds allowances to emit not less than the unit's total annual emissions for each of the two years of the period of extension. The extension application must contain evidence, including an executed contract, that the affected unit will be modified to employ a qualifying Phase I emissions reduction technology or that the owner/operator will transfer its Phase I emissions reduction obligation to a unit employing a qualifying Phase I technology. A qualifying Phase I technology is defined as a technological system of continuous emissions reduction which achieves a 90 percent reduction in emissions of sulfur dioxide from the emissions which would have resulted from the use of fuels which were not subject to treatment prior to combustion.

Under the 1990 amendments, electric utilities can earn emissions allowance "credits" by employing qualifying energy conservation measures or qualifying renewable energy. A qualifying energy conservation measure is a cost effective measure, identified by EPA in consultation with the Department of Energy, that increases the efficiency of the use of electricity provided by an electric utility to its customers. Qualified renewable energy is energy derived from biomass, solar, geothermal, or wind, as identified by EPA together with the Department of Energy.

Based on the Act's listed Phase I reductions, by December 31, 1991 EPA is to calculate the estimated total tonnage of reductions in the emissions of sulfur dioxide from all utility units in calendar year 1995, and is to establish from this amount a "reserve" of allowances not to exceed 3.50 million tons. Extensions from the Phase I limitations as discussed above are limited by the amount of allowances in the reserve. To the extent any amount of allowances remains in the reserve following EPA's review of the extension petitions, EPA may award "excess" allowances to affected units for calendar years 1997, 1998, and 1999.

In addition to the basic Phase I allowances allocated to the listed units, EPA is also to allocate excess allowances to utility plants located in Illinois, Indiana, or Ohio for the years 1995-1999. These allowances are to be excluded from the reserve discussed in the preceding paragraph.

## 9.3 Phase II Requirements

Section 405 sets forth the procedures for implementation of the Phase II sulfur dioxide limitations, which go into effect after January 1, 2000. As with the Phase I allocation "pool," EPA is authorized to set up a pool of "reserve" or "bonus" Phase II allowances for the years 2000-2009.[172] States heavily dependent on coal -- Illinois, Indiana, Ohio, Georgia, Alabama, Missouri, Pennsylvania, West Virginia, Kentucky and Tennessee --are to receive bonus Phase II allowances from the reserve.

The specific Phase II limitations applicable to each unit are to be calculated by EPA according to a formula which takes into account the capacity factor and output of the utility unit. For example, according to section 405(b), existing utility units (in commercial operation as of November 1990) serving generators with nameplate capacities of 75 MWe or greater and an actual 1985 emission rate of 1.20 lbs/mmBtu or greater may not exceed annual sulfur dioxide tonnage emissions equal to the product of the unit's baseline multiplied by an emission rate of 1.20 lbs/mmBtu, divided by 2000. This permissible rate may be further varied according to the location of the unit and the type of coal burned. Section 405 contains similar formulas for calculating the allowances for coal or oil-fired units below 75 MWe nameplate capacity, as well as other lower capacity units.

Finally, the act authorizes EPA to allocate extra Phase II allowances for units in "high growth states." A high-growth state is one which experienced a growth in population in excess of 25 percent between 1980 and 1988 according to "State Population and Household Estimates: 1981-1988," as allocated by the United States Department of Commerce, and which had an installed electrical generating capacity of more than 30,000 Megawatts in 1988.

### 9.4 Nitrogen Oxides Emissions Reduction Program

By May of 1992, EPA must establish annual allowable emission limitations for nitrogen oxides for utility boilers as follows:

1.  Tangentially-fired boilers: emissions not to exceed 0.45 lb/mmBtu;

2.  Dry bottom wall-fired boilers (other than units applying cell burner technology): emissions not to exceed 0.50 lb/mmBtu;[173]

By January 1, 1997, EPA must also establish emission limitations for (1) wet bottom wall-fired boilers; (2) cyclones; (3) units applying cell burner technology; and (4) all other types of utility boilers. The rate limitations are to be based on the degree of reduction achievable through retrofit application

---

[172] At the election of the State Governor, states with a state-wide annual average of sulfur dioxide emissions less than 0.80 lbs/mmBtu may receive allowances from the reserve calculated on a state-wide basis in lieu of other bonus allowances under the Act.

[173] EPA may set a higher rate if the agency finds that the maximum listed rate for each boiler type cannot be achieved using low nitrogen oxide burner technology.

of the best system of continuous emission reduction, taking into account available technology, costs, and energy and environmental impacts, and comparability to the costs of controls for tangentially-fired and dry bottom wall-fired boilers. Finally, by January 1, 1993, EPA is to propose revised standards of performance under Section 111 of the act for fossil-fuel fired steam generating units.

The owner or operator of a utility boiler may petition EPA for application of an alternative emission standard. For tangentially-fired and dry bottom wall-fired boilers, the petitioner must show that the unit cannot meet the applicable limitation using low nitrogen oxide burner technology; for the other types of units, the petitioner must demonstrate that the unit cannot meet the applicable limitation using the technology on which EPA based the limitation. Owner/operators of multiple units may also petition under section 405 for an emission level applicable to all units as a group controlled by the owner/operator. This total emissions level cannot exceed the sum of the individual applicable allowances for each unit in the group.

## 9.5 Repowered Sources and Clean Coal Technology Incentives

Units subject to the Phase II sulfur dioxide requirements are eligible for a three-year extension of the compliance date to January 1, 2003, if they demonstrate that the unit is to be repowered by a qualifying clean coal technology. The term "repowering" means replacement of an existing coal-fired boiler with one of the following technologies: atmospheric or pressurized fluidized bed combustion, integrated gasification combined cycle, magneto-hydrodynamics, direct and indirect coal-fired turbines, integrated gasification fuel cells. To make this demonstration, the unit's owner or operator must submit to EPA a binding contract for the majority of the equipment necessary to repower the unit. A derivative technology or other technology may qualify as repowering if EPA and the Department of Energy determine the alternative technology to be capable of controlling multiple combustion emissions simultaneously with improved boiler or generation efficiency, together with significantly greater waste reduction relative to the performance of technology in widespread commercial use as of November 1990.

"Clean coal technology" is defined as any technology, including technologies applied at the precombustion, combustion or post combustion stage, at a new or existing facility which will achieve significant reductions in the air emissions of sulfur dioxide or oxides of nitrogen associated with the use of coal in the generation of electricity, process steam, or industrial products, which was not in widespread use as of November 1990. As incentive to develop and employ clean coal technology, the amendments provide for partial federal funding for temporary (of a duration of five years or less) or permanent clean coal demonstration projects, as well as an exemption for the unit from section 111.[174]

### 9.5 Permit and Enforcement Procedures

Section 408 establishes a permitting procedure for affected units in order to police and keep track of the emissions allowance system. The permit will prohibit emissions of sulfur dioxide and oxides of nitrogen in excess of the allowances established pursuant to the act, and is to be enforced in accordance with the permit procedures established under Title V. Separate permits will be issued for the Phase I and Phase II requirements.

The initial permit application must include a compliance plan for the source to comply with the requirements of Title IV. In addition, the permit application must include a certificate of representation identifying the unit's "designated representative," which is the responsible person or official authorized by the owner or operator of the unit to represent the owner/operator in matters pertaining to the holding, transfer, or disposition of allowances allocated to the unit. Section 408 gives EPA six months to review each compliance plan for conformity with the act; regulations governing the submission and review process are to be promulgated by EPA by May of 1992. Permits are to be issued for a period of five years, and recordation by EPA of allowance transfers will automatically amend existing permits.

Section 411 provides for penalties for emissions in excess of the permitted amount. The financial penalty is calculated by multiplying the number of excess tons over the applicable allowances by $2000. In addition, the excess emissions must be offset against the allowance for the particular unit for the subsequent year in accordance with a plan submitted to and approved by EPA. By November of 1993, owners and operators subject to the Phase I emission requirements must install continuous emission monitoring systems ("CEMS") which comply with regulations to be promulgated by EPA. All other units must have qualifying monitoring technology by January 1, 1995. EPA must also establish regulations governing the reporting and recordkeeping of emission compliance.

### 9.6 The Allowance Auction System

For independent power producers not listed as affected units under the act, and who may be unable to purchase allowances from public utilities, EPA is to establish a special reserve of allowances to be sold by the agency. This

---

[174] Section 413 of the Amendments also authorizes the necessary appropriations for funding of at least 50 percent of a clean coal demonstration project to design, construct and test a technology system for a cyclone boiler to serve as a model for future systems. The unit selected for this project shall be in a utility plant that (1) is among the top 10 emitters of sulfur dioxide in the country; (2) has three or more units, two of which are cyclone boiler units; and (3) has no existing scrubbers.

Special Allowance Reserve shall consist of 2.8 percent of the annual allocation of allowances for both the Phase I and Phase II periods. The price shall be $1500 per ton of allowance, to be adjusted according to the Consumer Price Index.

### 9.7 Special Report Requirements

The acid rain provisions of the 1990 amendments require EPA to undertake a variety of studies and report back to Congress. These include a report on the feasibility and effectiveness of acid deposition standards to protect sensitive aquatic and terrestrial resources, creation of a National Acid Lakes Registry, and a report on Canada's progress in reducing sulfur dioxide and oxides of nitrogen emissions. EPA also must submit to Congress, every five years beginning in 1995, a report containing an inventory of national annual sulfur dioxide emissions from industrial sources. Where the report indicates emissions expected to rise over 5.60 million tons per year, EPA is authorized to take emergency action, including revising emission standards, to reduce the amount below the cap.

### 10.0 AIR PERMIT PROGRAMS

Until the 1990 amendments, the Clean Air Act lacked a uniform federal permit program for major sources of air pollution. Though there were permit requirements for new sources and for emitters of hazardous air pollutants, the absence of a federal permit program addressing most major sources of air pollution handicapped much enforcement and made imposition of revised regulations cumbersome and difficult. The only means to change requirements was to revise the state implementation plan (SIP), an elaborate and unsatisfactory means to make source-by-source adjustments in requirements.

The 1990 amendments added a new Title V to the Clean Air Act, imposing a federal permit program for major sources. In many important respects, this program parallels the National Pollutant Discharge Elimination System (NPDES) permit program under section 402 of the Clean Water Act. There are also significant differences, some reflecting political compromises, others reflecting the different physical and fiscal realities confronting Congress in 1990 than when it first enacted section 402 of the Clean Water Act in 1972. Thus the Clean Water Act NPDES program may provide important guidance in establishing and interpreting the clean air permit program, but that guidance will often not be dispositive.

The key questions to be addressed for those affected by the permit program are these:

What are the sources governed by Title V's permit program requirements?

What conditions must permits contain under Title V, in addition to the substantive requirements the permit is meant to implement?

What are the legal effects of a permit?

When must permit applications be filed and permits obtained under Title V?

What do state programs have to do·in order to satisfy Title V requirements, and what happens if states fail to devise adequate permit programs?

What about permit fees, and how are they to be calculated?

How is the permit process supposed to work under Title V, and what are the roles of the applicant, the state, EPA, the public, and adjacent states?

## 10.1 Stationary Sources Requiring Permits

Section 502(a) of the act makes it illegal for a source requiring a permit to operate without one, or to operate in violation of the permit and its conditions. In this respect, section 502 is similar to the Clean Water Act, which makes it unlawful for a "point source" to discharge to surface waters without a discharge permit.

Unlike the Clean Water Act permit program, which has no size threshold for small point source discharges, the Clean Air Act permit program does contain some thresholds. Two rules of thumb may be applied to determine whether most sources are included or not. If the source emits more than 100 tons of any air pollutant per year, then it will need a permit. If the source emits less than 100 tons per year, but emits or has the potential to emit 10 or more tons per year of any hazardous air pollutant (or 25 tons of any combination of hazardous air pollutants), it will be required to obtain a permit. If a source is in a nonattainment area, it may need a permit, depending upon the severity of the nonattainment problem, if it emits more than 10 tons per year of a criteria pollutant.

Under section 502, and the definitions in section 501, the following source categories must obtain permits in order to continue to operate legally:

(1) major stationary sources, meaning those which emit, or have the potential to emit more than 100 tons per year of any air pollutant;[175]

(2) major sources under the hazardous air pollutant provision, section 112. These sources are those which emit, or have the potential to emit, more than 10 tons per year of a hazardous air pollutant. If the source does emit or has the potential to emit more than 10 tons per year of any single hazardous air pollutant, a permit is still required if the

---

[175] §§ 502(a), 302(j).

source emits, or has the potential to emit, more than 25 tons per year of any combination of hazardous air pollutants regulated under section 112;[176]

(3) other sources regulated under section 112. This language will require area sources under section 112 to obtain permits.

(4) sources regulated under section 111. These include not only new and modified sources of air pollution in the source categories for which EPA has established new source performance standards (most of which would meet the definition of major stationary source in section 302(j)), but also existing sources of air pollution regulated under section 111(d), sources such as fertilizer and aluminum manufacturing, which emit pollutants which are not regulated as hazardous air pollutants under section 109, or hazardous air pollutants under section 112.

(5) sources required to have permits under the Prevention of Significant Deterioration (PSD) provisions in Subtitle C of Title I. Ordinarily, these will be new or modified major stationary sources of sulfur dioxide, nitrogen oxide, and/or particulates. These would probably be required to obtain permits by the definition of major stationary sources anyway, so this provision may not add many sources to the permit program.

(6) sources required to have permits under the nonattainment provisions in subtitle D of Title I. Usually these will be new or modified sources of air pollutants (or precursors such as volatile organic compounds), but the thresholds may be lower than the definition of major stationary source under section 302(j).

(7) Affected sources under Title IV, the acid rain provisions. These will be the 111 coal or oil-fired electric power plants listed in Title IV, as well as other sources which may opt for coverage under Title IV's requirements as part of an emission trading program. These sources also would be addressed by the 100 ton threshold for major stationary source in section 302(j).

(8) Other categories of sources designated by the administrator.

The administrator has the authority to exempt some categories of sources from permitting requirements, but under no circumstances may the administrator exempt "major sources," meaning those above the 100 ton

---

[176] The definition of major source for hazardous air pollutant purposes is found in § 112(a).

threshold for criteria or other non-hazardous pollutants, and those above the 10 ton (or 25 ton combination) threshold for hazardous air pollutants. The administrator may exempt source categories because permit requirements are impractical, infeasible, or unnecessarily burdensome for such source categories.

In calculating thresholds for inclusion in the permit program, the language of section 112(a) and 302(j) discusses not only actual emissions, but potential to emit. In the past, EPA has calculated potential to emit on the basis of emissions from the source when it is in continuous operations over the course of the year with its emission control equipment functioning.[177] This definition was challenged and partially invalidated in *Wisconsin Electric Power Company v. EPA*,[178] and is now the subject of an EPA rulemaking proceeding. This definition will be critical to many small and medium-sized operations, particularly for sources which are batch processors, or which have seasonal operations, such as certain canneries or other food processors.

### 10.2. Required Permit Conditions and Effects of Permit

A stationary source which meets the permit program definitions, usually the 100 or 10 ton thresholds discussed above, becomes subject to the permit program when EPA approves the state program, or if EPA does not approve it, when EPA initiates a federal permit program for that state.[179] If a source does not meet the size thresholds at the time the permit program becomes effective, it may later become subject to the permit program if it increases in size, or if it is built or modified after the permit program is approved, or if the permit program changes to include it.

A source subject to the permit program has one year from the program's effective date in which to prepare and submit a permit application,[180] unless the state sets an earlier filing deadline. If the act is implemented on schedule, sources will become subject to permit programs in November 1994, and will have until November 1995 in which to submit permit applications satisfying

---

[177] This language results from the D.C. Circuit's decision in *Alabama Power v. Costle*, 636 F.2d 323 (D.C. Cir. 1980) (Alabama Power II).

[178] 893 F.2d 901 (7th Cir. 1990). The court held that where a plant has never operated on a continuous basis, but rather was used for peak-load power supply, it was inappropriate for EPA to calculate potential to emit on the assumption that the plant was operated continuously. *Id.* 916-18. The court went on, however, to hold that any actual emission increase caused by a reconstruction of the boiler and increase in its power production capacity would trigger the application of PSD and NSPS requirements as a major modification. *Id.* at 907-10.

[179] § 503(a).

[180] § 503(c).

federal requirements. The state will have 18 months in which to act on the application, but section 503(c) allows the state to set up a phased processing schedule for the initial round of permit applications. This phased schedule may stretch out the processing period another six months.

For an existing source, a timely and complete permit application will satisfy the requirement that a source have a permit until the permitting agency acts on the permit application.[181] The permit application must be accompanied by a compliance plan including a "schedule of compliance," a defined term under section 501(3):

> a schedule of remedial measures, including an enforceable sequence of actions or operations leading to compliance with an applicable implementation plan, emission standard, emission limitation, or emission prohibition.

The compliance schedule must require periodic progress reports to the state, and such periodic reports must be made at least every six months, and more frequently if the state requires.[182] Additionally, the permit must require periodic compliance certifications, meaning at least annually.[183] Moreover, prompt reports must be made to the permitting authorities of "any deviations from permit requirements."[184]

The permit application and compliance schedule must be signed by a responsible corporate officer, and certified by that officer as accurate.[185] Permit applications, compliance plans, compliance schedules, permits, compliance certifications, emissions or compliance reports, must be publicly available.[186] This requirement complements similar requirements in section 114, and is intended to help foster citizen suits against violators of permits.

Under section 504, the permit must include the following provisions:

(1) enforceable emission limitations and standards;

(2) a schedule of compliance;

---

[181] § 503(d).

[182] § 503(b)(1).

[183] § 503(b)(2).

[184] *Id.*

[185] § 503(c).

[186] § 503(e).

(3) periodic monitoring reports submitted to the permitting authority, at least every six months;

(4) language addressing inspections, entry, monitoring, compliance certification, and reporting requirements;

(5) certification of reports by responsible corporate officials.

States are free to include other provisions in permits, as long as these are not inconsistent with the Clean Air Act.[187]

Continuous monitoring is preferred but not necessarily required under the permit program (although it is under the acid rain provisions in Title IV). Rather, under section 504(b), EPA's monitoring regulations need not require continuous monitoring if it finds that alternate means are available that provide sufficiently reliable and timely information to determine compliance.

The permit "shield" provision proved highly controversial as Congress worked to pass the 1990 amendments. The resulting provision, section 504(f), is a compromise. It provides that compliance with a permit issued under Title V constitutes compliance with section 502. Depending on the permit rules promulgated by EPA, the states *may* write permits to provide that compliance with the permit constitutes compliance with other applicable provisions of the Clean Air Act, *if*:

-- the permit includes applicable requirements from those provisions, or

-- the permitting authority determines the other provisions are inapplicable and the permit includes such a determination.

The administrator retains the authority to override such permits in emergencies under section 303.

From the point of view of an industrial manager, interested in stable permit requirements for orderly financial planning, the effectiveness of the shield provision is undercut by section 502(b)(9). Under this provision, states are required to show that for major source permits of three years duration or longer (the longest authorized permit term is five years), that revised regulations will be incorporated into existing permits within 18 months of the effective date of new requirements. This retroactive adjustment of permit requirements may prove most important in the hazardous air pollutant area where EPA must promulgate a great many new regulations, a process which will certainly take longer than the permitting programs are supposed to under Title V.

The new provisions do provide the permitting authorities some flexibility to address multiple or unusual sources. Under section 502(c), authorization is

---

[187] § 506(a).

given to issue a single permit for multiple sources at a single facility. This provision may facilitate the use of the "bubble" approach to compliance, particularly for a large, integrated manufacturing plant with many sources. For temporary sources, specific permitting authority is provided in section 504(e), allowing a single permit for a source which will be transferred to multiple temporary locations. This provision may make it easier for mobile incinerators to be permitted, though RCRA incinerator requirements are usually the more difficult permitting hurdle.

Where permitting authorities are faced with many similar sources, section 504(d) expressly authorizes the issuance of general permits after notice and opportunity for a public hearing. Presumably general permits will be used where many small sources are similarly situated, and the administrative burden on permittees and the permitting agency is disproportionate to the environmental benefit. In these circumstances, a general permit, outlining the terms and conditions under which a class of sources must operate makes considerable sense.

These permits, however, must comply with the minimum permit conditions outlined above, and permittees still must file a permit application. Unless the permit application requirements are considerably relaxed for sources covered by general permits, e.g. making the application a short-form notification of coverage, the benefits of general permits for permittees will prove minimal.

## 10.3. State Permit Program Requirements and Timing

The Clean Air Act now contemplates, just as the Clean Water Act has done for nearly two decades, that the states (or in some cases interstate agencies) will be the permitting authorities. Section 502(b) requires EPA to promulgate, by November 1991, the rules defining the minimum requirements for state clean air permitting programs. States will have until November 1993 in which to develop their permitting programs and submit them to EPA for approval. EPA will have one year -- November 1994 -- in which to review and approve (or disapprove) the permitting program. Upon such approval, the program will become effective for the purposes of stationary sources submitting permit applications, which will be due in November 1995.

Experience with the Clean Water Act's NPDES program suggests that the program is unlikely to work as smoothly or quickly as the drafters of Title V anticipated. Even now, nearly two decades after the NPDES permit program began, there are about fifteen states and territories which do not have approved programs. Moreover, the integration of state water pollution permit programs into the NPDES permit program in the 1970s was frequently a bumpy process, with frequent occasions for disputes between state and federal regulatory agencies. EPA often viewed state agencies as provincial and spineless in dealing with dischargers; states often viewed EPA as high-handed, dogmatic, and impractical. Unfortunately, there was often a factual basis for both views. As similar political dynamics will be at work in the new clean air permit program, similar friction between the state agencies and EPA also seems likely.

Under section 502(b), the regulations for state clean air permit programs set forth the minimum elements of an approvable state program. In order to obtain such approval, the state must show that its program has:

(1) A standard permit application form, and formal criteria for promptly determining when an application is complete.[188] A frequent complaint against permitting authorities are decisions late in the permitting process that the application is somehow incomplete, requiring the applicant to start over. This often occurs when an agency is unable to meet deadlines or is seeking to avoid a difficult political decision on an application.

(2) Adequate monitoring and reporting requirements.[189] Though these could be modelled on federal regulations, considerable leeway is provided for local variations.

(3) A permit fee program which will raise enough money to make the permitting program self-sufficient.[190] These elaborate requirements are discussed separately below, but the theory is to make the permittees, and not the taxpayers, pay the full costs of the permit program, including overhead. EPA grants supply much of the funding of state air pollution control agencies, and in the current budgetary climate, Congress would like to phase out such support.

(4) Assurances of adequate personnel and funding.[191] This is obviously related to the permit fee program, but also reflects sad experience over the last two decades in which state environmental programs have been gutted for budgetary reasons. Frequently EPA ends up funding the shortfall.

(5) The permitting agency must show it has adequate authority to administer and properly to enforce the program and permit requirements.[192] In particular, the agency must show it has authority to:

(A) issue permits with a fixed term, not longer than five years;

---

[188] § 502(b)(1).

[189] § 502(b)(2).

[190] § 502(b)(3).

[191] § 502(b)(4).

[192] § 502(b)(5).

(B) incorporate SIP requirements into permits on issuance or renewal;

(C) terminate, revoke, or modify permits for cause;

(D) enforce permits, fee requirements, and the obligation to obtain a permit. This authority must include authority to obtain civil penalties of up to $10,000 per day of violation, and appropriate criminal penalties;

(E) assure that no permit is issued if the EPA administrator makes a timely objection.

(6) Adequate procedures to assure that timely decisions are made, public notice given and an opportunity for public comments and hearings provided, and an opportunity for judicial review of the final permit in state court by the applicant and those who commented about the permit application.[193] Procedures must assure the public availability of permit applications, and related data, including monitoring data.[194] Procedures also must assure that changes which do not constitute source modifications within the meaning of Title I and do not increase emissions above permit limits do not require permit revisions, as long as seven days notice is given to the permitting agency.[195]

Experience with SIPs as well as experience with state NPDES programs suggests that EPA will give unqualified approval to rather few state programs. Thus instead of approval of state programs in November 1994, EPA may conclude its review of state programs with many partial disapprovals, which will give states another 180 days to correct the deficiencies found by EPA.[196] Alternatively, EPA may grant interim approval to a state program which substantially meets the requirements of Title V, but requires improvements.[197] EPA is to specify the improvements needed, and may grant up to two years for the state to make the needed changes.

Experience with SIPs and with the NPDES program also suggests that EPA will be hard-pressed to meet the statutory deadlines to review state programs.

---

[193] §§ 502(b)(6), (7).

[194] § 502(b)(8).

[195] § 502(b)(10).

[196] § 502(d)(1).

[197] § 502(g).

The statute obligates EPA to impose nonattainment area sanctions under section 179(b) if a state does not have an approved program within 18 months of the time it submitted its program.[198] The use of this mandatory language will permit citizen suits to force the imposition of such sanctions if EPA does not act to do so.

If no approved permit program is in place within two years of submission of a state program, EPA is to administer the permit program for that state.[199] As interim approvals of state programs suspend EPA's obligation to impose sanctions or to administer the permit program,[200] interim approvals are likely to be EPA's preferred method of dealing with deficiencies in state programs. This preference is reinforced because partial permit programs do *not* suspend the obligation to impose sanctions or to take over the disapproved portion of the state program within two years.

Section 502(f) does place limits on the approval of partial permit programs, and presumably, interim approvals as well. In order for a partial permit program to be approved, it must at least address Title IV (acid rain) affected sources, major, area and new sources under section 112 (for hazardous air pollutants), and other Title I requirements.[201]

If a state program becomes deficient after it is approved, either in administration or enforcement, EPA may make a formal finding to that effect under section 502(i).[202] If it does make such a finding, it is authorized to impose nonattainment area sanctions. If the deficiencies persist more than 18 months, sanctions become mandatory. If they are not corrected within two years, EPA must take over administration of the state program.

As a practical matter, EPA will seldom act under section 502(i) unless the deficiencies are very grave. EPA has similar authority to take back administration of state NPDES programs, which it has never exercised, though it has occasionally made informal threats to do so. The political consequences of such EPA action are difficult for the agency, and EPA will seldom have adequate resources to make a credible threat to take over a state permit program.

### 10.4. Permit Fees and State Programs

State clean air programs have often been hamstrung by inadequate resources. Imposition of a federal clean air permit program on the states

---

[198] § 502(d)(2)(B).

[199] § 502(d).

[200] § 502(g).

[201] § 502(f).

[202] § 502(i).

without making some provision for adequate financial resources to administer the program would have been a prescription for failure, especially in the current economic and budgetary climate.

The permit fee program found in section 502(b)(3) is Congress' effort to address that resource problem, by shifting the financial burden of the permit program to the permittees. The theory behind this provision is that permittees obtain the benefit of the permit program, and thus should pay for it through user fees. In practice, permittees often have a contentious relationship with state environmental agencies, and the requirement to pay one's antagonist adds insult to injury. In the House of Representatives, this (and other) fee provisions looked to many like emissions taxes rather than user fees, and sparked a jurisdictional fight in which the Ways and Means Committee argued unsuccessfully that this was a tax. In practice, there will be much to support the view that these fees are indeed taxes.

In order for a state to obtain approval of its permit program, it must show that it has a permit fee program in place under which the permittees will pay an annual fee sufficient to cover the reasonable direct *and indirect* costs of the permit program. Reasonable costs to be covered include the cost of:

(A) reviewing and acting on permit applications;

(B) implementing and enforcing the terms and conditions of permits (other than costs and attorney's fees of enforcement actions);

(C) emissions and ambient monitoring;

(D) modelling and analysis costs;

(E) preparing and updating emission inventories.[203]

The state must show that the permit fee program will raise in aggregate $25 per ton per year of regulated pollutant emitted, or such other amount as EPA determines adequately reflects the reasonable costs of the permit program. Fees are to be charged on the first 4000 tons of each regulated pollutant emitted by a source. Thus the total annual fee for a permittee emitting 4000 tons of a regulated pollutant will be $100,000. Moreover, if the source emits more than one regulated pollutant, and most do, the costs increase accordingly. Regulated pollutants mean:

-- volatile organic compounds;

-- each pollutant regulated under section 111, governing new source

---

[203] § 502(b)(3)(A)(i)-(vi).

-- each pollutant regulated under section 112, governing the list of 189 hazardous air pollutants;

-- criteria pollutants under section 109, except carbon monoxide.

Money collected by the state under the fee program is to be used solely to cover all reasonable (direct and indirect) costs of the permit program.[204]

The fees collected under the permit programs are to be adjusted upward each year in accordance with the consumer price index published by the Department of Labor. If EPA determines that a fee program is inadequate or improperly administered, it may collect the fees from the sources. EPA will retain the money it collects to administer permit programs. If sources do not pay the EPA imposed fees, they will face a penalty equal to 50% of the fee amount, plus interest.[205] Additionally, there are criminal penalties provided now in section 113(c) for willful failures to pay fees owed under the Clean Air Act.

These permit fee requirements are likely to prove extremely controversial as the economic impacts on sources are easily calculated and significant. Given the unhappy experience many companies have had with federal cost accounting under Superfund, it may be wisest for them to try to keep the permit fee program at the state level where overhead may be less and the impact of the fees on sources immediately apparent.

### 10.5. Role of EPA, Adjacent States, and the Public in Permitting

Once a state has an approved permit program, Title V gives the state considerable leeway to process the application as it sees fit. Section 505, however, does provide a role for EPA, adjacent states, and the public in reviewing permit applications.

Each state with an approved program is to transmit a copy of the permit application, proposed permits, and final permits to EPA for review.[206] Additionally, the application, proposed, and final permits are to be transmitted to all states whose air quality might be affected by the source, and which are contiguous to the permitting state, or which are within 50 miles of the source.[207] If another state objects, it is to submit written recommendations concerning the permit and its terms or conditions. If these recommendations

---

[204] § 502(b)(3)(C)(iii).

[205] § 502(b)(3)(C)(ii).

[206] § 505(a)(1).

[207] § 505(a)(2).

are not accepted, the objecting state is to be notified and the reasons for the decision provided.

EPA *must* object to a proposed permit which fails to comply with the act or the state implementation plan. If EPA objects within 45 days of receipt of the application, or within 45 days of receipt of another state's objection, then the permitting state may not issue the permit unless it is revised to conform to EPA's objections.[208] If the permitting state does not act within 90 days of receipt of EPA's objection, then EPA may issue or deny the permit.[209]

If a permit has already been issued, and EPA determines that there is cause to terminate, modify, or revoke and reissue the permit, EPA is to notify the permitting state and the source of that determination. The permitting state must take appropriate action within 90 days, which may be extended for another 90 days if a new application or additional information from the source is needed. If the state fails to act within 90 days, or if EPA objects to the proposed revision and the objection is not resolved, EPA may, after notice and "in accordance with fair and reasonable procedures," probably including a hearing, act to terminate, modify, or revoke and reissue the permit.[210]

If EPA fails to object to a permit within 45 days of receipt of the permit or of another state's objections, any person may petition EPA within the next 60 days to take such action.[211] The petition must be served on the applicant and on the permitting state. The petition must be based on objections raised with reasonable specificity during the course of the permit application proceeding before the state, unless the grounds for the objection arose later. EPA has 60 days to act on the petition. The filing of such a petition does not stay the effectiveness of any permit issued in the interim.

Unlike most provisions of the act, the EPA administrator may not delegate the petition requirements of section 505(b)(2). As a practical matter, most such petitions will be denied by default as the administrator will not have time to review more than a few in the time provided.

If the administrator determines that the petition is meritorious, the administrator must issue an objection to the permit or proposed permit as the case may be. If the permit has not been issued, then the permitting state has 90 days to revise the permit accordingly. If the permit has already issued, EPA is to modify, terminate, or revoke and reissue the permit.

Petitioners may obtain judicial review of an EPA decision to deny a

---

[208] §§ 505(b)(1),(3).

[209] § 505(c).

[210] § 505(e).

[211] § 505(b)(2).

petition in the court of appeals under section 307.[212] Presumably, disappointed permit applicants could also seek review under section 307 in the court of appeals, though no express provision is made for such review.

EPA may waive this review and objection process for categories of minor sources.[213] This waiver may have to be exercised because of the short time frames for EPA to review permit applications, and because the review language is written in mandatory terms.

## 11.0 MOBILE SOURCE EMISSION CONTROL REQUIREMENTS

The Clean Air Act regulates motor vehicle emissions and fuel and fuel additives through a certification and registration program. The 1990 amendments greatly strengthen regulation of motor vehicles -- particularly trucks, urban buses, and fleet vehicles -- as well as permissible components of vehicle fuel. The 1990 amendments, as discussed below, also place a substantial regulatory burden on EPA, as the agency is tasked with developing a wide variety of implementing regulations within a very short time frame.

### 11.1 Control of Vehicle Emissions

Since 1965, the federal government has had authority to set emission standards applicable to new motor vehicles and engines. Standards are to be set for pollutants which EPA determines ". . . cause, or contribute to, air pollution which may reasonably be anticipated to endanger public health and welfare." Limitations on emissions of hydrocarbons and carbon monoxide were applied to 1968 model year vehicles and all subsequent model years. An emission standard for oxides of nitrogen went into effect beginning with 1973.

In the belief that motor vehicle pollutants constituted the single most difficult air pollution problem facing the nation, Congress in 1970 took the unusual step of actually prescribing the numerical level of auto emission standards. The law[214] required a 90 percent reduction of hydrocarbons and carbon monoxide from 1970 levels, and a 90 percent reduction in nitrogen oxides emissions from levels attained in 1971 model year vehicles. The 90 percent reductions in HC and CO were to be achieved in 1975, and the $NO_x$ reductions in 1976. In each case, EPA was permitted to suspend for one additional year the 90 percent reduction requirement on finding, after public hearing, that the needed technology was not available, and that the

---

[212] § 505(b)(2).

[213] § 505(d).

[214] Section 202(a)(1) and (2); 42 U.S.C. §§ 7521(a)(1) and (a)(2).

manufacturer applying for the suspension had made good faith efforts to meet the standards.[215]

In the 1977 amendments, Congress enacted what amounted to another postponement of what were once the 1975 statutory standards. The hydrocarbon standard was set back to model year 1980; the carbon monoxide level deferred to 1981 with the potential of an administrative suspension for two more years. For oxides of nitrogen Congress went further and significantly loosened the stringent number originally set for the 1976 models. Section 202 prescribed a 1.0 gram per vehicle mile standard beginning in model year 1981. Each of the standards postponed or loosened by the 1977 amendments has now been achieved on production vehicles.

In the 1977 amendments, Congress for the first time also took charge of standard setting for heavy duty vehicles, i.e., larger trucks and motorcycles, fields previously left to EPA's discretion. EPA was left with the authority to substitute standards reflecting what the best available technology can achieve, if the statutory standards prove infeasible.

EPA was supposed to adopt standards for heavy-duty vehicles in time for manufacturers to comply during the 1985 model year. EPA, however, failed to promulgate such regulations until early 1985, setting standards for nitrogen oxides and particulate matter effective for the 1988 model year, with progressively tightened standards effective for the 1991 and 1994 model years. These regulations were upheld in 1986 against challenges by environmentalists and industry.[216]

---

[215] Manufacturers applied for the suspension of the 1975 standards in January 1972. After EPA determined that the manufacturers had failed to prove that technology was not available and denied the one-year suspension. The manufacturers took their case to the United States Court of Appeals for the District of Columbia Circuit, which reversed the decision, finding that EPA had not adequately supported its conclusion that the standards could be met. *International Harvester v. Ruckelshaus*, 478 F.2d 615 (D.C. Cir. 1973). Specifically, EPA had not adequately considered whether the available technology, catalytic mufflers, would be available for a sufficient variety of model lines or in sufficient quantities to meet market demands.

Subsequent to the decision, EPA held new hearings and granted a suspension. Then, in accordance with the statutory mandate, EPA set interim standards which (although not equal to the 90 percent reduction desired by Congress) were quite stringent. Renewed suspensions were granted in 1975 after an amendment to the law had made them available.

[216] *Natural Resources Defense Council v. Thomas*, 805 F.2d 410 (D.C. Cir. 1986).

### 11.1.1 1990 Amendments: Heavy-Duty Trucks

The 1990 amendments change section 202 to authorize EPA to revise emission standards applicable to emissions of hydrocarbons, carbon monoxide, oxides of nitrogen, and particulate matter from heavy-duty vehicles or engines manufactured during or after model year 1983.[217] These revised standards must reflect the "greatest degree of emission reduction achievable" through the application of technology that EPA determines will be available for the model year to which such standards apply. In developing these standards, EPA is to give consideration to cost, energy and safety factors associated with the application of such technology. The new standards are to become applicable no earlier than the model year commencing four years after the revised standard is promulgated.[218]

### 11.1.2. Vehicle Refueling Controls for Light-Duty Vehicles

By November 1991 EPA must promulgate rules mandating that new light-duty vehicles be equipped with vehicle-based ("onboard") systems for the control of vehicle refueling emissions. These rules first apply to vehicles made in the fourth model year (1995 or 1996) after the model year in which the standards are promulgated. These standards are to be further phased in over a three-year period. They must require that such onboard systems provide a minimum evaporative emission capture efficiency of 95 percent.

### 11.1.3. Emission Standards for Conventional Motor Vehicles

Manufacturers of light-duty trucks (up to 6000 lbs. gross vehicle weight) and light-duty vehicles must reduce emissions of nonmethane hydrocarbons, carbon monoxide, oxides of nitrogen and particulate matter in accordance with a phased-in schedule beginning in 1994. Sections 202(g) and (h), as added by the 1990 amendments, set forth the specific emission standards required for light-duty trucks and light-duty vehicles and the percentages of the

---

[217] Under the Act, "model year" is defined as the manufacturer's annual production period which includes January 1 of such calendar year. The term "heavy duty vehicle" means a truck, bus, or other vehicle manufactured primarily for use on public roads (not including railways) which has a gross vehicle weight in excess of six thousand pounds.

[218] The 1990 Amendments also require EPA to study the practice of rebuilding heavy-duty engines and the impact of rebuilding on engine emissions. On the basis of this study, EPA is authorized to prescribe requirements to control rebuilding practices and emissions from any rebuilt heavy-duty engines.

manufacturers' sales volumes of such trucks and vehicles that must comply with the required emission standards by the specified model years.

Section 202(i) also directs EPA to study whether or not further reductions in emissions from light-duty vehicles and light-duty trucks should be required. The study must consider whether to establish, with respect to model years commencing after January 1, 2003, even more stringent standards for light-duty vehicles and light-duty trucks. EPA is to submit the results of this study to Congress, and, based on the study, must promulgate more stringent emission standards, if there is a need for further reduction in emissions, the technology for meeting more stringent emission standards will be available, and obtaining further reductions in emissions will be cost effective. Any such standards are to take effect no earlier than model year 2003, but not later than model year 2006.[219]

### 11.1.4 Carbon Monoxide Emissions at Cold Temperatures

EPA additionally must promulgate regulations applicable to emissions of carbon monoxide from 1994 and later model light-duty vehicles and light-duty trucks when operated at 20 degrees Fahrenheit. The regulations must contain standards providing that emissions of carbon monoxide from light-duty vehicles when operated at 20 degrees Fahrenheit may not exceed 10.0 grams per mile; the standards applicable to light-duty trucks must be comparable in stringency. The amendments require that a certain percentage of each manufacturer's sales volume of light-duty vehicles and light-duty trucks must comply with the required emission standards by specified model years.[220]

### 11.1.5 Evaporative Emissions

Section 202(k) was added by the 1990 amendments. It requires EPA to regulate evaporative emissions of hydrocarbons from all gasoline-fueled motor

---

[219] Section 202(g) additionally extends the useful life of light-duty vehicles and engines, which is significant because the concept of "useful life" is used in setting the durability standards for certifying a vehicle model and in establishing the period during which vehicle families are subject to recall for failure to conform to emission standards. S. Rep. No. 228, 101st Cong., 1st Sess. 102 (1989).

[220] Section 202(j) as added by the 1990 amendments. Moreover, EPA must study the need for further reductions in emissions of carbon monoxide and the maximum reductions in such emissions achievable from model year 2001 and later model year light-duty vehicles and light-duty trucks when operated at 20 degrees Fahrenheit. If, as of June 1, 1997, six or more nonattainment areas have a carbon monoxide design value of 9.5 parts per million or greater, the regulations applicable to cold temperature emissions of carbon monoxide from model year 2002 and later model year light-duty vehicles and trucks must contain the more stringent standards specified in the act.

vehicles both (1) during operation and (2) during periods of nonuse lasting two or more days during ozone-prone summertime conditions. These regulations must require the greatest degree of emission reduction by means reasonably expected to be available for production during any model year to which the regulations apply, giving consideration to fuel volatility, and to cost, energy, and safety factors associated with the application of the appropriate technology. EPA is to begin this rulemaking process by November 1991.

### 11.1.6. Mobile Source-Related Air Toxics

In addition to developing the regulations specifically addressed by the 1990 amendments, EPA must study the need for, and the feasibility of, controlling emissions of toxic air pollutants associated with motor vehicles and motor vehicle fuels. This study is to focus on the categories of emissions posing the greatest risk to human health or about which significant uncertainties remain, including emissions of benzene, formaldehyde, and 1,3 butadiene. The study must be completed by April 1992 and, by April 1995, EPA is to promulgate regulations controlling those hazardous air pollutants from motor vehicles and motor vehicle fuels which the study identifies. The regulations must contain standards for vehicles or fuels, or both, that reflect the greatest degree of emission reduction achievable through the application of technology that will be available, taking into consideration, *inter alia,* the availability and costs of the technology, and noise, energy and safety factors, and lead time. The regulations must, at a minimum, apply to emissions of benzene and formaldehyde.

### 11.1.7 Emission Control Diagnostics Systems

By April 1992 EPA must promulgate rules requiring manufacturers to install diagnostic systems on all new light-duty vehicles and trucks. These systems must be capable of identifying (for the vehicle's useful life) emission-related systems deterioration or malfunction and alerting the vehicle's owner to maintain or to repair emission-related components or systems. EPA may also require manufacturers to install such on-board diagnostic systems on heavy-duty vehicles and engines. These regulations are to take effect in model year 1994.[221]

### 11.2. Motor Vehicle Testing, Certification, and Compliance

### 11.2.1 Inspection Procedures

Under Section 206(a), EPA is to test new motor vehicles and engines submitted by manufacturers to determine whether the equipment complies with the act's emission limitations and to issue certificates of conformity. As revised by the 1990 amendments, this section now directs EPA to revise the regulations previously promulgated under subsection 206(a) of the Clean Air

---

[221] Section 202(m), as added by the 1990 amendments.

Act for motor vehicle testing.[222]   The revised regulations must add test procedures capable of determining whether model year 1994 and later light-duty vehicles and light-duty trucks will pass the inspection methods and procedures established for that model year, under conditions reasonably likely to be encountered in the conduct of inspection and maintenance programs. (These conditions include fuel characteristics, ambient temperature, and short waiting periods before tests are conducted.)   EPA cannot grant a certificate of conformity under subsection 206(a) for any 1994 or later model year vehicle or engine that cannot pass these revised test procedures.[223]

### 11.2.2. Auto Warranties

The Clean Air Act's imposition of statutory warranties was perhaps a "first" in the history of regulatory legislation.   Section 207(a) required the manufacturer to warrant to the owner that the vehicle is designed, built, and equipped to conform at the time of sale with applicable standards, and that it is free from defects in materials and workmanship which would cause noncompliance.   Both of these warranties carry with them rather substantial problems of proof for the owner, and have not proved to be effective remedies.

Section 207(b) provided a potentially more important check on emissions. It required a manufacturer to warrant that the vehicle "if properly maintained and used" will perform in compliance with the applicable standards for its useful life.[224]

One controversial section of the 1990 amendments amended section 207 to impose specific requirements for the duration of motor vehicle warranties.[225] Section 207(i) now applies to new light-duty trucks and new light-duty vehicles and engines manufactured in model year 1995 and thereafter, and requires a warranty period of the earlier of first two years or 24,000 miles of use,

---

[222] Section 206(a)(4).

[223] Section 207(c) of the Clean Air Act, under which EPA tests light duty vehicles and trucks to determine compliance with emissions standards when they are in actual use, was changed by the 1990 amendments to establish intermediate standards applicable to in use light-duty trucks and light-duty vehicles.   These interim standards apply until more stringent final in-use standards take effect beginning in 1995. Section 207(c)(4)-(6).

[224] Section 207(c) gave EPA authority to order manufacturers to recall and repair or modify groups of vehicles which exceed the emission standards when in actual use.   The manufacturer has the right to a hearing to contest EPA's finding that its vehicles do not meet standards.   These are formal hearings before an administrative law judge.

[225] Section 207(i).

whichever first occurs. However, in the case of specified major emission control components (which include catalytic converters, electronic emissions control units and onboard emissions diagnostic devices), the warranty period for new light-duty trucks and new light-duty vehicles and engines manufactured starting in model year 1995 is eight years or 80,000 miles of use.

### 11.2.3  Information Collection

Section 208 was rewritten by the 1990 amendments. It requires manufacturers of new motor vehicles, engines and component parts to establish and maintain records, allow access to such records, perform tests, and make reports and provide information the agency may require to determine whether the manufacturer is acting in compliance with the act. EPA further is authorized to inspect the records, files, papers, processes, controls and facilities to ensure compliance.

### 11.3.  Fuel Requirements

The 1990 amendments expand and strengthen EPA's regulation of motor vehicle fuel and fuel additives. The Clean Air Act generally authorizes EPA to regulate the manufacture or sale of motor vehicle fuels or additives, on finding that the additives will impair, to a significant degree, the performance of an existing or proposed emission control device. Fuel additives must be registered with the government.

EPA determined that in order to attempt to meet the 1975 emission standards, automobile manufacturers primarily intended to rely on the catalytic converter -- a device which is "poisoned," i.e., rendered ineffective, by lead. As a result of this finding, the agency had promulgated regulations,[226] which require one grade of unleaded gasoline to be generally available throughout the country at the larger gasoline stations.[227]

EPA also was given authority to control the use of fuel additives if they "endanger the public health or welfare." EPA determined that lead emitted from automobiles as a result of the use of leaded gasoline posed an endangerment to public health, particularly among urban children. In 1973,[228] EPA adopted regulations that required the gradual phasing down of the amount of lead used in leaded gasoline by 1979. In 1982 and 1985 EPA further tightened the lead phase-down regulations.

---

[226]  40 C.F.R. Part 80.

[227]  In addition to various labeling requirements, the Part 80 regulations require that the unleaded gasoline be dispensed from a special nozzle, and that cars with catalytic converters have gasoline inlets designed to mate with the special nozzles.

[228]  40 C.F.R. 80.20.

The 1990 amendments prohibit the introduction by any person of leaded gasoline into motor vehicles designed for the use of unleaded gasoline. After December 31, 1995, motor vehicle gasoline cannot contain lead or lead additives. Similarly, new section 218 prohibits, after model year 1992, the manufacture or sale of motor vehicle engines or nonroad vehicle engines that require leaded gasoline.

Beginning October 1, 1993, use, manufacturing or sale of motor vehicle diesel fuel containing a concentration of sulfur in excess of .05 percent or failing to meet a cetane index minimum of 40 is similarly prohibited.[229]

Because of concern that fuel volatility had increased since the early 1970s, in part because of the lead phasedown, Section 216 directs EPA quickly to promulgate rules prohibiting sale during the high ozone season, of gasoline with a Reid Vapor Pressure in excess of nine pounds per square inch. EPA has been working with states since 1987 to promulgate similar rules; many have already been adopted. These regulations, which are to be promulgated by April 1991, must also establish more stringent Reid Vapor Pressure standards in nonattainment areas. EPA's new requirements under this section must take effect not later than the high ozone season -- spring and summer -- of 1992. The Reid Vapor pressure limitations established under this section are less stringent for fuel blends containing gasoline and 10% ethanol.

### 11.3.1. Reformulated Gasoline and Oxygenated Gasoline

By November 1991, EPA must establish rules for reformulated gasoline for use in gasoline-fueled vehicles in specified nonattainment areas. These regulations must require the greatest reduction in emissions of ozone-forming volatile organic compounds (VOCs) and emissions of toxic air pollutants achievable through the reformulation of conventional gasoline. In making these rules EPA must consider the cost of achieving such emission reductions, any nonair-quality and other air-quality related health and environmental impacts, and energy requirements. New sections 211(k)-(m) set forth in detail the requirements (*e.g.*, oxygen content, benzene content, heavy metals content, nitrogen oxide emissions) with which all reformulated gasoline must comply. EPA also must establish procedures for certification of reformulated gasoline as complying with EPA's requirements.

Beginning January 1, 1995, section 211 prohibits the sale or dispensing of conventional gasoline to ultimate consumers in any of nine specified ozone nonattainment areas. States may, moreover, elect to apply such prohibition in other areas with ozone pollution problems.

Section 211 also establishes a credit program, under which persons subject to the reformulated gasoline requirements will be allowed to pool gasoline sold in a given nonattainment area for purposes of determining compliance with the requirements governing reformulated gasoline. Under the credit program, a person may earn credit for gasoline with a higher oxygen content, lower

---

[229] Section 211(i), as added by the 1990 amendments.

aromatic hydrocarbon content, or lower benzene content than otherwise required. Such credits, once earned, may be used in the same nonattainment area in which they were earned to offset the sale or use of gasoline with a lower oxygen content, higher aromatic hydrocarbon content, or higher benzene content than otherwise required. However, credits may not be used to the extent that such use would result in an average gasoline oxygen, aromatic hydrogen or benzene content in a covered nonattainment area that is less stringent than would occur without a credit program.

### 11.4. Nonroad Engines and Vehicles

Section 213 as amended now requires EPA to study by November 1991, emissions from nonroad engines and nonroad vehicles (other than locomotives and locomotive engines).[230] EPA then is to develop regulations based on the study results. By November 1995, EPA must publish rules controlling emissions from new locomotives and new locomotive engines.[231]

### 11.5 Urban Buses

Section 219 was added by the 1990 amendments. It requires EPA to regulate the emissions from urban buses beginning in model year 1994. These standards must be based on the best technology that can reasonably be anticipated to be available at the time such measures are to be implemented, taking costs, safety, energy, lead time, and other relevant factors into account. The particulate standards must be cut by half from the 1990 standard for heavy-duty vehicles manufactured as of 1994.

Section 219 further authorizes EPA to conduct annual tests of a sample of operating urban buses subject to the particulate matter standards. If these tests show that urban buses do not comply with the particulate matter standards, EPA is to revise the standards applicable to such buses to require that new urban buses must be capable of operating and must be exclusively

---

[230] Nonroad vehicles do not include vehicles used solely for competition. Section 211(a) as amended also expands EPA's authority to regulate fuels and fuel additives used exclusively in nonroad engines or nonroad vehicles.

[231] The standards promulgated under section 213 must generally achieve the greatest degree of emission reduction achievable through the application of technology that the Administrator determines will be available for the engines, vehicles or locomotives, to which such standards apply, giving consideration to the cost of applying such technology within the period of time available to manufacturers and to noise, energy, and safety factors associated with the application of such technology. Standards under this section are to take effect at the earliest possible date considering the lead time necessary to permit the development and application of the requisite technology, giving appropriate consideration to the cost of compliance within such period and energy and safety.

operated on low-polluting fuels, such as methanol, ethanol, propane or natural gas.

## 11.6 Clean-Fuel Vehicles

The 1990 amendments added a new subpart C to Title II concerning clean-fuel vehicles. First, EPA has two years to develop regulations containing clean-fuel vehicle standards for the specified clean-fuel vehicles. The act specifically sets forth: (1) phase I (beginning in model year 1996) and phase II (beginning in model year 2001) emission standards for clean-fuel light-duty vehicles and certain light-duty trucks; (2) emissions standards for clean-fuel light-duty trucks of more than 6,000 lbs. gross vehicle weight rating, beginning in model year 1998; and (3) nonmethane organic gas emission standards for vehicles weighing not more than 8,500 lbs. gross vehicle weight rating that are capable of operating on more than one fuel ("flexible" or "dual" fueled vehicles), beginning in model year 1996.[232]

Subpart C also establishes standards for heavy-duty (gross vehicle weight rating above 8,500 up to 26,000 lbs.) clean-fuel vehicles, beginning for model year 1998.

This subpart additionally includes a program for fleet vehicles, under which fleet vehicles would be substantially cleaner than conventional vehicles. States in which covered areas (specified ozone and carbon monoxide nonattainment areas) are located must, by April 1994 submit a SIP revision to establish a clean-fuel vehicle program for fleets. This SIP revision must require that at least a specified percentage of all new covered fleet vehicles in model year 1998 and thereafter purchased by each covered fleet operator in each covered area be clean-fuel vehicles and use clean alternative fuels when operating in the covered area. A table in the act specifies the percentage of fleet vehicles that must be clean-fuel vehicles in model years beginning in 1998.[233] The state plans must also provide for the issuance by the states of appropriate credits to fleet operators for purchasing more clean-fuel vehicles than required or purchasing clean-fuel vehicles meeting more stringent standards than required; the use of such credits is described in detail in the act. Covered fleet vehicles owned or operated by an agency, department or instrumentality of the United States are also regulated under this subpart.

## 11.7 Mobile Source Enforcement

The 1990 amendments broaden EPA's mobile source and fuels enforcement authority in several ways. Sections 203, 205, and 211 are amended. These

---

[232] If, however, the state of California promulgates vehicle regulations that are at least as protective of public health as the vehicle standards described immediately above, then the California standards will apply to the clean-fuel vehicles in lieu of the standards otherwise applicable.

[233] Section 246(b).

amendments (1) change sections 203, 205 and 211 to conform to the new provisions, such as the recordkeeping and reporting requirements; (2) extend liability for tampering with vehicle emission controls; (3) raise from $10,000 to $25,000 the maximum civil penalty that can be levied for violation of certain vehicle requirements; (4) provide new authority to the administrator to assess administrative penalties of up to $200,000;[234] (5) replace the mandatory forfeiture penalty of $10,000 per day for violations of fuels regulations with a civil penalty of up to $25,000 per day for each violation and the amount of economic benefit or savings resulting from the violation; and (6) provide injunctive authority to restrain violations of fuels regulations (as is already available for violations of vehicle and stationary source requirements).

### 11.8 Aircraft Emission Standards

Section 231 empowers the administrator to establish emission standards for aircraft engines, following the regulatory pattern set forth in Section 202(a) for motor vehicles. EPA has established emission standards for most classes of new aircraft and aircraft engines and for the most significant emitters among existing aircraft and engines.[235]

These standards, which can be issued only if the Secretary of Transportation agrees that they do not create safety problems, are required by the act to be enforced by the Department of Transportation, which has issued regulations for that purpose.

### 12.0 OZONE PROTECTION

In 1975, scientists began to announce the results of studies on depletion of the ozone layer in the stratosphere. Ozone ($O_3$), which at a ground level is considered a criteria pollutant, and a key component in smog, is essential at twenty miles or higher in the stratosphere to screen out harmful ultraviolet radiation. That radiation can cause skin cancers and reduce crop yields if exposures become excessive.

The chemical agents implicated in ozone depletion are the halogenated compounds known as "halocarbons" or chlorofluorocarbons (CFCs). Though stable in the lower atmosphere, scientists believe they become unstable in sunlight at higher levels and react with ozone, forming new compounds, thereby depleting the ozone available for screening. These CFCs are in wide-

---

[234] The procedure to be followed by the administrator in assessing an administrative penalty and the factors to be considered by the administrator in determining the amount of an administrative penalty are set forth in detail in the act. They are similar to the procedures to be followed for stationary sources.

[235] 40 C.F.R. Part 87.

spread use, as aerosol propellants, in cleaning and manufacturing electronic equipment, as refrigerants and foaming agents, and they are released in the atmosphere when aerosol-packaged products are used and through leakage or destruction of refrigeration equipment.

Congress initially reacted to these concerns by adding Subtitle B of the Clean Air Act in 1977. The 1990 amendments repealed Subtitle B, replacing it with a new Title VI, providing more elaborate EPA regulatory authority. Prior to the 1990 amendments, the key thrust of EPA's efforts had been to negotiate (through the State Department) the Montreal Protocol on Substances that Deplete the Ozone Layer.[236] That agreement was reached in 1987, and EPA adopted implementing regulations,[237] part of which became effective in September 1988, the remainder of which become effective 90 days after ratification by eleven signatory countries. The regulations provide for a 50 percent reduction in the production and consumption of CFCs by June 1998.

In response to recent scientific evidence suggesting that the ozone depletion caused by CFCs and halons is worse than anticipated, the United States has moved beyond the 50 percent reduction in the production and consumption of CFCs mandated by the Montreal Protocol. Title VI to the 1990 amendments requires a complete phase-out by the year 2030 of the production and consumption of substances, including CFCs, halons and hydrochlorofluoro-carbons (HCFCs), that are believed to contribute to the depletion of ozone in the stratosphere.[238] Title VI is meant to supplement the terms and conditions of the Montreal Protocol and, accordingly, in the case of any conflict between the two, the more stringent provision shall govern.

The statute establishes a comprehensive schedule for the complete phase-out of ozone-depleting chemicals, with certain exceptions, over the next 40 years. In addition, the statute provides for a national recycling program of such harmful substances and sets forth a policy requiring companies to replace banned substances with safe substitutes that reduce risks to human health and the environment. Also, products containing or manufactured with any ozone-depleting chemicals are required to have warning labels identifying the particular substance and its danger to the environment.

## 12.1 Production and Consumption Phase-out Schedule

The list of substances that are to be phased out under Title VI consists of two separate classes. Class I contains substances believed to be the most damaging to the ozone layer, namely CFCs, halons, carbon tetrachloride, methyl chloroform, and all isomers of these substances, with the exception of

---

[236] The Protocol is reprinted at 52 Fed. Reg. 47515 (December 1987).

[237] 40 C.F.R. Part 82.

[238] Subtitle B to Title I of the prior Clean Air Act, sections 150 to 159, is repealed by the new Title VI.

1,1,2-trichloroethane. Class II contains HCFCs and all of their isomers, chemicals that are believed to be less damaging to the ozone layer and were once considered possible substitutes for CFCs. However, the list of substances is not comprehensive; EPA has the power to add any substance that is found to contribute significantly to harmful effects on the ozone layer.

Pursuant to section 604 of the act, production[239] and consumption of all Class I substances must be terminated by January 1, 2000 (except methyl chloroform, which must be terminated by January 1, 2002). Further, for the years leading up to termination, reductions in production of Class I substances must conform to the schedule set forth in Table One.

## TABLE ONE[240]

| Date | Carbon Tetrachloride | Methyl Chloroform | Other Class I Substances |
|------|---------------------|-------------------|--------------------------|
| 1991 | 100% | 100% | 85% |
| 1992 | 90% | 100% | 80% |
| 1993 | 80% | 90% | 75% |
| 1994 | 70% | 85% | 65% |
| 1995 | 15% | 70% | 50% |
| 1996 | 15% | 50% | 40% |
| 1997 | 15% | 50% | 15% |
| 1998 | 15% | 50% | 15% |
| 1999 | 15% | 50% | 15% |
| 2000 | -- | 20% | -- |
| 2001 | -- | 20% | -- |

Production of all substances listed in Class II, which are less damaging than CFCs to the ozone layer, must be frozen in 2015 at a level equal to the production level during the baseline year, which is to be determined by EPA.

---

[239] "Production" is statutorily defined as the manufacture of a substance from any raw material or feedstock chemical. Trace quantities manufactured where a substance is used in a chemical manufacturing process, and recycled substances, are excluded from this definition.

[240] The percentages in Table One refer to the maximum allowable production as a percentage of the quantity of the substance produced by the person concerned in the "baseline year." For carbon tetrachloride, methyl chloroform and certain CFCs listed in group III of Class I, the baseline year is 1989. For all other Class I substances, which are listed in groups I and II, the baseline year is 1986.

Effective January 1, 2030, production of all Class II substances must be terminated.

In a number of circumstances, however, EPA is required to accelerate the above schedules for freezes and bans on production. EPA must establish more stringent production and consumption phase-outs of Class I and Class II substances if (1) the schedule under the Montreal Protocol is tightened so that production is reduced more rapidly than under this statute's schedule; (2) EPA determines that, based on credible current scientific information, a more stringent schedule is necessary to protect human health and the environment; or (3) EPA determines that a more stringent schedule is practicable due to the availability of substitutes, taking into account technological achievability, safety and other relevant factors. In addition, the statute provides a mechanism whereby public interest groups may petition EPA to promulgate regulations accelerating the reduction and termination of these substances.

## 12.2 Exceptions to Phase-out Schedule

Sections 604 and 605 of the statute provide various exceptions to the production phase-out schedules of Class I and Class II substances. Production of methyl chloroform after January 1, 2002 is allowed for use in essential applications, such as nondestructive metal fatigue and corrosion testing of airplane engines and parts. A medical device exception allows production of Class I and Class II substances after their respective termination dates solely for use in medical devices if deemed necessary by the Food and Drug Administration. Limited production of halons is allowed for necessary aviation safety purposes if the Federal Aviation Administration determines no safe and effective substitute is available. The production of Class I and Class II substances under these exceptions, however, cannot exceed 10 percent of that produced during the baseline year.

A further exception is allowed for the limited production of Class I and Class II substances to satisfy the basic domestic needs of developing countries that are operating under Article 5 of the Montreal Protocol. For Class I substances, annual production is limited to the schedule's specified percentage plus 10 percent of baseline production through the year 1999 (2001 for methyl chloroform) and, for 10 years thereafter, production is capped at 15 percent of baseline production. For Class II substances, production under this exception cannot exceed 110 percent of baseline production between the years 2015 and 2030 and cannot exceed 15 percent of baseline production from 2030 to 2040.

A national security exception allows the President to order production of halons and CFC-114 if necessary to protect national security interests of the United States. And finally, production of halons for purposes of fire suppression and explosion prevention can exceed the specified percentage under the schedule, provided no safe and effective substitute has been developed.

## 12.3 Nonessential Products

By November 1992, it will be unlawful to sell any nonessential consumer product, excluding medical devices, that releases Class I substances into the environment.[241] In determining whether a product is nonessential, EPA must consider the purpose or intended use of the product, the technological availability of substitutes for the product and the Class I substances, safety, health and other relevant factors. In addition, a product falls into this category if it releases Class I substances during manufacture, use, storage or disposal.

At a minimum, however, EPA must prohibit the sale of CFC-propelled party streamers and noise horns and CFC-containing cleaning fluids for non-commercial electronic and photographic equipment. Further, by 1994, the sale or distribution of aerosol products or pressurized dispensers containing Class II substances will be prohibited, with the exception of uses determined by EPA to be essential.

### 12.4 Exchanges of Production Allowances

As currently provided under EPA regulations implementing the Montreal Protocol, the transfer of Class I and Class II production allowances between producers is allowed, provided the transfer involves substances within the same class. EPA regulations implementing the new exchange authority, however, must insure that any such transfer will result in greater total reductions of annual production than would occur in that year in the absence of such transfer.

The statute also provides for international trading of production allowances between the United States and other Parties to the Montreal Protocol. As a condition, however, one must show that the transfer will reduce the aggregate domestic production of the substance or substances involved.

### 12.5 Recycling

Effective July 1, 1992, EPA must promulgate rules to regulate the use and disposal of Class I and Class II substances used in appliances and for industrial process refrigeration.[242] The regulations must prohibit anyone who maintains, services, repairs or disposes of appliances from venting or releasing any such substances used as refrigerants. Further, effective 5 years after enactment of this statute, it shall be unlawful to vent, release or dispose of any environmentally harmful refrigerant substitute for a Class I or Class II substance. The regulations must also provide for a reduction in the use and emission of Class I and Class II substances used as refrigerants to the lowest achievable level and maximize the recycling of such substances.

By November 1991, EPA must promulgate rules to regulate those persons who service motor vehicle air conditioners and require them to be properly

---

[241] § 610.

[242] Clean Air Act, § 608.

trained and certified to perform such work.[243] Those persons must also be required to use refrigerant recycling equipment that is approved for such use by EPA.

## 12.6 Labeling Requirements

Section 611 of the act requires that by April 1993 warning labels must be affixed to all containers as well as certain products that contain Class I and Class II substances. The labels must identify the particular substances and state that the substance harms public health and the environment by destroying ozone. These labeling requirements do not create a defense to product liability claims, however, nor does compliance with them provide a basis to reduce damages in such cases.

Products that contain Class I substances must have warning labels. Products manufactured using a Class I substance must also have warning labels, unless EPA determines that there are no substitute products or manufacturing processes that (1) do not rely on the use of such Class I substance, (2) reduce the overall risk to human health and the environment, and (3) are currently or potentially available.

In contrast, products containing or manufactured with a Class II substance do not require warning labels, unless EPA determines that substitute products or manufacturing processes exist that (1) do not rely on the use of such Class II substance, (2) reduce the overall risk to human health and the environment, and (3) are currently or potentially available. Effective 2015, all products containing or manufactured with Class II substances must have warning labels.

## 12.7 Safe Alternatives

The statute also establishes a policy to ensure that banned substances are not replaced with chemicals that are harmful to health or the environment, when viable safe alternatives exist. Within two years of enactment, EPA must prohibit the replacement of any Class I or Class II substance with a substitute that EPA determines may present adverse effects to human health or the environment, but only if an alternative to such substitute has been identified by EPA that reduces overall risk to human health and the environment and is currently or potentially available. EPA must publish a list of safe alternatives and of prohibited unsafe substitutes for particular uses.

EPA must establish an overall policy of promoting research to identify safe alternatives to Class I and Class II substances and manufacturing processes that use these substances. In conjunction with this policy, EPA must maintain a public clearinghouse of alternative chemicals and manufacturing processes. EPA must also recommend federal research programs to identify alternatives, recommend changes in federal procurement policy to promote the use of safe

---

243 Clean Air Act, § 609.

alternatives, and require producers of alternatives to submit health and safety studies on such substances.

## 13.0 ENFORCEMENT, INFORMATION GATHERING, CITIZEN SUITS & JUDICIAL REVIEW

The 1990 amendments drastically overhauled the enforcement provisions of the act in order to make it far easier for EPA to bring enforcement action and to extract severe penalties from violators. These changes brought the Clean Air Act into conformity with the enforcement pattern set under the Clean Water Act and RCRA, providing criminal penalties for negligent offenses, knowing offenses, and knowing endangerment offenses, as well as for falsification of data or tampering with monitors. Additionally, a potent administrative penalty mechanism is now provided for lesser violations. The citizen suit provision should become a major factor in the enforcement calculus because of the new permit program and its monitoring provisions, as well as the new compliance certification powers under section 114.

### 13.1. Enforcement Powers

The 1990 amendments rewrote most of section 113, modernizing it and bringing it into conformity with the dramatic changes made in other parts of the act. The provision governs all enforcement except that conducted under Title II, concerning mobile sources.

As Congress has rewritten the provision, it now gives EPA a broad array of enforcement powers similar to those EPA enjoys under the Clean Water Act and RCRA. Though much of the new provision parallels enforcement under RCRA and the Clean Water Act, there are also some significant differences, reflecting experience under these other statutes and some different policy concerns under the Clean Air Act.

Under the prior version of the act, knowing violations of clean air requirements, including SIP requirements, could be punished criminally by up to one year in prison and a $25,000 fine. These criminal provisions were most often used for violations of hazardous air pollution requirements, especially in the asbestos area, where improper asbestos abatement has been widespread. Criminal penalties were also provided for tampering with monitors and falsification of data.

Under the new version of section 113(c), there are now four classes of criminal offenses: (1) negligent, (2) knowing, (3) knowing endangerment, and (4) tampering with monitors, falsification, and failure to make required reports.

### 13.1.1. Negligent Endangerment

For the first time under the Clean Air Act, negligent acts can now be the basis for criminal liability. Unlike the Clean Water Act where this is also true, however, the Clean Air Act restricts such negligent offenses to the negligent release of hazardous air pollutants or extremely hazardous substances of EPCRA. In order to be a criminal offense, the negligent release must place another person in imminent danger of death or serious bodily injury. It is a defense to such a charge if the release was authorized by a permit. Upon conviction, the violator may be imprisoned for up to one year; repeat violations can result in imprisonment for up to two years.

This negligent release language effectively criminalizes the release of the 189 hazardous air pollutants designated under section 112, as well as the 360 or so extremely hazardous substances designated under section 302(a) of the Emergency Planning and Community Right-to-Know Act (EPCRA). Though there is much overlap between the two lists, over 400 substances will be covered.

The "imminent danger of death or serious bodily injury" language is less of a limitation on these prosecutions than may first seem to be the case. Any release which requires the evacuation of people from an area will probably meet the statutory standards, unless shown to the contrary by the defendant. Additionally, the statute does not exclude employee exposures so that occupational exposures to high concentrations of contaminants which injure employees could lead to such prosecutions. The statute's requirement that the release be to the ambient air, however, will probably mean that indoor exposures to such substances will not be covered under the Clean Air Act.

### 13.1.2. Knowing Offenses

Most criminal prosecutions under the act will continue to have to show that the violation complained of was committed "knowingly."[244] Unlike the prior version of the statute, however, the penalties are now five years' imprisonment upon conviction, with a doubling upon conviction for a repeat offense. Fines are to be assessed under the general criminal code, Title 18, and are likely to be much higher, especially for corporations, than the $25,000 per day of violation previously provided.

Interpretations of the "knowledge" requirement of this provision will likely parallel the interpretation given similar language in RCRA. As discussed in the liability chapter of this book, the courts have interpreted the knowledge

---

[244] Section 113(c)(1) applies to violations of the state implementation plan during periods of federally assumed enforcement or 30 days after a notice of violation has issued, to violations of other administrative orders, to violations of new source performance standards, national emission standards for hazardous air pollutants, to the new solid waste combustion provisions, to preconstruction requirements under the PSD provisions, to emergency orders under section 303, to permit requirements under Title V, to the acid rain provisions of Title IV, and to the ozone protection requirements under Title VI. This provision also applies to non-payment of fees owed under the Act (other than under Title II), and to permits, waivers, orders, and rules promulgated under the listed provisions.

requirement to mean "known or should have known," for those who operate in a highly regulated area, such as those subject to RCRA or the Clean Air Act.

Section 113(c)(3) also makes it a criminal offense to "knowingly" fail to pay any fee owed the United State under Titles I, III, IV, V, or VI, all of the Act's provisions except for mobile sources and fuel regulation. The punishment for such offenses is up to one year of imprisonment and a fine set under Title 18 of the U.S. Code. As is the case for other offenses under the Clean Air Act, the penalties double for repeat offenses.

### 13.1.3. Knowing Endangerment

The 1990 amendments added a knowing endangerment provision which closely parallels the similar provisions of RCRA and the Clean Water Act.[245] Under section 113(c)(5), "knowing endangerment" means (1) knowingly releasing into the ambient air any hazardous air pollutant listed under section 112 or any extremely hazardous substance designated under section 302 of the Emergency Planning and Community Right-to-Know Act, *and* (2) knowingly placing another person in imminent danger of death or serious bodily injury. The penalty for knowing endangerment is up to fifteen years imprisonment, and for an organization, a fine of up to $1,000,000. Penalties double for repeat offenses.

Releases in accordance with permit conditions do not constitute offenses. Moreover, knowledge is not to be attributed to individuals except that circumstantial evidence can be used to show knowledge, including evidence that a person took affirmative steps to be shielded from relevant information.

### 13.1.4. Falsifications, Failures to Report, and Tampering

Section 113(c)(2) penalizes knowing actions to falsify reports, to fail to keep necessary monitoring records, and material omissions from such reports and records. The provision also penalizes knowing failures to report or notify as required by the act, and tampering or failure to properly install the monitoring equipment required by the act. Similar provisions were in the prior version of section 113, but the penalty is now up to two years' imprisonment. Moreover, the failure to make reports and notifications was not expressly spelled out as a criminal offense in the prior provision.

### 13.1.5. Contractor Listing

For companies which are convicted of criminal offenses under the Clean Air Act, there is an additional sanction provided in section 306: debarment of the offending facility from contracting with the federal government until EPA certifies that the condition giving rise to the violation has been corrected. A similar provision is found in the Clean Water Act, and most federal contracts require certifications by the contractor that they have not been convicted of

---

[245] The Clean Air Act provision is § 113(c)(5); the similar provision in the Clean Water Act is § 309(c)(3), and in RCRA, §§ 3008(e),(f).

criminal violations of the Clean Air or Clean Water Act. The 1990 amendments increased the potency of this sanction by allowing EPA to extend the debarment to other facilities owned or operated by the convicted party. This new sanction may allow EPA to debar entire companies from contracting with the federal government as opposed to single facilities. For some large companies, this may prove a very harsh sanction.

### 13.1.6. Civil Enforcement

Though EPA has now been given a potent new array of criminal enforcement powers, it is likely that EPA will continue to use civil actions for the bulk of its judicial enforcement efforts. The civil penalty provisions of the act were not significantly changed by the 1990 amendments. The civil penalty level remains at $25,000 per day, the same level as is also provided under the Clean Water Act. Each day of violation constitutes a separate offense, as is true under the other clean air act provisions. Significant penalties have been recovered under this civil penalty provision, in one PSD case over $6,000,000.[246]

Section 120 of the act allows EPA to recover the economic benefit of noncompliance. It has been amended to apply not only to violations of SIP requirements and NSPS and NESHAP provisions, but to PSD, emergency order, acid rain, ozone protection requirements and to violations of permits.[247] Usually this is calculated as the interest on foregone capital investment needed to come into timely compliance with the act's provisions, or with requirements of state implementation plans. EPA's regulations were issued in 1980, and upheld in 1983.[248] To date, these rules have seen little use, in part because of their complexity, and in part because the $25,000 per day penalty is usually sufficient to address the calculated economic benefit of noncompliance. The fine is to be calculated using a complicated computer model, a model which requires information on fifteen different variables from the company proposed to be penalized.

### 13.1.7. Administrative Enforcement

The 1990 amendments overhauled EPA's administrative order authority under the Clean Air Act and expanded it greatly. The administrative penalty mechanism now resembles the Clean Water Act's system, but has some important differences, specifically the provision for issuance of field citations for violations observed in the field.

---

[246] *U.S. v. Chevron,* 639 F.Supp. 770 (N.D. Tex. 1985).

[247] Clean Air Act Amendments of 1990, § 710, amending § 120 of the Clean Air Act.

[248] 40 C.F.R. Part 66. These rules were upheld in *Duquesne Light Co. v. EPA,* 698 F.2d 456 (D.C. Cir. 1983).

As under the prior version of the statute, if EPA finds that there are violations of SIP requirements, it may issue a notice of violation (NOV) to the affected source and the state. After the expiration of 30 days, EPA may issue administrative orders (AOs) requiring compliance with SIP provisions, issue an AO assessing a civil penalty, or take civil enforcement action.[249] The thirty day notice is for the benefit of the affected state, not for the affected source. The state is thus given an opportunity to enforce its own SIP requirements without federal intervention.

In the event EPA finds that the state has such widespread violations that the state has failed to enforce the SIP, EPA may take over direct enforcement of the SIP,[250] as was true in the prior version of the act, and as is also true under the Clean Water Act. Where EPA believes a state is not properly implementing or enforcing NSPS requirements, EPA may by order prohibit construction or modification of major stationary sources.[251]

EPA's new administrative enforcement powers allow the Agency to initiate an administrative penalty proceeding for current or past violations. Compliance is to be required under such orders "as expeditiously as practicable," but not later than one year after the date the order is issued.[252] These orders are not renewable, and thus are not to be a backdoor means by which compliance deadlines are extended.

The 1990 amendments added a new section 113(d) authorizing EPA to assess civil penalties through administrative penalty orders and proceedings. This provision is modelled very closely on section 309(g) of the Clean Water Act. Like that CWA provision, penalties may be assessed after an opportunity for a hearing on the record in conformity with section 554 and 556 of the Administrative Procedure Act. This means that the alleged violator will have the right to be heard before an administrative law judge (ALJ), to summon and cross-examine witnesses, be represented by counsel, and in general, have its due process rights protected.

A violator may challenge the determination of the ALJ by filing an action in U.S. District Court within thirty days following the date when the order becomes final. This action is not to be a retrial of the administrative proceeding; rather, the court is to review the administrative record to

---

[249] § 113(a)(1).

[250] § 113(a)(2).

[251] § 113(a)(5).

[252] § 113(a)(4).

determine if there is substantial evidence in the record to uphold the ALJ's decision.[253]

If a violator fails to pay or appeal a final administrative penalty order, the government may bring a collection action in district court. Failure to pay a final penalty will subject the person refusing to pay to an additional civil penalty of ten percent per quarter that the non-payment persists, the United States' attorney's fees and court costs, and interest at the statutory rate.[254] The validity of the underlying penalty may not be reviewed in the collection action.

Section 113(d) places an upper dollar limit on penalties which may be administratively assessed. The limit is $200,000; the limit may be waived by agreement between EPA and the Justice Department. There is also a time limit: EPA is to bring administrative penalty proceedings within a year of the violation. This time limit, like the dollar limit, may be waived by agreement with the Justice Department. The time limit should probably not be understood as a statute of limitation, because section 113(a)(1) makes specific reference to the general five year statute of limitations on civil penalty actions in 28 U.S.C. § 2462.[255]

Administrative penalties may be sought for violations of SIP requirements more than thirty days after a notice of violation, and for any violation of other requirements of the act, rules issued under it, or permits, other than requirements relating to mobile sources.[256] Thus virtually any stationary source violation may be subject to administrative penalty orders. Moreover, administrative penalties are not a bar to other EPA enforcement action, or to

---

[253] This administrative record review may be subject to constitutional challenge under *Tull v. United States*, 481 U.S. 412 (1987), which held that an alleged violator had a Seventh Amendment right to a jury trial to determine liability where the government sought to obtain civil penalties.

[254] § 113(d)(5)(B).

[255] There is divided case law about the application of 28 U.S.C. § 2462 to administrative penalty proceedings. The Fifth Circuit has held that such proceedings must be initiated, concluded, and a collection action brought within five years of the alleged violation. *United States v. Core Laboratories, Inc.*, 759 F.2d 480 (5th Cir. 1985). The First Circuit has declined to follow this rule. *United States v. Meyer*, 808 F.2d 912 (1st Cir. 1987). The Fifth Circuit case may be distinguishable by the United States in the Clean Air Act context because the statute involved there, the Export Administration Act, provided for a right of de novo review in federal district court, a review that means working from a clean slate. Under the Clean Air Act, the review is to be based on the administrative record, using a substantial evidence test.

[256] § 113(d)(1)(A).

citizen suits. The latter point is a departure from the clean water act model, where an administrative penalty proceeding does bar citizen suits, but citizens have the right to intervene in the proceeding.[257]

Section 113(d)(3) of the act now provides for a program of field citations for minor violations. Under this program, penalties of up to $5,000 per day may be assessed by designated EPA officers or employees for violations observed in the field. Presumably these field citations are to be used like traffic tickets, issued at the time an inspector observes a violation. These citations may be contested through an informal hearing, not subject to the administrative procedure act requirements governing the more elaborate administrative penalty orders. The statutory language limits this power to EPA officers and employees; thus contractors which EPA sometimes uses for inspections may not have this power. Assessment or payment of field citations is not a bar to other enforcement action.

### 13.1.8. Other Penalty and Enforcement Issues

The penalties and other sanctions available to EPA and the courts under the Clean Air Act are quite powerful. The potency of these provisions is increased further by several statutory presumptions. Under section 113(e)(2), in a civil or administrative case, once the plaintiff, usually an enforcement agency, makes out a prima facie case that the violation likely persisted from the time of the notice of violation, the presumption arises that the violation was ongoing from the time of the notice of violation until the defendant shows that the violation abated, or for those intervening days where it can show no violation occurred, e.g. periods of plant shutdown. As each day of a violation is a separate offense,[258] this presumption rapidly increases the civil penalty exposure of violators to very high levels.

Section 113(e)(1) directs courts and EPA to consider a set of factors in assessing penalties. These factors are:

-- size of the business;

-- economic impact of the penalty on the business;

-- the violator's full compliance history and good faith efforts to comply;

-- the duration of the violation as established by any credible evidence (including evidence other than the applicable test method);

-- payment of penalties previously assessed for the same violation;

---

[257] Clean Water Act, §§ 309(g)(4),(6).

[258] § 113(e)(1).

-- the economic benefit of noncompliance;

-- the seriousness of the violation; and

-- other factors justice may require.

These factors are very similar to what the Clean Water Act directs EPA and courts to consider, and to EPA's previous penalty policy. Before such settlements are submitted to the court for approval they are subject to public comment under the Justice Department's public participation policy and now under section 113(g) for settlements not covered by that policy.

### 13.2. Emergency Powers

The Clean Air Act gives EPA broad authority to act in emergency situations to protect public health and the environment. This emergency authority is much broader than the considerable powers EPA is granted to act under normal circumstances. These powers were expanded by the 1990 amendments.

Section 303 now authorizes EPA to bring a civil action or issue an administrative order to immediately restrain any source or combination of sources (including mobile sources) to stop the emissions causing or contributing to the emergency. The 1990 amendments expanded the bases for taking such action from threats to public health to include threats to public welfare or the environment. Orders may now be issued by EPA for up to 60 days rather than 48 hours. Such administrative orders may be extended for up to 14 additional days if EPA initiates a suit for injunctive relief during the 60 day period of the order; the court may extend such an order further during the pendency of such a suit. Violation of such administrative orders may subject the violator to the act's severe civil and criminal penalties.

Prior to the 1990 amendments, these emergency powers had been used only once, in Birmingham, Alabama against the steel industry in the early 1970s. EPA has prepared to take similar action in several other cities in air pollution emergencies, but not had to invoke the powers, in part because sources will often voluntarily curtail operations in response to EPA requests or threats of action under section 303. The 1990 amendments will likely increase the use of section 303, and make such use far easier to defend.

### 13.3. Information Gathering Authority

Congress has granted EPA powers to compel sources of air pollution and manufacturers of air pollution control equipment to make and maintain records, to sample air pollution emissions, and to report this information to EPA.

EPA may also enter the premises of a source to conduct its own emission testing or inspect other aspects of the source's operations.[259]

These powers are broad in keeping with the breadth of EPA's enforcement authority under the act, and they were strengthened by the 1990 amendments. Among other changes, EPA may now compel manufacturers of air pollution control or process equipment to provide information about the performance parameters of the equipment.

The 1990 amendments added a new requirement for compliance certifications by major stationary sources. Under section 114(a)(3), the administrator must obtain compliance certifications and enhanced monitoring from owners and operators of major stationary sources, and may require such certifications and enhanced monitoring from owners and operators of other air pollution sources. These certifications must include identification of:

-- the applicable requirements that are the basis for the certification;

-- the method used to determine compliance status;

-- the compliance status;

-- whether compliance is continuous or intermittent; and

-- other facts EPA may require.

EPA is to promulgate rules for such enhanced monitoring and compliance certifications by November 1992.

The data submitted under section 114 are to be publicly available with the exception of trade secrets. Section 307(a) and case law under section 114 makes clear that emission data are not to be considered trade secrets because of their importance to the operation of the Clean Air Act's citizen suit provisions.[260]

Section 307(a) was also amended in 1990 to broaden EPA's subpoena powers to extend to any investigation, monitoring, requirement, entry,

---

[259] EPA will obtain search warrants where permission to enter is refused, as required by *Marshall v. Barlow*, 436 U.S. 307 (1978), in which the Supreme Court read a warrant requirement into similar language under the Occupational Safety and Health Act. The Court has upheld EPA's right under section 114 to conduct aerial photography of a source without a warrant to do so. *Dow Chemical Co. v. United States*, 476 U.S. 227 (1986). The *Dow* case may become more important as remote sensing technologies such as lidars improve, allowing off-site inspectors to check the composition of emissions.

[260] Eg. in the *Natural Resources Defense Council v. EPA*, 478 F.2d 875, 893 (1st Cir. 1973).

compliance inspection, or administrative enforcement proceeding under the act. These subpoena powers are enforceable in district court. The penalty assessment criteria expressly provide that penalties are not to be assessed for noncompliance with administrative subpoenas or actions under section 114 where the violator had sufficient cause to violate or fail or refuse to comply with such subpoena or action.[261]

This standard would appear to require the violator to have a colorable defense to a subpoena or certification demand if it is to avoid penalties. Thus in responding to agency information requests, companies should make sure they have a principled legal basis to object, seek to comply to the extent they do not object to the request, and seek to narrow areas of disagreement with EPA over the scope of such orders. Presumably the district courts, drawing on requirements frequently imposed in civil discovery disputes, will expect at least that much effort by objecting parties to resolve differences if they are to avoid the imposition of sanctions. The stakes are potentially much higher-- $25,000 per day -- for noncompliance with such administrative subpoenas or certifications than is normally the case for noncompliance with civil discovery requests in federal district court.

### 13.4. Citizen Suits

When Congress passed the Clean Air Act of 1970, it wrote a citizen suit provision into section 304. That section became the model for citizen suits in most federal environmental statutes. This provision was an unusual enforcement approach, enlisting private citizens into the effort to help bring sources into compliance and to guard against EPA failures to act. The legislative history of section 304 remains influential in interpreting the citizen suit provisions of the other environmental statutes.

Section 304(a) allows citizens to bring enforcement actions against any person alleged to be violating "emission standards" under the act, against persons constructing or proposing to construct new sources in violation of PSD or nonattainment provisions or permits, and against EPA to compel the administrator to take non-discretionary actions. "Emission standards" are broadly defined in section 304(f) to include most of the act's substantive requirements, as well as permits, orders, SIP and permit requirements and conditions implementing these substantive requirements. These actions may be brought against federal agencies operating sources of air pollution as well as against states, localities and private parties owning or operating such sources.

To date, the citizen suit provision of the Clean Air Act has received much less use against alleged violators of the act than has the comparable Clean Water Act provision. There are a number of reasons for this dearth of citizen suits, but the lack of a uniform federal permit program under the Clean Air Act, together with the lack of uniform continuous monitoring and reporting requirements for stationary sources, are probably the main reasons.

---

[261] § 113(e)(1).

The changes in the monitoring and compliance certification provisions, together with the addition of Title V's federal permit program, seem likely to greatly increase the number of citizen enforcement actions against stationary sources.

Information concerning violations should be readily available to interested citizens, especially now that the permit program has been added to the statute, and now that the monitoring and compliance certification provisions in section 114 have been strengthened. Additionally, section 110(a)(2)(f) requires that sources periodically report emission data to the state, and that such reports must be available to the public. Section 114, which authorizes the administrator to inspect sources and require reports, specifically exempts "emission data"[262] from information which might be withheld from the public on the grounds that it constitutes a trade secret. Again, in Section 208, emission data on motor vehicles is excluded from restrictions which might otherwise allow it to be withheld from public disclosure.

In order to initiate citizen enforcement actions, a written notice must be sent to the alleged violator, EPA, and the state in which the violation is occurring at least 60 days before the action is to be filed. Likewise, in suits to force EPA to perform its nondiscretionary duties, at least 60 days notice must be given to EPA before the suit is begun. If the United States or a state brings or is already bringing a diligent enforcement action, then the citizen suit is barred, but the citizen has a right to intervene in the state or federal enforcement action. Unlike the situation under the Clean Water Act, the pendency of an administrative penalty proceeding is *not* a bar to a citizen suit.

The 1990 amendments now require that the action also be served on the United States and that the United States have 45 days in which to present its views to the court about any proposed settlement. The United States has the right to intervene in any citizen suit brought under section 304.

The 1990 amendments changed section 304(a) to make clear that citizen suits can be brought to recover civil penalties for past violations if there is evidence that the alleged violation has been repeated. The Bush Administration objected to this change, apparently on the view that citizen suits should only be available for ongoing violations. The 1990 amendments also clarified that citizen suits could be brought to recover civil penalties, not just injunctive relief; the prior version of the statute did not expressly authorize citizen suits for civil penalties.

The 1990 amendments now require civil penalties assessed under section 304 be paid to the U.S. Treasury and deposited in a special penalty fund for use by EPA in financing enforcement activities. The court has the discretion to direct that up to $100,000 of the civil penalties assessed be spent instead on beneficial mitigation projects to enhance public health or the environment. The role of environmentally beneficial expenditures has been controversial in settling enforcement cases under the Clean Water Act and other environmental

---

[262] Section 114(c).

statutes. It is normally in the interest of an alleged violator to spend money for such projects instead of penalties, because there are arguments that expenditures for such projects are a deductible business expense, where the Internal Revenue Code clearly prohibits any tax deduction for the payment of penalties, including payments to settle a civil penalty action.

Though suits against violators are far less common under the Clean Air Act than the Clean Water Act, the citizen suit provision has proven extremely important to EPA's implementation of the act. Section 304(a)(2) allows action to compel the EPA administrator to perform a non-discretionary duty. This provision has been frequently invoked to force EPA to act, particularly where deadlines to promulgate regulations have expired. Noteworthy cases to compel EPA action include the Sierra Club's 1972 case to invalidate all SIPs because of EPA's failure to require non-degradation provisions to be included,[263] and a citizen suit to compel EPA to set an ambient air quality standard for lead.

The 1990 amendments amended section 304(a) to make clear that citizen suits may be brought to compel agency action which has been unreasonably delayed. In such actions, the citizen bringing the action must give 180 days notice to EPA of the intention to bring such an action. As a practical matter, this may have the effect of extending most deadlines in the statute for promulgating regulations by 180 days. By the same token, it may suggest that any delay beyond 180 days after the statutory deadline is unreasonable.

## 13.5. EPA Rulemaking and Judicial Review

Because of the potential importance and the controversial nature of EPA regulatory decisions implementing the Clean Air Act, many decisions are challenged in court by environmentalists, by industry or both. To expedite the judicial review of EPA's regulations, in view of the short statutory deadlines, Congress provided for direct review of all "final" regulations in the United States Courts of Appeals and required that challenges by brought within certain time limits. Under the 1990 amendments, this includes final decisions by the administrator to defer a nondiscretionary action to a later time.

The act requires persons challenging an agency action to file a petition for review in the appropriate court of appeals within sixty days after the action was taken. The courts have upheld this time limit on judicial review by dismissing late petitions. In order to obtain judicial review after the deadline, a person must petition the agency for reconsideration and demonstrate that information is available which was not available when the EPA action was being developed.

The appropriate court of appeals to challenge regulations of national applicability is the District of Columbia Circuit; challenges to SIPs are to be brought in the Court of Appeals for the circuit in which the affected state is

---

[263] *Sierra Club v. Ruckelshuas,* 344 F.Supp. 253 (D.D.C. 1972), *affirmed without opinion by an equally divided court sub. nom. Fri v. Sierra Club,* 412 U.S. 541 (1973).

located. Regulations may not be attacked as invalid in enforcement proceedings if the issue could have been raised in a court of appeals challenge.

Section 307(d)(9) sets forth the bases for reversing EPA actions reviewed under section 307:

-- if the EPA action is arbitrary, capricious, an abuse of discretion, or otherwise not in accordance with law;

-- contrary to constitutional right, power, privilege, or immunity;

-- in excess of statutory jurisdiction, authority, or limitations, or short of statutory right; or

-- without observance of procedure required by law, provided that such failure was arbitrary and capricious.

In order to obtain a reversal on procedural grounds, the challenger must also show that the procedural objection was raised with reasonably specificity during the proceedings, and that the errors were so serious and related to matters of such central relevance to the rule that there is a substantial likelihood that the rule would have been significantly changed if such errors had not been made. This standard for procedural reversals is extremely hard to meet, and there have been few such reversals since Congress wrote these standards into section 307 in 1977.

The standards for reversal on substantive grounds closely track those in the Administrative Procedure Act, and are also quite difficult to satisfy, especially after the Supreme Court's opinion in *Chevron, U.S.A., Inc. v. Natural Resources Defense Council,*[264] made clear that the arbitrary and capricious standard under the Clean Air Act was to be applied in a deferential manner to EPA decision-making. Though courts do generally defer both to EPA policy choices and to EPA views of the law, they have often insisted on a substantial explanation by EPA of the legal and policy considerations that led to the agency's decision.[265]

The courts of appeals conduct their review of EPA's decisions on the basis of the record made before EPA during the rulemaking process. Ordinarily this process is conducted pursuant to section 553 of the Administrative Procedure Act, where notice of the proposed rule and its basis is published in the Federal Register, and an opportunity for comment is provided before the rule becomes final.

---

[264] 467 U.S. 837 (1984).

[265] *Portland Cement Ass'n v. Ruckelshaus,* 486 F.2d 375 (D.C.Cir. 1973) (Leventhal, J.).

Section 307(d) codified the record requirements for EPA rulemaking, requirements which had been largely imposed by the courts in decisions prior to 1977. Congress did not amend section 307(d) in the 1990 amendments so there is some question whether EPA is required to follow these provisions in promulgating rules under many of the new provisions of the Clean Air Act. Additionally under the 1990 amendments it is unclear when or whether some EPA decisions are reviewable. As EPA is under considerable time pressure to promulgate rules under the amendments, there may also be pressure to relax some of the procedural restrictions on EPA. The 1990 amendments did clarify that the filing of a petition for reconsideration does not stay the effectiveness of the rule, and does not extend the time for the filing of a petition for judicial review. This change may allow EPA to move somewhat faster in promulgating its new rules.

## CONCLUSION

Implementation of the 1990 Clean Air Amendments by EPA and the states will be one of the most costly, complicated and difficult environmental programs to understand and comply with for the 1990s. This situation is a change from the past decade, when Congress' failure to amend the act, and the Reagan administration's failure to implement it aggressively, made clean air regulation a relatively quiet area of environmental law. The regulated community, the public, and EPA will now have to invest far more time and resources into clean air compliance. As is usually true with a program as complicated as the Clean Air Act, the potential for expensive mistakes in formulating regulations and in complying with them is very high. The costs of noncompliance have also dramatically increased, placing a premium on careful, timely, and well-funded compliance efforts.

Congress has made the judgment that the environmental and health improvements are worth these inevitable problems and costs. It is now up to EPA, states, the regulated community, and environmentalists to make Congress' complicated gamble on clean air pay off in actual health and environmental benefits.

# APPENDIX A

| CAS Number | Chemical Name |
|---|---|
| 75070 | Acetaldehyde |
| 60355 | Acetamide |
| 75058 | Acetonitrile |
| 98862 | Acetophenone |
| 53963 | 2-Acetylaminofluorene |
| 107028 | Acrolein |
| 79061 | Acrylamide |
| 79107 | Acrylic acid |
| 107131 | Acrylonitrile |
| 107051 | Allyl chloride |
| 92671 | 4-Aminobiphenyl |
| 62533 | Aniline |
| 90040 | 0-Anisidine |
| 1332214 | Asbestos |
| 71432 | Benzene (including benzene from gasoline) |
| 92875 | Benzidine |
| 98077 | Benzotrichloride |
| 100447 | Benzyl chloride |
| 92524 | Biphenyl |
| 117817 | Bis(2-ethylhexyl)phthalate (DEHP) |
| 542881 | Bis(chloromethyl)ether |
| 75252 | Bromoform |
| 106990 | 1,3-Butadiene |
| 156627 | Calcium cyanamide |
| 105602 | Caprolactam |
| 133062 | Captan |
| 63252 | Carbaryl |
| 75150 | Carbon disulfide |
| 56235 | Carbon tetrachloride |
| 463581 | Carbonyl sulfide |
| 120809 | Catechol |
| 133904 | Chloramben |
| 57749 | Chlordane |
| 7782505 | Chlorine |
| 79118 | Chloroacetic acid |

| | |
|---|---|
| 532274 | 2-Chloroacetophenone |
| 108907 | Chlorobenzene |
| 510156 | Chlorobenzilate |
| 67663 | Chloroform |
| 107302 | Chloromethyl methyl ether |
| 126998 | Chloroprene |
| 1319773 | Cresols/Cresylic acid (isomers and mixture) |
| 95487 | o-Cresol |
| 108394 | m-Cresol |
| 106445 | p-Cresol |
| 98828 | Cumene |
| 94757 | 2,4-D, salts and esters |
| 3547044 | DDE |
| 334883 | Diazomethane |
| 132649 | Dibenzofurans |
| 96128 | 1,2-Dibromo-3-chloropropane |
| 84742 | Dibutylphthalate |
| 106467 | 1,4-Dichlorobenzene(p) |
| 91941 | 3,3-Dichlorobenzidene |
| 111444 | Dichloroethyl ether (Bis(2-chloroethyl)ether) |
| 542756 | 1,3-Dichloropropene |
| 62737 | Dichlorvos |
| 111422 | Diethanolamine |
| 121697 | N,N-Diethyl aniline (N,N-Dimethylaniline) |
| 64675 | Diethyl sulfate |
| 119904 | 3,3-Dimethoxybenzidine |
| 60117 | Dimethyl aminoazobenzene |
| 119937 | 3,3-Dimethyl benzidine |
| 79447 | Dimethyl carbamoyl chloride |
| 68122 | Dimethyl formamide |
| 57147 | 1,1-Dimethyl hydrazine |
| 131113 | Dimethyl phthalate |
| 77781 | Dimethyl sulfate |
| 534521 | 4,6-Dinitro-o-cresol, and salts |
| 51285 | 2,4-Dinitrophenol |
| 121142 | 2,4-Dinitrotoluene |
| 123911 | 1,4-Dioxane (1,4-Diethyleneoxide) |
| 122667 | 1,2-Diphenylhydrazine |
| 106898 | Epichlorohydrin (1-Chloro-2,3-epoxypropane) |
| 106887 | 1,2-Epoxybutane |
| 140885 | Ethyl acrylate |
| 100414 | Ethyl benzene |
| 51796 | Ethyl carbamate (Urethane) |
| 75003 | Ethyl chloride (Chloroethane) |
| 106934 | Ethylene dibromide (Dibromoethane) |

107062 . . . . . . . . . . . . . Ethylene dichloride (1,2-Dichloroethane)
107211 . . . . . . . . . . . . . Ethylene glycol
151564 . . . . . . . . . . . . . Ethylene imine (Aziridine)
75218 . . . . . . . . . . . . . Ethylene oxide
96457 . . . . . . . . . . . . . Ethylene thiourea
75343 . . . . . . . . . . . . . Ethylidene dichloride (1,1-Dichloroethane)
50000 . . . . . . . . . . . . . Formaldehyde
76448 . . . . . . . . . . . . . Heptachlor
118741 . . . . . . . . . . . . . Hexachlorobenzene
87683 . . . . . . . . . . . . . Hexachlorobutadiene
77474 . . . . . . . . . . . . . Hexachlorocyclopentadiene
67721 . . . . . . . . . . . . . Hexachloroethane
822060 . . . . . . . . . . . . . Hexamethylene-1,6-diisocyanate
680319 . . . . . . . . . . . . . Hexamethylphosphoramide
110543 . . . . . . . . . . . . . Hexane
302012 . . . . . . . . . . . . . Hydrazine
7647010 . . . . . . . . . . . . . Hydrochloric acid
7664393 . . . . . . . . . . . . . Hydrogen fluoride (Hydrofluoric acid)
123319 . . . . . . . . . . . . . Hydroquinone
78591 . . . . . . . . . . . . . Isophorone
58899 . . . . . . . . . . . . . Lindane (all isomers)
108316 . . . . . . . . . . . . . Maleic anhydride
67561 . . . . . . . . . . . . . Methanol
72435 . . . . . . . . . . . . . Methoxyclor
74839 . . . . . . . . . . . . . Methyl bromide (Bromomethane)
74873 . . . . . . . . . . . . . Methyl chloride (Chloromethane)
71556 . . . . . . . . . . . . . Methyl chloroform (1,1,1-Trichloroethane)
78933 . . . . . . . . . . . . . Methyl ethyl ketone (2-Butanone)
60344 . . . . . . . . . . . . . Methyl hydrazine
74884 . . . . . . . . . . . . . Methyl iodide (iodomethane)
108101 . . . . . . . . . . . . . Methyl isobutyl ketone (Hexone)
624839 . . . . . . . . . . . . . Methyl isocyanate
80626 . . . . . . . . . . . . . Methyl methacrylate
1634044 . . . . . . . . . . . . . Methyl tert butyl ether
101144 . . . . . . . . . . . . . 4,4-Methylene bis(2-chloroaniline)
75092 . . . . . . . . . . . . . Methylene chloride (Dichloromethane)
101688 . . . . . . . . . . . . . Methylene diphenyl diisocyanate (MDI)
101779 . . . . . . . . . . . . . 4,4-Methylenedianiline
91203 . . . . . . . . . . . . . Naphthalene
98953 . . . . . . . . . . . . . Nitrobenzene
92933 . . . . . . . . . . . . . 4-Nitrobiphenyl
100027 . . . . . . . . . . . . . 4-Nitrophenol
79469 . . . . . . . . . . . . . 2-Nitropropane
684935 . . . . . . . . . . . . . N-Nitroso-N-methylurea
62759 . . . . . . . . . . . . . N-Nitrosodimethylamine
59892 . . . . . . . . . . . . . N-Nitrosomorpholine

56382 . . . . . . . . . . . . . Parathion
82688 . . . . . . . . . . . . . Pentachloronitrobenzene (Quintobenzene)
87865 . . . . . . . . . . . . . Pentachlorophenol
108952 . . . . . . . . . . . . Phenol
106503 . . . . . . . . . . . . p-Phenylenediamine
75445 . . . . . . . . . . . . . Phosgene
7803512 . . . . . . . . . . . . Phosphine
7723140 . . . . . . . . . . . . Phosphorus
85449 . . . . . . . . . . . . . Phthalic anhydride
1336363 . . . . . . . . . . . . Polychlorinated biphenyls (Aroclors)
1120714 . . . . . . . . . . . . 1,3-Propane sultone
57578 . . . . . . . . . . . . . beta-Propiolactone
123386 . . . . . . . . . . . . Propionaldehyde
114261 . . . . . . . . . . . . Propoxur (Baygon)
78875 . . . . . . . . . . . . . Propylene dichloride (1,2-Dichloropropane)
75569 . . . . . . . . . . . . . Propylene oxide
75558 . . . . . . . . . . . . . 1,2-Propylenimine (2-Methyl aziridine)
91225 . . . . . . . . . . . . . Quinoline
106514 . . . . . . . . . . . . Quinone
100425 . . . . . . . . . . . . Styrene
96093 . . . . . . . . . . . . . Styrene oxide
1746016 . . . . . . . . . . . . 2,3,7,8-Tetrachlorodibenzo-p-dioxin
79345 . . . . . . . . . . . . . 1,1,2,2-Tetrachloroethane
127184 . . . . . . . . . . . . Tetrachloroethylene (Perchloroethylene)
7550450 . . . . . . . . . . . . Titanium tetrachloride
108883 . . . . . . . . . . . . Toluene
95807 . . . . . . . . . . . . . 2,4-Toluene diamine
584849 . . . . . . . . . . . . 2,4-Toluene diisocyanate
95534 . . . . . . . . . . . . . o-Toluidine
8001352 . . . . . . . . . . . . Toxaphene (chlorinated camphene)
120821 . . . . . . . . . . . . 1,2,4-Trichlorobenzene
79005 . . . . . . . . . . . . . 1,1,2-Trichloroethane
79016 . . . . . . . . . . . . . Trichloroethylene
95954 . . . . . . . . . . . . . 2,4,5-Trichlorophenol
88062 . . . . . . . . . . . . . 2,4,6-Trichlorophenol
121448 . . . . . . . . . . . . Triethylamine
1582098 . . . . . . . . . . . . Trifluralin
540841 . . . . . . . . . . . . 2,2,4-Trimethylpentane
108054 . . . . . . . . . . . . Vinyl acetate
593602 . . . . . . . . . . . . Vinyl bromide
75014 . . . . . . . . . . . . . Vinyl chloride
75354 . . . . . . . . . . . . . Vinylidene chloride (1,1-Dichloroethylene)
1330207 . . . . . . . . . . . . Xylenes (isomers and mixture)
95476 . . . . . . . . . . . . . o-Xylenes
108383 . . . . . . . . . . . . m-Xylenes
106423 . . . . . . . . . . . . p-Xylenes

0 . . . . . . . . . . . . . . . . . . Antimony Compounds
0 . . . . . . . . . . . . . . . . . . Arsenic Compounds
                             (inorganic including arsine)
0 . . . . . . . . . . . . . . . . . . Beryllium Compounds
0 . . . . . . . . . . . . . . . . . . Cadmium Compounds
0 . . . . . . . . . . . . . . . . . . Chromium Compounds
0 . . . . . . . . . . . . . . . . . . Cobalt Compounds
0 . . . . . . . . . . . . . . . . . . Coke Oven Emissions
0 . . . . . . . . . . . . . . . . . . Cyanide Compounds[1]
0 . . . . . . . . . . . . . . . . . . Glycol ethers[2]
0 . . . . . . . . . . . . . . . . . . Lead Compounds
0 . . . . . . . . . . . . . . . . . . Manganese Compounds
0 . . . . . . . . . . . . . . . . . . Mercury Compounds
0 . . . . . . . . . . . . . . . . . . Fine mineral fibers[3]
0 . . . . . . . . . . . . . . . . . . Nickel Compounds
0 . . . . . . . . . . . . . . . . . . Polycyclic Organic Matter[4]
0 . . . . . . . . . . . . . . . . . . Radionuclides (including radon)[5]
0 . . . . . . . . . . . . . . . . . . Selenium Compounds

---

Note: For all listings above which contain the word "compounds" and for glycol ethers, the following applies: Unless otherwise specified, these listings are defined as including any unique chemical substance that contains the named chemical (i.e., antimony, arsenic, etc.) as part of that chemical's infrastructure.

# Other Related Books Published by Government Institutes...

## Federal Environmental Laws

**Environmental Statutes, 1991 Edition**
All the major environmental laws incorporated into a single, convenient book! The complete text of each statute as currently amended is included with a detailed Table of Contents for your quick referral. Hardcover, 1,170 Pages, Code 252, Mar '91. ISBN: 0-86587-252-X

**Environmental Regulatory Glossary, 5th Edition**
This glossary records and standardizes more than 3,000 terms, abbreviations and acronyms, all compiled directly from the environmental statutes or the U.S. Code of Federal Regulations. Because their source is actual environmental legislation or regulations, these definitions are the official legal meanings. Hardcover, 544 Pages, Code 798, Mar '90. ISBN: 0-86587-798-X

**Natural Resources Law Handbook**
This is the first definitive handbook to cover the entire field of Natural Resources Law. Learn from 14 legal experts, as they explain the laws governing: Public Lands; Wildlife; Forests; Mining; Fisheries and Marine Resources; Oil, Gas and Coal Resources; Water Rights; and more! Softcover, approx. 375 pages, Code 243, Mar '91. ISBN: 0-86587-243-0

**Natural Resources Statutes**
Covers the complete text of 25 of the most important natural resources statutes based on the new U.S. Code. Includes statutes covering coastal zones, federal lands, fish and wildlife, forestry, minerals, soil and water, endangered species, and more. Softcover, approx. 600 pages, Code 241, Mar '91. ISBN: 0-86587-241-4

## General Environmental References

**Environmental Reporting and Recordkeeping Requirements**
Find out what to report, when to report, what written records are required, how long

you must retain those records, and more. These papers from our recent course, and other specially-authored papers have been combined into one comprehensive handbook that will help you to fully understand your obligations and improve your current system for reporting and recordkeeping under Clean Air, Clean Water, RCRA, CERCLA, SARA, TSCA, and OSHA. Softcover, 260 pages, Code 216, July '90. ISBN: 0-86587-216-3

### Environmental Audits, 6th Edition
Contains all the step-by-step guidance you need for conducting and managing your own environmental audit. You will learn the legal issues you face; the elements of a successful program; how to plan, conduct, or manage your audit; how to evaluate your results and implement the solutions; how to manage all the necessary data; and much more. Softcover, 592 Pages, Code 776, Nov.'89. ISBN: 0-86587-776-9

### Fundamentals of Environmental Compliance Inspections
Developed by EPA for their inspector training course, this manual allows you to get the same legal, technical and procedural insight into the basic underpinnings of all of EPA's compliance inspections. It covers the inspector's guidelines for facility entry, addressing confidential business information, taking photographs, collecting samples, reviewing records, conducting interviews, documenting evidence, and more! Softcover, 300 Pages, Code 782, July '89. ISBN: 0-86587-782-3

### Environmental, Health & Safety Manager's Handbook, 2nd Edition
Written by 15 top authorities in the field of corporate environmental management, law, and environmental consulting, this handbook is full of real-life solutions from today's top corporations on Organization and Management of Environmental Programs. Softcover, 242 Pages, Code 219, Aug '90. ISBN: 0-86587-219-8

### Environmental Communication and Public Relations Handbook
Practical guidance for communicating your environmental program to the news media, your employees, the government, and the community. E. Bruce Harrison Company, the foremost public relations firm in the environmental field, gives you the tools needed for managing the environmental disclosure requirements of OSHA and SARA. Softcover, 165 Pages, Code 748, July '88. ISBN: 0-86587-748-3

### Multi-Media Compliance Inspection Manual, 4th Edition
This EPA Office of Enforcement manual is used to guide its inspectors in conducting a multi-media compliance audit inspection of facilities that result in effluents, emissions, wastes or materials regulated under several laws such as the Clean Water Act, Clean Air Act, RCRA and TSCA. Softcover, 350 Pages, Code 779, July '89. ISBN: 0-86587-779-3

# Real Estate/Environment

### Environmental Laws and Real Estate Handbook, 2nd Edition
Learn to understand and minimize your liability under environmental law! The national law firm of Donovan Leisure Newton & Irvine provides detailed "liability checklists" of specific questions you should ask about the facility, and surveys state environmental legislation affecting real estate deals. Covers purchasers' and lenders' liability, insurance for environmental hazards, auditing the facility, and sample provisions to include in your next contract to limit your liability—plus much more! Softcover, 280 Pages, Code 753, Aug '88. ISBN: 0-86587-753-X

### Environmental Due Diligence Handbook, 2nd Edition
Learn how to establish the "Innocent Landowner Defense" to avoid liability at the time of acquisition, by being certain you've made every "reasonable inquiry" regarding the property! The law firm of Gage & Tucker provides lenders, buyers, sellers, real estate agents, brokers, attorneys and others involved with real estate and business acquisitions with clear explanations of the key elements of this new area. Softcover, 272 Pages, Code 245, Mar '91. ISBN: 0-86587-245-7

### Environmental Evaluations for Real Estate Transactions: A Technical and Business Guide
A practical "how-to" guide by Diagnostic Engineering, Inc. for evaluating the environmental risks involved with commercial real estate transfers. It covers business issues that must be considered; designing and managing preliminary and secondary evaluations; reviewing agency records; assessing hydrology and topography; where, how and what to test for; consultant's contracts and fees; reports to buyers, sellers and lenders—plus much more! Softcover, 250 Pages, Code 765, Mar '89. ISBN: 0-86587-765-3

### Wetlands and Real Estate Development Handbook
The law firm of Porter, Wright, Morris & Arthur provides insight on: drafting real estate clauses to minimize, avoid, and transfer wetlands liability; the wetland permit process; increasing court challenges by public interest groups; EPA's renewed interest in wetlands regulations; and "Applicant Information" for obtaining a wetlands permit! Softcover, 214 pages, Code 773, Apr '89. ISBN: 0-86587-773-4

### Wetlands Identification: Federal Manual for Identifying and Delineating Jurisdictional Wetlands
This government manual provides you with the mandatory technical criteria, field indicators, and other sources of information and recommended methods to determine whether an area is a jurisdictional wetland or not, and to delineate the upper

boundary of those wetlands. Softcover, 125 Pages, Code 787, Sep '89. ISBN: 0-86587-787-4

**Asbestos in Buildings, Facilities and Industry**
Legal and business authorities show you how to minimize liability and develop cost-effective asbestos abatement strategies. Learn how to minimize liability when buying or selling a building; business strategies for existing facilities; how to maximize insurance coverage; plan an inspection; and develop an asbestos management program. Softcover, 296 Pages, Code 727, Apr '87. ISBN: 0-86587-727-0

# State Environmental Law Compliance Center

**State Environmental Law Special Report, 1991 Edition**
Highly regarded law firms from 43 states highlight for each state the recent and forthcoming major events in hazardous and solid waste control, air and water pollution control, underground storage tanks, state superfunds, special land use regulations, and more. Covers: AL, AK, AZ, AR, CA, CO, CT, FL, GA, IL, IN, KS, KY, LA, ME, MD, MA, MI, MN, MS, MO, MT, NE, NV, NH, NJ, NM, NY, NC, OH, OK, OR, PA, PR, RI, SC, TN, UT, VA, WA, WV, WI and WY. Softcover, 418 Pages, Code 238, Jan '91. ISBN: 0-86587-238-4

## State Environmental Law Handbooks

Well respected law firms from every state have authored, or are currently preparing, State Environmental Law Handbooks for their state's environmental laws. Each of these comprehensive handbooks gives complete coverage of the state organizational structure, required permits and reports, hazardous and solid waste disposal, air, water and natural resources regulation, the relationship between federal and state regulations, and much more! The detailed handbooks are written by respected attorneys from each state, with hands-on experience in dealing daily with the maze of state and federal environmental regulations. For more information on available and forthcoming State Environmental Law Handbooks, please call Government Institutes -- (301) 251-9250.

# RCRA

**RCRA Hazardous Wastes Handbook, 8th Edition**
The Washington, D.C., law firm of Crowell & Moring analyzes all the current RCRA requirements to give you the insight you need to be sure you're in compliance. Also includes the RCRA law as currently amended. Softcover, 490 Pages, Code 778, May '89. ISBN: 0-86587-778-5

### RCRA Inspection Manual, 2nd Edition
Covers all details of a RCRA inspection, from facility entry to closing discussion with the owner/operator, including a synopsis of the regulations and the corresponding inspection procedures. Softcover, 401 Pages, Code 762, Feb '89. ISBN: 0-86587-762-9

### RCRA Compliance Implementation Guide
The detailed checklists in this new guide will help you accurately identify your RCRA requirements, and then provide you with step-by-step guidance for developing an effective management program! An experienced Regulatory Analyst and an Environmental Engineer clearly explain the procedures for handling contingency plans, permits, labeling, EPA notification, employee training, and much more! Softcover, 206 Pages, Code 211, Jun '90. ISBN: 0-86587-211-2

### Corrective Action Response Guide for Leaking Underground Storage Tanks
Minimize your expenses and liabilities by planning ahead with these sound guidelines for investigating, confirming and correcting a leaking underground storage tank. Albert D. Young of McLaren/Hart Environmental Management Corp. clearly explains Detection of Tank Failure; Corrective Action, Cleanup and Product Recovery; Tank Owner Response Procedures; Legal, Safety, Environmental and Public Relations; Communications and Records; Tank Failure Prevention; and Coping with UST Regulations. Includes Field Procedure Checklists; and more! Softcover, 150 Pages, Code 209, May '90. ISBN: 0-86587-209-0

### Treatment Technologies
This new EPA manual explains 26 methods for treating hazardous wastes -- including thermal, chemical and physical treatments -- in one easy-to-follow format which enables readers to quickly compare the benefits and drawbacks of individual technologies, explained in terms of Applicability, Underlying Principles of Operation, Description of the Process, Waste Characteristics Affecting Performance, and Design and Operating Parameters. Softcover, 232 Pages, Code 220, Aug '90. ISBN: 0-86587-220-1

### Transportation of Hazardous Materials: A Management Guide for Generators and Manufacturers
The Washington, D.C. law firm of Rea, Cross & Auchincloss provides in this comprehensive guide an overview of hazardous materials regulation, alternative shipping methods for generators, and useful approaches for achieving compliance. Softcover, 300 Pages, Code 792, Dec '89. ISBN: 0-86587-792-0

### Aboveground Storage Tank Management: A Practical Guide
Whether you are a current tank owner, or considering a switch from underground

to aboveground storage, this manual will provide you with a review of what regulations are on the horizon, and help you evaluate how to cost-effectively design, build, manage, operate and maintain an aboveground tank system that meets your storage needs and complies with all federal and state codes and regulations. Softcover, 220 Pages, Code 202, Feb '90. ISBN: 0-86587-202-3

**Underground Storage Tank Management: A Practical Guide, 3rd Edition**
Let the environmental engineering firm of McLaren/Hart Environmental Management Corp. bring you up-to-date on the latest in tank design, how to predict tank leaks, test tank integrity, avoid costly tank replacement through low-cost retrofit and maintenance techniques, and how to respond to leaks. Softcover, 400 Pages, Code 759, Jan '89. ISBN: 0-86587-759-9

**Medical Waste Incineration Handbook**
Generators of medical waste can turn to this comprehensive new reference for guidance on tough state regulations, new requirements for the tracking of medical waste, and solving the problem of the reluctance of landfills to accept medical waste. Includes the current emission standards for medical waste incinerators in all 50 states, addresses and phone numbers of manufacturers of medical waste incinerators and of air pollution control equipment. Softcover, 270 Pages, Code 223, Nov '90. ISBN: 0-86587-223-6

**Used Oil: Disposal Options, Management Practices
and Potential Liability, 3rd Edition**
Don't take chances with improper disposal of your used oil! Let the President of the National Oil Recyclers Association, and the Washington, D.C., law firm of Schmeltzer, Aptaker & Sheppard detail for you: precautions for generators; steps to assure regulatory compliance; the disposal options of recycling and re-refining; how and why you should investigate your recycler; what your contract with your recycler must cover; your civil and criminal liability; and crucial insurance coverage issues. Includes a national list of qualified recyclers—and much more! Softcover, 321 Pages, Code 234, Dec. '90. ISBN: 0-86587-234-1

# CERCLA/Superfund

**Superfund Manual: Legal and Management Strategies, 4th Edition**
The Washington, D.C., law firm of Crowell & Moring presents a comprehensive analysis of federal, state, and common law that will give you a workable compliance strategy. This manual clearly explains Hazardous Substance Release Reporting; Governmental Response Authority and Duties; Liability and Enforcement; Natural Resource Damages; The National Contingency Plan and the NPL; Response

Strategies; Uses of the Superfund; and Community Right-to-Know. Includes a current copy of the Superfund Law. Softcover, 442 Pages, Code 229, Oct. '90. ISBN: 0-86587-229-5

### SARA Title III Law and Regulations, 3rd Edition
Get the complete picture—the law, the lists, and an authoritative analysis of what they mean to you! This thorough manual by the respected Washington, D.C., law firm of Patton, Boggs & Blow gives you a clear, concise analysis of all the legal and regulatory requirements of the Emergency Planning and Community Right-to-Know Act. Softcover, 310 Pages, Code 760, Feb '89. ISBN: 0-86587-760-2

# Waste Minimization

### Waste Minimization Opportunity Assessment Manual
This EPA manual contains step-by-step procedures for identifying waste minimization opportunities. Takes you from the initial assessment phase, through technical and economic feasibility analysis, to actual implementation. Softcover, 106 Pages, Code 752, Oct '88. ISBN: 0-86587-752-1

### Waste Minimization Manual
The complete picture on the current status of waste reduction. Selected papers from our late 1986 and 1987 Hazardous and Solid Waste Minimization seminars bring you the critical elements of a waste reduction plan and audit. Includes actual case studies on waste minimization at DOW, Chevron, DuPont and others. Softcover, 181 Pages, Code 731, Sep '87. ISBN: 0-86587-731-9

# Pesticides

### Pesticides Inspection Manual
Written for EPA inspectors conducting pesticides inspections, this manual provides all of the necessary guidance to carry out the standard field procedures. Softcover, 231 Pages, Code 784, Sep '89. ISBN: 0-86587-784-X

### Pesticide Poisonings Handbook: The Recognition and Management of Pesticide Poisonings, 4th Edition
This EPA handbook lists 1,750 active ingredients and brand names and gives you step-by-step treatment procedures. Provides current information on health hazards of pesticides and concensus recommendations for management of poisonings. Each chapter covers a major group of pesticides, listing for each group the main active

ingredients and brand names, the basic toxicology, methods to confirm exposure, principal symptoms and signs of poisoning. Softcover, 207 Pages, Code 785, Sep '89. ISBN: 0-86587-785-8

### Regulation of Pesticides: Science, Law and the Media

Insight from industrial, regulatory, scientific, and media experts to help you better manage the risks of pesticides! Proceedings from the symposium of the Agrochemical Division of the American Chemical Society focus on the real problems facing the regulatory process—risk perception and risk communication, good laboratory practices, the weighing of risks and benefits, plus much more! Softcover, 204 Pages, Code 740, Apr '88. ISBN: 0-86587-740-8

# Toxics

### TSCA Handbook, 2nd Edition

The national law firm of McKenna, Conner & Cuneo details existing chemical regulation under TSCA; EPA's program for evaluating and regulating new chemical substances; PMN preparations and follow through; civil and criminal liability; inspections and audits; required testing of chemical substances and mixtures; exemptions from PMN requirements; the TSCA Chemical Inventory; reporting and retention of information; and special obligations of importers/exporters. Contains charts, figures, tables, and multiple indexes. Softcover, 490 Pages, Code 791, Nov '89. ISBN: 0-86587-791-2

### Toxicology Handbook

Get a basic understanding of toxicological principles and have the relevant EPA Guidance and Implementation Documents highlighted for quick and easy reference. Contains a list of key acronyms, glossary of terms, and chapters on Fundamental Concepts; Toxicity Assessments; Protocols in Toxicology Studies; Exposure Assessment; Risk Assessment; Dioxins; and much more. Softcover, 180 Pages, Code 714, Sep '86. ISBN: 0-86587-142-6

### Risk Assessment Guidelines and Information Directory

EPA guidelines and key information sources pulled together in one comprehensive volume. Contains both EPA's guidance on the conduct of EPA risk assessments, as well as information on EPA and non-EPA data bases, environmental and dose response models, manuals, directories, and periodicals applicable to each major element of risk assessment. Softcover, 291 Pages, Code 755, Nov '88. ISBN: 0-86587-755-6

### Good Laboratory Practice Compliance Inspection Manual

Make sure your laboratory inspection procedures comply with TSCA and FIFRA!

The questions EPA will ask when conducting laboratory inspections of facilities, techniques, recordkeeping, safety and quality assurance programs are detailed in this manual. Softcover, 116 Pages, Code 584, Aug '85. ISBN: 0-86587-043-8

### TSCA Inspection Manual, Part I
Developed by EPA to support its field inspections, this manual covers such topics as EPA inspectors' authorities and responsibilities; TSCA inspection procedures; post-inspection activities for the inspector; special procedures; forms; samples; PCBs enforcement program; and more. Softcover, 341 Pages, Code 541, Oct '82. ISBN: 0-86587-056-X

### TSCA Inspection Manual, Part II
Used by EPA to support its field inspections, Part II explains the complex details of EPA's PMN, CFC, Dioxin, TSCA Level A, Asbestos, and Asbestos in Schools inspections. Softcover, 216 Pages, Code 715, Sep '86. ISBN: 0-86587-143-4

# Clean Air

### Clean Air Handbook
F. William Brownell, attorney from the law firm of Hunton & Williams, provides a clear explanation of the Clean Air Act including the 1990 Clean Air Act Amendments and how they will affect businesses. This handbook covers: regulatory issues and the nonattainment puzzle; NAAQ standards; emerging air quality issues; source performance standards; air toxics regulations; permits and pre-construction review; stationary and mobile source regulations; and more! Softcover, approx. 206 pages, Code 239, Feb '91. ISBN: 0-86587-239-2

### Acid Rain: The View from the States
Get an authoritative overview of state acid rain activities! In these proceedings of this national conference sponsored by the Acid Rain Information Clearinghouse, 25 experts present a complete update of state activities, as well as technological developments and a look at the federal-state connection. Softcover, 181 Pages, Code 754, Sep '88. ISBN: 0-86587-754-8

# Clean Water

### Clean Water Handbook
This authoritative handbook was written by attorneys from the highly regarded Washington, D.C., law firm of Patton, Boggs & Blow, along with a team of other legal and technical experts. In it, they offer straightforward, nonlegalese explana-

tions of Enforcement; Toxics; Water Quality Standards; Effluent Limitations; NPDES; Stormwater & Nonpoint Discharge Control. Softcover, 446 Pages, Code 210, May '90. ISBN: 0-86587-210-4

### Oil Pollution Act of 1990: Special Report

This report frames a comprehensive prevention, response, liability, and compensation system for dealing with vessel and facility caused oil pollution. Covers liability under the new act, the Oil Spill Liability Trust Fund, financial responsibility and related arrangements, industry response, compliance challenges for facilities and the transportation industry, and much more! Softcover, 210 pages, Code 240, Mar '91. ISBN: 0-86587-240-6

### Drinking Water Treatment Technologies: Comparative
### Health Effects Assessment

This EPA report evaluates the relative benefits and risks of each of the common types of drinking water treatment technologies. It includes an assessment of raw water quality, an overview of drinking water treatment, and analysis of each treatment technology and its associated health risks from substances either added or recovered during treatment. Softcover, 206 Pages, Code 217, Aug '90. ISBN: 0-86587-217-1

### Industrial User Permitting Guidance Manual

Get an "inside look" at how industrial user (IU) permits are written! With this EPA manual, designed to help POTWs draft and issue IU permits, you can see exactly what EPA advises POTWs to include in your permit! Softcover, 292 Pages, Code 204, Apr '90. ISBN: 0-86587-204-X

### NPDES Permit Handbook

Written by experts at the Washington, D.C., law firm of Swidler & Berlin, this comprehensive book gives you details on what a permit is; who needs one; how to apply and renew; establishing effluent limits; compliance deadlines and schedules; special provisions; permitting procedures; enforcement; and more. Softcover, 240 Pages, Code 774, Apr '89. ISBN: 0-86587-774-2

### NPDES Compliance Inspection Manual, 2nd Edition

Learn to spot the same potential problems that EPA inspectors look for, and correct them before the inspector arrives! Chapters describe the NPDES program, provide basic guidance on inspection procedures, and give a wealth of specific technical information for accurate compliance. Get EPA's requirements for recordkeeping, reporting, facility site review, sampling, and more. Softcover, 234 Pages, Code 751, Oct '88. ISBN: 0-86587-751-3

### Ground Water Handbook

EPA's comprehensive technical guide for assessing and monitoring ground water contamination. Over 165 charts, tables and illustrations highlight chapters on Ground Water Contamination; Use of Models in Managing Ground Water Protection Programs; Ground Water Restoration; Ground Water Quality Investigations; Basic Hydrogeology; Monitoring Well Design and Construction; Ground Water Sampling; Ground Water Tracers; and Basic Geology. Softcover, 230 Pages, Code 761, Jan '89. ISBN: 0-86587-761-0

### Pretreatment Compliance Monitoring and Enforcement Guidance

Developed by EPA for Publicly Owned Treatment Works (POTWs), this manual (issued July 1986 and still current) gives POTWs detailed inspection guidance on: establishing monitoring requirements for Industrial Users (IUs); sampling and inspecting IUs; reviewing IU reports; determining IU compliance status; responding to IU noncompliance; and setting priorities for enforcement actions against IUs. Industrial facilities can use this manual to prepare in advance for a POTW compliance inspection and sampling visit by knowing how the inspector will proceed and what the POTW's enforcement options are! Softcover, 138 Pages, Code 789, Oct '89. ISBN: 0-86587-789-0

### Pretreatment Compliance Inspection and
### Audit Manual for Approval Authorities

Developed for EPA Regional Offices and States to use in verifying the compliance status of Publicly Owned Treatment Works (POTWs), this manual (issued July 1986 and still current) focuses primarily on the POTW's compliance monitoring and enforcement activities regarding its industrial users. POTWs can use this manual to better prepare for a pretreatment compliance inspection by EPA, often scheduled as an adjunct to an NPDES inspection. Industrial users can use this manual to get an "inside look" at exactly how EPA wants the POTWs to run their pretreatment programs, and then plan their business strategies accordingly! Softcover, 111 Pages, Code 790, Oct '89. ISBN:0-86587-790-4

# OSHA

### OSHA Handbook, 2nd Edition

This practical, non-legalese guide, written by a former OSHA official, will put you on the right track toward meeting your OSHA requirements. Covers OSHA Standards; The General Duty Clause; Recordkeeping, Imminent Dangers and Discrimination Complaints; Compliance; OSHA Inspections; Citations and Penalties; Hearing and Adjudication; Hazard Communication/Right-to-Know; Civil/Criminal Liabilities and Remedies. Includes a 76-page section of "Suggested Forms, Practices and Programs." Softcover, 400 Pages, Code 769, Mar '89. ISBN: 0-86587-769-6

**OSHA Field Operations Manual, 3rd Edition**
This step-by-step manual, developed by OSHA for use by its own Compliance Safety and Health Officers in carrying out their inspections, will show you *where* the inspectors will look, *what* they'll look for, *how* they'll evaluate your working conditions, and *how* they'll actually proceed once inside your facility. Softcover, 440 Pages, Code 788, Nov '89. ISBN: 0-86587-788-2

**OSHA Technical Manual**
Used by Compliance Safety and Health Officers (CSHOs) in performing inspections, this update of the Industrial Hygiene Technical Manual covers Personal Sampling Techniques and Procedures for Air and Surface Contaminants; Heat Stress (with Heat Disorders and Health Effects, Investigation Guidelines, Sampling Methods, etc.); Noise Measurement (with definitions, inspection data, program evaluation, etc.); Back Disorders in Industry; and much more! Softcover, 100 Pages, Code 205, Mar '90. ISBN: 0-86587-205-8

**OSHA Regulated Hazardous Substances: Industrial Exposures and Control Technologies**
This comprehensive work contains over 600 OSHA regulated substances and was developed by OSHA from over a dozen commercial and government databases expressly for employers responsible for workers who are potentially exposed to these substances. It offers a wealth of specific information on each substance including Toxicity/OSHA Exposure Limits; CAS Number; Synonyms; Trade Names; Health Effects; Industry Use Data; Engineering Controls; Personal Protective Equipment; and Storage. Softcover, 2,400 Pages, Code 795, Mar '90. ISBN: 0-86587-795-5

**Hazard Communication Standard Inspection Manual, 2nd Edition**
OSHA's own inspection procedures covering your Hazard Communication Program, Hazard Determination Procedures, employee information and training, labeling, trade secrets, MSDS completeness, and the instances in which OSHA inspectors are instructed to issue citations—plus more! Includes OSHA's 24-Question "Guide for MSDS Completeness." Softcover, 150 Pages, Code 770, Mar '89. ISBN: 0-86587-770-X

**OSHA Systems Safety Inspection Guide**
These inspection procedures, used by OSHA, focus on overall management of any operation in which hazardous chemicals are handled. Contains inspection guidelines covering management programs, maintenance, repair, equipment calibration, training, chemical hazard assessment, piping systems, process sewers, general plant controls, emergency systems and response procedures, fire protection systems, and more! Softcover, 100 Pages, Code 764, Mar '89. ISBN: 0-86587-764-5

# Information Resources

**How the Environmental Legal & Regulatory System Works:**
**A Business Primer**
Aaron Gershonowitz, noted attorney from the nationally-recognized law firm of Rivkin, Radler, Bayh, Hart & Kremer, explains how the regulatory system works and how it affects you and your business. Chapters include: where environmental laws come from; conflicts between Federal, State and Local laws; how laws and regulations are made; how the regulated community can affect the development of regulations; the environmental regulatory agencies; how environmental laws are enforced; what regulations apply to what business activities; effects of the environmental regulatory process on contracts; choosing environmental counsel; and sources of further information on environmental law. Softcover, 128 pages, Code 244, Mar '91. ISBN: 0-86587-244-9

**Directory of Environmental Information Sources, 3rd Edition**
Now you can save time and effort by beginning and ending your search for environmental information sources all in one place! Details hard-to-find Federal and State Government Resources; Professional, Scientific, and Trade Organizations; Newsletters, Magazines, Periodicals; and an Expanded Section on Databases. Softcover, 288 Pages, Code 221, Sep '90. ISBN: 0-86587-221-X

**EPA Organization and Functions Manual**
This convenient reference makes it easier to do business with EPA by providing detailed descriptions of exactly which office, division, support staff, lab, etc. within EPA is responsible for what functions. Includes a comprehensive organization chart for each office. Softcover, Approx. 230 Pages, Code 228, Jan '90. ISBN: 0-86587-228-7

**Book of Lists for Regulated Hazardous Substances**
Contains 54 of the most frequently referenced lists for environmental compliance and regulatory information -- compiled from a variety of sources including current CFRs, federal registers, and government agencies. The "Red Book" provides quick reference to the RCRA, CERCLA, CAA, CWA, SDWA, and OSHA lists you need. Softcover, 265 Pages, Code 213, Jun '90. ISBN: 0-86587-213-9

**Environmental Engineering Dictionary**
This comprehensive work, compiled by C.C. Lee, Ph.D., clearly defines over 6,000 engineering terms relating to pollution control technologies, monitoring, risk assessment, sampling and analysis, quality control, permitting, and environmen-

tally- related engineering and science. Softcover, 630 Pages, Code 786, Sep '89. ISBN: 0-86587-786-6

**1990 -1991 Environmental Telephone Directory**
This handy directory contains extensive EPA information; complete addresses and phone numbers for all Senators and Representatives with their Environmental Aides, full information on Senate and House Committees and Subcommittees and Federal and Executive agencies dealing with environmental issues; and detailed information on state environmental agencies. Softcover, 256 Pages, Code 781, Nov '89. ISBN: 0-86587-781-5

**Chemical Information Manual**
This manual – used by government inspection officers – presents in concise form a wide variety of useful data on over 1,200 chemical substances, including: Proper Identification; OSHA Exposure Limits; Description and Physical Properties; Carcinogenic Status; Health Effects and Toxicology; Sampling and Analysis. Softcover, 265 Pages, Code 746, May '88. ISBN: 0-86587-746-7

# Video Distribution Service

Government Institutes' videotape service offers in one place a wide range of timely videotapes to help you meet your training and compliance neeeds. Contact Government Institutes at (301) 251-9250 on these and other available topics on videotape:

>Environmental Law Fundamentals and Regulations
>Emergency Planning and Community Right-to-Know
>Drugs in the Workplace
>Environmental Site Assessments
>Radon
>Hazard Communication Program for Employees
>Key Elements of an MSDS
>Waste Minimization Programs
>Groundwater Monitoring Wells
>Transportation of Hazardous Waste